KREITNER   KINICKI   COLE   DIGBY

Third Canadian Edition

OB

Key Concepts, Skills, and Best Practices

McGraw-Hill Ryerson

Connect. Learn. Succeed.

McGraw-Hill Ryerson
Connect. Learn. Succeed.

Organizational Behaviour: Key Concepts, Skills, and Best Practices
Third Canadian Edition

ISBN-13: 978-0-07096739-7
ISBN-10: 0-07-096739-3

2 3 4 5 6 7 8 9 10 CTPS 1 9 8 7 6 5 4 3 2 1

Statistics Canada information is used with the permission of Statistics Canada. Users are forbidden to copy this material and/or redisseminate the data, in an original or modified form, for commercial purposes, without the expressed permission of Statistics Canada. Information on the availability of the wide range of data from Statistics Canada can be obtained from Statistics Canada's Regional Offices, its World Wide Web site at http://www.statcan.ca and its toll-free access number 1-800-263-1136.

Printed and bound in China

Care has been taken to trace ownership of copyright material contained in this text; however, the publisher will welcome any information that enables them to rectify any reference or credit for subsequent editions.

Vice President, Editor-in-Chief: Joanna Cotton
Senior Sponsoring Editor: Kim Brewster
Marketing Manager: Cathie Lefebvre
Developmental Editor: Leslie Mutic/Rachel Horner
Senior Editorial Associate: Christine Lomas
Permissions Editor: Katherine Goodes, My Editor Inc.
Supervising Editor: Graeme Powell
Copy Editor: Janice Dyer
Production Team Lead: Jennifer Hall
Cover Design: Sarah Orr, ArtPlus Ltd.
Interior Design: Sarah Orr, ArtPlus Ltd.
Page Layout: ArtPlus Ltd.
Printer: China Translation & Printing Services Ltd.

Cover Images: In the letter "O": ©iStockphoto.com/falcatraz; ©iStockphoto.com/Xaviarnau; ©iStockphoto.com/Andresr; ©iStockphoto.com/Peterclose; ©iStockphoto.com/Yuri_Arcurs; ©iStockphoto.com/francisblack. In the letter "B": ©iStockphoto.com/H-Gall; ©iStockphoto.com/ Yuri_Arcurs; ©iStockphoto.com/jsmith; ©iStockphoto.com/aldomurillo; ©iStockphoto.com/mstay; ©iStockphoto.com/webphotographeer

Library and Archives Canada Cataloguing in Publication

Organizational behaviour : key concepts, skills, and best practices / Robert Kreitner ... [et al.].—3rd Canadian ed.

Includes index.
Previous ed. by Robert Kreitner, Angelo Kinicki and Nina Cole.
ISBN 978-0-07-096739-7

1. Organizational behavior—Textbooks. I. Kreitner, Robert

HD58.7.O7315 2009   658   C2009-905400-0

Victoria Digby, BA, MA is a full-time business professor at Fanshawe College—Kinlin School of Business in London, Ontario. For the past 25 years, Victoria has taught over two dozen assorted business courses at various levels, including community college and university undergraduate programs, industry accreditation programs offered through university continuing education, and corporate training workshops. As a result of this broad scope of teaching, she has developed an understanding of the degree of interconnectedness of many of the business courses, and has thus created rich applications to enhance students' learning experiences.

Before stepping into academics, Victoria worked for eight years in U.S. and Canadian business, and has continued corporate consultation over the last 22 years.

Over the last dozen years, Victoria has been the course master for strategic management, leadership, and OB-related courses, responsible for curriculum development and design. This role includes working closely with industry accreditation organizations—like CGA, PMAC, and CHRP—who look for a certain level of rigour in courses to grant equivalencies. Victoria has also been a contributing editor for various American and Canadian industry and textbook publishers, allowing her to strengthen her writing abilities and apply her knowledge of practical business experiences.

In 2006, Victoria won the President's Distinguished Teacher Award at Fanshawe College. In 2007, Victoria was the recipient of the Association of Canadian Community Colleges Teaching Excellence Award. In 2008, she was granted a year's sabbatical to work on this organizational behaviour textbook for McGraw-Hill. Also in 2008–09, Victoria was contracted to be an undergraduate lecturer in organizational behaviour at the Social Science Management and Organizational Studies Program at the University of Western Ontario.

Robert Kreitner, PhD (pictured left) is a professor emeritus of management at Arizona State University and a member of ASU's W P Carey School of Business Faculty Hall of Fame. Prior to joining ASU in 1975, Bob taught at Western Illinois University. He also taught organizational behaviour at Thunderbird. Bob is a popular speaker who has addressed a diverse array of audiences worldwide on management topics. Bob has authored articles for journals such as *Organizational Dynamics, Business Horizons*, and *Journal of Business Ethics*. He also is the co-author (with Fred Luthans) of the award-winning book *Organizational Behavior Modification and Beyond: An Operant and Social Learning Approach*, and the author of *Management*, 10th edition, a best-selling introductory management text.

Among his consulting and executive development clients have been American Express, SABRE Computer Services, Honeywell, Motorola, Amdahl, the Hopi Indian Tribe, State Farm Insurance, Goodyear Aerospace, Doubletree Hotels, Bank One–Arizona, Nazarene School of Large Church Management, US Steel, and Allied-Signal. In 1981–82 he served as chairman of the Academy of Management's Management Education and Development Division. Bob grew up in western New York state. After a four-year enlistment in the US Coast Guard, including service on the icebreaker EASTWIND in Antarctica, Bob attended the University of Nebraska–Omaha on a football scholarship. Bob also holds an MBA from the University of Nebraska–Omaha and a PhD from the University of Nebraska–Lincoln. While working on his PhD in business at Nebraska, he spent six months teaching management

courses for the University in Micronesia. In 1996, Bob taught two courses in Albania's first-ever MBA program (funded by the US Agency for International Development and administered by the University of Nebraska–Lincoln). He taught a summer leadership program in Switzerland from 1995 to 1998. Bob and his wife, Margaret, live in Phoenix with their two cats. They enjoy world travel, lots of hiking, and a little fishing.

Angelo Kinicki is a professor of management at the W P Carey School of Business at Arizona State University. He was awarded the Weatherup/Overby Chair in Leadership in 2005. He has held his current position since receiving his doctorate in organizational behaviour from Kent State University in 1982.

Angelo is recognized for both his teaching and research. As a teacher, Angelo has been the recipient of several awards, including the John W Teets Outstanding Graduate Teacher Award (2004–05), Graduate Teaching Excellence Award (1998–99), Continuing Education Excellence Award (1991–92), and Undergraduate Teaching Excellence Award (1987–88). He also was selected into *Who's Who of American Colleges and Universities* and *Beta Gamma Sigma*. He has published more than 80 articles in a variety of leading academic and professional journals and has coauthored six college textbooks (19 including revisions). His textbooks have been used by hundreds of universities around the world and have been translated into multiple languages. Angelo's experience as a researcher resulted in his selection to serve on the editorial review boards for

the *Academy of Management Journal*, the *Journal of Management*, and the *Journal of Vocational Behavior*. He also received the All-Time Best Reviewer Award from the *Academy of Management Journal* for the period of 1996 to 1999. Angelo's current research interests include the study of leadership, organizational culture, and coping with organizational change and involuntary job loss.

Angelo is an active international consultant who works with management groups to create organizational change aimed at increasing organizational effectiveness and profitability. He enjoys delivering a variety of executive development programs on many topics related to organizational behaviour. He has worked with many *Fortune* 500 firms as well as numerous entrepreneurial organizations in diverse industries. His work on leadership development led to the creation of a 360-degree leadership feedback instrument called the Performance Management Leadership Survey (PMLS) that has been used by companies throughout the United States and Europe.

One of Angelo's strengths is his ability to teach students at all levels within a university. He uses an interactive environment to enhance undergraduates' understanding about management and organizational behavior. He focuses MBAs on applying management concepts to solve complex problems; PhD students learn the art and science of conducting scholarly research.

Angelo and his wife, Joyce, have enjoyed living in the beautiful Arizona desert for 25 years but are natives of Cleveland, Ohio. They enjoy travelling, golfing, and spoiling Nala, their golden retriever.

A MESSAGE TO PROFESSORS:

Kinicki, Kreitner, Cole, and Digby's *Organizational Behaviour: Key Concepts, Skills, and Best Practices* (3rd Cdn. Ed.) is a Canadian adaptation of a successful textbook that originated out of the United States. There is a need for this kind of OB textbook for the Canadian undergraduate college and university market because it satisfies the requirements for research-based rigour, supported by contemporary Canadian applications, statistics, and information. As OB professors, we know it is critical to dispel myths or misconceptions within initial classroom dialogues that OB is just common sense knowledge applied in a business setting. It is important to establish an appreciation for behavioural models and systems-based structures that have been studied by experts over many years and further supported by empirical research. We're sure you would also agree that as higher-educational leaders, we have an obligation to our students to provide such content using the language and literature from our Canadian cultural environment. This third edition builds upon your students' previous work experience, and also fills the gap for international students who have never experienced life in Canada (let alone worked here), by using colourful illustrations and examples.

This textbook is the culmination of the work by all the contributing authors, who have a combined 85 years of teaching experience and research of organizational behaviour and management in Canada, the United States, the Pacific Rim, and Europe. Thanks to detailed feedback from students, professors, and business practitioners, this 3rd edition is more encompassing, effectively organized, and graphically enhanced. Many changes have been made in this edition to reflect new research evidence, new behavioural techniques for the workplace, and the fruits of our own learning process.

Organizational Behaviour (3rd Cdn. Ed.) is user driven as a result of carefully listening to our readers. It was developed through close teamwork between the authors and the publisher, and is the product of continuous improvement. This approach has helped us achieve a balance between conflicting needs; i.e., a balance between theory and practice, between solid content and interesting coverage, and between instructive detail and readability. Our efforts to achieve this balance are demonstrated by many new topics, 941 source material references in the appendix (the vast majority dated 2005–2009), many new real-life examples, timely new cases, new feature box inserts, and unique end-of-chapter experiential exercises for both individual and group learning applications. More specifically, for those professors using multi-media, hybrid, and/or laptop delivery models, the *Google Searches* allow for students to research up-to-date material on their own, the *Presentation Assistant* brings the lesson to life through secular means, and the *SmartBoard Exercises* in the instructor's manual are unlike any currently offered in the industry. The package of ancillary materials that accompanies this third edition is comprehensive and complete in servicing the broad needs of the instructional panel. We trust it will meet your expectations and enhance your delivery of OB curricula.

—The Authors

A NOTE TO STUDENTS:

Kinicki, Kreitner, Cole, and Digby's *Organizational Behaviour: Key Concepts, Skills and Best Practices* (3rd Cdn. Ed.) has been modified significantly from the 2nd edition. Students often ask, "Can I just use the old edition that my roommate used when he/she took the course last year?" The answer is clearly "no"—if you do, you will be at a significant disadvantage because the content has changed so much. Specifically, chapters have been dropped or replaced, current examples have been added that are relevant to the new market conditions, and new theory, models, and end-of-chapter material have been added. In addition, if your professor pulls test questions from the Test Bank, then using an old edition text to study from will not provide you with the necessary knowledge to successfully attempt a test.

This textbook has been revised with the student in mind. It provides as many contemporary Canadian business examples as possible. Although the language may be challenging at times, do not shy away from it; rather, embrace it, understand it, and learn it—future employers expect their employees to know current business language. Upon graduation, you will be at a disadvantage if you don't understand the words used in everyday business meetings. Throughout the text, we have placed synonyms in parentheses next to relevant words, ( ), to assist your understanding. It's our way of helping you learn the language of business.

Each chapter includes feature boxes for your broader knowledge. It's important that you see applications beyond the OB theory you are studying and that you clearly identify themes that run through every OB chapter topic. In this case:

- **Ethics & Law** What are the legal or ethical implications of this OB topic within the Canadian work environment?

- **Diversity** How is this OB topic affected by diversity in the workforce?

- **International Globalization** How does this OB topic relate to what is happening in other countries?

- **Best Practices** How do Canadian organizations actually apply this OB topic to their own business environment?

- **Self-Assessment Exercises** What are your skills with or knowledge of this OB topic?

Professors often ask students to complete some sort of group activity, project, or semester assignment. In this day and age of added scrutiny (inspection) by professors to ensure that the work you are completing is indeed new and unique, we have provided new cases, new activities for group work, and new exercises at the end of every chapter.

If your professor assigns an end-of-semester presentation but you don't have a topic, just go to the back of any chapter and review the *Presentation Assistant* section. This chart provides three topics with specific relevant resources, including YouTube videos, movies, books, Web sites, popular episodes from TV shows, and even ice breaker activities to begin! We have provided these resources to help get you begin; they are not comprehensive. However, they will definitely get you started on an awesome multi-media presentation!

Got a laptop in class? This is a powerful learning tool because at the end of each chapter you'll find three interesting and fun *Google Search* exercises to show you real-life, current applications of the topic you're studying. By completing these exercises, you will have just-in-time facts related to the current lesson at your fingertips, ready to impress your professor and classmates.

You'll notice that we mention specific research methodology throughout the text. We encourage you to go to the *Appendix* and read the explanations provided prior to reading the text. Also in the *Appendix*, you'll find a helpful section on *Case Study Analysis—A Framework*, which provides nine simple steps to follow to complete a case analysis. This will be a good resource to use if your professor assigns any of the many cases included in this textbook.

One last note: Have fun and enjoy this wonderful course. It's one of the most relevant courses you'll probably take during your years of higher learning. This textbook is just one tool in your learning toolkit; we encourage you to read contemporary business literature and trade publications, talk to industry professionals, and share your insights with others as you journey through the world of OB. If at any time you need to see the big picture of what you have studied and where it fits into the course, just turn to the *OB At A Glance* diagram located on the inside cover of this textbook. This textbook is designed to serve you and your learning needs—write in it, mark it up, and highlight it to help you to learn! We wish you all the best and success in your course.

—*The Authors*

BRIEF TABLE OF CONTENTS

TABLE OF CONTENTS

03 UNIT 3 ▶ MANAGING GROUP AND TEAM BEHAVIOUR

CHAPTER 6

CHAPTER 7

UNIT 5 ▶ MANAGING CHANGE AND CHANGE AGENTS THAT AFFECT BEHAVIOUR

CHAPTER 13

CHAPTER 14

PREFACE

Less is more! That famous adage is what we kept in mind for the latest edition of *Organizational Behaviour: Key Concepts, Skills, and Best Practices*. We have kept the same great information that will guide students through the dynamic world of organizational behaviour, but have created new ways for busy students to engage with the material.

CONTINUED EXCELLENCE

Kreitner, Kinicki, Cole, and Digby's *Organizational Behaviour: Key Concepts, Skills, and Best Practices* (3rd Cdn. Ed.) builds upon the solid foundation laid in previous editions. The mantra of creating "a short, up-to-date, practical, user-friendly, interesting, and engaging introduction to the field of organization behaviour" has guided this revision. The authors have continued to use compelling pedagogical features and up-to-date cases and examples to provide rich coverage of a variety of important topics in organizational behaviour. In addition, the authors have updated OB examples and theories with the most recent research and studies. Most noticeably, the design of the book has also been changed to encompass the authors' philosophy.

NEW DESIGN

Organizational Behaviour has evolved with students; a new layout and four-colour design similar to a magazine-style text allows for portability, eye-catching graphics, and an affordable price. The third Canadian edition has been renewed with a fresh approach to colour and layout that will engage students and appeal to instructors who prefer a more traditional textbook.

CONCISE AND FLEXIBLE STRUCTURE

The new design of the third Canadian edition has maintained the adaptability of the text to a traditional 12- or 13-week academic term, summer and inter-sessions, management development seminars, and distance learning programs via the Internet. The flow of the text guides students and instructors through OB from individual to groups and teams, through to organizations, starting out small and ending with how all of these smaller elements comprise the metaphorical big picture. We encourage you to mix and match chapters in various combinations to get the most out of your OB learning/teaching experience.

ENGAGING PEDAGOGY

Organizational behaviour is a subject that deals with the intriguing realities of working in modern organizations. Insight about how and why people behave as they do in the workplace is not only useful, but can be a provocative and exciting course of study. To facilitate active and interactive learning, *Organizational Behaviour: Key Concepts, Skills, and Best Practices* includes the following features to encourage students and teachers to engage with the material on a variety of levels:

- Learning Objectives at the beginning of each chapter help students and instructors see the focus of the content—this can be a great feature to use for easily creating study and lesson plans.

- Opening cases and photos make connections between the theoretical and real world applications of what students are learning in their coursework.

- Special boxed features include Skills and Best Practices, Law and Ethics at Work, and Focus on Diversity.

- International OB, another boxed feature, highlights current international trends in OB.

- Summary of Learning Objectives is a tool that is perfect for studying for tests and exams or as a refresher before a class discussion.

- Personal Awareness and Growth Exercises follow each chapter and help the reader personalize and expand upon key concepts.

- Google Searches help students make use of familiar technology to research topics with groups or as individuals.

- The Presentation Assistants, Experiential Exercises, and Ethical Dilemma Cases help students work through a concept by creating presentations, exploring a variety of resources, and through critical analysis.

- OB in Action Case Studies present more options for instructors who prefer to teach using cases. Each chapter includes an "OB in Action Case Study" and a group of additional cases, varying in length and scope, are located at the end of the text.

ACTIVE LEARNING

The authors have developed this text to provide efficient coverage of topics such as diversity in organizations, ethics, and globalization, which are recommended by AACSB International—the Association to Advance Collegiate Schools of Business. Up-to-date chapter-opening cases, learning outcomes, a wealth of skill building experiential end-of-chapter materials, four-colour presentation, a lively writing style, and real-world, in-text examples are all used to enhance this overall educational package.

The author team has collectively designed your text to facilitate active learning by relying on the following pedagogical features:

CHAPTER PEDAGOGY

CHAPTER 8

Conflict and Negotiation

Workplace Bullying At Any Level Is Unacceptable

The belief that office bullying starts at the top of an organization and works its way downward throughout the rest of the workplace is a misread of the situation.

While there are many reported cases of managers bullying non-managerial employees, there is growing evidence that bullying takes place at all levels throughout the organization. According to Marilyn Noble, community co-chair of the research team on workplace bullying at the Muriel McQueen Fergusson Centre for Family Violence Research at the University of New Brunswick in Fredericton, this includes

HR Reporter
Published by Thomson Reuters Canada Ltd.

employee to employee, employee to customer, and patron to employee bullying situations. In fact, there have been incidences of "receptionists holding an entire organization hostage with their behaviour," says Noble.

Interpersonal aggression to the point of bullying can show up at the office in different forms, from social isolation to excessive criticism. Psychological violence is much more prevalent and pervasive in the workplace than physical violence, according to Gerry Smith, Toronto-based vice-president of organizational solutions and training at Shepell-fgi. "We're human beings and we all have our bad days. But when someone's bad day is becoming a bad month and a bad year, that's really an abuse of the safety of the workplace," says Smith. The evolving notion that a workplace distracted by interpersonal conflict is an indication of an unsafe work environment is receiving more attention from HR directors.

Patti Boucher, vice-president of client and consulting services at the Toronto-based Ontario Safety Association for Community and Healthcare, believes enforced policies around workplace harassment and bullying are critical. If there isn't a company policy supported by a network of formal response strategies for the victims (e.g., reporting mechanisms, procedures, and reports), then workers will be reluctant to report. They'll figure it's not worth their time, and that the company doesn't care. Boucher says that such strategies are key because feeling safe at work is "huge" to combat the fears of ongoing conflict from the office bully in the form of retaliation, and to serve as notice to office bullies that if caught, they will be reprimanded by those in authority. Creating and maintaining a safe work environment from both a physical and psychological point of view is very important.

In times of economic uncertainty, many firms are required to lay off employees, making the workplace ripe for conflict and aggression as managers feel the pressure to use their legitimate power to stay on top of employee productivity, by force if necessary. But resolving conflict by force is not always the answer, as it can escalate the conflict.

So, what is the answer?

HR experts suggest that to prevent workplace bullying and to cope with complaints, employers should ensure they have an effective, formal response that includes training, counselling, coaching, policies, peer support, proper infrastructure for reporting, proper documentation of incidents, and transition strategies for resetting behaviour standards to get both the victim and the bully back into the workplace.

SOURCES: S. Dotson, "Tackling the Bullies, Conflict Management," *Canadian HR Reporter,* March 9, 2009, p 13.

Brief Chapter Opening Cases

For real-world context, these cases use contemporary topics that are timely and relevant to actual life situations.

Special Boxed Features

Each chapter contains updated boxed features called Law and Ethics at Work, Skills & Best Practices, Focus on Diversity, and International OB to highlight examples of real companies, personalities, and issues to offer students practical experience.

Skills & Best Practices

The Effective Manager's Skill Profile

1. **Clarifies goals and objectives** for everyone involved.
2. **Encourages participation,** upward communication, and suggestions.
3. **Plans and organizes** for an orderly work flow.
4. **Has technical and administrative expertise** to answer organization-related questions.
5. **Facilitates work** through team building, training, coaching, and support.
6. **Provides feedback** honestly and constructively.
7. **Keeps things moving** by relying on schedules, deadlines, and helpful reminders.
8. **Controls details** without being overbearing.
9. **Applies reasonable** pressure for goal accomplishment.
10. **Empowers and delegates** key duties to others while maintaining goal clarity and commitment.
11. **Recognizes good performance** with rewards and positive reinforcement.

SOURCE: Adapted from material in F. Shipper, "A Study of the Psychometric Properties of the Managerial Skill Scales of the Survey of Management Practices," *Educational and Psychological Measurement,* June 1995, pp 468–79; and C. L. Wilson, *How and Why Effective Managers Balance Their Skills: Technical, Teambuilding, Drive* (Columbia, Maryland: Rockatech Multimedia Publishing, 2003).

LAW AND ETHICS at Work

EMPLOYMENT EQUITY ACT IN CANADA

In Canada, legislation covering federal workers and those in some provinces requires employers to actively pursue employment equity. Employment equity involves working to increase the number of employees from groups that have historically been underrepresented in an organization's workforce. In particular, the legislation requires that steps be taken to increase the representation of qualified women, visible minorities, Aboriginal people, and persons with disabilities at all levels of an organization. The Canadian Human Rights Commission is responsible for ensuring compliance with the Act. To this end, the Commission conducts audits to determine whether employers meet the statutory requirements of the Act.

SOURCE: The Government of Canada Employment Equity Act: http://www.chrc-ccdp.ca/employment_equity/default-en.asp

FOCUS ON Diversity

HIRING EMPLOYEES BASED ON THEIR GENETIC QUALITIES

Consider the following futuristic scenario: **ABC Company Inc.** advertises for an elite group of applicants to work for their organization based on genetic code testing results. All applicants must agree to submit blood and skin sample reports, along with their resumé, to be considered for an interview. The organization is looking for certain unique employee qualities that they believe will prove more effective on the job.

Sound ridiculous? It is already legal in Canada under certain circumstances to run drug and alcohol tests on potential new employees. Further, police checks, HIV, urine and hair follicle testing are more common today than they were ten years ago. Now consider that the Human Genome Project, a 50-year project, has finally been completed by scientists from around the world. In their efforts to write the sequence of all the genes in the DNA molecule, their focus from the beginning was on identifying the faulty genes responsible for diseases such as diabetes, cancer, leukaemia, eczema, and heart disease. However, researchers are currently using such information to track down the specific genes involved in very complicated constructs like intelligence, personality, and human behaviour. Over the next several years, ". . . there are going to be a lot of behavioural studies involved and they will yield up some pretty interesting discoveries," says Dr. Francis Collins, one of the leading scientists who worked on the project. The supporters of diversity in the workplace will find such science offensive and threatening, as certain types of people become preferred over others. What do you think?

Sources: BBC News, Scientists complete DNA 'Book of Life,' April 14, 2003; Genome's knowledge 'avalanche,' March 9, 2006; website: http://newsvote.bbc.co.uk/mpapps/pagetools/print/news.bbc.co.uk/2/hi/science/nature/4772114.stm and http://news.bbc.co.uk/cbbcnews/hi/sci_tech/newsid_2946000/2946419.stm. K. Davies, PBS Nova Online, "Cracking The Code of Life," Nature vs. Nurture Revisited, April 2001, http://www.pbs.org/wgbh/nova/genome/debate.html

INTERNATIONAL OB

WHAT PART OF THE SOCIAL NETWORK SITE DOES THE EMPLOYER OWN?

A U.K. court recently ordered an ex-employee of a recruitment firm to disclose details of his profile, business contacts, and emails at his social networking site, LinkedIn, to his former employer. The ex-employee had invited his employer's customers to join his network while he was still in their employ. The employer claimed those contacts belonged to them. He allegedly used his LinkedIn network to approach customers for his own rival business, which had been set up a few weeks before the end of his employment. The starting point is that customer lists are the employer's property, and employees and former employees should use them for their employer's purposes, not personal gain. The situation is not unlike information in a company database, or whether duplicates are kept by the employee on a social network site or by some means not controlled by the company. The blurring of work and personal via social network sites makes it difficult to determine who owns what. The lesson in this case is for all to think about how employees use social media for business purposes, and for employers to consider communicating the expectations that go along with it.

EXCERPT: D. Canton, "Who Owns Your Facebook Friends?" Today's Business Law, *The London Free Press,* September 8, 2008, Business, p 10.

END-OF-CHAPTER PEDAGOGY

Are You Intrinsically Motivated at Work?

INSTRUCTIONS: The following survey was designed to assess the extent to which you are deriving intrinsic rewards from your current job. If you are not working, use a past job or your role as a student to complete the survey. There are no right or wrong answers to the statements. Circle your answer by using the rating scale provided. After evaluating each of the survey statements, complete the scoring guide.

	STRONGLY DISAGREE	DISAGREE	NEITHER AGREE or DISAGREE	AGREE	STRONGLY AGREE
1. I am passionate about my work.	1	2	3	4	5
2. I can see how my work tasks contribute to my organization's corporate vision.	1	2	3	4	
3. I have significant autonomy in determining how I do my job.	1	2	3		
4. My supervisor/manager delegates important projects/ tasks to me that significantly impact my department's overall success.	1	2			
5. I have mastered the skills necessary for my job.	1	2			
6. My supervisor/manager recognizes when I competently perform my job.	1	2			
7. Throughout the year, my department celebrates its progress toward achieving its goals.	1	2			
8. I regularly receive evidence/information about my progress toward achieving my overall performance goals.	1	2	3		

Scoring Key

Sense of meaningfulness (add items 1–2) _____

Sense of choice (add items 3–4) _____

Sense of competence (add items 5–6) _____

Sense of progress (add items 7–8) _____

Overall score (add all items) _____

Arbitrary Norms

For each intrinsic reward, a score of 2–4 indicates low intrinsic motivation, 5–7 represents moderate intrinsic motivation, and 8–10 indicates high intrinsic motivation. For the overall score, 8–19 is low, 20–30 is moderate, and 31–40 is high.

Self-Assessment Exercises

This feature allows students to evaluate their own behaviour and how it relates to concepts and theories within the text.

Discussion Questions

1. What are your thoughts about the opening vignette firm, High Road Communications, and their approach to creating a pleasant workplace? If you pay people enough money to work, isn't that enough to keep them satisfied?
2. Why do you think a store manager would have greater impact on employee turnover than the actual neighbourhood location of the store?
3. Imagine that you work with a fellow employee who continues to take credit for work you complete. You decide to approach the person and give him or her a piece of your mind! The final decision to behave this way toward someone gives you a bad attitude. Explain which of the three behavioural components of attitude you are exhibiting at this time.
4. Use Ajzen's theory of planned [behaviour]... to analyze how managers can reduce voluntary turn[over]... managers can do to affect each aspect of t...

Discussion Questions

These sets of review questions cover key concepts of the chapter and are a great discussion-starter in the classroom or a helpful tool for individual review.

Google Searches

1. **Google Search:** "Big Five Personality S... Personality Type Assessment" Complete... assessments to determine your persona... share with members of your group. Do you... your response.
2. **Google Search:** "The Luck Factor—Change Your ... a few paragraphs of what Professor Wiseman's research ... 'lucky' individuals. How do lucky people cope with disappointment or bad luck? Are you a lucky person? Working with a partner, answer the following question: Would you say that lucky people have a high or low internal locus on control? Explain.
3. **Google Search:** "What is Your Emotional Intelligence Quotient?" and complete an online self-assessment. What did you score? Do you agree with the EQ results? Explain your response. Compare your results with group members and discuss the differences between people

Google Searches

By using an Internet search engine that most students are familiar with, the text shows different ways to use technology as it applies to course work.

Summary of Learning Objectives

1. **Define power, social power, and socialized power.** Power is the ability to influence others to develop a dependent relationship. Social power is the ability to get things done with human, informational, and material resources. Socialized power is when power is directed to helping others.

   [Ident]ify and briefly describe French and Raven's five bases of power, relating [t]actics used and work outcomes (e.g., job performance, job [...and turnover].) French and Raven's five bases of power are reward [...compliance], coercive power (punishing non-compliance), [...relying on formal authority), expert power (providing needed

Summary of Key Concepts

A handy review tool for all users, the summary of key concepts includes responses to learning objectives in each chapter.

Experiential Exercise

Tuckman's Stages of Group Development Exercise

PURPOSE: This exercise is meant to assist you with the specifics of group development by combining Tuckman's model with other factors related to effective group performance. Review Figure 6.2 before beginning this exercise. Approx. Timing: 25 minutes.

ACTIVITY ASSIGNMENT:
■ Form small groups and answer the questions below.
■ Share your group's responses with the rest of the class after 10 minutes.

Experiential Exercises

These exercises are designed to sharpen users' skills by either recommending how to apply a concept, theory, or model, or giving an exemplary corporate application. Students will benefit from the applied experience and direct skill-building opportunities.

The **Presentation** Assistant

Here are possible topics and sources related to this chapter that can be further explored by student groups looking for ideas.

	SOURCES OF CONFLICT IN THE OFFICE—EXAMPLES AND HOW TO RESOLVE THEM USING THE TECHNIQUES FROM CHAPTER	THE LANGUAGE OF CONFLICT—IS IT THE SAME IN ALL CULTURES?	WHEN CONFLICT ESCALATES INT... VIOLENCE—CA... AND PREVENT...

YouTube Videos	• Terry Tate the Office Linebacker for Resolving Conflict
	• Russel Peters – Business With Chinese
	• Angry Boss with Will Ferrell
		• Russel Peters –How To Become A Canadian Citizen
		• Creating Healthy Community Patterns – Canadian Aboriginal Conflict Resolution
		• Bush Comes Under Shoe Attack In Baghdad
			• Workplace Vio...
			• Gunman Open...
			  German Schoo...
			• Angry Employe...
			  Boss's Car

TV Shows or Movies to Preview	• *The Office* (Season 2) – "Conflict Resolution Episode" • *30 Rock* – "Fight The Power Episode"	• *Outsourced* (Movie) • *Boiler Room* • *Rush Hour 2*	• *Office Space* (Movie)
Internet Searches	• Canadian Centre for Occupational Health and Safety	• *Cross Cultural Conflict* (by D. Elmer) • *Cross Cultural Conflict*	• Canadian Safety Council, Psychological Violence • Canadian Initiative ...

Presentation Assistants

The Presentation Assistant helps students structure a group or individual presentation on the chapter material. This feature includes ideas for guiding class discussions and resources for further research.

Ethical OB Dilemmas

This feature offers students a scenario where they must evaluate their ethical decision-making and critical thinking skills. Questions help guide users through material and discussion.

OB in Action Case Study

Design a Motivating Job Using The JCM

Kareem Padawan is 17 years old and works at Chapters bookstore in the West Edmonton Mall. Kareem has worked at Chapters for two months, earning the standard minimum wage. In the short time he has worked at the bookstore, Kareem has noticed that there is a tremendous turnover of employees, but doesn't fully understand the possible reasons for it. However, he does know a few things. For example, Kareem knows that: workers like himself are paid minimum wage; must be willing to work at least four five-hour shifts for a total of 20 hours per week; must wear a uniform that is purchased from the company at $40/shirt and pants; and are assigned to work in a specifically designated area. In this case, Kareem is paid and trained to be an inventory/stock person—unloading trucks when they come in, unpacking boxes, and carrying the boxes out to the front for processing by the clerks. When the boxes are empty, Kareem breaks them down and packs them up for the garbage. He was getting bored with that job, so Kareem applied for... ...clerk, which would allow him to use the store computer syste... ...be processed from the back and placed on shelves... ...the front to help out at the customer service ...the clerk's job. Instead, he was given the

Ethical OB Dilemma

The Motivation to Cheat

You are taking a college course. The tests and quizzes are online through the class Web site. The professor gives you a three-day window and you take the tests in your personal time. The professor has strict guidelines about cheating. At the beginning of the semester, the professor told all of you that the tests and quizzes will be timed so you will not have enough time to look the answers up in the book. You are in the computing commons taking one of the quizzes and notice a group of your classmates huddled around a computer. They are taking the quiz as well. One student is looking up the answers in the book, one is taking the quiz, and the other is recording the answers. You wonder what would motivate students to behave in such a way.

As a student, what would you do?

Consider the following options:

1. You conclude that these students are liars and deserve to be punished for their unethical behaviour. You immediately contact your professor about what ...

OB in Action Cases

Students can see key concepts in action with an end-of-chapter case, complete with follow-up questions.

UNIT 1

Introduction to Organizational Behaviour

A RUNNING SUCCESS (CEOTV.COM) ⏱ 3:38

This video is an interview with John Stanton, President of Running Room, Inc., a... enthusiastic entrepreneur who started this successful Canadian business back... 1984 in the living room of an old renovated Edmonton home. As a veteran runne... Stanton wasn't satisfied with the kind of service he received nor the quality of equipment typically found in sporting goods stores. He wanted to start a busine... to provide top quality athletic running wear sold by knowledgeable sales personn... Today Stanton oversees a growing enterprise that has become North America's... largest chain of specialty stores for walkers and runners, with over 90 stores in bo... Canada and the U.S. John Stanton's philosophy and personal commitment drive... this organization. As stated on their Web site: "We are not just selling shoes and equipment, we are selling a commitment to active living."

Video Cases

This resource offers the opportunity for situational analysis in the classroom or individual study. The instructor's package, including a DVD and questions for discussion and videos, is available at Connect, www.mcgrawhillconnect.ca The video case studies are featured at the end of the text in the Appendix section.

END-OF-TEXT PEDAGOGY

Additional Cases

An appendix containing additional cases is great for more in-depth individual study or group assignments.

JESSICA CASSERRA'S TASK FORCE: HOSPITAL INTEGRATION IN THE REGION OF ERIE[1]

CASE STUDIES

Jessica Casserra stretched back from the monitor and rubbed her eyes. Technology had made it possible to be home in the evenings with her family, but as they pointed out, that didn't mean they saw much of her. For the past two months, most evenings and weekends had been spent pouring over internal reports, briefs, governmental documents, spreadsheets, and consulting studies concerning the integration of hospital services in the Region of Erie.

The taxpayers of the Region had received far more than their fair share of her time, but she wasn't sure that it... ...nslating into added value. Budgeting, control,

Metropolitan was located in the major urban area (population = 90,000) in the region. It was surrounded by agricultural and tourist areas and a number of smaller municipalities. Five of these towns hosted 20 to 50 bed hospitals, offering limited services to residents in the immediate area.

Each of the hospitals in the region had strong local support and good reputations for the quality of care and services they provided. In recent years this support had been tested as waiting periods for medical procedures increased, and emergency care lineups lengthened. Shortages of funds and health care workers (nurses,

VIDEO CASES

Each unit includes current and relevant video cases from CEO TV and other sources, helping instructors highlight such important topics as flextime, motivating employees, and diversity. Video teaching notes are available in the Instructor's Resource Manual and are downloadable from the Instructor section of Connect™.

INSTRUCTOR SECTION OF CONNECT OB
(www.mcgrawhillconnect.ca)

Connect™ is a Web site that follows the text chapter by chapter, with additional materials and quizzes that enhance the text and/or classroom experience. A secured Instructor Resource Centre stores essential course materials and saves prep time before class. This area houses all the Instructor supplements needed for your OB course: An Instructor's Resource Manual, written by the text author; PowerPoint® Presentations, EZ Test Computerized Test Bank, and Video Notes and teaching material.

MANAGEMENT ASSET GALLERY

McGraw-Hill Ryerson, in conjunction with McGraw-Hill/Irwin Management, is excited to provide a one-stop-shop for our wealth of assets, allowing instructors to quickly and easily locate specific materials to enhance their course. The Asset Gallery includes our non-text-specific management resources (Self-Assessments, Test Your Knowledge exercises).

MANAGER IN THE HOT SEAT
RESOURCES (www.mhhe.com/mhs)

In today's workplace, managers are confronted daily with issues such as ethics, diversity, working in teams, and the virtual workplace. The Manager's Hot Seat is an interactive online resource that allows students to watch as 15 real managers apply their years of experience to confront these issues.

GROUP AND VIDEO RESOURCE MANUAL:
AN INSTRUCTOR'S GUIDE TO AN ACTIVE CLASSROOM
(www.mhhe.com/mobmanual)

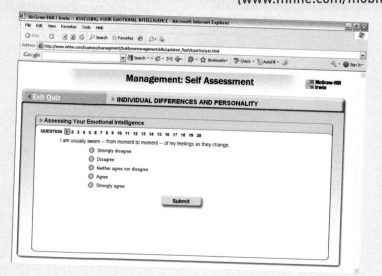

This manual, created for instructors, contains everything needed to integrate activities successfully into the classroom. It includes a menu of items to use as teaching tools in class. All of our interactive Self-Assessment Exercises, Test Your Knowledge quizzes, Group Exercises, and Manager's Hot Seat segments are located in this one manual, along with teaching notes and PowerPoint slides to use in class. Group exercises include everything you might need to use the exercise in class—handouts, figures, etc. This manual is organized into 25 topics including ethics, decision making, change, and leadership for easy inclusion in your lecture. A matrix appears at the front of the manual that references each resource by topic.

INTEGRATED LEARNING (*i*LEARNING)

Your Integrated Learning (*i*Learning) Sales Specialist is a McGraw-Hill Ryerson representative who has the experience, product knowledge, training, and support to help you assess and integrate any of our products, technology, and services into your course for optimum teaching and learning performance. Whether it's using our test bank software, helping your students improve their grades, or putting your entire course online, your *i*Learning Sales Specialist is there to help you do it. Contact your local *i*Specialist today to learn how to maximize all of McGraw-Hill Ryerson's resources!

TEACHING, TECHNOLOGY, & LEARNING CONFERENCE SERIES

The educational environment has changed tremendously in recent years, and McGraw-Hill Ryerson continues to be committed to helping you acquire the skills you need to succeed in this new milieu. Our innovative Teaching, Technology, & Learning Conference Series brings faculty together from across Canada with 3M Teaching Excellence award winners to share teaching and learning best practices in a collaborative and stimulating environment. Pre-conference workshops on general topics, such as teaching large classes and technology integration, are also offered. We will also work with you at your own institution to customize workshops that best suit the needs of your faculty.

CONNECT OB

McGraw-Hill Connect™—Available 24/7 with instant feedback so you can study when you want, how you want, and where you want. Take advantage of the Study Plan—an innovative tool that helps you customize your learning experience. You can diagnose your knowledge with pre- and post-tests, identify the areas where you need help, search the entire learning package for content specific to the topic you're studying, and add these resources to your personalized study plan. Visit **www.mcgrawhillconnect.ca** to register—take practice quizzes, search the e-book, and much more.

FOR STUDENTS:

Developed in partnership with Youthography, a Canadian youth research company, and hundreds of students from across Canada, McGraw-Hill Connect™ embraces diverse study behaviours and preferences to maximize active learning and engagement.

With McGraw-Hill Connect™, students complete pre- and post-diagnostic assessments that identify knowledge gaps and point them to concepts they need to learn. McGraw-Hill Connect™ provides students the option to work through recommended learning exercises and create their own personalized study plan using multiple sources of content, including a searchable e-book, multiple-choice and true/false quizzes, chapter-by-chapter learning goals, interactivities, personal notes, videos, and more. Using the copy, paste, highlight and sticky note features, students collect, organize and customize their study plan content to optimize learning outcomes.

FOR INSTRUCTORS:

McGraw-Hill Connect™ assessment activities don't stop with students! There is material for instructors to leverage as well, including a personalized teaching plan where instructors can choose from a variety of quizzes to use in class, assign as homework, or add to exams. They can edit existing questions and add new ones; track individual student performance—by question, assignment, or in relation to the class overall—with detailed grade reports; integrate grade reports easily with Learning Management Systems such as WebCT and Blackboard; and much more. Instructors can also browse or search teaching resources and text specific supplements and organize them into customizable categories. All the teaching resources are now located in one convenient place.

*McGraw-Hill Connect™—helping instructors and students **Connect, Learn, Succeed!***

ACKNOWLEDGEMENTS

My intent for this 3rd edition was to make it as Canadian and current as possible for the learner. I tried to find as many contemporary applications for complex OB theory as possible; also, I wanted to include never-before seen end-of-chapter exercises and activities to make the classroom experience interesting but also fun. My vision of what this textbook would look like has been supported, guided, and enabled by the professional editors and assistants at McGraw-Hill Ryerson. I have been overwhelmed at times by the high level of cooperation and encouragement offered by the Whitby team, including Becky Walker, Arlene Bautista, Christine Lomas, Alison Derry, Leslie Mutic and Rachel Horner—it has truly been appreciated. My thanks to Elda Giardelli, the best sales rep, for making this dream come true. A big thanks to the behind-the-scenes efforts of Katherine Goodes, permissions editor, for all her hard work securing the needed approvals on stories, pictures, and such. I especially want to thank Kim Brewster, Senior Sponsoring Editor who believed in me from the start and always made me feel included whenever decisions had to be made.

I also want to thank my family, Paul, Justin, and Drew Digby, for their patience, love, and support during the many months when I wasn't able to be there for lunch or dinner because I was too busy working on this book. I would like to dedicate this book to them. To my sister Carol Starr, for being there to pick up the slack when I wasn't able to drive down and help take care of my mother, Adele Plotinski, I would like to express my deep gratitude.

To the thirteen professors from across the country who reviewed both batches of the first draft—I owe them sincere thanks for their constructive comments and professional insight. While it was difficult at first to hear their comments, in the end I had to agree that most of the changes were needed, and indeed they were right. The enhancements that were made did significantly improve the manuscript. They pushed me to reach a higher level of professionalism, and for that I am grateful.

Clark Olson, *Sheridan College*
David Smiderle, *Conestoga College*
Debbie Gamracy, *Fanshawe College*
Debra Warren, *Centennial College*
Grace O'Farrell, *University of Winnipeg*
Jane Guzar, *Mohawk College*
Joan Condie, *Sheridan Institute of Technology and Advanced Learning*
Laura Jean Taplin, *Humber College*
Lorna Kaufman, *Vancouver Island University*
Louis Masson, *SAIT*
Michelle White, *Fanshawe College*
Sean MacDonald, *University of Manitoba*
Stan Arnold, *Humber College*
Wendi Adair, *University of Waterloo*

My thanks to the many OB students at Fanshawe College—Kinlin School of Business who throughout the years have allowed me to develop a transformational style of teaching by letting me know what worked and what didn't. They've told me my class helped change their lives, when in fact they helped to shape mine. What I present in this edition is a culmination of years of teaching OB to thousands of students who have sat through my lectures and shared their stories, opinions, and insights with me. What a joy they have been, and how lucky I have been to have had the opportunity to be their professor.

My thanks to the MOS2180-02 class at the University of Western Ontario who were my students the year I was on sabbatical to write this textbook. Their patience, sense of humour, and curiosity to learn OB allowed me to see what kind of material appealed to today's student and what didn't work. I know that what I am presenting in this edition works because I've tried it in my own class with 175 undergrad students.

—*Victoria Digby*
April 2009

> *"The way you see them is the way you treat them and the way you treat them is the way they often become."*
>
> *Zig Ziglar (Motivational Speaker)*

CHAPTER **1**

Organizational & Behaviour
People-Centred Management

The Transformation of the Canadian Workplace

As a student learning business principles, you are lucky to be studying during one of the most transformational times in Canadian business history. For the last three decades, the Canadian economy has been slowly shifting its economic dependency away from the traditional routine-oriented manufacturing base toward a knowledge- or idea-driven creative economy. According to a $2.2 million report compiled by a team of 30 staffers and 20 contractors under the direction of Roger Martin (Dean of the Rotman School of Management) and Richard Florida (Director of the Martin Prosperity Institute at the University of Toronto), the financial and economic problems of the early 21st century only accentuated the need for Canadians to take note of this shift and its importance to them.

But why the shift? Where are the jobs going? Photographer Edward Burtynsky and filmmaker Jennifer Baichwal captured this shift in their brilliant multi-award winning National Film Board of Canada documentary, *Manufactured Landscapes*. The opening scene showing thousands of employees working at an assembly-plant in China takes on greater significance when the viewer begins to see the enormous size of the facility, hear the daily corrective directions from the team leader, and witness the dominant age demographic of the average worker who must put in double-digit hours per day, sometimes six days per week, just to stay employed. Couple these factors with the extremely low cost of labour in China, and the evidence speaks for itself. It's difficult for Canadian manufacturing to compete.

This shift of routine manufacturing-based jobs away from Canada is also evident in India, Mexico, Central America, and so on. It's happening slowly, but have no doubt: it is happening, and Canadians need to take note. Naturally, the talent needed to fuel this new kind of creative-based economy will be offered to Canadians first, but if they are unable to adapt, conform, and be productive to the new expectations, then business will look elsewhere to fill the gap.

So, what can Canadians do to prepare? The report makes three main suggestions:

1. Gain greater understanding of how the Canadian workplace is changing and develop new skills through increased training and post secondary education.

2. Appreciate the need for reinvention and creativity when designing our jobs.

3. Support the development and promotion of unique Canadian talent from those who have been marginalized in the past—embrace the diversity they bring to the workplace.

This is only a small snapshot of the Canadian work environment today, but nonetheless it is a significant one. The challenge of building a creative economy that is more tech-savvy, inclusive, and sustainable is cause enough to make us all think hard about whether we're prepared to accept a role in this new transformed workplace.

Are you ready?

SOURCES: *The Globe and Mail.* "Economy In Transition." February 5, 2009, p1A. *The National Film Board of Canada.* "Manufactured Landscapes." 2007.

The business landscape is changing in Canada. Here an individual reads the electronic TSX tickerboard.

SOURCE: www.greatplacetowork.ca

LEARNING OBJECTIVES

After reading this chapter, you should be able to:

LO 1   **Define** *organizational behaviour* and *management*.

LO 2   **Explain** why OB is studied and what benefits it can bring to the workplace.

LO 3   **Discuss** the relevance of OB to the contemporary Canadian workplace by differentiating between managers from the past versus those of the future.

LO 4   **Summarize** the history of OB in a timeline by incorporating three significant landmarks of theory development, including distinguishing characteristics of each.

LO 5   **Infer** and predict the challenges that at least four contemporary OB issues may present to both non-managerial employees and management in the future.

The opening vignette asks a very important question: Are you ready? This is a significant question to reflect upon. As a future employee, you need to appreciate the environment that will surround your job, and identify which segments of that workplace can be influenced by your behaviour and which exist outside of your area of influence.

Studying organizational behaviour will help you understand the Canadian work environment, which is the first step in being better prepared for this new creative economy. Learning organizational behaviour is like placing your cupped hands against the window of a business and looking inside at all of the different behaviours that are occurring at the same time and wondering why .... Why are people behaving that way? Why does the company have those policies and procedures? Why don't these individuals get along? This text, the cases at the end of the book, and the exercises at the end of each chapter are designed to help you understand the possible meanings behind such behaviours, and the broad implications they can have on the entire organization. Further, organizational behaviour will clearly identify workplace expectations waiting for you upon completion of your studies.

We'll begin your journey by providing the fundamentals of organizational behaviour and move on from there. Keep in mind, if at any time you need to review the big picture of what you are studying and how it fits into the larger scheme of things, just open the inside front cover to regain perspective. We have included a flowchart there for you to review.

LO 1 What Is Organizational Behaviour?

Organizational Behaviour, commonly referred to as OB, investigates three interdependent systems—the individual, the group, and the combination of both individuals and groups within an organizational context—to develop a better understanding of the workplace, especially when managing people. OB involves the study of what people think and feel and the resulting effect on individual and group behaviour within organizations. Figure 1.1 uses the metaphor of three trees, with each tree representing an interdependent system. Deep in the ground, where the roots find nourishment, are research contributions from the behavioural sciences. At the base of each trunk are eight external factors, collectively acting as inputs. Notice how each tree has its own branches and leaves; this shows the many factors that help the transformation process between using the many inputs to create the positive outputs from each system. Overall, this metaphor models organizational behaviour.

Organizational Behaviour

A field of study that investigates three interdependent systems—the individual, the group, and the organizational context overall—to develop better understanding of the workplace, especially when managing people.

OB is more than common sense. It gains its credibility as an academic discipline by being research-driven (see Appendix Item #1). OB researchers investigate unanswered questions relating to effective **management** of behaviour in organizations, and the results are intended to be used by managers and other employees to improve workplace effectiveness. Research evidence indicates that people-centred practices are strongly associated with much higher profits and significantly lower employee turnover. In order for any team of managers and other employees to contribute to organizational goals and objectives, they must all work together and reinforce such practices.

OB is not an everyday job category such as accounting, marketing, or finance. Students of OB typically do not get jobs in organizational behaviour per se. OB is a horizontal discipline that cuts across virtually every job category, business function, and professional specialty.

Management

The process of working with and through others to achieve organizational objectives effectively, efficiently, and ethically.

▶ FIGURE 1.1 A Model of Organizational Behaviour

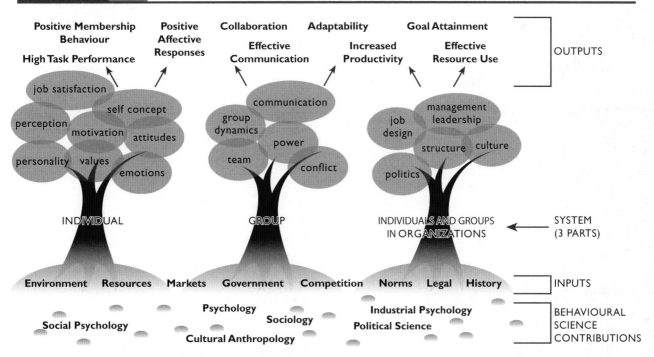

SOURCE: J. Kelly, JB. Prince &, B. Ashforth, *OB*, 2nd Ed., Prentice-Hall, Toronto (1991) p. 24.

LO 2 Why Study Organizational Behaviour?

Anyone who plans to make a living in a large or small, public or private, profit or not-for-profit organization needs to study organizational behaviour. OB provides the foundation for the steps to take when individuals need to foster greater satisfaction at their job. In addition, new knowledge can be applied directly and immediately, such as stress reduction techniques, to promote on-the-job satisfaction, which can lead to greater productivity. OB knowledge can help people have greater confidence knowing that their firm is moving in the right direction by understanding the policies and procedures that are reinforced.[1]

Other benefits for individuals studying OB include:

- The ability to identify and analyze fundamental behaviours that occur within the workplace—this can contribute to greater overall cooperation and understanding.

- The ability to evaluate and help other employees develop sensitivity toward organizational structure, corporate strategy, business culture, standard practices, and leadership—this can promote greater understanding, stimulate dialogue, and result in higher performance.

- The ability to identify and provide examples of best practices among those organizations that successfully demonstrate the knack to operate within an ethical, legal, and socially responsible context—this emphasizes the fact that people-friendly behaviours don't have to be sacrificed to accomplish corporate goals (i.e., make a profit).

But what about those employees who are offered a team-leadership opportunity or an entry-level supervisory position, or those who have clear managerial aspirations; why do they need to study OB? It is important for them to study OB because they'll need to know how to effectively manage others. Today's successful managers need to creatively envision and actively sell bold new directions in an ethical and sensitive manner (see The Effective Manager's Skill Profile in the Skills & Best Practices feature box). Professor Henry Mintzberg, a respected management scholar from McGill University, Montreal, observed that any kind of management role is vital to our society, as social institutions give them the authority to either serve us well or squander the talents and resources of the organization.[2]

It should be pointed out that we are discussing management in this chapter, not leadership. There is a difference, and we'll explore those differences later, in Chapter 9. For now, let us take a look at the skills that contemporary managers need to have in the workplace, and the future direction of management.

Skills & Best Practices

The Effective Manager's Skill Profile

1. **Clarifies goals and objectives** for everyone involved.

2. **Encourages participation**, upward communication, and suggestions.

3. **Plans and organizes** for an orderly work flow.

4. Has **technical and administrative expertise** to answer organization-related questions.

5. **Facilitates work** through team building, training, coaching, and support.

6. **Provides feedback** honestly and constructively.

7. **Keeps things moving** by relying on schedules, deadlines, and helpful reminders.

8. **Controls details** without being overbearing.

9. **Applies reasonable** pressure for goal accomplishment.

10. **Empowers and delegates** key duties to others while maintaining goal clarity and commitment.

11. **Recognizes good performance** with rewards and positive reinforcement.

SOURCE: Adapted from material in F. Shipper, "A Study of the Psychometric Properties of the Managerial Skill Scales of the Survey of Management Practices," *Educational and Psychological Measurement*, June 1995, pp 468–79; and C. L. Wilson, *How and Why Effective Managers Balance Their Skills: Technical, Teambuilding, Drive* (Columbia, Maryland: Rockatech Multimedia Publishing, 2003).

LO 3 The Transformation Toward People-Centred Management

It's important for all employees to understand how management is taking on new behaviours, as this will have a direct impact on the kinds of behaviours that individual employees will be expected to demonstrate on the job. As we've already discussed in broad terms, today's workplace is indeed undergoing immense and permanent changes.[3] Organizations are being "reengineered" for greater speed, efficiency, and flexibility.[4] Entrepreneurial spirit is needed in both small and large businesses. Teams are pushing aside the individual as the primary building block of organizations.[5] Costs are being managed by use of contract workers. Command-and-control management is giving way to participative management and empowerment, (we'll discuss these concepts in greater detail in Chapter 8).[6] Ego-centred leaders are being replaced by customer-centred leaders. Employees are increasingly being viewed as internal customers. Clearly such dynamic changes create a mandate for a new kind of manager in the 21st century. Table 1.1 contrasts the characteristics of past and future managers. This change in management style is not just a good idea; it is an absolute necessity in the new workplace.

Indeed, many elements of organizational behaviour are transforming, and we're going to discuss them in greater detail throughout the rest of this text. For now, let's remain focused on the wide-ranging aspects of OB. We can better understand where the field of organizational behaviour is today and where it appears to be headed by appreciating where it has been. This next section will examine the evolution of understanding and managing people.

The History of Organizational Behaviour

To understand behaviour in organizations, it is necessary to draw upon a diverse array of disciplines, including psychology, management, sociology, organization theory, social psychology, statistics, anthropology, general systems theory, economics, information technology, political science, vocational counselling, human stress management, psychometrics, ergonomics, decision theory, and ethics. This rich heritage has spawned many competing perspectives and theories about human work behaviour.

The Characteristics of Past Managers and Future Managers

	PAST MANAGERS	FUTURE MANAGERS
Primary role	Order giver, privileged elite, manipulator, controller	Facilitator, team member, teacher, advocate, sponsor, coach
Learning and knowledge	Periodic learning, narrow specialist	Continuous lifelong learning, generalist with multiple specialties
Compensation criteria	Time, effort, rank	Skills, results
Cultural orientation	Monocultural, monolingual	Multicultural, multilingual
Primary source of influence	Formal authority	Knowledge (technical and interpersonal)
View of people	Potential problem	Primary resource
Primary communication pattern	Vertical	Multidirectional
Decision-making style	Limited input for individual decisions	Broad-based input for joint decisions
Ethical considerations	Afterthought	Forethought
Nature of interpersonal relationships	Competitive (win–lose)	Cooperative (win–win)
Handling of power and key information	Hoard and restrict access	Share and broaden access
Approach to change	Resist	Facilitate

TABLE 1.1

LO 4

Let us examine three significant landmarks of OB theory development:

1. Scientific Management (late 1800s–1915)

2. The Human Relations Movement (1930s)

3. The Contingency Approach (1980–present)

SCIENTIFIC MANAGEMENT

The Industrial Revolution that started with the development of steam power and the creation of large factories in the late 18th century lead to significant changes in the production of textiles and other products.[7] The factories that evolved created tremendous challenges for organizations and management that had not been confronted before. Managing such large pools of material, people, and information over large distances created the need for methods for dealing with the new management issues.

Frederic Taylor began to create a science of management (commonly referred to as **scientific management**) that used research to determine the optimum degree of specialization and standardization of work tasks. His model was the machine with its cheap, interchangeable parts, each of which did one specific task. Taylor attempted to use the machine mind-set as a template to standardize individual work movements and breaks. This involved disassembling each task into its most minute unit and figuring out the one best way to do each job.

The overall goal of Taylor's research was to remove human variability. The results of his efforts were profound, as productivity increased dramatically. Of course, this did not come about without resistance. First, the old line managers resisted the notion that management was a science to be studied, not something one was born with (or inherited). Then, many workers resisted what some considered to be the "dehumanization" of work. Nevertheless, the industrial engineer with his stopwatch and clipboard, standing over employees measuring each little part of the job and their movements, became a hated figure and lead to much sabotage and group resistance.

> "... the industrial engineer with his stopwatch and clipboard, standing over employees measuring each little part of the job and their movements, became a hated figure and lead to much sabotage and group resistance."

Scientific Management
A body of research by Frederic Taylor (1856–1915) that involved systematically analyzing human behaviour at work to increase productivity and efficiency (e.g., time–motion studies).

The core elements of scientific management remain popular today as organizations remain focused on increasing the productivity of their workforce and striving to find the best way to manage an organization to achieve its goals. Some results of the scientific management movement include: the creation of a personnel department, implementation of quality control factors, introducing procedures for operations, striving for greater workplace efficiency, and recognizing the need for formalized management within an organizational structure.[8]

THE HUMAN RELATIONS MOVEMENT

A unique combination of factors during the 1930s fostered the human relations movement. First, following legalization of union–management collective bargaining in North America in the early 20th century, management began looking for new ways of handling employees. Until then, management was based on a scientific management approach that focused on the worker as a machine to be managed for maximum efficiency. Second, behavioural scientists conducting on-the-job research started calling for more attention to the "human" factor. Managers who had lost the battle to keep unions out of their factories heeded the call for better human relations and improved working conditions.

The **human relations movement** gathered momentum through the 1950s, as academics and managers alike made stirring claims about the powerful effect that individual needs, supportive supervision, and group dynamics apparently had on job performance.

Human Relations Movement
Research that started calling attention to the "human" factor within the workplace.

The Writings of Mayo and Follett

Essential to the human relations movement were the writings of Elton Mayo and Mary Parker Follett. Australian-born Mayo advised managers to attend to employees' emotional needs in his 1933 classic, *The Human Problems of an Industrial Civilization*. Follett was a true pioneer, not only as a woman management consultant in the male-dominated industrial world of the 1920s, but also as a writer who saw employees as complex combinations of attitudes, beliefs, and needs. Mary Parker Follett was way ahead of her time in telling managers to motivate job performance instead of merely demanding it, a "pull" rather than "push" strategy.[9]

McGregor's Theories In 1960, Douglas McGregor wrote a book entitled *The Human Side of Enterprise*, which has become an important philosophical base for the modern view of people at work. Drawing upon his experience as a management consultant, McGregor formulated two sharply contrasting sets of assumptions about human nature (see Table 1.2). His **Theory X** assumptions were pessimistic and negative and, according to McGregor's interpretation, typical of how managers traditionally perceived employees. To help managers break with this negative tradition, McGregor formulated his **Theory Y**, a modern and positive set of assumptions about people. McGregor believed managers could accomplish more through others by viewing them as self-energized, committed, responsible, and creative beings.

Theory X

Negative, pessimistic assumptions about human nature and its effect on productivity.

Theory Y

Positive assumptions about employees being responsible and creative.

New Assumptions about Human Nature Modern research methods have shown that the human relationists embraced some naive and misleading conclusions. Despite its shortcomings, the human relations movement opened the door to more progressive thinking about human nature. Rather than continuing to view employees as passive economic beings, managers began to see them as active social beings and took steps to create more humane work environments.

THE CONTINGENCY APPROACH

Since the 1980s, OB experts have focused their attention on emphasizing the fit between organizational processes and various characteristics of the situation. Throughout the later part of the 20th century, it became clear that there in fact was no one best way to approach a workplace; rather an appropriate style depended on the demands of the situation. Hence, the **contingency approach** calls for using management concepts and techniques in a situationally appropriate manner, instead of trying to rely on one best way. If, for example, we were trying to determine the most effective leadership style to use in a certain situation, we would have to consider the abilities of the followers; or, if we were trying to determine the appropriate level of pay increase for an employee, we would consider if productivity is contingent on the need for more money. Harvard's Clayton Christensen put it this way: "Many of the widely accepted principles of good management are only situationally appropriate."[10]

Contingency Approach

Using management tools and techniques in a situationally appropriate manner; avoiding the "one best way" mentality.

OB specialists embrace the contingency approach because it helps them realistically interrelate individuals, groups, and organizations. Moreover, the contingency approach sends a clear message to managers in today's global economy: Carefully read the situation and then apply lessons learned from published research studies.[11]

McGregor's Theory X and Theory Y

OUTDATED (THEORY X) ASSUMPTIONS ABOUT PEOPLE AT WORK	MODERN (THEORY Y) ASSUMPTIONS ABOUT PEOPLE AT WORK
1. Most people dislike work; they avoid it when they can.	1. Work is a natural activity, like play or rest.
2. Most people must be coerced and threatened with punishment before they will work. People require close direction when they are working.	2. People are capable of self-direction and self-control if they are committed to objectives.
3. Most people actually prefer to be directed. They tend to avoid responsibility and exhibit little ambition. They are interested only in security.	3. People generally become committed to organizational objectives if they are rewarded for doing so.
	4. The typical employee can learn to accept and seek responsibility.
	5. The typical member of the general population has imagination, ingenuity, and creativity.

▲ TABLE 1.2

SOURCE: Adapted from D. McGregor, *The Human Side of Enterprise* (New York: McGraw-Hill, 1960), Ch 4.

We can see how complex organizational behaviour can be and why it should be studied with great depth and scope.

LO 5 Contemporary Issues in OB

The field of OB is a dynamic work in progress, not static and in final form. As such, OB is being redirected and reshaped by various forces, both inside and outside the discipline. In this section, we explore four contemporary issues affecting OB:

- Workplace diversity
- The ethics challenge
- The Internet and e-business revolution
- Globalization

WORKPLACE DIVERSITY

How well do you appreciate and value diversity? Before we begin this section, you are encouraged to complete the Self-Assessment Exercise to better understand the concepts we're about to discuss. ***Diversity management*** is one of the most important social issues facing Canadian organizations today, as policies, activities, and organizational changes are developed and aimed at managing individual differences to enable all people to perform to their maximum potential. Statistics from the 2001 Census of Population predict that by 2017, the proportion of immigrants in Canada could equal that observed in the early 20th century; that would translate into possibly one Canadian in five being a visible minority individual. Now you can see why diversity management is of such interest to OB experts. We'll reference this Statistics Canada data again when we talk about globalization (Chapter 14).

Diversity represents the multitude of individual differences and similarities that exist among people.[12] Many different dimensions or components of diversity make all of us unique. Figure 1.2 shows the diversity wheel and its four layers. Personality is at the centre of the diversity wheel because it represents a stable set of characteristics that are responsible for a person's individual identity. The dimensions of personality are discussed further in Chapter 3.

The next layer of diversity consists of a set of internal dimensions such as age, race, and gender that are referred to as the primary dimensions of diversity.[13] These dimensions, for the most part, are not within our control, but strongly influence our attitudes, expectations, and assumptions about others, which in turn influence our behaviour.

Diversity

The host of individual differences that make people different from and similar to each other.

Diversity management

Policies, activities, and organizational changes aimed at managing individual differences to enable all people to perform up to their maximum potential.

▶ **FIGURE 1.2** The Four Layers of Diversity

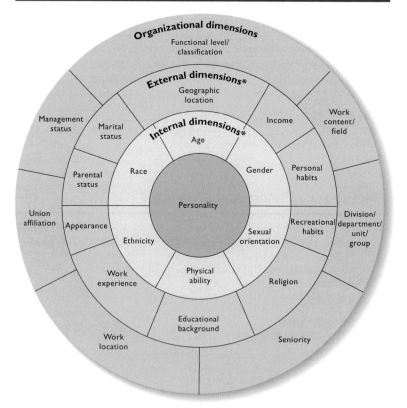

*Internal Dimensions and External Dimensions are adapted from Loden and Rosener, *Workforce America!* (Homewood, IL: Business One Irwin, 1991).

SOURCE: L. Gardenswartz and A. Rowe, *Diverse Teams at Work: Capitalizing on the Power of Diversity* (New York: McGraw-Hill, 1994), p 33. Copyright 1994. Reproduced with permission of The McGraw-Hill Companies.

Appreciating and Valuing Diversity

Here's a quick self-assessment to get you to think about diversity issues and to evaluate the behaviours you exhibit that reflect your level of appreciation of those who are different than you are.

		NEVER	SOMETIMES	REGULARLY
1.	Do you make a conscious effort not to think stereotypically (stereotyping example: that person is blonde, therefore she must be dumb)?	1	3	5
2.	Do you listen with interest to the ideas of people who don't think like you do?	1	3	5
3.	Do you respect other people's opinions, even when you disagree?	1	3	5
4.	Do you spend time with individuals who are different from you with regard to age, race, gender, ability, economic status, education, etc.?	1	3	5
5.	Do you believe your way is not the only way?	1	3	5
6.	Do you adapt well to change and new situations?	1	3	5
7.	Do you enjoy travelling, seeing new places, eating different foods, and experiencing other cultures?	1	3	5
8.	Do you try not to offend or hurt others?	1	3	5
9.	Do you allow extra time to communicate with someone whose first language is not yours?	1	3	5
10.	Do you consider the effect of cultural differences on the messages you send and adjust them accordingly?	1	3	5

Feedback

50/50

Your score of 50 out of a possible 50 point total indicates you understand the importance of valuing diversity and exhibit some behaviours that support your appreciation of diversity.

30/50

Your score of 30 out of a possible 50 point total indicates you have a basic understanding of the importance of valuing diversity and exhibit some behaviours that support that understanding.

10/50

Your score of 10 out of a possible 50 point total indicates you appear to lack an understanding of valuing diversity and exhibit few, if any, behaviours of an individual who appreciates and values diversity.

Please refer to the OLC (www.mcgrawhill.ca/olc/kreitner) for more information regarding the five types of behaviour associated with appreciating and valuing diversity.

The next layer of diversity is composed of external, or secondary, dimensions such as religion and marital status. They represent individual differences that we have a greater ability to influence or control. These dimensions also exert a significant influence on our perceptions, behaviour, and attitudes. The final layer of diversity includes organizational dimensions such as job title, union affiliation, and seniority. The Royal Bank of Canada encourages this aspect of diversity by encouraging staff mobility within the bank. Every year, 25 percent of employees assume new work roles.[14]

One of the most well-known problems faced by women and visible minorities in the workplace is the *glass ceiling*. The glass ceiling represents an invisible barrier that blocks certain workers, primarily qualified women and visible minorities, from advancing into top management positions. It can be particularly de-motivating because employees can look up and see coveted top management positions through the transparent ceiling, but are unable to obtain them. One study found that the barrier is much greater for minorities, and called it a "concrete ceiling."[15]

Diversity management involves activities aimed at managing individual differences to enable people to perform up to their maximum potential, including but not limited to those required for employment equity (see Law and Ethics feature box). It focuses on changing an organization's culture, policies, and procedures such that employees can perform at their highest level of productivity. To attract and retain the best workers,

Glass ceiling

Invisible barrier blocking qualified women and minorities from top management positions.

Ann Walker (front left) and Sheena Yaseen (front right) with colleagues at Scarborough Hospital, a large urban health care centre where new nurses must attend a two-hour diversity workshop.

companies need to adopt policies and programs that meet the needs of a diverse group of workers. Programs such as daycare, eldercare, flexible work schedules, less rigid relocation policies, and mentoring programs are likely to assist workers from all backgrounds to perform their job duties at an optimal level.

A landmark study of the diversity practices used by 16 organizations that successfully manage diversity uncovered 52 different practices, 20 of which were used by the majority of the companies sampled. The practices were classified into three main types: accountability, developmental, and recruitment.[16] Table 1.3 shows the top practices associated with each type. We discuss them in relative order of importance.

Accountability Practices Accountability practices relate to managers' responsibility to treat diverse employees fairly. Table 1.3 reveals that companies predominantly

LAW AND ETHICS *at Work*

EMPLOYMENT EQUITY ACT IN CANADA

In Canada, legislation covering federal workers and those in some provinces requires employers to actively pursue employment equity. Employment equity involves working to increase the number of employees from groups that have historically been underrepresented in an organization's workforce. In particular, the legislation requires that steps be taken to increase the representation of qualified women,

visible minorities, Aboriginal people, and persons with disabilities at all levels of an organization. The Canadian Human Rights Commission is responsible for ensuring compliance with the Act. To this end, the Commission conducts audits to determine whether employers meet the statutory requirements of the Act.

SOURCE: The Government of Canada Employment Equity Act: http://www.chrc-ccdp.ca/employment_equity/default-en.asp.

Common Diversity Practices

TABLE 1.3

ACCOUNTABILITY PRACTICES	DEVELOPMENT PRACTICES	RECRUITMENT PRACTICES
1. Top management's personal intervention	1. Diversity training programs	1. Targeted recruitment of non-managers
2. Internal advocacy groups	2. Networks and support groups	2. Key outside hires
3. Emphasis on employment equity statistics, profiles	3. Development programs for all high-potential managers	3. Extensive public exposure to diversity
4. Inclusion of diversity in performance evaluation goals, ratings	4. Informal networking activities	4. Corporate image as liberal, progressive, or benevolent
5. Inclusion of diversity in promotion decisions, criteria	5. Job rotation	5. Partnerships with educational institutions
6. Inclusion of diversity in management succession planning	6. Formal mentoring program	6. Recruitment incentives such as cash supplements
7. Work and family policies	7. Informal mentoring program	7. Internships
8. Policies against racism, sexism	8. Entry development programs for all high-potential new hires	8. Publications or PR products that highlight diversity
9. Internal audit or attitude survey	9. Internal training (such as personal safety or language)	9. Targeted recruitment of managers
10. Active employment equity committee, office	10. Recognition events, awards	10. Partnership with non-traditional groups

SOURCE: Abstracted from Tables A.10, A.11, and A.12 in A.M. Morrison, *The New Leaders: Guidelines on Leadership Diversity in America* (San Francisco: Jossey-Bass, 1992). Reprinted with permission of John Wiley & Sons, Inc.

accomplish this objective by creating administrative procedures aimed at integrating diverse employees into the management ranks (practices numbered 3, 4, 5, 6, 8, 9, and 10). In contrast, work and family policies (practice 7) focus on creating an environment that fosters employee commitment and productivity. Moreover, organizations are increasingly attempting to build an accountability component into their diversity programs to motivate managers to effectively manage diversity.

Developmental Practices The use of developmental practices to manage diversity is relatively new compared with the historical use of accountability and recruitment practices. Developmental practices focus on preparing diverse employees for greater responsibility and advancement. These activities are needed because most non-traditional employees have not been exposed to the types of activities and job assignments that develop effective leadership and social networks.[17] Table 1.3 indicates that diversity training programs, networks and support groups, and mentoring programs are among the most frequently used developmental practices.

Recruitment Practices Recruitment practices focus on attracting diverse job applicants at all levels who are willing to accept challenging work assignments. This focus is critical because people learn the leadership skills needed for advancement by successfully accomplishing increasingly responsible work assignments. As shown in Table 1.3, targeted recruitment of non-managers (practice 1) and managers (practice 9) are commonly used to identify and recruit workers in groups that are often underrepresented in the workforce. This is particularly relevant to the Canadian medical community, where recruitment of hospital staff outside of Canada is becoming a reality (see Focus on Diversity feature box). For example, the Clinician Assessment for Practice Program (CAPP) affiliated with the College of Physicians and Surgeons of Nova Scotia has established a two-day assessment session for foreign-trained physicians who believe they are ready to enter family practice without extra training in Canada and who are legally permitted to work in Nova Scotia, Canada.

In summary, effective workforce diversity management requires a number of OB skills, including managing change (Chapter 13), understanding cultural differences when communicating (Chapter 7), avoiding misunderstandings that lead to conflict (Chapter 8), managing the challenges around political issues (Chapter 8), and most of all, exhibiting strong leadership skills (Chapter 10). Understanding diversity is an underlying theme that runs throughout every chapter of this text. It will resurface again when we discuss globalization (Chapter 14).

THE CHALLENGES AROUND DIVERSITY

In 2008, five million Canadians, approximately 15 percent of the population, did not have a family doctor. The Fraser Institute predicts that by 2015, the number of doctors per capita in Canada will decline even more. Why the shortage? Several reasons were cited in the Institute report: cutbacks, natural attrition, and the lure of higher salaries to other countries. However, another radical effect is having a profound impact on supply and demand: female doctors who are leaving medicine altogether. Fifty-two percent of doctors under age 35 are now women. And the majority of students at nearly all of Canada's 17 medical schools are female. Why is this problem? Because, according to Dr. Brian Day, president of the Canadian Medical Association (CMA), for various reasons female doctors will not work the same hours nor have the same lifespan of contributions to the medical system as male doctors. To avoid burnout, they choose to leave their profession early.

Assuming medical schools maintain their current enrolment targets, there is only one logical solution according to the Fraser Institute: allow more foreign-trained doctors to practise in Canada. Should such action occur, the Canadian medical community can expect a far greater level of diversity in the future.

SOURCE: "Canada's doctor shortage to worsen without changes: Fraser Report," CBC News website: www.cbc.ca/health/story/2006/08/28/doctor-shortage.html; *Maclean's Magazine*, "Canada's Doctor Shortage Worsening," January 14, 2008, website: http://www.macleans.ca/science/health/article.jsp?content=20080102_122329_6200.

THE ETHICS CHALLENGE

Here are four good reasons to care about business ethics:

1. Bernard Ebbers, the Canadian ex-patriot and former CEO of WorldCom, is serving a 25 year sentence for fraud and conspiracy.

2. Conrad Black, the former Canadian media baron and CEO of Hollinger International Inc., is serving a 6½ year sentence for obstruction of justice and three counts of mail fraud.

3. Mike Lazaridis and James Balsillie, co-CEOs of Research In Motion (Blackberry), are paying $68-million back to the company in a settlement resulting from improprieties over stock-option backdating.

4. Garth Drabinsky, the former head of live theatre company Livent Inc. and his partner, were found guilty of financial irregularities and fraud against shareholders and are paying close to $40-million.

Thanks to the highly-publicized criminal acts of these and other executives, corporate officers in Canada, as well as those involved with public trading in the U.S., are now subject to high accountability standards and harsh penalties from the likes of the RCMP, the Ontario Securities Commission, the Securities and Exchange Commission, and Revenue Canada.

Everyone needs to join in the effort to stem this tide of unethical conduct. A variety of individual and organizational factors contribute to unethical behaviour. At an individual level, ethics is a unique combination of personality characteristics, values, and moral principles. At the organizational level, ethics is guided by ethical codes (or lack thereof), culture, size, structure, perceived pressure for results, and corporate strategy.[18] OB is an excellent vantage point for better understanding and improving workplace ethics. If OB can provide insights about managing human work behaviour, then it can teach us something about avoiding misbehaviour.

Ethics involves the study of moral issues and choices. It is concerned with right versus wrong, good versus bad, and the many shades of grey in supposedly black-and-white issues. Moral implications spring from virtually every decision, both on and off the job. All employees are challenged to have more imagination and the courage to do the right thing to make the world a better place.

Ethics

Study of moral issues and choices.

In the final analysis, ethics come down to individual motivation. Organizational climate, role models, structure, and rewards can all point employees in the right direction. But individuals must want to do the right thing. Bill George, the respected former CEO of Medtronic, the maker of life-saving devices such as heart pacemakers, gave us this call to action: "Each of us needs to determine ... where our ethical boundaries are and, if asked to violate (them), refuse ... If this means refusing a direct order, we must be prepared to resign."[19] Rising to this challenge requires strong personal values (more about values in Chapter 4) and the courage to adhere to them during adversity.[20]

Since ethics is such an important issue today, it is worth noting that feature boxes dedicated to law and ethics at work are provided throughout each chapter of this textbook. Further, we'll continue our discussion about ethics when discussing decision making in Chapter 8.

THE INTERNET AND E-BUSINESS REVOLUTION

Experts on the subject draw an important distinction between e-commerce (buying and selling goods and services over the Internet) and **e-business**, using the Internet to facilitate every aspect of running a business.[21] Says one industry observer: "Strip away the highfalutin talk, and at bottom, the Internet is a tool that dramatically lowers the cost of communication. That means it can radically alter any industry or activity that depends heavily on the flow of information."[22]

E-business

Running an entire business via the Internet.

Relevant information includes everything from customer needs and product design specifications, to prices, schedules, finances, employee performance data, and corporate strategy. Intel has taken this broad view of the Internet to heart. This builder of human capital is striving to become what it calls an e-corporation, one that relies primarily on the Internet to not only buy and sell things, but to facilitate all business functions, exchange knowledge among its employees, and build partnerships with outsiders as well. Intel is on the right track, according to this survey finding: "Firms that embraced the Internet averaged a 13.4 percent jump in productivity . . . compared with 4.9 percent for those that did not."[23]

E-business has significant implications for OB because it eventually will seep into every corner of life, both on and off the job. Thanks to the Internet, individuals are able to make quicker and better decisions because of speedy access to vital information (discussed in greater detail in Chapter 7). The Internet also allows individuals to seemingly defy the laws of physics by being in more than one place at the same time. For example, employees can be sitting in their home office while receiving emails on their Blackberry, while at the same time participating in an online net-meeting with colleagues from around the world. In short,

organizational life will never be the same because of email, e-learning,[24] e-management, e-leadership, virtual teams, and virtual organizations. You will learn more about email, virtual teams, and virtual organizations in later chapters.

GLOBALIZATION

Globalization refers to the major trend whereby firms are extending their operations to new markets abroad. When we speak of operations, we need to consider the inclusion of human capital as well, since talent can be exported or imported to meet the human resource needs of a firm (see International OB feature box). This poses many challenges. For example, it is very likely that the future Canadian labour force will be comprised of many different people from many different cultures other than Canada (we'll discuss this in greater detail in Chapters 13 and 14). The implication for the workplace is that foreign employees with Canadian workplace visas or newly-acquired Canadian citizenship papers may not be aware of Canadian national values, cultural traditions, or workplace behaviours. The chances for misunderstanding and conflict in the workplace are increased under such conditions.

Globalization

The extension of business operations to markets around the globe.

In the case of exporting Canadian human capital, expatriate managers struggle to find effective methods of managing employees in countries as diverse as Kazakhstan, Bangladesh, and the Philippines. Cross-cultural training is essential, and specific knowledge regarding motivation, decision making, communication, and leadership practices in the country of operation is required to assist in maintaining smooth day-to-day operations. Globalization means that organizations manage people all over the world—people speaking different languages, governed by different political systems, under widely differing social, ethical, and behavioural norms. This situation has created a major challenge for managers from Western countries who are deployed in other parts of the world. Managerial approaches based on OB knowledge from North America will not necessarily apply in other cultures. One general research finding of great importance in global management relates back to our earlier discussion about the contingency theory. There is rarely one best way to manage people; the specific situation must be considered.

> " . . . the Internet is a tool that dramatically lowers the cost of communication. That means it can radically alter any industry or activity that depends heavily on the flow of information."

IMPORTING TALENT FROM AROUND THE WORLD

Global campus placements have become fairly common in premier business and technology schools, but it's a fairly new trend in the field of law. "It's all a part of globalization," explains Alex Pease, a London-based partner at one of the world's largest corporate law firm, Allen & Overy. "We've been hiring lawyers with a Common Law background from Canada, New Zealand, and Australia for 20 years. Now we're recruiting from India." Take Rohan Menon, for example. This 23-year-old student recently flew from Hyderabad, India to London, England at his own expense to appear for a series of tests at a certain law firm, that ended with an interview with the firm's partners. Menon emerged with flying colours. Within a few months, Menon was earning an annual salary of 40,000 pounds as a trainee solicitor, to be increased to 63,000 pounds once his training period was complete in two years. "I was one of the first from my law school to apply abroad," he said. "In the current batch, more than half the students are joining foreign firms."

The workforce of the future will see opportunities far beyond the borders of the country where they were initially trained—either formally or on the job. It will take a flexible mindset to appreciate the vast array of opportunities that exist beyond the Canadian market, and to seize these experiences with great enthusiasm since they can broaden perspective and make for a far more interesting curriculum vitae.

SOURCES: Adapted from "Premier Law Schools To Export Talent Abroad," *The Economic Times*, February 22, 2008. A. Letourneau "So You Want To Be A Lawyer, Eh?" *Law School in Canada*, 2nd Edition, Writing on Stone Press Inc., October 2007.

Overall, today's managers need considerable knowledge of organizational behaviour to effectively manage the individuals and groups they are responsible for. Business realities such as the Internet, e-business, workforce diversity, ethical business practices, and globalization all have a major impact on the behaviour of employees, both individually and in groups, and even on the behaviour of organizations themselves.

A Road Map to Learning OB

OB is a broad and growing field, and we have a lot of ground to cover. To make the trip as instructive and efficient as possible, we will use a theory–research–practice strategy. For virtually all major topics in this text, we begin by presenting the underlying theoretical framework (often with graphical models showing key variables and how they relate) and defining key terms. Next, we explore the latest research findings for valuable insights. Finally, we round out the discussion with illustrative practical examples and, when applicable, how-to-do-it advice. The Brief Contents page located at the beginning of this textbook before the Table of Contents can be a useful reference; it allows you to see an overview of this OB textbook on one page.

Summary of Learning Objectives

1. **Define *organizational behaviour* and *management.*** Organizational behaviour (OB) is a field of study dedicated to better understanding and managing people at work, both individually and in groups. Management is the process of working with and through others to achieve organizational objectives efficiently and ethically.

2. **Explain why OB is studied and what benefits it can bring to the workplace.**

   OB can assist individual development toward positive membership behaviour and positive affective responses, and can encourage greater task performance. OB can assist groups by helping them communicate better and work in collaboration more effectively, and as a result, have greater productivity. OB can assist the entire organization by facilitating the adaptation to change process, ensuring that resources are used effectively and helping achieve corporate goals.

3. **Discuss the relevance of OB to the contemporary Canadian workplace by differentiating between managers from the past versus those of the future.**

   Managers from the past were primarily order-givers, the privileged elite with a primary role to control and manipulate. Their primary means for influencing others was to use their formal authority. In contrast, the contemporary manager is more participative in nature, inviting employees into the decision-making process. They are interpersonal and knowledgeable, believing people to be their greatest resource.

4. **Summarize the history of OB in a timeline incorporating three significant landmarks of theory development, including distinguishing characteristics of each.**

   - Scientific management (late 1800s–1915)—Involved systematically analyzing human behaviour at work to increase productivity and efficiency. Frederic Taylor's research played a significant role during this phase (e.g., time–motion studies).

   - The human relations movement (1930s)—Recognized the powerful effect that individual needs, supportive supervision, and group dynamics apparently have on job performance. This movement called attention to the human factor that exists in the workplace.

   - The contingency approach (1980–present)—Uses management tools and techniques in a situationally appropriate manner; avoids the "one best way" mentality.

5. **Infer and predict the challenges that at least four contemporary OB issues may present to both non-managerial employees and management in the future.**

   - Workplace diversity—Diversity is the host of individual differences that make people different from each other. Integration of women, visible minorities, Aboriginal people, and person's with disabilities into the Canadian workforce is something that organizations will continue to strive for in the future. Non-managerial employees will find themselves working alongside people of diversity who speak differently, who may not understand Canadian values or appreciate the corporate values, who may not identify with the behaviours of the corporate culture, and who may be unaware of Canadian employment laws. This could create more opportunity for misunderstanding and conflict in the workplace. Managers may find themselves having to educate non-managerial employees on how to get along in a more diverse work environment. Managers themselves may need training in the same area. Raising sensitivities toward diversity is going to be an ongoing challenge for all levels of the Canadian workforce.

   - Ethics in the workplace—With the media giving so much attention to prominent CEOs who have been found guilty of cons, schemes, tax evasion, or conspiracy to commit fraud, there is a clear need for greater awareness of business ethics. Individuals need to realize that ethics starts from within. When faced with pressure from certain people or groups, individuals need to have the character to say no and instead do the ethical thing. Organizations need to live up to their vision and values statements, have better corporate governance, and hire people who value ethical behaviour.

- E-business and the Internet—E-business involves using the Internet to more effectively and efficiently manage every aspect of a business. The Internet is reshaping how people communicate. The ability to be in two places at one time allows for multi-tasking and time savings. Individuals will need training and support; management will be expected to provide both. In the long run, organizations will be forced to provide the latest resources that support e-business and the Internet so that the organization will be able to compete.
- Globalization—Globalization is the extension of business operations to markets around the globe. The contingency approach to OB is particularly relevant here, as it suggests that it is better to use management tools and techniques in a situationally appropriate manner than to rely on one best way to manage. The importing and exporting of human capital into and out of the Canadian market will allow individuals to explore new worlds and strengthen their skills. In the future we will see more, not less, globalization. As the world's labour force becomes more intermingled, there will be a need for more customized people-solutions to fit the situation as values between people in different markets will vary.

Discussion Questions

1. How would you respond to a fellow student who says each of the following: *OB is just a bunch of common sense, why do I need to buy a book or attend a class?*; *OB means being nice to everyone on the job!*

2. Have you ever worked with a Theory X manager (see Table 1.2)? What sorts of experiences did you witness on the job when the manager disciplined others? Communicated with others? In the end, how did this manager make you feel?

3. How has technology changed the skills and role of the employee? The manager?

4. Describe some of the demands that a diverse workforce and increased global operations make on managers. What are some of the opportunities that these trends offer to an organization?

5. If the Canadian government enforced more criminal laws against CEOs and if Revenue Canada cracked down more on tax fraud, do you think we would see more ethical behaviour in business? Is making more rules and laws the answer?

Google Searches

1. **Google Search:** "the best workplaces in Canada 20__" and "Canada's best diversity employers" Review the top 25 organizations on both lists. Do any organizations appear on both lists? What does it take to make the best place to work list? What criteria are used to make the best diversity employer list?

2. **Google Search:** "Conference Board of Canada—employability skills 2000+" Review the three areas for skill development: Fundamental, Personal Management, and Teamwork. How can OB assist an individual to achieve these skills?

3. **Google Search:** "Canadians working overseas 20__" and "What you need to know to work overseas" Based on what you find, do you believe that Canada is the only country experiencing large exchanges of labour to and from other countries? Explain your answer based on the evidence from your search.

Experiential Exercise

TV Group Exercise

PURPOSE: This exercise will help familiarize you with organizational behaviour concepts. It demonstrates OB concepts within contemporary settings and familiar pop culture shows to help you to relate to and understand the concepts.

Approx. Timing: two 15-minute segments

ACTIVITY ASSIGNMENT:
- Work in small groups.
- Choose a popular television show from the list below.
- For homework, individually watch the agreed-upon show, take notes, and be prepared to share your observations with your other group members on the following:
  1. A brief plot summary and situation description
  2. A list of the main characters
  3. Examples of individual workplace behaviour, group behaviour, contemporary organizational situations and responses, and any other OB-related concepts discussed in Chapter 1
- Share your observations with one another, and create a master list of observations.
- Distribute the master list to the entire class.

POSSIBLE TV SHOWS				
Family Guy	House	The Office	CSI	24
Dirty Jobs	The Nature of Things	30 Rock	Corner Gas	Flashpoint

Discussion Questions

1. Given this exercise, how pervasive would you say organizations are in our society? Do you think this has always been the case?
2. Predict what role organizations will play in our future society.
3. Are the situations shown in the TV shows realistic, or are they distorted for entertainment purposes?
4. What possible danger can people run into if they assume that what they see on TV is in fact the way people behave in real life when working?

The **Presentation** Assistant

Here are possible topics and corresponding sources related to this chapter that can be further explored by student groups looking for ideas.

	WORKPLACE TRENDS— THE WORLD OF WORK FROM 1900–2025. WHAT WILL THE FUTURE WORKPLACE LOOK LIKE?	CANADA 2017—IF ⅕TH OF THE CANADIAN POPULATION IS A VISIBLE MINORITY, WHAT CHALLENGES ARE AHEAD?	GENERATIONAL DIFFERENCES: BOOMERS, GEN X AND DIGITALS. ARE THEY SO DIFFERENT?
YouTube Videos	• Dr. Patrick Dixon – Futurist • Emerging Market Business Trends • Malcom Gladwell – Tipping Point	• Molson "I Am Canadian" • Diversity In Canada – NPA 2008 • Ethnic Job Discrimination	• Managing Generation Y • Max Valiquette & Youthography
TV Shows or Movies to Preview	• The Corporation (the evolution of corporations) • Gung Ho (unionism) • Fast Times (managers and managing)	• *Inside Man* • *Due South* • *Family Man* • Archie Bunker and *All In The Family*	• *Bye Bye Birdie* • What's the Matter With Kids Today? • *Freaky Friday*
Internet Searches	• *The Tipping Point* (by Malcom Gladwell) • Canadian workplace trends	• Canadian Centre For Diversity • Statistics Canada Diversity Facts	• Future Search Richard Worzel – What's Next For Canada • *Grown Up Digital* (by D. Tapscott)
Ice Breaker Classroom Activity	• Ask students: How have (1) organizational structure, (2) employees, and (3) general purpose changed over the last 100 years? Have students divide a paper in half and label one side title "Traditional" and the other side title "Contemporary." Have students find two characteristics for each side. Share responses with the class.	• Ask students to predict what effects more diversity will have on the Canadian workplace. What sorts of changes and challenges will organizations face? Have students find two characteristics for each side that correspond to the three factors mentioned above Share responses with class.	• Have students write down their own personal experiences when they've witnessed generational differences in the workplace. What happened? Did it cause a problem between employees?

OB in Action Case Study

Managing the Winter Games

What takes years to plan and needs 1,200 full-time employees, 3,500 temporary employees, and 25,000 volunteers? The Vancouver 2010 Olympic and Paralympic Winter Games (VANOC). That's a huge increase from the initial 275 employee team lead by VANOC CEO John Furlong. To prepare for this massive national employment effort, VANOC's management team selected Workopolis as the exclusive Official Supplier of Online Recruitment for the Vancouver Games. Professionals are needed who are passionate about hosting the world in 2010, and "VANOC is building a huge enterprise in just over three years," commented Patrick Sullivan, President of Workopolis.

According to plans, as the organization grew during the expansion phase, the executive team identified the key divisions that would have to be managed:

- CEO's office
- Sport, Paralympic Games, Venue Management, and Technology and Systems
- Games, Services, Operations, and Ceremonies
- Venue Development
- Revenue, Marketing, and Communications
- Human Resources and Sustainability
- Finance and Legal

The Vancouver 2010 mission is to touch the soul of the nation and inspire the world by creating and delivering an extraordinary Olympic and Paralympic experience with lasting legacies. With the support of dozens of sponsors and partners, VANOC will look after the planning, organizing, financing, and stage portions of the XXI (21st) Olympic Winter Games and the X (10th) Paralympic Winter Games. The Winter Games are staged in Vancouver and Whistler from February 12–28, 2010. Vancouver and Whistler host the Paralympic Winter Games from March 12–21, 2010.

Discussion Questions

1. Refer to Table 1.1. How do you think managing the 21st Olympic Winter Games in Vancouver would differ from managing the very first Olympic Winter Games in 1924, held in the French Alps for 11 days?

2. How is VANOC's decision to use Workopolis for their recruitment efforts consistent with the contemporary issues mentioned in the chapter?

3. Do you believe that VANOC should be focused on recruiting as diverse a workforce as possible for the Winter Games in 2010? Explain.

SOURCE: VANOC website: www.vancouver2010.com; City of Vancouver Media Release, October 3, 2006, www.boardoftrade.com.

Ethical OB Dilemma

Behaviour and Integrity towards Policy

Situation #1: On the first day of his fourth-year physics class, University of Ottawa professor Denis Rancourt announced to his students that he was going to give every student a grade of A+. He explained that he did not think his job was to rank their skills for future employers, or train them to be "information transfer machines," regurgitating facts on demand. Within months of his classroom announcement, the senior physicist was suspended from teaching, locked out of his laboratory, and told that the administration was recommending he be terminated and banned from campus because of his violation of university policy. When he appeared on campus two months into the ban, Rancourt was led away in handcuffs by police and charged with trespassing. Rancourt continued to receive his pay while awaiting a final decision from the university.

Situation #2: First year Ryerson University student, Chris Avenir, was charged with 146 counts of academic misconduct for cheating and helping others cheat—a clear violation of university policy—after it was discovered that he helped run a Facebook study group. The 18-year-old, studying computer engineering in Toronto, decided to join and later became an administrator of an online chemistry study group called "Dungeons/Mastering Chemistry Solutions." Avenir stated that the group was essentially a site on Facebook where students could ask questions about homework assignments. In time, 146 students used the group to help each other with homework. The professor who taught the chemistry course found out about the group. At first he gave Avenir a B grade, but later changed the mark to F. During the disciplinary panel investigation, it was learned that the chemistry professor had stipulated that take-home assignments were to be done independently. However, Avenir invited students to "input solutions" to the questions so the answers could be shared on the Facebook site. In the end, Avenir was not expelled from the school and his passing grade in the course was reinstated, although he was given a zero on the 10 percent portion of the mark for homework. He was also expected to complete a workshop on academic integrity.

SOURCES: *The Globe and Mail*, "Professor Makes His Mark, But It Costs Him His Job," February 6, 2009, pA1. The *Toronto Star*, "Cheating Is Cheating," March 20, 2008. CBC News Online, March 6, 2008, http://www.cbc.ca/canada/toronto/story/2008/03/06/facebook-study.html.

Discussion Questions

1. If ethics is a study of right from wrong, and these individuals were disciplined for doing something wrong, can you identify what they did that was unethical?
2. Did the punishments fit the "crimes"? Would you recommend harsher treatment for such behaviours?
3. If these individuals are so quick to dismiss policy, how do you think they will behave in response to other dilemmas they may encounter in the workplace, especially when deciding right from wrong?
4. Would you trust these individuals if they worked for you?

Visit www.mcgrawhillconnect.ca to register.

McGraw-Hill Connect™—Available 24/7 with instant feedback so you can study when you want, how you want, and where you want. Take advantage of the Study Plan—an innovative tool that helps you customize your learning experience. You can diagnose your knowledge with pre- and post-tests, identify the areas where you need help, search the entire learning package for content specific to the topic you're studying, and add these resources to your personalized study plan. Visit **www.mcgrawhillconnect.ca** to register—take practice quizzes, search the e-book, and much more.

> "Do not wait; the time will never be 'just right.' Start where you stand, and work with whatever tools you may have at your command, and better tools will be found as you go along."
>
> *Napoleon Hill (Motivational Speaker)*

Social Perception

& Attribution Factors Influencing Individual Behaviour

The Questionable Truth Behind Our Perceptions

For years there has been a perception that the so-called "toxic" work environment in the Canadian public sector is on the rise as more employees become stressed, burned out, and depressed. But a six-year survey spanning 65 federal departments and agencies challenges this perception. Findings suggest that fewer employees are seeking counselling for work-related issues (about eight percent of the workforce in 2006-07, down from more than 10 percent six years earlier). The trend is down, not up. The report's findings were

Global Business and Economic Roundtable on **Addiction** and **Mental Health**

determined by calculating how often public servants used employee assistance programs or EAPs. In addition, researchers measured what kinds of complaints were raised during the first visit to a workplace counsellor. The statistics were drawn from a wide range of departments, employing several hundred thousand workers.

But not all experts agree. Bill Wilkerson, Chair of the Global Business and Economic Rountable on Addiction and Mental Health, states, "We are seeing absences, disability rates, and illness among public sector organizations that beg a national evaluation of what it is about these workplaces that creates such high levels of distress." As a former business executive, CEO, author, and political advisor, Wilkerson co-founded the federal non-profit corporation with the hope of reducing disabilities due to (health) disorders in the labour force. Called the "working wounded," Canadians are suffering from severe depression, bipolar disorder, and schizophrenia in the community and at work, not in the hospital. Every day, 500,000 Canadians are absent from work due to psychiatric problems, the most recent estimate pegging the annual economic burden of mental illness at a staggering $51 billion.

There you have it: two perspectives on the same topic. Which do you agree with—an internal federal study based on EAP statistics, or statistics from an independent mental health organization? Whatever your response to this question, your opinion is based on your perception that comes from both internal factors and external influencers, which will guide your behaviour. We'll be studying the topic of social perception in this chapter.

> "We are seeing absences, disability rates, and illness among public sector organizations that beg a national evaluation of what it is about these workplaces that creates such high levels of distress."

SOURCES: D. Beeby, "Fewer Federal Workers Seek Counselling," *London Free Press*, July 7, 2008; A. Picard, "The Working Wounded," *The Globe and Mail*, June 23, 2008; The Global Business and Economic Roundtable on Addiction and Mental Health website: www.mentalhealthroundtable.ca.

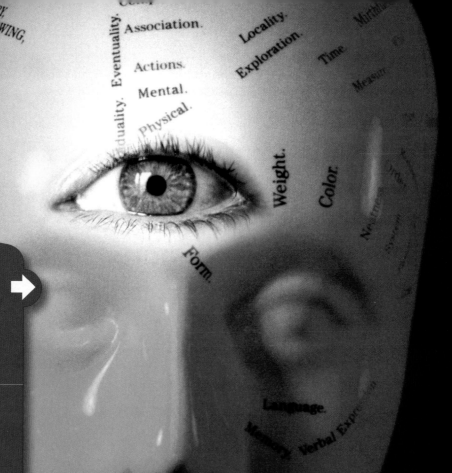

LEARNING OBJECTIVES →

After reading this chapter, you should be able to:

LO 1 **Define** *social perception* and *causal attributions*.

LO 2 **Explain** *perception* in terms of the four-stage social cognition processing sequence.

LO 3 **Illustrate** six managerial implications of social perceptions.

LO 4 **Examine** the managerial challenges and recommendations of sex-role, age, racial/ethnic, and disability stereotypes.

LO 5 **Compare and contrast** *fundamental attribution bias* and *self-serving bias*.

Assessing Your Perception Taking

If you read Harper Lee's novel, *To Kill a Mockingbird*, you may remember the character of Atticus Finch. He is a prominent attorney in Maycomb, Alabama, and an Alabama state legislator. A widower, Atticus devotes himself to his children and stands as one of literature's strongest and most positive father figures. In the 1962 film version, Gregory Peck won his only Best Actor Oscar playing the role of Atticus, and the film itself was nominated for eight Academy Awards, including Best Picture.

If you've read the book or seen the movie, you will recall the story is narrated by the adult version of one of the main characters of the story—six-year-old Jean Louise "Scout" Finch, the younger of Atticus' two children. Through Scout's telling of her story, she reveals her father's strong moral character in how he teaches his children and his community to stand up against prejudice and ignorance as he defends a black man, Tom Robinson, wrongfully accusing of raping a white woman.

One of the most famous lines from this classic work—and one that gives the reader great insight into explaining why Atticus lives his life the way he does—is taken from a scene where Atticus is having a heart-to-heart talk with his daughter, Scout, where he tells her: "If you can learn a simple trick, Scout, you'll get along a lot better with all kinds of folks. You never really understand a person until you consider things from his point of view—until you climb into his skin and walk around in it."

That's what this assessment will help you find out: Do you have the skill to consider things from others' points of view, to climb into their skin and walk around in it?

Indicate the extent to which you agree or disagree with each statement. Perspective taking skills play a big part in your ability to lead others, to get along with others, to communicate effectively, and to have satisfying interpersonal relationships in both your personal and professional lives. For how to keep score, see question #1.

1 Before criticizing somebody, I try to imagine how I would feel if I were in his/her place.
- ❏ Does not describe me at all (*score 1 point*)
- ❏ Does not describe me well (*score 2 points*)
- ❏ Describes me somewhat (*score 3 points*)
- ❏ Describes me well (*score 4 points*)
- ❏ Describes me very well (*score 5 points*)

2 If I'm sure I'm right about something, I don't waste much time listening to other people's arguments.
- ❏ Does not describe me at all
- ❏ Does not describe me well
- ❏ Describes me somewhat
- ❏ Describes me well
- ❏ Describes me very well

3 I sometimes try to understand my friends better by imagining how things look from their perspective.
- ❏ Does not describe me at all
- ❏ Does not describe me well
- ❏ Describes me somewhat
- ❏ Describes me well
- ❏ Describes me very well

4 I believe that there are two sides to every question and try to look at them both.
- ❏ Does not describe me at all
- ❏ Does not describe me well
- ❏ Describes me somewhat
- ❏ Describes me well
- ❏ Describes me very well

5 I sometimes find it difficult to see things from the other person's point of view.
- ❏ Does not describe me at all
- ❏ Does not describe me well
- ❏ Describes me somewhat
- ❏ Describes me well
- ❏ Describes me very well

6 I try to look at everybody's side of a disagreement before I make a decision.
- ❏ Does not describe me at all
- ❏ Does not describe me well
- ❏ Describes me somewhat
- ❏ Describes me well
- ❏ Describes me very well

7 When I'm upset at someone, I usually try to "put myself in his/her shoes" for a while.
- ❏ Does not describe me at all
- ❏ Does not describe me well
- ❏ Describes me somewhat
- ❏ Describes me well
- ❏ Describes me very well

Scoring Key

Sense of meaningfulness
(use score for #1–2) _____

Sense of choice (use score for #3–4) _____

Sense of competence
(use score for #5–6) _____

Sense of progress (use score for #7–8) _____

Overall score (add all items) _____

Arbitrary Norms

The range of possible scores is from 7 to 35 (low perspective taking: 7-15; moderate perspective taking: 16-25; high perspective taking: 26-35). The average score in recent studies across Canadian groups of people is approximately 20. Also keep in mind that women tend to score about 1.5 points higher than men on this perspective-taking scale.

SOURCES: M.H. Davis, "A multidimensional approach to individual differences in empathy," J*SAS Catalog of Selected Documents in Psychology, 10* (1980), 85.

H. Lee, *To Kill a Mockingbird*, (United States: Harper Collins, 1960).

By completing the self-assessment on perspective taking, you have begun the process of uncovering the importance of considering things from different points of view and the role such consideration plays in understanding individual behaviour. So how important is the perception process? It can be the source of communication distortion and conflict between people from different cultures. Our perceptions and feelings are influenced by information we receive from newspapers, magazines, television, Internet, Facebook, radio, family, and friends. We all use information stored in our memories to interpret the world around us, and our interpretations, in turn, influence how we respond and interact with others.

What Is Perception?

As human beings, we constantly strive to make sense of our surroundings. The resulting knowledge influences our behaviour and helps us navigate our way through life. Think of the perceptual process that occurs when you meet someone for the first time. Your attention is drawn to the individual's physical appearance, mannerisms, actions, and reactions to what you say and do. You ultimately arrive at conclusions based on your perceptions of this social interaction. The brown-haired, green-eyed individual turns out to be friendly and fond of outdoor activities. You further conclude that you like this person and then ask him or her to go to a concert, calling the person by the name you stored in memory.

The reciprocal process of perception, interpretation, and behavioural response also applies at work. Consider the experience of Lisa Bromiley-Meier after losing her job at Enron. Just a short recap: In 2001, Enron Corporation was one of the largest energy companies in the world; however, due to unethical business practices orchestrated by its leader, Kenneth Lay, the firm filed for bankruptcy in December, 2001. (Note: this case proves significant because Enron was the largest corporate failure in business history at the time.) Bromiley-Meier told a reporter from *Business Week* that "she endured six months of potential employers asking her the same question: 'So, were you corrupt or were you stupid?'"[1] Interviewers apparently assumed or perceived that Lisa was either a crook or stupid because she worked for Enron. They could not have been more wrong. Today Lisa is the COO of Flotek Industries, Inc., a maker of chemicals and drilling tools for the oil industry.

Social cognition

How people perceive one another.

The perception process influences much more than the impressions people make about each other. For example, companies use their knowledge about perceptions when marketing their products, and political candidates use it to get elected.[2]

Moreover, inaccurate perceptions and stereotypes can influence whether or not you get hired, promoted, or fired. Perceptions also impact the grade you receive when giving an oral presentation in class, and whether or not a person wants to date or marry you. The point we are trying to make is that the perception process influences a host of managerial activities, organizational processes, and quality-of-life issues. In this chapter, you will gain a fundamental understanding of how perception works and how you can use it to enhance your future personal and professional success.

Let us begin our exploration of the perceptual process and its associated outcomes. In this chapter we focus on (1) an information-processing model of perception, (2) stereotypes, and (3) how causal attributions are used to interpret behaviour.

AN INFORMATION-PROCESSING MODEL OF PERCEPTION

LO 1

Perception is a cognitive process that enables us to interpret and understand our surroundings. One of this process's major functions is recognition of objects. For example, both people and animals recognize familiar objects in their environments. You would recognize a picture of your best friend; dogs and cats can recognize their food dishes or a favourite toy. Reading involves recognition of visual patterns representing letters in the alphabet. People must recognize objects to meaningfully interact with their environment.[3] But since OB's principal focus is on people, the following discussion emphasizes social perception rather than object perception.

Perception

The process of interpreting one's environment.

The study of how people perceive one another has been labelled **social cognition** and *social information processing*. In contrast to the perception of objects, social cognition is the study of how people make sense of other people and themselves. It focuses on how ordinary people think about people. Research on social cognition also goes beyond naive psychology. The study of social cognition entails a fine-grained analysis of how people think about themselves and others, and it leans heavily on the theory and methods of cognitive psychology.[4]

Let us now examine the fundamental processes underlying perception.

LO 2 FOUR-STAGE SEQUENCE

Perception involves a four-stage information-processing sequence, as illustrated in Figure 2.1. The first three stages in this model describe how specific social information is observed and stored in memory. The fourth stage involves turning mental representations into real-world judgments and decisions.

Stage 1: Selective Attention/Comprehension People are constantly bombarded by physical and social stimuli in the environment. Since they do not have the mental capacity to fully comprehend all this information, they selectively perceive subsets of environmental stimuli. This is where attention plays a role. **Attention** is the process of becoming consciously aware of something or someone. Attention can be focused on information either from the environment or from memory. Regarding the latter situation, if you sometimes find yourself thinking about totally unrelated events or people while reading a textbook, your memory is the focus of your attention.

Attention
Being consciously aware of something or someone.

Salient Stimuli Research has shown that people tend to pay attention to salient stimuli. Something is *salient* when it stands out from its context. For example, a 250-pound man would certainly be salient in a women's aerobics class, but not at a meeting of the Canadian Football League Players' Association. One's needs and goals often dictate which stimuli are salient. For a driver whose gas gauge is on empty, a Petro-Canada sign is more salient than a McDonald's or Tim Horton's sign. The reverse would be true for a hungry driver with a full gas tank. Moreover, research shows that people have a tendency to pay more attention to negative than positive information. This leads to a negativity bias.[5] This bias helps explain the gawking factor that slows traffic to a crawl following a car accident.

Stage 2: Encoding and Simplification Observed information is not stored in memory in its original form; encoding is required. Encoding means interpreting or translating raw information into mental representations. To accomplish this, perceivers assign pieces of information to cognitive categories. "By category we mean a number of objects that are considered equivalent. Categories are generally designated by names, e.g., dog, animal."[6] People, events, and objects are interpreted and evaluated by comparing their characteristics with information contained in schemata (or schema in singular form).

> If you are reading this textbook late at night after hours of intense homework, this photo might have caught your attention before anything else on the page. It's an example of salient stimuli, or something that stands out from its context. The context for this hamburger picture is the text on this page.

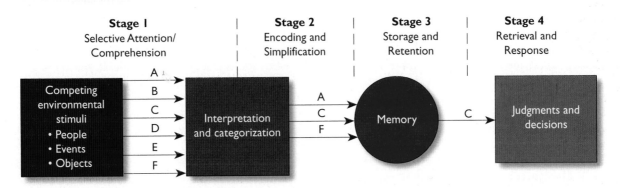

▶ FIGURE 2.1   Social Perception Model

Stage 1 Selective Attention/ Comprehension	**Stage 2** Encoding and Simplification	**Stage 3** Storage and Retention	**Stage 4** Retrieval and Response
Competing environmental stimuli · People · Events · Objects → A B C D E F →	Interpretation and categorization → A C F →	Memory → C →	Judgments and decisions

SOURCE: Adapted in part from B.J. Pannett and S. Withane, "Hofstede's Value Survey Module: To Embrace or Abandon?," *Advances in International Comparative Management*, vol 5, ed S.B. Prasad (Greenwich, CT: JAI Press, 1990), pp 69–89.

Schemata A **schema** represents a person's mental picture or summary of a particular event or type of stimulus. Cognitive-category labels are needed to make schemata meaningful. For example, picture your image of a sports car. Does it contain a smaller vehicle with two doors? Is it red? If you answered yes, you would tend to classify all small, two-door, fire-engine-red vehicles as sports cars because this type of car possesses characteristics that are consistent with your "sports car schema."

Schema

Mental picture of an event or object.

Encoding Outcomes We use the encoding process to interpret and evaluate our environment. Interestingly, this process can result in differing interpretations and evaluations of the same person or event. Varying interpretations of what we observe occur due to four key reasons.

First, people possess different information in the schemata used for interpretation. For instance, a recent meta-analysis of 62 studies revealed women and men had different opinions about what type of behaviours constituted sexual harassment. Women defined a broader range of behaviours as harassing.[7] Second, our moods and emotions influence our focus of attention and evaluations of others.[8] For example, you are likely to forget the full name of a new classmate that your friend just introduced you to if you are preoccupied with a $200 traffic ticket that a police officer served to you a few hours earlier. Third, people tend to apply recently-used cognitive categories during encoding. For example, you are more likely to interpret a neutral behaviour exhibited by a professor as positive if you were recently thinking about positive categories and events.[9]

Fourth, individual differences influence encoding. Pessimistic or depressed individuals, for instance, tend to interpret their surroundings more negatively than optimistic and happy people do. The point is that we should not be surprised when people interpret and evaluate the same situation or event differently. Researchers are currently trying to identify the host of factors that influence the encoding process.

Stage 3: Storage and Retention This phase involves storage of information in long-term memory. Long-term memory is like an apartment complex consisting of separate units connected to one another. Although different people live in each apartment, they sometimes interact. In addition, large apartment complexes have different wings (such as A, B, and C). Long-term memory similarly consists of separate but related categories. Like the individual apartments inhabited by unique residents, the connected categories contain different types of information. Information also passes among these categories. Finally, long-term memory is made up of three compartments (or wings) containing categories of information about events, semantic materials, and people.[10]

Event Memory This compartment is composed of categories containing information about both specific and general events. These memories describe appropriate sequences of events in well-known situations, such as going to a restaurant, going on a job interview, going to a food store, or going to a movie.

Semantic Memory Semantic memory refers to general knowledge about the world. In so doing, it functions as a mental dictionary of concepts. Each concept contains a definition (e.g., a good leader) and associated traits (outgoing), emotional states (happy), physical characteristics (tall), and behaviours (works hard). Just as there are schemata for general events, concepts in semantic memory are stored as schemata. It's worth mentioning here that there can be

Is this consistent with your "sports car schema?" If it is, you'll likely classify all small, two-door, red vehicles as sports cars. Can you think of another example of a common schema in today's culture?

cultural differences in the type of information stored in semantic memory. For example, if you were to ask Chinese factory workers to describe their mental picture in terms of gender for the word *boss*, they would probably respond with *male* because in China, it is far more common to have a male as a direct supervisor or a boss than a female.

Person Memory Categories within this compartment contain information about a single individual (a peer) or groups of people (the support staff). These memories help a person evaluate and compare characteristics of a new person or object to the information stored in memory.

Stage 4: Retrieval and Response People retrieve information from memory when they make judgments and decisions. These judgments and decisions are based on either (i) the process of drawing on, interpreting, and integrating categorical information stored in long-term memory, or (ii) retrieving a summary judgment that was already made. For instance, consider how you would feel after your closest colleague at work tells you in confidence that eight years ago your new boss was accused (but not found guilty) of workplace bullying. How long would you hold on to that information in your head? Do you think that you would always have that knowledge sitting there in the background every time you had to deal with your new boss, just waiting to see any evidence of similar behaviour? You trust your friend, and even though there is no evidence of what happened eight years ago in a different office, you pay attention to a judgment that was made years ago.

LO 3 MANAGERIAL IMPLICATIONS

Social cognition is the process through which we all observe, interpret, and prepare our responses to people and events. A wide variety of managerial activities, organizational processes, and quality-of-life issues are thus affected by perception. Let's consider the effects of perception on hiring, performance appraisal, leadership, communication, interpersonal influence, workplace aggression, bullying and antisocial behaviour, as well as overall physical and psychological well-being.

Hiring Interviewers make hiring decisions based on their impression of how an applicant fits the perceived requirements of a job. Unfortunately, many of these decisions are made on the basis of implicit cognition. *Implicit cognition* represents any thoughts or beliefs that are automatically activated from memory without our conscious awareness. The existence of implicit cognition leads people to make biased decisions without an understanding that it is occurring.[11] This tendency has been used as an explanation for alleged discriminatory behaviour at FedEx, Johnson & Johnson, Cargill, and Walmart. (In the case involving Walmart, gender bias claims were made on behalf of more than one million women—certainly a problem worth addressing.) Experts recommend two solutions for reducing this problem.[12]

First, train managers to understand and reduce this type of hidden bias. For example, one study demonstrated that training improved interviewers' ability to obtain high-quality, job-related information and to stay focused on the interview task. Trained interviewers

Implicit cognition

Any thought or belief that is automatically activated without conscious awareness.

provided more balanced judgments about applicants than did non-trained interviewers.[13] Second, you can reduce bias by using structured as opposed to unstructured interviews, and by relying on evaluations from multiple interviewers rather than just one or two people.

Performance Appraisal Faulty perceptions about what constitutes good versus poor performance can lead to inaccurate performance appraisals, which erode work motivation, commitment, and loyalty. Therefore, it is important for managers to accurately identify the employee behaviours and results indicative of good performance at the beginning of a performance review cycle. These characteristics can then serve as the benchmarks for evaluating employee performance. Managers are advised to use more objectively-based measures of performance as much as possible because subjective indicators are prone to bias and inaccuracy. In those cases where the job does not possess objective measures of performance, however, managers have to use subjective evaluations. For example, if your supervisors wanted to assess the strength of your work ethic, they could look at your attendance pattern (i.e., late arrival times in the morning and early leave requests). These are quantifiable facts and therefore considered to be objective in nature. But what if your organization does not measure qualitative factors like cooperative nature, pleasant disposition, eagerness to assist others, and positive attitude? These factors are much harder to measure. If there is no mechanism in place to effectively monitor or assess these behaviours, then it can be left to personal interpretation by the supervisor and is therefore subjective in nature. Such assessment can be filled with bias and political intent (office politics will be discussed in greater detail in Chapter 9). Because memory for specific instances of employee performance deteriorates over time, anyone in a position of evaluating another individual (a work team or a supervisor) needs a mechanism for accurately recalling employee behaviour (work teams where employees evaluate each other will be discussed in Chapter 6). Research reveals that individuals can be trained to more accurately rate performance.[14]

Leadership Research demonstrates that employees' evaluations of leader effectiveness are influenced strongly by their schemata of good and poor leaders. Leaders will have a difficult time influencing employees when they exhibit behaviours contained in employees' schemata of poor leaders. A team of researchers investigated the behaviours contained in our schemata of good and poor leaders. Good leaders were perceived as exhibiting the following behaviours: (1) assigning specific tasks to group members; (2) telling others that they had done well; (3) setting specific goals for the group; (4) letting other group members make decisions; (5) trying to get the group to work as a team; and (6) maintaining definite standards of performance. In contrast, poor leaders were perceived to exhibit these behaviours: (1) telling others that they had performed poorly; (2) insisting on having their own way; (3) doing things without explaining themselves; (4) expressing worry over the group members' suggestions; (5) frequently changing plans; and (6) letting the details of the task become overwhelming.[15]

Communication and Interpersonal Influence Managers must remember that social perception is a screening process that can distort communication, both coming and going. Because people interpret oral and written communications by using schemata developed through past experiences, your ability to influence others is affected by information contained in others' schemata regarding age, gender, ethnicity, appearance, speech, mannerisms, personality, and other personal characteristics. It is important to keep this in mind when trying to influence others or when trying to sell your ideas. The Skills & Best Practices feature box identifies four behavioural tendencies that are negatively perceived by others when trying to pitch or sell them an idea. Avoiding these tendencies can help you to achieve greater acceptance of your ideas or opinions.

Workplace Aggression, Bullying, and Antisocial Behaviour Research revealed that aggressive, bullying, and antisocial behaviour at work were based on employees' perceptions of the work environment. Employees behaved aggressively toward co-workers and displayed antisocial behaviours such as swearing, making fun of someone, and taking home organizational property without consent when they believed that they were treated unfairly.[16] It is very important for managers to treat employees fairly, remembering that perceptions of fairness are in the eye of the beholder.

Physical and Psychological Well-Being The negativity bias can lead to both physical and psychological problems. Specifically, research shows that perceptions of fear, harm, and anxiety are associated with the onset of illnesses such as asthma and depression.[17] Attempt to avoid the tendency of giving negative thoughts too much attention.

Stereotypes and other Perceptual Errors

LO 4

While it is often true that beauty is in the eye of the beholder, perception does result in some predictable outcomes. Organizations with employees who are aware of the perception process and its outcomes enjoy a competitive edge. The Walt Disney Company, for instance, takes full advantage of perceptual tendencies

Skills & Best Practices

Avoid Four Behavioural Tendencies That Are Negatively Perceived When Trying To Influence Others.

1 Being a pushover. This tendency involves giving up on an idea rather than defending it. Be prepared to defend your ideas with facts, figures, and passion. Do not simply drop an idea because someone questions it.

2 Being a robot. This tendency involves a communication style and approach that is too rigid. When answering questions about your ideas, do not use canned answers. Rather, first try to understand the other individual's point of

view or source of confusion/resistance. You then can provide an answer that specifically responds to the person's concerns.

3 Being a used-car sales associate. This tendency involves being pushy, close-minded, and argumentative. Remember, you can catch more bees with honey than with vinegar.

4 Being a charity case. This tendency is characterized by desperation and pleading.

SOURCE: Reprinted by permission of *Harvard Business Review*. This information was derived from K.D. Elsbach, "How to Pitch a Brilliant Idea," *Harvard Business Review*, September 2003, p 119. Copyright © 2003 by Harvard Business School Publishing Corporation; all rights reserved.

to influence customers' reactions to waiting in long lines at its theme parks:

- At Disney-MGM Studios in Orlando, visitors waiting to get into a Muppet attraction watch tapes of Kermit the Frog on TV monitors.

- At the Magic Kingdom, visitors to the Extra-Terrestrial Alien Encounter attraction are entertained by a talking robot before the show.

- At some rides, the company uses simple toys, like blocks, to help parents keep small children busy and happy during the wait.[18]

These examples illustrate how the focus of one's attention influences the perception of standing in long lines.

Likewise, managers can use knowledge of perceptual outcomes to help them interact more effectively with employees. For example, Table 2.1 describes five common perceptual errors that can occur in an educational setting. Since these perceptual errors often distort the evaluation of job applicants and of employee performance, managers need to guard against them. Can you think of common office examples where these same perceptual errors could apply?

We'll now examine one of the most important and potentially harmful perceptual outcomes associated with person perception: stereotypes. After exploring the process of stereotype formation and maintenance, we will discuss sex-role stereotypes, age stereotypes, race stereotypes, disability stereotypes, and the managerial challenge to avoid stereotypical biases.

STEREOTYPE FORMATION AND MAINTENANCE

Stereotype

Beliefs about the characteristics of a group.

"A *stereotype* is an individual's set of beliefs about the characteristics or attributes of a group."[19] Stereotypes are not always negative. For example, the belief that engineers are good at math is certainly part of a stereotype. Stereotypes may or may not be accurate. Engineers may in fact be better at math than the general population. In general, stereotypic characteristics are used to differentiate a particular group of people from other groups.[20]

It is important to remember that stereotypes are a fundamental component of the perception process and we use them to help process the large amount of information that bombards us daily. As such, it is not immoral or bad to possess stereotypes. That said, however, inappropriate use of stereotypes can: lead to

Commonly Found Perceptual Errors

PERCEPTUAL ERROR	DESCRIPTION	EXAMPLE
Halo	A rater forms an overall impression about an object and then uses that impression to bias ratings about the object.	Rating a professor high on the teaching dimensions of ability to motivate students, knowledge, and communication because he or she is punctual in getting to class.
Leniency	A personal characteristic that leads an individual to consistently evaluate other people or objects in an extremely positive fashion.	Rating a professor high on all dimensions of performance regardless of his or her actual performance. Hesitating to say negative things about others.
Central tendency	The tendency to avoid all extreme judgments and rate people and objects as average or neutral.	Rating a professor average on all dimensions of performance regardless of his or her actual performance.
Recency effects	The tendency to remember recent information. If the recent information is negative, the person or object is evaluated negatively.	Evaluating a professor negatively because lectures over the last three weeks were done poorly, although he or she has given good lectures for 12 to 15 weeks.
Contrast effects	The tendency to evaluate people or objects by comparing them with characteristics of recently observed people or objects.	Rating a good professor as average because you compared his or her performance with three of the best professors you have ever had in university, from whom you are currently taking courses.

▲ TABLE 2.1

poor decisions; create barriers for women, older individuals, people of colour, or people with disabilities; and undermine loyalty and job satisfaction. In other words, negative stereotyping can lead to workplace barriers through discrimination. When this happens, then personal prejudice occurs, meaning that a shortcut in judgment is made about someone without being fair. Can you see how negative stereotyping can lead to discrimination because of personal prejudices? When this happens in the workplace, opportunities are not equal to all who apply for jobs, and that is not only unethical, but also illegal (see Law and Ethics at Work feature box). It's important to recognize errors in perception and shortcuts to processing our perceptions as they can lead to dangerous practices within an organization— especially when they unconsciously evolve into formalized policies and procedures.

Stereotyping is a four-step process. It begins by categorizing people into groups according to various criteria, such as gender, age, race, and occupation. Next, we infer that all people within a particular category possess the same traits or characteristics (e.g., all women

> "Every individual . . . has the right to the protection and equal benefit of the law . . . without discrimination based on race, national or ethnic origin, colour, religion, sex, age, mental or physical disability."

are nurturing, older people have more job-related accidents, and all professors are absentminded). Then, we form expectations of others and interpret their behaviour according to our stereotypes. Finally, stereotypes are maintained by overestimating the frequency of stereotypic behaviours exhibited by others, incorrectly explaining expected and unexpected behaviours, and differentiating minority individuals from oneself.[21] It is hard to stop people from using stereotypes because these four steps are self-reinforcing. The good news, however, is that researchers have identified a few ways to break the chain of stereotyping.

Research shows that the use of stereotypes is influenced by the amount and type of information available to individuals and their motivation to accurately process information.[22] People are less apt to use stereotypes to judge others when they encounter salient information that is highly inconsistent with a stereotype. For instance, you are unlikely to assign stereotypic "professor" traits to a new professor you have this semester if she rides a Harley-Davidson, wears leather pants to class, and has a pierced nose.

LAW AND ETHICS at Work

CANADA'S BARRIER-REMOVAL LEGISLATION

When it comes to offering jobs or promotional opportunities to visible minorities, the Canadian Charter of Rights and Freedoms provides clear protection for all from discriminating business practices. But that wasn't always the case. When the Charter was first drafted in the early 1980s, persons with disabilities were not included among the protected classes of persons enumerated in section 15. As a result of an intense and effective lobbying effort by a number of groups, the government relented and added the category "mental and physical disability." Section 15 now reads:

> *Every individual is equal before and under the law and has the right to the protection and equal benefit of the law without*

discrimination and, in particular, without discrimination based on race, national or ethnic origin, colour, religion, sex, age, mental or physical disability.

Today, employees with disabilities as well as all visible minorities can find protection under the Charter or Canadian Human Rights Legislation. Do you think it was necessary to modify Section 15?

SOURCE: Adapted from the Council of Canadians with Disabilities, *Law Reform Analysis*, May 14, 1999, website: www.ccdonline.ca; Canadian Human Rights Commission website: http://www.chrc-ccdp.ca/legislation_policies/human_rights_act-en.asp; The Canadian Charter of Rights and Freedoms – The Canadian Encyclopedia website: http://www.thecanadianencyclopedia.com/index.cfm?PgNm=TCE&Params=A1ARTA0001270.

People also are less likely to rely on stereotypes when they are motivated. Let's consider, for example, a situation where you are looking for a job and you really need the money badly because of all of the school debt you've incurred. To your delight, an opening comes up at a company in your town that involves working alongside another individual. After a successful interview, where you claim to be a team player, they offer you the position. On the first day, you're introduced to your new colleague, a female Canadian Aboriginal. You've never worked with an Aboriginal individual before. This has you seriously concerned and cautious because of stereotype comments made by colleagues, friends, and/or family over the years. Rather than quit because of this, you decide to give the job a chance. After one week, you decide to stay at the job. Working alongside your new colleague turns out to be a non-issue because the motivation to earn money to pay off debts takes precedence over your possibly stereotypical behaviour.

We'll now turn our attention to four common forms of stereotypes: sex-role, age, racial and ethnic, as well as disability. It's important for students learning OB to become familiar with these different stereotypes so they can avoid them in their own behaviour, and also be aware in case they witness such behaviour in a future work environment.

Sex-Role Stereotypes

A *sex-role stereotype* is the belief that differing traits and abilities make men and women particularly well suited to different roles. A recent survey of 61,647 people—50 percent female and 50 percent male—sheds light on common sex-role stereotypes. Results revealed that women were labelled as moody, gossipy, emotional, and catty. A similar set of negative stereotypes was not uncovered when it came to perceptions about men. When asked who would be more likely to lead effectively, males were preferred by a two-to-one margin by both men and women.[23] Researchers suggest that this pattern of results is related to gender-based expectations or stereotypes that people have about men and women.[24] The key question, however, is whether or not these stereotypes influence the hiring, evaluation, and promotion of people at work.

A meta-analysis of 19 studies comprising 1,842 individuals found no significant relationships between applicant gender and hiring recommendations.[25] A second meta-analysis of 24 experimental studies revealed that men and women received similar performance ratings for the same level of task performance. Stated differently, there was no pro-male bias. These experimental results were further supported in a field study of female and male professors.[26] Unfortunately, results pertaining to promotion decisions

Sex-role stereotype

Beliefs about appropriate roles for men and women.

are not as promising. A field study of 682 employees in a multinational Fortune 500 company demonstrated that gender was significantly related to promotion potential ratings. Men received more favourable evaluations than women, in spite of controlling for age, education, organizational tenure, salary grade, and type of job.[27] Another study of 448 upper-level managers showed that gender bias influenced the performance ratings and promotional opportunities for women, particularly when women worked in non-traditional jobs. The researchers conducting this study concluded that sex-role stereotypes partially explained these findings.[28]

Age Stereotypes

Age stereotypes reinforce age discrimination because of their negative orientation. For example, long-standing age stereotypes depict older workers as less satisfied, not as involved with their work, less motivated, not as committed, less productive than younger co-workers, and more apt to be absent from work. Older employees are perceived as being more accident prone. As with sex-role stereotypes, these age stereotypes are based more on fiction than fact, as Dr. Michael DeBakey's story shows (see Focus On Diversity feature box).

OB researcher Susan Rhodes sought to determine whether age stereotypes were supported by data from 185 different studies. She discovered that as age increases, so does employees' job satisfaction, job involvement, internal work motivation, and organizational commitment. Moreover, older workers were not more accident prone.[30] Results are not as clear-cut regarding job performance. A meta-analysis of 96 studies representing 38,983 people and a cross-section of jobs revealed that age and job performance were unrelated.[31] Some OB researchers, however, believe that this finding does not reflect the true relationship between age and performance. They propose that the relationship between age and performance changes as people grow older.[32] This idea was tested on data obtained from 24,219 individuals. In support of this hypothesis, results revealed that age was positively related to performance for younger employees (25 to 30 years of age) and then plateaued: older employees were not less productive. Age and experience also better predicted performance for more complex jobs than other jobs, and job experience had a stronger relationship with performance than age.[33] Another study examined memory, reasoning, spatial relations, and dual tasking for 1,000 doctors, ages 25 to 92, and 600 other adults. The researchers concluded "that a large proportion of older individuals scored as well or better on aptitude tests as those in the prime of life. We call these intellectually vigorous individuals 'optimal agers.' "[34]

WOULD YOU LET A 96-YEAR-OLD DOCTOR PRACTISE MEDICINE ON YOU?

D r. Michael DeBakey was a world-renowned heart surgeon, innovator, medical educator, and international medical statesman. In 1939, he was one of the first physicians to find a relationship between smoking and cancer. In 1953, he performed the first successful carotid endarterectomy (artery bypass surgery). In the 1960s, DeBakey and his team of surgeons were among the first to record surgeries on film. To the amazement of his colleagues and patients, DeBakey continued to practise medicine at an age well after most others have retired. In 2004, he was interviewed by a reporter from *The Wall Street Journal* to determine his secrets of health; he was still working at the age of 96. Here is what the reporter wrote:

Entering the room, Dr. DeBakey looked only slightly older than he did in photographs taken decades ago ... Whatever subject I broached, his response reflected a quality that aging experts say is common among the long lived: optimism. Avian flu doesn't worry him: "We're lucky now to pick up those threats early," he says. But here is what Dr. DeBakey sees as the real secret to his longevity: work. He rises at five each morning to write in his study for two hours before driving to the hospital at 7:30 am, where he stays until 6 pm. He returns to his library after dinner for an additional two to three hours of reading or writing before going to bed after midnight. He sleeps only four to five hours a night, as he always has.[29]

Dr. DeBakey's work ethic supports the findings of OB researcher Susan Rhodes, who attempted to disprove the long-standing age stereotype depicting older workers as less able than their younger co-workers. What is your perspective toward aging employees?

SOURCES: Adapted from Dr. DeBakey website: www.debakeydepartmentofsurgery.org; Kreitner, R. & Kinicki, A., *Organizational Behaviour*, 8th Edition, p 194; www.wikipedia.org/wiki/Michael_E._DeBakey.

What about turnover and absenteeism? A meta-analysis containing 45 samples and a total of 21,656 individuals revealed that age and turnover were negatively related.[35] That is, older employees quit less often than younger employees quit. Similarly, another meta-analysis of 34 studies encompassing 7,772 workers indicated that age was inversely related to both voluntary (a day at the beach) and involuntary (sick day) absenteeism.[36] Contrary to stereotypes, older workers are ready and able to meet their job requirements. Moreover, results from the two meta-analyses suggest that managers should focus more attention on the turnover and absenteeism among younger workers than among older workers.

Racial and Ethnic Stereotypes There are many different racial and ethnic stereotypes. They are so common that well-known Canadian comic Russell Peters has built a successful comedy career poking fun at the amusing stereotypes. As he explains, his comedy is rooted in the reality of growing up "brown"

Stand-up comedian Russell Peters is well known for his routines that poke fun at racial and ethnic stereotypes.

in a "white" Canadian society. Other examples of racial and ethnic stereotypes include Asians as quiet, introverted, smarter, and more quantitatively oriented; Hispanics as family-oriented and religious; and Arabs as angry.[37] Racial and ethnic stereotypes are particularly problematic because they are automatically triggered and lead to racial bias without our conscious awareness.[38] These stereotypes are often activated by looking at someone's facial features or skin colour.[39] This behaviour became the topic of conversation post 9-11 Canada when accusations were made that law enforcement and border customs officers were using racial profiling on the job. The media picked up on it, but the accusations were denied by government officials, saying their actions were legitimate in fighting the war on terrorism.

Negative racial stereotypes are still apparent in many aspects of life. Consider the experience of Eldrick (Tiger) Woods. Tiger was raised in two different cultures: his mother was from Thailand and his father was African-American. Since becoming a professional golfer in 1996, Tiger has won 90 tournaments and he has more career victories than any other active player on the PGA Tour. He also is the only golfer in history to hold the title for all four major tournaments at the same time.[40] Unfortunately, Tiger has experienced a host of racial stereotypes and biases. "I grew up in the 1980s and still had incidents," Woods remembers. In 1994, Woods was 18 years old and practising before the U.S. Amateur championship when he recalled, ". . . Some guy just yelled over the fence and used the N-word numerous times at me."[41]

According to Statistics Canada Census data, despite being more highly educated than non-visible minorities, visible minorities have higher unemployment rates than their counterparts, namely 9.5 percent to 7.1 percent. As a follow-up to the census data, The Canadian Centre for Justice Statistics in Ottawa compiled a report from their own study and found that the proportion of visible minorities who felt they had experienced discrimination was twice that of non-visible minorities. Overall, 81 percent of visible minorities who felt that they had experienced discrimination believed that it was because of their race or ethnic origin.[42] Workplace stereotyping resulting in discrimination is not unique to Canada nor North America. In fact, the European Union is taking action as well to identify similar occurrences through awareness and educational initiatives that such business practices are wrong and must be addressed (see International OB feature box).

When it comes to ethnic stereotyping within organizations, it becomes harder to prove that higher unemployment rates are a direct result of stereotyping. Many anecdotal stories suggest that it may be occurring, but on a subtle level. Take, for instance, the case involving the United Parcel Service (UPS) at their Mississauga, Ontario sorting plant. The UPS manager claimed that he had to fire eight Muslim women because they refused to follow the dress code that was put into place for health and safety reasons. The women, all part-time workers, refused to hike their ankle-length skirts above the knee over their long pants. The UPS manager told the Human Rights tribunal that was investigating the complaint that the way the women dressed was a safety hazard, as workers were expected to climb ladders up to six metres high. The women claimed their dismissal was more than that. The discrimination case was settled with the mediation assistance of both the tribunal and the Worker's Action Centre organization, but the terms of the agreement were kept secret.[43]

EUROPEAN UNION FIGHTING PERCEPTUAL ERRORS

Issues born out of stereotyping, such as harassment, discrimination, and victimization, are being addressed in the European Union (EU) by their Fundamental Rights Agency that was created to provide assistance and expertise in addressing such issues. Recently, the European Commission created a "Guide for Victims of Discrimination," summarizing new Europe-wide legislation banning discrimination. This guide provides practical advice about what citizens can do if they believe they have been denied employment due to their age, disability, ethnicity, sexual orientation, or religion. For example, it asks the question, "Have you felt that decisions about participation in training, your work conditions, pay, or promotion were based on who you are rather than how well you perform?" Many European countries already have legislation against discrimination, but the new laws aim to give a consistent set of rights across Europe.

SOURCE: The European Union Agency for Fundamental Rights (FRA) website: www.eumc.at/eumc/index.php, "What You Can Do If You Have Suffered Discrimination" a guide for victims. More information on the EU-wide campaign "For Diversity. Against Discrimination." website: www.stop-discrimination.info.

In a recent UN report, Canada was cited as not doing enough in the area of racial and aboriginal issues, including training and employment opportunities.[44] John Sims, deputy minister of the Department of Justice, was the head of the 20-person delegation that presented Canada's case in Geneva. In his response, Sims said, "Canada recognized that no country, including Canada, has a perfect human rights record." He acknowledged Canada's efforts and challenges when it came to areas like Native rights.[45]

On a more positive note, a recent paper by Professor Krishna Pendakur, of Simon Fraser University, suggests that changes in visible minority labour market performance across cities will fare well in Canada's future. As more natural integration takes place, barriers to employment opportunities because of racial and ethnic stereotyping will decrease.[46]

Disability Stereotypes People with disabilities not only face negative stereotypes that affect their employability, but they also can be stigmatized by the general population. These trends create a host of problems for people with disabilities. For example, Canadians with disabilities are more likely to be unemployed, and they are also far more likely to be living at the bottom of the income scale. Among adults aged 25 to 54 with disabilities, 47 percent have a personal income below $15,000, compared with only 25 percent of those without disabilities. Lower income and high unemployment rates are largely the result of lower educational attainment among adults with disabilities. In fact, Canadian adults with a disability are nearly two times less likely to obtain university credentials as compared to those without a disability. In 2001, about 25 percent of working-aged Canadians had completed a university education; in contrast, just 14 percent of Canadians with disabilities had achieved the same. Although postsecondary participation has increased among young adults, the education gap remains. Half (51 percent) of young people with a disability (aged 15 to 24) have not even completed high school, compared with 42 percent of those without disabilities.[47]

Causal Attributions

Another very important perception relates to the causes of observed behaviour. Attributions are perceptions regarding the causes of observed behaviour. Rightly or wrongly, we constantly formulate cause-and-effect explanations for our own and others' behaviour. Attributional statements such as the following

Causal attributions

Suspected or inferred causes of behaviour.

are common: "Joe drinks too much because he has no willpower; but I need a couple of drinks after work because I'm under a lot of pressure." Formally defined, **causal attributions** are the perceived causes of behaviour. It is important to understand how people formulate attributions, because they profoundly affect organizational behaviour. For example, a supervisor who attributes an employee's poor performance to a lack of effort might reprimand that individual. However, training might be deemed necessary if the supervisor attributes the poor performance to a lack of ability.

Generally speaking, people formulate causal attributions by considering the events preceding an observed behaviour. Attribution theory proposes that behaviour can be attributed either to internal factors within a person (such as ability), or to external factors within the environment (such as a difficult task). People make causal attributions after gathering information about three dimensions of behaviour: consensus, distinctiveness, and consistency.[48] These dimensions vary independently, thus forming various combinations and leading to differing attributions.

- *Consensus* involves a perceiver comparing an individual's behaviour with that of his or her peers. There is high consensus when the individual acts like the rest of the group and low consensus when the individual acts differently.

- *Distinctiveness* is determined by a perceiver comparing an individual's behaviour on one task with the individual's behaviour on other tasks. High distinctiveness means the individual has performed the task in question in a significantly different manner than he or she has performed other tasks. Low distinctiveness means stable performance or quality from one task to another.

- *Consistency* is determined when a perceiver judges if an individual's performance on a given task is consistent over time. High consistency implies that the individual performs a certain task the same, time after time. Unstable performance of a given task over time would mean low consistency.

It is important to remember that consensus relates to other *people*, distinctiveness relates to other *tasks*, and consistency relates to *time*. The question now is: How does information about these three dimensions of behaviour lead to internal or external attributions?

People attribute behaviour to external causes (environmental factors) when they perceive high consensus, high distinctiveness, and low consistency. Internal attributions (personal factors) tend to be made when observed behaviour is characterized by low consensus, low distinctiveness, and high consistency. So, for example, when all employees are performing poorly (high consensus), when the poor performance occurs on only one of several tasks (high distinctiveness), and the poor performance occurs during only one time period (low consistency), a supervisor will probably attribute an employee's poor performance to an external source such as peer pressure or an overly difficult task. In contrast, performance will be attributed to an employee's personal characteristics (an internal attribution) when only the individual in question is performing poorly (low consensus), when the inferior performance is found across several tasks (low distinctiveness), and when the low performance has persisted over time (high consistency). Many studies support this predicted pattern of attributions.[49]

ATTRIBUTIONAL TENDENCIES

Researchers have uncovered two attributional tendencies that distort one's interpretation of observed behaviour—*fundamental attribution bias* and *self-serving bias*.

Fundamental attribution bias

Ignoring environmental factors that affect behaviour.

Fundamental Attribution Bias The *fundamental attribution bias* reflects one's tendency to attribute behaviour to personal characteristics, as opposed to situational factors. This bias causes perceivers to ignore important environmental forces that often significantly affect behaviour. For example, consider a scenario involving a sales clerk we'll call Pat at a retail store, who is being evaluated by his supervisor two weeks before Christmas. Let's say there is a shortage of help because of a firing and another clerk is expected to be away ill for the next week, leaving no one to straighten up the merchandise on the floor or circulate around asking "may I help you" kinds of questions to potential customers. The clerks who are scheduled, including Pat, pick up the slack and do the best they can under the circumstances. It doesn't come as a surprise when customer complaints around poor customer service and messy merchandise presentations are received. If the supervisor attributes these complaints solely to Pat's personal characteristic deficiencies, then he or she has ignored all the situational factors that played a role during this time period. Such a fundamental attribution bias is not an accurate judgment of the situation.

Self-serving bias

Taking more personal responsibility for success than failure.

Self-Serving Bias The *self-serving bias* represents one's tendency to take more personal responsibility for success than for failure. Employees tend to attribute their successes to internal factors (high ability and/or hard work) and their failures to uncontrollable external factors (tough job, bad luck, unproductive co-workers, or an unsympathetic boss).[50] For example, if you were to go for a job interview and not get the job, would you blame the interview questions as being too difficult or unfair? The timing of the interview disadvantaged you? If this happened, then you would be using self-serving bias to explain the situation, especially if you were out the night before partying, were unable to answer questions during the interview because you didn't do any research prior to the visit, wore ripped jeans and a ball cap on your head, and answered your cell phone during the interview! Instead, you blame the lack of a job offer from this firm on factors you believe could not be controlled; you believe you were a victim of someone else's bias.

But what if you are offered a promotion at your job? If you believe you have earned the promotion because of your hard work and good work ethic, then telling you that no one else applied or wanted the job wouldn't be a factor for consideration. Instead, you attribute the promotion to the fact that you were the best candidate for the job. You believe you controlled all the variables in this situation.

MANAGERIAL APPLICATION AND IMPLICATIONS

Attribution models can be used to explain how managers handle poorly performing employees. One study revealed that managers gave employees more immediate, frequent, and negative feedback when they attributed their performance to low effort. This reaction was even more pronounced when the manager's success was dependent on an employee's performance. A second study indicated that managers tended to transfer employees whose poor performance was attributed to a lack of ability. These same managers also decided to take no immediate action when poor performance was attributed to external factors beyond an individual's control.[51]

The preceding situations have several important implications for managers. First, managers tend to disproportionately attribute behaviour to internal causes.[52] This can result in inaccurate evaluations of performance, leading to reduced employee motivation. No one likes to be blamed because of factors they perceive to be beyond their control. Further, because managers' responses to employee performance vary according to their attributions, attributional biases may lead to inappropriate managerial actions, including promotions, transfers, layoffs, and so forth. This can dampen motivation and performance. Attributional training sessions for managers are in order. Basic attributional processes can be explained, and managers can be taught to detect and avoid attributional biases. Finally, employees' attributions for their own performance have dramatic effects on subsequent motivation, performance, and personal attitudes such as self-esteem. For instance, people tend to give up, develop lower expectations for future success, and experience decreased self-esteem when they attribute failure to a lack of ability. In contrast, employees are more likely to display high performance and job satisfaction when they attribute success to internal factors such as ability and effort.[53] Fortunately, attributional realignment can improve both motivation and performance. The goal of attributional realignment is to shift failure attributions away from ability and toward attributions of low effort or some other external cause (e.g., lack of resources).

→ Summary of Learning Objectives

1. **Define *perception* and *causal attributions*.** Perception is a cognitive process that enables us to interpret and understand our surroundings. It is possible that during the cognitive process of gathering information, certain external variables can have a salient stimuli effect, or perhaps internal bias can cause errors in judgement. Causal attributions are suspected or inferred causes of behaviour. Attribution theory is based on the premise that people attempt to infer causes for observed behaviour. Rightly or wrongly, we constantly formulate cause-and-effect explanations for our own and others' behaviour.

2. **Explain *perception* in terms of the four-stage social cognition processing sequence.** Social perception, also referred to as social cognition, is the study of how people perceive one another, and it is best explained with a four-stage process. The four stages are selective attention/comprehension, encoding and simplification, storage and retention, and retrieval and response. During social cognition, salient stimuli are assigned to cognitive categories and stored in long-term memory.

3. **Illustrate six managerial implications of social perceptions.** Social perception affects hiring decisions, performance appraisals, leadership perceptions, communication processes, workplace aggression and antisocial behaviour, and physical and psychological well-being. Inaccurate schemata or racist and sexist schemata may be used to evaluate job applicants. Similarly, faulty schemata about what constitutes good versus poor performance can lead to inaccurate performance appraisals. Invalid schemata need to be identified and replaced with appropriate schemata through coaching and training. Further, managers are advised to use objective rather than subjective measures of performance. With respect to leadership, leaders will have a difficult time influencing employees when they exhibit behaviours contained in employees' schemata of poor leaders. Because people interpret oral and written communications by using schemata developed through past experiences, an individual's ability to influence others is affected by information contained in others' schemata regarding age, gender, ethnicity, appearance, speech, mannerisms, personality, and other personal characteristics. It is very important to treat employees fairly, as perceptions of unfairness are associated with aggressive and antisocial behaviour.

4. **Examine the managerial challenges and recommendations of sex-role, age, racial/ethnic, and disability stereotypes.** The key managerial challenge is to reduce the extent to which stereotypes influence decision making and interpersonal processes throughout the organization. Training can be used to educate employees about the problem of stereotyping and to equip managers with the skills needed to handle situations associated with managing employees with disabilities. Because mixed-group contact reduces stereotyping, organizations should create opportunities for diverse employees to meet and work together in cooperative groups of equal status. Hiring decisions should be based on valid individual differences, and managers can be trained to use valid criteria when evaluating employee performance. Minimizing differences in job opportunities and experiences across groups of people can help alleviate promotional barriers. It is critical to obtain top management's commitment and support to eliminate stereotyping and discriminatory decisions.

5. **Compare and contrast *fundamental attribution bias* and *self-serving bias*.** Fundamental attribution bias involves emphasizing personal factors more than situational factors while formulating causal attributions for the behaviour of others. Self-serving bias involves personalizing the causes of one's successes and externalizing the causes of one's failures.

Discussion Questions

1. Why is it important for managers to have a working knowledge of perception and attribution?

2. Have you ever been stereotyped by someone? If so, what were the conditions under which you experienced it and how did it make you feel?

3. Can you think of an example of salient stimuli?

4. Can you think of an example of someone you know who has used self-serving bias? Try and recall the situation for your classmates.

5. Is it possible for individuals NOT to constantly formulate cause-and-effect explanations for their own and others' behaviour? Explain.

Google Searches

1. **Google Search:** "common stereotypes of Canadians" Identify at least three stereotypes and share them with your classmates. Discuss how such stereotypes make people feel.

2. **Google Search:** "self serving bias" Identify at least two examples from various sites that can help clarify this concept. Share your examples with the rest of the class.

3. **Google Search:** Compare and contrast Section 15 of the "Canadian Charter of Rights and Freedoms" to the purpose of the Canadian Human Rights Act under the "Canadian Human Rights Commission." How do these documents support one another?

Experiential Exercise

Perception Group Exercise

PURPOSE   This exercise is meant to help familiarize you with the OB concept of social perception. Approx. Timing: 20 minutes.

GIVEN SITUATION   In 2009, the number of Canadian corporations filing for bankruptcy soared to double-digit levels, the TSX reflected higher unemployment rates as the recession took a deeper hold on the economy, and tens upon thousands of layoffs were announced across the country as a result of the global financial crisis. Production cut backs, pay freezes, and wage rollbacks were a common occurrence. No one could have predicted the extraordinary decline of the domestic automobile industry.

ACTIVITY ASSIGNMENT:
- Work in teams of four members each.
- Read the Given Situation.
- Describe the Given Situation from each of the following perspectives listed below. Consider how your interpretations of the same event(s) will differ.
  1. An unemployed CAW auto worker
  2. A 75-year-old retired factory worker
  3. A 19-year-old full-time business student
  4. A 24-year-old recent business student graduate
  5. The owner(s) of a 65-year-old Canadian manufacturing firm that just filed for bankruptcy
  6. The HR Department of the City of Winnipeg looking to hire 250 people for seasonal summer work

The Presentation Assistant

Here are possible topics and corresponding sources related to this chapter that can be further explored by student groups looking for ideas.

	PREJUDICE, NEGATIVE STEREOTYPING, AND DISCRIMINATION IN THE WORKPLACE—HOW ARE THEY DIFFERENT?	TRICKING OUR SENSES AND THE ROLE OF PERCEPTION—IS WHAT WE SEE ACCURATE?	SELF-SERVING BIAS IN THE WORKPLACE—CAN IT BE AVOIDED?
YouTube Videos	• Discrimination, prejudice in the office • Age discrimination • Disability Discrimination • Russell Peters Live	• Criss Angel Walks On Water • The World of Optical Illusions • Magic Moving Images • Look at things from a different perspective	• Employee Evaluations • Employee Performance Reviews • Bias Perspective • (Call in sick or late) work excuses
TV Shows or Movies to Preview	• (Harvey) *Milk* • *Remember The Titans* • *Crash* • *The Office* – "Diversity Episode"	• *Vantage Point* • *Mind Freak*	• *The Office* – "Performance Review Episode" • *The Apprentice* – "You're Fired"

Internet Searches	• Hate Crimes In Canada • 3 Canadian Cops Arrested For Hate Crimes Against Muslims • *Visible Minorities In Canadian Workplaces* (by Prof. Krishna Pendakur)	• Paradigms • The Perception of Truth • Observation, Truth, Ethics and Judgment • People Performance – Can you believe what you see?	• Self Serving Bias In The Workplace • Barriers To Productive Work • The Dysfunctional Workplace
Ice Breaker Classroom Activity	• Ask the students if any of them have ever been discriminated against or omitted from a team when no one picked them. Once identified, ask these people how it made them feel. Share responses around the room.	• Ask the students to view several optical illusion graphics and see if they can shift their perspective back and forth to see all possible images.	• Go to Table 2.1 and have the students relate these concepts to the world of work by identifying examples of each.

OB In Action Case Study

Portrait of a Canadian Advisor

Results of this study provide a revealing portrait of the Canadians who work as advisors on Canadian International Development Agency (CIDA)-sponsored projects. From interviews with advisors, spouses, colleagues, and national counterparts, the following profile emerges of a typical Canadian advisor.

The typical Canadian advisor is a male between the ages of 40 and 50. He was born in Canada, where he has lived at least five years of his life. His mother tongue is English (47 percent) or French (44 percent) and he is well-educated, having at least one university degree. He is married and is accompanied on this assignment by his spouse.

Our advisor is a professional working for a private Canadian firm that is under contract to CIDA. No stranger to the developing world, he has had at least one previous overseas posting, and has spent at least two years working in developing countries. On this assignment, he is working in an urban setting as part of a team, working directly with a counterpart from the country of assignment in a management capacity. He sees his role as an advisory one involving training and the transfer of skills and knowledge.

Our advisor approaches this assignment with confidence. His interest in the host country is high, and he is not worried about his ability to adapt. He is confident that he will do well on the assignment and that he can make a significant contribution to development efforts in the country. He feels he has better than average interpersonal and communication skills. And although he considers himself to have a high sense of adventure and altruism, he is concerned about his security and puts a high value on upward mobility.

A desire to give and/or learn lies behind our advisor's acceptance of the overseas assignment. His attitudes on development are fairly conservative, and he views the transfer of technology as the key to improving economic prosperity in developing countries and to narrowing the gap between rich and poor nations. He sees no need for the developed world to limit its standards of living and supports Canada's policy of "tied aid," which requires that the majority of our development dollars be spent on the purchase of Canadian good and services.

On assignment, our advisor expresses a great deal of satisfaction in his personal, family, and professional life, and experiences a high degree of involvement in the local culture. In his mind, the process of adaptation has been a smooth one involving little culture shock, and he feels more satisfaction with his life overseas than he did previously in Canada.

On the job, he feels that his terms of reference are well-defined and understood, and that both he and his colleagues have been highly effective in the task of transferring skills and knowledge to their national counterparts.

Although status differences exist between himself and his counterpart, he does not see this inhibiting their working relationship. And while he feels that his living conditions are generally less comfortable than those in Canada, he does not see this as an impediment to his assignment.

DIFFERING REALITIES

The views and attitudes expressed above are the advisor's perceptions of himself. A different and less optimistic portrait emerges from field interviews with spouses, colleagues, and counterparts, as well as observations made by field researchers. As seen by others, our advisor had minimal involvement with the local culture, preferring instead to spend his leisure and social time in the company of other Canadians and expatriates. He has made little effort to learn the local language, and is likely to spend little time outside the job with his counterpart of other nationals. Although he is able to accurately identify the key factors that promote success on a development assignment, he is less able to actually demonstrate the required skills and interest in his own behaviour. What people say and what they do are often inconsistent. How an individual sees and assesses himself often bears little resemblance to how he is seen and assessed by others.

Discussion Questions

1. Why is the gap between the typical Canadian advisor's self-perception and the perception of him by others likely to be greater in a foreign environment? Would similar gaps exist in a domestic environment?

2. How is this gap likely to affect the advisor's performance?

3. What measures would you recommend to improve the accuracy of the advisor's self-perception and performance?

SOURCE: D.J. Kealey, "Cross-Cultural Effectiveness—A Study of Canadian Technical Advisors Overseas," (Hull, QC: Canadian International Development Agency, 1990), pp 32–33. Reproduced by permission of CIDA Briefing Centre, Hull, QC and D.J. Kealey. In R. Hoffman and F. Ruemper, *Organizational Behaviour: Canadian Cases and Exercises*, 5th ed, (Concord, ON: Captus Press, 2005), pp 194–195.

↴ Ethical OB Dilemma

Can We Talk About Your Body Art?

As tattoos and piercings gain popularity with a younger generation of employees, interviewers and supervisors are developing new dress code criteria.

While there are industries and companies that are tolerant of body art, it is still more common for businesses to hold a hard line, especially in jobs that require frequent customer interaction or those with health and safety concerns; some just don't like it. For example, according to Cindy Truong, image consultant, "(They) should be kept out of the office at all times; you can show them off on your own time. You're representing the company. Tattoos are seen as rebellious and they send the wrong message to older generations."

On the other hand, some have much more acceptance of tattoos. For example, Anne Sowden, the past president of the Association of Image Consultants

International, points out that it is possible to find up to four generations of co-workers in a typical office, resulting in a less anti-tattoo environment.

"If the company has a written or stated dress code," . . . [says an employment attorney], then "the company gets to determine what constitutes a professional image or appearance."

SOURCE: A. Verner, "Tattoos Not Taboo For Professionals Looking To Make Indelible Impression," *The Globe & Mail,* August 5, 2007.

Which of the following statements best describes how you feel employers should deal with self-expression through body art?

1. "Many businesses have carefully cultivated images to protect, so they have a moral responsibility to their shareholders to monitor their employees' appearance." Explain.
2. "Companies may have the legal right to force people to look a certain way, but they don't have the moral right to stifle self-expression in arbitrary ways." Explain.
3. "The style of a new generation calls for new employment policies by organizations on employee appearance." Explain.
4. "The business case for diversity declares that an organization's employees should look like its customer base. If a growing number of customers have body art, why can't employees? It all depends on the industry." Explain.
5. "Today's discrimination against those with body art is equivalent to now-illegal racial and gender discrimination years ago." Explain.

Self Concept,
Personality, and Emotions

Canadian Students Have High Self-Esteem and Believe They Deserve More

What kind of person are you? What sorts of abilities do you have? What expectations do you have for a job upon graduation? Ask your friends these three questions and you'll probably get a variety of answers. That's because individuals have different self-concepts, abilities, and expectations. What we think of ourselves (self-esteem) and what we think we deserve in this world become the foundation of our goals (*I want this because I know I can achieve it!*) and how we'll accomplish them.

Some students expect they'll have to work hard for many years before earning an annual salary above the Canadian average for individuals (approximately $30,000 average income after tax, according to Statistics Canada). Others expect it within months of graduation. One recent computer science graduate expressed it this way, "I did not spend all that money and years in school to make $12 per hour working phone support and resetting passwords all day!"

> "I did not spend all that money and years in school to make $12 per hour working phone support and resetting passwords all day!"

According to a recent Canadian Policy Research Networks (CPRN) study, nearly a quarter of young Canadians are working at low-paying jobs beneath their skill level—such as pouring coffee and answering phones—the highest rate among the 16 nations that belong to the Organization for Economic Co-operation and Development. "There appears to be a mismatch between what young Canadians are being trained for and the jobs that are offered," says the survey report.

According to Amanda Aziz, national chairwoman of the Canadian Federation of Students, the cost for post secondary education is the highest it has ever been in this country. Therefore, it is not unreasonable to expect higher than average salaries upon graduation. Aziz believes there is an unfair societal attitude toward the current generation of students, labelling them as spoiled. But Aziz takes exception to this belief. Are Canadian students spoiled or just individuals with high self-esteem who know what they want?

SOURCES: *The Canadian Press*, April 17, 2008, "1 in 4 young Canadians overqualified for jobs: report," www.cbc.ca/canada/story/2008/04/17/bc-youth-labour; Statistics Canada: Income after tax by economic family types, http://www40.statcan.ca/l01/cst01/famil21a.htm.

What students think of themselves drives their behaviour when accomplishing personal goals.

→ LEARNING OBJECTIVES

After reading this chapter, you should be able to:

LO 1 Define *self-esteem* and *self-efficacy*.

LO 2 **Explain** what is meant by self-monitoring and discuss how it relates to the social learning model of self-management.

LO 3 **Relate** the one Big Five personality dimension that is most positively correlated with job performance .

LO 4 **Compare and contrast** internal and external locus of control.

LO 5 **Summarize** the theory of emotional intelligence and explain how it relates to appreciating individual differences between people.

Thanks to a vast array of individual differences, modern organizations have a rich and interesting human texture. On the other hand, individual differences make the manager's job endlessly challenging. In fact, according to research, "variability among workers is substantial at all levels but increases dramatically with job complexity. In life insurance sales, for example, unevenness in performance is around six times as great as in routine clerical jobs."[1] Growing workforce diversity compels managers to view individual differences in a fresh new way. Rather than limiting diversity, as in the past, today's managers need to better understand and accommodate employee diversity and individual differences.[2]

This chapter explores the following important dimensions of individual differences: (1) self-concept, (2) personality traits, (3) mental abilities, and (4) emotions. The conceptual model in Figure 3.1 shows the relationship between self-concept (how you view yourself), personality (how you appear to others), and key forms of self-expression. Considered as an integrated package, these factors provide a foundation for better understanding yourself and others as unique and special individuals.

Understanding Self-Concept

Self is the core of one's conscious existence. Awareness of self is referred to as one's self-concept. Individualistic North American cultures have been called self-centred. Not surprisingly, when people ages 16 to 70 were asked in a recent survey what they would do differently if they could live life over again, 48 percent chose the response category "Get in touch with self."[3] To know more about self-concept is to understand more about life in general.[4]

Sociologist Viktor Gecas defines **self-concept** as "the concept the individual has of himself as a physical, social, and spiritual or moral being."[5] In other words, because you have a self-concept, you recognize yourself as a distinct human being. A self-concept would be impossible without the capacity to think. This brings us to the role of cognitions. **Cognitions** represent "any knowledge, opinion, or belief about the environment, about oneself, or about one's behaviour."[6] Among many different types of cognitions, those involving anticipation, planning, goal setting, evaluating, and setting personal standards are particularly relevant to OB.

Importantly, ideas of self and self-concept vary from one historical era to another, from one socio-economic group to another, and from culture to culture.[7] How well one detects and adjusts to different cultural notions of self can spell the difference between success and failure in international dealings. Keeping this cultural qualification in mind, we will explore three topics invariably mentioned when behavioural scientists discuss self-concept: self-esteem, self-efficacy, and self-monitoring.

SELF-ESTEEM

LO 1

Self-esteem is beliefs about one's own self-worth based on an overall self-evaluation.[8] Self-esteem is measured by having survey respondents indicate their agreement or disagreement with both positive and negative statements. A positive statement on one general self-esteem survey is: "I feel I am a person of worth, the equal of other people."[9] Among the negative items is: "I feel I do not have much to be proud of."[10] Those that agree with the positive statements and disagree with the negative statements have high self-esteem. They see themselves as worthwhile, capable, and acceptable. People with low self-esteem view themselves in negative terms. They do not feel good about themselves and are hampered by self-doubts.[11]

Employment and Self-Esteem What researchers call *organization-based self-esteem* makes paid employment a prime determinant of overall self-esteem in modern life.[12] Identifying oneself with a collective group of individuals who are gainfully employed can be very rewarding and fulfilling, especially when others around you are out of work. Consequently, unemployment can have a devastating impact on one's self-esteem. Look around and reflect on the tens of thousands of individuals who lost their jobs during the economic downturn in the early 2000s and again during the latest correction that began in late 2008 and carried over into 2009. Imagine how low their self-esteem must be, knowing that finding a career job in the near future will be a very difficult task. They may learn from Arthur J. Fiacco, a 56-year-old executive who was laid off without any warning during the tech downturn in 2001:

> *I had never felt so lonely and helpless. I had been working since I was 16 years old .... A job isn't just about working. A job helps define who we are. It is what we talk with our neighbours about. It is the place we go. It is how we are introduced. It is one of the first things people ask about when we meet them. And most important, we measure ourselves from our very first job onward. Without a job, I felt I had lost my identity.*[13]

Self-concept

A person's self-perception as a physical, social, spiritual being.

Cognitions

A person's knowledge, opinions, or beliefs.

Self-esteem

One's overall self-evaluation.

▶ **FIGURE 3.1** **Studying Individual Differences**

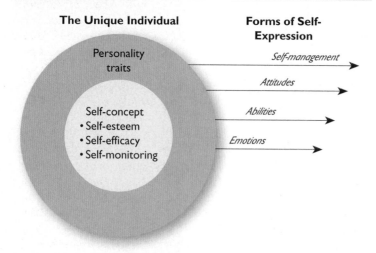

The Unique Individual

Personality traits

Self-concept
- Self-esteem
- Self-efficacy
- Self-monitoring

Forms of Self-Expression

Self-management

Attitudes

Abilities

Emotions

Fiacco eventually turned things around by building a successful consulting business. He says now, "I am making a contribution and feel good . . . . I have learned to listen to what others are trying to tell me."[14]

www.cartoonbank.com

IT'S ALWAYS 'GOOD DOG'- NEVER 'GREAT DOG'.

A Cross-Cultural Perspective What are the cross-cultural implications for self-esteem, a concept that has been called uniquely Western? In a survey of 13,118 students from 31 countries worldwide, a moderately positive correlation was found between self-esteem and life satisfaction. But the relationship was stronger in individualistic cultures (e.g., Canada, New Zealand, Netherlands, and the United States) than in collectivist cultures (e.g., Korea, Kenya, and Japan). The researchers concluded that individualistic cultures socialize people to focus more on themselves, while people in collectivist cultures "are socialized to fit into the community and to do their duty. Thus, how a collectivist feels about him- or herself is less relevant to . . . life satisfaction."[15] Global managers and employees working in multi-cultural work environments, whether in Canada or abroad, need to remember to de-emphasize self-esteem when doing business in collectivist ("we") cultures, as opposed to emphasizing it in individualistic ("me") cultures.[16]

Can General Self-Esteem Be Improved? The short answer is yes. More detailed answers come from research. In one study, youth-league baseball coaches who were trained in supportive teaching techniques had a positive effect on the self-esteem of young boys. A control group of untrained coaches had no such

positive effect.[17] Another study led to this conclusion: "Low self-esteem can be raised more by having the person think of desirable characteristics possessed rather than of undesirable characteristics from which he or she is free."[18] Yet another comprehensive study threw cold water on the popular view that high self-esteem is the key to better performance. The conclusion:

> . . . self-esteem and school or job performance are correlated. But long overdue scientific scrutiny points out the foolishness of supposing that people's opinion of themselves can be the cause of achievement. Rather, high-esteem is the result of good performance.[19]

This is where self-efficacy comes to the forefront.

SELF-EFFICACY ("I CAN DO THAT.")

Have you noticed how those who are confident about their ability tend to succeed, while those who are preoccupied with failing tend to fail? **Self-efficacy** is a person's belief about his or her chances of successfully accomplishing a specific task. According to one OB writer, "Self-efficacy arises from the gradual acquisition of complex cognitive, social, linguistic, and/or physical skills through experience."[20]

Self-efficacy

Belief in one's ability to do a task.

Helpful nudges in the right direction from parents, role models, and mentors are central to the development of high self-efficacy. Consider, for example, how Earl Woods used his military tough-love style to build his son Tiger's self-efficacy on the golf links:

> Long after Tiger Woods is finished playing golf, people will study Earl Woods. They will want to hear the stories of exactly how he raised this generation's most popular athlete . . . .
> "I tried to break him down mentally, tried to intimidate him verbally, by saying. 'Water on the right, OB [out of bounds] on the left,' just before his downswing," Earl Woods once told the Associated Press. "He would look at me with the most evil look, but he wasn't permitted to say anything . . . one day I did all my tricks, and he looked at me and smiled. At the end of the round, I told him, 'Tiger, you've completed the training.' And I made him a promise. 'You'll never run into another person as mentally tough as you.' He hasn't. And he won't."[21]

Pro golfer Tiger Woods has a high level of self-efficacy on the golf links.

The relationship between self-efficacy and performance is a cyclical one. Efficacy–performance cycles can spiral upward toward success or downward toward failure.[22] Researchers have documented a strong link between high self-efficacy expectations and success in widely varied physical and mental tasks, anxiety reduction, addiction control, pain tolerance, illness recovery, and avoidance of seasickness in naval cadets.[23] In contrast, those with low self-efficacy expectations tend to have low success rates. Chronically low self-efficacy is associated with a condition called learned helplessness, the severely debilitating belief that one has no control over one's environment.[24] Although self-efficacy sounds like some sort of mental magic, it operates in a very straightforward manner, as the following model will show.

Mechanisms of Self-Efficacy   A basic model of self-efficacy is displayed in Figure 3.2. It draws upon the work of psychologist Albert Bandura.[25] Let us explore this model with a simple illustrative task. Imagine you have been told to prepare and deliver a 10-minute talk to an OB class of 50 students on the workings of

▶ FIGURE 3.2   Self-Efficacy Beliefs Pave the Way for Success or Failure

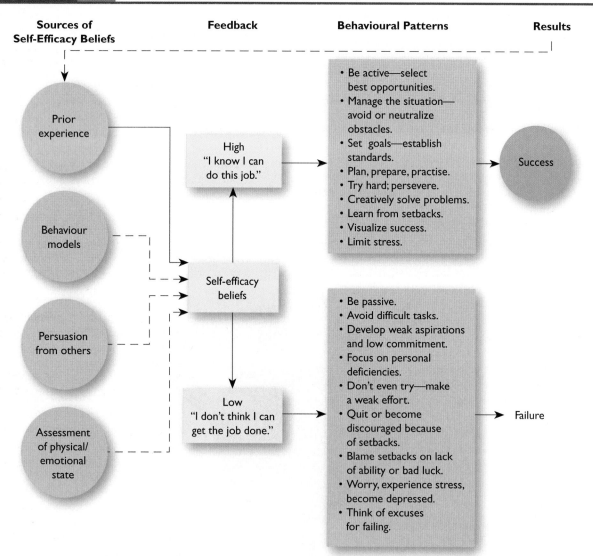

SOURCES: Adapted from discussion in A. Bandura, "Regulation of Cognitive Processes through Perceived Self-Efficacy," *Developmental Psychology*, September 1989, pp 729–35; and R. Wood and A. Bandura, "Social Cognitive Theory of Organizational Management," *Academy of Management Review*, July 1989, pp 361–84.

the self-efficacy model in Figure 3.2. Your self-efficacy assessment would involve thinking and reviewing the interaction between your perceived abilities and those opportunities and obstacles around you.

As you begin to prepare for your presentation, the four sources of self-efficacy beliefs come into play. Because prior experience is the most potent source, according to Bandura, it is listed first and connected to self-efficacy beliefs with a solid line.[26] Past success in public speaking would boost your self-efficacy. But bad experiences with delivering speeches would foster low self-efficacy. Regarding behaviour models as a source of self-efficacy beliefs, you would be influenced by the success or failure of your classmates in delivering similar talks. Their successes would tend to bolster you (or perhaps their failure would if you were very competitive and had high self-esteem). Likewise, any supportive persuasion from your classmates that you will do a good job would enhance your self-efficacy. Physical and emotional factors also might affect your self-confidence. A sudden case of laryngitis or a bout of stage fright could cause your self-efficacy expectations to plunge. Your cognitive evaluation of the situation then would yield a self-efficacy belief—ranging from high to low expectations for success. Importantly, self-efficacy beliefs are not merely boastful statements based on bravado; they are deep convictions supported by experience.

Moving to the *behavioural patterns* portion of Figure 3.2, we see how self-efficacy beliefs are acted out. In short, if you have high self-efficacy about giving your 10-minute speech you will work harder, more creatively, and longer when preparing for your talk than will your low self-efficacy classmates. The results would then take shape accordingly. People program themselves for success or failure by enacting their self-efficacy expectations. Positive or negative results subsequently become feedback for one's base of personal experience. Bob Schmonsees, a software entrepreneur, is an inspiring example of the success pathway through Figure 3.2:

A contender in mixed-doubles tennis and a former football star, Mr Schmonsees was standing near a ski lift when an out-of-control skier rammed him. His legs were paralyzed. He would spend the rest of his life in a wheelchair. Fortunately, he discovered a formula for his different world: Figure out the new rules for any activity, then take as many small steps as necessary to master those rules. After learning the physics of a tennis swing on wheels and the geometry of playing a second bounce (standard rules), he became the world's top wheelchair player over age 40.[27]

Managerial Implications On-the-job research evidence encourages managers to nurture self-efficacy, both in themselves and in others. In fact, a meta-analysis encompassing 21,616 subjects found a significant positive correlation between self-efficacy and job performance.[28] To illustrate this point, let's take the case example discussed in the Law and Ethics at Work feature box, where a manager receives information suggesting employees waste time on the job. That translates into money being wasted in the mind of the manager and prompts a reaction; in this instance, it's critical for the manager not to overreact with coercive tactics. To get people back on track, management should reflect on the best way to help the employees understand the need for behaviour change. By providing employees with the right tools, employees can monitor their own behaviour and thus maintain positive self-efficacy, which in turn will lead to better job performance.

Self-efficacy requires constructive action in each of the following managerial areas:

1. **Recruiting/selection/job assignments** Design interview questions to probe job applicants' general self-efficacy as a basis for determining orientation and training needs. Pencil-and-paper tests for self-efficacy are not in an advanced stage of development and validation. Take care to not hire solely on the basis of self-efficacy, because studies have detected below-average self-esteem and self-efficacy among women and protected minorities.[29]

2. **Job design** Complex, challenging, and autonomous jobs tend to enhance perceived self-efficacy.[30] Boring, tedious jobs generally do the opposite.

3. **Training and development** Improve employees' self-efficacy expectations for key tasks through guided experiences, mentoring, and role modelling.[31]

4. **Self-management** Systematic self-management training involves enhancement of self-efficacy expectations.[32]

5. **Goal setting and quality improvement** Goal difficulty needs to match the individual's perceived self-efficacy.[33] As self-efficacy and performance improve, goals and quality standards can be made more challenging.

6. **Creativity** Supportive managerial actions can enhance the strong linkage between self-efficacy beliefs and workplace creativity.[34]

7. **Coaching** Those with low self-efficacy need lots of constructive pointers and positive feedback. [35]

8. **Leadership** Leadership talent emerges when top management gives high self-efficacy managers a chance to prove themselves under pressure.

9. **Rewards** Small successes need to be rewarded as stepping-stones to a stronger self-image and greater achievements.

LO 2 SELF-MONITORING

Consider these contrasting scenarios:

1. You are rushing to an important meeting when a co-worker pulls you aside and starts to discuss a personal problem. You want to break off the conversation, so you glance at your watch. He keeps talking. You say, "I'm late for a big meeting." He continues. You turn and start to walk away. The person keeps talking as if he never received any of your verbal and non-verbal signals that the conversation was over.

2. Same situation. Only this time, when you glance at your watch, the person immediately says, "I know, you've got to go. Sorry. We'll talk later."

Self-monitoring

Observing one's own behaviour and adapting it to the situation.

In the first all-too-familiar scenario, you are talking to a "low self-monitor." The second scenario involves a "high self-monitor." But more is involved here than an irritating situation: a significant and measurable individual difference in self-expression behaviour, called self-monitoring, is highlighted. *Self-monitoring* is the extent to which people observe their own self-expressive behaviour and adapt it to the demands of the situation.[36]

Experts on the subject offer this explanation:

Individuals high in self-monitoring are thought to regulate their expressive self-presentation for the sake of desired public appearances, and thus are highly responsive to social and interpersonal cues of situationally appropriate performances. Individuals low in self-monitoring are thought to lack either the ability or the motivation to so regulate their expressive self-presentations. Instead, their expressive behaviours are thought to functionally reflect their own enduring and momentary inner states, including their attitudes, traits, and feelings.[37]

LAW AND ETHICS *at Work*

EMPLOYERS NEED TO FIND WAYS TO BUILD EMPLOYEE SELF-EFFICACY

Imagine you are a manager and you've just read a recent Gallup poll stating that employees acknowledged that they wasted an average of about one hour a day at work. This has you concerned. Are your employees wasting hours at work each week or are they being productive? You decide to ask a colleague his opinion on how to monitor such activity in the workplace. He suggests installing NetVizor, the latest software that lets employers secretly monitor all computer and Internet activities of every employee on their network. But is it legal?

In banking, insurance, telecommunications, and travel, as many as 80 percent of employees may be subject to some level of monitoring. While it is an offence under the Criminal Code in Canada to intercept private communications, the Personal Information Protection and Electronic Documents Act (PIPEDA) introduced in 2004 makes it clear that Canadian companies have to

justify surveillance and have written policies regarding Internet and phone use or face a possible civil lawsuit before the federal court.

Several decisions from the Canadian federal privacy commissioner clearly identify that employers must act in compliance with the purposes and limited collection provisions of PIPEDA that allow individuals the right to privacy so as to, in essence, monitor their own behaviour without coercive means from management.

SOURCES: A. Gahtan, "Big Brother or Good Business?," *WebWorld*, March 1997, p. 24; J. Allinson, "Companies Will Have To Justify Surveillance," *London Free Press*, December 27, 2003; J. Allinson, "Written Policies are must for Internet, phone use," *London Free Press*, January 8, 2004; M. Cywinski, "Management Tip – employees acknowledged in Self-Monitoring 2007 that they wasted an average of about an hour a day at work, but . . .," *Canadian Management Centre PodCast Series*, January 24, 2008, (http://www.cmctraining.org/wordpress/?author=2).

How Good Are You at Self-Monitoring?

INSTRUCTIONS: In an honest self-appraisal, mark each of the following statements as True (T) or False (F), and then consult the scoring key.

_____ **1.** I guess I put on a show to impress or entertain others.

_____ **2.** In a group of people I am rarely the centre of attention.

_____ **3.** In different situations and with different people, I often act like very different persons.

_____ **4.** I would not change my opinions (or the way I do things) in order to please someone or win their favour.

_____ **5.** I have considered being an entertainer.

_____ **6.** I have trouble changing my behaviour to suit different people and different situations.

_____ **7.** At a party I let others keep the jokes and stories going.

_____ **8.** I feel a bit awkward in public and do not show up quite as well as I should.

_____ **9.** I can look anyone in the eye and tell a lie with a straight face (if for a right end).

_____ **10.** I may deceive people by being friendly when I really dislike them.

Scoring Key

Score one point for each of the following answers:
1. T; 2. F; 3. T; 4. F; 5. T; 6. F; 7. F; 8. F; 9. T; 10. T

Score: _____

1–3 = Low self-monitoring

4–5 = Moderately low self-monitoring

6–7 = Moderately high self-monitoring

8–10 = High self-monitoring

SOURCE: Excerpted and adapted from M. Snyder and S. Gangestad, "On the Nature of Self-Monitoring: Matters of Assessment, Matters of Validity," *Journal of Personality and Social Psychology*, July 1986, p 137.

In organizational life, both high and low self-monitors are subject to criticism. High self-monitors are sometimes called chameleons, who readily adapt their self-presentation to their surroundings. Low self-monitors, on the other hand, often are criticized for being on their own planet and insensitive to others. Importantly, within an OB context, self-monitoring is like any other individual difference—not a matter of right or wrong or good versus bad, but rather a source of diversity that needs to be adequately understood.

A Matter of Degree   Self-monitoring is not an either–or proposition; it is a matter of degree, a matter of being relatively high or low in terms of related patterns of self-expression. If you haven't done so already, complete the Self-Assessment Exercise to determine how good you are at self-monitoring. It is meant to help you better understand yourself. Review your score. Does it surprise you in any way? Are you unhappy with the way you present yourself to others? What are the ethical implications of your score (particularly with regard to items 9 and 10)?

Research Insights and Practical Recommendations According to field research, there is a positive relationship between high self-monitoring and career success. Among 139 MBA graduates who were tracked for five years, high self-monitors enjoyed more internal and external promotions than did their low self-monitoring classmates.[38] Another study of 147 managers and professionals found that high self-monitors had a better record of acquiring a mentor (someone to act as a personal career coach and professional sponsor).[39] These results mesh well with an earlier study that found managerial success (in terms of speed of promotions) was tied to political savvy (knowing how to socialize, network, and engage in organizational politics).[40]

The foregoing evidence and practical experience lead us to make these practical recommendations:

- *For high, moderate, and low self-monitors:* Become more consciously aware of your self-image and how it affects others.

- *For high self-monitors:* Don't overdo it by turning from a successful chameleon into someone who is widely perceived as insincere, dishonest, phoney, and untrustworthy. You cannot be everything to everyone.

- *For low self-monitors:* You can bend without breaking, so try to be a bit more accommodating while being true to your basic beliefs. Don't wear out your welcome when communicating. Practise reading and adjusting to non-verbal cues in various public situations. If your conversation partner is bored or distracted, stop—he or she is not really listening.

SELF-MANAGEMENT: A SOCIAL LEARNING MODEL

Albert Bandura, the expert psychologist introduced earlier, extended his self-efficacy concept into a comprehensive model of human learning. According to Bandura's *social learning theory*, an individual acquires new behaviour through the interplay of environmental cues and consequences and cognitive processes.[41] When you consciously control this learning process yourself, you are engaging in self-management. Bandura explains:

> *[A] distinguishing feature of social learning theory is the prominent role it assigns to self-regulatory capacities. By arranging environmental inducements, generating cognitive supports, and producing consequences for their own actions, people are able to exercise some measure of control over their own behaviour.*[42]

In other words, to the extent that you can control your environment and your cognitive representations of your environment, you are the master of your own behaviour. The practical model displayed in Figure 3.3 is derived from social learning theory. The two-headed arrows reflect dynamic interaction among all factors in the model. Each of the four major components of this self-management model requires a closer look. Since the focal point of this model is behaviour change, let us begin by discussing the behaviour component in the centre of the triangle.[43]

Changing Your Behaviour In today's fast-paced Internet age, corporate hand-holding is pretty much a thing of the past when it comes to career management. Employees are told things such as, "You own your own employability." They must make the best of themselves and any opportunities that may come along. A brochure at one large company tells employees: "No one is more interested or qualified when it comes to evaluating your individual interests, values, skills, and goals than you are."[44] The new age of career self-management challenges you to do a better job of setting personal goals, having clear priorities, being well organized, skilfully managing your time, and developing a self-learning program.[45]

> "By arranging environmental inducements, generating cognitive supports, and producing consequences for their own actions, people are able to exercise some measure of control over their own behaviour."

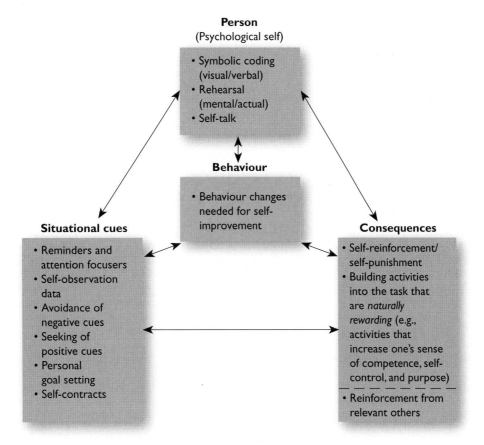

Person
(Psychological self)

- Symbolic coding (visual/verbal)
- Rehearsal (mental/actual)
- Self-talk

Behaviour

- Behaviour changes needed for self-improvement

Situational cues

- Reminders and attention focusers
- Self-observation data
- Avoidance of negative cues
- Seeking of positive cues
- Personal goal setting
- Self-contracts

Consequences

- Self-reinforcement/ self-punishment
- Building activities into the task that are *naturally rewarding* (e.g., activities that increase one's sense of competence, self-control, and purpose)
- Reinforcement from relevant others

SOURCE: Adapted in part from B.J. Pannett and S. Withane, "Hofstede's Value Survey Module: To Embrace or Abandon?," *Advances in International Comparative Management*, vol 5, ed S.B. Prasad (Greenwich, CT: JAI Press, 1990), pp 69–89.

Fortunately, Stephen R. Covey, in his best-selling books *The 7 Habits of Highly Effective People* and *The 8th Habit*, has given us a helpful agenda for improving ourselves (see Table 3.1). Covey refers to the eight habits practised by truly successful people, as "principle-centered, character-based."[46] The first step for putting the model in Figure 3.3 to work is to pick one or more of the eight habits that are personal trouble spots and translate them to specific behaviours. For example, "think win–win" might remind a conflict-prone person to practise cooperative teamwork behaviours with co-workers. Habit number five might prompt another person to stop interrupting others during conversations. Next, a supportive environment is needed for the target behaviour.

Managing Situational Cues When people try to give up a nagging habit such as smoking, the cards are stacked against them. Many people (friends who smoke) and situations (after dinner, when under stress at work, or when relaxing) serve as subtle yet powerful cues telling the

individual to light up. If the behaviour is to be changed, the cues need to be rearranged so they trigger alternative behaviour. Six techniques for managing situational cues are listed in the left column of Figure 3.3.

Reminders and attention focusers do just that. For example, many students and employees cue themselves about deadlines and appointments with notes stuck all over their work areas, refrigerators, and dashboards. Self-observation data, when compared against a goal or standard, can be a potent cue for improvement. Those who keep a weight chart near their bathroom scale will attest to the value of this tactic. Successful self-management calls for avoiding negative cues while seeking positive cues. Managers in Northwestern Mutual Life Insurance Company's new business department appreciate the value of avoiding negative cues: "On Wednesdays, the department shuts off all incoming calls, allowing workers to speed processing of new policies. On those days, the unit averages 23 percent more policies than on other days."[47]

Covey's Eight Habits: An Agenda for Self-Improvement

1. Be proactive. Choose the right means and ends in life, and take personal responsibility for your actions. Make timely decisions and make positive progress.

2. Begin with the end in mind. When all is said and done, how do you want to be remembered? Be goal-oriented.

3. Put first things first. Establish firm priorities that will help you accomplish your mission in life. Strike a balance between your daily work and your potential for future accomplishments.

4. Think win–win. Cooperatively seek creative and mutually beneficial solutions to problems and conflicts.

5. Seek first to understand, then to be understood. Strive hard to become a better listener.

6. Synergize. Because the whole is greater than the sum of its parts, you need to generate teamwork among individuals with unique abilities and potential. Value interpersonal differences.

7. Sharpen the saw. "This is the habit of self-renewal, which has four elements. The first is mental, which includes reading, visualizing, planning, and writing. The second is spiritual, which means value clarification and commitment, study, and meditation. Third is social/emotional, which involves service, empathy, synergy, and intrinsic security. Finally, the physical element includes exercise, nutrition, and stress management."

8. "Find your voice and inspire others to find theirs." Take your life to a higher level by seeking fulfillment, doing things passionately, and making a significant contribution.

SOURCES: Adapted from discussion in S.R.Covey, *The 7 Habits of Highly Effective People* (New York: Simon & Schuster, 1989). Excerpt in No. 7 from "Q & A with Stephen Covey," *Training*, December 1992, p 38. Eighth habit quoted and adapted from C. Lee, "Stephen Covey Talks About the 8th Habit: Effective Is No Longer Enough," *Training*, February 2005, pp 17–19 (emphasis added).

Arranging Support for the Psychological Self Referring to the person portion of the self-management model in Figure 3.3, three cognitive supports for behaviour change are symbolic coding, rehearsal, and self-talk. These amount to psychological, as opposed to environmental, cues. Yet, according to Bandura, they prompt appropriate behaviour in the same manner. Each requires a brief explanation:

- **Symbolic coding** From a social learning theory perspective, the human brain stores information in visual and verbal codes. For example, a sales manager could use the visual picture of a man chopping down a huge tree to remember Woodman, the name of a promising new client. In addition, people commonly rely on acronyms to recall names, rules for behaviour, and other information. An acronym (or verbal code) that is often heard in managerial circles is the KISS principle, standing for "Keep It Simple, Stupid."

- **Rehearsal** While it is true that practice often makes perfect, mental rehearsal of challenging tasks can also increase one's chances of success. Importantly, experts draw a clear distinction between systematic visualization of how one should proceed and daydreaming about success:

  The big difference between daydreaming and visualizing is that "visualizing is much more specific and detailed," says consultant Judith Schuster. "A daydream typically has gaps in

it—we jump immediately to where we want to wind up. In visualization, we use building blocks and, step-by-step, construct the result we want."[48]

Experts recommend using this sort of visualization when involved with strategic planning.[49] Individuals also stand to learn a great deal about mental rehearsal and visualization from successful athletes. Kim Woodring, an all-star volleyball player, is a good example. She effectively combines visualization and self-talk:

"I'm always positive," she says. "Even if I'm losing. I talk positively to myself. I go on with the next play and don't worry about the last one. When I visualize, I always see the perfect pass, perfect hit, perfect set, perfect kill, perfect result."[50]

Job-finding seminars for students are very popular on campuses today because they typically involve mental and actual rehearsal of tough job interviews. This sort of manufactured experience can build the confidence and self-efficacy necessary for real-world success.[51]

- **Self-talk** According to an expert on the subject, "*self-talk* is the set of evaluating thoughts that you give yourself about facts and events that happen to you."[52] Personal experience

Self-talk

Evaluating thoughts about oneself.

tells us that self-talk tends to be a self-fulfilling prophecy. Negative self-talk tends to pave the way for failure, whereas positive self-talk often facilitates success. Replacing negative self-talk ("I'll never get a raise") with positive self-talk ("I deserve a raise and I'm going to get it") is fundamental to better self-management. One business writer, while urging salespeople to be their own cheerleaders, offered this advice for handling difficult situations:

Tell yourself there's a positive side to everything and train yourself to focus on it. At first your new self-talk will seem forced and unnatural, but stick with it. Use mental imagery to help you concentrate on the benefits of what you think is a bad situation. If you don't like cold calling, for example, think of how good you'll feel when you're finished, knowing you have a whole list of new selling opportunities. Forming a new habit isn't easy, but the effort will pay off.[53]

Consequences The completion of self-contracts and other personal achievements calls for self-reinforcement. According to Bandura, three criteria must be satisfied before self-reinforcement can occur:

1. The individual must have *control over desired reinforcers*.

2. Reinforcers must be *self-administered on a conditional basis*. Failure to meet the performance requirement must lead to self-denial.

3. *Performance standards must be adopted* to establish the quantity and quality of target behaviour required for self-reinforcement.[54]

In view of the following realities, self-reinforcement strategies need to be resourceful and creative:

Self-granted rewards can lead to self-improvement. But as failed dieters and smokers can attest, there are short-run as well as long-run influences on self-reinforcement. For the overeater, the immediate gratification of eating has more influence than the promise of a new wardrobe. The same sort of dilemma plagues procrastinators. Consequently, one needs to weave a powerful web of cues, cognitive

Athletes, such as Olympic gold medal winner Lori-Ann Muenzer, use a combination of visualization and self-talk techniques when competing. This is a way of supporting themselves during a challenging time.

supports, and internal and external consequences to win the tug-of-war with status-quo payoffs. Primarily because it is so easy to avoid, self-punishment tends to be ineffectual. As with managing the behaviour of others, positive instead of negative consequences are recommended for effective self-management.[55]

In addition, it helps to solicit positive reinforcement for self-improvement from supportive friends, co-workers, and relatives.

Personality Dynamics

Individuals have their own way of thinking and acting, their own unique style or *personality*. **Personality** is defined as the combination of stable physical and mental characteristics that give individuals their identity. These characteristics or traits—including how one looks, thinks, acts, and feels—are the product of interacting genetic and environmental influences.[56] In this section, we introduce the Big Five personality dimensions and discuss key personality dynamics, including locus of control, attitudes, intelligence, and mental abilities.

Personality

Stable physical and mental characteristics responsible for a person's identity.

THE BIG FIVE PERSONALITY DIMENSIONS

When it comes to personality, the Big Five identifies the following key five dimensions: extraversion, agreeableness, conscientiousness, emotional stability, and openness to experience (see Table 3.2 for descriptions). Standardized personality tests determine how positively or negatively a person scores on each of the Big Five. For example, someone scoring negatively on extraversion would be an introverted person prone to shy and withdrawn behaviour.[57] Someone scoring negatively on emotional stability would be nervous, tense, angry, and worried. A person's scores on the Big Five reveal a personality profile as unique as fingerprints.

But one important question lingers: Are personality models ethnocentric and unique to the culture in which

TABLE 3.2

The Big Five Personality Dimensions

STABLE PHYSICAL AND MENTAL CHARACTERISTICS RESPONSIBLE FOR A PERSON'S IDENTITY	
1. Extraversion	Outgoing, talkative, sociable, assertive
2. Agreeableness	Trusting, good-natured, cooperative, soft-hearted
3. Conscientiousness	Dependable, responsible, achievement-oriented, persistent
4. Emotional stability	Relaxed, secure, unworried
5. Openess to experience	Intellectual, imaginative, curious, broad-minded

SOURCE: Adapted from M.R. Barrick and M.K. Mount, "Autonomy as a Moderator of the Relationships between the Big Five Personality Dimensions and Job Performance," *Journal of Applied Psychology*, February 1993, pp 111–18.

they were developed? At least as far as the Big Five model goes, crosscultural research evidence points in the direction of "no." Specifically, the Big Five personality structure held up very well in a study of women and men from Canada, Russia, Hong Kong, Poland, Germany, and Finland.[58]

Another research question relates to personality and gender: Are the personalities of men and women the same? As illustrated in the International OB feature box, psychologist David P. Schmitt set out to clarify the roles of the modern-day male and female, and what he found seems almost counter to what contemporary researchers think. So unbelievable were the first set of research findings, Schmitt crunched new data from 40,000 men and women on six continents. He concluded that, as wealthy modern societies level external barriers between women and men, some ancient internal differences are being revived. In other words, some of the old stereotypes (discussed in Chapter 2) keep reappearing. More researchers have decided to explore this area of gender and personality. As their findings continue to spur discussion and questions, the likelihood of men and women completely understanding each other won't be happening soon!

Personality and Job Performance Those interested in OB want to know the connection between the Big Five and job performance. Ideally, Big Five personality

LO 3

INTERNATIONAL OB

CROSS-CULTURAL DIFFERENCES BETWEEN MEN AND WOMEN

A series of research teams recently analyzed personality tests taken by men and women in more than 60 countries around the world. For evolutionary psychologists, the findings show that the size of the gender gap in personality varies among cultures. For social-role psychologists, the bad news is that the variation is going in the wrong direction. It looks as if personality differences between men and women are smaller in traditional cultures, like in India or Zimbabwe, than in Canada or the Netherlands. A husband and a stay-at-home wife in a patriarchal Botswanan clan seem to be more alike than a working couple in Canada or France. The more the two genders have equal rights and similar jobs, the more their personalities seem to diverge.

The study suggests that as wealthy modern societies level external barriers between women and men, some ancient internal differences are being revived. The biggest changes recorded by the researchers involved the personalities of men, not women. Men in traditional agricultural societies and poorer countries seem more cautious and anxious, less assertive, and less competitive than men in the most progressive and rich countries of North America and Europe.

SOURCE: Adapted from J. Tierney, "As Barriers Disappear, Some Gender Gaps Widen," *The New York Times*, September 9, 2008, http://www.nytimes.com/2008/09/09/science/09tier.html?_r=2&em=&pagewanted=print&oref=slogin&oref=slogin.

dimensions that correlate positively and strongly with job performance would be helpful in the selection, training, and appraisal of employees. A meta-analysis of 117 studies involving 23,994 subjects from many professions offers guidance.[59] Among the Big Five, *conscientiousness* had the strongest positive correlation with job performance and training performance. According to the researchers, "those individuals who exhibit traits associated with a strong sense of purpose, obligation, and persistence generally perform better than those who do not."[60] So it comes as no surprise that British researchers recently found that people scoring *low* on conscientiousness tended to have significantly more accidents both on and off the job.[61]

Another expected finding was that extraversion (an outgoing personality) was associated with success for managers and salespeople. Also, extraversion was a stronger predictor of job performance than agreeableness, across all professions. The researchers concluded, "It appears that being courteous, trusting, straightforward, and soft-hearted has a smaller impact on job performance than being talkative, active, and assertive."[62] Not surprisingly, in a recent study, a strong linkage between conscientiousness and performance was found among those with polished social skills.[63] As an added bonus for extraverts, a recent positive psychology study led to this conclusion: "All you have to do is act extraverted and you can get a happiness boost."[64] So the next time you are on the job, go initiate a conversation with someone and be more productive and happier!

The Proactive Personality As suggested by the above discussion, someone who scores high on the Big Five dimension of conscientiousness is probably a better and safer worker. Researchers Thomas S. Bateman and J. Michael Crant took this important linkage an additional step by formulating the concept of the ***proactive personality***. They define and characterize the proactive personality in these terms: "Someone who is relatively unconstrained by situational forces and who effects environmental change. Proactive people identify opportunities and act on them, show initiative, take action, and persevere until meaningful change occurs."[65] In short, people with proactive personalities are "hardwired" to change the status quo. In a review of relevant studies, Crant found

Proactive personality

Action-oriented person who shows initiative and perseveres to change things.

the proactive personality to be positively associated with individual, team, and organizational success.[66]

Successful entrepreneurs exemplify the proactive personality.[67] In his book, *The Formation of Entrepreneurial Intentions*, David S. Summers decided to expand upon the earlier findings of Bateman and Crant and apply the proactive personality research to his own career choices.[68] As he explains in the preface of the book:

> "... the thought of being independent and the chance to build something of value, combined with a unique set of life's circumstances, influenced my decision [to become an entrepreneur]."

For over twenty years I have been fascinated with the idea of being an entrepreneur. I have owned my own wholesale and retail merchandising firm, been an independent real estate agent, developed a management consulting business, and taught 'would be' entrepreneurs the joys and skills of starting a business. In all these years, however, I never really knew why someone would choose to be in a business for themselves. For me the thought of being independent and the chance to build something of value, combined with a unique set of life's circumstances, influenced my decision. I wanted to know if others felt the same way.

His findings suggest that Bateman and Crant were correct in that "people who were inclined to control their environment so they could get what they wanted were likely to start new businesses." People with proactive personalities truly are valuable *human capital*. Those wanting to get ahead would do well to cultivate the initiative, drive, and perseverance of someone with a proactive personality.

There Is No "Ideal Employee" Personality A word of caution is in order here. The Big Five personality dimensions of conscientiousness and extraversion and the proactive personality are generally desirable in the workplace, but they are not a panaceas (cure-all). Given the complexity of today's work environments, the diversity of today's workforce, and recent research evidence,[69] the quest for an ideal employee personality profile is sheer folly. Just as one shoe does not fit all people, one personality profile does not fit all job situations. Good management involves taking the time to get to know each employee's unique combination of personality traits, abilities, and potential and then creating a productive and satisfying person–job fit.

Personality Assessment Instrument While there are several assessment instruments available on the market to identify employee personality type, the Myers-Briggs Type Indicator (MBTI) is a fairly popular instrument often used by business. With assistance from Psychometrics Canada, Inc., the Canadian distributor of the instrument, organizations can have a trained professional arrive on-site to work with employees or to help screen new applicants. The results of the test can help individuals understand their own preferences, biases, and behaviour. If team-orientation is desired by the firm, then test results can be used to help facilitate a better transition between members. To determine your own MBTI personality type, go to the end of this chapter and review the Google search exercise #1.

LO 4   LOCUS OF CONTROL: SELF OR ENVIRONMENT?

Individuals vary in terms of how much personal responsibility they take for their behaviour and its consequences. Julian Rotter, a personality researcher, identified a dimension of personality he labelled *locus of control* to explain these differences. He proposed that people tend to attribute the causes of their behaviour primarily to either themselves or environmental factors,[70] producing different behaviour patterns.

People who believe they control the events and consequences that affect their lives are said to possess an **internal locus of control**. For example, these people tend to attribute positive outcomes, such as getting a passing grade on an exam, to their own abilities. Similarly, an "internal" tends to blame negative events, such as failing an exam, on personal shortcomings—not studying hard enough, perhaps. Many entrepreneurs eventually succeed because their *internal* locus of control helps them overcome setbacks and disappointments.

Internal locus of control

Attributing outcomes to one's own actions.

On the other side of this personality dimension are those who believe their performance is the product of circumstances beyond their immediate control. These individuals are said to possess an **external locus of control** and tend to attribute outcomes to environmental causes, such as luck or fate. Unlike internals, an "external" would attribute a passing grade on an exam to something external (an easy test or a good day), and attribute a failing grade to an unfair test or problems at home.

External locus of control

Attributing outcomes to circumstances beyond one's control.

Research Lessons Researchers have found important behavioural differences between internals and externals:

- Internals display greater work motivation.

- Internals have stronger expectations that effort leads to performance.

- Internals exhibit higher performance on tasks involving learning or problem solving, when performance leads to valued rewards.

- There is a stronger relationship between job satisfaction and performance for internals than for externals.

- Internals obtain higher salaries and greater salary increases than externals.

- Externals tend to be more anxious than internals.[71]

Tempering an Internal Locus of Control with *Humility*
Do you have an internal locus of control? Odds are high that you do, judging from the "typical" OB student we have worked with over the years. Good thing, because it should pay off in the workplace with opportunities, raises, and promotions. But before you declare yourself Grade A executive material, here is one more thing to toss into your tool kit: a touch of humility. **Humility** is "a realistic assessment of one's own contribution and the recognition of the contribution of others, along with luck and good fortune that made one's own success possible."[72] Humility has been called the silent virtue. How many truly humble people brag about being humble? Two OB experts recently offered this instructive perspective:

Humility

Considering the contributions of others and good fortune when gauging one's success.

Humble individuals have a down-to-earth perspective of themselves and of the events and relationships in their lives. Humility involves a capability to evaluate success, failure, work, and life without exaggeration. Furthermore, humility enables leaders to distinguish the delicate line between such characteristics as healthy self-confidence, self-esteem, and self-assessment, and those of over-confidence, narcissism, and stubbornness. Humility is the mid-point between the two negative extremes of arrogance and lack of self-esteem. This depiction allows one to see that a person can be humble and competitive or humble and ambitious at the same time, which contradicts common—but mistaken—views about humility.[73]

HIRING EMPLOYEES BASED ON THEIR GENETIC QUALITIES

Consider the following futuristic scenario: *ABC Company Inc.* advertises for an elite group of applicants to work for their organization based on genetic code testing results. All applicants must agree to submit blood and skin sample reports, along with their resumé, to be considered for an interview. The organization is looking for certain unique employee qualities that they believe will prove more effective on the job.

Sound ridiculous? It is already legal in Canada under certain circumstances to run drug and alcohol tests on potential new employees. Further, police checks, HIV, urine and hair follicle testing are more common today than they were ten years ago. Now consider that the Human Genome Project, a 50-year project, has finally been completed by scientists from around the world. In their efforts to write the sequence of all the genes in the DNA molecule, their focus from the beginning was on identifying the faulty genes responsible for diseases such as diabetes, cancer, leukaemia, eczema, and heart disease. However, researchers are currently using such information to track down the specific genes involved in very complicated constructs like intelligence, personality, and human behaviour. Over the next several years, ". . . there are going to be a lot of behavioural studies involved and they will yield up some pretty interesting discoveries," says Dr. Francis Collins, one of the leading scientists who worked on the project. The supporters of diversity in the workplace will find such science offensive and threatening, as certain types of people become preferred over others. What do you think?

Sources: BBC News, *Scientists complete DNA 'Book of Life,'* April 14, 2003; Genome's knowledge "avalanche," March 9, 2006; website: http://newsvote.bbc.co.uk/mpapps/pagetools/print/news.bbc.co.uk/2/hi/science/nature/4772114.stm and http://news.bbc.co.uk/cbbcnews/hi/sci_tech/newsid_2946000/2946419.stm. K. Davies, PBS Nova Online, "Cracking The Code of Life," *Nature vs. Nurture Revisited*, April 2001, http://www.pbs.org/wgbh/nova/genome/debate.html

Abilities (Intelligence) and Performance

Although experts do not agree on a specific definition, *intelligence* represents an individual's capacity for constructive thinking, reasoning, and problem solving.[74] When employers engage in hiring potential candidates, traits such as these become of interest as the right person is sought after and selected. But what is the best way to find such candidates to hire? Historically, intelligence was believed to be an innate capacity, passed genetically from one generation to the next. So, for example, if a firm hired the son or daughter of a prominent business person, then it was assumed that the child would perform at the same successful level as the parent. Of course, such a hiring practice is riddled with bias and discourages diversity. The Focus on Diversity feature box takes this discussion of genetics, intelligence, and bias a bit further.

For now, contemporary research shows that intelligence (like personality) goes beyond genetics and is also a function of environmental influences, such as sleep deprivation and nutrition.[75] Organic factors have more recently been added to the formula as a result of mounting evidence of the connection between alcohol and drug abuse by pregnant women and intellectual development problems in their children.[76]

Researchers have produced some interesting findings about abilities and intelligence in recent years. A unique five-year study documented the tendency of people to "gravitate into jobs commensurate with their abilities."[77] This prompts the vision of the labour market acting as a giant sorting or sifting machine, with employees tumbling into various ability bins. Meanwhile, a steady and significant rise in average intelligence among those in developed countries has been observed over the last 70 years. Why? Experts at a North American psychology conference concluded, "Some combination of better schooling, improved socioeconomic status, healthier nutrition, and a more technologically complex society might account for the gains in IQ scores."[78] So if you think you're smarter than your parents and your teachers, you're probably right!

Intelligence

Capacity for constructive thinking, reasoning, and problem solving.

Two Types of Abilities By examining the relationships between measures of mental abilities and behaviour using an empirical approach, researchers have statistically isolated major components of intelligence. Using this procedure, pioneering psychologist Charles Spearman proposed in 1927 that all cognitive performance is determined by two types of abilities. The first can be characterized as a general mental ability needed for all cognitive tasks. The second is unique to the task at hand. For example, an ability to complete crossword puzzles is a function of broad mental abilities, as well as the specific ability to perceive patterns in partially completed words.

Seven Major Mental Abilities Through the years, much research has been devoted to developing and expanding Spearman's ideas on the relationship between cognitive abilities and intelligence.[79] One research psychologist listed 120 distinct mental abilities. Table 3.3 defines the seven most frequently cited mental abilities. Of the seven abilities, personnel selection researchers have found verbal ability, numerical ability, spatial ability, and inductive reasoning to be valid predictors of job performance for both minority and majority applicants. Also, according to a recent comprehensive research review, standard intelligence (IQ) tests do a good job of predicting both academic achievement and job performance.[80] This contradicts the popular notion that different cognitive abilities are needed for school and work.

DO WE HAVE MULTIPLE INTELLIGENCES?

Howard Gardner, a world-renown professor of education, offered a new paradigm for human intelligence in his 1983 book, *Frames of Mind: The Theory of Multiple Intelligences*.[81] He has subsequently identified eight different intelligences that vastly broaden the longstanding concept of intelligence. Gardner's concept of multiple intelligences (MI) includes not only cognitive abilities, but also social and physical abilities and skills:

- **Linguistic intelligence** Potential to learn and use spoken and written languages.

- **Logical-mathematical intelligence** Potential for deductive reasoning, problem analysis, and mathematical calculation.

- **Musical intelligence** Potential to appreciate, compose, and perform music.

- **Bodily-kinesthetic intelligence** Potential to use mind and body to coordinate physical movement.

- **Spatial intelligence** Potential to recognize and use patterns.

- **Interpersonal intelligence** Potential to understand, connect with, and effectively work with others.

- **Intrapersonal intelligence** Potential to understand and regulate oneself.

- **Naturalist intelligence** Potential to live in harmony with one's environment.[82]

TABLE 3.3	Mental Abilities Ability Description	
	STABLE PHYSICAL AND MENTAL CHARACTERISTICS RESPONSIBLE FOR A PERSON'S IDENTITY	
	1. Verbal comprehension	The ability to understand what words mean and to readily comprehend what is read.
	2. Word fluency	The ability to produce isolated words that fulfill specific symbolic or structural requirements (such as all words that begin with the letter b and have two vowels).
	3. Numerical	The ability to make quick and accurate arithmetic computations such as adding and subtracting.
	4. Spatial	Being able to perceive spatial patterns and to visualize how geometric shapes would look if transformed in shape or position.
	5. Memory	Having good rote memory for paired words, symbols, lists of numbers, or other associated items.
	6. Perceptual speed	The ability to perceive figures, identify similarities and differences, and carry out tasks involving visual perception.
	7. Inductive reasoning	The ability to reason from specifics to general conclusions.

SOURCE: Adapted from M.D. Dunnette, "Aptitudes, Abilities, and Skills," in *Handbook of Industrial and Organizational Psychology*, ed. M.D. Dunnette (Skokie, IL: Rand McNally, 1976), pp 478–83.

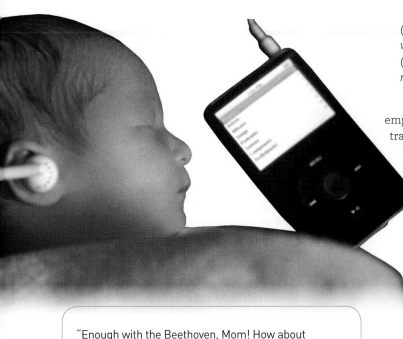

"Enough with the Beethoven, Mom! How about some Jay-Z?" Some parents strive to develop their baby's multiple intelligences by exposing them to unconventional stimuli. Here, a sleeping newborn baby (7 days old) is listening to classical music on an iPod.

(shaping), or finding a new environment within which to work (selection). One uses these skills to (a) manage oneself, (b) manage others, and (c) manage tasks.[83]

Others believe MI has important implications for employee selection and training.[84] One-size-fits-all training programs fall short when MI diversity is taken into consideration. We look forward to breakthroughs in this area as MI attracts OB researchers and practicing managers.

Emotions: An Emerging OB Topic

In the ideal world of management theory, employees pursue organizational goals in a logical and rational manner; emotional behaviour is seldom factored into the equation. Yet day-to-day organizational life shows us how prevalent and powerful emotions can be. Anger and jealousy, both potent emotions, often push aside logic and rationality in the workplace. Managers use fear and other emotions to both motivate and intimidate. For example, consider Microsoft CEO Steve Ballmer's management style prior to his recent efforts to become a kinder, gentler leader: "Ballmer shouts when he gets excited or angry—his voice rising so suddenly that it's like an electric shock . . . by the early 1990s, Ballmer had to have throat surgery to fix problems brought on by shouting."[85]

Less noisy, but still emotion laden, is John Chambers's tightrope act as CEO of Cisco Systems:

Many educators and parents have embraced MI because it helps explain how a child could score poorly on a standard IQ test yet be obviously gifted in one or more ways (e.g., music, sports, relationship building). Moreover, they believe the concept of MI underscores the need to help children develop their own unique way and at their own pace. They say standard IQ tests deal only with the first two intelligences on Gardner's list. Meanwhile, most academic psychologists and intelligence specialists continue to criticize Gardner's model as being too subjective and poorly integrated.

They prefer the traditional model of intelligence as a unified variable measured by a single test. While the academic debate continues, we can draw some practical benefits from Gardner's notion of MI. In the final section of this chapter, you will encounter the concept of emotional intelligence. Psychologist Robert J. Sternberg recently applied Gardner's "naturalist intelligence" to the domain of leadership under the heading *practical intelligence*. He explains,

Practical intelligence is the ability to solve everyday problems by utilizing knowledge gained from experience in order to purposefully adapt to, shape, and select environments. It thus involves changing oneself to suit the environment (adaptation), changing the environment to suit oneself

Any company that thinks it's utterly unbeatable is already beaten. So when I begin to think we're getting a little bit too confident, you'll see me emphasizing the paranoia side. And then when I feel that there's a little bit too much fear and apprehension, I'll just jump back to the other side. My job is to keep those scales perfectly balanced.[86]

These corporate leaders would not have achieved what they have without the ability to be logical and rational decision makers *and* be emotionally charged. Too much emotion, however, could have spelled career and organizational disaster for either one of them.

In this final section, our examination of individual differences turns to defining emotions, reviewing a typology of 10 positive and negative emotions, and discussing the topics of emotional contagion, emotional labour, and emotional intelligence.

POSITIVE AND NEGATIVE EMOTIONS

Richard S. Lazarus, a leading authority on the subject, defines **emotions** as "complex, patterned, organismic reactions to how we think we are doing in our lifelong efforts to survive and flourish and to achieve what we wish for ourselves."[87] The word *organismic* is appropriate because emotions involve the *whole* person—biological, psychological, and social. Importantly, psychologists draw a distinction between *felt* and *displayed* emotions.[88] For example, you might feel angry (felt emotion) at a rude co-worker, but not make a nasty remark in return (displayed emotion). Emotions play roles in both causing and adapting to stress and its associated biological and psychological problems. The destructive effect of emotional behaviour on social relationships is all too obvious in daily life.

Lazarus's definition of emotions centres on a person's goals. Accordingly, his distinction between positive and negative emotions is goal-oriented. Some emotions are triggered by frustration and failure when pursuing one's goals. Lazarus calls these *negative* emotions. They are said to be goal incongruent. For example, which of the six negative emotions in Figure 3.4 are you likely to experience if you fail the final exam in

> **Emotions**
>
> Complex human reactions to personal achievements and setbacks that may be felt and displayed.

a required course? Failing the exam would be incongruent with your goal of graduating on time. On the other hand, which of the four *positive* emotions in Figure 3.4 would you probably experience if you graduated on time and with honours? The emotions you would experience in this situation are positive because they are congruent (or consistent) with an important lifetime goal. The individual's goals, it is important to note, may or may not be socially acceptable. Thus, a positive emotion, such as love/affection, may be undesirable if associated with sexual harassment. Oppositely, slight pangs of guilt, anxiety, and envy can motivate extra effort. On balance, the constructive or destructive nature of a particular emotion must be judged in terms of both its intensity and the person's relevant goal.

GOOD (AND BAD) MOODS ARE CONTAGIOUS

Have you ever had someone's bad mood sour your mood? That person could have been a parent, supervisor, co-worker, friend, or someone serving you in a store or restaurant. Appropriately, researchers call this emotional contagion. We, quite literally, can catch another person's good or bad mood or displayed emotions. This effect has been documented in two separate studies. UBC OB Professor Peter Frost talked about it in his book *Toxic Emotions At Work* (we'll be discussing this later in Chapter 8), as well as in a study involving 131 bank tellers (92 percent female) and 220 exit interviews with their customers. In the latter study, tellers who expressed positive emotions tended to have more satisfied customers.[89] Two field studies with nurses and accountants as subjects found a strong linkage between the work group's collective mood and the individual's mood.[90] Both foul moods and good moods turned out to be contagious. Perhaps more managers should follow the lead of orchestra director Lorin Maazel:

> *I have noticed in my long career that if I am really tired or I have a flu coming on that it's felt. Everybody gets into that mode, and pretty soon, they're playing as sluggishly as I'm conducting. I have learned to come to rehearsal fresh, energetic, projecting enthusiasm and go-go-go. It's got to be irresistible. If I don't think I'm up to it, I take a cold shower. That's my*

> ▶ **FIGURE 3.4** **Positive and Negative Emotions**

Negative Emotions (Goal incongruent)

Positive Emotions (Goal congruent)

Anger · Happiness/joy · Fright/anxiety · Pride · Guilt/shame · Love/affection · Sadness · Envy/jealousy · Relief · Disgust

SOURCE: Adapted from discussion in R.S. Lazarus, *Emotion and Adaptation* (New York: Oxford University Press, 1991), Chapters 6, 7.

job—to energize people. If they grind it out and couldn't care less, then they wind up hating you and themselves because it's not why they practised all of their lives. Emotion is what it's all about. Music making without emotion and passion is nothing.[91]

EMOTIONAL LABOUR (IT HAS *NOT* BEEN A PLEASURE SERVING YOU!)

Although they did not have the benefit of a catchy label or a body of sophisticated research, generations of managers have known about the power of emotional contagion in the marketplace. "Smile, look happy for the customers," employees are told over and over again. But what if the employees are having a rotten day? What if they have to mask their true feelings and emotions? What if they have to fake it?

Emotional labour

Management of feeling to create a publicly observable facial and bodily display.

Researchers have begun studying the dynamics of what they call ***emotional labour***. Sociologist Arlie Hochschild defines emotional labour as management of feeling to create a publicly observable facial and bodily display.[92] Other OB researchers have considered the complexities around emotional labour, and here is what they conclude:

> *Emotional labour can be particularly detrimental to the employee performing the labour and can take its toll both psychologically and physically. Employees ... may bottle up feelings of frustration, resentment, and anger, which are not appropriate to express. These feelings result, in part, from the constant requirement to monitor one's negative emotions and express positive ones. If not given a healthy expressive outlet, this emotional repression can lead to a syndrome of emotional exhaustion and burnout.*[93]

Interestingly, a pair of laboratory studies found no gender difference in *felt* emotions, but the women were more emotionally expressive than the men.[94] This stream of research on emotional labour has major practical implications for productivity and job satisfaction, as well as for workplace anger, aggression, and violence. Taking a lead from Lorin Maazel, who we mentioned earlier, managers need to be attuned to (and responsive to) the emotional states and needs of their people. They need to understand how emotions affect people and how their own personal emotions affect others in a contagious way. This understanding can be achieved through emotional intelligence.

EMOTIONAL INTELLIGENCE

LO 5

In 1995, Daniel Goleman, a psychologist turned journalist, created a stir in education and management circles with the publication of his book, *Emotional Intelligence*. As a result, an obscure topic among positive psychologists became mainstream. According to Goleman, traditional models of intelligence (IQ) are too narrow, failing to consider interpersonal competence. Goleman's broader agenda includes "abilities such as being able to motivate oneself and persist in the face of frustrations; to control impulse and delay gratification; to regulate one's moods and keep distress from swamping the ability to think; to empathize and to hope."[95] Thus, ***emotional intelligence*** is the ability to manage oneself and one's relationships in mature and constructive ways. Referred to by some as EI and others as EQ, emotional intelligence is said to have four key components: self-awareness, self-management, social awareness, and relationship management.[96] The first two constitute personal competence; the second two feed into social competence (see Skills & Best Practices feature box).

Emotional intelligence

Ability to manage oneself and interact with others in mature and constructive ways.

These emotional intelligence skills need to be well polished in today's pressure-packed workplaces:

> *Unanticipated hot spots often flare up during important meetings. Show patience, career experts say. Take deep breaths, compose your thoughts, restate the question—and use humour to defuse tension. If you avoid blurting out the first thing that comes to mind, "people will see your demeanour as cool and professional," observes [executive and author] David F D'Alessandro.*
>
> *Most people don't do well with the unexpected because they lack a script, notes Dr. [Dory] Hollander. The workplace psychologist recommends acting classes for her clients.*
>
> *A year of lessons helped one female client advance into the executive ranks at a big technology company. The woman used to perform poorly when colleagues tossed out unforeseen questions after presentations. "She looked like she was in pain," Dr. Hollander recalls.*
>
> *Today, the former middle manager acts confident and appears to enjoy herself even when she lands on the hot seat. "It really is theatre," her coach concludes.*[97]

Self-assessment instruments supposedly measuring emotional intelligence have appeared in the popular management literature. Sample questions include: "I believe I can stay on top of tough situations,"[98] and "I

Skills & Best Practices

Developing Emotional Intelligence

Personal Competence: These capabilities determine how we manage ourselves.

Self-Awareness

- *Emotional self-awareness:* Reading one's own emotions and recognizing their impact; using "gut sense" to guide decisions.
- *Accurate self-assessment:* Knowing one's strengths and limits.
- *Self-confidence:* A sound sense of one's self-worth and capabilities.

Self-Management

- *Emotional self-control:* Keeping disruptive emotions and impulses under control.
- *Transparency:* Displaying honesty and integrity; trustworthiness.
- *Adaptability:* Flexibility in adapting to changing situations or overcoming obstacles.
- *Achievement:* The drive to improve performance to meet inner standards of excellence.
- *Initiative:* Readiness to act and seize opportunities.
- *Optimism:* Seeing the upside in events.

Social Competence: These capabilities determine how we manage relationships.

Social Awareness

- *Empathy:* Sensing others' emotions, understanding their perspective, and taking active interest in their concerns.
- *Organizational awareness:* Reading the currents, decision networks, and politics at the organizational level.
- *Service:* Recognizing and meeting follower, client, or customer needs.

Relationship Management

- *Inspirational leadership:* Guiding and motivating with a compelling vision.
- *Influence:* Wielding a range of tactics for persuasion.
- *Developing others:* Bolstering others' abilities through feedback and guidance.
- *Change catalyst:* Initiating, managing, and leading in a new direction.
- *Conflict management:* Resolving disagreements.
- *Building bonds:* Cultivating and maintaining a web of relationships.
- *Teamwork and collaboration:* Cooperation and team building.

SOURCE: Reprinted by permission of Harvard Business School Press. D. Goleman, R. Boyatzis, and A. McKee, *Primal Leadership: Realizing the Power of Emotional Intelligence* (Boston: Harvard Business School Press, 2002), p 39. Copyright © 2002 by the Harvard Business School Publishing Corporation; all rights reserved.

am able to admit my own mistakes."[99] Recent research, however, casts serious doubt on the reliability and validity of such instruments[100] Even Goleman concedes, "It's very tough to measure our own emotional intelligence, because most of us don't have a very clear sense of how we come across to other people . . . ."[101] Honest feedback from others is necessary. Still, the area of emotional intelligence is useful for teachers and organizational trainers because, unlike IQ, social problem solving and the ability to control one's emotions can be taught and learned. Scores on emotional intelligence tests definitely should *not* be used for making hiring and promotion decisions until valid measuring tools are developed.

Summary of Learning Objectives

1. **Define *self-esteem* and *self-efficacy*.** Self-esteem is an overall evaluation of oneself, one's perceived self-worth. Self-efficacy is the belief in one's ability to successfully perform a task.

2. **Explain what is meant by self-monitoring and discuss how it relates to the social learning model of self-management.** High self-monitors strive to make a good public impression by closely monitoring their behaviour and adapting it to the situation. Low self-monitors do the opposite by acting out their momentary feelings, regardless of their surroundings. According to the social learning model of self-management, behaviour results from interaction among four components: (a) situational cues, (b) the person's psychological self, (c) the person's behaviour, and (d) consequences. Effective behaviour, such as Covey's eight habits of highly effective people, can be developed by relying on supportive cognitive processes such as mental rehearsal and self-talk. Carefully arranged cues and consequences also help in the self-improvement process.

3. **Relate the one Big Five personality dimension that is most positively correlated with job performance.** The Big Five personality dimensions are extraversion (social and talkative), agreeableness (trusting and cooperative), conscientiousness (responsible and persistent), emotional stability (relaxed and unworried), and openness to experience (intellectual and curious). Conscientiousness is the best predictor of job performance.

4. **Compare and contrast internal and external locus of control.** People with an internal locus of control, such as entrepreneurs, believe they are masters of their own fate. Those with an external locus of control attribute their behaviour and its results to situational forces. In an empowered workplace, a manager would want to hire people with a high internal locus of control because they would be more likely to "blame" themselves rather than others for poor work performance, thus self-managing themselves to higher productivity.

5. **Summarize the theory of emotional intelligence and explain how it relates to appreciating individual differences between people.** Emotional intelligence (EI) is the ability to manage oneself and interact with others in mature and constructive ways. The four key components of EI are self-awareness and self-management (personal competence), and social awareness and relationship management (social competence). Someone with high EI has the ability to see the connection between emotions and behaviour in the workplace—first their own, and then those of others. Since EI goes beyond traditional intelligence, it provides a deeper understanding of individual human behaviour. Old school assumptions around hiring people who have certain personalities or intelligences need to be enriched with a more contemporary understanding of EI so that a more complete picture of how people differ is considered.

Discussion Questions

1. How is someone you know with low self-efficacy, relative to a specified task, "programming himself/herself for failure"? How could that individual develop high self-efficacy?

2. What importance do you attach to self-talk in self-management? Explain.

3. On a scale of 1 (low) to 10 (high), how would you rate yourself on the Big Five personality dimensions? Is your personality profile suitable for your current (or chosen) line of work? Explain.

4. What benefit would there be to employers if they pre-screened all job applicants with a combination of personality assessments and instruments measuring EI levels?

5. Which of the four key components of emotional intelligence is (or are) your strong suit? Which is (or are) your weakest? What are the everyday implications of your EI profile?

Google Searches

1. **Google Search:** "Big Five Personality Self-Assessments" and "My MBTI Personality Type Assessment" Complete one or two of the online self-assessments to determine your personality type. Record your results and share with members of your group. Do you agree with the results? Explain your response.

2. **Google Search:** "The Luck Factor—Change Your Luck, Change Your Life" Read a few paragraphs of what Professor Wiseman's research discovered about 'lucky' individuals. How do lucky people cope with disappointment or bad luck? Are you a lucky person? Working with a partner, answer the following question: Would you say that lucky people have a high or low internal locus on control? Explain.

3. **Google Search:** "What is Your Emotional Intelligence Quotient?" and complete an online self-assessment. What did you score? Do you agree with the EQ results? Explain your response. Compare your results with group members and discuss the differences between people.

Experiential Exercise

Managing Situational Cues

PURPOSE   This exercise is meant to strengthen student understanding of the Social Learning Model of Self-Management (Figure 3.3). Approx. Timing: 15 minutes.

ACTIVITY ASSIGNMENT
- The two individuals described below want to achieve a new goal.
- Working in groups, help the individuals through the various factors of the Social Learning Model to achieve a successful outcome.
- Review the Social Learning Model (Figure 3.3) while working through the two situations.

1. SHAKIRA

SCENARIO: Shakira's family doctor says that she is in poor health, 60 pounds overweight, and is a strong candidate for diabetes. The doctor has ordered Shakira to start eating properly, exercise daily, and lose the weight over the next 12 months or face taking medication every day for the rest of her life.

BEHAVIOUR CHANGE: Shakira decides to set a goal of taking her health more seriously—starting now.

SITUATIONAL CUES: Identify at least six cues that have to be rearranged for Shakira to achieve her goal.

CONSEQUENCES: List at least three consequences (or rewards) that Shakira can implement.

2. XIN (pronounced "Shin")

SCENARIO: Xin works 50–60 hours per week, on average. Sometimes there is so much to do that the only time work can get done is for Xin to stay late at night or work on weekends to get caught up. Xin is getting concerned about being able to sustain such a level of performance; besides, no one else in the office works the same kind of hours. One day, a colleague in the next office mentions to Xin that the HR Department is offering a time management seminar. Xin wonders if attending this seminar might help decrease the number of hours spent at the office each week.

BEHAVIOUR CHANGE: Xin decides to set a goal to decrease the number of hours spent working each week.

SITUATIONAL CUES: Identify at least six cues that have to be rearranged for Xin to achieve this goal.

CONSEQUENCES: List at least three consequences (or rewards) that Xin can implement.

www.mcgrawhill.ca/olc/kreitner

The **Presentation** Assistant

Here are possible topics and corresponding sources related to this chapter that can be further explored by student groups looking for ideas.

	PERSONALITY TEST —WHAT IS THE MBTI PROFILE OF YOUR CLASS AND DO YOU AGREE WITH THE RESULT?	BEYOND IQ—HOW MANY MULTIPLE INTELLIGENCES ARE THERE?	STUDENTS WITH HIGH SELF-ESTEEM—HOW MUCH ARE YOU WORTH?
YouTube Videos	• Psychometric Tests • Personality Profiling • Personality Evaluation • MBTI	• Multiple Intelligences • Howard Gardner	• Grad Jobs and Salary • Hiring New Graduates
TV Shows or Movies to Preview	• *Sybil* • *The United States of Tara*	• *Numbers* • *A Beautiful Mind* • *Jack Ass The Movie*	• *Graduation Movie* • *Friends*
Internet Searches	• MBTI Online Testing and Assessment • Psychometrics Canada	• What is IQ? • How Is IQ Traditionally measured? • Are IQ Tests Biased?	• Statistics Canada Education in 2000–20__ (the most recent publication) • *Canadian HR Reporter* – Students wishing they studied more • Kelly Global Workforce Index, Kelly Services • Try your own school placement office
Ice Breaker Classroom Activity	• Ask each person in the room to complete the online assessment. Once completed, have everyone write their type on a 3 × 5 card and hand it in. Compile all the cards and place the profile on the front board. What is the dominant type of the students?	• Ask the students to find practical examples of people who demonstrate each of Howard Gardner's Multiple Intelligences. For example, "Which intelligence would Wayne Gretzky score high on?"	• Ask each student to write down how much they believe they are worth to an employer upon graduation. What is their expected salary? Share responses with the class.

Who Should We Hire?

Consider the following scenario:

Bob Sharkey and Phay Sing are both middle managers who work at TriCom Inc., a toy manufacturing facility in Vancouver, B.C. On this particular morning, Bob and Phay are standing in the office lobby waiting for the elevator to arrive. They are in the midst of a discussion about a new hire for the office. Here is their conversation on what kind of person should be hired for the office in the near future:

BOB: *I am so tired of the people that HR sends us. I need someone who will take direction and not give me a hard time when I ask him or her to do something.*

PHAY: *What are you talking about? HR pre-screens all our employees so that we get the kind of applicants that will fit in. When you say you want someone to take direction, are you looking for a slave or an employee?*

BOB: *What do you mean by that? I just want people who take direction from their superior and want to work in this office. You see, I believe that whenever possible, managers should hire people who know their place, don't ask stupid questions, and keep to themselves! Is that so hard?*

PHAY: *Personally, I would much rather have someone work with me rather than for me . . . I prefer people who can think on their own, provide valuable insight or input to an issue, and let me know whether my thinking is accurate or not.*

BOB: *Oh boy, are we ever going to agree on this issue? I doubt it!*

PHAY: *That depends on whether we can get you into the 21st Century with your thinking!! Come on . . . I'll buy you lunch and I'll even let you decide what you want to order!*

BOB: *Gee – thanks!*

Just as they both began to laugh, the elevator door opened in front of them. "Going down?" asked the person inside. "Yeah," said Bob, "First floor please."

Discussion Questions

1. Is Bob looking for a high or low self-monitoring employee?
2. What type of locus of control does Bob want his new hire to have? Explain.
3. Do you believe Bob's actions will screen out a certain type of (proactive) employee? Is this what he wants?
4. Name two managerial implications for employees who have a high degree of external locus of control. Can you think of an example?
5. Name two managerial implications for those employees who have a high degree of internal locus of control. Can you think of an example?

Ethical OB Dilemma

www.mcgrawhill.ca/olc/kreitner

When Emotional Intelligence Is Lacking, Job Satisfaction Can Suffer

Consider the following scenario:

Shamir is a 21-year-old student working at a local Canadian Tire store as a customer sales associate. He joined the company two weeks ago as a part-time seasonal employee. He enjoys the training, the people, and the atmosphere of the store. "There is so much to learn but I know I can do it!" he tells his roommate. After the two week training period, Shamir is scheduled to work 20 hours by the assistant store manager in charge of scheduling. This displeases Shamir very much as he was hoping for more hours. On his break he goes into the lunchroom to review the posted hours for all the shifts, and notices that other employees are getting a lot more hours than he is. He goes up to one of his sales colleagues and begins to complain about how management made up the hours unfairly; the colleague tells him to go talk to the boss directly. Not satisfied with that response, Shamir starts complaining to a customer standing near by; the customer pretends not to hear and walks away. Finding no support at work, Shamir completes his shift, drives home angry, and immediately types out a 500 word email to the assistant store manager expressing the unfairness of the shift schedule. "**Dear Asst. Store Manager, My name is Shamir and I . . .**"

Emotional Intelligence is now being taught in business schools around the country. According to the Social Science and Humanities Research Council of Canada, the way a person handles their emotions on the job may affect their chances at corporate success.

SOURCE: The Business of Emotions, *Winning Research, Social Sciences and Humanities Research Council of Canada,* http://www.sshrc.ca/web/winning/story_e.asp?story_id=98

Discussion Questions

1. Identify the behaviours that Shamir exhibited on the job that would suggest that he may have low emotional intelligence.
2. Do you agree with Shamir's decision to write an email to his boss? Explain.
3. How do you think Shamir handles emotions on the job?
4. Is it possible for a person to be competent with high IQ, but be unable to work with others because of low EQ? Explain.
5. How do you feel about organizations screening potential employees on their emotional intelligence prior to an interview?

 **Visit www.mcgrawhillconnect.ca to register.**

McGraw-Hill Connect™ —Available 24/7 with instant feedback so you can study when you want, how you want, and where you want. Take advantage of the Study Plan—an innovative tool that helps you customize your learning experience. You can diagnose your knowledge with pre- and post-tests, identify the areas where you need help, search the entire learning package for content specific to the topic you're studying, and add these resources to your personalized study plan. Visit www.mcgrawhillconnect.ca to register—take practice quizzes, search the e-book, and much more.

4

Values, Attitudes, & Job Satisfaction

Setting The Standard at High Road Communications

When 29-year-old executive Mia Wedgbury and two of her colleagues decided to leave the PR firm Hill & Knowlton to start High Road Communications in 1996, her boss said, "You're way too young. You don't have the experience to make this happen."

Today, High Road is the largest tech-specific PR firm in Canada, with 63 employees and offices in Vancouver, Toronto, Ottawa, and Montreal. High Road's clients include SIRIUS, Canon, Microsoft, MSN, and Disney Interactive Studios. In 2006, it was ranked as one of the 20 best small companies to work for in Canada, according to a survey compiled by Queen's School of Business and Hewitt Associates. What makes the High Road workplace so special?

Their success is attributed to a set of core values: provide career opportunities for employees; ensure caring senior management; and maintain strong leadership in Wedgbury, who has a vision for the company. A combination of factors much more fundamental than salary and wages have created highly productive workers who ranked High Road the highest of any other firm in the survey. In an industry where workers frequently move around, High Road has a turnover rate of only 4 percent—which translates into high job satisfaction for its workers.

Having such an impressive standard attracts potential employees who have similar values. Who wouldn't want to be part of a successful company where employees actually enjoy coming to work? Over a ten year period, High Road reported losing only two employees to competitors. To improve communication, the firm has developed initiatives such as Operation Lunch Hour, which encourages VPs to take employees who they don't normally work with out for lunch. Receptive management and open communication is what it's all about at High Road Communication.

This story reminds us that job satisfaction for employees goes beyond salary. Clearly, when individual values systems are congruent with those of the organization, a harmonious and productive workplace is possible.

SOURCES: S. Brearton, *The Globe and Mail/Report on Business*, "The 20 best small companies to work for in Canada," April 25, 2006, http://www.reportonbusiness.com/servlet/story/RTGAM.20060425.gtrosb1best/BNStory/specialSmallBusiness . High Road Communication website: www.highroad.com.

Mia Wedgbury is President and Co-founder of High Ridge Communications.

E mployees quit their jobs for a variety of reasons. That said, research
indicates, however, that employees are less likely to quit when their
personal values are consistent with the organization's values, when
they have positive attitudes about the work environment, and when they are
satisfied with their jobs.[1] This is why progressive companies like Genentech,
Container Store, Network Appliance, and Microsoft offer programs and benefits such as daycare, flexible work schedules, paternal leaves, generous tuition
reimbursement, wellness programs, telecommuting, concierge services, and
mentoring to a wider segment of the workforce.[2]

The overall goal of this chapter is to continue our investigation of individual
behaviour, started in Chapter 3, so that you get a better idea of how managers and
organizations can use knowledge of individual differences to attract, motivate,
and retain quality employees. We explore and discuss the impact of personal
values and attitudes on important outcomes such as job satisfaction, performance, and turnover. To prepare for these topics, you are invited to complete the
"What Do You Value?" Self-Assessment Exercise at the beginning of this chapter.

LEARNING OBJECTIVES

After reading this chapter,
you should be able to:

LO 1 **Define** *value system*,
terminal values, and
instrumental values.

LO 2 **Describe** three types
of value conflicts.

LO 3 **Identify** the three
components of attitude.

LO 4 **Relate** organizational
commitment to
psychological contract.

LO 5 **Compare and
discriminate** between
eight variables that
have a relationship with
job satisfaction.

What Do You Value?

There are 16 items in the list below. Rate how important each one is to you on a scale of 0 (not important) to 100 (very important). Write a number between 0 and 100 on the line to the left of each item.

NOT IMPORTANT				SOMEWHAT IMPORTANT				VERY IMPORTANT		
0	10	20	30	40	50	60	70	80	90	100

_____ 1. An enjoyable, satisfying job.

_____ 2. A high-paying job.

_____ 3. A good marriage.

_____ 4. Meeting new people; social events.

_____ 5. Involvement in community activities.

_____ 6. My religion.

_____ 7. Exercising, playing sports.

_____ 8. Intellectual development.

_____ 9. A career with challenging opportunies.

_____ 10. Nice cars, clothes, home, and so on.

_____ 11. Spending time with family.

_____ 12. Having several close friends.

_____ 13. Volunteer work for non-profit organizations, such as the Canadian Cancer Society.

_____ 14. Meditation, quiet time to think, pray, and so on.

_____ 15. A healthy, balanced diet.

_____ 16. Educational reading, television, self-improvement programs, and so on.

Scoring Key

Transfer the numbers for each of the 16 items to the appropriate column; then add up the 2 numbers in each column.

Professional	Financial	Family	Social
1. ____	2. ____	3. ____	4. ____
9. ____	10. ____	11. ____	12. ____
TOTALS ____	____	____	____

Community	Spiritual	Physical	Intellectual
5. ____	6. ____	7. ____	8. ____
13. ____	14. ____	15. ____	16. ____
TOTALS ____	____	____	____

The higher the total in any value dimension, the higher the importance you place on that value set. The closer the numbers are in all eight dimensions, the more well-rounded you are.

SOURCE: RN. Lussier, *Human Relations in Organizations: A Skill Building Approach*, 2nd ed. (Homewood, IL: Richard D. Irwin, 1993). Reprinted by permission of the McGraw-Hill Companies, Inc.

LO 1 Personal Values

Values are an individual's strong, enduring beliefs of a mode of conduct or desired end-state. Accordingly, pioneering values researcher Milton Rokeach defined a person's **value system** as an "enduring organization of beliefs concerning preferable modes of conduct or end-states of existence along a continuum of relative importance."[3] For some, a value system can be very strong and intense throughout their lives. Others may have a weaker set of personal values that are therefore not a driving force at all. In this chapter, our focus is on personal values; in Chapter 11, we'll shift that focus to collective or shared values when we discuss organizational culture.

Values
Enduring belief in a mode of conduct or desired end-state.

Value system
The organization of one's beliefs about preferred ways of behaving and desired end-states.

Extensive research supports Rokeach's contention that differing value systems go a long way toward explaining individual differences in behaviour. Value–behaviour connections have been documented for a wide variety of behaviours, ranging from weight loss, shopping selections, and political party affiliation, to religious involvement and choice of a college major.[4]

We will learn more about personal values by distinguishing between instrumental and terminal values, discussing three types of value conflict, and examining the timely value-related topic of work versus family life conflicts.

INSTRUMENTAL AND TERMINAL VALUES

Rokeach proposed that personal values can be categorized along two dimensions: terminal and instrumental.[5] **Terminal values**, such as a sense of accomplishment, happiness, pleasure, salvation, and wisdom, are desired end-states or life goals. These values represent the things we want to achieve or accomplish during our lives. For example, if you value family more than career success, you are more likely to work fewer hours and to spend more time with your family than someone who values career success. Can values change? The answer is yes, but with a strong caveat; typically it takes a life-altering experience, such as surviving a horrendous life-threatening disease, living through an unforgiving natural disaster, or miraculously avoiding a fatal terrorist attack to change an entire value system. An average working day consisting of driving down the same street, at the same time, in the same car, and waiting in line at the same Tim Horton's is not enough to alter a value system. Generally speaking, values stay constant

Terminal values
Personally preferred end-states of existence.

throughout our lives; however, our preferences and interests can shift during various stages, depending on our needs or motivations for change.[6] So when you see your 50-year-old professor driving up to class on her Harley-Davidson motorbike, don't assume that her values have changed. Instead, consider the possibility that her interests have changed and she just wants to have fun doing something she used to do many years ago.

Instrumental values are alternative behaviours or means by which we achieve our terminal values or desired end-states. Sample instrumental values include ambition, honesty, independence, love, and obedience. The key thing to remember about instrumental values is that they direct us in determining how we should behave in the pursuit of our goals. For example, someone who values the instrumental value of honesty is less likely to lie and cheat to accomplish a terminal value associated with a sense of accomplishment than someone who does not value honesty.

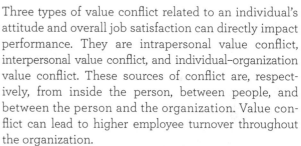

Instrumental values
Personally preferred ways of behaving.

VALUE CONFLICTS

Three types of value conflict related to an individual's attitude and overall job satisfaction can directly impact performance. They are intrapersonal value conflict, interpersonal value conflict, and individual–organization value conflict. These sources of conflict are, respectively, from inside the person, between people, and between the person and the organization. Value conflict can lead to higher employee turnover throughout the organization.

Intrapersonal Value Conflict Inner conflicts that lead to stress are typically experienced when highly ranked instrumental and terminal values pull the individual in different directions. Because the locus of influence stems from what an individual desires, intrapersonal value conflict can present a huge challenge for some individuals. For individuals who want balance in their life, a stressful conflict arises when they value, for example, "being highly ambitious and wanting the fancy urban job" (instrumental value), and at the same time want to "be happy in the end while spending time with family and friends" (terminal value)—all at the same time. A few years ago, Dan Rosensweig, the ex-chief operating officer at Yahoo!, expressed having intrapersonal value conflict to a reporter from *Fast Company* by noting that his "biggest challenge was giving your job everything you have because it deserves it, but at the same time recognizing and appreciating the most important things in your life," for example your family. He commented on feeling "envious of people who were able to find better balance between work and personal life."[7] In general, people are happier and less stressed when their personal values are aligned.

Interpersonal Value Conflict   This type of value conflict is often at the core of personality conflicts, and such conflicts can negatively affect one's career. Consider the case of a former newspaper publisher, Jeffrey Johnson, who was fired by the owner when his values collided with those of senior management. Senior management wanted Johnson to improve the paper's financial results by cutting costs. Johnson was then asked to eliminate employees from the payroll. The conflict for Mr. Johnson was that he did not believe that the newspaper's problems would be solved by employee layoffs. He wanted to improve the newspaper's financial status by exploring creative ways to generate revenue as opposed to cutting costs.[8] This example highlights how important it is to carefully evaluate the pros and cons of handling interpersonal value conflicts with your superiors.

Today someone called me pompous, overpaid, and out of touch. I think it's beginning to happen for me."

HARVARD BUSINESS REVIEW

Individual–Organization Value Conflict   Companies actively seek to embed certain values into their corporate cultures. Conflict can occur when values espoused and enacted by the organization collide with employees' personal values. OB researchers refer to this type of conflict as value congruence or person–culture fit.[9] **Value congruence** or **person–culture fit** reflects the similarity between an individual's personal values and the cultural value system of an organization. This is an important type of conflict to consider when accepting future jobs, because positive outcomes such as satisfaction, commitment,

Value congruence or person–culture fit

The similarity between personal values and organizational values.

performance, career success, reduced stress, and lower turnover intentions are realized when an individual's personal values are similar or aligned with organizational values.[10]

Handling Value Conflicts through Values Clarification   For intrapersonal conflict, a Toronto management writer and consultant recommends getting out of what she calls "the busyness trap" by asking these questions:

- *Is your work really meeting your most important needs?*
- *Are you defining yourself purely in terms of your accomplishments?*
- *Why are you working so hard?*
- *Are you making significant sacrifices in favour of your work?*
- *Is your work schedule affecting other people who are important in your life?*[11]

Another approach for dealing with all forms of value conflict is a career-counselling and team-building technique called values clarification. The goal of this technique is to reduce value conflict through discussion. Conflicting parties are encouraged to identify and talk about personal values to establish common ground as a basis for teamwork and conflict avoidance/resolution (we'll talk more about conflict in Chapter 8).

WORK VS. FAMILY LIFE CONFLICT

A complex web of demographic and economic factors makes the balancing act between job and life very challenging for most of us. Demographically, there are more women in the workforce, more dual-income families, more single working parents, more international travel, and an aging population that gives mid-career employees daycare and/or eldercare responsibilities.[12] On the economic front, years of downsizing and corporate cost-cutting have given employees heavier workloads.

In this section, we seek to better understand work versus family life conflict by introducing a values-based model and discussing practical research insights. Importantly, our goal here is to get a firmer grasp on this difficult area, not offer quick-and-easy solutions with little chance of success.

A Values-Based Model of Work/Family Conflict   Building upon the work of Rokeach, Pamela L Perrewé and Wayne A. Hochwarter constructed the model in Figure 4.1. This model is meant to help you understand the causes of work/family conflict. Let's start on the left box of the model; here we see one's *general life values* feeding into one's family-related values and work-related values. Family values involve enduring beliefs about the

SOURCE: P.L. Perrewé and W.A. Hochwarter, "Can We Really Have It All? The Attainment of Work and Family Values," *Current Directions in Psychological Science*, February 2001, p 30. Published by Blackwell Publishers, Inc. © American Psychological Society.

importance of family and who should play key family roles (e.g., child rearing, housekeeping, and income earning). Work values centre on the relative importance of work and career goals in one's life.

From here, the model splits in two. *Value similarity* relates to the degree of consensus among family members about family values. While work may be a symptom of conflict between family members, the real cause stems from competing values between family members. For example, if a homemaker launches a business venture despite her spouse's desire to be the sole breadwinner, lack of family value similarity will cause work/family conflict. *Value congruence*, on the other hand, involves the amount of value agreement between employee and employer. In this instance, it's the demands of the job and the expectations of the employer that are the cause of conflict. If, for example, refusing to go on a business trip to stay home for a child's birthday is viewed as disloyalty to the company, then lack of value congruence can trigger work/family conflict within the employee.

At this point, the model converges into actual work/life conflicts. Notice how these "work-family conflicts can take two distinct forms: (1) work interference with family, or (2) family interference with work."[13] For example, suppose two managers in the same department have daughters playing on the same soccer team. One manager misses the big soccer game to attend a last-minute department meeting; the other manager skips the meeting to attend the game. Both may experience work/family conflict, but for different reasons.

The last two boxes in the model—value attainment and job and life satisfaction—are a package deal. Satisfaction tends to be higher for those who stay true to themselves by living their life according to their values, and lower for those who do not. Overall, this model reflects much common sense. How does your life track through the model? Sadly, for many it is often a painful trip.

Practical Research Insights about Work/Family Conflict
This is a new but very active area of OB research. The evidence typically comes from field surveys of real people in real jobs, rather than from contrived laboratory studies. Recent practical findings include:

■ *Work/family balance begins at home.* Historically, women shouldered the majority of the standard household chores and child-rearing responsibilities. Fortunately, there is some data suggesting that men are beginning to share more of the work associated with running a home. A national survey revealed that male Gen-Xers, born between 1965 and 1979, were equally involved with spouses in taking care of children. Males were also more focused on spending time with family.[14] This is a promising result in light of a recent study of 223 men and 113 women, where findings showed that people had greater life satisfaction when they were committed to their marriage and to their children.[15]

- *An employer's family-supportive philosophy is more important than specific programs.* Many employers offer family-friendly programs, including child and elder daycare assistance, parental leave, telecommuting, and flexible work schedules. However, if employees are afraid or reluctant to take advantage of those programs because the organization's culture values hard work and long hours above all else, families will inevitably suffer. To be truly family-friendly, the organization needs to provide programs and back them up with a family-supportive philosophy and culture.[16]

- *Informal flexibility in work hours as well as allowing people to work at home is essential to promoting work/family balance.* Quite simply, flexibility allows people to cope more effectively with competing demands across their personal and work lives. Dell Inc., for example, allows some work teams to eliminate "firm office hours and hands employees control over when and how they achieve goals." Bristol-Myers Squibb similarly tries to enhance worker flexibility by enabling people to choose one of six different work schedules.[17]

- *Mentors can help.* According to a field survey of 502 respondents (63 percent men), "The results indicate that having a mentor is significantly related to lower levels of work-family conflict ... Such findings suggest another potential benefit of mentoring: a source of social support to reduce employee stress caused by conflicts between the work and family domains."[18]

- *Take a proactive approach to managing work/family conflict.* Two recent meta-analyses of more than 60 different studies and 43,000 people demonstrated that employees' personal lives spill over to their work life and vice versa. This means that employees' job satisfaction, organizational commitment, and intentions to quit are significantly related to the amount of work/family conflict that exists in their lives.[19] We thus encourage you to identify and manage the sources of work/family conflict.

- *Being your own boss is no panacea (ultimate solution).* Self-employment turns out to be a good news/bad news proposition when compared to standard organizational employment. Among the benefits of being self-employed are a stronger sense of autonomy (independence), a higher level of job involvement, and greater job satisfaction. But self-employed people also report higher levels of work/family conflict and lower levels of family satisfaction.[20]

Organizational Response to Work/Family Issues

Organizations have implemented a variety of family-friendly programs and services aimed at helping employees balance the interplay between their work and personal lives. Although these programs are positively received by employees, experts now believe that such efforts are partially misguided because they focus on balancing work/family issues rather than integrating them. Balance is needed for opposites, and work and family are not opposites. Rather, our work and personal lives should be a well-integrated whole. A team of researchers arrived at the following conclusion regarding the need to integrate versus balance work/life issues:

> Great companies recognize that the ability to take care of family concerns is an important part of an employee's job satisfaction. How can a company's policies reflect a family-supportive philosophy?

Gendered assumptions and stereotypes based in the separation of [occupational and family] spheres constrain the choices of both women and men. Our vision of gender equity is to relax these social norms about separation so that men and women are free to experience these two parts of their lives as integrated rather than as separate domains that need to be "balanced." Integration would make it possible for both women and men to perform up to their capabilities and find satisfaction in both work and personal life, no matter how they allocate their time commitment between the two. To convey this goal, we speak of integrating work and personal life rather than balancing. This terminology expresses our belief in the need to diminish the separation between these two spheres of life in ways that will change both, rather than merely reallocating—or "balancing"—time between them as they currently exist.[21]

One last consideration to the discussion around organizational response to values should also include religious accommodation, which plays a major role in the lives of some employees. If, for example, your organization has a significant number of Muslim male employees, it would be wise not to schedule a staff meeting at noon every Friday—the time they go to prayer. Out of respect for employees who practise their faith, some organizations have built prayer rooms on site, which translates into less time spent away from the office,[22] resulting in a win–win situation. As illustrated in the Law and Ethics at Work feature box, it benefits the entire organization when values are mutually respected.

Attitudes

Hardly a day goes by without the media reporting the results of another attitude survey, designed to take the pulse of public opinion. What do we think about candidate X, terrorism, the war on drugs, gun control, or abortion? In the workplace, meanwhile, managers conduct attitude surveys to monitor such things as job and pay satisfaction. All this attention on attitudes is based on the realization that our attitudes influence our behaviour. For example, research demonstrated that seniors with a positive attitude about aging had better memory, better hearing, and lived longer than those with negative attitudes.[23] In a work setting, a recent meta-analysis involving more than 50,000 people revealed that overall job attitudes were positively related to performance and negatively associated with indicators of withdrawal—lateness, absenteeism, and turnover.[24] In this section, we discuss the components of attitudes and examine the connection between attitudes and behaviour.

THE NATURE OF ATTITUDES

An **attitude** is defined as "a learned predisposition to respond in a consistently favourable or unfavourable manner with respect to a given object."[25] Consider your attitude toward chocolate ice cream. You are more likely to purchase a chocolate ice cream cone if you have a positive attitude toward chocolate ice cream. In contrast, you are more likely to purchase some other flavour, say vanilla caramel swirl, if you have a positive attitude toward vanilla and a neutral or negative attitude toward chocolate ice cream. Now consider a work example. If you have a positive attitude about your job (i.e., you like what you are doing), you are likely to be more willing to extend yourself at work by working longer and harder.

> **Attitude**
>
> Learned predisposition toward a given object.

LAW AND ETHICS *at Work*

OBSERVING RELIGIOUS ACCOMMODATION IN THE WORKPLACE

The Canadian Human Rights Act (1985) spells out the legal expectations of preventing discrimination, but in many ways it can be likened to articulating Canadian values on a broad national level. In response to the Act, each province has enacted their own Human Rights Code that outlines specific behaviours and/or responsibilities on the part of all persons and organizations operating within their jurisdiction. As Canada becomes more diverse, there is greater momentum at the organizational level to comply with the Code as it relates to accommodating individuals on the basis of religious beliefs.

Some religious celebrations are widely recognized in all sectors of Canadian business and present no personal/work conflict. But that is not the case for all individual religions. That is why it is recommended that organizations prepare a policy for observing religious values. With the assistance of provincial multi-faith councils, many organizations have gone so far as to create a calendar of religious accommodation, which outlines over a dozen pages of recognized religions, an explanation of each major holy day throughout the year, and the specific date of each celebration. Such action keeps individual religious values from competing with corporate values.

If a manager receives a request from an employee for time off to observe a religious celebration and the manager is not familiar with the celebration, it is imperative for both sides to understand the process. The employee needs to be sensitive to work demands by ensuring a reasonable timeline to place the request. The manager needs to understand the legal and ethical obligations to accommodate when and if possible.

SOURCE: The Canadian Human Rights Act website: http://www.chrc-ccdp.ca/legislation_policies/human_rights_act-en.asp; Ontario Human Rights Commission website: www.ohrc.on.ca; 2008–2009 Academic Year Calendar of Religious Accommodation, A summary prepared by Equity & Human Rights Services, The University of Western Ontario, http://www.uwo.ca/equity/docs/mfcalendar.htm.

These examples illustrate that attitudes propel us to act in a specific way in a specific context. That is, attitudes affect behaviour at a different level than do values. While values represent global beliefs that influence behaviour across all situations, attitudes relate only to behaviour directed toward specific objects, persons, or situations. Values and attitudes generally, but not always, are in harmony. For example, a manager who strongly values helpful behaviour may have a negative attitude toward helping an unethical co-worker. The difference between attitudes and values is clarified by considering the three components of attitudes: affective, cognitive, and behavioural.[26] It is important to note that your overall attitude toward someone or something is a function of the combined influence of all three components.

LO 3 **Affective Component** The *affective component* of an attitude includes the feelings or emotions one has about a given object or situation. For example:

■ *I don't like working with bossy people because they make me feel inferior.*

Cognitive Component The *cognitive component* of an attitude reflects the beliefs or ideas one has about an object or situation. For example:

■ *I work with a person named Pat who I believe is a bossy person.*

Behavioural Component The *behavioural component* refers to how one intends or expects to act toward someone or something. Attitude Theory suggests that your ultimate behaviour in this situation is a function of all three attitudinal components. For example:

■ *I avoid working with Pat (behavioural) because I believe that Pat is bossy (cognitive) and I don't like working with bossy people who make me feel inferior (affective).*

So, while we observe individual behaviour around the office, we need to understand the two steps that took place before the person acted them out. Greater understanding of behaviour will occur once a clearer picture unfolds around the feelings and beliefs that went before it. If the desire is to correct a person's behaviour, then don't start at the behaviour; rather, go back two steps and clarify the factors that prompted it.

Affective component

The feelings or emotions one has about an object or situation.

Cognitive component

The beliefs or ideas one has about an object or situation.

Behavioural component

How one intends to act or behave toward someone or something.

WHAT HAPPENS WHEN ATTITUDES AND REALITY COLLIDE? COGNITIVE DISSONANCE

What happens when a strongly held attitude is contradicted by reality? Suppose you are extremely concerned about getting AIDS, which you believe is transferred from contact with body fluids, including blood. Then you find yourself in a life-threatening accident in a foreign country and need surgery and blood transfusions—including transfusions of blood from a blood bank with unknown quality control. Would you reject the blood to remain consistent with your beliefs about getting AIDS? According to social psychologist Leon Festinger, this situation would create cognitive dissonance.

Many business students probably recall learning about cognitive dissonance from their marketing class when discussing consumer behaviour. But it also applies to OB; in this instance, *cognitive dissonance* represents the psychological discomfort people experience when their attitudes or beliefs are incompatible with their behaviour.[27] Festinger proposed that people are motivated to maintain consistency between their attitudes and beliefs and their behaviour. When faced with such situations around the office, employees will try and minimize the dissonance because it is so upsetting to them personally. If ignored, it can paralyze performance. Managers need to be sensitive to such an occurrence and help employees through these situations by discussing alternative options, finding new resources, or considering other possible solutions to overcome the anxiety.

Festinger theorized that people will seek to reduce the "dissonance" or psychological tension through one of three main methods:

Cognitive dissonance

Psychological discomfort experienced when attitudes and behaviour are inconsistent.

1. **Change your attitude or behaviour, or both** This is the simplest solution when confronted with cognitive dissonance. Let's take an example of a person who is anti-smoking. What will this employee do if the company she works for co-sponsors a sporting event with Imperial Tobacco Group and she is expected to attend the event on behalf of the company? If the employee attends, she will feel like a hypocrite (two-faced). If she refuses to attend, it could mean a reprimand (discipline) from

the employer. What to do? To avoid the dissonance, the employee changes her attitude toward cigarette smoking, saying that people have the right to smoke if they want to. The employee considers that perhaps she has been *overreacting toward the whole thing*.

2. **Belittle the importance of the inconsistent behaviour** This happens all the time. In our example, the employee could belittle the belief that attending the event means supporting cigarette smoking. *It's a sporting event, not a smoking event, and besides, it's just a one-time thing.*

3. **Find consonant elements that outweigh dissonant ones** This approach entails rationalizing away the dissonance. The employee attends the sporting event because she believes there are no other options. *After all, it could mean the employee's job and she can't afford to lose this great paying job because of family obligations and responsibilities.*

HOW STABLE ARE ATTITUDES?

In one landmark study, researchers found the job attitudes of 5,000 middle-aged male employees to be very stable over a five-year period. Positive job attitudes remained positive; negative ones remained negative. Even those who changed jobs or occupations tended to maintain their prior job attitudes.[28] More recent research suggests the foregoing study may have overstated the stability of attitudes because it was restricted to a middle-aged sample. This time, researchers asked: What happens to attitudes over the entire span of adulthood? General attitudes were found to be more susceptible to change during early and late adulthood than during middle adulthood. Three factors accounted for middle-age attitude stability: (1) greater personal certainty, (2) perceived abundance of knowledge, and (3) a need for strong attitudes. Thus, the conventional notion that general attitudes become less likely to change as the person ages was rejected. Elderly people, along with young adults, can and do change their general attitudes because they are more open and less self-assured.[29]

Because our cultural backgrounds and experiences vary, our attitudes and behaviour vary. Attitudes are translated into behaviour via behavioural intentions. Let us examine an established model of this important process.

ATTITUDES AFFECT BEHAVIOUR VIA INTENTIONS

Building on Leon Festinger's work on cognitive dissonance, Icek Ajzen and Martin Fishbein delved further into understanding the reason for discrepancies between individuals' attitudes and behaviour. Ajzen ultimately developed and refined a model focusing on intentions as the key link between attitudes and planned behaviour. His theory of planned behaviour in Figure 4.2 shows three separate but interacting determinants of one's intention (a person's readiness to perform a given behaviour) to exhibit a specific behaviour.

Importantly, this model only predicts behaviour under an individual's control, not behaviour due to circumstances beyond one's control. For example, this model can predict the likelihood of someone skipping work if the person says his or her intention is to stay in bed tomorrow morning. But it would be a poor model for predicting getting to work on time, because uncontrolled circumstances such as traffic delays or an accident could intervene.

▶ **FIGURE 4.2** Ajzen's Theory of Planned Behaviour

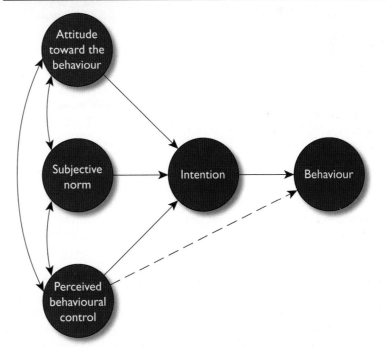

SOURCE: Reprinted from I. Ajzen, "The Theory of Planned Behaviour," *Organizational Behaviour and Human Decision Processes*, Figure 1, p 182. Copyright 1991, with permission from Elsevier Science.

Determinants of Intention   Ajzen explains the nature and roles of the three determinants of intention as follows:

> *The first is the* attitude toward the behaviour *and refers to the degree to which a person has a favourable or unfavourable evaluation or appraisal of the behaviour in question. The second predictor is a social factor termed* subjective norm; *it refers to the perceived social pressure to perform or not to perform the behaviour. The third antecedent of intention is the degree of* perceived behaviour control, *which ... refers to the perceived ease or difficulty of performing the behaviour and it is assumed to reflect past experience as well as anticipated impediments and obstacles.*[30]

To bring these three determinants of intention to life, let us return to our lazy soul who chose to stay in bed rather than go to work. This person feels overworked and underpaid, and thus has a favourable attitude about skipping work occasionally. The person's perceived subjective norm is favourable because he sees co-workers skipping work with no ill effects (in fact, they collect sick pay). Regarding perceived behaviour control, this person is completely in charge of acting on his intention to skip work today. So the person turns off the alarm clock and pulls the covers over his head. Sweet dreams!

Intentions and Behaviour Research Lessons and Implications   According to Ajzen's model of planned behaviour, someone's intention to engage in a given behaviour is a strong predictor of that behaviour. For example, the quickest and possibly most accurate way of determining whether individuals will quit their job is to have an objective third party ask if they intend to quit. A meta-analysis of 34 studies of employee turnover involving more than 83,000 employees validated this direct approach. The researchers found stated behavioural intentions to be a better predictor of employee turnover than job satisfaction, satisfaction with the work itself, or organizational commitment.[31] A recent study took these findings one step further by considering whether or not job applicants' intention to quit a job before they were hired would predict voluntary turnover six months after being hired. Results demonstrated that intentions to quit significantly predicted turnover.[32] Perhaps now you can understand why your summer employer always asked you if you planned on returning to school in the fall. Your stated intention was an accurate indicator of your future behaviour.

Research has demonstrated that Ajzen's model accurately predicts intentions to buy consumer products, have children, and choose a career versus becoming a homemaker. Weight loss intentions and behaviour, voting for political candidates, using Internet services to facilitate the shipping of products, nurses' willingness to work with older patients, attending on-the-job training sessions, and condom use have also been predicted successfully by the model.[33] In addition, the theory of planned behaviour explains the behaviour of people from Turkey and the Netherlands.[34] Understanding this simple model can help you succeed while studying at school. For example, you might want to consider using it when establishing a working group for your next project.

Before forming a group, you may want to ask each potential member what their final grade intention is for the project. Asking the questions, "What grade do you want to earn on this project?" or "How many hours per week do you plan on working on this project?" may actually provide you with a clearer picture of how a fellow student is going to behave over the next few months.

From a practical standpoint, Ajzen's theory of planned behaviour has important managerial implications. Managers are encouraged to use prescriptions derived from the model to implement intervention techniques aimed at changing employees' behaviour. According to this model, changing behaviour starts with the recognition that behaviour is modified through intentions, which in turn are influenced by three different determinants (see Figure 4.2). Managers can thus influence behavioural change by doing or saying things that affect the three determinants of employees' intentions to exhibit a specific behaviour.[35] For example, if full-time employees are paranoid that they are going to lose their job because of downsizing, then they may act out with hostility toward part-time workers. As a case in point, a study showed that employees had lower perceptions of job security and more negative attitudes toward temporary workers when they had the behavioural belief that temporary workers posed a threat to their jobs.[36] Ultimately, a manager would want to intervene by first asking the full-time workers, *"How do you feel about having temporary workers on site?"* Once

> The three determinants of intention are "... the degree to which a person has a favourable or unfavourable evaluation of the behaviour ..., the perceived social pressure to perform or not to perform the behaviour ..., and the perceived ease or difficulty of performing the behaviour ..."

this attitude is confirmed, then the manager could ask, *"Do you believe your job security to be threatened by temporary workers? If so, in what way(s)?"* This second question gets to the heart of the subjective norms and beliefs. Finally, to help change behaviour, the manager could ask the full-timers, *"What experiences have you had in the past being replaced by temporary workers? Are you aware that your performance at work is being negatively affected by your beliefs toward temporary workers? Is this what you want? Is this your intention? If not, then your behaviour needs to change. What can I do to help?"*

Employee beliefs can be influenced by the information management provides on a day-by-day basis, organizational cultural values, role models, and rewards that are targeted to reinforce certain beliefs. If a manager wants employee participation in decision making, then inviting them into the process by providing ongoing information and relevant data would be beneficial in maintaining favourable attitudes toward the process. In another example, management can foster the belief that teamwork is valued by setting and rewarding team-based goals instead of individual goals. Beliefs can also be modified through education and training.

Three Key Work Attitudes

Work attitudes such as organizational commitment, job involvement, and job satisfaction have a dual interest to managers. On the one hand, they represent important outcomes that managers may want to enhance. On the other, they are indicative of other potential problems. For example, low job satisfaction may be a symptom of an employee's intention to quit. It is therefore important for managers to understand the causes and consequences of key work attitudes. What is your attitude toward work? Is work something meaningful that defines and fulfills you, or is it just a way to pay the bills? People have a multitude of attitudes about things that happen to them at work, but OB researchers have focused on a limited number of them. This next section specifically examines two work attitudes—organizational commitment and job involvement—that have important practical implications. Then the third work attitude, job satisfaction, is thoroughly discussed in the final section of this chapter.

CHUCK CAROTHERS AND IRENE TSE COMMIT TO THEIR JOBS, CAREERS, AND THE THRILL OF ACHIEVEMENT

In the realm of extreme sports, Chuck Carothers is a champ. One of the world's leading motocross riders, he has broken 21 bones in his career. Yet he keeps competing, describing the rush he gets from sailing through the air on a motorbike as a "complete addiction." In a weird way, Irene Tse, the 34-year-old head of the government bond-trading desk at Goldman Sachs, understands Carothers's passion. "I've done this for 10 years," she says, "And I can count on the fingers of one hand the number of days in my career when I didn't want to come to work. Every day I wake up and I can't wait to get here."

Working at one of the largest global investment and banking firms and overseeing a desk that trades billions of dollars daily, with profits and losses in the millions—an experience equivalent to Carothers's famous flying barrel roll—can be hair-raising. "There are days when you make a lot, and other days where you lose so much you're just stunned by what you've done," Tse admits. But the exhilaration of her work, and the challenge of figuring out what forces are likely to next roil the markets, has kept her motivated through a decade of 80-hour weeks.

Indeed, there's an addictive quality to her work that has rewired her body. There are no broken bones, but Tse says she hasn't slept through the night in years, typically getting up two or three times to check on global market activity. "Through time, your body clock just wakes up when London opens," she says.

What drives Chuck and Irene's commitment?

SOURCE: Excerpted and adapted from L. Tischler, "Extreme Jobs," *Fast Company*, April 2005, p 56. © 2005 Gruner & Jahr USA Publishing. First published in *Fast Company* Magazine. Reprinted with permission.

ORGANIZATIONAL COMMITMENT

Before discussing a model of organizational commitment, it is important to consider the meaning of the term *commitment*. What does it mean to commit? Common sense suggests that commitment is an agreement to do something for yourself or another individual, group, or organization.[37] Is it possible for different people working in separate careers to express their commitment in different ways, yet be equally committed to whatever they are doing? Chuck Carothers and Irene Tse are good examples of two individuals who work in totally different industries, are different genders, and yet exhibit equally high degrees of commitment (see Focus on Diversity feature box). Formally, OB researchers define commitment as "a force that binds an individual to a course of action of relevance to one or more targets."[38] This definition highlights that commitment is associated with behaviour and can be aimed at multiple targets or entities. For example, people can be committed to their job, family, girl- or boyfriend, faith, friends, career, organization, or a variety of professional associations. Let us now consider in greater depth the application of commitment to a work organization.

Organizational commitment reflects the extent to which an individual identifies with an organization and is committed to its goals. It is an important work attitude because committed individuals are expected to display a willingness to work harder to achieve organizational goals and a greater desire to stay employed at an organization. Figure 4.3 presents a model of organizational commitment that identifies its causes and consequences.

A Model of Organizational Commitment Examine Figure 4.3. It looks complicated, but we're going to thoroughly dissect this model to make sense of it.

The centre of Figure 4.3 shows that organizational commitment is composed of three separate but related

> *Organizational commitment*
>
> Extent to which an individual identifies with an organization and its goals.

▶ **FIGURE 4.3**   A Model of Organizational Commitment

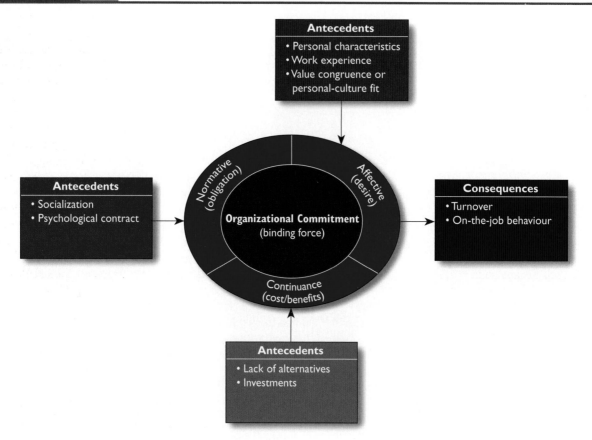

SOURCE: Adapted from J.P. Meyer and L. Herscovitch, "Commitment in the Workplace: Toward a General Model," *Human Resource Management Review*, Autumn 2001, p 317.

components: (1) affective commitment, (2) normative commitment, and (3) continuance commitment. John Meyer and Natalie Allen, a pair of commitment experts, define these components as follows:

- *Affective commitment* refers to the employee's emotional attachment to, identification with, and involvement in the organization. Employees with a strong affective commitment continue employment with an organization because they want to do so (strong desire).

- *Continuance commitment* refers to an awareness of the costs associated with leaving the organization. Employees whose primary link to the organization is based on continuance commitment remain because they need to do so (too costly to leave job).

- *Normative commitment* reflects a feeling of obligation to continue employment. Employees with a high level of normative commitment feel that they ought to remain with the organization (feel an obligation to stay).[39]

Figure 4.3 also reveals that these three components combine to produce a *binding force* that influences the consequences (the box on the far right in the model) of employee turnover and on-the-job behaviour such as performance, absenteeism, and organizational citizenship, which is discussed later in this chapter.

Going back to the model—notice how each of the three components of commitment has its own separate set of antecedents that influence it. In the current context, an antecedent is something that causes the component of commitment to occur. So, for example, *affective commitment* (the desire to stay at a job) is related to a variety of personal characteristics such as personality and locus of control (recall our discussion in Chapter 3), past work experience, and value congruence, which was discussed earlier in this chapter.[40]

Continuance commitment (can't afford to leave the job because of high cost) reflects a ratio of the costs and benefits associated with leaving an organization. Antecedents are anything that affects the costs and benefits of leaving. Examples are a lack of job/career alternatives and the amount of real and psychological investments a person has in a particular organization or community. Continuance commitment would be high if individuals have no job alternatives, have many friends in the community, and don't want to leave or can't afford to leave a job because they need the extended health benefits.

LO 4

Finally, *normative commitment* (the feeling that they have to stay at their job out of obligation) is influenced by the socialization process and what is termed the psychological contract. *Psychological contracts* represent an individual's perception about the terms and conditions of a reciprocal exchange between herself and another party.[41] In a work environment, the psychological contract represents employees' beliefs about what they are entitled to receive in return for what they provide to the organization.

Psychological contract

An individual's perception about the terms and conditions of a reciprocal exchange with another party.

Research and Practical Applications

Organizational commitment matters. A meta-analysis of 183 studies and almost 26,000 individuals uncovered a significant and strong positive relationship between organizational commitment and job satisfaction.[42] This finding encourages managers to increase job satisfaction to elicit higher levels of commitment. In turn, another meta-analysis involving 26,344 individuals revealed organizational commitment was significantly correlated with job performance.[43] This is an important finding because it implies managers can increase productivity by enhancing employees' organizational commitment.

Finally, a third meta-analysis summarizing results across 67 studies and 27,500 people uncovered a significant negative relationship between organizational commitment and turnover.[44] This finding underscores the importance of paying attention to employees' organizational commitment, because high commitment helps reduce the costs of employee turnover. In summary, managers are encouraged to focus on improving employees' organizational commitment.

So, how can companies increase employees' organizational commitment? Interestingly, they use a variety of methods. Consider the different approaches used by Genentech and the Container Store. Genentech provides employees with a six-week paid sabbatical for every six years of service, and the Container Store pays employees 50 percent to 100 percent more than the industry average. The Container Store also relies on a flexible schedule that allows parents to drop off and pick up their children at daycare or school.[45] All told, people are more likely to be committed to their organizations when they believe that the organization truly cares about their welfare and well-being.

Managers can also increase each of the three components of employee commitment through the following activities:

- *Enhance affective commitment* by hiring people whose personal values are consistent with the organization's values. A positive, satisfying work environment should also increase employees' desire to stay. Harley-Davidson is following this advice. "Employee surveys show 90 percent strongly identify with the company's riding culture. Some employees get to work at biker rallies at Harley's expense."[46]

■ *Enhance continuance commitment* by offering employees a variety of progressive benefits and human resource programs. For instance, Aflac will pay up to $20,000 per year in tuition reimbursement for an employee's college-age children or grandchildren who maintain a GPA of 2.5 or higher. QuikTrip also has a policy of promoting from within, and it provides part-time employees with tuition reimbursement and health coverage.[47] Can you think of some examples through your own work experience where the organization offered incentives to stay with the firm?

■ *Increase normative commitment* by making sure that management follows up on its commitments and by trying to enhance the level of trust throughout the organization. We provide specific recommendation for building and maintaining trust in Chapter 6. Have you ever felt this level of commitment toward an organization—for example, your old Scouts' club, a church group, or a former employer?

JOB INVOLVEMENT

Job involvement is defined as "the degree to which one is cognitively preoccupied with, engaged in, and concerned with one's present job."[48] This work attitude manifests itself through the extent to which people are immersed in their job tasks. Think of the passion you have toward your job—do you feel emotionally connected to the work? Physically engaged so much so that even if you're not feeling great, you still show up for work because it actually helps make you feel better in the end? Cognitively engaged enough to feel like you make a difference when you work? If you answered yes to all three of these questions, then you have a high level of job involvement.

Take Vinton Studios' animators/directors Sean Burns and Doug Aberle, for example. Vinton Studios trademarked an animation process known as Claymation®. The process has been used in television commercials involving the California Raisins and M&Ms, and the television series *The PJs*. Sean says, "This is a great place to work. We work on truly interesting and cutting-edge stuff. Plus I get to work on things that interest me. Each project is a new situation every time. We suggest interesting twists, new ideas."[49] Doug is also involved in his work: "At the end of the day, you've never been so tired—or had so much fun! There's a lot of variety in working on a TV show. There's something different

Job involvement

Extent to which individuals are immersed in their present job.

Although this little Claymation character seems a bit sceptical, the artists at Vinton Studios exhibit high job involvement. They love working on creative projects that hold their interest and turn hard work into fun. Task variety also is a big plus. An added bonus: their uncooperative subjects can be tossed back into the clay bucket.

every day."[50] This suggests it is important for managers to understand the causes and consequences of job involvement because of its association with motivation and satisfaction.

The results from a meta-analytic study involving thousands of people provide more information about job involvement.[51] In this study, job involvement was positively associated with job satisfaction, organizational commitment, and intrinsic motivation, and negatively related to intentions to quit. There are three key managerial implications associated with these results:

1. Managerial attempts to improve either of the two work attitudes discussed in this section are likely to positively affect the other work attitude.

2. Managers can increase employees' job involvement by providing work environments that fuel intrinsic motivation. We discuss specific recommendations for doing this in the section on intrinsic motivation in Chapter 5.

3. Improving job involvement can reduce employee turnover.

Job Involvement and Performance Past results pertaining to the relationship between job involvement and performance are controversial. While an earlier meta-analysis failed to uncover a significant relationship between job involvement and performance, poor measures of job involvement used in past studies may have biased the results. A more recent study corrected this problem and found a positive relationship between job involvement and performance.[52] Managers are thus encouraged to increase employees' job involvement as a viable strategy for improving job performance.

Results from three recent studies shed additional insight about the importance of job involvement. First, job involvement was found to remain relatively stable over five years. This suggests that managers may want to include an assessment of an individual's job involvement during the hiring process.[53] Second, job involvement was negatively associated with employees' psychological detachment from their work.[54] Individuals are thus more likely to stay productive and focused at work when they possess high job involvement. Finally, job involvement was significantly associated with absenteeism when employees were dissatisfied with their jobs.[55] This finding underscores the importance of the interrelationship among key work attitudes. Managers are encouraged to consider the interplay among organizational commitment, job involvement, and job satisfaction when trying to motivate and retain employees. Let us now turn our attention to job satisfaction, the work attitude that is most frequently investigated by OB researchers.

JOB SATISFACTION

Job satisfaction essentially reflects the extent to which individuals like (or dislike) their job. Formally defined, *job satisfaction* is an emotional response toward various facets of one's job. This definition implies that people can be relatively satisfied with one aspect of their job and dissatisfied with one or more other aspects. For example, you may like your job because of the people you work with, but dislike the office work environment which, in your opinion, is inefficient and in need of major change. Although researchers do not have consensus about the exact number of dimensions that constitute job satisfaction, they do agree that it has five predominant causes. It is important to understand these various causes because each one offers a different solution toward stopping the decline in job satisfaction uncovered in recent employee surveys.[56] We believe that knowledge about the causes of job satisfaction can assist managers in using a multi-faceted approach toward increasing this key work attitude. Let us now examine the five major causes of job satisfaction.

Job satisfaction

An affective or emotional response to one's job.

THE FIVE MAJOR CAUSES OF JOB SATISFACTION

The five predominant models of job satisfaction focus on different causes: (1) need fulfillment, (2) discrepancy, (3) value attainment, (4) equity, and (5) dispositional/genetic components. The distinctions between them can be very small at times, but a brief review of each model should provide greater insight into the variety of methods that can be used to increase employees' job satisfaction.[57]

Need Fulfillment These models propose that satisfaction is determined by the extent to which the characteristics of a job allow employees to fulfill their needs. Organizations are aware of the premise associated with this model of satisfaction and have responded by providing creative benefits to help satisfy employees' needs. A recent survey of 975 employers, for example, revealed the percentage of companies that provided the following services on the premises to make employees' lives easier: ATM (41 percent), banking services (24 percent), dry cleaning/laundry service (21 percent), credit union (19 percent), travel services (18 percent), company store (16 percent), entertainment discounts and ticket purchase (15 percent), and mail services (14 percent).[58] Although need fulfillment models generated a great degree of controversy, it is generally accepted that need fulfillment is correlated with job satisfaction.[59] What sorts of services have you experienced at a job that you felt were very convenient and that you liked?

Discrepancies These models propose that satisfaction is a result of *met expectations*. Met expectations represent the difference between what people expect to receive from a job, such as good pay and promotional opportunities, and what they actually receive. When expectations are greater than what is received, people will be dissatisfied. In contrast, this model predicts that employees will be satisfied when they attain outcomes above and beyond expectations. If realistic expectations are stated during the interview and hiring stages, then clearly employees know what to expect when they start the job. But if the employer fails to clarify expectations of the job or if employees fail to clarify their understanding of the expectations of the job, then a discrepancy occurs causing job dissatisfaction. A meta-analysis of 31 studies that included 17,241 people demonstrated that met expectations were significantly related to job satisfaction.[60] Many companies use employee attitude or opinion surveys to assess employees' expectations and concerns (see International OB feature box). Do you think these kinds of employee surveys are an accurate indicator of satisfaction? On a similar note, have you ever accepted a job expecting one thing, but ending up experiencing something different? How did that make you feel and did it affect your level of job satisfaction?

Met expectations

The extent to which one receives what one expects from a job.

Value attainment

The extent to which a job allows fulfillment of one's work values.

Value Attainment The idea underlying *value attainment* is that satisfaction results from the perception that a job allows for fulfillment of

COMMERCIAL SYSTEMS DISTRIBUTION UNIT USES SURVEYS TO ASSESS EMPLOYEES' JOB SATISFACTION

John Conover, president of Trane's Commercial Systems Distribution unit, says the survey process his company uses yields information about managers that they may not enjoy hearing . . . and once you get the feedback, he says, you have to move on it. "If associates give you the input and see you doing something about it, reacting to it, that's powerful; it will have a strong impact."

Dan Tyler, HR leader for Trane's Latin American Territory, was surprised at the relative ease with which many of the managerial shortcomings revealed on the Human Capital Capability Scorecard (HCCS) could be addressed. "It was low-hanging fruit; there were things we could do easily that will improve the scores next time. For example, in Santiago, Chile, within the Leadership Practices index, we scored low on communications; employees said there was too much isolation. The solution was easy; we instituted a newsletter to keep people informed."

SOURCE: Excerpted from R.J. Grossman, "Measuring the Value of HR," *HR Magazine*, December 2006, p 47.

---

an individual's important work values.[61] For example, a survey by Salary.com showed that 53 percent of the respondents valued time off more than a raise of $5,000. These results suggest that organizations should stop measuring productivity in terms of the number of hours people work, and that they should encourage employees to take their vacations and turn off the technology while at home.[62]

In general, research consistently supports the prediction that value fulfillment is positively related to job satisfaction. Managers can thus enhance employee satisfaction by structuring the work environment and its associated rewards and recognition to reinforce employees' values. A bit confused? Think of *value attainment* as those psychological rewards felt from the job itself—for example, flex time when requested, or leaving early once the job is completed, or the freedom of discretion to come and go on the job without asking permission. On the other hand, think of *needs fulfillment* as those creative benefit packages that an organization develops for all the employees in the entire organization to take advantage of, regardless of the job or position.

Equity In this model, satisfaction is a function of how fairly an individual is treated at work. Satisfaction results from one's perception that work outcomes, relative to inputs, compare favourably with a significant other's outcomes/inputs. A meta-analysis involving 190 studies and 64,757 people supported this model. Employees' perceptions of being treated fairly at work were highly related to overall job satisfaction.[63] Managers are therefore encouraged to monitor employees' fairness perceptions and to interact with employees in such a way that they feel equitably treated. Naturally, the problem with fairness is that it is very subjective. As a result, it's wise to assess reality from the employees' perspective. In other words, how an individual defines fair management treatment is the starting point for discussion, not the other way around. Do you think the *equity model* sounds similar to *discrepancy*? If so, this may help: Not all discrepancies are a result of feeling a lack of fairness. When an individual feels something isn't fair, it may have nothing to do with unfulfilled expectations or false promises that were made at the time of hiring. It's a fine distinction, but nonetheless an important one.

Dispositional/Genetic Components Have you ever noticed that some of your co-workers or friends appear to be satisfied across a variety of job circumstances, whereas others always seem dissatisfied? This model of satisfaction attempts to explain this pattern.[64] Specifically, the dispositional/genetic model is based on the belief that job satisfaction is partly a function of both personal traits and genetic factors. As such, this model implies that stable individual differences are just as important in explaining job satisfaction as are characteristics of the work environment. Although only a few studies have tested these propositions, results support a positive, significant relationship between personal traits and job satisfaction over time periods ranging from two to 50 years.[65] Genetic factors were also found to significantly predict life satisfaction, well-being, and general job satisfaction.[66] Overall, researchers estimate that 30 percent of an individual's job satisfaction is associated with dispositional and genetic components.[67]

Pete and Laura Wakeman, founders of Great Harvest Bread Company, have used this model of job satisfaction while running their company for more than 25 years:

> Our hiring ads say clearly that we need people with "strong personal loves as important as their work." This is not a little thing. You can't have a great life unless you have a buffer of like-minded people all around you. If you want to be nice, you can't surround yourself with crabby people and expect it to work. You might stay nice for a while, just because—but it isn't sustainable over years. If you want a happy company, you can do it only by hiring naturally happy people. You'll never build a happy company by "making people happy"—you can't really "make" people any way that they aren't already. Laura and I want to be in love with life, and our business has been a good thing for us in that journey.[68]

Although Pete and Laura's hiring approach is consistent with the dispositional and genetic model of job satisfaction, it is important to note that hiring "like-minded"

These employees appear to be enjoying their jobs. Research suggests that they are more likely to enjoy their job if they are predisposed to being happy, based on genetic factors and personal traits.

people can potentially lead to discriminatory decisions. Managers are advised not to discriminate on the basis of race, gender, religion, colour, national origin, and age.

THE RELATIONSHIP BETWEEN JOB SATISFACTION AND EIGHT OTHER FACTORS

LO 5

Thousands of studies have examined the relationship between job satisfaction and other organizational variables, making it an area with significant managerial implications. Because it is impossible to examine them all, we will consider a subset of the more important variables from the standpoint of managerial relevance. The following eight key variables have a strong, moderate, or weak relationship with job satisfaction.

1. **Motivation** A recent meta-analysis of nine studies and 1,739 workers revealed a significant positive relationship between motivation and job satisfaction. Because satisfaction with supervision was also significantly correlated with motivation, managers are advised to consider how their behaviour affects employee satisfaction.[69] Managers can potentially enhance employees' motivation through various attempts to increase job satisfaction.

2. **Job Involvement** Job involvement represents the extent to which employees are personally involved with their work role. A meta-analysis involving 27,925 individuals from 87 different studies demonstrated that job involvement was moderately related with job satisfaction.[70] Managers are thus encouraged to foster satisfying work environments to fuel employees' job involvement.

3. **Organizational Citizenship Behaviour** *Organizational citizenship behaviours (OCBs)* consist of employee behaviours that are beyond the call of duty. Examples include "such gestures as constructive statements about the department, expression of personal interest in the work of others, suggestions for improvement, training new people, respect for the spirit as well as the letter of housekeeping rules, care for organizational property, and punctuality and attendance well beyond standard or enforceable levels."[71] Managers certainly would like employees to exhibit these behaviours. A meta-analysis covering 7,031 people and 21 separate studies revealed a significant and moderately positive relationship between organizational citizenship behaviours and job satisfaction.[72] Moreover, additional research demonstrated that employees' citizenship behaviours were determined more by leadership

Organizational citizenship behaviours (OCBs)

Employee behaviours that exceed work-role requirements.

and characteristics of the work environment than by an employee's personality.[73] It thus appears that managerial behaviour significantly influences an employee's willingness to exhibit citizenship behaviours. This relationship is important to recognize because employees' OCBs were positively correlated with their conscientiousness at work, organizational commitment, performance ratings and promotions.[74] Another recent study demonstrated a broader impact of OCBs on organizational effectiveness. Results revealed that the number of OCBs exhibited by employees working in 28 regional restaurants was significantly associated with each restaurant's corporate profits one year later.[75] Because employees' perceptions of being treated fairly at work are related to their willingness to engage in OCBs, managers are encouraged to make and implement employee-related decisions in an equitable fashion. More is said about this topic in Chapter 9.

4. **Absenteeism** Absenteeism is not always what it appears to be, and it can be costly. For example, a survey of 700 managers indicated that 20 percent of them called in sick because they simply did not feel like going to work that day. The top three reasons given for the bogus excuse of being sick were doing personal errands, catching up on sleep, and relaxing.[76] While it is difficult to provide a precise estimate of the cost of absenteeism, one study projected it to be $789 per employee.[77] This would suggest that absenteeism costs $236,700 for a company with 300 employees. Imagine the costs for a company with 100,000 employees! Because of these costs, managers are constantly on the lookout for ways to reduce it (see Skills and Best Practice feature box for a description of what McDonald's is doing). One recommendation

Withdrawal cognitions

Overall thoughts and feelings about quitting a job.

has been to increase job satisfaction. If this is a valid recommendation, there should be a strong negative relationship between satisfaction and absenteeism. In other words, as satisfaction increases, absenteeism should decrease. A researcher tracked this prediction by synthesizing three separate meta-analyses containing a total of 74 studies. Results revealed a weak negative relationship between satisfaction and absenteeism.[78] It is unlikely, therefore, that managers will realize any significant decrease in absenteeism by increasing job satisfaction. Remember, here we are talking about a relationship between job satisfaction and absenteeism . . . earlier we were talking about job involvement and absenteeism. Be clear in your understanding about the differences between these two types of work attitudes. It may be beneficial to review the distinctions between them.

5. **Withdrawal Cognitions** Although some people quit their jobs impulsively or in a fit of anger, most go through a process of thinking about whether or not they should quit.[79] *Withdrawal cognitions* encapsulate this thought process by representing an individual's overall thoughts and feelings about quitting. What causes employees to think about quitting their job? Job satisfaction is believed to be one of the most significant contributors. For example, a study of managers, salespersons, and auto mechanics from a national automotive retail store chain demonstrated that job dissatisfaction caused employees to begin the process of thinking about quitting. In turn, withdrawal cognitions had a greater impact on employee turnover than job satisfaction in this sample.[80] Results from this study imply that managers can indirectly help to reduce employee turnover by enhancing employee job satisfaction.

Skills & Best Practices

McDonald's Creative Approach for Reducing Absenteeism

To help reduce absenteeism and turnover—chronic problems for fast-food managers—McDonald's is testing an unusual program at some of its 1,250 British restaurants. Employees from the same immediate family can fill in for one another without clearing it with the boss—a new twist on job-sharing—according to Mercer Human Resources Consulting.

The so-called Family Contract is a response to surveys in which workers described juggling work and other duties as stressful. It permits family members—including same-sex partners—to sign on in pairs and take each other's shifts.

Do you see any problems with the approach being used by McDonald's? Discuss.

SOURCE: Excerpted from M. Arndt, "The Family that Flips Together . . .," *BusinessWeek*, April 17, 2006, p 14.

6. **Turnover** Recent statistics show that turnover is on the rise for managers, salespeople, manufacturing workers, and chief financial officers.[81] This is a problem because turnover disrupts organizational continuity and is very costly. Costs of turnover fall into two categories: separation costs and replacement costs.

> *Separation costs may include severance pay, costs associated with an exit interview, outplacement fees, and possible litigation costs, particularly for involuntary separation. Replacement costs are the well-known costs of a hire, including sourcing expenses, HR processing costs for screening and assessing candidates, the time spent by hiring managers interviewing candidates, travel and relocation expenses, signing bonuses (if applicable), and orientation and training costs.*[82]

Experts estimate that the cost of turnover for an hourly employee is roughly 30 percent of annual salary, whereas the cost can range up to 150 percent of yearly salary for professional employees.[83]

Although there are various things a manager can do to reduce employee turnover, many of them revolve around attempts to improve employees' job satisfaction.[84] This trend is supported by results from a meta-analysis of 67 studies covering 24,556 people. Job satisfaction had a moderate negative relationship with employee turnover.[85] Given the strength of this relationship, managers are advised to try to reduce employee turnover by increasing employee job satisfaction.

7. **Perceived Stress** Stress can have very negative effects on organizational behaviour and an individual's health. Stress is positively related to absenteeism, turnover, coronary heart disease, and viral infections. Based on a meta-analysis of 32 studies covering 11,063 individuals, perceived stress has a strong negative relationship with job satisfaction.[86] Managers should attempt to reduce the negative effects of stress by improving job satisfaction.

8. **Job Performance** One of the biggest controversies within OB research centres on the relationship between job satisfaction and job performance. Although researchers have identified eight different ways in which these variables are related, the dominant beliefs are either that satisfaction causes performance, or performance causes satisfaction.[87] A team of researchers recently attempted to resolve this controversy through a meta-analysis of data from 312 samples involving 54,417 individuals.[88] There were two key findings from this study. First, job satisfaction and performance are moderately related. This is an important finding because it supports the belief that employee job satisfaction is a key work attitude managers should consider when attempting to increase employees' job performance. Second, the relationship between job satisfaction and performance is much more complex than originally thought. It is not as simple as satisfaction causing performance or performance causing satisfaction. Rather, researchers now believe both variables indirectly influence each other through a host of individual differences and work-environment characteristics.[89]

There is one additional consideration to keep in mind regarding the relationship between job satisfaction and job performance. Researchers believe the relationship between satisfaction and performance is understated due to incomplete measures of individual-level performance. For example, if performance ratings used in past research did not reflect the actual interactions and interdependencies at work, inaccurate measures of performance served to lower the reported relationships between satisfaction and performance. Examining the relationship between aggregate measures of job satisfaction and organizational performance is one way to correct this problem.

In support of these ideas, a team of researchers recently conducted a meta-analysis of 7,939 business units in 36 companies. Results uncovered significant positive relationships between business-unit-level employee satisfaction and business-unit outcomes of customer satisfaction, productivity, profit, employee turnover, and accidents.[90] As a result, it appears that managers can positively affect a variety of important organizational outcomes, including performance, by increasing employee job satisfaction.

> "Separation costs may include severance pay, costs associated with an exit interview, outplacement fees, and possible litigation costs . . . . Replacement costs are . . . the costs of a hire, including sourcing expenses, HR processing costs . . ., time spent for interviewing, travel and relocation expenses, signing bonuses, and orientation and training costs."

1. **Define** *value system*, *terminal values*, **and** *instrumental values.* A value system is an enduring organization of one's personal beliefs about preferred ways of behaving and desired end-states. An individual can have an intense value system or a weak value system. Personal values can be categorized in two dimensions: terminal and instrumental values. A terminal value is an enduring belief about a desired end-state (e.g., happy, full of wisdom). An instrumental value is an enduring belief about how one should behave (e.g., obedient, honest).

2. **Describe three types of value conflicts.** (1) Intrapersonal value conflict can be likened to the internal conflict individuals feel when they are torn between two opposite desires/feeling (e.g., "I want a high paying job because I value large amounts of money, but I don't want to work nights or weekends because I'll miss time with my family, whom I love"). (2) Interpersonal value conflict occurs when the values that an individual is feeling conflict with external values from another individual (e.g., "My boss tells me to bury the costs so that our bottom line looks more positive, but that goes against my personal values of being an ethical accountant"). (3) Individual–organizational value conflict is classic whistle-blower behaviour (e.g., if an employee sees that the organizational culture is moving toward dishonesty and infectious greed, then he will feel compelled to blow the whistle by going to the board of directors or the media).

3. **Identify the three components of attitude.** The three components of attitude are affective, cognitive, and behavioural. The affective component represents the feelings or emotions one has about a given object or situation. The cognitive component reflects the beliefs or ideas one has about an object or situation. The behavioural component refers to how one intends or expects to act toward someone or something.

4. **Relate organizational commitment to psychological contract.** Organizational commitment reflects how strongly a person identifies with an organization and is committed to its goals. Organizational commitment is composed of three related components: affective commitment, continuance commitment, and normative commitment. In turn, each of these components is influenced by a separate set of antecedents. An antecedent is something that causes the component of commitment to occur. Once an individual feels strong commitment toward the organization, it will be easier to establish a psychological contract between the two parties. A psychological contract represents employees' beliefs about what they are entitled to receive in return for what they provide to the organization.

5. **Compare and discriminate between eight variables that have a relationship with job satisfaction.** Eight major variables that have a relationship with job satisfaction are: motivation (moderate positive relationship), job involvement (moderate positive), organizational citizenship behaviour (moderate positive), absenteeism (weak negative), withdrawal cognitions (strong negative), turnover (moderate negative), perceived stress (strong negative), and job performance (moderate positive). Strong relationships imply that managers can significantly influence the variable of interest by increasing job satisfaction.

Discussion Questions

1. What are your thoughts about the opening vignette firm, High Road Communications, and their approach to creating a pleasant workplace? If you pay people enough money to work, isn't that enough to keep them satisfied?

2. Why do you think a store manager would have greater impact on employee turnover than the actual neighbourhood location of the store?

3. Imagine that you work with a fellow employee who continues to take credit for work you complete. You decide to approach the person and give him or her a piece of your mind! The final decision to behave this way toward someone gives you a bad attitude. Explain which of the three behavioural components of attitude you are exhibiting at this time.

4. Use Ajzen's theory of planned behaviour (Figure 4.2) to analyze how managers can reduce voluntary turnover. Be sure to explain what managers can do to affect each aspect of the theory.

5. "What's the matter with today's generation? They just don't have the same ambition or work ethic like the employees we hired 50 years ago. Their personal values are clashing with our corporate values." How does this quote make you feel? Do you agree or disagree with the statement? Explain your response.

Google Searches

1. **Google Search:** "Honda and Keays" The long awaited Supreme Court of Canada decision was finally reached in 2008. After reading about the case, do you agree with the final court decision? Could Mr. Keays control his absenteeism or was he discriminated against when Honda fired him?

2. **Google Search:** "Equity and Human Rights Services Religious Accommodation" Notice how many post-secondary educational institutions in Canada have produced a calendar of religious accommodation. Go to one of the sites and review the organizational policy recognizing diverse faiths and their respective holy dates. Are you familiar with all these religious faiths and their celebrations? What are your impressions of an organization having a policy for such occasions?

3. **Google Search:** "Turban Sikh RCMP officer" In 1996, the Canadian Supreme Court dismissed the appeal to ban turbans from the RCMP uniform. Read about the case, watch the CBC streamed video regarding the case, and discuss how cultural values are crossing over into the workplace. Do you agree with the Supreme Court decision? How much, if any, should the Canadian workplace flex to accommodate different cultural values?

Experiential Exercise

Student Values vs. Corporate Values Exercise

PURPOSE: This exercise is to help familiarize you with your own personal values and then consider how they may differ from corporate values.
Approx. Timing: 20 minutes.

ACTIVITY ASSIGNMENT:
The Rokeach Model was discussed in this chapter under the subhead of "values." Basically, there are two types of categories of values: terminal and instrumental.

- Independently write down at least two terminal and two instrumental values that you subscribe to in life.
- Independently write down the kind of organization you want to work for by describing it in terms of values (e.g., "I want to work for a company that values _____"). Try and identify at least 3–5 values that the desired company subscribes to.
- When completed, work in small groups to share responses and address the following questions:

  1. Is there a common set of values that most organizations subscribe to? If so, what would they be?
  2. Can your group identify an occupation for each member that is congruent with that person's set of values?
  3. Can your group name a specific organization that would "fit" each member's individual set of values?
  4. Can your group list those organizations that would not "fit" each member's set of values? Explain your reasoning.

The Presentation Assistant

Here are possible topics and corresponding sources related to this chapter that can be further explored by student groups looking for ideas.

	FOUR DIFFERENT GENERATIONS IN THE WORKFORCE—HOW DO THEIR VALUES DIFFER?	COGNITIVE DISSONANCE AT WORK—HAS THIS EVER HAPPENED TO YOU?	JOB SATISFACTION—WHAT MAKES YOU SATISFIED AT YOUR JOB?
YouTube Videos	• Baby Boomers • Retirement and Gen X • Managing Gen Y • Digitals	• Cognitive Dissonance • Expectations and Disappointment at Work • Enron Corporate Whistle-blowers	• Job Satisfaction

TV Shows or Movies to Preview	• Boomers watched *Archie Bunker*, *Tonight Show* with Johnny Carson • Gen X's watched *The Brady Bunch*, *Friends*, *90210*, *Tonight Show* with Jay Leno • Gen Y's watched *The Hills*, *Family Guy*, *Tonight Show* with Conan O'Brien • Digitals watch *Daily Show* and the *Unique You Tube Videos*	• *Enron The Movie* • *Standard Operating Procedure* (Following Orders)	• *The Presidio* • *I Really Hate My Job* • *Worst Jobs In History* • *Dirty Jobs* TV–Mike Rowe
Internet Searches	• *Boom, Bust, Echo* (by Dr. David Foot) • Population Pyramids • *Gen X T.V.* (by Rob Owen) • Generations In the Workplace	• How Following Orders Can Harm Your Career • Famous Whistleblower – Watkins at Enron • Shiv Chopra – Canadian Microbiologist whistleblower	• *Three Signs of a Miserable Job (A Fable For Managers)* (by Patrick Lencioni) • I Need a New Job • My Job's Giving Me a Heart Attack – CNN News
Ice Breaker Classroom Activity	• Ask the students to break into groups and write down at least two values of their generation that are distinctively associated with them. Ask them to do the same with the Baby Boomer generation.	• Ask the students to think of an example where they were asked to do something at work that they didn't feel comfortable doing. What was the result? Did they get in trouble from the manager? Share responses.	• Ask the students to list one thing that makes them feel satisfied at their job. Ask them to identify at least one factor that makes them feel less satisfied. Share their comments with the class.

OB In Action Case Study

Valuing Work: Life Balance

According to professor, author, and lecturer Catherine Middleton, the latest communication devises issued by employers are causing major conflict in their employees' lives. Middleton reports in her book, *Mobility and Technology in the Workplace*, that family and friends of BlackBerry users are often referred to as "BlackBerry orphans," which clearly demonstrates the level of disruption these devises can cause people in their social and family life.

One woman recounts how she caught her husband emailing a client under the table during their Valentine Day's dinner. Another says her companion checked his BlackBerry email during their first date.

"In the past, work-life balance meant there was some sort of separation between your personal and work life. But with the BlackBerry, it allows you to bring your work home with you," says Middleton. "Subscribers to BlackBerrys think this gives them more time to spend with their families and friends, but to those around these users, they are still at work."

Over a period of several years, Middleton conducted her own research on the behaviour of BlackBerry users and the reaction of their family and friends. Her findings are quite interesting. For example:

- People are using their BlackBerrys while in the shower, at funerals, at their children's soccer match, and while on vacation.
- Users claim they feel better able to manage the demands of their jobs by staying connected 24/7 to their emails.
- Family and friends tend to want to toss the "BlackBerry out the window" or "Throw it off the boat when [they] were on [their] honeymoon."

With the introduction of satellite phone, employers may be able to reach their employees virtually anywhere at anytime. From the perspective of an employer, the possibilities are exciting. Can the same be said from the employee's point of view?

SOURCE: "BlackBerry's hurt work-life balance: Professor." *Canadian HR Reporter*, Nov. 28, 2007, http://www.hrreporter.com/loginarea/members/viewing.asp?ArticleNo=5651&subscriptionType=Print.

Discussion Questions

1. Identify the terminal and instrumental values that BlackBerry users in all probability adhere to.
2. To employees striving for balance in their lives, does the BlackBerry create intra- or interpersonal conflict? Explain.
3. What sort of organizational response would you recommend for firms whose employees are experiencing the challenge of balancing work and life?
4. Looking into the future, do you think work-life balance will become more or less of an issue for employees? Explain.

Ethical OB Dilemma

Valuing Truth on the Job

Do you value truth and expect others who you work with to tell the truth? Consider the following scenario:

> Joe Shmoe misled his employer about his qualifications and prior work experience. The organization didn't discover the deceit until after Joe was hired. If they had known prior to his hiring, they would not have done so. Joe stated on his resumé that he was still working for a large packaged food company and, wanting to avoid relocation, he was looking for a new job. In fact, Joe had been fired months earlier. Joe also stated that he had a degree in business, but once again, had lied. Eventually the organization caught up to Joe's lies and fired him immediately for just cause.

Falsification on a resumé, according to one Canadian legal expert, can be as high as 50 percent of all resumés—from little lies to giant whoppers. When it comes to full blown lying on your resumé, the truth is that you can be fired.

SOURCE: Daniel Lublin, lawyer, practises employment and human rights law in Toronto. "Lying on Resumé" past stories, 2006, – http://www.toronto-employmentlawyer.com/news_extra_6.shtml.

Discussion Questions

1. Do you value the truth in business? Do you think organizations should?
2. Why do you suppose people lie on their resumés?
3. Do you agree with the organization for firing Joe once they learned the truth?
4. Do you think this was Joe's first time lying? Explain your response as it relates to this chapter's topic of personal values/beliefs.

Visit www.mcgrawhillconnect.ca to register.

McGraw-Hill Connect™ —Available 24/7 with instant feedback so you can study when you want, how you want, and where you want. Take advantage of the Study Plan—an innovative tool that helps you customize your learning experience. You can diagnose your knowledge with pre- and post-tests, identify the areas where you need help, search the entire learning package for content specific to the topic you're studying, and add these resources to your personalized study plan. Visit www.mcgrawhillconnect.ca to register—take practice quizzes, search the e-book, and much more.

5

Foundations *of* Motivation

Motivating During Troubled Times

The last several quarters in 2008 and almost all of 2009 were difficult, with global financial markets experiencing great volatility causing significant economic uncertainty; all of which eventually gave way to tough times in the Canadian labour market. The challenge for many managers during such turbulent times was how to maintain productivity. Under these circumstances, motivation became difficult as employees turned their attention toward their own job security over output.

What sorts of things can motivate employees during troubled times?

"The best way to motivate any group when things are in turmoil is to say: 'Things happen. Dust yourself off and make a plan for moving forward,'" says Leo Houle, the former Chief Talent Officer of BCE Inc. & Bell Canada. Having spent 40 years as a human resource manager, Houle advises managers to be straightforward and honest with their employees during tough times. "While it sounds harsh, bald facts are what people are looking for in troubled times. All people are looking for is honesty."

Here are nine tips from experts for how managers can keep their staff motivated:

- Stick to a routine—maintain normal work habits so as not to provoke fear of change
- Communicate often—suppress rumours by being open about events
- Be straightforward—tell it like it is; efforts to suppress bad news will only make employees resentful if they find out after the fact
- Encourage discussion—formally set aside time for employees to ask questions
- Get support from the top—senior management need to be involved in staff town hall discussions to show that all parties are trying to find solutions
- Stay visible—management need to be seen on the floor, present and able to respond to concerns
- Give lots of feedback—hold discussions around career options and performance reviews to focus on progress and moving forward
- Offer outside help—invite experts in to speak on innovation, motivation, and support services available for employees
- Be reasonable—encourage employees to get back to being productive, but don't expect 100 percent of their focus to be on work

ADAPTED: W. Immen, "Tough Love For Tough Times," *The Globe and Mail*, October 8, 2008, section C, page 1.

Employers can use the interview process to identify potential employer needs and motivations.

E ffective employee motivation has long been one of management's most difficult and important duties. As you will read in this chapter, an employee's motivation is a function of several components, including an individual's needs, the extent to which a work environment is positive and supportive, perceptions of being treated fairly (creating a strong relationship between performance and the receipt of valued rewards), the use of accurate measures of performance, and the setting of specific goals. As you study the various theories of motivation discussed in this chapter, keep in mind that each one offers different recommendations about how to motivate employees.

LO 1

The term *motivation* derives from the Latin word *movere*, meaning "to move." In the present context, **motivation** represents "those psychological processes that cause the arousal, direction, and persistence of voluntary actions that are goal directed."[1] Researchers have proposed two general **theories of motivation** to explain the psychological processes underlying employee motivation: content theories and process theories. **Content theories of motivation** focus on identifying internal factors such

Motivation

Psychological processes that arouse and direct goal-directed behaviour.

Theories of motivation

Two psychological processes: content & process.

Content theories of motivation

Identify internal factors influencing motivation.

→ **LEARNING OBJECTIVES**

After reading this chapter, you should be able to:

LO 1 **Define** *motivation* and *theories of motivation*.

LO 2 **Contrast** Maslow's, Alderfer's, and McClelland's need theories.

LO 3 **Explain** Vroom's expectancy theory, and review its practical implications.

LO 4 **Explain** how goal setting motivates an individual, and review the four practical lessons from goal-setting research.

LO 5 **Summarize** the various approaches to job design, including mechanistic, motivational, biological, and perceptual-motor.

as instincts, needs, satisfaction, and job characteristics that energize employee motivation. These theories do not explain how motivation is influenced by the dynamic interaction between individuals and the environment in which they work. This limitation led to the creation of process theories of motivation. **Process theories of motivation** focus on explaining the process by which internal factors and cognitions influence employee motivation.[2] We'll explore both of these theories in greater detail over the next several sections, but first let's discuss the content theories of motivation.

Process theories of motivation

Identify the process by which internal factors and cognitions influence motivation.

LO 2 Content Theories of Motivation

Most content theories of motivation revolve around the notion that an employee's needs influence motivation. **Needs** are physiological or psychological deficiencies that arouse behaviour. They can be strong or weak, and are influenced by environmental factors. Thus, human needs vary over time and place. The general idea behind need theories of motivation is that unmet needs motivate people to satisfy them. Conversely, people are not motivated to pursue a satisfied need. Let us now consider four popular content theories of motivation: (1) Maslow's need hierarchy theory, (2) Alderfer's ERG theory, (3) McClelland's need theory, and (4) Herzberg's motivator-hygiene model.

Needs

Physiological or psychological deficiencies that arouse behaviour.

MASLOW'S NEED HIERARCHY THEORY

In 1943, psychologist Abraham Maslow published his now-famous **need hierarchy theory** of motivation. Although the theory was based on his clinical observation of a few individuals, it has subsequently been used to explain the entire spectrum of human behaviour. Maslow proposed that motivation is a function of five basic needs. These needs are:

Need hierarchy theory

Five basic needs—physiological, safety, love (belonging), esteem, and self-actualization influence behaviour.

1. **Physiological** Basic need entails having enough food, air, and water to survive.

2. **Safety** The need to be safe from physical and psychological harm. This need has become a real priority in today's workplace (see Law & Ethics At Work feature box for more details).

3. **Love (belonging)** The desire to be loved and to love. Includes the needs for affection and belonging.

4. **Esteem** Need for reputation, prestige, and recognition from others. Also includes need for self-confidence and strength. Some organizations threaten such needs with inappropriate office practices (see International OB feature box for details).

5. **Self-actualization** The desire for self-fulfillment—to become the best one is capable of becoming.

Maslow said these five needs are arranged in the hierarchy shown in Figure 5.1. In other words, he believed human needs generally emerge in a predictable stair-step fashion. Accordingly, when one's physiological needs are relatively satisfied, one's safety needs emerge, and so on up the need hierarchy, one step at a time. Once a need is satisfied, it activates the next higher need in the hierarchy. This process continues until the need for self-actualization is activated.[3]

Although research does not clearly support this theory of motivation, two key managerial implications of Maslow's theory are worth noting. First, it is important for managers and team leaders to focus on satisfying employee needs related to self concepts—self-esteem and self-actualization—because their satisfaction is significantly associated with a host of important outcomes such as academic achievement, physical illness, psychological well-being (e.g., anxiety disorders,

▶ **FIGURE 5.1** Maslow's Need Hierarchy

IS A SAFE WORK ENVIRONMENT FULFILLING WORKER NEEDS?

Workplace drug-testing policies are not new to Canada. The Canadian Human Rights Commission allows various kinds of testing in a workplace if an employer can demonstrate there are bona fide occupational requirements to doing so. But some Canadians view this sort of treatment as an infringement of their personal right to privacy, or management's attempt to control employee behaviour . . . even intimidation. To other employees, such testing is welcomed as it speaks to their right for a safe workplace and their personal need for job satisfaction by way of health and safety on the job.

As part of a safe work environment, unionized construction workers in British Columbia are now required to take a drug or alcohol test after an accident or near-miss as a result of an unprecedented agreement that was signed between the Construction Labour Relations Association (CLRA) of B.C. and the Bargaining Council of B.C. Building Trades Unions. According to Clyde Scollan, President of the Vancouver-based CLRA, which represents 350 construction contractors, "Employers have an obligation to provide a safe work site. Drug and alcohol testing is recognized as part and parcel of that." If management believes that there is reasonable suspicion of on-the-job impairment, the employee must agree to be tested. Do you agree that a safe workplace fulfills employee needs?

SOURCE: S. Kile, "Unions, contractors agree to drug testing in B.C.—Workers to be tested following work site accident or near miss," *Canadian HR Reporter*, September 22, 2008, www.hrreporter.com.

depression), criminal convictions, drug abuse, marital satisfaction, money and work problems, and performance at work.[4]

Second, a satisfied need may lose its motivational potential. Therefore, managers and team leaders are advised to motivate others by devising programs or practices aimed at satisfying emerging or unmet needs. Many companies have responded to this recommendation by offering employees targeted benefits that meet their specific needs.[5] Results from a nationwide survey conducted by the Society for Human Resource Management can help in this pursuit. Findings revealed that employee wants and desires vary by age. Table 5.1 summarizes the survey results by presenting the top five things employees are looking for from their jobs across three different age groups. Managers and team leaders are encouraged to use customized surveys to assess the specific needs of employees.[6]

ALDERFER'S ERG THEORY

Clayton Alderfer developed an alternative theory of human needs in the late 1960s. Alderfer's theory differs from Maslow's in three major respects. First, a smaller set of core needs is used to explain behaviour. From lowest to highest level, they are existence needs (E)—the desire for physiological and materialistic well-being; relatedness needs (R)—the desire to have meaningful relationships with significant others; and growth needs (G)—the desire to grow as a human being and to use one's abilities to their fullest potential; hence, the label **ERG theory**. Second, ERG theory does not assume needs are related to each other in a stair-step hierarchy as does Maslow. Alderfer believes that more than one need may be activated at a time. Finally, ERG theory contains a frustration-regression component. That is, frustration of higher-order needs can influence the desire for lower-order needs.[7] For example, employees may demand higher pay or better benefits (existence needs) when they are frustrated or dissatisfied with the quality of their interpersonal relationships (relatedness needs) at work.

Research on ERG theory has provided mixed support for some of the theory's key propositions.[8] That said, however, there are two key managerial implications associated with ERG. The first revolves around the frustration-regression aspect of the theory. Managers and team leaders should keep in mind that employees may be motivated to pursue lower-level needs because they are frustrated with a higher-order need. For instance, the solution for a stifling work environment may be a request for higher pay or better benefits.

ERG theory

Three basic needs—existence, relatedness, and growth—influence behaviour.

TABLE 5.1

Employees' Needs and Desires Vary by Age

	TOP FIVE NEEDS AND DESIRES
35 and younger	Compensation Other benefits Health care/medical benefits Job security Flexibility to balance work-life issues
36 to 55	Compensation Health care/medical benefits Retirement benefits Other benefits Job security
56 and older	Feeling safe in the work environment Retirement benefits Other benefits Health care/medical benefits Meaningfulness of job

SOURCE: Data were reported in E. Esen, *SHRM 2006 Job Satisfaction Survey Report* (Alexandria, VA: Society for Human Resource Management, 2006).

Second, ERG theory is consistent with the finding that individual and cultural differences influence our need states (see Focus On Diversity feature box). People are motivated by different needs at different times in their lives. This implies that managers should customize their reward and recognition programs to meet employees' varying needs. Consider how Marc Albin, CEO of Albin Engineering Services, Inc., handles this recommendation.

INTERNATIONAL OB

TRUSTING EMPLOYEES IS DIFFICULT FOR SOME FIRMS

National prosecutors alleged that certain individuals at Deutsche Telekom, the German telecommunication company, illegally monitored some of its staff's phone calls during 2005–2006. The allegations claim that an outside agency was hired by Deutsche Telecom to monitor contacts between members of its supervisory board and journalists at a time when the company was laying off workers. The company partially admitted to prosecutors that spying was conducted in hopes of finding out who was leaking information to the press. However, the CEO at the time, Rene Obermann, denied any knowledge of such actions, preferring to push the violation blame onto the company's own security department.

According to legal expert Thomas Hoeren, it is becoming more common in Germany for companies to watch their employees, which unto itself is not against the law. However, when privacy laws are broken for whatever reason, as in this case for alleged security breach reasons, then it becomes an area of concern. In your opinion, is it acceptable for employers to spy on their employees? Does such action threaten employee esteem needs?

SOURCES: "Rene Obermann Profile on People," *Forbes Magazine* online, www.forbes.com. Digital Civil Rights In Europe, "Deutsche Telekom Under Investigation For Spying On Its Employees," June 4, 2008 www.edri.org/edrigram/number6.11/deutsche-telekomp-spying-employees.

GIVING PEOPLE A CHANCE BY ACCOMMODATING THEIR DIFFERENCES CAN BE MOTIVATING AND ADVANTAGEOUS

Organizations that hire people with diverse backgrounds provide a motivating work environment because it sends a clear message of hope to all those current employees who could be categorized as "different." The message? It's okay to be different. In fact, diversity is celebrated, supported, and promoted within the organization. According to Anne Lamont, CEO and President of Career Edge, a Toronto based not-for-profit organization that arranges internships, "if (Canadian) companies are really going to do what's right for their organization and for the Canadian economy, then they have to be more creative and open-minded to looking at different candidates."

"Traditionally, employers don't think of going to (immigrants or people with disabilities), because of preconceived notions that the talent isn't there," says Bill Young, President of Social Capital Partners, a non-profit organization in Toronto. But Young is adamant about the need to support these people, and his organization is committed to helping them find employment. Often they are motivated and willing to try and prove themselves, but no one is willing to give them a chance.

Jane Lewis, human resource manager at Procter & Gamble (Toronto) states, "We see diversity as a competitive advantage. We have a fundamental belief that a diverse company will outperform a homogenous company." The accounting firm of Ernst & Young would agree; 1,026 of the firm's 4,099 employees are skilled immigrants and most of them are in (global) client-serving positions at the supervisory level.

SOURCES: M. Harman, "Outlook 2008 (The Watch List): Labour." *Canadian Business Online* http://www.canadianbusiness.com/managing/strategy/article.jsp?content=20071219_00020_000020. "Strategic Efforts to Integrate Immigrants—TRIEC awards highlight competitive advantage for employers that hire skilled immigrants." *Canadian HR Reporter*, February 9, 2009.

To identify which parts of individual employees' egos need scratching, Albin takes an unconventional approach.

"My experience in managing people is, they're all different," says Albin. "Some people want to be recognized for their cheerful attitude and their ability to spread their cheerful attitude. Some want to be recognized for the quality of their work, some for the quantity of their work. Some like to be recognized individually; others want to be recognized in groups."

Consequently, at the end of each employee-orientation session, Albin emails his new hires and asks them how and in what form they prefer their strokes.

"It helps me understand what they think of themselves and their abilities, and I make a mental note to pay special attention to them when they're working in that particular arena," he says. "No one has ever said, 'Just recognize me for anything I do well.'"[9]

Need for achievement

Desire to accomplish something difficult.

McCLELLAND'S NEED THEORY

In the late 1940s, David McClelland, a well-known psychologist, studied the relationship between needs and behaviour. Although he is most recognized for his research on the need for achievement, he also investigated the needs for affiliation and power. Let us consider each of these needs.

The Need for Achievement The **need for achievement** is defined by the following desires:

To accomplish something difficult. To master, manipulate, or organize physical objects, human beings, or ideas. To do this as rapidly and as independently as possible. To overcome obstacles and attain a high standard. To excel one's self. To rival and surpass others. To increase self-regard by the successful exercise of talent.[10]

Achievement-motivated people share three common characteristics: (1) they prefer working on tasks of moderate difficulty; (2) they prefer situations in which performance is due to their efforts rather than other factors, such as luck; and (3) they desire more feedback on their successes and failures than do low achievers.

The Need for Affiliation People with a high *need for affiliation* prefer to spend more time maintaining social relationships, joining groups, and wanting to be loved. Individuals high in this need are not the most effective managers or leaders because they have a hard time making difficult decisions without worrying about being disliked.[11]

Need for affiliation

Desire to spend time in social relationships and activities.

The Need for Power The *need for power* reflects an individual's desire to influence, coach, teach, or encourage others to achieve. People with a high need for power like to work and are concerned with discipline and self-respect. There is a positive and negative side to this need. The negative face of power is characterized by an "if I win, you lose" mentality. In contrast, people with a positive orientation to power focus on accomplishing group goals and helping employees obtain the feeling of competence. Chapter 9 provides more information about the two faces of power. Because effective managers must positively influence others, McClelland proposes that top managers should have a high need for power coupled with a low need for affiliation. He also believes that individuals with high achievement motivation are not best suited for top management positions. Several studies support these propositions.[12]

Need for power

Desire to influence, coach, teach, or encourage others to achieve.

Managerial Implications Given that adults can be trained to increase their achievement motivation,[13] organizations should consider the benefits of providing achievement training for employees. Moreover, achievement, affiliation, and power needs can be considered during the selection process, for better placement. For example, a study revealed that individuals' need for achievement affected their preference to work in different companies. People with a high need for achievement were more attracted to companies that had a pay-for-performance environment than were those with a low achievement motivation.[14] Finally, managers should create challenging task assignments or goals because the need for achievement is positively correlated with goal commitment and job involvement.[15] Moreover, challenging goals should accompany a

more autonomous work environment and employee empowerment to capitalize on the characteristics of high achievers.

HERZBERG'S MOTIVATOR–HYGIENE THEORY

Frederick Herzberg's theory is based on a landmark study in which he interviewed 203 accountants and engineers.[16] These interviews sought to determine the factors responsible for job satisfaction and dissatisfaction. Herzberg found separate and distinct clusters of factors associated with job satisfaction and dissatisfaction. Job satisfaction was more frequently associated with achievement, recognition, characteristics of the work, responsibility, and advancement. These factors were all related to outcomes associated with the content of the task being performed. Herzberg labelled these factors *motivators* because each was associated with strong effort and good performance. He hypothesized that motivators cause a person to move from a state of no satisfaction to satisfaction (see Figure 5.2). Therefore, Herzberg's theory predicts managers can motivate individuals by incorporating motivators into an individual's job.

Motivators

Job characteristics associated with job satisfaction.

▶ **FIGURE** **5.2** Herzberg's Motivator–Hygiene Model

Motivators

No Satisfaction ⟶ Satisfaction
Jobs that do not offer achievement, recognition, stimulating work, responsibility, and advancement.
Jobs offering achievement, recognition, stimulating work, responsibility, and advancement.

Hygiene factors

Dissatisfaction ◀— No Dissatisfaction
Jobs with poor company policies and administration, technical supervision, salary, interpersonal relationships with supervisors, and working conditions.
Jobs with good company policies and administration, technical supervision, salary, interpersonal relationships with supervisors, and working conditions.

SOURCE: Adapted in part from D. A. Whitsett and E. K. Winslow, "An Analysis of Studies Critical of the Motivator–Hygiene Theory," *Personnel Psychology*, Winter 1967, pp 391–415.

Jesse Kiefer (right) finds many rewards in his job as a gumologist for Cadbury Schweppes, maker of Trident gum.

Jesse Kiefer, a gumologist, is a good example of someone who is energized by the motivators contained in his job. Here is what he said to a reporter from *Fortune* about his job.

Some days I don't blow any bubbles. Other days I have to blow a lot. It depends on what stage we are in the project. A piece of gum weighs just one to seven grams, but it's packed with a lot of different technology. It has to deliver a burst of flavour, a lot of sweetness, and a lot of tartness if it's a fruit gum. Our team figures out how to combine all those. For example, Trident Splash Strawberry with Lime—it's not easy to pick lime and strawberry flavours that complement each other . . . When we work on the gum in its raw form, sometimes we use a hatchet to chop it up. I did my graduate work as a chemical engineer, and I started out working on detergent and soaps. But with gum there's just so many flavours! I find the job very stimulating.[17]

Herzberg found job dissatisfaction to be associated primarily with factors in the work context or environment. Specifically, company policy and administration, technical supervision, salary, interpersonal relations with one's supervisor, and working conditions were most frequently mentioned by employees expressing job dissatisfaction. Herzberg labelled this second cluster of factors ***hygiene factors***. He further proposed that they were not motivational. At best, according to Herzberg's interpretation, individuals will experience no job dissatisfaction when they have no grievances about hygiene factors (refer to Figure 5.2). In contrast, employees like Katrina Gill are likely to quit when poor hygiene factors lead to job dissatisfaction.

Hygiene factors

Job characteristics associated with job dissatisfaction.

Katrina Gill, a 36-year-old certified nursing aide, worked in a long-term care facility. From 10:30 PM to 7 AM, she was on duty alone, performing three rounds on the dementia ward, where she took care of up to 28 patients a night for $9.32 an hour. She monitored vitals, turned for bedsores, and changed adult diapers. There were the constant vigils over patients like the one who would sneak into other rooms, mistaking female patients for his deceased wife. Worse was the resident she called "the hitter" who once lunged at her, ripping a muscle in her back and laying her flat for four days. Last month, Gill quit and took another job for 68¢ an hour more, bringing her salary to $14,400 a year.[18]

The key to adequately understanding Herzberg's motivator–hygiene theory is recognizing that he believes that satisfaction is not the opposite of dissatisfaction. Herzberg concludes that "the opposite of job satisfaction is not job dissatisfaction, but rather no job satisfaction; and similarly, the opposite of job dissatisfaction is not job satisfaction, but no dissatisfaction."[19] Herzberg thus asserts that the dissatisfaction–satisfaction continuum contains a zero midpoint at which dissatisfaction and satisfaction are absent. Conceivably, an organization member who has good supervision, pay, and working conditions but a tedious and unchallenging task with little chance of advancement would be at the zero midpoint. That person would have no dissatisfaction (because of good hygiene factors) and no satisfaction (because of a lack of motivators).

Herzberg's theory has generated a great deal of research and controversy.[20] Research does not support the two-factor aspect of his theory nor the proposition that hygiene factors are unrelated to job satisfaction. On the positive side, however, Herzberg correctly concluded that people are motivated when their needs for achievement, recognition, stimulating work, and advancement are satisfied.[21] As you will learn in a later section of this chapter, Herzberg's theory has important implications for how managers and team leaders can motivate employees through job design.

Process Theories of Motivation

Earlier in the chapter we discussed the differences between content theories of motivation, which focused on the impact of internal factors on motivation. Now we'll discuss process theories that go one step further in explaining motivation by identifying the process by which various internal factors influence motivation. These models are also cognitive in nature. That is, they are based on the premise (idea) that motivation is a function of employees' perceptions, thoughts, and beliefs. We now explore the three most common process theories of motivation: (1) equity theory, (2) expectancy theory, and (3) goal-setting theory.

EQUITY THEORY OF MOTIVATION

Equity theory

Holds that motivation is a function of fairness in social exchanges.

Defined generally, **equity theory** is a model of motivation that explains how people strive for fairness and justice in social exchanges or give-and-take relationships. As a process theory of motivation, equity theory explains how an individual's motivation to behave in a certain way is fuelled by feelings of inequity or a lack of justice. Psychologist J. Stacy Adams pioneered application of the equity principle to the workplace. Central to understanding Adams's equity theory of motivation is an awareness of key components of the individual–organization exchange relationship. This relationship is essential in the formation of employees' perceptions of equity and inequity.

The Individual–Organization Exchange Relationship

Adams points out that two primary components are involved in the employee–employer exchange, *inputs* and *outcomes*. Employees' inputs, for which they expect a just return, include education/training, skills, creativity, seniority, age, personality traits, effort expended, and personal appearance. On the outcome side of the exchange, the organization provides such things as pay/ bonuses, fringe benefits, challenging assignments, job security, promotions, status symbols, and participation in important decisions.

Negative inequity

Comparison in which another person receives greater outcomes for similar inputs.

Negative and Positive Inequity

On the job, feelings of inequity revolve around people's evaluation of whether they receive adequate rewards to compensate for their contributions. People perform these evaluations by comparing the perceived fairness of their employment exchange to that of relevant others. This comparative process, which is based on an equity norm, was found to generalize across countries.[22] People tend to compare themselves to other individuals with whom they have close interpersonalties (such as friends) or to similar others (such as people performing the same job or individuals of the same gender or educational level) rather than dissimilar others. For example, do you consider the average top-100 CEO in Canada a relevant comparison person to yourself? If not, then you should not feel inequity because Canada's 100 best paid CEOs make an average of $8,528,304.[23] For someone working at minimum wage, the contrast is beyond extreme. By 1:04 p.m. New Year's Day, the best paid CEOs pocket what takes a minimum wage worker the entire year to earn. Every four hours and four minutes, the best-paid 100 CEOs keep pocketing the annual income of a full-time full-year minimum wage worker.[24]

Three different equity relationships are illustrated in Figure 5.3: (1) equity, (2) negative inequity, and (3) positive inequity. Try and think of a time when you found out that a person at work was earning more than you per hour—even though you two had pretty much the same job. How did that make you feel? To understand this situation, refer to Figure 5.3 as we walk you through the theory. In the example, assume the two people in each of the equity relationships have equivalent backgrounds (equal education, seniority, and so forth), and perform identical tasks. Only their hourly pay rates differ. Equity exists for people when their ratio of perceived outcomes to inputs is equal to the ratio of outcomes to inputs for a relevant co-worker (part A in Figure 5.3). Because equity is based on comparing *ratios* of outcomes to inputs, inequity will not necessarily be perceived just because someone else receives greater rewards. If the other person's additional outcomes are due to greater inputs, a sense of equity may still exist. However, if the comparison person enjoys greater outcomes for similar inputs, **negative inequity** will be perceived (part B in Figure 5.3). On the other hand, a person will experience **positive inequity** when the outcome to input ratio is greater than that of a relevant co-worker (part C in Figure 5.3).

Positive inequity

Comparison in which another person receives lesser outcomes for similar inputs.

Dynamics of Perceived Inequity

Managers can derive practical benefits from Adams's equity theory by recognizing that (1) people have varying sensitivities to perceived equity and inequity, and (2) inequity can be reduced in a variety of ways.

Thresholds of Equity and Inequity

Have you ever noticed that some people become very upset over the slightest inequity, whereas others are not bothered at all? Research has shown that people respond differently to the same level of inequity due to an individual difference called equity sensitivity. **Equity sensitivity** reflects an individual's "different preferences for, tolerances for, and reactions to the level of equity associated with any given situation."[25] Equity sensitivity spans across a continuum. On one side would be those people who have a *higher tolerance* for negative inequity (Figure 5.3 B); they prefer their outcome/input ratio to be lower than ratios from the other person who they are comparing themselves against. In contrast, along the same continuum, some other people are more

Equity sensitivity

An individual's tolerance for negative and positive equity.

A. An Equitable Situation

B. Negative Inequity

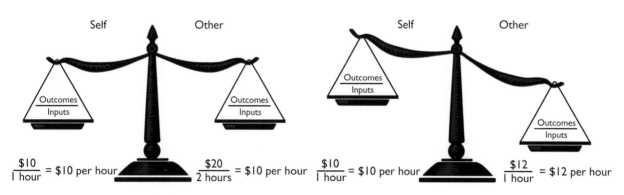

$\dfrac{\$10}{1\ hour}$ = $10 per hour $\dfrac{\$20}{2\ hours}$ = $10 per hour $\dfrac{\$10}{1\ hour}$ = $10 per hour $\dfrac{\$12}{1\ hour}$ = $12 per hour

C. Positive Inequity

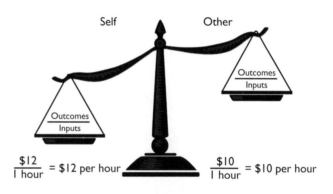

$\dfrac{\$12}{1\ hour}$ = $12 per hour $\dfrac{\$10}{1\ hour}$ = $10 per hour

sensitive because of their loyalty to a strict norm of reciprocity (this task earns this reward always, no matter who does it) and are quickly motivated to resolve both negative and positive inequity (either Figure 5.3 B or C). And finally, on the complete opposite side of the continuum are those people who have *no tolerance* for negative inequity (Figure 5.3 B). They actually expect to obtain greater output/input ratios than others and become upset when this is not the case.[26]

Reducing Inequity If people perceive inequity, then only they can alter it. Equity ratios can be changed by attempting to alter outcomes or adjusting inputs. For example, negative inequity might be resolved by asking for a raise or a promotion (i.e., raising outputs) or by reducing inputs (i.e., working fewer hours or exerting less effort). It is also important to note that equity can be restored by altering equity ratios behaviourally or cognitively, or both. A cognitive

strategy entails psychologically distorting perceptions of one's own or one's comparison person's outcomes and inputs (e.g., conclude that the other person you're comparing yourself to has more experience or works harder). You may recall we talked about cognitive dissonance in Chapter 4.

EXPECTANCY THEORY

LO 3

Expectancy theory holds that people are motivated to behave in ways that produce desired combinations of expected outcomes. Generally, expectancy theory can be used to predict motivation and behaviour in any situation in which a choice between two or more alternatives must be made. For instance, it can be used to predict whether to quit or stay at a job; whether to exert substantial or minimal effort at a task; and whether to major in IT, human resources, insurance, finance, marketing, accounting, or general business.

Expectancy theory

Holds that people are motivated to behave in ways that produce valued outcomes.

Victor Vroom formulated a mathematical model of expectancy in his 1964 book, *Work and Motivation*.[27] Vroom's theory has been summarized as follows:

The strength of a tendency to act in a certain way depends on the strength of an expectancy that the act will be followed by a given consequence (or outcome) and on the value or attractiveness of that consequence (or outcome) to the actor.[28]

Motivation, according to Vroom, boils down to the decision of how much effort to exert in a specific task situation. This choice is based on a two-stage sequence of expectations (effort → performance, and performance → outcome). First, motivation is affected by an individual's expectation that a certain level of effort will produce the intended performance goal. For example, if you do not believe increasing the amount of time you spend studying will significantly raise your grade on an exam, you probably will not study any harder than usual. Motivation is also influenced by employees' perceived chances of getting various outcomes as a result of accomplishing their performance goal. Finally, individuals are motivated to the extent that they value the outcomes received.

Vroom used a mathematical equation to integrate the above concepts into a model of motivational force or strength. For our purposes however, it is sufficient to define and explain the three key concepts within Vroom's model—*expectancy*, *instrumentality*, and *valence*.

Expectancy

Expectancy An *expectancy*, according to Vroom's terminology, represents an individual's belief that a particular degree of effort will be followed by a particular level of performance. In other words, it is an effort → performance expectation. For example, suppose you have not memorized the keys on a computer keyboard. No matter how much effort you exert, your perceived probability of typing 30 error-free words per minute likely would be zero. If you decided to memorize the letters on a keyboard as well as practise a couple of hours a day for a few weeks (high effort), you should be able to type 30 words per minute without any errors. In contrast, if you do not memorize the letters on a keyboard and only practise an hour or two per week (low effort), there is a very low probability (say, a 20 percent chance) of being able to type 30 words per minute without any errors.

Expectancy

Belief that effort leads to a specific level of performance.

Instrumentality

Instrumentality

A performance → outcome perception.

Instrumentality An *instrumentality* is a performance → outcome perception. It represents a person's belief that one lower level outcome leads to another higher level outcome occurring. In other words, a particular outcome is contingent on accomplishing a specific level of performance. Performance is instrumental when it leads to something else. For example, passing exams with the necessary grade level is instrumental to graduating; or, completing all required tasks as directed by the boss is instrumental to securing a pay raise. Hopefully, one outcome leads to another with greater certainty.

The concept of instrumentality can be seen in practice by considering the national debate regarding CEO pay. Amid complaints that CEOs make too much money, especially if their firm is losing tens of millions of dollars, more corporate boards are linking CEO pay to specific performance targets.

Valence

Valence As Vroom used the term, *valence* refers to the positive or negative value people place on outcomes. Valence mirrors our personal preferences. For example, most employees have a positive valence for receiving additional money or recognition. In contrast, job stress and being laid off would likely result in negative valence for most individuals.

Valence

The value of a reward or outcome.

Farcus

by David Waisglass
Gordon Coulthart

© 1994 Farcus Cartoons   WAISGLASS/COULTHART

www.farcus.com

"Frankly, I didn't think they'd go for this performance incentive stuff."

This is rather complicated, to say the least, and you might be asking yourself: Do people really think this way? Do they consciously look at expectancy, percentage chances of achieving certain performances or outcomes and then measure the valence of a reward or outcome? Simply stated—probably not. It's more likely that people take all three into consideration when living their lives. Use yourself as an example: Think about the kinds of expectancies you have about your own school achievement. You probably have an idea of what sorts of opportunities will come your way if you achieve what you set out to do, and of the value of such opportunities for yourself.

Vroom's Expectancy Theory in Action   Vroom's expectancy model of motivation can be used to analyze a real-life motivation program. Consider the following performance problem described by Frederick W. Smith, founder and chief executive officer of Federal Express Corporation:

[W]e were having a helluva problem keeping things running on time. The airplanes would come in and everything would get backed up. We tried every kind of control mechanism that you could think of, and none of them worked. Finally, it became obvious that the underlying problem was that it was in the interest of the employees at the cargo terminal—they were college kids, mostly—to run late, because it meant that they made more money. So what we did was give them all a minimum guarantee and said, "Look, if you get through before a certain time, just go home, and you will have beat the system." Well, it was

unbelievable. I mean, in the space of about 45 days, the place was way ahead of schedule. And I don't even think it was a conscious thing on their part.[29]

How did Federal Express get its young-adult aged cargo handlers to switch from low effort to high effort? According to Vroom's model, the student workers originally exerted low effort because they were paid on the basis of time, not output. It was in their best interest to work slowly and accumulate as many hours as possible. By offering to let the student workers *go home early if and when they completed their assigned duties*, Federal Express prompted high effort. This new arrangement created two positively valued outcomes: guaranteed pay plus the opportunity to leave early. The motivation to exert high effort became greater than the motivation to exert low effort.

Judging from the impressive results, the student workers had both high effort → performance expectancies and positive performance → outcome instrumentalities. Moreover, the guaranteed pay and early departure opportunity evidently had strong positive valences for the student workers.

Research on Expectancy Theory and Managerial Implications   Many researchers have tested expectancy theory. In support of the theory, a meta-analysis of 77 studies indicated that expectancy theory significantly predicted performance, effort, intentions, preferences, and choice.[30] Another summary of 16 studies revealed that expectancy theory correctly predicted occupational or organizational choice 63.4 percent of the time, significantly better than chance predictions.[31]

Managerial and Organizational Implications of Expectancy Theory

IMPLICATIONS FOR MANAGERS	IMPLICATIONS FOR ORGANIZATIONS
Determine the outcomes employees value.	Reward people for desired performance, and do not keep pay decisions secret.
Identify good performance so appropriate behaviours can be rewarded.	Design challenging jobs.
Make sure employees can achieve targeted performance levels.	Tie some rewards to group accomplishments to build teamwork and encourage cooperation.
Link desired outcomes to targeted levels of performance.	Reward managers for creating, monitoring, and maintaining expectancies, instrumentalities, and outcomes that lead to high effort and goal attainment.
Make sure changes in outcomes are large enough to motivate high effort.	Monitor employee motivation through interviews or anonymous questionnaires.
Monitor the reward system for inequities.	Accommodate individual differences by building flexibility into the motivation program.

TABLE 5.2

Nonetheless, expectancy theory has been criticized for a variety of reasons. For example, the theory is difficult to test, and the measures used to assess expectancy, instrumentality, and valence have questionable validity.[32] In the final analysis, however, expectancy theory has important practical implications for individual managers and organizations as a whole (see Table 5.2).

Managers are advised to enhance effort that leads to performance expectancies by helping employees accomplish their performance goals. Managers can do this by providing support and coaching, and by increasing employees' self-efficacy. It is also important for managers to influence employees' instrumentalities and to monitor valences for various rewards. This raises the issue of whether organizations should use monetary rewards as the primary method to reinforce performance. Although money is certainly a positively valent reward for most people, there are many issues to consider when deciding on the relative balance between monetary and non-monetary rewards. For example, research shows that some workers value interesting work, recognition, and group welfare more than money.[33]

In summary, there is no one best type of reward. Individual differences and need theories tell us that people are motivated by different rewards. Managers should therefore focus on linking employee performance to valued rewards regardless of the type of reward used to enhance motivation. The Skills & Best Practices feature box discusses how one company, the Jamba Juice Co., allocates different rewards for various levels of performance.

MOTIVATION THROUGH GOAL SETTING

Regardless of the nature of their specific achievements, successful people tend to have one thing in common: their lives are goal oriented. As a process model of

Goal
What an individual is trying to accomplish.

motivation, goal-setting theory explains how the simple behaviour of setting goals activates a powerful motivational process that leads to sustained, high performance. This section explores the theory and research pertaining to goal setting.

Goals: Definition and Background   Edwin Locke, a leading authority on goal setting, and his colleagues define a *goal* as "what an individual is trying to accomplish; it is the object or aim of an action."[34] The motivational effect of performance goals and goal-based reward plans has been recognized for a long time. At the turn of the century, Frederick Taylor attempted to scientifically establish how much work of a specified quality an individual should be assigned each day. He proposed that bonuses be based on accomplishing those output standards. More recently, goal setting has been promoted through a widely used management technique called *management by objectives* (MBO).

How Does Goal Setting Work?   Despite abundant goal-setting research and practice, goal-setting theories are surprisingly scarce. An instructive model was formulated by Locke and his associates. According to Locke's model, goal setting has four motivational mechanisms: (1) directs attention, (2) regulates effort, (3) increases persistence, and (4) helps to foster development and application of strategies and plans.

Goals Direct Attention   Goals direct one's attention and effort toward goal-relevant activities and away from goal-irrelevant activities. If, for example, you have a term project due in a few days, your thoughts and actions tend to revolve around completing that project.

Goals Regulate Effort   Not only do goals make us selectively perceptive, they also motivate us to act. The instructor's deadline for turning in your term project

LO 4

Skills & Best Practices

Jamba Juice Company Links Performance and Rewards

The 7,500-employee company bases its annual distribution of merit raises on established performance-ratings categories for employees. Performance is simply ranked as being outstanding, exceeding requirements, meeting requirements, or falling below requirements. The higher the rating, the higher the raise.

Those employees who rate below requirements do not receive a merit increase and are disqualified for any bonus opportunity as well.

Team members understand how they will be evaluated, and the company has made clear how their overall performance will correlate to their merit increase.

SOURCE: Excerpted from S. J. Wells, "No Results, No Raise," *HR Magazine*, May 2005, pg 79.

would prompt you to complete it, as opposed to going out with friends, watching television, or studying for another course. Generally, the level of effort is proportionate to the difficulty of the goal.

Goals Increase Persistence Within the context of goal setting, persistence represents the effort on a task over an extended period of time: It takes effort to run 100 metres; it takes persistence to run a 26-mile marathon. Persistent people tend to see obstacles as challenges to be overcome rather than as reasons to fail. A difficult goal that is important to an individual is a constant reminder to keep giving effort in the appropriate direction. Annika Sorenstam is a great example of someone who persisted at her goal of being the best female golfer in the world. She has won 69 tournaments since starting the LPGA tour in 1994. She has already qualified for the LPGA and World Golf Halls of Fame, has won a career Grand Slam, shot the only round of 59 in women's pro golf, and has won eight Player of the Year Titles.[35] Just like Tiger Woods, major titles and a single-season Grand Slam have become her focus. "Nobody else has done it, so I think that says it all," she said, "but I like to set high goals, I like to motivate myself. If you believe it in your mind, I think you can do it."[36]

Goals Foster the Development and Application of Task Strategies and Action Plans If you are here and your goal is out there somewhere, you face the problem of getting from here to there. For example, the person who has resolved to lose 20 pounds must develop a plan for getting from "here" (present weight) to "there" (20 pounds lighter). Goals can help because they encourage people to develop strategies and action plans that enable them to achieve their goals. By virtue of setting a weight-reduction goal, the dieter may choose a strategy of exercising more, eating less, or some combination of the two.

Practical Lessons from Goal-Setting Research Research consistently has supported goal setting as a motivational technique. Setting performance goals increases individual, group, and organizational performance. Further, the positive effects of goal setting were found in six other countries or regions outside of Canada: Australia, the Caribbean, England, West Germany, the United States, and Japan. Goal setting works in different

Annika Sorenstam persisted to become the best female golfer in the world.

cultures. Reviews of the many goal-setting studies conducted over the past few decades have given managers four practical insights.

1. Specific high goals lead to greater performance *Goal specificity* pertains to the quantifiability of a goal. For example, a goal of selling nine cars a month is more specific than telling a salesperson to do his best. Results from more than 1,000 studies entailing over 88 different tasks and 40,000 people demonstrated that performance was greater when people had specific high goals.[37]

Goal specificity

Quantifiability of a goal.

2. Feedback enhances the effect of specific, difficult goals Feedback plays a key role in all of our lives. Feedback lets people know if they are headed toward their goals or if they are off course and need to redirect their efforts. Goals plus feedback is the recommended approach.[38] Goals inform people about performance standards and expectations so that they can channel their energies accordingly. In turn, feedback provides the information needed to adjust direction, effort, and strategies for goal accomplishment. While face-to-face feedback may be something past generations preferred, future generations (who have grown up with interactive technology) will expect instant and continuous feedback for their just-in-time performance reviews.

3. Participative goals, assigned goals, and self-set goals are equally effective Both managers and researchers are interested in identifying the best way to set goals. Should goals be cooperatively set, assigned, or set by the employee? A summary of goal-setting research indicated that no single approach is consistently more effective than others in increasing performance.[39] Managers are advised to use a contingency approach by picking a method that seems best suited for the individual and situation at hand.

4. Goal commitment and monetary incentives affect goal-setting outcomes *Goal commitment* is the extent to which an individual is personally committed to achieving a goal. In general, individuals are expected to persist in attempts to accomplish a goal when they are committed to it. Researchers believe that goal commitment moderates the relation-ship between the difficulty of a goal and performance. That is, difficult goals lead to higher performance only when employees are committed to their goals. Conversely, difficult goals are hypothesized to lead to lower performance when people are not committed to their goals. A meta-analysis of 21 studies based on 2,360 people supported these predictions.[40] It is also important to note that people are more likely to commit to high goals when they have high self-efficacy about successfully accomplishing their goals.

Goal commitment
Amount of commitment to achieving a goal.

Like goal setting, the use of monetary incentives to motivate employees is seldom questioned. Unfortunately, research uncovered some negative consequences when goal achievement is linked to individual incentives. Empirical (observed data) studies demonstrated that goal-based bonus incentives produced higher commitment to easy goals and lower commitment to difficult goals. People were reluctant to commit to high goals that were tied to monetary incentives. People with high goal commitment offered less help to their co-workers when they received goal-based bonus incentives to accomplish difficult individual goals. Individuals also neglected aspects of the job that were not covered in the performance goals.[41]

These findings underscore some of the dangers of using goal-based incentives, particularly for employees in complex, interdependent jobs requiring cooperation. Managers need to consider the advantages, disadvantages, and dilemmas of goal-based incentives prior to implementation.

LO 5 Motivating Employees Through Job Design

Job design is used when a manager suspects that the type of work an employee performs or characteristics of the work environment are causing motivational problems. *Job design*, also referred to as *job redesign*, "refers to any set of activities that involve the alteration of specific jobs or interdependent systems of jobs with the intent

Job design
Changing the content or process of a specific job to increase job satisfaction and performance.

of improving the quality of employee job experience and their on-the-job productivity."[42] A team of researchers examined the various methods for conducting job design and integrated them into an interdisciplinary framework that includes four major approaches: (1) mechanistic, (2) motivational, (3) biological, and (4) perceptual-motor.[43] As you will learn, each approach to job design emphasizes different outcomes. This section discusses these four approaches to job design and focuses most heavily on the motivational methods.

THE MECHANISTIC APPROACH

The mechanistic approach draws from Frederick Taylor's research in industrial engineering and *scientific management* (see History of OB in Chapter 1). Taylor, a mechanical engineer, developed the principles of scientific management while working at both Midvale Steel Works and Bethlehem Steel in Pennsylvania. He observed very little cooperation between management and workers, and found that employees were underachieving by engaging in output restriction, which Taylor called "systematic soldiering." Taylor's interest in scientific management grew from his desire to improve upon this situation.

Because jobs are highly specialized and standardized when they are designed according to the principles of scientific management, this approach to job design targets efficiency and employee productivity. An assembly line worker whose job is predictable day in and day out would be an example of a person who works at a mechanistic type of job. The tasks and expectations of the job do not change over time and therefore the employee's proficiency completing the task is high. The job itself is designed for repetitious routine types of work.

Designing jobs using the principles of scientific management has both positive and negative consequences. Positively, employee efficiency and productivity are increased. On the other hand, research reveals that simplified, repetitive jobs also lead to job dissatisfaction, poor mental health, higher levels of stress, and low sense of accomplishment and personal growth.[44] These negative consequences paved the way for the motivational approach to job design.

MOTIVATIONAL APPROACHES

The motivational approaches to job design attempt to improve employees' affective and attitudinal reactions such as job satisfaction and intrinsic motivation, as well as a host of behavioural outcomes such as absenteeism, turnover, and performance. We discuss four key motivational techniques: (1) job enlargement, (2) job enrichment, (3) job rotation, and (4) a contingency approach called the job characteristics model.

Job Enlargement This technique was first used in the late 1940s in response to complaints about tedious and overspecialized jobs. *Job enlargement* involves putting more variety into a worker's job by combining specialized tasks of comparable difficulty. Some call this *horizontally loading* the job. Researchers recommend using job enlargement as part of a broader approach that uses multiple motivational methods, because it does not have a significant and lasting positive effect on job performance by itself.[45] An example of job enlargement would be a contemporary customer service representative for a packaged good firm who loads up the SUV in the morning with boxes of product, drives to retail stores to meet with clients, notices if stock is low on store shelves and replenishes it, places an electronic order to head office on behalf of the retailer for a larger future shipment, and then issues the paperwork for signature and payment purposes. Traditionally, several employees would have completed these tasks: one person loaded trucks with boxes, another employee delivered boxes to retailers, another employee acted as the customer rep taking orders from clients, and then another employee back in the office issued the paperwork. Job enlargement significantly improves work efficiency and flexibility.

Job enlargement

Putting more variety into a job.

Job Rotation As with job enlargement, job rotation's purpose is to give employees greater variety in their work. *Job rotation* calls for moving employees from one specialized job to another. Rather than performing only one job, workers are trained and given the opportunity to perform two or more separate jobs on a rotating basis. By rotating employees from job to job, managers believe they can stimulate interest and motivation while providing employees with a broader perspective of the organization. Other proposed advantages of job rotation include increased worker flexibility and easier scheduling, because employees are cross-trained to perform different jobs. Organizations also use job rotation as a vehicle to place new employees into jobs of their choice. The idea is that turnover is reduced and performance increases because people self-select their jobs. Ability Beyond Disability, an 800-person firm that provides health care for people with disabilities in more than 100 locations, is a good example.

Job rotation

Moving employees from one specialized job to another.

Within days after an interview, a successful applicant is on the payroll, undergoing extensive training and visiting the employer's group homes to see the real world of caring for people with disabilities. For about two months, sometimes three, the new hires—called intern floaters—are exposed to a wide variety of jobs in a variety of settings before they commit to a particular post . . . . New hires have choices and are urged to "try different areas" within the organization, to sample many types of direct care before taking a regular post.[46]

> "New hires have choices and are urged to "try different areas" within the organization, to sample many types of direct care before taking a regular post."

Managers at Ability Beyond Disability are happy with the results from the rotation program. Employee retention is up, turnover is down, and there is a reduction in staffing needs.

Despite positive experiences from companies like Ability Beyond Disability, it is not possible to draw firm conclusions about the value of job rotation programs because they have not been adequately researched.

Job Enrichment Job enrichment is the practical application of Frederick Herzberg's motivator–hygiene theory of job satisfaction that we discussed earlier in this chapter. Specifically, *job enrichment* entails modifying a job such that an employee has the opportunity to experience achievement, recognition, stimulating work, responsibility, and advancement. These characteristics are incorporated into a job through vertical loading. Rather than giving employees additional tasks of similar difficulty (horizontal loading), vertical loading consists of giving workers more responsibility. In other words, employees take on tasks normally performed by their supervisors. Going back to our earlier example, if we wanted to also enrich the job of the contemporary customer service representative for a packaged good firm, we could have that same person responsible for assessing the efficiency of the entire supply chain for that particular client. If the client had a problem, the customer service rep would have the authority to approach the delivery truck driver directly or even call the warehouse supervisor and make inquiries.

Job enrichment

Building achievement, recognition, stimulating work, responsibility, and advancement into a job.

The Job Characteristics Model Two OB researchers, J. Richard Hackman and Greg Oldham, played a central role in developing the job characteristics approach. These researchers tried to determine how work can be structured so that employees are internally or intrinsically

Intrinsic motivation

Motivation caused by positive internal feelings.

motivated. To determine your own preference, you may want to complete the Self-Assessment Exercise, "Are You Intrinsically Motivated At Work?" *Intrinsic motivation* occurs when an individual is "turned on to one's work because of the positive internal feelings that are generated by doing well, rather than being dependent on external factors (such as incentive pay or compliments from the boss) for the motivation to work effectively."[47] These positive feelings power a self-perpetuating cycle of motivation. As shown in Figure 5.4, internal work motivation is determined by three psychological states. In turn, these psychological states are fostered by the presence of five core job dimensions. The object of this approach is to promote high intrinsic motivation by designing jobs that possess the five core job characteristics shown in Figure 5.4. Let us examine the core job dimensions.

In general terms, *core job dimensions* are common characteristics found to a varying degree in all jobs. Three of the job characteristics shown in Figure 5.4 combine to determine the experienced meaningfulness of work, which includes:

Core job dimensions

Job characteristics found to various degrees in all jobs.

- **Skill variety** The extent to which the job requires individuals to perform a variety of tasks that require them to use different skills and abilities.

- **Task identity** The extent to which the job requires individuals to perform a whole or completely identifiable piece of work. In other words, task identity is high when people work on a product or project from beginning to end and see a tangible result.

- **Task significance** The extent to which the job affects the lives of other people within or outside the organization.

- **Autonomy** The extent to which the job enables individuals to experience freedom, independence, and discretion in both scheduling and determining the procedures used in completing the job.

- **Feedback** The extent to which individuals receive direct and clear information about how effectively they are performing the job.[48]

Hackman and Oldham recognized that everyone does not want a job containing high amounts of the five core job characteristics. They incorporated this conclusion into

▶ **FIGURE 5.4** The Job Characteristics Model

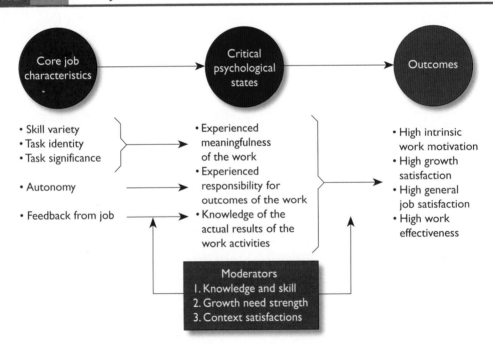

SOURCE: From J. R. Hackman and G. R. Oldham, *Work Redesign*, © 1980, p 90. Reprinted by permission of Pearson Education, Inc., Upper Saddle River, NJ.

Are You Intrinsically Motivated at Work?

INSTRUCTIONS: The following survey was designed to assess the extent to which you are deriving intrinsic rewards from your current job. If you are not working, use a past job or your role as a student to complete the survey. There are no right or wrong answers to the statements. Circle your answer by using the rating scale provided. After evaluating each of the survey statements, complete the scoring guide.

	STRONGLY DISAGREE	DISAGREE	NEITHER AGREE or DISAGREE	AGREE	STRONGLY AGREE
1. I am passionate about my work.	1	2	3	4	5
2. I can see how my work tasks contribute to my organization's corporate vision.	1	2	3	4	5
3. I have significant autonomy in determining how I do my job.	1	2	3	4	5
4. My supervisor/manager delegates important projects/tasks to me that significantly impact my department's overall success.	1	2	3	4	5
5. I have mastered the skills necessary for my job.	1	2	3	4	5
6. My supervisor/manager recognizes when I competently perform my job.	1	2	3	4	5
7. Throughout the year, my department celebrates its progress toward achieving its goals.	1	2	3	4	5
8. I regularly receive evidence/information about my progress toward achieving my overall performance goals.	1	2	3	4	5

Scoring Key

Sense of meaningfulness (add items 1–2) _____

Sense of choice (add items 3–4) _____

Sense of competence (add items 5–6) _____

Sense of progress (add items 7–8) _____

Overall score (add all items) _____

Arbitrary Norms

For each intrinsic reward, a score of 2–4 indicates low intrinsic motivation, 5–7 represents moderate intrinsic motivation, and 8–10 indicates high intrinsic motivation. For the overall score, 8–19 is low, 20–30 is moderate, and 31–40 is high.

their model by identifying three attributes that affect how individuals respond to job enrichment. These attributes are concerned with the individual's knowledge and skill, growth need strength (representing the desire to grow and develop as an individual), and context satisfactions (see the box labelled Moderators in Figure 5.4). Context satisfactions represent the extent to which employees are satisfied with various aspects of their job, such as satisfaction with pay, co-workers, and supervision.

Several practical implications are associated with using the job characteristics model to enhance intrinsic motivation. Managers may want to use this model to increase employee job satisfaction. Research overwhelmingly demonstrates a moderately strong relationship between job characteristics and satisfaction.[49] Employee job satisfaction can occur as a result of designing more autonomy into employees' jobs; for example, allowing employees to select from a variety of work schedules that meet their needs, or flexible hours using compressed work weeks and telecommuting from home.[50] Research supports this investment, as autonomy is positively associated with job performance and pro-active work behaviours.[51]

Moreover, research suggests that managers can enhance employees' intrinsic motivation, initiative, creativity, innovation, and commitment to their performance goals by increasing the core job characterstics.[52] Two separate meta-analyses also support the practice of using the job characteristics model to help managers reduce absenteeism and turnover.[53] On the negative side, however, job redesign appears to reduce the quantity of output just as often as it has a positive effect. Caution and situational appropriateness are advised. For example, one study demonstrated that job redesign works better in less complex organizations (small plants or companies).[54] Nonetheless, managers are likely to find noticeable increases in the quality of performance after a job redesign program. Results from 21 experimental studies revealed that job redesign resulted in a median increase of 28 percent in the quality of performance.[55]

BIOLOGICAL AND PERCEPTUAL-MOTOR APPROACHES

We've grouped the last two approaches together: biological and perceptual-motor. First, the biological approach to job design is based on research from biomechanics, work physiology, and ergonomics, and focuses on designing the work environment to reduce employees' physical strain, fatigue, and health complaints. For example, a host of companies, including Google and Sprint Nextel Corporation, are experimenting

with work station practices by allowing employees to sit away from their desks, opting instead for alternative furniture over traditional chairs. To date, researchers have identified both pros (e.g., improved concentration) and cons (e.g., lower back strain, no arm support) for such work stations.[56]

These Google employees seem to be enjoying their new work stations. Would you like to work in this type of office environment?

The perceptual-motor approach is derived from research that examines human factors engineering, perceptual and cognitive skills, and information processing. This approach to job design emphasizes the reliability of work outcomes by examining error rates, accidents, and workers' feedback about facilities and equipment.[57] IBM and Steelcase are jointly developing a new interactive office system, labelled BlueSpace, which is based on this method of job design. Its features include:

- **BlueScreen** A touch screen that sits next to a user's computer monitor and puts users in control of their heat or cooling, ventilation, and light.

- **Everywhere Display** A video projector that displays information on walls, floors, desktops, and other surfaces.

- **Monitor rail** A moving rail that consists of a work surface that travels the length of a work space and a dual monitor arm that rotates to nearly a complete circle, allowing users be positioned almost anywhere.

- **Threshold** An L-shaped partial ceiling and wall on wheels that provides on-demand visual and territorial privacy to a user.[58]

The frequency of using both the biological and perceptual-motor approaches to job redesign is increasing in light of the number of workers who experience injuries related to overexertion or repetitive motion. ***Repetitive motion disorders (RMDs)*** are a family of muscular conditions that result from repeated motions performed in the course of normal work or daily activities. "RMDs include carpal tunnel syndrome, bursitis, tendonitis, epicondylitis, ganglion cyst, tenosynovitis, and trigger finger. RMDs are caused by too many uninterrupted repetitions of an activity or motion, unnatural or awkward motions such as twisting the arm or wrist, overexertion, incorrect posture, or muscle fatigue."[59]

Data from the Canadian Centre for Occupational Health and Safety (CCOHS) shows that RMDs (sometimes referred to as work-related musculoskeletal disorders or WMSDs) are recognized as leading causes of significant human suffering, loss of productivity, and

Repetitive motion disorders (RMDs)

Muscular disorder caused by repeated motions.

economic burdens on society. Although available Canadian data on RMDs is limited, this does not diminish its importance nor represent the magnitude of the problem; there is a great deal of under-reporting of these types of injuries. For example, several years ago over 20,000 Ontario workers received compensation for new cases of work-related musculoskeletal disorders, accounting for about 600,000 days of lost work.

In British Columbia, over half the industrial disease claims are due to similar problems. A Simon Fraser University survey of cashiers throughout B.C. indicated that over 30 percent of the work force surveyed suffered a form of physical ailment, such as RMDs. CCOHS will take more of an interest in this topic as more injuries are reported.[60]

Summary of Learning Objectives

1. **Define *motivation* and *theories of motivation*.** Motivation represents psychological processes that arouse and direct goal-directed behaviour. There are two theories of motivation: need and process. Need theories attempt to pinpoint internal factors that energize behaviour. Process theories go one step further in explaining motivation by identifying the process by which various internal factors influence motivation. These models are also cognitive in nature. That is, they are based on the premise that motivation is a function of employees' perceptions, thoughts, and beliefs.

2. **Contrast Maslow's, Alderfer's, and McClelland's need theories.** Maslow proposed that motivation is a function of five basic needs arranged in a prepotent (greater in power) hierarchy. The concept of a stair-step hierarchy has not stood up well under research. Alderfer concluded that three core needs explain behaviour—existence, relatedness, and growth (ERG). He proposed that more than one need can be activated at a time, and frustration of higher-order needs can influence the desire for lower-level needs. McClelland argued that motivation and performance vary according to the strength of an individual's need for achievement. High achievers prefer tasks of moderate difficulty, situations under their control, and a desire for more performance feedback than low achievers. Top managers have a high need for power coupled with a low need for affiliation.

3. **Explain Vroom's expectancy theory and review its practical implications.** Expectancy theory assumes motivation is determined by one's perceived chances of achieving valued outcomes. Vroom's expectancy model of motivation reveals how effort → performance expectancies and performance → outcome instrumentalities influence the degree of effort expended to achieve desired (positively valent) outcomes. Managers are advised to enhance

effort → performance expectancies by helping employees accomplish their performance goals. With respect to instrumentalities and valences, managers should attempt to link employee performance and valued rewards.

4. **Explain how goal setting motivates an individual, and review the four practical lessons from goal-setting research.** Four motivational mechanisms of goal setting are as follows: (1) goals direct one's attention, (2) goals regulate effort, (3) goals increase one's persistence, and (4) goals encourage development of goal-attainment strategies and action plans. Research identifies four practical lessons about goal setting. First, specific high goals lead to greater performance. Second, feedback enhances the effect of specific, difficult goals. Third, participative goals, assigned goals, and self-set goals are equally effective. Fourth, goal commitment and monetary incentives affect goal-setting outcomes.

5. **Summarize the various approaches to job design, including mechanistic, motivational, biological, and perceptual-motor.** Job design is changing the content or process of a specific job to increase job satisfaction and performance. The mechanistic approach is based on industrial engineering and scientific management and focuses on increasing efficiency, flexibility, and employee productivity. Motivational approaches aim to improve employees' affective and attitudinal reactions and behavioural outcomes. Job enlargement, job enrichment, job rotation, and a contingency approach called the job characteristics model are motivational approaches to job design. The biological approach focuses on designing the work environment to reduce employees' physical strain, fatigue, and health complaints. The perceptual-motor approach emphasizes the reliability of work outcomes.

Discussion Questions

1. Why should the average manager be well versed in various motivational theories?

2. Which of the four types of job design is most likely to be used in the future? Explain your rationale.

3. Could managers' attempts to treat their employees as equals still lead to misperceptions of inequity? Explain.

4. Goal-setting research suggests that people should be given difficult goals. How does this prescription fit with expectancy theory? Explain where these two concepts could possibly disagree.

5. There are many media stories recounting the unethical behaviour of various organizations' employees. In your opinion, what do you believe is the motivation for these people to behave in such a manner? Try relating your answer to one of the two motivational theories: need or process.

Google Searches

1. **Google Search:** "The Canadian Centre for Occupational Health and Safety—work-related musculoskeletal disorders (WMSDs)" Review the risk factors for WMSDs. For each risk factor, try to determine the type of occupation/job that would cause such an injury. Share your responses with the class. Continue to read prevention techniques for each.

2. **Google Search:** "Globe and Mail Executive Compensation Survey 200_" Review the compensation paid in fiscal 200_ to the CEOs of the 100 largest companies. How does this information make you feel when compared to the annual salary of a minimum wage earner? Do you feel a sense of positive or negative inequity with these figures? Explain.

3. **Google Search:** "Best Employers In Canada 200_" This annual survey is conducted by several organizations, including *The Globe & Mail.* A list has been published each year since 2000. Review the latest list and compare the top five firms that appear to those that have made the top five over the last few years. Are there any repeats? If so, who? Read through the Web site to determine how a company is nominated for such a list. If the company you worked for appeared on this list, would you find it motivating enough to perform at a higher level overall? Explain.

Experiential Exercise

Intrinsic Motivation and Extrinsic Rewards Exercise

PURPOSE   This exercise is meant to help you understand the differences between intrinsic motivation and extrinsic rewards. Approx. Timing: 12 minutes.

ACTIVITY:

- Individually complete the chart below.
- After a few minutes, form a small group for discussion purposes.
- Share your responses with the other group members. Try and come to a consensus.
- Share your group's responses with the rest of the class.

	IS THIS AN INTRINSIC MOTIVATING FACTOR OR AN EXTRINSIC REWARD?
Pay	
Job Security	
Personal Expression	
Enjoyment	
Praise From Peers	
Lack of Frustration	
Knowledge Gain	
Bonus	
Promotion	
Skill Development	
Lack of Anxiety	

Here are possible topics and sources related to this chapter to consider that can be further explored by student groups looking for ideas.

	MOTIVATING EMPLOYEES— WHAT'S THE BEST WAY?	EMPLOYEES' NEEDS AND DESIRES VARY BY AGE—EXAMPLES FOR EMPLOYERS TO APPLY AT WORK	EMPLOYEES' NEEDS AND DESIRES VARY BY CULTURAL GROUP— COMPARISONS BETWEEN ABORIGINALS, FRENCH AND ANGLO CANADIANS, AND OTHERS
YouTube Videos	• Motivating employees (funny) or comedy • 40 great movies inspirational speeches in 2 minutes	• Anthony Robbins Human Needs • Managing Digital Generation • Managing Baby Boom Generation • Managing Gen X • Managing Gen Y	• Dance Me Outside— Ceremony Scene • Frozen River—Zuguide Trailer • Canada: French Culture in Canada • *This Hour Has 22 Minutes*
TV Shows or Movies to Preview	• Talladega Nights (motivational speech) • Al Pacino—Any Given Sunday Speech • *The Office*—"Performance Review Episode," Season 2	• Gen X Movies • The BBHQ Boomer Movie Quiz • Movies of Gen Y • *American Pie*	• *Dances With Wolves* • *North of 60* • *Legends of the Fall* • *Videodrome* • Top 10 Films From Canada
Internet Searches	• *Fish—Catch The Energy & Release Potential* (by Charthouse International Learning Corporation) • *The Speed of Trust* (by S. Covey)	• *Boom Bust Echo* (by Dr. D. Foot) • *Workforce Crisis* (by R. Morison) • *Growing Up Digital* (by Don Tapscott) • *Society for Human Resources 2008*—Job Satisfaction Survey Report	• Urban Society for Aboriginal Youth • Aboriginal People of Canada: A demographic Profile (Stats Can) • French Speaking Canadians Demographic
Ice Breaker Classroom Activity	• Ask the students to share their greatest motivating speech—who gave it, where, when, and how did it make them feel?	• Ask the students to identify the four generations currently in the workplace. Then ask them to list at least one motivating factor that differs between each group. Share results with the class.	• Ask the students to identify at least one motivating factor that differs between each of the groups mentioned in the title. Share their responses with the class.

Design a Motivating Job Using The JCM

Kareem Padawan is 17 years old and works at Chapters bookstore in the West Edmonton Mall. Kareem has worked at Chapters for two months, earning the standard minimum wage. In the short time he has worked at the bookstore, Kareem has noticed that there is a tremendous turnover of employees, but doesn't fully understand the possible reasons for it. However, he does know a few things. For example, Kareem knows that: workers like himself are paid minimum wage; must be willing to work at least four five-hour shifts for a total of 20 hours per week; must wear a uniform that is purchased from the company at $40/shirt and pants; and are assigned to work in a specifically designated area. In this case, Kareem is paid and trained to be an inventory/stock person—unloading trucks when they come in, unpacking boxes, and carrying the boxes out to the front for processing by the clerks. When the boxes are empty, Kareem breaks them down and packs them up for the garbage. He was getting bored with that job, so Kareem applied for a position as clerk, which would allow him to use the store computer system so that the books could be processed from the back and placed on shelves.

Clerks are sometimes called to the front to help out at the customer service counter when needed. Kareem didn't get the clerk's job. Instead, he was given the job of store greeter. Kareem liked his new role at the beginning because it got him out from the back of the store and talking to customers up front. But after two weeks of being a full-time greeter, he began to get bored with the job. He found the public difficult to work with. He talked to his friends in the back all the time, but they were bored too. All they did was complain to each other every time they worked. Kareem decided to take his concerns to management.

The next day, Kareem made an appointment to speak to the store manager about what he believed to be the primary reason so many employees were leaving their jobs. "It has to do with the lack of motivation on the job," said Kareem. "Is that so?" stated the store manager, "And what do you suggest we do to correct the problem?" The store manager welcomed Kareem's comments and asked him for input as to how the jobs could be made more interesting and in the long-run decrease the employee turnover rate at the store.

Discussion Questions

1. In your opinion, what is the problem at the bookstore? Do you agree with Kareem? Explain.

2. Identify at least three of the various factors to consider when designing a motivating job.

3. Imagine that you are Kareem. Use the Job Characteristics Model—JCM (see Figure 5.4) to create at least five new approaches to solving the problem that he and the other employees are having with their job.

www.mcgrawhill.ca/olc/kreitner

Ethical OB Dilemma

The Motivation to Cheat

You are taking a college course. The tests and quizzes are online through the class Web site. The professor gives you a three-day window and you take the tests in your personal time. The professor has strict guidelines about cheating. At the beginning of the semester, the professor told all of you that the tests and quizzes will be timed so you will not have enough time to look the answers up in the book. You are in the computing commons taking one of the quizzes and notice a group of your classmates huddled around a computer. They are taking the quiz as well. One student is looking up the answers in the book, one is taking the quiz, and the other is recording the answers. You wonder what would motivate students to behave in such a way.

As a student, what would you do?

Consider the following options:

1. You conclude that these students are liars and deserve to be punished for their unethical behaviour. You immediately contact your professor about what is going on. It is unfair to the rest of your classmates if these three get away with cheating.

2. You conclude these students are motivated by creativity and therefore decide to form a similar test group of your own so you'll be perceived as being creative, too. The professor never specifically said you couldn't complete the tests in groups.

3. You conclude that such an incident does not involve you and therefore decide to ignore the group's behaviour and continue completing the test on your own. You are sure these three will be caught eventually and at least have the satisfaction of knowing that you earned your grade.

4. You reflect on their behaviour and how it makes you feel, noting your own equity sensitivity. This becomes an interesting thing to reflect upon but you don't feel any need to act.

5. You decide to behave differently. Explain.

Visit www.mcgrawhillconnect.ca to register.

McGraw-Hill Connect™ —Available 24/7 with instant feedback so you can study when you want, how you want, and where you want. Take advantage of the Study Plan—an innovative tool that helps you customize your learning experience. You can diagnose your knowledge with pre- and post-tests, identify the areas where you need help, search the entire learning package for content specific to the topic you're studying, and add these resources to your personalized study plan. Visit www.mcgrawhillconnect.ca to register—take practice quizzes, search the e-book, and much more.

> "When employees and employers, even coworkers, have a commitment to one another, everyone benefits. I have people who have been in business with me for decades. I reward their loyalty to the organization and to me. I know that they'll always be dedicated to what we're trying to accomplish."
>
> Donald Trump (Entrepreneur & Business Person)

Fundamental Concepts *of* Group Behaviour

Hewlett-Packard (HP) Uses Virtual Teams

HP is among the world's largest information technology companies, operating in more than 170 countries around the world, with almost a dozen offices scattered throughout Canada. While some organizations are only beginning to appreciate the value of having virtual teams, HP has been on the leading edge for many years, using the tools, developing techniques, training management, and building the culture necessary to make it work.

In the late 1990s, HP faced the challenge of having an expanding business with diverse interests and a supply chain that routinely spanned the globe, and requiring its managers to build and run teams whose members rarely worked face to face. When virtual teams first began at HP, relatively routine tasks, such as scheduling a meeting, became complex and fraught with interpersonal friction—especially when one member of the team was beginning the day wanting to talk about budgeting or strategic planning, and another was ending the day on the opposite side of the globe. Simple email exchanges became the catalyst for misinterpretations as cultures and languages clashed. The lack of a mechanism to allow for information-sharing caused productivity to slow down. Something had to be done.

HP reports that 60 percent of their employees are not in the same location as their supervisor, so managing a virtual team is a vital skill taken seriously by the organization. Some of the tools HP has in place include:

- **Virtual Classroom** This Web-based portal enables teams to conduct virtual meetings in real time, view documents simultaneously, and share important files.
- **On-line Depository** A dedicated Web site is used for archiving files.
- **IM** Instant messaging facilitates communication on a virtual team.
- **Podcasting** Live video chats can be streamed to team leaders using podcasts, and they can also be used to show slide presentations.

With the availability of satellite cell phones, wireless email, Intranets, Web-based presentations, and video-conferencing, dispersed teams can easily distribute large quantities of data around the world, collaborate on corporate initiatives, and actively participate in file sharing.

But virtual teams are not without their problems. Some members may experience a sense of isolation and feelings of frustration from the lack of cohesiveness, which could potentially affect work performance in a negative way. The long distance factor, coupled with a high need for coordination, can set back any virtual team. HP's executive vice president of HR says, "I think at the end of the day, it's the frequency of interaction, regardless if you have them face to face or on the phone. Frequency is very critical."

Could you work on a virtual team?

SOURCES: Canadian Management Centre PodCast Series, *Leadership Tip – Building Virtual Teams at Hewlett-Packard (HP)*, January 11, 2008, http://www.cmctraining.org/wordpress/?author=2.

J. Hawkrigg, "Virtual Teams Need Human Touch," *Canadian HR Reporter*, March 12, 2007, http://www.hrreporter.com. Hewlett-Packard corporate website: www.hp.com.

B. Snyder, "Teams That Span Time Zones Face New Work Rules," *Stanford Business Magazine*, May 2003, http://www.gsb.stanford.edu/news/bmag/sbsm0305/feature_virtual_teams.shtml.

LEARNING OBJECTIVES →

After reading this chapter,
you should be able to:

LO 1 **List and define** the five stages of Tuckman's theory of group development.

LO 2 **Contrast** *roles* and *norms*, emphasizing reasons why norms are enforced in organizations.

LO 3 **Examine** the process of how a work group becomes a team, emphasizing various teamwork competencies.

LO 4 **Explain** why trust is a key ingredient to building an effective team, referring to both self-managed and virtual teams.

LO 5 **Summarize** at least two threats to group and team effectiveness.

This chapter begins Unit 3, which shifts the focus away from individual behaviour toward group behaviour. It's important to recognize that we don't study OB in a vacuum; it is the study of the organization and its members in a social environment. Any student who has had to work with others on a school project will know the challenges that working with others can bring. Not everyone appreciates the value of teamwork or understands the value in what it can bring to improving the final product.

This chapter will help you see the value of teamwork, how it's being applied throughout the work world, and how it can assist the organization overall. Our discussions will first look at the fundamental building blocks behind formal and informal groups, then we'll move on to how groups develop, followed by the various roles and norms that exist within groups. Since some people believe that groups and teams are the same, we'll spend time explaining the differences, specifically discussing self-managed teams and the more contemporary virtual teams (see the opening vignette about Hewlett-Packard). To wrap things up, we'll explain what factor(s) nurture teamwork, as well as those that can threaten team effectiveness.

Fundamentals of Group Behaviour

Group

Two or more freely interacting people with shared norms and goals and a common identity.

Drawing from the field of sociology,[1] we define a **group** as two or more freely interacting individuals who share collective norms and goals and have a common identity.[2] Organizational psychologist Edgar Schein shed light on this concept by drawing helpful distinctions between a group, a crowd, and an organization:

The size of a group is thus limited by the possibilities of mutual interaction and mutual awareness. Mere aggregates of people do not fit this definition because they do not interact and do not perceive themselves to be a group even if they are aware of each other as, for instance, a crowd on a street corner watching some event. A total department, a union, or a whole organization would not be a group in spite of thinking of themselves as "we," because they generally do not all interact and are not all aware of each other. However, work teams, committees, subparts of departments, cliques, and various other informal associations among organizational members would fit this definition of a group.[3]

Take a moment now to think of various groups of which you are a member. Does each "group" satisfy the four criteria in Figure 6.1?

▶ **FIGURE 6.1** Four Sociological Criteria of a Group

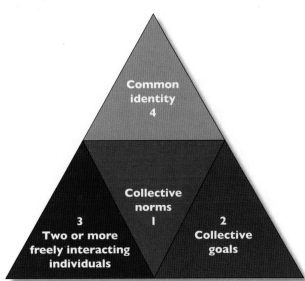

FORMAL AND INFORMAL GROUPS

Individuals join groups, or are assigned to groups, to accomplish various purposes. If the group is formed by a manager to help the organization accomplish its goals, then it qualifies as a **formal group**. Within an organization, formal groups typically wear such labels as work group, team, committee, or task force. An example of a formal group would be a corporate board responsible for governing an organization; it has legitimate authority and assigned responsibilities, and the decisions it makes affect the organization directly (see International OB feature box). An **informal group** exists when the members' overriding purpose of getting together is friendship.[4] Formal and informal groups often overlap, such as when a team of corporate auditors heads for the tennis courts after work. A recent survey of 1,385 office workers found 71 percent had attended important events with co-workers, such as weddings and funerals.[5] Indeed, friendships forged on the job can be strong enough to outlive the job itself in an era of job hopping, reorganizations, and mass layoffs.

Formal group

Formed by the organization.

Informal group

Formed by friends.

Many employees are finding that leaving their employer doesn't always mean saying goodbye. Membership in organized corporate "alumni" groups is increasingly in vogue. There are now alumni groups for hundreds of companies, including Hewlett-Packard, Ernst & Young, and Yahoo (who alone lists more than 500 such ex-employee groups). Some groups are started by former employees, while others are formally sanctioned by employers as a way to stay in touch, creating a potential pool of boomerang workers that employers can draw from when hiring picks up.[6]

The desirability of overlapping formal and informal groups has its problems.[7] Some managers firmly believe personal friendship fosters productive teamwork on the job, while others view workplace "bull sessions" as a serious threat to productivity. Both situations are common, and it is the manager's job to strike a workable balance, based on the maturity and goals of the people involved.

Researchers point out that formal groups fulfill two basic functions: *organizational* and *individual*.[8] The various functions are listed in Table 6.1.

BOARDS ARE FORMAL GROUPS

The Boards of Directors for European multi-national corporations (MNCs) have evolved into formal global teams responsible for a wide-range of governing issues. As reported in the Singapore Management Review, the findings from three exploratory studies showed that European MNCs have a large proportion of internationally qualified personnel on their boards of directors. This is an important finding. Since boards oversee the governing responsibilities that cover broad issues related to organizations, their perspective must cut across cultural divides, and their legitimate authority requires them to be taken seriously as their decisions impact many.

SOURCES: T. Palmer & I. Vamer, "A Comparison of the International Diversity on Top Management Teams of Multi-national firms based . . .," *Singapore Management Review*, January 1, 2007. *All Business online*, a Dun & Bradstreet Company, http://www.allbusiness.com/public-administration/national-security-international/4019164-1.html.

LO 1 THE GROUP DEVELOPMENT PROCESS

Groups and teams in the workplace go through a maturation process, such as one would find in any life-cycle situation (e.g., humans, organizations, products). While there is general agreement among theorists that the group development process occurs in identifiable stages, they disagree about the exact number, sequence, length, and nature of those stages.[9]

One model often referred to is the one proposed in 1965 by educational psychologist Bruce W. Tuckman. His original model involved only four stages (forming, storming, norming, and performing). The five-stage model in Figure 6.2 evolved when Tuckman and a doctoral student added "adjourning" in 1977.[10] A word of caution is in order. Somewhat akin to Maslow's need hierarchy theory, Tuckman's theory has been repeated and taught so often and for so long that many have come to view it as documented fact, not merely a theory. Even today, it is good to remember Tuckman's own caution that his group development model was derived more from group

therapy sessions than from natural-life groups. Still, many in the OB field like Tuckman's five-stage model of group development because of its easy-to-remember labels and common sense appeal.

Let us briefly examine each of the five stages in Tuckman's model. Notice in Figure 6.2 how individuals give up a measure of their independence when they join and participate in a group.[11] Also, the various stages are not necessarily of the same duration or intensity. For instance, the storming stage may be practically non-existent or painfully long, depending on the clarity of the goal and the commitment and maturity of the members. Since the model is not static, it's theoretically possible to go backwards, especially for those groups that make it to the performing stage but experience a significant change. Consider a group that added a new member or perhaps lost a member; in this case, the group would theoretically be forced back into the forming stage all over again, and yet still be expected to perform as if nothing changed. This situation would become a

TABLE 6.1 Formal Groups Fulfill Organizational and Individual Functions

ORGANIZATIONAL FUNCTIONS	INDIVIDUAL FUNCTIONS
1. Accomplish complex, interdependent tasks that are beyond the capabilities of individuals.	1. Satisfy the individual's need for affiliation.
2. Generate new or creative ideas and solutions.	2. Develop, enhance, and confirm the individual's self-esteem and sense of identity.
3. Coordinate interdepartmental efforts.	3. Give individuals an opportunity to test and share their perceptions of social reality.
4. Provide a problem-solving mechanism for complex problems requiring varied information and assessments.	4. Reduce the individual's anxieties and feelings of insecurity and powerlessness.
5. Implement complex decisions.	5. Provide a problem-solving mechanism for personal and interpersonal problems.
6. Socialize and train newcomers.	

SOURCE: Adapted from E.H. Schein, *Organizational Psychology*, 3rd ed (Englewood Cliffs. NJ: Prentice-Hall, 1980), pp 149–51.

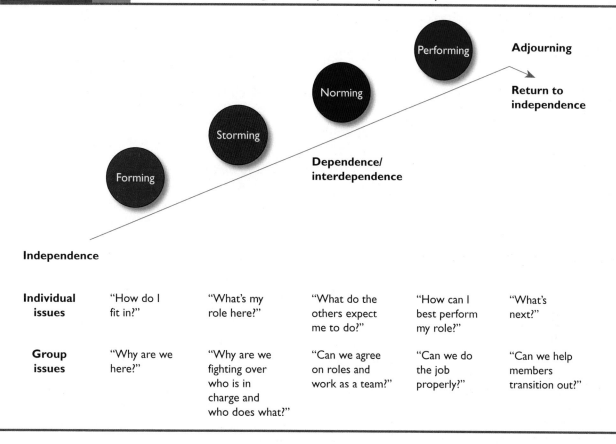

Individual issues	"How do I fit in?"	"What's my role here?"	"What do the others expect me to do?"	"How can I best perform my role?"	"What's next?"
Group issues	"Why are we here?"	"Why are we fighting over who is in charge and who does what?"	"Can we agree on roles and work as a team?"	"Can we do the job properly?"	"Can we help members transition out?"

complicated challenge for members of the group as adjustments would have to be made, but it would also be a time of patience for management, who would have to understand the dynamics the group is experiencing at a possibly demanding time.

You can make this five-step process come to life by relating the various stages to your own experiences with work groups, committees, athletic teams, social or religious groups, or class project teams. Some group happenings that surprised you when they occurred may now make sense, or strike you as inevitable, when seen as part of a natural development process.

Stage 1: Forming During this "ice-breaking" stage, group members tend to be uncertain and anxious about such things as their roles, who is in charge, and the group's goals. Mutual trust is low, and there is a good deal of holding back to see who takes charge and how. In life-and-death situations, such as those sometimes faced by surgical teams and airline cockpit crews, the period of uncertainty can be dangerous. If the formal leader (e.g., a supervisor) does not assert authority, an emergent leader will eventually step in to fulfill the group's need for leadership and direction. Leaders typically mistake this honeymoon period as a mandate for permanent control. But later problems may force a leadership change.

Stage 2: Storming This is a time of testing. Individuals test the leader's policies and assumptions as they try to determine how they fit into the power structure.[12] Subgroups take shape, and subtle forms of rebellion, such as procrastination, occur. Many groups stall in stage 2 because power politics erupts into open rebellion.

Stage 3: Norming Groups that make it through stage 2 generally do so because a respected member, other than the leader, challenges the group to resolve its power struggles so something can be accomplished. Questions about authority and power are resolved through unemotional, matter-of-fact group discussion. A feeling of team spirit is experienced because members believe they have found their proper roles. *Group cohesiveness*, defined as the "we feeling" that binds members of a group together, is the principal by-product of stage 3.[13]

Group cohesiveness

A "we feeling" binding group members together.

Stage 4: Performing Activity during this vital stage is focused on solving task problems. As members of a mature group, contributors get their work done without hampering others. There is a climate of open communication, strong cooperation, and lots of helping behaviour. Conflicts and job boundary disputes are handled constructively and efficiently.[14] Cohesiveness and personal commitment to group goals help the group achieve more than any one individual acting alone could.

Stage 5: Adjourning The work is done; it's time to move on to other things. Having worked so hard to get along and get something done, many members feel a compelling sense of loss. The return to independence can be eased by rituals celebrating "the end" and "new beginnings." Parties, award ceremonies, graduations, or mock funerals can provide the needed punctuation at the end of a significant group project. Leaders need to emphasize valuable lessons learned in group dynamics to prepare everyone for future group and team efforts.

> "Calling a set of people a team or (pressuring) them to work together is insufficient ... action must be taken to establish a team's boundaries, to define the task as one for which members are collectively responsible and accountable, and to give members the authority to manage."

PATTERNS ESTABLISHED EARLY

The initial time spent on upfront planning and organizing the opening stages of team development are well worth the effort, since it is here where core patterns and agreements are determined. At least theoretically, the team will try and abide by such terms until a crisis midpoint occurs and the group members realize they have to start working harder if a deadline is to be met. This point is well illustrated in the 1988 research conducted by professor and OB expert Connie Gersick, who identified a sequence of behaviour a bit different from Tuckman's, and perhaps more appropriate for projects and student teams where meeting a deadline is very important.[15] She called it the ***punctuated equilibrium model*** of group development because of the time spent by the group experiencing stable equilibrium with a punctuated (interruption) period that causes a disturbance to the group. Once resolved, the group progresses on to the deadline. Gersick's research found that from the opening moments of a group's existence, its members try to do two things: (1) develop strategies to complete a task, and (2) develop the structure and processes for interpersonal relationships. Gersick reported:

> *... lasting patterns can appear as early as the first few seconds of a group's life ... The sheer speed*

with which recurring patterns appear suggest that they're influenced by material established before the group convenes. Such material includes members' expectations about the task, each other and the context and their repertoire of behaviour routines and performance strategies.

Management Implications No one wants to be part of a group that is set up for failure before it even starts. That is why managers need to create the right sort of conditions for team members from the outset so they can generate team identity and loyalty, such as establishing open communication, building camaraderie, and developing trust. This can be accomplished if management philosophically supports the team process by giving them the opportunity to self-manage, puts into place the necessary resources that create a healthy working climate, and provides time for the team to develop group cohesiveness. By planning early on, managers prepare the necessary conditions for positive interpersonal interaction that will also facilitate future decision-making around tasks. As psychology researcher J. Richard Hackman puts it, "To reap the benefits of teamwork, one must actually build a team. Calling a set of people a team or (pressuring) them to work together is insufficient ... action must be taken to establish a team's boundaries, to define the task as one for which members are collectively responsible and accountable, and to give members the authority to manage."[16]

GROUP MEMBER ROLES

LO 2

Four centuries have passed since William Shakespeare had his character Jacques speak the following memorable lines in Act II of *As You Like It*: "All the world's a stage, And all the men and women merely players; They have their exits and their entrances; And one man in his time plays many parts ..." This intriguing notion of all people as actors in a universal play was not lost on 20th-century sociologists, who developed a complex theory of human interaction based on ***roles***. According to an OB scholar, "roles are sets of behaviours that persons expect of occupants of a position."[17]

As described in Table 6.2, both task and maintenance roles need to be performed if a work group is to accomplish anything.[18]

Punctuated equilibrium model
Group development process consisting of stable periods interrupted by punctuated situations.

Roles
Expected behaviours for a given position.

Task versus Maintenance Roles *Task roles* enable the work group to define, clarify, and pursue a common purpose. Meanwhile, *maintenance roles* foster supportive and constructive interpersonal relationships. In short, task roles keep the group on track, while maintenance roles keep the group together. A project team member is performing a task function when the member says at an update meeting, "What is the real issue here? We don't seem to be getting anywhere." Another individual who says, "Let's hear from those who oppose this plan," is performing a maintenance function. Importantly, each of the various task and maintenance roles may be played in varying combinations and sequences by either the group's leader or any of its members.

Checklist for Managers The task and maintenance roles listed in Table 6.2 can serve as a handy checklist for managers and group leaders who wish to ensure proper group development. Roles that are not always performed when needed, such as those of coordinator, evaluator, and gatekeeper, can be performed in a timely manner by the formal leader or assigned to other members. The task roles of initiator, orienter, and energizer are especially important because they are goal-directed roles. Research studies on group goal setting confirm the motivational power of challenging goals. As with individual goal setting, difficult but achievable goals are associated with better group results.[19] Also in line with individual goal-setting theory and research, group goals are more effective if group members clearly understand them and are both individually and collectively committed to achieving them. Initiators, orienters, and energizers can be very helpful in this regard.

International managers need to be sensitive to cultural differences regarding the relative importance of task and maintenance roles. In Japan, for example,

Task roles

Task-oriented group behaviour.

Maintenance roles

Relationship-building group behaviour.

Functional Roles Performed by Group Members

TASK ROLES	DESCRIPTION
Initiator	Suggests new goals or ideas.
Information seeker/giver	Clarifies key issues.
Opinion seeker/giver	Clarifies pertinent values.
Elaborator	Promotes greater understanding through examples or exploration of implications.
Coordinator	Pulls together ideas and suggestions.
Orienter	Keeps group headed toward its stated goal(s).
Evaluator	Tests group's accomplishments with various criteria such as logic and practicality.
Energizer	Prods group to move along or to accomplish more.
Procedural technician	Performs routine duties (e.g., handing out materials or rearranging seats).
Recorder	Performs a "group memory" function by documenting discussion and outcomes.
MAINTENANCE ROLES	**DESCRIPTION**
Encourager	Fosters group solidarity by accepting and praising various points of view.
Harmonizer	Mediates conflict through reconciliation or humour.
Compromiser	Helps resolve conflict by meeting others half way.
Gatekeeper	Encourages all group members to participate.
Standard setter	Evaluates the quality of group processes.
Commentator	Records and comments on group processes/dynamics.
Follower	Serves as a passive audience.

TABLE 6.2

SOURCE: Adapted from discussion in K.D. Benne and P. Sheats, "Functional Roles of Group Members," *Journal of Social Issues*, Spring 1948, pp 41–49.

cultural tradition calls for more emphasis on maintenance roles, especially the roles of harmonizer and compromiser:

> *Courtesy requires that members not be noticeable or disruptive in a meeting or classroom. If two or more members discover that their views differ—a fact that is tactfully taken to be unfortunate—they adjourn to find more information and to work toward a stance that all can accept. They do not press their personal opinions through strong arguments, neat logic, or rewards and threats. And they do not hesitate to shift their beliefs if doing so will preserve smooth interpersonal relations. (To lose is to win.)*[20]

GROUP NORMS

Norm

Shared attitudes, opinions, feelings, or actions that guide social behaviour.

Norms are more encompassing than roles. While roles involve behavioural expectations for specific positions, norms help organizational members determine right from wrong and good from bad. According to one respected team of management consultants: "A **norm** is an attitude, opinion, feeling, or action—shared by two or more people— that guides their behaviour."[21] Although norms are typically unwritten and seldom discussed openly, they have a powerful influence on group and organizational behaviour.[22] For instance, consider Alberta-Pacific (Al-Pac) Forest Industries Inc. in Boyle, Alberta. A norm at their pulp facility equates team productivity with physical activity. Voted one of Canada's top 100 employers, Al-Pac encourages its employees to enjoy the outdoors whenever possible. On any given day, if the weather permits, employees can be observed fishing on their lunch hour in the trout pond located right on the 16-hectare property site, or organizing an informal baseball game on the company ball field, or participating with others in a daily health-walk around the many groomed trails.[23]

At Al-Pac and elsewhere, group members positively reinforce those who adhere to current norms with friendship and acceptance. On the other hand, non-conformists often experience criticism and even rejection by group members. Anyone who has experienced the "silent treatment" from a group of friends knows what a potent social weapon ostracism (isolation) can be.[24] Norms can be put into proper perspective by understanding how they develop and why they are enforced.

How Norms Are Developed   Experts say norms evolve in an informal manner as the group or organization determines what it takes to be effective. Norms can affect performance either positively or negatively. Generally speaking, norms develop in various combinations of the following four ways:

1. **Explicit statements by supervisors or co-workers** For instance, a group leader might explicitly set norms about not drinking alcohol at lunch.

2. **Critical events in the group's history** At times there is a critical event in the group's history that establishes an important precedent. For example, a key recruit may have decided to work elsewhere because a group member said too many negative things about the organization. Hence, a norm against such "sour grapes" behaviour might evolve.

3. **Primacy** The first behaviour pattern that emerges in a group often sets group expectations. For example, this is how Paul Pressler set the norm for informality, creativity, and questioning when he took over as CEO of Gap Inc., the clothing retailer that owns the Old Navy and Banana Republic stores: "On his first day at work, speaking to 400 employees in Gap's first-floor auditorium, Pressler said, 'I've got a gazillion ideas, many of which are really stupid. But what the hell—you'll let me know!'"[25]

4. **Carryover behaviours from past situations** Such carryover of individual behaviours from past situations can increase the predictability of group members' behaviours in new settings and facilitate task accomplishment. For instance, students and professors carry fairly constant sets of expectations from class to class.[26]

Enforcing Norms   Norms tend to be enforced by group members when they:

- Help the group or organization survive
- Clarify or simplify behavioural expectations
- Help individuals avoid embarrassing situations
- Clarify the group's or organization's central values and/or unique identity[27]

Working examples of each of these four situations are presented in Table 6.3.

Teams, Teamwork, and Trust

The team approach to managing organizations is having diverse and substantial impacts on organizations and individuals. Teams promise to be a cornerstone of progressive management for the foreseeable future. General Electric's CEO, Jeffrey Immelt, offers this blunt overview: "You lead today by building teams and placing

Four Reasons Norms Are Enforced

NORM	REASON FOR ENFORCEMENT	EXAMPLE
"Make our department look good in top management's eyes."	Group/organization survival	After vigorously defending the vital role played by the Human Resources Management Department at a divisional meeting, a staff specialist is complimented by her boss.
"Success comes to those who work hard and don't make waves."	Clarification of behavioural expectations	A senior manager takes a young associate aside and cautions him to be a bit more patient with co-workers who see things differently.
"Be a team player, not a star."	Avoidance of embarrassment	A project team member is ridiculed by her peers for dominating the discussion during a progress report to top management.
"Customer service is our top priority."	Clarification of central values/ unique identity	Two sales representatives are given a surprise Friday afternoon party for having received prestigious best-in-the-industry customer service awards from an industry association.

others first. It's not about you."[28] This means that virtually all employees will need to polish their team skills.

The trend toward teams has a receptive audience today. Both women and younger employees, according to research, can thrive in team-oriented organizations.[29] One negative reality in this otherwise positive picture involves a perception gap between upper management and non-management. In a survey of 293,377 employees at 13 companies, 65 percent of upper managers agreed with the statement, "Teamwork and cooperation exist among departments."[30] Meanwhile, only 48 percent of the non-managers agreed. The resulting 17 percent perception gap challenges managers to "walk the talk" when it comes to teamwork.

In the next section we define the term team, look at teamwork competencies and team building, discuss trust as a key to real teamwork, and explore two evolving forms of teamwork—self-managed teams and virtual teams.

A TEAM IS MORE THAN JUST A GROUP   LO 3

Jon R. Katzenbach and Douglas K. Smith, management consultants at McKinsey & Company, say it is a mistake to use the terms group and team interchangeably. After studying many different kinds of teams—from athletic to corporate to military—they concluded that successful teams tend to take on a life of their own. Katzenbach and Smith define a *team* as "a small number of people with complementary skills who are committed to a common purpose, performance goals, and approach for which they hold themselves mutually accountable."[31]

Team

Small number of people with complementary skills who hold themselves mutually accountable for common purpose, goals, and approach.

Teams serve many purposes at Whole Foods Market, where all employees belong to teams. In each of their six Canadian stores, team members share equally in the selection of employee benefits, they share any savings achieved for the company, and they collectively vote on whether newcomers will be permanently hired.

Thus, a group becomes a team when the following criteria are met:

1. *Leadership* becomes a shared activity.

2. *Accountability* shifts from strictly individual to both individual and collective.

3. The group develops its own *purpose* or mission.

4. *Problem solving* becomes a way of life, not a part-time activity.

5. *Effectiveness* is measured by the group's collective outcomes and products.[32]

Relative to Tuckman's theory of group development covered earlier—forming, storming, norming, performing, and adjourning—teams are task groups that have matured to the *performing* stage. Because of conflicts over power and authority and unstable interpersonal relations, many work groups never become an effective team.[33] Katzenbach and Smith clarified the distinction this way: "The essence of a team is common commitment. Without it, groups perform as individuals; with it, they become a powerful unit of collective performance."[34]

When Katzenbach and Smith refer to "a small number of people" in their definition, they mean between two and 25 team members. They found effective teams to typically have fewer than 10 members. This conclusion was echoed in a survey of 400 workplace team members in Canada and the United States: "The average North American team consists of 10 members. Eight is the most common size."[35]

DEVELOPING TEAMWORK COMPETENCIES

Forming workplace teams and urging employees to be good team players are good starting points on the road to effective teams. But by themselves, they are not enough; teams need to develop certain abilities, called "competencies," that will help them to perform at higher levels. The five critical team competencies are:[36]

1. **Orients team to problem-solving situation**   Can the team arrive at a common understanding of the situation or problem?

2. **Organizes and manages team performance**   Can the team establish specific, challenging, and accepted team goals?

3. **Promotes a positive team environment**   Can the team create and reinforce norms of tolerance, respect, and excellence?

4. **Facilitates and manages task conflict**   Can the team encourage desirable conflict and discourage undesirable team conflict?

5. **Appropriately promotes perspective**   Can the team defend stated preferences, withstanding pressure to change position for another that is not supported by knowledge-based arguments?

Teamwork skills and competencies need to be modelled and taught. For example, when faced with disagreement, does management force their position onto others without consultation, or is a model of welcoming diverse opinion, open discussion, and compromise practised? The team will quickly learn the norms of tolerance when opinions differ and compromise is practised around the office.

It is also important to reward teamwork competencies. For example, consider what has taken place at Internet equipment maker Cisco Systems:

> "[CEO John] Chambers . . . made teamwork a critical part of top executives' bonus plans. He told them 30 percent of their bonuses for the 2003 fiscal year would depend on how well they collaborated with others."

[CEO John] Chambers took . . . steps to rein in Cisco's Wild West culture during 2002. Most pointedly, he made teamwork a critical part of top executives' bonus plans. He told them 30 percent of their bonuses for the 2003 fiscal year would depend on how well they collaborated with others. "It tends to formalize the discussion around how can I help you and how can you help me," says Sue Bostrom, head of Cisco's Internet consulting group.[37]

SELF-MANAGED TEAMS

Have you ever thought you could do a better job than your boss? Well, if the trend toward self-managed work teams continues to grow in Canada as it has grown in the U.S., then it's very possible that you just may get your chance. Entrepreneurs and artisans often boast of not having a supervisor. In general, the same cannot be said for employees working in offices and factories. But things are changing in North America. It's common business knowledge that self-managed work teams exist in U.S.-owned firms located in offices across Canada—such as Kraft Foods Inc., 3M, and Quaker Canada—but current statistics on the depth and scope of use across this country is very limited. However, according to U.S. facts, an estimated half of the employees at *Fortune 500* companies are working on teams,[38] and a growing share of those teams are self-managing. For example, at a General Mills cereal plant, "teams . . . schedule, operate, and maintain machinery so effectively that the factory runs with no managers present during the night shift."[39] More typically, managers are present to serve as trainers and facilitators. Self-managed teams come in every conceivable format today, some more autonomous (independent) than others (see Self-Assessment Exercise).

Self-managed teams are defined as groups of workers who are given administrative oversight for their task domains. Administrative oversight involves delegated activities such as planning, scheduling, monitoring, and staffing. These chores are normally performed by managers. In short, employees in these unique work groups act as their own supervisor. Accountability is maintained *indirectly* by outside managers and leaders. According to a recent study of a company with 300 self-managed teams, 66 "team advisors" relied on these four indirect influence tactics:

Self-managed teams

Groups of employees granted administrative oversight for their work.

- **Relating** Understanding the organization's power structure, building trust, showing concern for individual team members

- **Scouting** Seeking outside information, diagnosing teamwork problems, facilitating group problem solving

- **Persuading** Gathering outside support and resources, influencing team to be more effective and to pursue organizational goals

- **Empowering** Delegating decision-making authority, facilitating a team decision-making process, coaching[40]

Self-managed teams are variously referred to as semi-autonomous work groups, independent work groups, and super-teams.

Managerial Resistance Something much more complex is involved than what this apparently simple label suggests. The term *self-managed* does not mean simply turning workers loose to do their own thing. Indeed, an organization embracing self-managed teams should be prepared to undergo revolutionary changes in management philosophy, structure, staffing and training practices, and reward systems. Moreover, the traditional notions of managerial authority and control are turned on their heads. Not surprisingly, many managers strongly resist giving up the reins of power to people they view as subordinate (not equivalent). They see self-managed teams as a threat to their job security. We spoke earlier of the kinds of roles members of a team have to assume to accomplish a task. Within that model is a change of roles for management, as well. The new role assumes more of a supporter position for the team.

Cross-Functionalism A common feature of self-managed teams, particularly among those above the shop-floor or clerical level, is **cross-functionalism.**[41] In other words, specialists from different areas are put on the same team. Mark Stefik, a manager for a large research centre, explains the wisdom of cross-functionalism:

Cross-functionalism

Team made up of technical specialists from different areas.

Something magical happens when you bring together a group of people from different disciplines with a common purpose. It's a middle zone, the breakthrough zone. The idea is to start a team on a problem—a hard problem, to keep people motivated. When there's an obstacle, instead of dodging it, bring in another point of view: an electrical engineer, a user interface expert, a sociologist, whatever spin on the market is needed. Give people new eyeglasses to cross-pollinate ideas.[42]

Cross-functionalism is seeping down into college and university programs as well, to help students see the big picture and polish their team skills.[43] The world does not operate in a vacuum, and neither should the learning process. So, by encouraging students from programs that serve different functional areas of an organization to work together on projects or assignments, they are being better prepared for the real-world work environment.

Are Self-Managed Teams Effective? The Research Evidence Among companies with self-managed teams, the most commonly delegated tasks are work scheduling and dealing directly with outside customers. The least common team chores are hiring and firing.[44] Most of today's self-managed teams remain bunched at the shop-floor level in factory settings. Experts predict growth of the practice in the managerial ranks and in service operations.[45] Much of what we know about self-managed teams comes from testimonials and case studies. Fortunately, a body of higher-quality field research is slowly developing across North America. A review of three meta-analyses covering 70 individual studies concluded that self-managed teams had:

- A positive effect on productivity

- A positive effect on specific attitudes relating to self-management (e.g., responsibility and control)

- No significant effect on general attitudes (e.g., job satisfaction and organizational commitment)

- No significant effect on absenteeism or turnover[46]

How Autonomous Is Your Work Group?

INSTRUCTIONS: Think of your current (or past) job and work group. Characterize the group's situation by selecting one number on the following scale for each statement. Add your responses for a total score:

STRONGLY DISAGREE						STRONGLY AGREE
1	2	3	4	5	6	7

Work Method Autonomy

1. My work group decides how to get the job done. _____

2. My work group determines what procedures to use. _____

3. My work group is free to choose its own methods when carrying out its work. _____

Work Scheduling Autonomy

4. My work group controls the scheduling of its work. _____

5. My work group determines how its work is sequenced. _____

6. My work group decides when to do certain activities. _____

Work Criteria Autonomy

7. My work group is allowed to modify the normal way it is evaluated so some of our activities are emphasized and some de-emphasized. _____

8. My work group is able to modify its objectives (what it is supposed to accomplish). _____

9. My work group has some control over what it is supposed to accomplish. _____

Total score = _____

NORMS

9–26 = Low autonomy
27–45 = Moderate autonomy
46–63 = High autonomy

SOURCE: Adapted from an individual autonomy scale in J.A. Breaugh, "The Work Autonomy Scales: Additional Validity Evidence," *Human Relations*, November 1989, pp 1033–56.

In a recent review of 28 studies, Dutch researchers found a positive relationship between self-managed teamwork and job satisfaction.[47] Although encouraging, these results do not qualify as a sweeping endorsement of self-managed teams. Nonetheless, experts say the trend toward self-managed work teams will continue in North America because of a strong cultural bias in favour of direct participation. Managers need to be prepared for the resulting shift in organizational administration.

VIRTUAL TEAMS

Virtual teams are a product of modern times. They take their name from *virtual reality* computer simulations, where "it's almost like the real thing." Thanks to evolving information technologies such as the Internet, email, video conferencing, groupware, and fax machines, you can be a member of a work team without really being there.[48] Traditional team meetings are location specific. Team members are either physically present or absent. Virtual teams, in contrast, convene electronically with members reporting in from different locations, different organizations, and even different time zones. *BusinessWeek* recently offered this broad perspective:

> *More and more, the creative class is becoming post-geographic. Location-independent. Office-agnostic. Demographers and futurists call this trend the rise of "the distributed workforce." Distributed workers are those who have no permanent office at their companies, preferring to work in home offices, cafés, airport lounges, high school stadium bleachers, client conference rooms, or some combination of what [author Richard] Florida calls the "no-collar workplace." They are people who do team projects over the Web and report to bosses who may be thousands of miles away ... [one expert] predicts that 40% of the workforce will be distributed by 2012. "We're at a tipping point."[49]*

Because virtual teams are so new, there is no agreed-upon definition. Our working definition of a **virtual team** is a physically dispersed task group that conducts its business through modern information technology.[50] Advocates say virtual teams are very flexible and efficient because they are driven by information and skills, not by time and location.[51] People with needed information and/or skills can be team members, regardless of where or when they actually do their work. Hewlett-Packard is an example of a company using virtual teams (see the chapter opening vignette). On the negative side, lack of face-to-face interaction not only diminishes need for human interaction, but it can weaken trust, communication, and accountability.

Research Insights As one might expect with a new and ill-defined area, research evidence to date is a bit spotty. Here is what we have learned so far from recent studies of computer-mediated groups:

- Virtual groups formed over the Internet follow a group development process similar to that for face-to-face groups.[52]

- Internet chat rooms create more work and yield poorer decisions than face-to-face meetings and telephone conferences.[53]

- Successful use of groupware, software that facilitates interaction among virtual group members (e.g., Net Meeting, Webex), requires training and hands-on experience.[54]

- Inspirational leadership has a positive impact on creativity in electronic brainstorming groups.[55]

Practical Considerations Virtual teams may be in fashion, but they are not a cure-all. In fact, they may be a giant step backward for those not well versed in modern information technology and group dynamics.[56] Managers who rely on virtual teams agree on one point: *Meaningful face-to-face contact, especially during early phases of the group development process, is absolutely essential.* Virtual group members need "faces" in their minds to go with names and electronic messages.[57] It may be advantageous to approach this type of group first as a self-managed team. Additionally, virtual teams cannot succeed without some old-fashioned factors such as top-management support, hands-on training, a clear mission, specific objectives, effective leadership, organized schedules, and deadlines.[58]

TEAM BUILDING HELPS TEAMWORK

Team building is a catch-all term for a host of techniques aimed at improving the internal functioning of work groups. Whether conducted by company trainers or hired consultants (and done on-site or off-site), team-building workshops strive for greater cooperation, better communication, and less dysfunctional conflict. Team builders discourage lectures and routine classroom discussions; they prefer active versus passive learning. They also place greater emphasis on how work groups get the job done, rather than on the task itself. Experiential learning techniques

Virtual team

Information technology allows group members in different locations to conduct business.

Team building

Experiential learning aimed at improving internal functioning of groups.

Seagate Technology celebrated their 8th annual Eco Seagate teambuilding week in New Zealand, where each 17-hour day started off with yoga, followed by painstaking competitions between corporate teams.

such as interpersonal trust exercises, conflict role-play sessions, and competitive games are common.[59] Some prefer off-site gatherings to get participants away from their work and out of their comfort zones. An exotic (and expensive) case in point is Seagate Technology:

Plenty of companies try to motivate the troops, but few go as far as Seagate Technology. Since 2001, the $12.7 billion maker of computer storage hardware has flown 200 staffers to New Zealand for their annual Eco Seagate—an intense week of team-building, topped off by an all-day race in which Seagaters kayak, hike, bike, swim, and rappel down a cliff. The tab? $2 million . . . participants volunteer and train for this annual event, which is meant to break down barriers, boost confidence, and, yes, make staffers better team players.[60] Employee and past Eco Seagate participant Rob Hyrkas wrote on his blog, "The race was fantastic. The weather was perfect. Seagate has spared no expense to make this event the incredible experience it is. It felt like a world-class event, really. Incredible!"

The bottom line: Without clear goals, proper leadership, careful attention to details, and transfer of learning back to the job, both on-site and off-site team-building sessions can become an expensive disappointment.[61] You don't want people returning to their desks the day after a teambuilding activity wondering why they had to attend or thinking what a waste of time it was. As reported in *Fast Company* magazine,[62] when planning off-site team building activities, try and adhere to the following five principles:

1. **Articulate your goals**   Be sure to identify what it is you want accomplished in the end; there must be a purpose to pulling people away from the regular work environment.

2. **Make the location exotic**   Make the event special to heighten participant interest and anticipation; enthusiasm can go a long way.

3. **Plan a signature moment**   Plan for the 'ah ha' moment when participants see the big picture and what they should be collectively moving toward.

4. **Hangovers happen**   Don't begin meetings at 8 a.m.; participants will socialize, so give them a break by planning all the important activities later on in the day.

5. **Review your progress**   Provide continuous feedback on how goals are being accomplished; ask people via formal short surveys, "What do you think?," and informally ask participants questions during breaks; gauge attendance at events.

TRUST: A KEY INGREDIENT OF TEAMWORK   `LO 4`

These have not been good times for trust in the corporate world. Years of mergers, layoffs, bloated executive bonuses, and corporate criminal proceedings have left many of us justly cynical about trusting management. According to *Canadian Business Magazine*, which conducts an annual Best Workplace survey, "trust is tops."[63] Building a caring and trusting workplace culture is often mentioned by employees when asked what made their organization such a great place to work. Here are some principles that have emerged from the survey:[64]

1. Determine where your organization is on the trust continuum. Is it relatively easy to have open conversations about how business decisions affect employee trust, or is trust simply not talked about at the executive table?

2. Managers need to understand that every interaction is an opportunity to build trust, and that missteps can quickly break trust.

3. Focus on a few key trust-building changes and pursue these consistently and relentlessly, recognizing that transforming a culture is evolutionary, not revolutionary.

Three Dimensions of Trust *Trust* is defined as reciprocal faith in others' intentions and behaviour.[65] Experts on the subject explain the reciprocal (give-and-take) aspect of trust as follows:

> When we see others acting in ways that imply that they trust us, we become more disposed to reciprocate by trusting in them more. Conversely, we come to distrust those whose actions appear to violate our trust or to distrust us.[66] In short, we tend to give what we get: Trust begets trust; distrust begets distrust.

Trust is expressed in different ways. Three dimensions of trust are: (1) *overall trust* (expecting fair play, the truth, and empathy); (2) *emotional trust* (having faith that someone will not misrepresent you to others or betray a confidence); and (3) *reliableness* (believing that promises and appointments will be kept and commitments met).[67] These different dimensions contribute to a wide and complex range of trust, from very low to very high. Building trust within a team, especially if it is a virtual team, can be difficult. As illustrated in the Law & Ethics At Work feature box, there has to be a balance between trusting members and monitoring their performance. Trust is something that has to be earned over time; it can't be demanded, and it doesn't necessarily come easily to many.

Trust

Reciprocal faith in others' intentions and behaviour.

How to Build Trust Management professor/consultant Fernando Bartolomé offers the following six guidelines for building and maintaining trust:

1. **Communication** Keep team members and employees informed by explaining policies and decisions and providing accurate feedback. Be candid about one's own problems and limitations. Tell the truth.[68]

2. **Support** Be available and approachable. Provide help, advice, coaching, and support for team members' ideas.

3. **Respect** Delegation, in the form of real decision-making authority, is the most important expression of managerial respect. Actively listening to the ideas of others is a close second. Empowerment is not possible without trust.[69]

4. **Fairness** Be quick to give credit and recognition to those who deserve it. Make sure all performance appraisals and evaluations are objective and impartial.

5. **Predictability** Be consistent and predictable in your daily affairs. Keep both expressed and implied promises.

6. **Competence** Enhance your credibility by demonstrating good business sense, technical ability, and professionalism.[70]

LAW AND ETHICS *at Work*

SOCIAL DEVIANCE IN VIRTUAL TEAMWORK

If a member of a self-managed work team decides to work from home, how do the other members of the team back in the office know in fact that to be true? In the age of the moveable workplace, where employees do much from home or "on the road," the issue of trustworthiness among team members raises an interesting ethical dilemma. There is a body of research that suggests that the communication tools routinely used between virtual team members can actually promote untrustworthy social behaviour (e.g., email versus telephone). In other words, the lack of trust that can develop between members may be functionally determined by the type of communication tool preferred and the frequency of its use, and not incidentally as some believe. But let's take this even further: What if a team member visits a personal friend in the evening on a business trip; is that being socially deviant, and is there a need for the rest of the team to be aware of this? Does the private life of members diminish once they become part of a virtual team, since it's possible for the employee to cast an indirect light on the company/team? These questions speak to the issue of how much autonomy and privacy one should expect when working for a virtual team-oriented organization.

SOURCES: R. Sainsbury and R. Baskerville, "Distrusting Online: Social Deviance in Virtual Teamwork," *System Sciences*, volume 6, issue 4, January 2006, pg 121a. R. Audi, *Business Ethics and Ethical Business*, Oxford University Press, 2009, pg 88–89.

LO 5 Threats to Group and Team Effectiveness

No matter how carefully managers staff and organize task groups and teams, group dynamics can still go haywire. Here we discuss two major threats to group effectiveness—groupthink and social loafing—and we provide information that can help managers and team members alike take necessary preventive steps.

GROUPTHINK

Modern managers can all too easily become victims of groupthink, just like professional politicians, if they passively ignore the danger. Professor and OB expert Irving Janis defines **groupthink** as "a mode of thinking that people engage in when they are deeply involved in a cohesive in-group, when members' strivings for unanimity (harmony) override their motivation to realistically appraise alternative courses of action."[71] He adds, "Groupthink refers to a deterioration of mental efficiency, reality testing, and moral judgment that results from in-group pressures."[72] Members of groups victimized by groupthink tend to be friendly and tightly knit.

According to Janis's model, there are eight classic symptoms of groupthink. The greater the number of symptoms, the higher the probability of groupthink:

1. **Invulnerability** An illusion that breeds excessive optimism and risk taking.

2. **Inherent morality** A belief that encourages the group to ignore ethical implications.

3. **Rationalization** Protects pet assumptions.

4. **Stereotyped views of opposition** Causes the group to underestimate opponents.

5. **Self-censorship** Stifles critical debate.

6. **Illusion of unanimity** Silence is interpreted to mean consent.

7. **Peer pressure** Loyalty of dissenters is questioned.

8. **Mindguards** Self-appointed protectors against unpleasant information.[73]

Groupthink

Janis's term for a cohesive in-group's unwillingness to realistically view alternatives.

In short, policy- and decision-making groups can become so cohesive that strong-willed executives are able to gain unanimous support for poor decisions.

Janis believes that prevention is better than cure when dealing with groupthink (see Skills & Best Practices feature box for his preventive measures).[74]

"Our last meeting started out with everyone, except Mr. Simms, heartily laughing at Mr. Baine's joke . . ."

Skills & Best Practices

How to Prevent Groupthink

1 Assign each member of the group to the role of critical evaluator. This role involves actively voicing objections and doubts.

2 Do not use policy committees to rubber-stamp decisions that have already been made.

3 Have different groups with different leaders explore the same policy questions.

4 Use subgroup debates and outside experts to introduce fresh perspectives.

5 Give someone the role of devil's advocate when discussing major alternatives. This person tries to uncover every conceivable negative factor.

6 Once a consensus has been reached, encourage everyone to rethink their position to check for flaws.

SOURCE: Adapted from discussion in I.L. Janis, *Groupthink*, 2nd ed. (Boston: Houghton Mifflin, 1982), ch 11.

SOCIAL LOAFING

Is group performance less than, equal to, or greater than the sum of its parts? For example, can three people working together accomplish less than, the same as, or more than they would working separately? An interesting study conducted more than a half century ago by a French agricultural engineer named Ringelmann found the answer to be "less than."[75] In a rope-pulling exercise, Ringelmann reportedly found that three people pulling together could achieve only two and a half times the average individual rate. Eight pullers achieved less than four times the individual rate. This tendency for individual effort to decline as group size increases has come to be called *social loafing*.[76] Let us briefly analyze this threat to group effectiveness and synergy with an eye toward avoiding it.

Social loafing

Decrease in individual effort as group size increases.

Social Loafing Theory and Research   Among the theoretical explanations for the social loafing effect are: (1) equity of effort ("Everyone else is goofing off, so why shouldn't I?"); (2) loss of personal accountability ("I'm lost in the crowd, so who cares?")—this point is illustrated in the Focus on Diversity feature box; (3) motivational loss due to the sharing of rewards ("Why should I work harder than the others when everyone gets the same reward?"); and (4) coordination loss as more people perform the task ("We're getting in each other's way.").

Laboratory studies refined these theories by identifying situational factors that moderated the social loafing effect.

360-degree feedback

Comparison of anonymous feedback from one's superior, subordinates, and peers with self-perceptions.

Social loafing occurred when

- The task was perceived to be unimportant, simple, or not interesting[77]
- Group members thought their individual output was not identifiable[78]
- Group members expected their co-workers to loaf[79]

But social loafing did *not* occur when group members in two laboratory studies expected to be evaluated.[80] Also, research suggests that self-reliant "individualists" are more prone to social loafing than are group-oriented "collectivists." But individualists can be made more cooperative by keeping the group small and holding each member personally accountable for results.[81]

Practical Implications   These findings demonstrate that social loafing is not an inevitable part of group effort. Management can curb this threat to group effectiveness by making sure the task is challenging and perceived as important. Additionally, it is a good idea to hold group members personally accountable for identifiable portions of the group's task.[82] A few strategies worth considering when monitoring for social loafing include implementing self-assessments ("Do you think your contributions are having a positive effect on the team?"), paying for performance ("In order to get this reward, you must produce this outcome"), or using a *360-degree feedback* evaluation (secure anonymous feedback on team performance from all members of team, as well as the manager, subordinates, clients, peers, etc.).

IS IT SOCIAL LOAFING OR JUST BEING EXCLUDED?

FOCUS ON Diversity

Researchers Elizabeth Mannix and Margaret A. Neale study team diversity, and their research supports the intuitive belief that when teams are comprised of diverse members, they will have the ability to exploit a variety of resources and to bring them "to the table." When it comes to innovation and brainstorming, a diverse group is better than a homogeneous group. The evidence is clearly positive for both the organization and the team. But there is also a side finding to their research that shows that some people from diverse backgrounds are not always able to fit into the group, and may in fact feel like outcasts. While this is not always the case, it is possible. Because such a possibility exists, it is important for the team leader and management to identify whether the performance of a given team member is related to social loafing or to other reasons. One of the lessons to learn from this research is that when a team grows and becomes more diverse in membership, it becomes necessary for the team leader to watch for cues, and if necessary to step in to assist with developing identity and sharing minority opinions whenever possible.

Source: D.A. Kravitz, "Diversity in Teams, A Two-Edged Sword Requires Careful Handling." George Mason University. Printed in the *American Psychological Society Newsletter Editorial 2005*, Volume 6, Number 2.

1. **List and define the five stages of Tuckman's theory of group development.** The five stages in Tuckman's theory are forming (the group comes together), storming (members test the limits and each other), norming (questions about authority and power are resolved as the group becomes more cohesive), performing (effective communication and cooperation help the group get things done), and adjourning (group members go their own way).

2. **Contrast roles from norms, emphasizing reasons why norms are enforced in organizations.** While roles are specific to the person's position, norms are shared attitudes that differentiate appropriate from inappropriate behaviour in a variety of situations. Norms evolve informally and are enforced because they help the group or organization survive, clarify behavioural expectations, help people avoid embarrassing situations, and clarify the group's or organization's central values.

3. **Examine the process for how a work group becomes a team, emphasizing various teamwork competencies.** A team is a mature group where leadership is shared, accountability is both individual and collective, the members have developed their own purpose, problem solving is a way of life, and effectiveness is measured by collective outcomes. Five teamwork competencies are (1) orients team to problem-solving situations; (2) organizes and manages team performance; (3) promotes a positive team environment; (4) facilitates and manages task conflict; and (5) appropriately promotes perspective.

4. **Explain why trust is the key ingredient to building an effective team, referring to both self-managed and virtual teams.** Trust contributes to teambuilding by allowing a reciprocal faith in others' intentions and behaviour. By having trust, the internal functioning of work groups is improved. Self-managed teams need to have built-in trust with one another because they have administrative oversight for their task domains; there is no manager per se to turn to for answers. They must have trust in one another as they rely less on management and become more co-dependent. Mutual trust among the membership will allow for open communication, especially during stressful times. Virtual teams need trust to get work done, since they don't have the physical cues to indicate that work is getting done as promised. Dividing up the work within a virtual team assumes that all members are competent and able to complete their portion of a task. That assumption can sometimes be based on blind trust.

5. **Summarize at least two threats to group and team effectiveness.** Two major threats to group and team effectiveness are groupthink and social loafing. Groupthink results when people are deeply involved in a cohesive in-group, when members' strivings for harmony override their motivation to realistically appraise alternative courses of action. This can be dangerous because it can blind the group to minority opinion from dissenters, lead the group to rationalize their behaviour on the basis of false assumptions, and act as a type of censorship that stifles debate. One possible technique to use to minimize groupthink is to assign a member the role of devil's advocate or critical evaluator. Social loafing results when individual effort decreases within a group as the group itself gets larger. This is particularly applicable when intuition would lead us to believe that more is better when applied to assigning membership to a group. Social loafing is a threat to group effectiveness because it leads members to false expectations that authority and responsibility to perform is equally felt throughout the group. This may not be the case, and therefore sets the team up for disappointment. Ongoing assessment and evaluation can minimize social loafing.

Discussion Questions

1. Relative to the chapter-opening vignette, how important is trust in the smooth functioning of a virtual IT team? Explain.
2. What is your opinion about managers being friends with the people they supervise (in other words, overlapping formal and informal groups)?
3. In your personal relationships, how do you come to trust someone? How fragile is that trust? Explain.
4. Are virtual teams likely to be a passing fad? Why or why not?
5. Have you ever witnessed groupthink or social loafing firsthand? Explain the circumstances and how things played out.

Google Searches

1. **Google Search:** "Stanford Prison Experiment" What is this research study about? What happens to individual behaviour when groups are formed? Was there evidence of groupthink among the guards? Can you draw a parallel to the workplace—do you think some employees feel hopeless/powerless as they become intimidated by authority, thus lowering their self esteem? Why was it so hard for the prisoners to resist or quit? Do you think that we are the sole determinants of our behaviour?
2. **Google Search:** "Beijing Olympics—Canada's Eight Rowing Team" Read the final standing of the Canadian men's rowing team at the Beijing Summer Olympics. How did they place? What were some of the challenges this team faced in preparation of their race? Would you consider this team of eight a work group or a high performing team? Explain your response.
3. **Google Search:** "Banff Team Building" or "Fun Canadian Team Building Activities" or "Eco Seagate Team Building" Search the various sites and record five of your favourite team building retreats/activities. Share your responses with the class.

Experiential Exercise

Tuckman's Stages of Group Development Exercise

PURPOSE: This exercise is meant to assist you with the specifics of group development by combining Tuckman's model with other factors related to effective group performance. Review Figure 6.2 before beginning this exercise. Approx. Timing: 25 minutes.

ACTIVITY ASSIGNMENT:
- Form small groups and answer the questions below.
- Share your group's responses with the rest of the class after 10 minutes.

For each of the five stages of Tuckman's model (forming, storming, norming, performing, adjourning), answer the following questions:

1. What are two possible questions that can be asked by individual members of the group? (For example: Forming – How do I fit in?; Storming – What's my role here?; Norming – What do the others expect from me?; Performing – How can I best perform my role?; Adjourning – What's next?)

2. What are two possible questions that can be asked by the group overall? (For example: Forming – Why are we here?; Storming – What are we fighting over?; Norming – How can we work together?; Performing – Can we do the job properly?; Adjourning – What do we do to disband the group?)

3. What level of trust is needed at each stage?

4. What level of social loafing is possible at each stage (low, medium, or high)?

5. What strategy can the group use at each stage to ensure work is being completed?

6. What initiative can management use at each stage to assist the group in achieving goals?

The **Presentation** Assistant

Here are possible topics and sources related to this chapter that can be further explored by student groups looking for ideas.

	SPORTS TEAMS—WHAT FACTORS AND BEHAVIOURS DIFFERENTIATE A SUCCESSFUL TEAM FROM A NON-SUCCESSFUL TEAM?	TEAMBUILDING ACTIVITIES FOR CORPORATE DEVELOPMENT—WHAT ARE THEY, HOW DO THEY ENHANCE COMMUNICATION AND CONTRIBUTE TO BUILDING AN EFFECTIVE TEAM?	TYPES OF WORK TEAMS AND THEIR CHARACTERISTICS— WHAT ARE EXAMPLES OF COMBINATIONS OF MEMBER EXPERTISE, LEVEL OF INTEGRATION WITH OTHER WORK UNITS, AND LENGTH OF THE WORK CYCLE?
YouTube Videos	• 2002 Team Canada Hockey Gold • NBA Chicago Bulls Dynasty 1990s • Manchester United Soccer Club	• Corporate team building activities • PIT Instruction and Training (Pit Crew Team Building) • Eco Seagate Team Building	• Xbox 360 Assembly Line • Overseas Heart Surgery Team • Boeing Contract Negotiations
TV Shows or Movies to Preview	• *Rudy* (Ruettiger) • *Remember The Titans*	• *300* • *The Dirty Dozen* • *13 going on 30*	• *Lucy, Lucy, Lucy* (assembly worker) • *The Apprentice* (Committee)
Internet Searches	• Guinness World Records Most Successful Sports Teams • Top 10 Characteristics of a Successful Team • *Successful Team Building – A Worksmart Book* (by T. Quick) • *The Five Dysfunctions of a Team* (by P. Lencioni)	• *The Speed of Trust* (by, S. Covey) • *Instant Team Building* (by B. Sugars) • NASCAR University • Banff Centre – Team building Seminars • Seagate Technologies	• Work Teams – *American Psychologist 1990* (by Sundstrom) • Negotiating As a Team – *Harvard Business Journal* • Province of Ontario Negotiating Team – Algonquin Land Claims (committees)

| Ice Breaker Classroom Activity | • Split the students into two teams. Give each team the same task of passing a role of toilet paper throughout their team. The team that successfully passes the unrolling toilet paper without it breaking wins. Ask the students to identify how one side won—What did they do that the other side didn't? | • Split the students into small teams. Give each team the same kind and quantity of Lego pieces. Allow 1 minute for the groups to plan. Allow 2 minutes for the groups to build. Put in a change condition of 'cost cuts': each team has to give up two pieces. Allow 1 minute for the groups to build under these new conditions. Compare the results of team building based on beauty, height, and using all pieces. The winning team gets a prize. | • Write four headings on the board: Advice, Production or Service, Project, Organized Action. Ask the students to list as many different types of work groups that they can think of for each of these four types of work. As answers are given, write them on the board under the corresponding heading. |

 # OB In Action Case Study

Let's Get Together

In many management classes, students are required to work together on group assignments. This case describes four meetings of this type of group. You may find yourself identifying with the experiences of the individuals described.

Meeting 1

The first time Dan, Lisa, Michelle, Paula, and Stavros met was at the end of their second management systems class. Their instructor had assigned them to work together to perform a critical analysis of the management philosophies at a local company, and to provide recommendations for improvement. Their analysis was to be based largely on data from a case and their results were to be presented to the class. Their instructor suggested that some form of example or illustration of the problem, as well as class discussion, would help result in a good grade. Furthermore, they were told that the presentation would be graded on an individual basis. The group members did not know each other previously, so their first task was to introduce themselves.

   Following the introductions, Dan initiated a discussion about the requirements of their presentation, scheduled in four weeks. He informed the other members of the group that his uncle had worked for the organization they were studying, and would therefore be able to give him all the information they needed about its management practices. A few minutes into the discussion, Stavros scribbled his phone number on some paper and announced that he didn't have time to talk things over at the moment. After Stavros' abrupt exit, Michelle attempted to refocus the others' attention by reminding them that their instructor had urged them to start working on their project right away. Paula added that she felt they could all benefit from reading their textbook chapter on management philosophies, and offered to research the background of the company at the local library and on the Internet. Lisa volunteered to go to the library with Paula, noting that it would be more fun to work as a team. This first meeting concluded with a tentative agreement to meet again the following week at the same time.

Meeting 2

A week later, all the group members except Dan met again at the student centre. The meeting started out with a spirited exchange about the previous night's hockey game between the Montreal Canadiens and the Edmonton Oilers. After discussing hockey for a few minutes, Paula initiated a discussion about the presentation. Paula said Dan had told her that his uncle probably couldn't help them after all, because he had left the organization under something of a cloud. However, he had an idea for a class exercise that could be part of the presentation. Eventually the conversation drifted to the subject of presentation styles and a debate developed about the style the group should use. Stavros felt that the group should present a formal, serious, professional image, to impress the instructor. Paula agreed that they should have a professional image, but also felt that some humour and lightheartedness would make the presentation more interesting to the class. Lisa said that she would go along with whatever the other group members decided, while Michelle tried to prevent the others from getting into a heated argument. The discussion finally ended with Michelle saying that she would speak to their instructor and ask which presentation style was recommended. Paula went on to show the others the information she and Lisa had found at the library over the weekend. Lisa invited the group to meet at her house the following Saturday afternoon, offering to make popcorn and order a pizza. The others agreed, and so the second meeting was concluded.

Meeting 3

All the group members were able to meet at Lisa's house the following Saturday. All except Dan had done the background reading, and the group proceeded to discuss the content of the presentation. Michelle reported that the instructor had encouraged them to make the presentation interesting, adding that humour was fine as long as they didn't stray too far from their topic. She suggested that a short skit demonstrating some management philosophies in action might be a good way to conclude their presentation. Dan also pointed out that, with the presentation date only two weeks away, the group needed to give the go-ahead on his exercise as soon as possible. After some discussion, they decided that Michelle would write up a short script for a skit, while Dan would prepare a class participation exercise. Paula and Lisa would write up the bulk of the information needed for the presentation, while Stavros would use his computer to make any handouts needed, and also a banner to hang at the front of the classroom. Conflicting points of view arose regarding the number of people who would be involved in the skits. However, this was quickly settled when Michelle pointed out they were all being marked separately for their part in the presentation, and the more each person did, the more material the instructor would have to use to assess each of them. After settling a few more details, the group members agreed to meet again the following week to tie everything together.

Meeting 4

At the fourth meeting, Stavros explained to the others that he had not been able to prepare any handouts because he had lost the folder with his rough notes. As he began collecting information from Lisa and Paula, Michelle distributed copies of the skit. After they read it through as a group, Dan described his participation exercise. A difficulty became apparent when they practised the exercise and realized that it would take almost 20 minutes to complete. Paula told Dan that, with the amount of information they were going to cover, there was no way they could devote half their time to a class exercise. Dan argued that he had based the exercise on a past work situation, and could not shorten it without taking away from its meaning and its effect on the class. Lisa tried to help by suggesting that the class be divided into groups so they could work through different parts of the exercise simultaneously. Dan continued to react strongly, emphasizing that he had spent a great deal of time preparing this part of the presentation and could not believe that all the others could do was criticize him. Michelle calmly tried to explain that since they were each being marked separately, it was only fair that they all get the same time to present. At this point, Dan told them that if they didn't want his help he wouldn't give it to them, and he stormed out of the student centre. The others were silent for a few moments, somewhat shocked by Dan's performance. Eventually Michelle brought the group back to focus by saying that Dan would realize how self-centred he had been when he had had a chance to cool off. She suggested that it would be best if they continued to work out the details for the remainder of the presentation. The group wondered if they would be able to work things out with Dan before their presentation day, and they began to contemplate what to do next and how to resolve the situation.

WHAT NEXT?

Teamwork is an integral part of the working world, so it is a skill that must be developed as soon as possible. Schools, especially business schools, often aim to develop these skills in their students, often in the manner illustrated in the above case. You may find that the problems experienced by Dan, Lisa, Michelle, Paula, and Stavros are all too familiar.

SOURCE: T. Cawsey and G. Deszca, *Cases in Organizational Behaviour*, 1st ed (Toronto: McGraw-Hill Ryerson, 2005), pp 65–67. © A Templer.

Discussion Questions

1. Imagine you are Dan. What is your perspective of the situation?
2. Image you are one of the other group members (but not Dan). What is your assessment of what led to the current situation?
3. What should the group do now, given that Dan has stormed out? For example, should the group present as they are (without Dan), speak to the professor and complain, or try to reason with Dan? What is the likelihood they can put the group back together before presentation day?
4. How would your group resolve the situation? What specific action steps would you take?
5. What can we learn from the analysis of this type of group process?
6. How common and applicable is this example to the world of work? Have you had any similar experiences, and how were they resolved?

Ethical OB Dilemma

Group Dynamics—Dare To Disagree

You work for Ideas, Inc. as a sales marketing director. This three-year-old company was founded by a wealthy Canadian entrepreneur who is always looking for new ideas. The director of strategic planning for the firm and the corporate president, Pat Wing, recently came across a new clothing line that they believe will "sell like crazy" here in Canada. Pat wants the company to have exclusive rights to this product. Arrangements are made to allow you and two others from the office to travel to Bogata, Columbia for further investigation. The fact-finding team going south includes the company lawyer from Ideas Inc., the director of finance (Peter Swarez), and you.

The team arrives at the corporate offices to meet with Miguel Caballero, who is walking around his company's showroom holding a .38-calibre revolver. "You—you want to be shot?" he asks the director of finance. He then points his finger at you and says, "You're next."

The director of finance wiggles nervously into an $850 brown suede winter jacket and zips it up to the collar. A foot or so away, the smiling Caballero lowers the weapon and takes aim.

"One!" Swarez takes a deep breath and stares up at the ceiling. "Two!" A deafening blast sends Swarez lurching backward—and then screaming out in relief, clutching at the hole in the jacket where the bullet has come to a safe stop.

No, this isn't some cruel corporate hazing ritual. For Caballero, founder and CEO of the company that carries his name, this is just a showy way of demonstrating his products. Caballero sells a line of armoured clothing that fits like Armani but deflects point-blank gunfire like the Pope-mobile. In 2005, the 38-year-old entrepreneur sold an estimated $7 million worth of bullet-proof trench coats, business suits, suede jackets, and denim casuals to executives, political leaders, undercover agents, and other VIPs—people who demand more than a bodyguard for protection and who don't like the bulk or SWAT-team look of flak jackets and vests. "There are hundreds of companies that make bullet-proof vests," Caballero says. "We make bullet-proof fashion."

You are outraged by the demonstration and can't believe Pat Wing wants to import this product into Canada. You look to the corporate lawyer who appears excited about the demonstration. Peter Swarez gets up off the floor and says out loud, "This is an amazing product; I think we've found a goldmine! The Canadian office is going to be thrilled when we bring this product up north!" You are feeling like the odd person out in this situation and are nervous about what to do next.

SOURCE: Excerpted from S. Brodzinsky, "Protects Like Armor, Fits Like Armani," *Business 2.0*, August 2006, p 60.

Consider the following statements. Which one best describes how you would respond?

1. You say nothing and go along with the rest of the team because of the pressure to conform.
2. You decline the demonstration offer and instead ask for evidence the product is safe 100 percent of the time. You assume your role on the team as the person who is going to uncover evidence from faulty research, and in the end save the team from making a bad decision.
3. You remind the others of the norms that your team has agreed to in the past; there must be consensus before agreements are made. You show outrage to the Ideas, Inc. team who you believe aren't thinking clearly.
4. You pick up your satellite cell phone and dial Pat Wing immediately to voice your concern about the product.
5. You would respond differently. Explain.

Effective Communication

Data Mining Your Communication History For All To See

How would you feel if your professor began reading your Facebook or MySpace blog out loud in class? What if that same professor began listing all of the Web sites that you subscribe to on the whiteboard for all to read? This is exactly what happened several months ago. A part-time professor at a large Ontario community college was excited about his first day teaching business students the power and sophistication of contemporary data systems. Being a recent university computer science graduate, the young professor thought his opening demonstration for the class would catch their attention and make his point.

Some students were amused; others complained to the administration. It's called "data mining"—a broader term is "knowledge management"—and it's causing many to think about the way they communicate with others. Think of data mining as a super in-depth intelligence search into the many layers of data on the Internet. Once found, it kicks back the requested information to whoever asks for it. The results can be quite intrusive.

For the purposes of screening new job applicants and minimizing a firm's exposure to the growing problem of employee fraud, Canadian HR experts are beginning to understand the value of having the explicit, and systematic management of vital knowledge. Multi-billion dollar high-tech firms like HP, Teradata, and IBM have invested huge amounts of resources into the growing demand for data-mining, -warehousing, and -retrieval systems: "[data mining] allows you the ability to really understand your employees," says Robert Carlyle, head of the consulting firm Aon-Intelligence Unit. As reported by Service Canada, recent literature on this topic suggests that HR specialists or trainers would be qualified candidates for using such processes in a firm.

You may be asking yourself, what about those social network sites that are supposedly password protected and "by invite" only? Well, with a bit of special knowledge, coupled with common search software available online for less than $35, these sites become easy to break into. This begs the question—isn't knowledge management a violation of Canadian privacy laws? Recent changes to Facebook's security and safeguard policies are an attempt to address such concerns. But remember, public Internet sites are open for all, the very essence of why the Internet was created to begin with: an open sharing of rich data easily accessible with little to no cost.

Bottom line: Whatever is placed on the Internet sits there for many years in some form, either in real time or cached. Users are well-advised to consider what they say about others, their boss, clients, and organizations. It's possible that such information could be used against them in the future.

SOURCES: *Knowledge Management*, Service Canada, HR for Employers/Government of Canada, http://hrmanagement.gc.ca/go1/hrmanagement/site.nsf/en/hr11573.html; *Employee Fraud*, HRM Guide, http://www.hrmguide.com/general/employee-fraud.htm; "HP Sees A Gold Mine In Data Mining," *BusinessWeek*, April 30, 2007, http://www.businessweek.com/print/magazine/content/07_18/b4032077.htm?chan=gl; S. Klie, "Guesses just don't cut it anymore," *Canadian HR Reporter*, March 24, 2008, http://www.canadianhrreporter.com/loginarea/members/viewing.asp?ArticleNo=5923; V. Tsang, "No more excuses—Poor hires can sink a company so HR should be diligent about conducting thorough background checks," *Canadian HR Reporter*, May 23, 2005, http://www.hreporter.com/loginarea/members/viewing.asp?article No=3829&viewwhat=Print&subscription.

LEARNING OBJECTIVES

After reading this chapter, you should be able to:

LO 1 **Illustrate** the various components of the perceptual process model of communication.

LO 2 **Describe** the various barriers to effective communication.

LO 3 **Contrast** the communication styles of assertiveness, aggressiveness, and non-assertiveness.

LO 4 **Explain** the formal and informal communication channels.

LO 5 **Summarize** the various factors involved in maintaining effective communication as organizations move toward using more electronic devices in the workplace.

In his best-selling book *The World Is Flat,* Thomas L. Friedman concluded that information technology is transforming and connecting people's lives around the world. The chapter-opening vignette reinforces that claim; it shows how the Internet is being used to instantaneously communicate all types of information to anyone with access to a computer.

Studying communication is important because every employee must be able to convey and receive ideas or concerns with other employees. But it's not just for internal purposes; employees are often expected to communicate with stakeholders outside of the organization, such as suppliers and clients. Every supervisory function and activity involves some form of direct or indirect communication. Decisions and organizational policies are ineffective unless they are understood by those responsible for enacting them. Consider, for example, how the communication process within Adecco SA, the world's largest temporary help company, negatively affected the company's stock price:

> *Eight days ago, the Swiss-based concern announced it wouldn't be able to release its year-end results on schedule in February and warned of "material weaknesses with internal controls" at its North American staffing business. But Adecco officials refused to elaborate on the terse statement, citing legal constraints. At the time, they wouldn't even confirm the identity of an independent counsel that Adecco's board has appointed to conduct its own investigation. The company's bunker mentality stirred anxiety among investors, who quickly dumped Adecco shares. Within a few hours, the company lost 35 percent of its market capitalization.*[1]

Ineffective communication clearly contributed to the drop in Adecco's share price. Effective communication is also critical for employee motivation and job satisfaction. For example, a recent polling of 336 organizations revealed that 66 percent of the respondents did not know or understand their organization's mission and business strategy, which subsequently led them to feel disengaged at work. The apparent lack of communication in these organizations is a problem because employee disengagement is associated with lower productivity and product quality, and higher labour costs and turnover.[2]

This chapter will help you understand how all employees can improve their communication skills and how management can design more effective communication programs. We discuss (1) basic dimensions of the communication processes, focusing on a perceptual process model and barriers to effective communication; (2) interpersonal communication; and (3) communicating in the age of information technology.

LO 1 Basic Dimensions of the Communication Process

Communication is defined as "the exchange of information between a sender and a receiver, and the inference (perception) of meaning between the individuals involved."[3] Employees who understand this process can analyze their own communication patterns

and managers can design communication programs that fit organizational needs. This section reviews a perceptual process model of communication and discusses the barriers to effective communication.

A PERCEPTUAL PROCESS MODEL OF COMMUNICATION

As we all know, communicating is not simple or clear-cut; it is fraught with miscommunication. While recognizing this, researchers have begun to examine communication as a form of social information processing in which receivers interpret messages by cognitively processing information. This view led to the development of a *perceptual model of communication* that depicts communication as a process in which receivers create meaning in their own minds. Let us briefly examine the elements of the perceptual process model shown in Figure 7.1.

Perceptual model of communication

Process in which receivers create their own meaning.

Sender The sender is an individual, group, or organization that desires or attempts to communicate with a particular receiver. A receiver may be an individual, a group, or an organization.

Communication

Interpersonal exchange of information and understanding.

Encoding Communication begins when a sender encodes an idea or thought. Encoding translates mental thoughts into a code or language that can be understood by others. People typically encode using words, numbers,

▶ FIGURE 7.1 **Communication Process in Action**

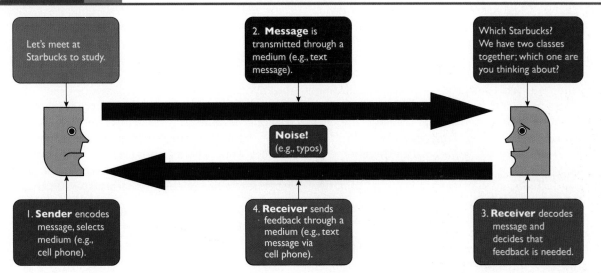

1. **Sender** encodes message, selects medium (e.g., cell phone).

Let's meet at Starbucks to study.

2. **Message** is transmitted through a medium (e.g., text message).

Noise! (e.g., typos)

3. **Receiver** decodes message and decides that feedback is needed.

Which Starbucks? We have two classes together; which one are you thinking about?

4. **Receiver** sends feedback through a medium (e.g., text message via cell phone).

gestures, non-verbal cues such as facial expressions, or pictures. Moreover, different methods of encoding can be used to portray similar ideas.

The Message   The output of encoding is a message. There are two important points to keep in mind about messages. First, they contain more than meets the eye. Messages may contain hidden agendas, as well as trigger affective or emotional reactions. Second, messages need to match the medium used to transmit them. How would you evaluate the match between the message of letting someone know he or she has been laid off and the communication medium used in the following example?

> Tower Snow was chairman of Brobeck, Phleger & Harrison, a leading law firm. Late Friday, as he got off his airplane flight, a gate agent handed him an envelope. Inside: a notice that Brobeck, his employer, had fired him.[4]

How would you feel if this happened to you? Surely there is a better way to let people know they are being fired. This example illustrates how thoughtless managers can be when they do not carefully consider the interplay between a message and the medium used to convey it. At the same time, it's important to understand the reasons why an employer would take the kind of action as in the case of Tower Snow. We explore such reasons in the Law & Ethics at Work feature box.

Selecting A Medium   People can communicate through a variety of media, including face-to-face conversations, telephone calls, electronic mail or email, voice mail, video conferencing, written memos or letters, photographs or drawings, meetings, bulletin boards, computer output, and charts or graphs. Choosing the appropriate media depends on many factors, including the nature of the message, its intended purpose, the type of audience, proximity to the audience, time horizon for disseminating (distributing) the message, personal preferences, and the complexity of the problem/situation at hand.

All media have advantages and disadvantages and should be used in different situations. Face-to-face conversations, for example, are useful for communicating sensitive or important issues that require feedback and intensive interaction. In contrast, telephones are convenient, fast, and private, but lack non-verbal cues. Although writing memos or letters can be time-consuming, they

LAW AND ETHICS *at Work*

EMPLOYERS MUST COMMUNICATE NOTICE TO AN EMPLOYEE

In Canada, an employer has two options when terminating an employee without cause: give the employee working notice of termination, or provide pay in lieu of notice. Employers may decide against working notice due to concerns about the terminated employee's access to sensitive information, the effect upon workplace morale, and possible sabotage of client relations. Canadian legislation uniformly requires employers to provide employees with notice of termination in the absence of just cause.

What some employers (and employees, for that matter) do not realize is that the legislated requirements for notice are supplemented by the common law, which can significantly increase the amount of notice required. For example, where notice is given, employees are required to continue to work during normal hours and perform their duties throughout the notice period. If the employer chooses to provide pay in lieu of notice, employees continue to receive wages and benefits for the same notice period, but are not required to work during that time. In other words, the employer pays the employee not to work. Some employers choose this action because there are potential disadvantages to continuing to employ someone during the notice period. If the notified employees are bitter and vindictive (wanting to get even) about the termination, they may try and sabotage the company in any number of ways. These concerns are even more real in the case of higher-level employees, like Tower Snow, who may have access to sensitive information or may regularly interact with clients. Because of this, employers perceive paying someone not to work as a justified expense to alleviate these concerns.

SOURCE: S.E. Rudner, "The perils of working notice termination," *Canadian HR Reporter*, July 14, 2003, http://www.hrreporter.com/loginarea/members/viewing.asp?ArticleNo=2636&viewwhat=Print&subscription.

are good media to use when it is difficult to arrange a meeting with another person, when formality and a written record are important, and when face-to-face interaction is not necessary to enhance understanding. Electronic communication, which is discussed later in this chapter, can be used to communicate with a large number of dispersed (widely placed) people and is potentially a very fast medium when recipients regularly check their email.[5]

Face-to-face communication is useful for delivering sensitive or important issues to others that require feedback, intensive interaction, or observation of non-verbal cues.

Thomas Swidarski used the benefits of email on the first day of his appointment as president and CEO of Diebold. He sent an email to Diebold's 14,500 employees inviting comments and outlining his priorities, including building customer loyalty by speeding the flow of products through the supply chain, and "providing quality products and outstanding service." He told them that leading Diebold "does not rest with one person—it rests with each and every one of us." He received more than 1,000 responses.[6]

Decoding   Decoding is the receiver's version of encoding. Decoding consists of translating verbal, oral, or visual aspects of a message into a form that can be interpreted. Receivers rely on social information processing to determine the meaning of a message during decoding. Decoding is a key contributor to misunderstanding in interracial and intercultural communication because decoding by the receiver is subject to social values and cultural values that may not be understood by the sender.

Creating Meaning   The perceptual model of communication is based on the belief that receivers create the meaning of a message in their head. A receiver's

interpretation of a message can thus differ from that intended by the sender. In turn, receivers act according to their own interpretations, not the communicator's.

Feedback   Have you ever been on your cell phone and thought that you lost your connection with the person you were talking to? If yes, something like the following probably occurred. "Hello, Joyce, are you there?" "Joyce, can you hear me?" The other person may say back, "Yes, I can hear you, but your voice is fading in and out." This is an example of feedback—the receiver expresses a reaction to the sender's message. The receiver's response to a message is the heart of the feedback loop. At this point in the communication process, the receiver becomes a sender. Specifically, the receiver encodes a response and then transmits it to the original sender. This new message is then decoded and interpreted.

Noise   *Noise* represents anything that interferes with the transmission and understanding of a message. It affects all linkages of the communication process. Sue Weidemann, director of research for a consulting company, investigated the impact of noise at a large law firm. Her results indicated that "the average number of times that people were interrupted by noise, visual distractions and chatty visitors prairie-dogging over a cube wall was 16 a day—or 21 a day including work-related distractions." She concluded that it takes 2.9 minutes to recover concentration after these disruptions, "meaning people spend more than an hour a day trying to refocus. And that doesn't even count the time drain of the distraction itself."[7] Noise includes factors such as a speech impairment, poor telephone connections, illegible handwriting, inaccurate statistics in a memo or report, poor hearing and eyesight, environmental noises, people talking or whistling, and physical distance between sender and receiver. Supervisors and managers can improve communication by encouraging employees to try to minimize the noise levels around their work stations, and reduce office distractions and noise.[8]

> *Noise*
>
> Interference with the transmission and understanding of a message.

BARRIERS TO EFFECTIVE COMMUNICATION   LO 2

Communication noise is a barrier to effective communication because it interferes with the accurate transmission and reception of a message. Table 7.1 identifies and explains common barriers at each level of the communication process. Awareness of these barriers is a good starting point to improve the communication process. There are three key barriers to effective communication: (1) personal barriers, (2) physical barriers, and (3) semantic barriers.

Barriers to Communication that Happen Within the Communication Process

- **Sender barrier—no message gets sent.** Have you ever had an idea but were afraid to voice it because you feared criticism? Then obviously no message got sent. But the barrier need not be for psychological reasons. Suppose as a new manager you simply didn't realize (because you weren't told) that supervising your subordinates' expense accounts was part of your responsibility. In that case, it may be understandable why you never call them to task about fudging their expense reports—why, in other words, no message got sent.

- **Encoding barrier—the message is not expressed correctly.** No doubt you've sometimes had difficulty trying to think of the correct word to express how you feel about something. If English is not your first language, perhaps, then you may have difficulty expressing to a supervisor, co-worker, or subordinate what it is you mean to say.

- **Medium barrier—the communication channel is blocked.** You never get through to someone because his or her phone always has a busy signal. The computer network is down and the email message you sent doesn't go through. These are instances of the communication medium being blocked.

- **Decoding barrier—the recipient doesn't understand the message.** Your boss tells you to "lighten up" or "buckle down," but because English is not your first language, you don't understand what the messages mean. Or perhaps you're afraid to show your ignorance when someone is throwing computer terms at you and says that your computer connection has "a bandwidth problem."

- **Receive barrier—no message gets received.** Because you were talking to a co-worker, you weren't listening when your supervisor announced today's work assignments, and so you have to ask him or her to repeat the announcement.

- **Feedback barrier—the recipient doesn't respond enough.** No doubt you've had the experience of giving someone street directions, but since they only nod their heads and don't repeat the directions back to you, you don't really know whether you were understood. The same thing can happen in many workplace circumstances.

SOURCE: A. Kinicki and B. Williams, *Management: A Practical Introduction*, 3rd ed. (Burr Ridge, IL: McGraw-Hill, 2008), p. 493.

Personal barriers

Any individual attribute that hinders communication.

Personal Barriers Have you ever communicated with someone and felt totally confused? This may have led you to wonder: is it them or is it me? *Personal barriers* represent any individual attributes that hinder communication. Let's examine nine common personal barriers that foster miscommunication.

1. **Variable skills in communicating effectively** Some people are simply better communicators than others. They have the speaking and listening skills, the ability to use gestures for dramatic effect, the vocabulary to alter the message to fit the audience, the writing skills to convey concepts in simple and concise terms, and the social skills to make others feel comfortable.[9] In contrast, others lack these skills. Don't worry, communication skills can be enhanced with training.[10]

2. **Variations in how information is processed and interpreted** Did you grow up in the country, in the suburbs, or in a city? Did you attend private or public school? What were your parents' attitudes toward you doing chores and playing sports? Are you from a loving home or one spoiled with fighting, yelling, and lack of structure? What is your gender? (See the Focus on Diversity feature box.) Answers to these questions are relevant because they make up the different frames of references and experiences people use to interpret the world around them. This means that these differences affect our interpretations of what we see and hear.

3. **Variations in interpersonal trust** Communication is more likely to be distorted when people do not trust each other. Rather than focusing on the message, a lack of trust is likely to cause people to be defensive and question the accuracy of what is being communicated.

4. **Stereotypes and prejudices** Stereotypes are over-simplified beliefs about specific groups of people. They potentially distort communication because their use causes people to misperceive and recall information. It is important for all of us to be aware of our potential stereotypes and to recognize that they may subconsciously affect the interpretation of a message.

5. **Big egos** Our egos, whether due to pride, self-esteem, superior ability, or arrogance, are a communication barrier. Egos can cause political battles, turf wars, and pursuit of power, credit, and resources. Egos influence how we treat others, as well as our receptiveness to being influenced by others. Have you ever had someone put you down in public? Then you know how ego can influence communication.

6. **Poor listening skills** How many times have you been in class when a student asks the same question that as asked minutes earlier? How about going to a party and meeting someone who only talks about himself or herself and never asks questions about you? This experience certainly doesn't make people feel important or memorable. It's hard to communicate effectively when one of the parties is not listening. We discuss listening skills in a later section of this chapter.

7. **Natural tendency to evaluate others' messages** What do you say to someone after watching the latest movie in a theatre? What did you think of the movie? The person might say, "It was great, best movie I've seen all year." You then may say, "I agree," or alternatively, "I disagree, that movie stunk." The point is that we all have a natural tendency, according to renowned psychologist Carl Rogers, to evaluate messages from our own point of view or frame of reference, particularly when we have strong feelings about the issue.[11]

8. **Inability to listen with understanding** Listening with understanding occurs when a receiver can "see the expressed idea and attitude from the other person's point of view, to sense how it feels to him, to achieve his frame of reference in regard to the thing he is talking about."[12] Try to listen with understanding; it will make you less defensive and can improve your accuracy in perceiving messages.

9. **Non-verbal communication** Communication accuracy is enhanced when facial expression and gestures are consistent with the intent of a message. Interestingly, people may not even be aware of this issue. More is said about this important aspect of communication later in this chapter.

Physical Barriers The distance between employees can interfere with effective communication. It is hard to understand someone who is speaking to you from 20 metres away. Time zone differences between the East

---

and West Coasts also represent physical barriers. Work and office noise are additional barriers. The quality of telephone lines or crashed computers represent physical barriers that impact our ability to communicate with information technology.

In spite of the general acceptance of physical barriers, they can be reduced. For example, employees from Atlantic Canada can agree to call their West Coast peers prior to leaving for lunch. In the case of small confining space that discourages communication, walls can be torn down; or if the office is too noisy, maybe doors can be installed or walls built to block it out. It is important that all employees attempt to manage the noise barrier around their work station or the situation in general by choosing a medium that optimally reduces the physical barrier at hand.

Semantic Barriers *Semantics* is the study of words. When your boss tells you, "We need to complete this project right away," what does it mean? Does "we" mean just you? You and your co-workers? Or you, your co-workers, and the boss? Does "right away" mean today, tomorrow, or next week? These are examples of semantic barriers. Semantic barriers show up as encoding and decoding errors because these phases of communication involve transmitting and receiving words and symbols. These barriers are partially fuelled by the use of slang ("that's cool!" means something is good) and acronyms ("I drive an SUV" means sports utility vehicle).[13]

Semantics
The study of words.

Jargon is another key semantic barrier. *Jargon* represents language or terminology that is specific to a particular profession, group, or company. The use of jargon has been increasing as our society becomes more technologically oriented. (For example, "The CIO wants the RFP to go out ASAP" means "The Chief Information Officer wants the Request for Proposal to go out as soon as possible.") It is important to remember that words that are ordinary to you may be mysterious to outsiders. If we want to be understood more clearly, it is important to carefully choose our language.

Jargon
Language or terminology that is specific to a particular profession, group, or company.

Semantic barriers are more likely in today's multicultural workforce. Their frequency is also fuelled by the growing trend to outsource customer service operations to foreign countries, particularly India. Unfortunately, some North Americans are incensed over having to communicate with customer-service employees working in such call centres. Consider the message that Mitul Pandley, a specialist working in a call centre located in India, received from a customer living in the U.S.: "I wish not to have anyone from India or any foreign country or anyone with an Indian accent or foreign accent continue handling my case."[14] Such shallow thinking as this presents a huge barrier to communication.

Semantic barriers also are related to the choice of words we use when communicating. Consider the case of using profanity at work.

> Ann Garcia had to thread the needle. On the one hand, the No. 1 executive at her former company hated the use of profanity, seeing it as a sign of not having learned to communicate effectively. On the other hand, the No. 2 executive appreciated a potty mouth now and then because it indicated passion. He "felt that if you weren't swearing, you probably didn't care enough," says Ms. Garcia. As it happened, there weren't clashes over profanity, so much as careful navigation of the office's language protocol. "When groups reported to the executive who was pro-profanity," it was acceptable, says Ms. Garcia. "With units who reported to the other one, things were very buttoned up."[15]

Also, it is important to note that the use of profanity is offensive to some people, and its use can create emotional responses that interfere with effective communication.

Choosing our words more carefully is the easiest way to reduce semantic barriers. This barrier can also be decreased by attentiveness to mixed messages and cultural diversity. Mixed messages occur when people's words imply one message while their actions or non-verbal cues suggest something different. Obviously, understanding is enhanced when a person's actions and non-verbal cues match the verbal message.

CHOOSING MEDIA: A CONTINGENCY PERSPECTIVE

In this section, we turn our attention to discussing the how of the communication process. Specifically, Figure 7.2 helps us examine how employees and managers can determine the best method or medium to use when communicating across the various formal and informal channels of communication.

Employees can choose from many different types of communication media (telephone, email, voice mail, cell phone, express mail, instant messaging, video, and so forth). Fortunately, research tells us that employees can help reduce information overload and improve communication effectiveness through their choice of communication media. If people use an inappropriate medium, then decisions may be based on inaccurate information, important messages may not reach the intended audience, and employees may become dissatisfied and unproductive. Consider Marnie Puritz Stone's reaction to the inappropriate use of email.

"All communications regarding hiring and firings were sent via email," Stone explains. Her managers may have felt they were being efficient, but she and her colleagues thought the managers were rude. *"I think that callousness with which [some] email delivers news—good or bad—is a poor way to show leadership,"* she says, *"And it creates a lot of resentment."*

Stone's manager created even more resentment when it came to providing feedback, which was done mostly through email. *"I was reprimanded via email, which was really bad,"* she recalls, *"Criticism via email leaves you very belittled since you can't respond."[16]*

This example illustrates that media selection is a key component of communication effectiveness. The following section explores a contingency model designed to help all employees select communication media in a systematic and effective manner. Media selection in this model is based on the interaction between information richness and difficulty of the problem/situation at hand.

> "I think that callousness with which [some] email delivers news—good or bad—is a poor way to show leadership . . . and it creates a lot of resentment."

Information Richness Respected organizational theorists Richard Daft and Robert Lengel define *information richness* in the following manner:

> *Richness is defined as the potential information-carrying capacity of data. If the communication of an item of data, such as a wink, provides substantial new understanding, it would be considered rich. If the (standard position) provides little understanding, it would be low in richness.[17]*

Information richness

Information-carrying capacity of data.

As this definition implies, alternative media possess levels of information richness that vary from rich to lean.

Information richness is based on four factors: (1) feedback (ranging from fast to very slow), (2) channel (ranging from the combined visual and audio characteristics of a video conference to the limited visual aspects of a computer report), (3) type of communication (ranging from personal to impersonal), and (4) language source (ranging from the natural body language and speech

▶ **FIGURE 7.2**   Contingency Model for Selecting Communication Media

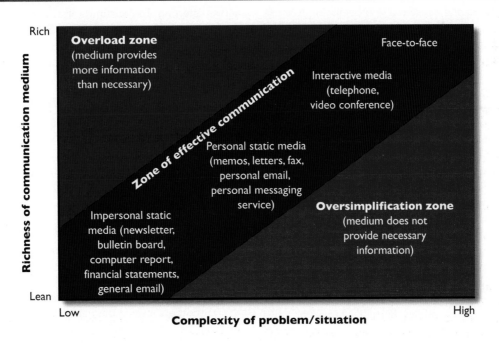

SOURCES: Adapted from R. Lengel and R.L. Daft, "The Selection of Communication Media as an Executive Skill," *Academy of Management Executive*, August 1988, p 226, and R.L. Daft and R.H. Lengel, "Information Richness: A New Approach to Managerial Behavior and Organization Design," *Research in Organizational Behavior*, eds B.M. Staw and L.L. Cummings (Greenwich, CT: JAI Press, 1984), p 199.

contained in a face-to-face conversation to the numbers contained in a financial statement).

Face-to-face is the richest form of communication. It provides immediate feedback and allows for the observation of multiple language cues, such as body language and tone of voice. Although high in richness, telephone and video conferencing are not as informative as the face-to-face medium. In contrast, newsletters, computer reports, and general email are lean media because feedback is very slow, the channels involve only limited visual information, and the information provided is generic or impersonal.

Contingency Recommendations The contingency model for selecting media is graphically shown in Figure 7.2. As shown, there are three zones of communication effectiveness. Effective communication occurs when the richness of the medium is matched appropriately with the complexity of the problem or situation. Media low in richness—impersonal static and personal static—are better suited for simple problems; media high in richness—interactive media and face-to-face—are appropriate for complex situations. Sun Microsystems, for example, followed this recommendation when communicating with employees about upcoming layoffs. The organization used a series of face-to-face sessions to deliver the bad news and provided managers with a set of slides and speaking points to help distribute the necessary information.[18]

On the other hand, ineffective communication occurs when the richness of the medium is either too high or too low for the complexity of the problem or situation. For example, district sales managers would fall into the overload zone if they communicated monthly sales reports through richer media. Conducting face-to-face meetings or telephoning each salesperson would provide excessive information and take more time than necessary.

The oversimplification zone represents another ineffective choice of communication medium. In this situation, media with inadequate richness are used to communicate complicated or emotional issues. For example, Radio Shack Corporation (store now called The Source) used email to notify 400 employees at its headquarters that they were being let go. Worse yet, a London-based body-piercing and jewellery store used a text message to fire an employee. This choice of medium is ineffective in this context because it does not preserve privacy and it does not allow employees to ask questions. Further, dismissing employees in this manner can lower morale among remaining employees and damage a company's image.[19]

Research Evidence The relationship between media richness and problem/situation complexity has not been extensively researched because the underlying theory is relatively new. Available evidence indicates that employees and managers used richer sources when confronted with ambiguous (can be interpreted more than one way) and complicated events, and miscommunication was increased when rich media were used to transmit information that was traditionally communicated through lean media.[20] Moreover, a meta-analysis of more than 40 studies revealed that media usage was significantly different across organizational levels. Upper-level executives/managers spent more time in face-to-face meetings than did lower-level managers.[21] This finding is consistent with recommendations that flow from the contingency model just discussed.

Interpersonal Communication

The quality of interpersonal communication within an organization is very important. People with good communication skills help groups to make more innovative decisions and are promoted more frequently than individuals with less developed abilities.[22] But what does it mean to have good communication skills? It can mean several things; there is no universally-accepted definition. Therefore, we are going to focus on the five factors that are under your control: assertiveness, aggressiveness, non-assertiveness, non-verbal communication, and active listening. To get things started, complete the Self-Assessment Exercise "What Is Your Business Etiquette?" Being sensitive to such items can be considered as a fundamental aspect of good communication.

ASSERTIVENESS, AGGRESSIVENESS, AND NON-ASSERTIVENESS

LO 3

The saying "You can attract more flies with honey than with vinegar" captures the difference between using an assertive communication style and an aggressive style. Research studies indicate that assertiveness is more effective than aggressiveness in both work-related and consumer contexts.[23] An **assertive style** is expressive and self-enhancing and is based on the "ethical notion that it is not right or good to violate our own or others' basic human rights, such as the right to self-expression or the right to be treated with dignity and respect."[24] In contrast, an **aggressive style** is expressive and self-enhancing, and strives to take unfair

Assertive style

Expressive and self-enhancing behaviour, but does not take advantage of others.

Aggressive style

Expressive and self-enhancing behaviour, but takes unfair advantage of others.

What Is Your Business Etiquette?

INSTRUCTIONS: Business etiquette is one component of communication competence. Test your business etiquette by answering the following questions. After circling your response for each item, calculate your score by reviewing the correct answers. Next, use the norms at the end of the test to interpret your results.

1. The following is an example of a proper introduction: "Ms. Boss, I'd like you to meet our client, Mr. Smith."

   True   False

2. If someone forgets to introduce you, you shouldn't introduce yourself, you should just let the conversation continue.

   True   False

3. If you forget someone's name, you should keep talking and hope no one will notice. This way you don't embarrass yourself or the person you are talking to.

   True   False

4. When shaking hands, a man should wait for a woman to extend her hand.

   True   False

5. Who goes through a revolving door first?

   a. Host   b. Visitor

6. It is all right to hold private conversations, either in person or on a cell phone, in office bathrooms, elevators, and other public spaces.

   True   False

7. When two Canadian businesspeople are talking to one another, the space between them should be approximately

   a. 0.5 metre   b. 1 metre   c. 2 metres

8. Business casual attire requires socks for men and hose for women.

   True   False

9. To signal that you do not want a glass of wine, you should turn your wine glass upside down.

   True   False

10. If a call is disconnected, it's the caller's responsibility to redial.

    True   False

11. When using a speakerphone, you should tell the caller if there is anyone else in the room.

    True   False

12. You should change your voice mail message if you are going to be out of the office.

    True   False

Answers

1. **False.** Clients always take precedence, and people with the greatest authority or importance should be introduced first.
2. **False.** You should introduce yourself. Say something like "My name is _____. I don't believe we've met."
3. **False.** It's OK to admit you can't remember. Say something like "My mind just went blank, your name is?" Or offer your name and wait for the other person to respond with his or hers.
4. **False.** Business etiquette has become gender neutral.
5. **a. Host.** This enables the host to lead his or her guest to the meeting place.
6. **False.** Not only is it rude to invade public areas with your conversation, but you never know who might hear details of your business transaction or personal life.
7. **b. 1 metre.** Closer than this is an invasion of personal space. Farther away forces people to raise their voices. Because communication varies from country to country, you should also inform yourself about cultural differences.
8. **True.** An exception to this would be if your company holds an event at the beach or the pool.
9. **False.** Just wave your hand over it when asked, or say "No thank you."
10. **True.** The person who initiated the call should redial if the connection is broken.
11. **True.** If you must use a speakerphone, you should inform all parties who's present.
12. **True.** You should record a greeting such as "I'm out of the office today, March 12. If you need help, please dial _____ at extension _____"

Arbitrary Norms

Low business etiquette (0–4 correct): Consider buying an etiquette book or hiring a coach to help you polish your professional image.

Moderate business etiquette (5–8 correct): Look for a role model or mentor, and look for ways you can improve your business etiquette.

High business etiquette (9–12 correct): Good for you. You should continue to practise good etiquette and look for ways to maintain your professional image.

SOURCE: Adapted from material contained in M. Brody, "Test Your Etiquette," *Training & Development*, February 2002, pp 64–66. Copyright © February 2002 from *Training & Development* by M. Brody. Reprinted with permission of American Society for Training & Development.

advantage of others. A ***non-assertive style*** is characterized by timid and self-denying behaviour. Non-assertiveness is ineffective because it gives the other person an unfair advantage.

Employees may improve their communication competence by trying to be more assertive and less aggressive or non-assertive. This can be achieved by using the appropriate non-verbal and verbal behaviours listed in Table 7.2. For instance, managers should attempt to use the non-verbal behaviours of good eye contact, a strong, steady, and audible voice, and selective interruptions. They should avoid non-verbal behaviours such as glaring or little eye contact, threatening gestures, slumped posture, and a weak or whiny voice. Appropriate verbal behaviours

include direct and unambiguous language and the use of "I" messages instead of "you" statements. For example, when you say, "Mike, I was disappointed with your report because it contained typographical errors," rather than "Mike, your report was poorly done," you reduce defensiveness. "I" statements describe your feelings about someone's performance or behaviour instead of laying blame on the person. We'll spend more time discussing the language of conflict, the "I" vs. "you" pronoun consideration, in the next chapter.

SOURCES OF NON-VERBAL COMMUNICATION

Non-verbal communication is "Any message, sent or received independent of the written or spoken word. [It] includes such factors as use of time and space, distance between persons when conversing

TABLE 7.2	**Communication Styles**		
COMMUNICATION STYLE	DESCRIPTION	NON-VERBAL BEHAVIOUR PATTERN	VERBAL BEHAVIOUR PATTERN
Assertive	Pushing hard without attacking; permits others to influence outcome; expressive and self-enhancing without intruding on others	• Good eye contact • Comfortable but firm posture • Strong, steady, and audible voice • Facial expressions matched to message	• Direct but not forceful and unambiguous language • No attributions or evaluations of other's behaviour • Appropriately serious tone • Selective interruptions to ensure understanding • Use of "I" statements and cooperative "we" statements
Aggressive	Taking advantage of others; expressive and self-enhancing at other's expense	• Glaring eye contact • Moving or leaning too close • Threatening gestures (pointed finger; clenched fist) • Loud voice • Frequent interruptions	• Swear words and abusive language • Attributions and evaluations of other's behaviour • Sexist or racist terms • Explicit threats or put-downs
Non-assertive	Encouraging others to take advantage of us; inhibited; self-denying	• Little eye contact • Downward glances • Slumped posture • Constantly shifting weight • Wringing hands • Weak or whiny voice	• Qualifiers ("maybe"; "kind of") • Fillers ("uh," "you know," "well") • Negaters ("It's not really that important"; "I'm not sure")

SOURCE: Adapted in part from J.A. Waters, "Managerial Assertiveness," *Business Horizons*, September–October 1982, pp 24–29.

(talking), use of colour, dress, walking behaviour, standing, positioning, seating arrangement, office locations and furnishings."[25]

Experts estimate that 65 percent to 90 percent of every conversation is partially interpreted through non-verbal communication.[26] It is therefore important to ensure that your non-verbal signals are consistent with your intended verbal messages. Because of the prevalence of non-verbal communication and its significant effect on organizational behaviour (including, but not limited to, perceptions of others, hiring decisions, work attitudes, turnover, and the acceptance of one's ideas in a presentation), it is important that all employees become consciously aware of the sources of non-verbal communication.

Body Movements and Gestures Body movements, such as leaning forward or backward, and gestures, such as pointing, provide additional non-verbal information that can either enhance or detract from the communication process. Open body positions, such as legs that are not crossed and arms relaxed along the side, communicate openness, warmth, and availability for communication. *Defensiveness* is communicated by gestures such as folded arms, crossed hands, and crossed legs. Although it is both easy and fun to interpret body movements and gestures, it is important to remember that body-language analysis is subjective, easily misinterpreted, and highly dependent on the context and cross-cultural differences.[27] As a result, all employees need to be careful when trying to interpret body movements. Inaccurate interpretations can create additional "noise" in the communication process.

Touch Touching is another powerful non-verbal cue. People tend to touch those they like. A meta-analysis of gender differences in touching indicated that women do more touching during conversations than men.[28] Touching conveys an impression of warmth and caring and can be used to create a personal bond between people. Be careful about touching people from diverse cultures, however, as norms for touching vary significantly around the world.[29]

Facial Expressions Facial expressions convey a wealth of information. Smiling, for instance, typically represents warmth, happiness, or friendship, whereas frowning conveys dissatisfaction or anger. Do you think these interpretations apply to different cross-cultural groups? A summary of relevant research revealed that the association between facial expressions and emotions varies across cultures.[30] A smile, for example, does not convey the same emotion in different countries. Therefore, managers, supervisors and team leaders need to be careful in interpreting facial expressions among diverse groups of employees.

Eye Contact Eye contact is a strong non-verbal cue that varies across cultures. Westerners are taught at an early age to look at their parents when spoken to. In contrast, Asians are taught to avoid eye contact with a parent or superior to show obedience and subservience.[31] Once again, supervisors should be sensitive to different orientations toward maintaining eye contact with diverse employees.

Practical Tips It is important to have good non-verbal communication skills in light of the fact that they are related to the development of positive interpersonal relationships. Communication experts offer the following advice to improve non-verbal communication skills:[32]

Positive non-verbal actions that help communication:

- Maintaining appropriate eye contact

- Occasionally using affirmative nods to indicate agreement

- Smiling and showing interest

- Leaning slightly toward the speaker

- Keeping your voice low and relaxed

- Being aware of your facial expressions

Actions to avoid:

- Licking your lips or playing with your hair or moustache

- Turning away from the person you are communicating with

- Closing your eyes and displaying uninterested facial expressions such as yawning

- Excessively moving in your chair or tapping your feet

- Using an unpleasant tone and speaking too quickly or too slowly

- Biting your nails, picking your teeth, or constantly adjusting your glasses

ACTIVE LISTENING

Some communication experts contend that listening is the keystone communication skill for employees involved in sales, customer service, or management. In support of this conclusion, listening effectiveness was positively associated with customer satisfaction and negatively associated with employee intentions to quit. Poor communication between employees and management was also cited as a primary cause of employee discontent and turnover.[33] Listening skills are particularly important for all of us because we spend a great deal of time listening to others.

Listening involves much more than hearing a message. Hearing is merely the physical component of listening. **Listening** is the process of *actively* decoding and interpreting verbal messages. Listening requires cognitive attention and information processing; hearing does not. With these distinctions in mind, we examine listening styles and offer some practical advice for becoming a more effective listener.

Listening

Actively decoding and interpreting verbal messages.

Listening Styles Communication experts believe that people listen with a preferred listening style. While people may lean toward one dominant listening style, we tend to use a combination of two or three. There are five dominant listening styles: appreciative, empathetic, comprehensive, discerning, and evaluative.[34] Let us consider each style.

Appreciative listeners listen in a relaxed manner, preferring to listen for pleasure, entertainment, or inspiration. They tend to tune out speakers who provide no amusement or humour in their communications. *Empathetic* listeners interpret messages by focusing on the emotions and body language being displayed by the speaker, as well as the presentation media. They also tend to listen without judging. *Comprehensive* listeners make sense of a message by first organizing specific thoughts and actions and then integrating this information by focusing on relationships among ideas. These listeners prefer logical presentations without interruptions. *Discerning* listeners attempt to understand the main message and determine important points. They like to take notes and prefer logical presentations. Finally, *evaluative* listeners listen analytically and continually formulate arguments and challenges to what is being said. They tend to accept or reject messages based on personal beliefs, ask a lot of questions, and can become interruptive.

You can improve your listening skills by first becoming aware of the effectiveness of the different listening styles you use in various situations. This awareness can then help you to modify your style to fit a specific situation. For example, if you are watching the comedy channel on TV, then an appreciative style would be appropriate. If you are a journalist hired to cover an upcoming debate between the candidates running for prime minister, then you may want to focus on using a comprehensive and discerning style. In contrast, an evaluative style may be more appropriate if you are listening to a sales presentation.[35]

Informal communication channel

Does not follow the chain of command or legitimate organizational structure.

Becoming a More Effective Listener Effective listening is a learned skill that requires effort and motivation. That's right; it takes energy and desire to really listen to others. Unfortunately, it may seem like there are no rewards for listening, but there are negative consequences when we don't. Think of a time, for example, when someone did not pay attention to you by looking at his or her watch or doing some other activity, such as typing on a keyboard. How did you feel? You may have felt put down, unimportant, or offended. In turn, such feelings can erode the quality of interpersonal relationships, as well as fuel job dissatisfaction, lower productivity, and result in poor customer service. Listening is an important skill that can be improved by avoiding the 10 habits of bad listeners, while cultivating the 10 good listening habits (see Table 7.3).

In addition, a communication expert suggests that we can all improve our listening skills by adhering to the following three fundamental recommendations:[36]

1. Attend closely to what's being said, not to what you want to say next.

2. Allow others to finish speaking before taking our turn.

3. Repeat back what you've heard to give the speaker the opportunity to clarify the message.

THE GRAPEVINE

LO 4

There are two types of communication channels within an organization: formal and informal. The formal channels are authorized and used by all employees in a common and open manner. Formal channels follow structural etiquette in a public manner; as a result, the process takes time to "get the message out." Examples include staff notices, public forums, minutes of meetings, client briefing reports, and all other types of documents approved and/or written by management. Information received through formal channels can be considered accurate.

An **informal communication channel** does not follow the chain of command; it skips management levels and bypasses lines of authority. The **grapevine** represents the unofficial communication system of the organization and covers all types of communication media. For example, people can just as easily pass along information with email, face-to-face conversations, or telephone calls. Although the grapevine can be a source of inaccurate rumours, it functions

Grapevine

Unofficial communication system that follows no chain of authority or formal structure.

The Keys to Effective Listening

KEYS TO EFFECTIVE LISTENING	THE BAD LISTENER	THE GOOD LISTENER
1. Capitalize on thought speed	Tends to daydream	Stays with the speaker, mentally summarizes the message, weighs evidence, and listens between the lines
2. Listen for ideas	Listens for facts	Listens for central or overall ideas
3. Find an area of interest	Tunes out dry speakers or subjects	Listens for any useful information
4. Judge content, not delivery	Tunes out dry or monotone speakers	Assesses content by listening to entire message before making judgments
5. Hold your fire	Gets too emotional or worked up by something said by the speaker and enters into an argument	Withholds judgment until comprehension is complete
6. Work at listening	Does not expend energy on listening	Gives the speaker full attention
7. Resist distractions	Is easily distracted	Fights distractions and concentrates on the speaker
8. Hear what is said	Shuts out or denies unfavourable information	Listens to both favourable and unfavourable information
9. Challenge yourself	Resists listening to presentations of difficult subject matter	Treats complex presentations as exercise for the mind
10. Use handouts, overheads, or other visual aids	Does not take notes or pay attention to visual aids	Takes notes as required and uses visual aids to enhance understanding of the presentation

TABLE 7.3

SOURCES: Derived from N. Skinner, "Communication Skills," *Selling Power*, July/August 1999, pp 32–34; and G. Manning, K. Curtis, and S. McMillen, *Building the Human Side of Work Community* (Cincinnati, OH: Thomson Executive Press, 1996), pp 127–54.

positively as an early warning signal for organizational changes, a way to create organizational changes and to embed organizational culture, a mechanism for fostering group cohesiveness, and a way to get employee and customer feedback. For example, research shows that employees and consumers use the grapevine as a frequent source of information. Its use has increased with the advent of the Internet and instant messaging. Marketing experts refer to this as word-of-mouth advertising.[37]

People who consistently pass along grapevine information to others are called *liaison individuals* or gossips:

> About 10 percent of the employees on an average grapevine will be highly active participants. They serve as liaisons with the rest of the staff members who receive information but spread it to only a few other people. Usually these liaisons are friendly, outgoing people who are in positions that allow them to cross departmental lines.[38]

Liaison individuals

Those who consistently pass along grapevine information to others.

Informal communication channels bypass formal lines of authority to exchange information. The grapevine is part of this informal channel.

Effective managers monitor the pulse of work groups by regularly communicating with known liaisons.

In contrast to liaison individuals, **organizational moles** use the grapevine for a different purpose. They obtain information, often negative, to enhance their power and status. They do this by secretly reporting their perceptions and hearsay about the difficulties, conflicts, or failure of other employees to people with influence within the organization. This enables moles to switch attention away from themselves and to position themselves as more capable than others. Management should attempt to create an open, trusting environment that discourages mole behaviour, because moles can destroy teamwork, create conflict, and impair productivity.

Although research activity on this topic has slowed in recent years, past research about the grapevine provided the following insights: (1) it is faster than formal channels; (2) it is about 75 percent accurate; (3) people rely on it when they are insecure, threatened, or faced with organizational changes; and (4) employees use the grapevine to acquire the majority of their on-the-job information.[39]

The key recommendation for all employees is to understand the grapevine and listen to what is going on within it to remain informed. However, do not participate in it, otherwise you become part of the problem. For managers, the same advice applies, plus one additional recommendation: Do not try and control the grapevine—there are too many variables to keep track of, and it's a waste of energy. Besides, there are other more important things to do for the organization.

Organizational moles

Those who use the grapevine to enhance their power and status.

Communication in the Age of Information Technology

The use of computers and information technology is dramatically affecting many aspects of organizational behaviour. Consider, for example, how Bill Gates, chairman and chief software architect at Microsoft, is using information technology to change the way he works.

On my desk I have three screens, synchronized to form a single desktop. I can drag items from one screen to the next. Once you have that large display area, you'll never go back, because it has a direct impact on productivity. The screen on the left has my list of emails. On the center screen is usually the specific email I'm reading and responding to. And my browser is on the right-hand screen. This setup gives me the ability to glance and see what new message has come in while I'm working on something, and to bring up a link that's related to an email and look at it while the email is still in front of me ... Paper is no longer a big part of my day.[40]

You might expect that someone as closely linked to paperless technology as Bill Gates, Chairman of Microsoft, would rely almost entirely on electric forms of communication. And you'd be right. Says Gates, "Paper is no longer a big part of my day."

Bill Gates is not the only person using information technology to improve his productivity. A recent study of 2,032 youth by the Kaiser Family Foundation suggests that young people are also multi-tasking and spending a great deal of time using electronics. Results revealed that "8- to 18-year-olds live media-saturated lives, spending 44.5 hours a week with electronics. The 6.5 hours a day compares with 2.25 hours spent with parents, 1.5 hours spent in physical activity, and just 50 minutes on homework."[41] These statistics have long-range implications: these young people will soon be the in workplace, and how they'll prefer to communicate will be far different from what is taking place now.

The age of information technology is radically changing communication patterns in both our personal and work lives. For example, recent statistics reveal that 69 percent of the population in North America uses the Internet. Cross-culturally, this percentage is higher than the percentage of the population using the Internet in Africa (3 percent), Asia (10 percent), Europe

(36 percent), Middle East (10 percent), Latin America/ Caribbean (14 percent), and Oceania/Australia (53 percent).[42] Interestingly, 30 percent of Internet users go online on any particular day simply to have fun or pass the time.[43] This section explores key components of information technology that influence communication patterns and management within a computerized workplace: Internet/intranet/extranet, electronic mail, hand-held devices, blogs, video conferencing, group support systems, and teleworking.

INTERNET/INTRANET/EXTRANET

Internet

A global network of computer networks.

The Internet, or more simply, the Net, is more than a computer network. It is a network of computer networks. The *Internet* is a global network of independently operating but interconnected computers. The Internet connects everything from supercomputers to large mainframes in businesses, government, colleges, and universities, to the personal computers in our homes and offices. An *intranet* is nothing more than an organization's private Internet. Intranets also have *firewalls* that block outside Internet users from accessing internal information. This is done to protect the privacy and confidentiality of company documents. In contrast to the internal focus of an intranet,

Intranet

An organization's private Internet.

Extranet

Connects internal employees with selected customers, suppliers, and strategic partners.

an *extranet* is an extended intranet that connects internal employees with selected customers, suppliers, and other strategic partners. Ford Motor Company, for instance, has an extranet that connects its dealers worldwide. Ford's extranet was set up to help support the sales and servicing of cars and to enhance customer satisfaction.

The primary benefit of the Internet, intranets, and extranets is that they can enhance the ability of employees to find, create, manage, and distribute information. The effectiveness of these systems, however, depends on how organizations set up and manage their intranet/extranet and how employees use the acquired information, because information by itself cannot solve or do anything. For example, communication effectiveness can actually decrease if a corporate intranet becomes a dumping ground for unorganized information. In this case, employees will find themselves drowning in a sea of information. To date, however, no rigorous research studies have been conducted that directly demonstrate productivity increases from using the Internet, intranets, or extranets.

ELECTRONIC MAIL

Electronic mail, or email, uses the Internet/intranet to send computer-generated text and documents between people. The use of email is on the rise throughout the world. Email is becoming a major communication medium because of four key benefits:

Electronic mail

Uses the Internet/intranet to send computer-generated text and documents.

1. Email reduces the cost of distributing information to a large number of employees.

2. Email is a tool for increasing teamwork. It enables employees to quickly send messages to colleagues on the next floor, in another building, or in another country.

3. Email reduces the costs and time associated with print duplication and paper distribution. One management expert estimated that these savings can total $9,000 a year per employee.[44]

4. Email fosters flexibility. This is particularly true for employees with a portable computer, because they can log onto email whenever and wherever they want. Wireless technology and handheld devices enhance the flexibility of email.

In spite of these positive benefits, there are also four key drawbacks to consider. First, sending and receiving email can lead to a lot of wasted time and effort, or it can distract employees from completing critical job duties. Second, people overestimate their ability to effectively communicate via email.[45] Further, people have a tendency to write things in an email that they would not say in person. This can lead to negative interactions and defensiveness.

Information overload is the third problem associated with the increased use of email: People tend to send more messages to others, and there is a lot of "spamming" going on (sending junk mail, bad jokes, chain letters, or irrelevant memos). Nucleus Research estimated that 75 percent of all email traffic in 2004 was spam.[46] Going through junk email clearly wastes a lot of productivity time for many employees. The Skills & Best Practices feature box contains suggestions for managing email overload.

Finally, preliminary evidence suggests that people are using electronic mail to communicate when they should be using other media, resulting in reduced communication effectiveness. A four-year study of communication patterns within an organization of higher learning demonstrated that the increased use of electronic mail was associated with decreased face-to-face interactions

Skills & Best Practices

Managing Your Email

1 Scan first, read second.

2 Learn to delete without reading. Over time, you will get a sense for low-value messages and you should be able to delete messages from unrecognizable addresses.

3 Group messages by topic. Read the first message in a series and then go to the most recent. This enables you to save time by skipping emails between the first and last message.

4 Once steps 1–3 are complete, prioritize your inbox and respond in order of the message's importance.

5 Stop the madness by asking people to stop sending you unimportant messages.

6 Rather than continuing to engage in ping-pong emailing, determine if a phone call can get to the heart of the matter.

7 Get off cc lists. Ask to be removed from distribution lists.

8 Only respond to a message when it is absolutely required.

9 Keep messages brief and clear. Use clear subject headings and state the purpose of your email in the first sentence or paragraph.

10 Avoid the "reply to all" feature.

11 If the message concerns a volatile or critical matter, email is probably the wrong medium to use. Consider using the phone.

SOURCE: These recommendations were taken from C. Cavanagh, *Managing Your E-Mail: Thinking Outside the Inbox*, Copyright © 2003 John Wiley & Sons, Inc. Reprinted with permission of John Wiley & Sons, Inc.

and with a drop in the overall amount of organization communication. Employees also expressed feelings of being less connected and less cohesive as a department as the number of emails increased.[47] This interpersonal "disconnection" may be caused by the trend of replacing everyday face-to-face interactions with electronic messages. It is important to remember that employees' social needs are satisfied through the many different interpersonal interactions that occur at work.

There are three additional issues to consider when using email: (1) email only works when the party you desire to communicate with also uses it—email may not be a viable communication medium in all cases; (2) the speed of getting a response to an email message is dependent on how frequently the receiver examines his or her messages—it is important to consider this issue when picking a communication medium; and (3) many companies do not have policies for using email, which can lead to misuse and potential legal liability (e.g., four female employees working at Chevron filed a suit claiming that they were sexually harassed through email; the company settled for $2.2 million, plus legal fees and court costs). Do not

> "He fires off emails, checks stock prices—and recently plowed through the novel *The DaVinci Code*. But staring at the two-inch screen is taking its toll on Mr. Kwak's eyes."

assume that your email messages are private and confidential. Organizations are advised to develop policies regarding the use of email.[48]

HANDHELD DEVICES

As Canadians, we have to be proud of our international reputation as the country that created the BlackBerry, sometimes called the "crackberry" because of its addictive quality. It's interesting to observe pictures in the media of world leaders, NBA superstars, and Hollywood actors using their Canadian-made BlackBerry. This handheld device, which is also referred to as a PDA (personal digital assistant), offers users the portability to do work from any location. It is used by millions of people and was designed to allow users to multi-task from any location. For example, you can use PDAs to make and track appointments, do word processing, crunch numbers on a spreadsheet, check out favourite tunes and video clips, receive and send email, organize photos, play games, and complete a variety of other tasks.[49] Research In Motion, the Waterloo-based manufacturer of the BlackBerry, together with other PDA manufacturers, claim that the combination of portability and multi-tasking features enable people to be more efficient and productive. The question from an OB perspective is whether or not these devices actually lead to higher productivity.

There are concerns over increased pressure to multi-task, and about the level of increased errors, shorter attention spans, greater stress, and general cognitive overload. In addition to drawbacks associated with multi-tasking, using handheld devices has produced physical ailments for some users. Consider the experiences of Chris Kwak and Helena Bell. Chris Kwak, a 31-year-old financial planner, spends several hours each day looking at his handheld computer. "He fires off emails, checks stock prices—and recently plowed through the novel *The Da Vinci Code*. But staring at the two-inch screen is taking its toll on Mr. Kwak's eyes. He regularly pops Tylenol to dull the headaches he gets from focusing on the tiny font he has chosen for his device." Twenty-four-year-old Helena Bell "says that even scrolling through an iPod song menu makes her eyes feel sore." She ultimately abandoned her handheld device because of eye strain.[50] Producers of these devices are currently experimenting with alternative ways to alleviate these eye problems.

Given these considerations, we wonder why sales of handheld devices continue to explode. Psychology professor David Meyer offers one potential explanation. He notes that the use of PDAs activates our dopamine-reward system, which induces a pleasurable state for approximately 6 percent of the population. Dr Meyer says that this effect is clinically addictive.[51] Alternatively, people may view these devices as one way to cope with increasing pressures to accomplish more in the face of ever-increasing informational demands. In the end, time and additional research will determine the actual value of handheld devices.

BLOGS AND SOCIAL NETWORKING

Blogs A *blog* is an online journal in which people write whatever they want about any topic. Blogging is one of the latest Internet trends. Experts estimate that there are around 23.7 million blogs in existence, and 70,000 new ones pop up every day.[52] Current technology also allows people to blog on cell phones. The benefits of blogs include the opportunity for people to discuss issues in a casual format. These discussions serve much like a chat group, and thus provide managers with insights from a wide segment of the employee and customer base, as well as the general public. Blogs give people the opportunity to air their opinions, grievances, and creative ideas. Fanshawe College President Dr. Howard Rundle has

Blog

Online journal in which people comment on any topic.

been using his management blog site since 2008 to discuss important work issues with community stakeholders, communicate new programming initiatives to parents and potential students, as well as boost morale and show support for faculty.[53] Companies with blogs include Microsoft, Hewlett-Packard, and Sun Microsystems, as well as *The Globe and Mail* (*Report on Business*), the CBC, and Scouts Canada.[54]

Blogs also have pitfalls. One entails the lack of legal and organizational guidelines regarding what can be posted online. For example, flight attendant Ellen Simonetti and Google employee Mark Jen were both fired as a result of the information they included on their blogs. Simonetti posted suggestive pictures of herself in uniform, and Jen commented about his employer's finances.[55] Another involves the potential for employees to say unflattering things about their employer and to leak confidential information. Finally, one can waste a lot of time reading silly and unsubstantiated postings. For example, a recent study showed that 25 percent of employees read blogs at work, losing approximately 9 percent of their work week.[56]

We encourage organizations to develop policies around blogging, and encourage executives to become more familiar with blogs as a tool for communicating with employees, shareholders, and the market. Overall, we cannot make any conclusions regarding the effectiveness of blogs as communication, marketing, or managerial tools, because no research has been done to date. Once again, time will tell.

Social Networking *Social networking* is a type of communication that allows people to exchange information, share common interests, and display their personal information with others on Web sites that are open to all or by invitation only. Facebook, MySpace, and LinkedIn are just three popular examples of literally dozens of such sites that now exist on the World Wide Web. Today, millions of individuals around the world use these network sites to connect to others for personal and business purposes. As we've discussed throughout the first two units of this text, professional relationships are established in many ways in the workforce. Social networking Web sites can assist and ease the development of these business relationships. However, the connections you make can blur the line between professional and personal. Because of this, and the extreme popularity of such sites, they are now getting the attention of employers and legal experts alike (see International OB feature box).

Social networking

Virtual communities of individuals who share common interests and personal information on Web sites open to all or by invitation only.

WHAT PART OF THE SOCIAL NETWORK SITE DOES THE EMPLOYER OWN?

A U.K. court recently ordered an ex-employee of a recruitment firm to disclose details of his profile, business contacts, and emails at his social networking site, LinkedIn, to his former employer. The ex-employee had invited his employer's customers to join his network while he was still in their employ. The employer claimed those contacts belonged to them. He allegedly used his LinkedIn network to approach customers for his own rival business, which had been set up a few weeks before the end of his employment. The starting point is that customer lists are the employer's property, and employees and former employees should use them for their employer's purposes, not personal gain. The situation is not unlike information in a company database, or whether duplicates are kept by the employee on a social network site or by some means not controlled by the company. The blurring of work and personal via social network sites makes it difficult to determine who owns what. The lesson in this case is for all to think about how employees use social media for business purposes, and for employers to consider communicating the expectations that go along with it.

EXCERPT: D. Canton, "Who Owns Your Facebook Friends?" Today's Business Law, *The London Free Press*, September 8, 2008, Business, p 10.

Sociologist professor Jeannette Sutton has identified an emerging trend among social networking sites as they become "a tool for people to instantly share their grief. What we've seen in disaster research for 60 years is that people converge to a disaster, but now we're seeing them converge online."[57] The networks are also helping communication during disasters as trapped employees within offices are communicating with outside friends and emergency personnel for rescue strategies; this was the case in the school shooting in Winnenden, Germany in 2009, as well as during the terrorist attacks in the financial capital of Mumbai, India in the fall of 2008. In addition, Toronto Mayor David Miller has been using Twitter for a while now; he says his city uses social media to add to the ways it already reaches citizens during emergencies.[58]

Once again, we recommend an overall organizational policy addressing the use of social network sites by employees.

VIDEO CONFERENCING

Video conferencing, also known as teleconferencing, uses video and audio links along with computers to enable people in different locations to see, hear, and talk with one another. This enables people from many locations to conduct a meeting without having to travel. Video conferencing can significantly reduce an organization's travel expenses. Many organizations set up special video conferencing rooms or booths with specially equipped television cameras. More recent equipment enables people to attach small cameras and microphones to their desks or computer monitors. This enables employees to conduct long-distance meetings and training classes without leaving their office or cubicle.

There are two major disadvantages to video conferencing. The first is the high cost; the video conferencing endpoints range from a pair of $50 web cams connected to PCs running Microsoft NetMeeting software, to $50,000 boardroom-based systems with multiple cameras and microphones. Then there is the cost of the service itself, which can vary from 50 cents per minute to monthly subscriptions costing hundreds of dollars per minute. Long distance and international calls run much higher. If your organization only holds a few meetings per year, this may be an expensive alternative.

The second disadvantage is the challenge of overcoming the lack of non-verbal cues and the real-time human factor. Will a camera pick up the eye contact of a participant located 3 metres from the table? What about picking up the subtle effects of posture, doodling with a pen, and the shallow breathing associated with anxiety … will the camera pick up on these cues? The benefit of person-to-person interaction cannot be duplicated by even the most sophisticated and expensive video conferencing system. A firm handshake, a sincere smile, and the easy conversation over a business lunch all go far in establishing trust and cementing business relations.[59]

TELEWORKING

Teleworking, also referred to as telecommuting, is a work practice in which employees do parts of their job in a remote location, typically at home, using a variety of information technologies. That said, any employee with

> **Teleworking**
>
> Doing office work from a remote location using different information technologies.

a laptop, Internet access, and a phone can work from almost anywhere. Recent years have seen an explosion of telework within virtual call centres in home offices across the country.[60] For example, a recent survey of 350 North American call centres revealed that 24 percent of the employees, or 672,000 workers, were working from home.[61] Experts estimate that 41 million people teleworked from home at least one day a week by 2008.[62] Telework is more common for jobs involving computer work, writing, and phone work that require concentration and limited interruptions. Proposed benefits of telework include:

1. Reduction of capital costs

2. Increased flexibility and autonomy for workers

3. Competitive edge in recruitment

4. Increased job satisfaction and lower turnover

5. Increased productivity

6. Tapping non-traditional labour pools[63]

Although telecommuting represents an attempt to accommodate employee needs and desires, it requires adjustments and is not for everybody. Many people thoroughly enjoy the social friendship that exists within an office setting. These individuals probably would not like to telecommute. Others lack the self-motivation needed to work at home. Finally, organizations must be careful to implement telecommuting in a non-discriminatory manner so that opportunities to participate are offered to all employees in a fair and equitable manner.

LO 5 SUSTAINING EFFECTIVE COMMUNICATION

The challenge that lies ahead for all contemporary organizations is how to maintain effective interpersonal communication while moving toward greater usage of electronic devices in the workplace. The notion of using capital assets (i.e., computers connected to the Internet, email systems, video conferencing equipment, PDAs) to enhance productivity has a clear accounting and economic advantage; however, the intrusive nature of some of these devises presents a balancing act that employees are going to have to either get used to or learn to control. Undoubtedly, the employer's mandate to find greater efficiencies in day-to-day operations will only continue, and at times compete with, the personal interests of employees who wish to keep their work lives somewhat separate from their personal lives. Being on call 24/7 may appeal to some, but not all, employees.

We're in a transitional phase between Baby Boomers who are holding on to many of the senior jobs in the workforce and who have witnessed the birth, evolution, and workplace application of these devises, and Generation Y adults who have grown up with these items and consider electronic communication devises as standard issue. In fact, to many in this age group, there is an unmistakable preference for instant communication—and why not? From their perspective, it's affordable, available, and desirable.

As the use of electronic communication devises increases, employers will have to find ways to assist some senior employees to overcome their feelings of fear and anxiety at using these items in the workplace. Developing and communicating policies around these issues, along with providing training, can certainly assist this effort. For younger employees, the challenge will be to rein in their behaviour so they can maintain focus on their job. Because using these devises is second nature to many, these employees will see a short email chat or text-message exchange as not at all distracting. Again, training workshops that identify organizational objectives and expectations should support such employees.

Summary of Learning Objectives

1. **Illustrate the various components of the perceptual process model of communication.** Communication is a process of consecutively linked elements. This model of communication depicts receivers as information processors who create the meaning of messages in their own mind. Because receivers' interpretations of messages often differ from those intended by senders, miscommunication is a common occurrence. The various components are: (1) the sender who encodes; (2) the message; (3) the medium; (4) the receiver who decodes; (5) create meaning; (6) feedback from receiver to sender; and (7) noise that can distort message.

2. **Describe at least eight barriers to effective communication.** Every element of the perceptual model of communication is a potential process barrier. Personal barriers that commonly influence communication include: (a) the ability to effectively communicate; (b) the way people process and interpret information; (c) the level of interpersonal trust between people; (d) the existence of stereotypes and prejudices; (e) the egos of the people communicating; (f) the ability to listen; (g) the natural tendency to evaluate or judge a sender's message; and (h) the inability to listen with understanding. Physical barriers pertain to distance, physical objects, time, and work and office noise. Semantic barriers show up as encoding and decoding errors because these phases of communication involve transmitting and receiving words and symbols. Cultural diversity is a key contributor to semantic barriers.

3. **Contrast the communication styles of assertiveness, aggressiveness, and non-assertiveness.** An assertive style of communication is expressive and self-enhancing and is based on the "ethical notion that it is not right or good to violate our own or others' basic human rights, such as the right to self-expression or the right to be treated with dignity and respect. In contrast, an aggressive style is expressive and self-enhancing, and strives to take unfair advantage of others. A non-assertive style is characterized by timid and self-denying behaviour. Non-assertiveness is ineffective because it gives the other person an unfair advantage. Employees may improve their communication competence by trying to be more assertive and less aggressive or non-assertive.

4. **Explain the formal and informal communication channels.** There are two types of communication channels: formal and informal. The formal channels are authorized and used by all employees in a common and open manner. Formal channels follow structural protocol in a public manner; as a result, the process takes time to "get the message out." Examples include all staff notices, public forums, minutes of meetings, client briefing reports, and all other types of documents approved and/or written by management. Information received through formal channels can be considered as accurate. An informal channel does not follow the chain of command; it skips management levels and bypasses lines of authority. The grapevine is an example of an unofficial communication channel. Information received through this channel travels quickly throughout the organization, it is estimated to be only about 75 percent accurate, and it is commonly referred to as office gossip.

5. **Summarize the various factors involved in maintaining effective communication as organizations move toward using more electronic devices in the workplace.** The challenge that lies ahead for all contemporary organizations is how to maintain effective interpersonal communication while moving toward greater use of electronic devices in the workplace. The notion of using capital assets (i.e., computers connected to the Internet, electronic mail, video conferencing equipment, PDAs) to enhance productivity has a clear accounting and economic advantage; however, the intrusive nature of some of these devises presents a balancing act that employees are going to have to either get used to or learn to control. As the use of electronic communication devises increases, employers will have to find ways to assist senior employees to overcome their feelings of fear and trepidation (cautionary behaviour) toward using these items in the workplace. Developing and communicating policies around these issues, along with training, can certainly assist this effort. For younger employees, the challenge will be to rein in their behaviour so they maintain focus on their job. Because use of these devices is second nature to younger employees, they will see a short email chat or text-message exchange as not distracting at all. Again, training workshops that identify organizational objectives and expectations should support these employees.

Discussion Questions

1. What are some sources of noise that interfere with communication during a class lecture, an encounter with a professor in his or her office, or during a movie?
2. Which barrier to effective communication is most difficult to reduce? Explain.
3. If the goal is to improve interpersonal communication in the workplace, why is it important for individuals to first know their own preferred style of communication?
4. What are the behaviour differences between hearing a song through your iPod and actively listening to a classroom presentation by your professor?
5. Review the "Practical Tips—Advice to Improve Non-Verbal Communication Skills" and explain the reasons behind avoiding each of the six negative behaviours. For example, what does it mean when a receiver looks away from the speaker?

Google Searches

1. **Google Search:** "Glove Girl Harvard Business Review Online" Read the abstract for this fictional case regarding employee blogging and how it can affect corporate activity. What are your thoughts about this employee? In your opinion, is Glove Girl a security risk? What does this case suggest about corporate policies on blogging? (You may want to refer to this chapter's International OB feature box.)
2. **Google Search:** "MP Ujjal Dosanjh Threatened On Facebook—CBC News" After reading the news article, summarize what this case is about. How has communication technology using email contributed to this situation? What does this case teach us about email and communicating on social network sites?
3. **Google Search:** "English Homonyms" and "Canadianisms Contrasted and Compared to the US" Review both fun and lengthy lists. Does the English language have built-in barriers to effective communication? If you were a recent immigrant to Canada and heard Canadians speaking, do you think you would be confused and misunderstand the intention of a message? Explain and give examples where possible.

Experiential Exercise

Teleworking vs. Video Conferencing Exercise

PURPOSE: In this exercise, you will identify the pros and cons of both teleworking and video conferencing from a practical employee perspective and also from management's perspective. Approx. Timing: 25 minutes.

ACTIVITY ASSIGNMENT
- Work in small teams to fill in the chart below.
- Allow 15 minutes for team discussion and then another 10 minutes for sharing team answers with the rest of the class.

	EMPLOYEE PERSPECTIVE		MANAGEMENT PERSPECTIVE	
	Pros	Cons	Pros	Cons
Teleworking – Doing office work from a remote location using different information technologies	1. 2. 3.	1. 2. 3.	1. 2. 3.	1. 2. 3.
Videoconferencing – Using video and audio links, along with computers, to enable people in different locations to see, hear, and talk with one another	1. 2. 3.	1. 2. 3.	1. 2. 3.	1. 2. 3.

The **Presentation** Assistant

Here are possible topics and sources related to this chapter that can be further explored by student groups looking for ideas.

	CULTURES COMMUNICATE DIFFERENTLY—COMPARE THE CANADIAN COMMUNICATION STYLE (INCLUDING NON-VERBAL) TO ABORIGINAL, CHINESE, AND INDIAN EMPLOYEES	NON-VERBAL COMMUNICATION—RESEARCH, EXAMPLES, AND CHALLENGES	COMMON DISTORTIONS TO THE COMMUNICATION PROCESS—EVERYDAY BUSINESS EXAMPLES
YouTube Videos	• Russell Peters (Indian culture) • Overview of Chinese Communication Symbols • Communication and Relationship Building (Pallium Project)—aboriginal communication style	• Non-verbal communication • How primates communicate • Body language	• Workplace communication • Fawlty Towers 07—Communication Problems • Noise in the Office • Fast Talker • Double Talker
TV Shows or Movies to Preview	• *Rush Hour* (Jackie Chan and Chris Tucker) • *Unrepentant: Kevin Annett and Canada's Genocide* (documentary)	• *The Science Show—ABC Radio National—*"Primate Communication" (Nov 1/08) • *Seinfeld Show—*"Puffy Shirt Low Talker"	• *The Terminal* • *Agent Cody Banks* • *Workplace Communication—What The Apprentice teaches us about communication skills*
Internet Searches	• CBC Aboriginal (Oct. 17, 2008) • Marketing to Chinese Canadians • Challenges Around Overseas Tech Support (India)	• Non-Verbal in Police Interrogation (in the line of duty) • Sales People Use Non-Verbal (job interview mistakes)	• *Talking 9–5* (by Deborah Tannen) • Workplace Communication • Ted.com—Evelyn Glennie Shows How To Listen
Ice Breaker Classroom Activity	• Ask the students to write down at least three specific characteristics of the "typical" Canadian communication style. After one minute, go around the room and share responses—place a list on the board.	• Ask the students to look at three different photos on the projector. Have students silently guess what the people in the photos were thinking or saying to each other at the time the photo was taken. When done, have them share responses, asking for reasons and visual cues.	• Ask the students to identify how the simple multi-step communication process can get so messed up by people. What sorts of things can happen in the workplace to make this simple process go so wrong?

OB In Action Case Study

Communication Barriers Everywhere

Eli Walki is the manager of a large electronic retail store with over 200 employees, some full-time, most part-time. Walki has two assistant managers who split their time at the store; one is the day assistant-manager and the other is the night assistant-manager. The following four situations occurred during the past week.

1. Monday is Walki's day off, but he forgot his iPhone at work and ends up dropping in to pick it up after lunch. While walking through the front doors of the store, he notices garbage on the floor that has not been picked up, and several merchandise displays are not up to standard. Shelves are a mess or empty, the music over the PA system is way too loud, and no one is standing at the checkout area. Walki doesn't say anything at the time because he is in a hurry, but he is very upset, to say the least. Walki plans on discussing this with the two assistant managers the following day.

2. Chris Kowalski, one of Walki's more experienced sales people, asks him to intervene with Pat Starr, the night assistant-manager. Lately, employees have been getting upset by Starr's hardnosed communication style and common use of profanity around customers. When Walki is not around, Kowalski claims that Starr is a bully and gets angry when things aren't to his liking. Yesterday, Starr yelled really loud and threw insults at another employee in front of other employees; the employee began yelling back. It was embarrassing, Kowalski admitted. Walki can see that Kowalski is concerned, but the problem is that no one else has complained about Starr before. He's been a good night manager for over six months, and while Starr does have his unusual ways, he's a good worker and Walki trusts him. Walki ponders a plan for how best to discuss the situation with Starr.

3. On Thursday afternoon at 1:30 p.m., Walki learns from his regional manager, via a telephone call, that the company has been bought out by another electronic big box retailer. The sale, totally unexpected, will be announced to the financial community tomorrow, and will likely make the morning paper. The regional manager knows little of the details, saying that Walki now knows as much as he does and should communicate this information to his employees ASAP.

4. Walki must communicate to his employees that a new overtime system will be implemented company-wide, effective in two months. In the past, managers contacted workers by seniority, either in person or by phone, to make sure that the most senior workers had the first opportunity for overtime. This was always slow and ineffective, since some senior workers consistently declined overtime. The new system should give each manager more flexibility in overtime assignments by getting monthly, advance overtime commitments from workers. While most employees will buy into the new system, Walki knows that several of the more senior people are likely to be upset.

Discussion Questions

1. What is the major communication barrier in each of the four scenarios above?
2. If you were Walki, what would your strategy be in each of the four scenarios? Be sure to explain your answer.

Ethical OB Dilemma

Open Communication or Censorship?

The videos have started popping up on YouTube and MySpace.

In one, secretly videotaped by a student, an angry teacher is caught losing his temper toward the class. In another, teenagers make fun of fellow students, who also appear to be unaware they are being taped.

YouTube, MySpace, and other Web sites are sprinkled with videos taken in higher level classrooms around the world, often, it seems, without permission of the subjects. One popular YouTube video, called *The Angry Teacher*, shows a male instructor smashing a student's cell phone that was answered during a lecture.

But policing these secret videos is proving to be a challenge for school administrators, who say they must balance protecting the rights of students to express themselves in this digital age, while preventing them from holding classmates and teachers up to ridicule.

How would you advise the school administration to respond to the students who posted the videos? What are the ethical implications?

As a school advisor, what would you do?

Consider the following options:

1. This is a new issue. I would advise the school administrators to take some time to study the situation and then determine an appropriate response, which may be no response.

2. I would urge the school administrators to find out who posted those videos and punish the guilty students.

3. I would strongly suggest school administrators notify the families if the guilty students are under age. If the students can be considered adults under the law, then call the police and lay charges.

4. I would recommend that school administration create a policy for cell phone use and other electronic media within the classroom. Once formalized, the policy needs to be publicized through the faculty and the students to inform them of the resulting penalty for disobedience.

5. You believe a different response is needed. Explain.

Visit www.mcgrawhillconnect.ca to register.

McGraw-Hill Connect™—Available 24/7 with instant feedback so you can study when you want, how you want, and where you want. Take advantage of the Study Plan—an innovative tool that helps you customize your learning experience. You can diagnose your knowledge with pre- and post-tests, identify the areas where you need help, search the entire learning package for content specific to the topic you're studying, and add these resources to your personalized study plan. Visit www.mcgrawhillconnect.ca to register—take practice quizzes, search the e-book, and much more.

CHAPTER 8

Conflict *and* Negotiation

Workplace Bullying At Any Level Is Unacceptable

The belief that office bullying starts at the top of an organization and works its way downward throughout the rest of the workplace is a misread of the situation.

While there are many reported cases of managers bullying non-managerial employees, there is growing evidence that bullying takes place at all levels throughout the organization. According to Marilyn Noble, community co-chair of the research team on workplace bullying at the Muriel McQueen Fergusson Centre for Family Violence Research at the University of New Brunswick in Fredericton, this includes

employee to employee, employee to customer, and patron to employee bullying situations. In fact, there have been incidences of "receptionists holding an entire organization hostage with their behaviour," says Noble.

Interpersonal aggression to the point of bullying can show up at the office in different forms, from social isolation to excessive criticism. Psychological violence is much more prevalent and pervasive in the workplace than physical violence, according to Gerry Smith, Toronto-based vice-president of organizational solutions and training at Shepell-fgi. "We're human beings and we all have our bad days. But when someone's bad day is becoming a bad month and a bad year, that's really an abuse of the safety of the workplace," says Smith. The evolving notion that a workplace distracted by interpersonal conflict is an indication of an unsafe work environment is receiving more attention from HR directors.

Patti Boucher, vice-president of client and consulting services at the Toronto-based Ontario Safety Association for Community and Healthcare, believes enforced policies around workplace harassment and bullying are critical. If there isn't a company policy supported by a network of formal response strategies for the victims (e.g., reporting mechanisms, procedures, and reports), then workers will be reluctant to report. They'll figure it's not worth their time, and that the company doesn't care. Boucher says that such strategies are key because feeling safe at work is "huge" to combat the fears of ongoing conflict from the office bully in the form of retaliation, and to serve as notice to office bullies that if caught, they will be reprimanded by those in authority. Creating and maintaining a safe work environment from both a physical and psychological point of view is very important.

In times of economic uncertainty, many firms are required to lay off employees, making the workplace ripe for conflict and aggression as managers feel the pressure to use their legitimate power to stay on top of employee productivity, by force if necessary. But resolving conflict by force is not always the answer, as it can escalate the conflict.

So, what is the answer?

HR experts suggest that to prevent workplace bullying and to cope with complaints, employers should ensure they have an effective, formal response that includes: training, counselling, coaching, policies, peer support, proper infrastructure for reporting, proper documentation of incidents, and transition strategies for resetting behaviour standards to get both the victim and the bully back into the workplace.

SOURCES: S. Dobson, "Tackling the Bullies, Conflict Management," *Canadian HR Reporter*, March 9, 2009, p 13.

LEARNING OBJECTIVES →

After reading this chapter, you should be able to:

LO 1 **Define** *conflict*, *functional conflict*, and *dysfunctional conflict*.

LO 2 **Identify** the various causes of conflict.

LO 3 **List** two approaches an employee or manager can take to respond to each of the following: personality conflicts, intergroup conflict, and cross-cultural conflicts.

LO 4 **Compare and contrast** the five alternative styles for handling conflict.

LO 5 **Assess** the value of having third party interventions for conflict resolution, including the ADR and two negotiation processes.

Make no mistake: conflict is an unavoidable aspect of modern life. The following major trends work together to make organizational conflict an expected part of the workplace:

- Constant change
- Greater employee diversity
- More teams (virtual and self-managed)
- Less face-to-face communication (more electronic interaction)
- A global economy with increased cross-cultural dealings

Dean Tjosvold, from Canada's Simon Fraser University, notes that "Change (leads to) conflict, conflict (leads to) change"[1] and challenges us to do better with this realistic global perspective:

Learning to manage conflict is a critical investment in improving how we, our families, and our organizations adapt and take advantage of change. Managing conflicts well does not insulate us from change, nor does it mean that we will always come out on top or get all that we want. However, effective conflict management helps us keep in touch with new developments and create solutions appropriate for new threats and opportunities.

Much evidence shows we often fail to manage our conflicts and effectively respond to change. High divorce rates, disheartening examples of sexual and physical abuse of children, the expensive failures of international joint ventures, and bloody ethnic violence have convinced many people that we do not have the abilities to cope with our complex interpersonal, organizational, and global conflicts.[2]

But respond we must. As outlined in this chapter, tools and solutions are available if we develop the ability and will to use them frequently. The choice is ours: Be aware of how to resolve conflict, or have conflict manage you.[3]

LO 1 Conflict: A Modern Perspective

A complete review of the conflict literature provides this consensus definition: "**conflict** is a process in which one party perceives that its interests are being opposed or negatively affected by another party."[4] The word *perceives* reminds us that sources of conflict can be real or imagined; the resulting conflict is the same. Conflict can escalate (strengthen) or de-escalate (weaken) over time. "The conflict process unfolds in a context, and whenever conflict, escalated or not, occurs, then the people arguing or third parties can attempt to manage it in some manner."[5] Therefore, current and future managers need to understand the dynamics of conflict and know how to handle it effectively (both as a person in an argument and as third parties). This call to action is supported by a recent survey asking employees what their manager's New Year's resolution should be. The number one response was, "Deal with workplace conflicts faster."[6]

Conflict

One party perceives its interests are being opposed or set back by another party.

THE LANGUAGE OF CONFLICT: METAPHORS AND MEANING

Conflict is a complex subject for several reasons. Primary among them is the reality that conflict often carries a lot of emotional baggage.[7] Fear of losing or fear of change quickly raises the emotional stakes in a conflict. Conflicts also vary widely in magnitude. Conflicts have both participants and observers. Some observers may be interested and active, others disinterested and passive. Consequently, the term *conflict* can take on vastly different meanings, depending on the circumstances and one's involvement. For example, consider these three metaphors and accompanying workplace expressions:

- Conflict as war: "We shot down that idea."

- Conflict as opportunity: "What are all the possibilities for solving this problem?"

- Conflict as journey: "Let's search for common ground."[8]

Anyone viewing a conflict as war will try to win at all costs and wipe out the enemy. For example, *BusinessWeek* recently quoted Donald Trump as saying, "In life, you have fighters and non-fighters. You have winners and losers. I am both a fighter and a winner."[9] Alternatively, those seeing a conflict as an opportunity and a journey will tend to be more positive, open-minded, and constructive. In a hostile world, combative and destructive war-like thinking often prevails. But typical daily workplace conflicts are *not* war. So when dealing with organizational conflicts, we are challenged to rely less on the metaphor and language of war, and more on the metaphors and language of *opportunity* and *journey*. We need to carefully monitor our choice of words in conflict situations.[10]

While explaining the three metaphors, conflict experts Kenneth Cloke and Joan Goldsmith made this observation that you should keep in mind for the balance of this chapter:

Conflict gives you an opportunity to deepen your capacity for empathy and intimacy with your opponent. Your anger transforms the "Other" into a stereotyped demon or villain. Similarly, defensiveness will prevent you from communicating openly with your opponents, or listening carefully to what they are saying. On the other hand, once you engage in dialogue with that person, you will resurrect the human side of their personality—and express your own as well.

Moreover, when you process your conflicts with integrity, they lead to growth, increased awareness, and self-improvement. Uncontrolled anger, defensiveness, and shame defeat these possibilities. Everyone feels better when they overcome their problems and reach resolution, and worse when they succumb and fail to resolve them. It is a bitter truth that victories won in anger lead to long-term defeat. Those defeated turn away, feeling betrayed and lost, and carry this feeling with them into their next conflict.

Conflict can be seen simply as a way of learning more about what is not working and discovering how to fix it. The usefulness of the solution depends on the depth of your understanding of the problem. This depends on your ability to listen to the issue as you would to a teacher, which depends on halting the cycle of escalation and searching for opportunities for improvement.[11]

In short, win–win beats win–lose in both conflict management and negotiation.

PLACING CONFLICT ON A SCALE

Ideas about managing conflict underwent an interesting evolution during the 20th century. Initially, scientific management experts such as Frederick W. Taylor believed all conflict ultimately threatened management's authority, and thus had to be avoided or quickly resolved. Later, human relationists recognized the inevitability of conflict and advised both employees and managers to understand it, but to learn to live with it. Emphasis remained on resolving conflict whenever possible, however.

Beginning in the 1970s, OB specialists realized conflict had both positive and negative outcomes, depending on its nature and intensity. This perspective introduced the revolutionary idea that organizations could suffer from *too little* conflict. Figure 8.1 illustrates the relationship between conflict intensity and outcomes.

Work groups, departments, or organizations experiencing too little conflict tend to be plagued by apathy, lack of creativity, indecision, and missed deadlines. Excessive conflict, on the other hand, can erode organizational performance because of political infighting, dissatisfaction, lack of teamwork, and turnover. Workplace aggression and violence can be results of excessive conflict.[12] Appropriate types and levels of conflict energize people in constructive directions.[13]

Dysfunctional conflict
Conflict that is counterproductive and threatens the interests of the organization.

Functional conflict
Conflict that contributes to a positive outcome by serving an organization's interests.

FUNCTIONAL VERSUS DYSFUNCTIONAL CONFLICT

The distinction between *functional conflict* and *dysfunctional conflict* revolves around whether the organization's interests are served. According to one conflict expert,

> Some [types of conflict] support the goals of the organization and improve performance; these are functional, constructive forms of conflict. They benefit or support the main purposes of the organization. Additionally, there are those types of conflict that hinder organizational performance; these are dysfunctional or destructive forms. They are undesirable and should be eliminated.[14]

Functional conflict is commonly referred to as constructive or cooperative conflict.[15] Often, a simmering conflict can be defused in a functional manner or driven to dysfunctional proportions, depending on how it is handled. To illustrate the differences between these two types of conflict, let's use an example of two employees who work side by side in the same office and find themselves always bickering, disagreeing, and being noncooperative. They obviously don't like each other, but must work alongside each other. By itself, the disagreements between these two individuals are no one else's business . . . until they interfere with work flow and customer service. This kind of interpersonal behaviour becomes dysfunctional conflict when customers complain that the office staffers prefer to argue rather than serve; or when office phones go unanswered as the two employees play mind-games with one another by pretending to be busy so that the other is forced to answer. When this kind of behaviour finds itself in the workplace, it must be eliminated.

On the other hand, if two employees who work side by side in the same office get along very well to the point of enabling each others' poor work habits, like leaving early, coming into work late, and making personal phone calls during company time—all of which leave less time for being productive on the job—then the office supervisor must step in and correct the lax behaviours. This may cause a temporary conflict between the supervisor and the support staff workers because no one likes to be corrected or told what to do; but in this case, it is necessary to restore office productivity. Hence, it is referred to as a functional conflict because the interests of the organization are upheld.

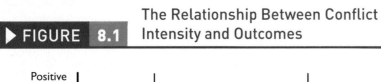

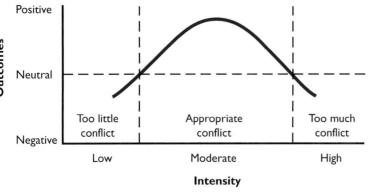

▶ FIGURE 8.1 The Relationship Between Conflict Intensity and Outcomes

SOURCE: L.D. Brown, *Managing Conflict at Organizational Interfaces*, 1st edition, © 1983, p 8. Reprinted by permission of Pearson Education, Inc., Upper Saddle River, NJ.

Layoff survivors typically complain about being overworked, thus paving the way for stress and conflict.

LO 2 CAUSES OF CONFLICT

Certain situations produce more conflict than others. By knowing the causes of conflict, individuals are better able to anticipate conflict and take steps to resolve it if it becomes dysfunctional. The following situations tend to produce either functional or dysfunctional conflicts:

- Incompatible personalities or value systems
- Overlapping or unclear job boundaries
- Competition for limited resources
- Inter-department/inter-group competition
- Inadequate communication
- Interdependent tasks (e.g., one person cannot complete his or her assignment until others have completed their work)
- Organizational complexity (conflict tends to increase as the number of hierarchical layers and specialized tasks increase)
- Unreasonable or unclear policies, standards, or rules
- Unreasonable deadlines or extreme time pressure
- Collective decision making (the greater the number of people participating in a decision, the greater the potential for conflict)
- Unmet expectations (employees who have unrealistic expectations about job assignments, pay, or promotions are more prone to conflict)
- Unresolved or suppressed conflicts[16]

Employees should be aware of these situations and avoid or resolve them. Proactive supervisors, managers, and team leaders should carefully read these early warnings and take appropriate action to manage them.

DESIRED CONFLICT OUTCOMES

Within organizations, conflict management is more than simply a mission to find agreement. If progress is to be made and dysfunctional conflict minimized, a broader agenda is in order. Tjosvold's cooperative conflict model (discussed in this chapter's introduction) calls for three desired outcomes:

1. **Agreement** But at what cost? Equitable and fair agreements are best. An agreement that leaves one party feeling exploited or defeated will tend to breed resentment and subsequent conflict.

2. **Stronger relationships** Good agreements enable conflicting parties to build bridges of goodwill and trust for future use. Moreover, conflicting parties who trust each other are more likely to keep their end of the bargain.

3. **Learning** Functional conflict can promote greater self-awareness and creative problem solving. Like the practice of management itself, successful conflict handling is learned primarily by doing. Knowledge of the concepts and techniques in this chapter is a necessary first step, but there is no substitute for hands-on practice. In a controversial world, there are plenty of opportunities to practise conflict management.[17]

Types of Conflict   LO 3

Certain causes of conflict deserve a closer look. This section explores the nature and organizational implications of three common forms of conflict: (1) personality conflict, (2) inter-group conflict, and (3) cross-cultural conflict. Our discussion of each type of conflict includes some practical tips.

PERSONALITY CONFLICTS

As discussed in Chapter 3, your *personality* is the package of stable traits and characteristics creating your unique identity. According to experts on the subject:

> *Each of us has a unique way of interacting with others. Whether we are seen as charming, irritating, fascinating, nondescript, approachable, or intimidating depends in part on our personality, or what others might describe as our style.[18]*

Given the many possible combinations of personality traits, it is clear why personality conflicts are inevitable. We define a ***personality conflict*** as interpersonal opposition based on personal dislike and/or disagreement.

Personality conflict

Interpersonal opposition driven by personal dislike or disagreement.

Workplace Incivility: Are You Part of the Problem?

How often have you engaged in these workplace behaviours during the past year?

		NEVER	OFTEN
1.	Paid little attention to a statement made by someone or showed little interest in their opinion.		1—2—3—4—5
2.	Made demeaning, rude, or derogatory remarks about someone.		1—2—3—4—5
3.	Made unwanted attempts to draw someone into a discussion of personal matters.		1—2—3—4—5
4.	Made fun of someone at work.		1—2—3—4—5
5.	Made an ethnic, religious, or racial remark or joke at work.		1—2—3—4—5
6.	Cursed at someone at work.		1—2—3—4—5
7.	Publicly embarrassed someone at work.		1—2—3—4—5
8.	Played a mean prank on someone at work.		1—2—3—4—5

Scoring Key

Add up your total points. Use the following "what-goes-around-comes-around" scale:

 8–16 = Good organizational citizen

17–31 = Careful, your mean streak is showing

32–40 = A real social porcupine—always needling the situation with argumentative behaviour that can escalate conflict.

SOURCE: Eight survey items excerpted from G. Blau and L. Andersson, "Testing a Measure of Instigated Workplace Incivility," *Journal of Occupational and Organizational Psychology*, December 2005, Table 1, pp 595–614.

Workplace Incivility: The Seeds of Personality Conflict

To better understand your own behaviour and the role it plays in conflicting experiences, you are encouraged to complete the Self-Assessment Exercise. Knowing your score may help you see some value in the lessons being taught in this chapter.

Somewhat like physical pain, chronic personality conflicts often begin with seemingly unimportant irritations. For instance, consider this situation:

The first thing Adam Weissman does when he arrives at his public relations job isn't to grab a cup of coffee or gab with his co-workers. Instead, the account executive with DBA Public Relations goes to his small office and turns on his iPod to listen to music through his speakers. For Weissman, some days he listens to mellow music (like surfer gone song-writer Jack Johnson). Other days it's (Jay-Z). He says the portable music player that stores his 3,600 songs keeps him focused when he's not on the phone. Not all his co-workers are singing the same tune. When he recently asked them what they thought of his office pastime, his colleagues admitted that sometimes it's annoying when Weissman drums on his desk or sings along.[19]

Sadly, scenarios such as this are all too common today, given the steady decline of civility in the workplace[20] (see Law and Ethics at Work feature box). To help develop civility behaviours, some organizations

BEING CIVIL HELPS MAINTAIN A SAFE WORKPLACE

Researchers view incivility as a self-perpetuating vicious cycle that can end in violence.[23] In 1999, the International Labour Organization declared physical and emotional violence to be one of the most serious problems facing the workplace in the new millennium.[24]

In 2000, a Canadian poll of labour unions revealed that more than 75 percent of those surveyed reported incidents of harassment and bullying at work.[25] The Canada Safety Council reports that 75 percent of workplace bullying victims leave their jobs. It also found that workplace bullying is four times more common than sexual harassment or workplace discrimination.[26]

Since 2008, the Ontario government has made considerable enhancements to workplace violence protection under the Occupational Health and Safety Act. "We want Ontario workers to enjoy safe and healthy workplaces," said Ontario Labour Minister Brad Duguid. "At the same time, we must make sure that our occupational health and safety legislation protects them from workplace violence in a balanced way that reflects the realities of today's workplaces."[27]

In the end, a civil workplace is a safe workplace, and that is not only ethical, but also supported by Canadian legislation.

---

have resorted to workplace etiquette training.[21] The Self-Assessment Exercise you took in Chapter 7 covered this very topic. Constructive feedback or skilful behaviour-shaping can keep a single irritating behaviour from becoming a full-blown personality conflict (or worse). Another promising tool for nipping workplace incivility in the bud is to offer the employee exhibiting incivility a *day of contemplation*, defined as: "a paid day off where an employee showing lack of dedication to the job is granted the opportunity to rethink their commitment to working at your company."[22] This tactic, also called decision-making leave, is not part of the organization's formal disciplinary process, nor is it a traditional suspension without pay. A day of contemplation is a one-time-only-per-employee option.

Dealing with Personality Conflicts Personality conflicts are a potential minefield for organizations. Traditionally, the workplace dealt with personality conflicts by either ignoring them or transferring one party.[28] These responses can lead to conflict escalation or even possible legal implications, such as accusations of harassment or discrimination. The Skills and Best Practices feature box presents practical tips for both non-managers and managers who are involved in or affected by personality conflicts. Our later discussions of handling dysfunctional conflict and alternative dispute resolution techniques also apply.

Day of contemplation

A one-time-only day off with pay to allow a problem employee to reflect and recommit to the organization's values and mission.

INTERGROUP CONFLICT

Conflict among work groups, teams, and departments is a common threat to organizational competitiveness. As we discussed in Chapter 6, cohesiveness—a "we feeling" binding group members together—can be a good or bad thing. A certain amount of cohesiveness can turn a group of individuals into a smooth-running team. Too much cohesiveness, however, can breed groupthink because a desire to get along pushes aside critical thinking. The study of in-groups by researchers has revealed a whole package of changes associated with increased group cohesiveness. Specifically,

- Members of in-groups view themselves as a collection of unique individuals, while they stereotype members of other groups as being "all alike."

- In-group members see themselves positively and as morally correct, while they view members of other groups negatively and as immoral.

- In-groups view outsiders as a threat.

- In-group members exaggerate the differences between their group and other groups. This typically involves a distorted perception of reality.[29]

Avid sports fans who simply can't imagine how someone would support the opposing team exemplify one form of in-group thinking. Also, this pattern of behaviour is a form *ethnocentrism* (i.e., looking at the world primarily from the perspective of one's own culture, which we will discuss in more detail in Chapter 14). Reflect for a moment on evidence of in-group behaviour in your life. Does your circle of friends make fun of others because of their race, gender, age, nationality, weight, sexual preference, or occupational program choice?[30]

In-group thinking is one more fact of organizational life that virtually guarantees conflict. Employees who are affected by such thinking need to become aware of it and try to avoid it by pointing it out to their group members. Managers cannot eliminate in-group thinking, but they certainly should not ignore it when handling inter-group conflicts.

Research Lessons for Handling Inter-Group Conflict
Sociologists have long recommended the contact hypothesis for reducing inter-group conflict. According to the contact hypothesis, the more the members of different groups interact, the less inter-group conflict they will experience. Those interested in improving race, international, and union–management relations typically encourage cross-group interaction. The hope is that any type of interaction, short of actual conflict, will reduce stereotyping and combat in-group thinking. But research has shown this approach to be naive and limited.

Inter-group friendships are still desirable, but they are readily overpowered by negative inter-group interactions. Thus, the number one priority for managers faced with inter-group conflict is to identify and root out specific negative linkages between (or among) groups. A single personality conflict, for instance, may contaminate the entire inter-group experience. The

same goes for an employee who voices negative opinions or spreads negative rumours about another group. Our updated contact model in Figure 8.2 is based on this and other recent research insights, such as the need to foster positive attitudes toward other groups.[31] Notice how conflict within the group and negative gossip from third parties are threats that need to be neutralized if inter-group conflict is to be minimized.

CROSS-CULTURAL CONFLICT

Doing business with people from different cultures is commonplace in our global economy, where world-wide

> Some cultural conflicts have resulted from the outsourcing of many jobs overseas to areas where labour is much cheaper than in Canada. This Ninestar location in India employs 850 people in three shifts, operating 24/7. What is your opinion about foreign outsourcing or "offshoring" of jobs?

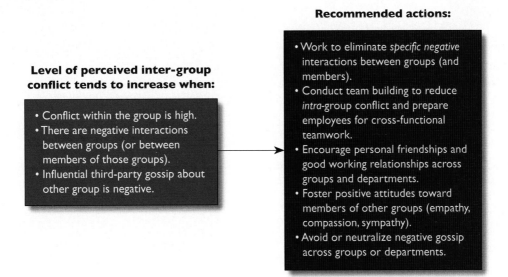

Level of perceived inter-group conflict tends to increase when:

- Conflict within the group is high.
- There are negative interactions between groups (or between members of those groups).
- Influential third-party gossip about other group is negative.

Recommended actions:

- Work to eliminate *specific negative* interactions between groups (and members).
- Conduct team building to reduce *intra*-group conflict and prepare employees for cross-functional teamwork.
- Encourage personal friendships and good working relationships across groups and departments.
- Foster positive attitudes toward members of other groups (empathy, compassion, sympathy).
- Avoid or neutralize negative gossip across groups or departments.

SOURCES: Based on research evidence in G. Labianca, D.J. Brass, and B. Gray, "Social Networks and Perceptions of Intergroup Conflict: The Role of Negative Relationships and Third Parties," *Academy of Management Journal*, February 1998, pp 55–67; C.D. Batson et al., "Empathy and Attitudes: Can Feeling for a Member of a Stigmatized Group Improve Feelings toward the Group?," *Journal of Personality and Social Psychology*, January 1997, pp 105–18; and S.C. Wright et al., "The Extended Contact Effect: Knowledge of Cross-Group Friendships and Prejudice," *Journal of Personality and Social Psychology*, July 1997, pp 73–90.

---

mergers, joint ventures, outsourcing, and alliances are the order of the day.[32] Because of differing assumptions about how to think and act, the potential for cross-cultural conflict is both immediate and huge. Success or failure, when conducting business across cultures, often hinges on avoiding and minimizing actual or perceived conflict. This is not a matter of who is right and who is wrong; rather it is a matter of accommodating cultural differences for a successful business transaction. Stereotypes also need to be identified and neutralized. Beyond that, cross-cultural conflict can be moderated by using international consultants and building cross-cultural relationships.

Using International Consultants   In response to broad demand, there is a growing army of management consultants specializing in cross-cultural relations. Competency and fees vary widely, of course. But a carefully selected cross-cultural consultant can be helpful, as this illustration shows:

> Last year, when electronics-maker Canon planned to set up a subsidiary in Dubai through its Netherlands division, it asked consultant Sahid Mirza of Glocom, based in Dubai, to find out how the two cultures would work together. Mirza sent out

the test questionnaires and got a sizable response. "The findings were somewhat surprising," he recalls. "We found that, at the bedrock level, there were relatively few differences. Many of the Arab (executives) came from former British colonies and viewed business in much the same way as the Dutch." But at the level of behaviour, there was a real conflict. "The Dutch are blunt and honest in expression, and such expression is very offensive to Arab sensibilities." Mirza offers the example of a Dutch executive who says something like, "We can't meet the deadline." Such a negative expression—true or not—would be gravely offensive to an Arab. As a result of Mirza's research, Canon did start the subsidiary in Dubai, but it first trained both the Dutch and the Arab executives.[33]

Consultants can also help untangle possible personality, value, and inter-group conflicts from conflicts rooted in differing national cultures. Note that although we have discussed basic types of conflict separately, they typically are encountered in complex, messy bundles. The work completed by researcher Rosalie L. Tung (see International OB feature box) provides some interesting insight into ways to build cross-cultural relationships.

WAYS TO BUILD CROSS-CULTURAL RELATIONSHIPS

Rosalie L Tung's study of 409 expatriates from Canadian and U.S. multinational firms is very helpful when building cross-cultural relationships.[34] Her survey sought to pinpoint success factors for expatriates (14 percent female) who were working in 51 different countries worldwide. Nine specific ways to facilitate interaction with host-country nationals, as ranked from most useful to least useful by the respondents, are listed below. Good listening skills topped the list, followed by sensitivity to others and cooperativeness rather than competitiveness.

BEHAVIOUR	RANK
Be a good listener	1
Be sensitive to needs of others	2
Be cooperative, rather than overly competitive	2 (Tie)
Advocate inclusive (participative) leadership	3
Compromise rather than dominate	4
Build rapport through conversations	5
Be compassionate and understanding	6
Avoid conflict by emphasizing harmony	7
Nurture others (develop and mentor)	8

SOURCE: Adapted from R.L. Tung, "American Expatriates Abroad: From Neophytes to Cosmopolitans," *Journal of World Business*, Summer 1998, Table 6, p 136.

LO 4 Managing Conflict

As we have seen, conflict has many faces and is a constant challenge for employees who are being given higher performance expectations and for managers who are responsible for reaching organizational goals.[35] Our attention now turns to the five alternative style for handling conflict and how third parties can deal effectively with conflict.

ALTERNATIVE STYLES FOR HANDLING CONFLICT

People tend to handle negative conflict in patterned ways, referred to as styles. Several conflict styles have been categorized over the years. A contemporary model has been designed by conflict specialist Afzalur Rahim, who identified five different conflict-handling styles and plotted them onto a 2 × 2 grid. High to low concern for self is found on the horizontal axis of the grid, while low to high concern for others forms the vertical axis (see Figure 8.3). Various combinations of these variables produce the five different conflict-handling styles: integrating, obliging, dominating, avoiding, and compromising.[36] It

▶ **FIGURE** **8.3** Five Conflict-Handling Styles

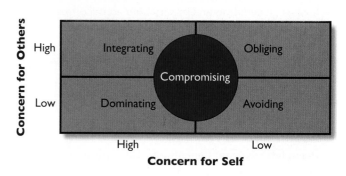

SOURCE: Reprinted by permission of Sage Publications Ltd from M.A. Rahim, "A Strategy for Managing Conflict in Complex Organizations," *Human Relations*, January 1985, p 84. Copyright © 1985 The Tavistock Institute.

is worth mentioning that although compromising sits in the centre of the model, it is not the ultimate style to use. Remember, there is no single best style; each has strengths and limitations, and is subject to "best fit" based on the situation.

Integrating (Problem Solving) In this style, the concern for self and others is high; therefore, the problem becomes the primary focus as interested parties take the time to confront an issue and cooperatively identify the problem, generate and weigh alternative solutions, and select a solution. Integrating is appropriate for complex issues plagued by misunderstanding. However, it is inappropriate for resolving conflicts rooted in opposing value systems. Its primary strength is its longer lasting impact, because it deals with the underlying problem rather than merely with symptoms. The primary weakness of this style is that it is very time-consuming.

Obliging (Smoothing) "An obliging person neglects his or her own concern to satisfy the concern of the other party."[37] This style, often called smoothing, involves more concern for others rather than for oneself. This is a style rooted in humility, as conflicting parties play down their differences while emphasizing what they have in common. Obliging may be an appropriate conflict-handling strategy when it is possible to eventually get something in return (for example, helping people when they need it and in turn asking for their help in the future when it is important to you). However, it is inappropriate for complex or worsening problems. Its primary strength is that it encourages cooperation. Its main weakness is that it's a temporary fix that fails to confront the underlying problem.

Dominating (Forcing) High concern for self and low concern for others encourages aggressive tactics where the other party's needs are largely ignored. This style is often called forcing because it relies on formal authority to force compliance. Dominating is appropriate when an unpopular solution must be implemented, the issue is minor, there are safety or security issues, or a deadline is very near. It is inappropriate in an open and participative climate. Speed is its primary strength. The primary weakness of this domineering style is that it often breeds resentment.[38]

Avoiding This style has low concern for both self and others' needs. This tactic may involve either passive withdrawal from the problem or active suppression of the issue. Avoidance is appropriate for trivial issues, when emotions are flared and things need to calm down, or when the costs of confrontation outweigh the benefits of resolving the conflict. It is inappropriate for difficult and worsening problems because it doesn't address the problem. The main strength of this style is that it buys time in emotionally charged or confusing situations. The primary weakness is that the tactic provides a temporary fix that sidesteps the underlying problem.

Compromising This is a give-and-take approach involving moderate concern for both self and others. Compromise is appropriate when parties have opposite goals or possess equal power. But compromise is inappropriate when overuse would lead to inconclusive action (e.g., failure to meet production deadlines). The primary strength of this tactic is that everyone gets something, but it's a temporary fix that can stifle creative problem solving.[39]

THIRD-PARTY INTERVENTIONS: ALTERNATIVE DISPUTE RESOLUTION

Disputes between employees, between employees and their employer, and between companies too often end up in lengthy and costly court battles. A more constructive, less expensive approach, called alternative dispute resolution, has enjoyed enthusiastic growth in recent years.[40] *Alternative dispute resolution (ADR)*, according to a pair of Canadian labour lawyers, "uses faster, more user-friendly methods of dispute resolution, instead of traditional, confrontational approaches."[41]

Alternative dispute resolution (ADR)

A conflict resolution strategy that involves assistance from a third party; used when both parties are unable find resolution on their own.

The following ADR techniques represent a progression of steps third parties can take to resolve organizational conflicts.[42] They are ranked from easiest and least expensive to most difficult and costly. A growing number of organizations have formal ADR policies involving an established sequence of various combinations of these techniques.

1. **Facilitation** A third party, usually a manager, informally urges disputing parties to deal directly with each other in a positive and practical manner.

2. **Conciliation** A neutral third party informally acts as a communication link between conflicting parties. This is appropriate when conflicting parties refuse to meet face to face. The immediate goal is to establish direct communication, with the broader aim of finding common ground and a constructive solution.

3. **Peer review** A panel of trustworthy co-workers, selected for their ability to remain objective, hears both sides of a dispute in an informal and private meeting. Any decision by the review panel may or may not be binding, depending on the company's ADR policy. Membership on the peer review panel often is rotated among employees.[43]

4. **Ombudsman** Someone who works for the organization, and is widely respected and trusted by his or her co-workers, hears grievances on a private basis and attempts to arrange a solution. This approach, more common in Europe than North America, permits someone to get help from an executive with ties to management without relying on the formal chain of command chain.

5. **Mediation** "The mediator—a trained, third-party neutral—actively guides the conflicting parties in exploring innovative solutions to the conflict. Although some companies have in-house mediators who have received ADR training, most also use external mediators who have no ties to the company."[44] Unlike an arbitrator, a mediator does not render a decision. It is up to the disputants to reach a mutually acceptable decision.

6. **Arbitration** Disputing parties agree ahead of time to accept the decision of a neutral arbitrator in a formal court-like setting, often complete with evidence and witnesses. Statements are classified. Decisions are based on legal merits. Trained arbitrators, typically from outside agencies such as the Arbitration and Mediation Institute of Canada, Inc., are versed in important laws and case precedents.

PRACTICAL LESSONS FROM CONFLICT RESEARCH

Laboratory studies, relying on college students as subjects, uncovered the following insights about organizational conflict:

- People with a high need to belong tended to rely on a smoothing (obliging) style while avoiding a forcing (dominating) style.[45] Thus, personality traits affect how people handle conflict.

- Disagreement expressed in a demeaning manner produced significantly more negative effects than the same sort of disagreement expressed in a reasonable manner.[46] In other words, how you disagree with someone is very important in conflict situations.

- Threats and punishment by one party in a disagreement tended to produce intensifying threats and punishment from the other party.[47] In short, aggression breeds aggression.

- As conflict increased, group satisfaction decreased. An integrative style of handling conflict led to higher group satisfaction than did an avoidance style.[48]

- Companies with mandatory or binding arbitration policies were viewed less favourably than companies without

such policies.[49] Apparently, mandatory or binding arbitration policies are a turn-off for job applicants who dislike the idea of being forced to do something.

Field studies involving real organizations have given us the following insights:

- Both intra-departmental and inter-departmental conflict decreased as goal difficulty and goal clarity increased. Thus, challenging and clear goals can smooth conflict.

- Higher levels of conflict tended to erode job satisfaction and internal work motivation.[50]

- Conflict tended to move around the organization in a case study of a public school system.[51] Thus, team leaders and managers need to be alert to the fact that conflict often begins in one area or level and becomes evident somewhere else. Conflict needs to be traced back to its source if there is to be lasting improvement.

- Samples of Japanese and German managers who were presented with the same conflict scenario preferred different resolution techniques. Japanese and German managers did not like the idea of integrating the interests of all parties. The Japanese tended to look upward to management for direction, whereas the Germans were more bound by rules and regulations. In cross-cultural conflict resolution, there is no one best approach. Culture-specific preferences need to be taken into consideration prior to beginning the conflict resolution process.[52]

As we transition from conflict to negotiation, take a short break from your reading and reflect on how you can better handle conflict in your daily life.

> Third party intervention is sometimes necessary to help conflicting parties find resolution. Several strategies are available, including mediation and arbitration techniques.

Negotiating

Formally defined, negotiation is a give-and-take decision-making process involving interdependent parties with different preferences.[53] Common examples include labour–management negotiations over wages, hours, and working conditions, and negotiations between supply chain specialists and vendors involving price, delivery schedules, and credit terms. Self-managed work teams with overlapping task boundaries also need to rely on negotiated agreements. Negotiating skills are more important today than ever.[54] In fact, in a recent survey of 625 small business owners, 30 percent said they needed to develop their negotiation skills.

TWO BASIC TYPES OF NEGOTIATION

Negotiation experts distinguish between two types of negotiation—*distributive* and *integrative*. Understanding the difference requires a change in traditional thinking:

> *A* distributive *negotiation usually involves a single issue—a "fixed-pie"—in which one person gains at the expense of the other. For example, haggling over the price of a rug in a bazaar is a distributive negotiation. In most conflicts, however, more than one issue is at stake, and each party values the issues differently. The outcomes available are no longer a fixed-pie divided among all parties. An agreement can be found that is better for both parties than what they would have reached through distributive negotiation. This is an* integrative *negotiation.*
>
> *However, parties in a negotiation often don't find these beneficial trade-offs because each assumes its interests directly conflict with those of the other party. "What is good for the other side must be bad for us" is a common and unfortunate perspective that most people have. This is the mindset we call the mythical "fixed-pie."*[55]

The "fixed-pie" metaphor has been associated with **distributive negotiation** because it involves win–lose thinking around a fixed amount of assets. This is illustrated by historical labour–management negotiations when settlements over wage increases seemed impossible. If you have survived a labour strike at your own college or university,

"In most conflicts, however, more than one issue is at stake, and each party values the issues differently . . . An agreement can be found that is better for both parties than what they would have reached through distributive negotiation."

Distributive negotiation

Two interdependent parties, each with their own opposite preference, seek to make a decision that will result in one party winning at the expense of the other.

the conflicting parties may decide to seek resolution from an arbitrator (see earlier discussion about ADR techniques).

On the other hand, ***integrative negotiation*** works under the belief that a resolution can be found that is mutually satisfying because it calls for a progressive win–win strategy.[56] Individuals can use integrative or added-value negotiation, for example, when they are trying to negotiate a settlement for themselves. Integrative negotiation is most appropriate for intergroup and inter-organizational conflict because of the numerous controversial issues on the table for discussion. It encourages joint cooperation and rich dialogue, hence more valued discussion. You can imagine the amount of time and money involved in reaching such resolution. In a laboratory study of joint venture negotiations, teams trained in integrative tactics achieved better outcomes for both sides than did untrained teams.[57]

North American negotiators generally are too short-term oriented and are poor relationship builders when negotiating in Asia, Latin America, and the Middle East.[58] The added-value negotiation techniques illustrated in Figure 8.4 are helpful during integrative negotiation; notice how dialogue expands under this model, as each side is encouraged to make a collective effort to make this agreement work. Refer back to Figure 8.3 and you can place integrative negotiation tactics on a line between integrating and avoiding, as negotiators use such tactics as reframing problems into opportunities, helping the other side save money, building trust during information exchanges to show sincerity

then you personally know the characteristics of distributive negotiation. Refer back to Figure 8.3 and you can place distributive negotiation tactics on a line between dominating and obliging as negotiators use such tactics as force, persuasion, promises, threats, or just digging in their heels (which can result in strike) to find resolution. If resolution is still not possible after such tactics, like in our example of a college or university labour issue, then

Integrative negotiation

Two interdependent parties with their own preferences and values seek a win–win resolution through greater dialogue and cooperation.

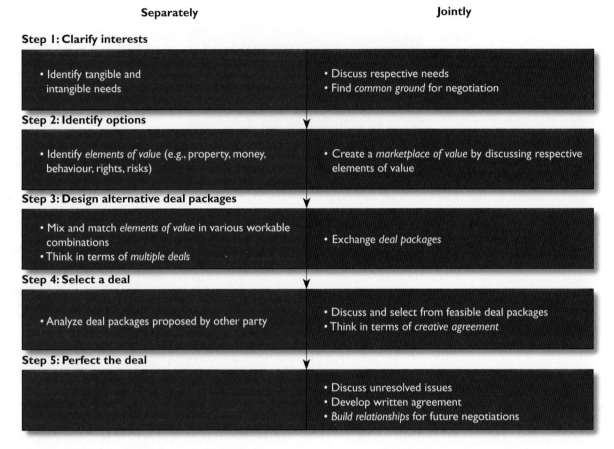

▶ **FIGURE** **8.4** An Integrative Approach: Added-Value Negotiation

Separately | **Jointly**

Step 1: Clarify interests

- Identify tangible and intangible needs

- Discuss respective needs
- Find *common ground* for negotiation

Step 2: Identify options

- Identify *elements of value* (e.g., property, money, behaviour, rights, risks)

- Create a *marketplace of value* by discussing respective elements of value

Step 3: Design alternative deal packages

- Mix and match *elements of value* in various workable combinations
- Think in terms of *multiple deals*

- Exchange *deal packages*

Step 4: Select a deal

- Analyze deal packages proposed by other party

- Discuss and select from feasible deal packages
- Think in terms of *creative agreement*

Step 5: Perfect the deal

- Discuss unresolved issues
- Develop written agreement
- *Build relationships* for future negotiations

SOURCE: Adapted from K. Albrecht and S. Albrecht, "Added Value Negotiating," *Training*, April 1993, pp 26–29. Used by permission of VNU Business Publications via The Copyright Clearance Center.

in bargaining in good faith, or maybe even helping the other side find more assets (expand the size of the pie). An example of integrative negotiation took place in 2009 between General Motors and the CAW to try and meet realistic wage/benefit targets as part of the conditions for government grants. The CAW understood the seriousness of GM's situation, so they agreed to concessions; on the other hand, GM respected the CAW's position on maintaining the wage and benefit gains received from previous agreements. Just weeks after GM's agreement, the CAW attempted to negotiate a similar deal with Chrysler, but was not as successful as both sides "dug in their heels."

Bringing It All Together If we were to compare and contrast these two types of negotiation styles, it would look like this:

Distributive negotiation:

- Goal: win-lose

- Amount of assets: fixed

- Tactics: force, persuasion, promises, threats, digging in heels

- Examples: historical labour-management wage disputes; haggling over prices with a street merchant

Integrative negotiation:

- Goal: win-win

- Amount of assets: expandable

- Tactics: dialogue, cooperation, reframing to find opportunities, cost cutting, and bargaining in good faith to build trust

- Example: more contemporary labour-management discussions

ETHICAL PITFALLS IN NEGOTIATION

The success of integrative negotiation, such as added-value negotiation, depends to a large extent on the *quality* of information exchanged, as researchers have documented.[59] Telling lies, hiding key facts, and engaging in the other potentially unethical tactics listed in Table 8.1 erode trust and goodwill. Without the benefits of trust and goodwill, a win–win resolution is not going to be possible.[60] An awareness of these dirty tricks can keep good faith bargainers from being unfairly exploited.[61] Unethical negotiating tactics need to be factored into organizational codes of ethics.

PRACTICAL LESSONS FROM NEGOTIATION RESEARCH

Laboratory and field studies have yielded these insights:

- Negotiators with fixed-pie expectations produced poor joint outcomes because they restricted and mismanaged information.[62]

- Personality characteristics can affect negotiating success. Negotiators who scored high on the Big Five personality dimensions of extraversion and agreeableness (refer back to Table 3.2) tended to do poorly with distributive (fixed-pie, win–lose) negotiations.[63]

Questionable/Unethical Tactics in Negotiation

TACTIC	DESCRIPTION/CLARIFICATION/RANGE
Lies	Subject matter for lies can include limits, alternatives, the negotiator's intent, authority to bargain, other commitments, acceptability of the opponent's offers, time pressures, and available resources.
Puffery	Among the items that can be puffed up are the value of one's payoffs to the opponent, the negotiator's own alternatives, the costs of what one is giving up or is prepared to yield, importance of issues, and attributes of the products or services.
Deception	Acts and statements may include promises or threats, excessive initial demands, careless misstatements of facts, or asking for concessions not wanted.
Weakening the opponent	The negotiator here may cut off or eliminate some of the opponent's alternatives, blame the opponent for his own actions, use personally abrasive statements to or about the opponent, or undermine the opponent's alliances.
Strengthening one's own position	This tactic includes building one's own resources, including expertise, finances, own position and alliances. It also includes presentations of persuasive rationales to the opponent or third parties (e.g., the public, the media) or getting mandates for one's position.
Non-disclosure	Includes partial disclosure of facts, failure to disclose a hidden fact, failure to correct the opponents' misperceptions or ignorance, and concealment of the negotiator's own position or circumstances.
Information exploitation	Information provided by the opponent can be used to exploit his weaknesses, close off his alternatives, generate demands against him, or weaken his alliances.
Change of mind	Includes accepting offers one had claimed one would not accept, changing demands, withdrawing promised offers, and making threats one promised would not be made. Also includes the failure to behave as predicted.
Distraction	These acts or statements can be as simple as providing excessive information to the opponent, asking many questions, evading questions, or burying the issue. Or they can be more complex, such as feigning weakness in one area so that the opponent concentrates on it and ignores another.
Maximization	Includes demanding the opponent make concessions that result in the negotiator's gain and the opponent's equal or greater loss. Also entails converting a win–win situation into win–lose.

TABLE 8.1

SOURCE: Reprinted from H.J. Reitz, J.A. Wall Jr., and M.S. Love, "Ethics in Negotiation: Oil and Water or Good Lubrication?," *Business Horizons*, May–June 1998, p 6. © 1998, with permission from Elsevier.

- Good and bad moods can have positive and negative effects, respectively, on negotiators' plans and outcomes.[64] So, wait until both you and your boss are in a good mood before you ask for a raise.

- In a recent study, subjects trained in goal setting and problem solving enjoyed more satisfying and hopeful dialogues on a controversial subject than did those with no particular strategy.[65] Practical implication: don't negotiate without being adequately prepared.

Research in the area of conflict, negotiation, and gender issues continues to draw attention and the results are rather interesting. See the Focus on Diversity feature box for more detail.

LO 5 **SUMMARIZING THE VALUE OF THIRD-PARTY INTERVENTION**

When conflicting parties are not able to find resolution on their own and need some assistance, third party intervention can help. ADR offers many different strategies to assist conflicting parties find resolution, including facilitation, conciliation, peer review, ombudsman, mediation, and arbitration. Negotiation differs from ADR as it is more of a give and take. Distributive negotiation is rooted in the assumption that there is a fixed amount of assets, so win–lose tactics include threats, promises, firmness, persuasion, or digging in heels to achieve the desired outcome. Integrative negotiation seeks a win–win resolution using tactics such as reframing problems into opportunities, helping the other side save money, building trust during information exchanges to show sincerity in bargaining in good faith . . . or maybe even helping the other side find more assets (expand the size of the pie).

Conflicting individuals are sometimes so focused on their own emotions that they have difficulty moving on to find a satisfying resolution. By inviting third-party intervention, unbiased parameters or ground rules for arguing can be determined so that a neutral perspective can guide discussion toward finding common interests.

A Contingency Approach to Conflict

Three realities exist around organizational conflict. First, various types of conflict are inevitable because they are triggered by different causes. Second, too little conflict may be as counterproductive as too much. Third, there is no single best way to avoid or resolve conflict. Conflict specialists recommend a contingency approach to managing conflict by monitoring causes of conflict and actual conflict. If signs of too little conflict—such as apathy or lack of creativity—appear, then functional conflict needs to be stimulated by looking for possible causes of conflict. On the other hand, when conflict becomes dysfunctional, the appropriate conflict-handling style needs to be used to find resolution and get the workplace back to a healthy place. Training involving role playing can prepare all employees to try alternative conflict-handling styles.

Third-party interventions are necessary when conflicting parties are unwilling or unable to engage in conflict resolution or integrative negotiation. Integrative or added-value negotiation is most appropriate for intergroup and inter-organizational conflict. The key is to get the conflicting parties to abandon traditional fixed-pie thinking and their win–lose expectations.

Summary of Learning Objectives

1. **Define *conflict, functional conflict,* and *dysfunctional conflict.*** Conflict is a process in which one party perceives that its interests are being opposed or negatively affected by another party. It is inevitable and not necessarily destructive. Too little conflict, as evidenced by apathy or lack of creativity, can be as great a problem as too much conflict. Functional conflict enhances organizational interests, while dysfunctional conflict is counterproductive.

2. **Identify the various causes of conflict.** Conflict can come from many different sources, including: incompatible personalities or value systems; overlapping or unclear job boundaries; competition for limited resources; inter-group or interdependent group competition; inadequate communication; unreasonable or unclear policies, standards, or rules; unreasonable deadlines; extreme time pressures; unmet expectations; unresolved or hidden conflicts that people are afraid to talk about; and the complexity of the organization.

3. **List two approaches an employee or manager can take to respond to each of the following: personality conflicts, inter-group conflict, and cross-cultural conflicts.** Personality conflicts involve interpersonal opposition based on personal dislike and/or disagreement (or as an outgrowth of workplace incivility). Care needs to be taken with personality conflicts in the workplace because of the legal implications of diversity, discrimination, and sexual harassment. This applies to all employees. As for managers, they should investigate and document personality conflicts, take corrective actions such as feedback or behaviour modification if appropriate, or attempt informal dispute resolution. Difficult or persistent personality conflicts need to be referred to human resource specialists or counsellors. Members of in-groups tend to see themselves as unique individuals who are more moral than outsiders, whom they view as a threat and stereotypically as all alike. In-group thinking is associated with a type of behaviour called *ethnocentrism,* which means looking at the world primarily from the perspective of one's own culture. International consultants can prepare people from different cultures to work effectively together. Cross-cultural conflict can be minimized by having expatriates build strong cross-cultural relationships with their hosts (primarily by being good listeners, being sensitive to others, and being more cooperative than competitive).

4. **Compare and contrast the five alternative styles for handling conflict.** The first conflict-handling style is *integrating (problem solving)*, which shows high concern for self and the other person's needs. The focus is directed to working the problem. This is a good style for generating a lot of alternative solutions around a complex conflict, but is very time consuming. *Obliging (smoothing)* is when people neglect their own concerns to satisfy the concerns of the other party. Differences between conflicting parties are played down and cooperation to assist the other side achieve their interests is preferred. This style is appropriate if you are involved with making a decision about something that is not of great priority to you. Obliging works on a cooperative model, but is usually used as a temporary fix, not a long-term solution. *Dominating (forcing)* is a style that has low concern for others' needs but high concern for oneself. This can cause the other party to become angry, as they feel they aren't having any say over the situation. Dominating styles work during contentious issues, when safety and security are at risk, and when a deadline is very near and a speedy solution is needed. However, it often breeds resentment. *Avoiding* is when there is low concern for self and others'

needs. This is a passive style and appropriate for calming emotionally charged situations, but it is a temporary fix as the real issues don't get addressed. *Compromising* is a give and take from both sides, involving moderate concern for both self and others. It works best if conflicting parties are from the same political level of the organization or have equal power. The strength of this strategy is that everyone gets something of value, but it does stifle creative problem solving. There is no single best style.

5. **Assess the value of having third party interventions for conflict resolution, including the ADR and two negotiation processes.** Sometimes conflicting parties are not able to find resolution on their own and need some assistance. A third party is brought in to help achieve a faster and more user-friendly resolution. ADR offers many different strategies to assist conflicting parties find resolution, including facilitation, conciliation, peer review, ombudsman, mediation, and arbitration. Negotiation differs from ADR as it is more of a give and take. There are two basic types of negotiation: distributive and integrative. Both involve people who are interdependent and have their own preferences, but the mindset is different. Distributive negotiation is rooted in the assumption that there is a fixed amount of assets. Here the win–lose tactics can include threats, promises, firmness, persuasion, or digging in heels to achieve desired outcome. This type of negotiation can be found on a line between the conflict-handling styles of dominating and obliging, and is usually associated with historical labour–management wage disputes. Integrative negotiation seeks a win–win resolution around many issues. The negotiators can use a range of tactics, such as reframing problems into opportunities, helping the other side save money, building trust during information exchanges to show sincerity in bargaining in good faith . . . or even helping the other side find more assets (expand the size of the pie). It is most appropriate for inter-group and inter-organizational conflict. Integrative negotiation can be found on a line between the conflict-handling styles of integrating and avoiding, as each side engages in dialogue to reach an agreement.

Discussion Questions

1. What examples of functional and dysfunctional conflict have you observed in organizations? What were the outcomes? What caused the dysfunctional conflict?

2. Which of the six ADR techniques appeals the most to you? Explain your response.

3. In your opinion, why would some individuals be reluctant to invite a third party to help resolve a conflict, while others are quick to drag as many people into the conflict as possible? Try to understand the behaviours of both types of people.

4. Why are some conflicting parties willing to stage a strike to get what they want?

5. Read, explain, and interpret the lesson to learn from the following statement:

   Corporations that have developed collaborative conflict management systems report significant litigation cost savings. Brown and Root reported an 80 percent reduction in outside litigation costs, Motorola reported a 75 percent reduction over a period of six years, NCR reported a 50 percent reduction and a drop of pending lawsuits from 263 in 1984 to 28 in 1993 (J. Ford, Workplace Conflict: Facts and Figures, *[online] Mediate.com website, July 2000).*

Google Searches

1. **Google Search:** "Cost of workplace conflict in Canada" or "CIM – the cost of workplace conflict" In business, activity that affects the bottom line gets the most attention. What is the cost of workplace conflict? Research information that quantifies the cost of workplace conflict on an annual basis in terms of dollars lost or lost productivity from increased absenteeism.

2. **Google Search:** "ADR Institute of Canada Inc." If you needed to find a third party to help resolve a conflict, who in your province is an available contact or affiliate?

3. **Google Search:** "BATNA – best negotiated agreement" and "walk away point of negotiation" Compare and contrast these two concepts. How do they relate to this chapter and the section on negotiation?

Experiential Exercise

Communicating in Conflict Exercise

PURPOSE: This exercise is to help familiarize you with communicating in conflict language, using the two pronouns "I" vs "You."   Approx. Timing: 20 minutes.

ACTIVITY ASSIGNMENT

Below are three statements. These are all true statements made to people at various times. Working with the student next to you, follow these directions:

- Underline and count the number of "you" (or your) words in each sentence.
- Circle the word(s) that make the sentence harsh and accusatory.
- Rewrite the statement using the word "I" so that the sentence isn't as likely to stir conflict. Try not to use the word "you."
- Share your new sentence with the rest of the class.
- Make corrections or enhancements to your rewritten sentence as necessary.

1. "Your position on customer service is twisted! How can you believe that customers are always right? They aren't! If we do what you want us to do by giving in to whatever the customer wants, we'll go broke!"

2. "Hey you moron . . . what are you doing? You aren't cleaning the work counters like you are supposed to. Didn't they teach you how to do it properly when you were being trained? Here, let me show you how to do it right!"

3. Joe says to Tia: "Last week in the meeting you 'shushed' me like a mother. In fact, you actually said, 'zip it' to me! You are not my parent. You have no right to tell me how to behave in a meeting. I'm a mature adult. If I want to talk, I will and you can't do anything about that! Don't you ever tell me to 'shush' up in a meeting again. Do you understand?"

   Tia says to Joe: "Yes, but you were talking and laughing so loud and for so long that I couldn't hear the speaker."

The **Presentation** Assistant

Here are possible topics and sources related to this chapter that can be further explored by student groups looking for ideas.

	SOURCES OF CONFLICT IN THE OFFICE—EXAMPLES AND HOW TO RESOLVE THEM USING THE TECHNIQUES FROM CHAPTER	THE LANGUAGE OF CONFLICT—IS IT THE SAME IN ALL CULTURES?	WHEN CONFLICT ESCALATES INTO VIOLENCE—CAUSES AND PREVENTION
YouTube Videos	• Terry Tate the Office Linebacker for Resolving Conflict • Russel Peters – Business With Chinese • Angry Boss with Will Ferrell	• Russel Peters –How To Become A Canadian Citizen • Creating Healthy Community Patterns – Canadian Aboriginal Conflict Resolution • Bush Comes Under Shoe Attack In Baghdad	• Workplace Violence • Gunman Opens Fire in German School • Angry Employee Destroys Boss's Car
TV Shows or Movies to Preview	• *The Office* (Season 2) – "Conflict Resolution Episode" • *30 Rock* – "Fight The Power Episode"	• *Outsourced* (Movie) • *Boiler Room* • *Rush Hour 2*	• *Office Space* (Movie)
Internet Searches	• Canadian Centre for Occupational Health and Safety • *Talking From 9–5 – Women and Men in the Workplace* (by D. Tannen) • *Getting To Yes* (by the Harvard Negotiation Project)	• *Cross Cultural Conflict* (by D. Elmer) • Cross Cultural Conflict Resolution In Teams	• Canadian Safety Council, Psychological Violence • Canadian Initiative on Workplace Violence • www.workplace.ca • *Canadian Security Magazine*
Ice Breaker Classroom Activity	• Ask students to identify one conflict they have personally experienced in their jobs. Have the class share these short vignettes and write a short summary title for each of them on the board to see if there is a pattern.	• Ask students if they are able to distinguish when a person from another culture is angry or upset. (To start the discussion, give the example of a person from Asia who shakes his or her head up and down in agreement – does this mean he or she admits guilt and agrees?)	• Ask the students if anyone has ever witnessed violence in the workplace. If so, how did it affect the productivity of those in the office, directly and indirectly?

OB In Action Case Study

How Should We Help Shelly?

SCENARIO: Jimmy Page is the Director of the IT department at ABC Inc. Jimmy prides himself in being a proactive manager in terms of policies and procedures. As well, Jimmy believes he's connected to his people and to the situations taking place within his department and in the organization.

Last week, Jimmy received an email from Shelly, a well-respected employee who has worked in sales at ABC Inc. for almost 15 years. Shelly is a seasoned vet when it comes to work experience and many people—including clients—like Shelly. Jimmy doesn't know Shelly personally, but knows of her. The email read as follows:

Hello Jim,

Something happened to me five weeks ago and I thought it may be something that warrants your involvement. I received a threatening and harassing email from one of our clients. The client was a 36-year-old male who threatened that if he didn't get the discount he wanted on a certain product, he was prepared to send notices to all our clients and suppliers about how bad the service is that we provided, what a terrible employee I was, and what a rip-off everything was at ABC Inc.

I complained to my immediate supervisor a few times about the client's behaviour and harassing emails, but I guess meeting sales targets each month was more important than my issue. Over the last several months, the client has been sending me dozens of flirtatious emails. I pretty much tried to politely ignore them, but when I refused his direct demands to go out with him on a date to dinner . . . well, that's when it got pretty bad. After I said no, then he became belligerent and argumentative every time we got into discussions, either face to face or in emails. He then began demanding that I give him better deals on our products, to sell our products below cost. I can understand his wanting a good deal, competitive pricing and all, but I believe he crossed the line with the personal attacks, profanity, and then personal threats: "Come on sweetie, I know what car you drive and where you live . . . no one will know about the f__ing deal . . . it'll be our secret." I considered contacting our security, but they typically only deal with trespassing and parking issues, not something of this magnitude. Instead, I was advised by a friend who is a lawyer to call the local police department to have him arrested for harassment and intent to do harm.

Over the last several weeks, I have learned that this client has bullied ABC Inc. employees for almost two years using three different email addresses, and everyone has either dismissed the threats as not being serious enough, or just tolerated or ignored the abuse. In fact, after reviewing past sales records, I discovered that he received deep discounts on our products dozens of times. I can't believe he has been allowed to behave in such a manner for so many years!!

I know that our customers are supposed to always be right and we're supposed to provide good service, but I think this client crossed the line. When I called the police, they agreed, but said that they couldn't do anything about his threats other than to give a warning because the client denied writing the emails—rather, he claimed that some other person at his office must have gotten ahold of his email account and wrote them! He denied ever asking me out on a date or flirting with me, and said that I must have misunderstood the intentions of his past emails.

My questions are simple—why was/is this client being allowed to harass and threaten us? Why wasn't something done before my complaint to the police last month? What constitutes improper client conduct as it relates to IT, computers, and email at ABC Inc? Is security the only ones who can request IT to block emails from certain clients? Is there anything that your office can do to make sure this sort of thing doesn't happen again?

Thank you,

Shelly Smith

Jimmy was surprised by this email. ABC Inc. clearly has many company policies regarding all of the issues raised in the email. Jimmy didn't know anything about this particular situation, nor had any complaints ever been received from any of the department managers over the last few years regarding client/supplier harassment. Jimmy needed time to reflect on what to do with Shelly's questions.

Discussion Questions

1. What do you believe are the causes of this conflict?
2. How has technology contributed to this conflict at ABC Inc.? Has it been a positive tool for the firm?
3. Is Shelly the wrong employee for ABC Inc.? Is there evidence to suggest she's incompetent?
4. What kind of training and development initiatives would you recommend for this organization?
5. Which employees or managers do you believe should attend such training?

Ethical OB Dilemma

Break It Up!

Imagine you are an OB consultant. A mid-manager from a local organization in your city has approached you for an opinion on what is happening at her firm. She says:

"At the company where I work—we make creative products for children—two of the top executives are at war with each other. They go off on rants, they use foul language, and from time to time they actually have shoving matches. Both of these people are top producers, I might add. What is causing this behaviour? And is there anything co-workers can do? We're appalled, but the boss won't step in."

What advice would you give the mid-manager about the ethical implications for this behaviour? Consider the following options:

1. These people are simply high-spirited thoroughbreds who kick up some dust while helping the firm win the race. Just stay out of their way.

2. The good results these people get are more than offset by the negative impact their feud has on company productivity and morale. A coalition of employees needs to confront the boss with the facts and recommend corrective action.

3. In this obvious clash of personalities, one of these bullies must be fired. Or should the company fire both? The boss is clueless, so someone needs to elevate the issue to the board of directors.

4. A brave co-worker who has the respect of these feuding people needs to take them aside for a little talk about workplace civility, to break the cycle of dysfunctional conflict. This would be a win–win option, where everyone could save face and upper management wouldn't be dragged into the fray.

5. Have employees take sides in this feud and fight it out until there's a clear winner and loser.

6. You decide to behave differently. Explain another option.

Visit www.mcgrawhillconnect.ca to register.

McGraw-Hill Connect™ —Available 24/7 with instant feedback so you can study when you want, how you want, and where you want. Take advantage of the Study Plan—an innovative tool that helps you customize your learning experience. You can diagnose your knowledge with pre- and post-tests, identify the areas where you need help, search the entire learning package for content specific to the topic you're studying, and add these resources to your personalized study plan. Visit www.mcgrawhillconnect.ca to register—take practice quizzes, search the e-book, and much more.

Power, Politics, & Decision Making

The Shift of Power— Decisions On Saving The Big Three

Throughout the early months of 2009, Federal Finance Minister of record Jim Flaherty was faced with a controversial decision: *Should the Canadian government bail out the struggling auto manufacturers?* The Big Three domestic automakers (GM, Ford, and Chrysler) were asking for $1 billion in loan guarantees to help tide over the sector until demand from Canada's biggest trading partner, the U.S., recovered for North American-produced vehicles. GM reported a $2.5 billion third-quarter loss and warned that its cash levels could fall below what was needed to run its business by the end of the year if the economy didn't turn around and if it didn't get government aid.

What was at stake? A threat to potentially hundreds of thousands of jobs, due to the multiplier effect, that could double unemployment and throw this country into an immediate recession the likes of which were being compared to the depression years of the 1930s. It was feared that the economy would not be able to tolerate such a shock and that the effects would be long lasting. Flaherty refused to rush into making a decision, and chose instead to continue discussions with Canada's Big Three on whether taxpayer money should be provided to bail out these large corporations.

The Canadian Auto Workers supported the bailout. As Chris Buckley, then president of CAW Local 222 in Oshawa, told *Canadian Business Magazine*, "...it's absolutely disgusting" that Flaherty says he's only monitoring the situation when immediate action is required. Buckley said Canada can't wait for the U.S. bailout decision. "We're asking Flaherty and (Prime Minister Stephen) Harper to react immediately." Ken Lewenza, then national CAW president, agreed that any money for the auto industry should not be viewed as a bailout, but rather as an investment in the Canadian economy.

But Flaherty was quick to respond with a counter-argument. He told a group of economists in Toronto that, "... in my own riding, where I was yesterday, in Whitby-Oshawa ... there are lots of people who say, 'Don't do anything. Don't use my tax money to bail out an enterprise that may not survive. These are not high falutin' rich people saying this to me—these are people on the street." Adam Taylor, the acting federal director of the Canadian Taxpayers Federation, clearly disagreed with a bailout by stating, "Taxpayers cannot afford to continue to bail out mismanaged companies that expect perpetual handouts in good and bad times." The federation claimed that between 2003 and 2008, the Big Three had already received a total of $782 million in loans and future commitments from Canadian taxpayers.

As Finance Minister, Flaherty had the legitimate power to authorize a loan, but granting a bailout of such sizable proportions without consultation would be a risky political move. Flaherty was faced with a difficult decision. What would you do if you were in Flaherty's place?

SOURCES: T. Burgmann and C. Thomas, "Flaherty, CAW spar over auto sector help; Clement wants long-term solution," *The Canadian Press*, November 12, 2008. Canadian Business Online: http://www.canadianbusiness.com/shared/print.jsp?content=b1112167A&adzone= markets/headline_news ; B. Saporito, "Is General Motors Worth Saving?," *Time Magazine*, November 13, 2008, http://www.time.com/time/printout/0,8816,1858702,00.html.

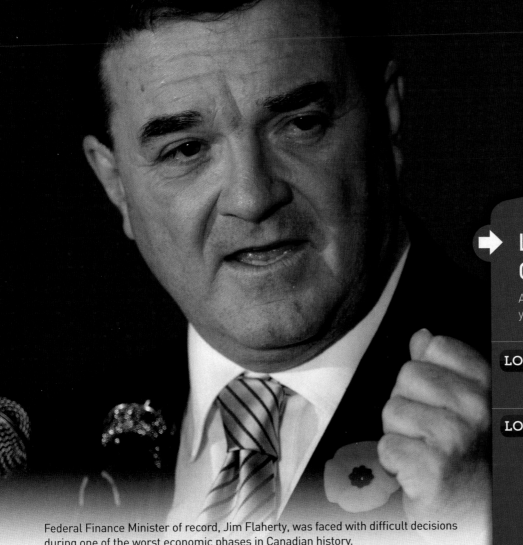

Federal Finance Minister of record, Jim Flaherty, was faced with difficult decisions during one of the worst economic phases in Canadian history.

The term *power* evokes mixed and often passionate reactions; just consider the keen positions taken in the chapter opening vignette involving corporate bailouts for the Big Three domestic automakers. Citing instances of government corruption and corporate misconduct, many observers view power as an evil force. To these cynics, Lord Acton's time-honoured statement that "power corrupts and absolute power corrupts absolutely" is as true as ever.[1] However, OB specialists remind us that, like it or not, power is a fact of life in modern organizations.

In fact, power can be a positive force in organizations to help collect the various resources available to get something done.[2] While power may be a mysterious concept to the casual observer, social scientists view power as having reasonably clear dimensions. We'll begin this chapter by discussing five fundamental dimensions of power: (1) power and dependency, (2) social power and the five bases of power, (3) research on tactics used and how power impacts outcomes, (4) employee empowerment, and (5) the need to use power ethically.

Our discussion of power will make the transition naturally into politics, as we see how one can influence the other. Understanding the role of politics within an organization is something that is rarely talked about in business classes, but it does exist and understanding the fundamentals around political action, building network contacts for support, and being aware of political tactics is important.

→ **LEARNING OBJECTIVES**

After reading this chapter, you should be able to:

LO 1 **Define** *power*, *social power*, and *socialized power*.

LO 2 **Identify** and briefly describe French and Raven's five bases of power, relating factors to tactics used and work outcomes (e.g., job performance, job satisfaction, and turnover).

LO 3 **Explain** how uncertainty can trigger the production of organizational politics, which can lead to the use of personalized power tactics.

LO 4 **Compare and contrast** the *rational model* of decision making to *bounded rationality*, *decision trees*, and *intuition*.

LO 5 **Infer** what causes an escalation of commitment and predict what type of outcome can result.

LO 6 **Summarize** the pros and cons of involving groups in the decision-making process.

We'll end our chapter discussions with decision making, because those with power who have the political influence are affecting organizational outcomes all the time. Other than using our "guts" to make decisions, there are several other models worth considering. In times of economic uncertainty, it's critical to emphasize the need for creative decision making to help find new solutions to complex problems ... and to keep in mind the need for an ethical base when doing so.

LO 1 The Fundamentals of Power

Power is often related to dependency, and is defined as the ability to influence others to develop a dependent relationship. For example, if employees depend on their manager to sign their paycheque, then the manager has power over the employees. If a manager only has one employee with the ability to complete a certain task and no one else in the entire organization has the same skill or ability, then the employee has power over the manager. Power exists throughout the entire organization, at all levels, and in all different sorts of positions.

Power

The ability to influence others to develop a dependent relationship.

Social and Socialized Power Recalling our discussion in Chapter 5 about motivation and McClelland's Need Theory, we learned that one of the basic human needs is for power. McClelland stated that this need for power is a learned behaviour, not something individuals are born with. Subsequently, throughout the last half century, researchers have been drawn to the notion of power and what it means to want it. To some, power is bad, and we'll talk more about this a bit later. But to others, power is necessary for doing something constructive. From this perspective, having **social power** is a good thing because it means the ability to get things done with human, informational, and material resources. So **socialized power** within an organization or by an individual is directed for the purposes of helping others. A series of interviews with 25 women elected to public office found a strong preference for socialized power. The following comments illustrate their desire to wield power effectively and ethically:

Social power

Ability to get things done with human, informational, and material resources.

Socialized power

Directed at helping others.

- "Power in itself means nothing ... I think power is the opportunity to really have an impact on your community."

- "My goal is to be a powerful advocate on the part of my constituents."[3]

The Focus on Diversity feature box explores in greater detail the differences in perspective on power between the genders.

THE FIVE BASES OF POWER   LO 2

A popular classification scheme for social power originated more than 46 years ago with the work of John French and Bertram Raven. They proposed that power arises from five different bases: reward power, coercive power, legitimate power, expert power, and referent power.[4] Notice how each of the four bases try to obtain compliance in some way, but the manner in which they approach influencing others differ greatly.

- **Legitimate power** This base of power is anchored to one's formal position or authority. Thus, individuals who obtain compliance primarily because of their formal authority to make decisions have **legitimate power**. Legitimate power may express itself in either a positive or negative manner. Here's an example of positive legitimate power that focuses constructively on job performance: *Pat, as the production coordinator on this project, I have to advise you that this material is late. I need your continued cooperation in the future because if ads are expected to run on time, then I'm going to need the approved copy no later than 24 hours before the deadline. OK? So, how's the family?"* Negative legitimate power tends to be threatening and demeaning to those being influenced. Its main purpose is to build the power holder's ego. For example, *I suggest you take my advice since I'm the Supervisor in charge of this unit ... I can make or break your career, you know!*

Legitimate power

Obtaining compliance through formal authority.

- **Reward power** People have **reward power** if they can obtain compliance by promising or granting rewards. This concept relates back to our discussions about Vroom's expectancy theory in Chapter 5. An example of reward power is a professor who encourages students to actively participate in class, and in return rewards students with bonus marks: *If you do this extra work, then I'd be pleased to take it into consideration when calculating your final mark!*

Reward power

Obtaining compliance with promised or actual rewards.

POWER FROM A GENDER VIEWPOINT

Is there a difference between the way women and men view power? In one study, a sample of 94 male and 84 female non-managerial and professional employees completed a psychological test. Results indicated that the male and female employees had similar needs for power, but the women had a significantly higher need for socialized power than did their male counterparts. This finding serves today's workplaces well, as women are playing an ever-greater administrative role. Unfortunately, as women gain power in the workplace, greater tension is observed between men and women.

According to an article published in *Training* magazine, the tension between women and men in the workplace is a natural outcome of power inequities between the genders. Social researchers argue that men still have most of the power and are resisting any change as a way to protect their power base. Consultant Susan L. Webb asserts that sexual harassment has far more to do with exercising power in an unhealthy way than with sexual attraction. Likewise, the glass ceiling, a metaphor for the barriers women face in climbing the corporate ladder to management and executive positions, is about power and access to power.

Accordingly, "powerful women were described more positively by women than by men" in a study of 140 female and 125 male college students in Sydney, Australia.

What is your perception of power, and is it consistent with the research discussed above?

SOURCES: B. Moses, "You Can't Make Change; You Have to Sell It," *Fast Company*, April 1999, p 101. Also see J. Kirby, "Just Trying to Help," *Harvard Business Review*, June 2006, pp 35–39; and J. Welch and S. Welch, "A Dangerous Division of Labor," *BusinessWeek*, November 6, 2006, p 122. B. Filipczak, "Is It Getting Chilly in Here?" *Training*, February 1994, p 27; Data from J. Onyx, R. Leonard and K. Vivekananda, "Social Perception of Power: A Gender Analysis," *Perceptual and Motor Skills*, February 1995, pp 291–296.

■ **Coercive power** Threats of punishment and actual punishment give an individual **coercive power.** For instance, consider this heavy-handed tactic by Wolfgang Bernhard, a Volkswagen executive. "A ruthless cost-cutter, Bernard has a favourite technique: He routinely locks staffers in meeting rooms, then refuses to open the doors until they've stripped $1,500 in costs from a future model."[5] Another example is, *Hey Hot Shot! If you don't want to do this job, then let me know and I'll inform the boss. I'm sure we can find ten other people in the unemployment office who would love to do this job at half the salary! So, what'll it be?*

Coercive power

Obtaining compliance through threatened or actual punishment.

■ **Expert power** Valued knowledge or information gives an individual **expert power** over those who need such knowledge or information. The power of supervisors is enhanced because they know about work schedules and assignments before their employees do. But employees who have a unique skill set that is the best in the region hold the power. In today's high-tech workplace, knowledge is power. For example, *I know Mitch is very hard to work with and can be difficult, but he writes better programs than any person in this province. We need him!*

■ **Referent power** Also called charisma, **referent power** comes into play when one's personality becomes the reason for compliance. Role models have referent power over those who identify closely with them.[6] They are liked— it's that simple. Certain kinds of leaders can have a lot of referent power over members of the organization (we'll talk more about this in the next chapter). But anyone in the organization who holds true to their word, is considerate of others, and treats people with respect and dignity will be given power by those who feel they deserve it. For example: *Fred is the best custodian we've ever had, he's competent, he's kind and very dependable. He's helpful to every employee in this building. If Fred says we're wasting too much energy, then I say we listen to him and start using more energy efficient bulbs!*

Referent power

Obtaining compliance through charisma or personal attraction.

Expert power

Obtaining compliance through one's knowledge or information.

RESEARCH FINDINGS: INFLUENCING TACTICS

Remember that power is the potential of influencing others—so how is this achieved? Research initiated by David Kipnis and his colleagues in 1980 revealed how people influence each other in organizations. Statistical refinements and replications by other researchers over a 13-year period eventually narrowed the findings down to nine influence tactics.[7] The nine tactics, ranked in diminishing order of use in the workplace, are as follows:

1. Rational persuasion (reason, logic, or facts)

2. Inspirational appeals (appeal to others emotions, ideals, or values)

3. Consultation (get others involved in process)

4. Ingratiation (use praise or flattery to make the other person more open to listening)

5. Personal appeals (friendship)

6. Exchange (making promises or trading favours)

7. Coalition tactics (get a third party to agree with you and convince others)

8. Pressure (threats)

9. Legitimating tactics (rules, policies, or rights)[8]

RESEARCH FINDINGS: INFLUENCING OUTCOMES

According to researchers, there are three possible influencing outcomes that can be expected when trying to have power over someone else: commitment, (agreement through buy in), compliance (completion of task without buy in), and resistance (no agreement). A re-analysis of 18 field studies that measured French and Raven's five bases of power uncovered "severe methodological shortcomings."[9] After correcting for these problems, the researchers identified the following relationships between power bases and work outcomes such as job performance, job satisfaction, and turnover:

- Expert and referent power had a *generally positive* impact on job performance and satisfaction, and lowered turnover. Using these types of power bases has a greater chance of getting *commitment* from others.

- Reward and positive legitimate power had only a *slightly positive* impact over the same variables. These types of power bases will likely result in getting others to be *compliant* with your requests.

- Coercive power had a *slightly negative* impact, meaning that this power base does not seem to enhance job performance or job satisfaction, and may in fact increase employee turnover. In this case, you can expect compliance, *resistance* from others in the form of excuses and arguments, or someone just saying "no."[10]

The goal for anyone seeking power is to try and make gains by using the expert and referent techniques first; do not rely upon the legitimate power a position may offer or the access to rich reward incentives. Using coercive power techniques to influence others is the weakest of all the bases and should therefore be avoided. Commitment is superior to compliance because it is driven by internal or intrinsic motivation.[11] Employees who merely comply require frequent "jolts" of power from team leaders, supervisors, or managers to keep them headed in a productive direction. Committed employees tend to be self-starters who do not require close supervision—a key success factor in today's flatter, team-oriented organizations.

In a follow-up study involving 251 employed business seniors, the same researcher looked at the relationship between influence styles and bases of power. This was a bottom-up study; it examined employee perceptions of managerial influence and power. Rational persuasion was found to be a highly acceptable managerial influence tactic. Why? Because employees perceived it to be associated with the three bases of power they viewed positively: legitimate, expert, and referent.[12] In the end, expert and referent power appear to get the best *combination* of positive results and favourable reactions from employees.[13]

EMPOWERMENT: FROM POWER SHARING TO POWER DISTRIBUTION

Empowerment is an exciting trend in today's organizations, which centres on giving employees authority and responsibility over tasks that were once held by their superiors. The movement toward more empowerment at all levels of an organization can be attributed to many factors, including skilled and knowledgeable employees wanting to self-manage, and also decades of cost cutting measures and structural downsizing that have resulted in losses of middle manager positions. This trend wears various labels, including "high-involvement management," "participative management," and "open-book management." Regardless of the preferred label, it is all about empowerment. While some OB textbooks emphasize it as a management tool, empowerment is really about increased job satisfaction demanded by those with high internal locus on control (see Chapter 3, Self Concept, Personality, and Emotions) who prefer to

Empowerment

Employees being assigned authority and responsibility over tasks once held by their superiors.

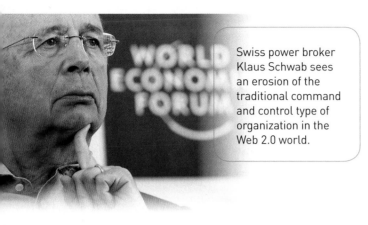

Swiss power broker Klaus Schwab sees an erosion of the traditional command and control type of organization in the Web 2.0 world.

A general issue will be the changing power equation, which means that everywhere in society and business, the power is moving from the centre to the periphery. Vertical command-and-control structures are being eroded and replaced by communities and different platforms. We are moving into the Web 2.0 world, and this has tremendous implications on the national level and on business models.[14]

manage themselves. Those who dismiss the employee empowerment trend as a passing fad need to see it as part of a much, much larger picture (see International OB feature box). Klaus Schwab, a respected Swiss businessman and philanthropist, recently offered this sweeping perspective:

Consultant and writer W. Alan Randolph offers this definition: "empowerment is recognizing and releasing into the organization the power that people already have in their wealth of useful knowledge, experience, and internal motivation."[15] A core component of this process is progressively pushing decision-making authority throughout the organization at all levels. Steve Kerr, who has served as the chief learning officer at General Electric and now Goldman Sachs, adds this important qualification: "We say empowerment is moving decision making

AZIM PREMJI, HEAD OF INDIA'S OUT-SOURCING GIANT WIPRO, IS NOT KING

INTERNATIONAL OB

Encouraging empowerment throughout an organization isn't just a North American phenomenon. One of Azim Premji's most important accomplishments has been creating a lean culture that thrives, even under intense competitive pressure. He established two core principles that are instrumental in building the character of his leadership team. The first is rare among India's family-controlled companies: *The chairman is not king.* While Premji owns a controlling stake in Wipro Technologies, the number one provider of integrated business in India, he shares authority and responsibility with his subordinates. The second key principle: *a zero-political culture.* At Wipro, backstabbing, playing favourites, and kissing up to the boss—tactics that sap employee energy—simply don't work. Open and honest disagreements are not only tolerated, but also required, of everyone.

The chairman's style isn't just to encourage his lieutenants to debate one another; Premji insists that they debate him as well, even take him to task for his decisions or actions. "The man takes frontal criticism, and it's celebrated. You can openly disagree with him," says Subroto Bagchi, a former Wipro executive.

For Premji, openness is more than a personal style; it's a strategy. "I find that people excel when they're provided a fair, free, and apolitical environment," he says. "At Wipro we strive to provide an open culture that encourages diversity of opinions. An organizational ability to encourage and harness diversity of thought is a significant competitive advantage."

Playing the game of business according to Premji's rules has worked well for Wipro. Over the last several years, at times its expanding revenues have reached some 30 percent annually, while the overall tech services industry is expanding at about 5 percent per year. Meanwhile, operating margins in its tech business top 20 percent—more than twice the level of large Western services outfits.

With so much evidence supporting the introduction of employee empowerment strategies, why do you think some work environments are still reluctant to introduce the concept? Is it because employees will resist, or because management wants to maintain control?

SOURCE : Excerpted from S. Hamm, "How This Tiger Got Its Roar," *BusinessWeek*, October 30, 2006, pp 92–100.

(throughout the operational levels) where a competent decision can be made."[16] Of course, it is naive and counterproductive to hand power over to unwilling or unprepared employees. There is an assumption that exists within an empowered work environment that all employees want to be empowered. We have done corporate training and can attest to the fact that some employees just want to do their job and go home. They don't want any more responsibility or authority; to them, a job is a job. This type of employee would resist the introduction of empowerment in the workplace, and would need to be shown the advantages of it through mentorship or development workshops.

A MATTER OF DEGREE

The concept of empowerment requires some adjustments in traditional thinking. Power is not a zero-sum situation where one person's gain is another's loss (you may recall our discussion of negotiation in the last chapter). Remember, the purpose of socialized power is to help others, so the possibility of gains is unlimited. Empowerment is an extension of socialized power and it requires win–win thinking. Frances Hesselbein, the woman credited with modernizing the Girl Guides organization, put it this way: "The more power you give away, the more you have."[17] People who prefer to maintain control over their organizational

territory will view empowerment as a threat to their personal power and are missing the point because of their win–lose thinking.

The second adjustment to traditional thinking involves seeing empowerment as a matter of degree, not as an either-or proposition.[18] Figure 9.1 illustrates how power can be shifted to the hands of non-managers, step by step, throughout all the functional areas of the organization. The overriding goal is to increase productivity and competitiveness in leaner organizations. Each step in this evolution increases the power of employees who traditionally were told what, when, and how to do things. A good role model for the spirit of empowerment is Motorola executive Greg Brown:

> *He boils his philosophy down to three words: listen, learn, lead. It means you need to understand your business down to the nuts and bolts, let your employees know you won't have all the answers, and focus on just a handful of truly crucial things, even though dozens seem as important.*[19]

USING POWER RESPONSIBLY AND ETHICALLY

There are two aspects of power responsibility worth mentioning here: the abuse of power as it relates to dependency, and violating the spirit of socialized power.

▶ FIGURE 9.1   The Evolution of Power: From Domination to Delegation

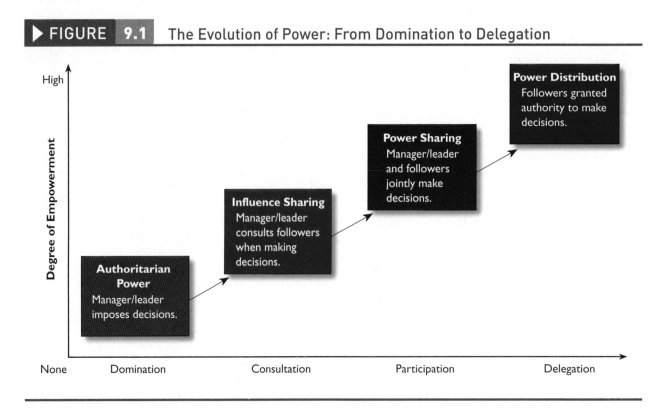

Abuse of Power As It Relates to Dependency When one person exerts power over another person in the office, and they do so through harassing and degrading means, then this is an abuse of power. Any type of harassing behaviour, including racial as well as sexual harassment, is about building up the impression of unstoppable power over another in a coercive demeaning way. Victims of this type of abuse in the office may not understand the method of these power games, but the intent is to belittle the self-worth of the person to the point of creating the illusion that success in the firm will only occur if total compliance is given over to the abuser. Today, most contemporary organizations have assigned personnel departments or other employee resources available for individuals reporting abuse; if not, then this type of behaviour is something that management must take seriously and remove from the workplace. If a person does not want to go to management to resolve this issue for whatever reason, then there are also outside government agencies in most major cities, like the Human Rights Commission, which will hear complaints on a confidential basis.

Abuse of Power by Violating the Spirit of Socialized Power People who have power but who do not use it for the purposes of helping others risk losing it. The media continue to cover stories of people in positions of power who misuse it for personal gain. You've probably heard the stories of Canadian ex-patriot Bernard Ebbers, the ex-CEO of WorldCom, or Conrad Black, the ex-CEO of Hollinger International, both of whom are serving time in jail for their misuse of power. But what about infamous Ponzi scheme investors, like Bernard Madoff or Montreal advisor Earl Jones, who are given power over the substantial cash assets of their clients; they mis-invest the money, lose it all, and yet still make money off the deal … isn't this an abuse of power? Or better yet, what about business people who ask for and receive financial assistance from taxpayers via government bailouts, only to pay themselves hefty bonuses while at the same time laying off other employees? Again, another example of power gone bad. These are all examples of a type of power quite different from socialized power, called ***personalized power***, and it is highly limiting. It also has the negative connotation of existing solely for the purposes of helping oneself win so that others may lose. People who have this type of power are not trusted, as their interests remain focused on themselves rather than on the collective interests of the organization.

Preoccupation with self-interest is understandable. When we came into this world, it was not out of wanting

Personalized power

Power directed at helping oneself.

to be a cooperating organization member, but as an individual with instincts for self-preservation. It took socialization in family, school, religious, sports, recreation, and employment settings to introduce us to the notion of mutuality of interest. Do you remember being taught as a child the idea of sharing with others, or to be kind and considerate of other people's things? In the corporate world, ***mutuality of interest*** involves win–win situations in which one's self-interest is served by cooperating actively and creatively with potential adversaries. A pair of organization development consultants offered this perspective of mutuality of interest:

Mutuality of interest

Balancing individual and organizational interests through win–win cooperation.

> *Nothing is more important than this sense of mutuality to the effectiveness and quality of an organization's products and services. Management must strive to stimulate a strong sense of shared ownership in every employee, because otherwise an organization cannot do its best in the long run. Employees who identify their own personal self-interest with the quality of their organization's output understand mutuality and strive to maintain it in their jobs and work relations.*[20]

Overall, the contemporary workplace seeks individuals in both managerial and non-managerial levels who are comfortable accepting the introduction of empowerment into the workplace. From an employee's perspective, they will benefit by having both responsibility and authority over their own work, which should translate into greater job satisfaction.

The Fundamentals of Organizational Politics

Employees are constantly challenged to achieve a workable balance between exercising personalized power that is self-serving, and socialized power that addresses the interests of the organization. If individuals spend too much energy enhancing their own position within the company, then it's safe to say you're dealing with people who understand the effect politics can have. We will use the following definition for our purposes when discussing politics: "***Organizational politics*** involves intentional acts of influence to enhance or protect the self-interest of an individual or group."[21] An emphasis on self-interest is key to

Organizational politics

Intentional acts of influence to enhance or protect the self-interest of an individual or group.

this concept. When a proper balance exists, the pursuit of self-interest may serve the organization's interests. Political behaviour becomes a negative force when self-interests erode or defeat organizational interests. For example, researchers have documented the political tactic of filtering and distorting information flowing up to the boss. This self-serving practice places the reporting employee in the best possible light.[22]

Most students of OB find the study of organizational politics intriguing. As we will see, however, organizational politics includes, but is certainly not limited to, dirty dealing. Organizational politics is an ever-present and sometimes annoying feature of modern work life. "Executives say that they spend 19 percent of their time dealing with political infighting with their staffs, according to a survey by OfficeTeam, a staffing services firm."[23] One expert recently observed, "Many 'new economy' companies use the acronym WOMBAT—or waste of money, brains, and time—to describe office politics."[24] On the other hand, organizational politics can be a positive force in modern work organizations. Skilful and well-timed politics can help you get your point across, neutralize resistance to a key project, or get a choice job assignment.

Roberta Bhasin, a telephone company district manager, put organizational politics into perspective by observing the following:

> *Most of us would like to believe that organizations are rationally structured, based on reasonable divisions of labour, a clear hierarchical communication flow, and well-defined lines of authority aimed at meeting universally understood goals and objectives.*
>
> *But organizations are made up of people with personal agendas designed to win power and influence. The agenda—the game—is called corporate politics. It is played by avoiding the rational structure, manipulating the communications hierarchy, and ignoring established lines of authority. The rules are never written down and seldom discussed.*
>
> *For some, corporate politics are second nature. They instinctively know the unspoken rules of the game. Others must learn. Managers who don't understand the politics of their organizations are at a disadvantage, not only in winning raises and promotions, but even in getting things done.*[25]

To that end, 32 percent of 3,447 middle and senior managers responding to an Internet survey said they needed coaching in how to be more politically savvy at work.[26]

We explore this important and interesting area by (1) identifying some basic triggers of political behaviour, (2) exploring the three levels of political action, and (3) discussing eight specific political tactics.

TRIGGERS OF POLITICAL BEHAVIOUR LO 3

Political manoeuvring is triggered primarily by uncertainty. Five common sources of uncertainty within organizations are:

1. Unclear objectives
2. Vague performance measures
3. Ill-defined decision processes
4. Strong individual or group competition[27]
5. Uncertainty that results from change

Regarding this last source of uncertainty, organization development specialist Anthony Raia noted, "Whatever we attempt to change, the political subsystem becomes active. Vested interests are almost always at stake and the distribution of power is challenged."[28]

Thus, we would expect a field sales representative striving to achieve an assigned quota to be less political than a management trainee working on a variety of projects. While some management trainees stake their career success on hard work, competence, and a bit of luck, many do not. These people attempt to gain a competitive edge through some combination of political tactics (to be discussed over the next few pages). Meanwhile, the salesperson's performance is measured in actual sales, not in terms of being friends with the boss or taking credit for others' work. Thus, the management trainee would tend to be more political than the field salesperson because of greater uncertainty about management's expectations.

Because employees generally experience greater uncertainty during the earlier stages of their careers, are junior employees more political than more senior ones? The answer is yes, according to a survey of 243 employed adults. In fact, one senior employee nearing retirement told the researcher: "I used to play political games when I was younger. Now I just do my job."[29]

It is easy to see how the management trainee would resort to as many personalized power tactics as possible to gain the kind of recognition desired, so let's discuss political action and tactics a bit more.

THREE LEVELS OF POLITICAL ACTION

Figure 9.2 illustrates three different levels of political action: the individual level, the coalition level, and the network level.[30] Each level has its distinguishing characteristics:

■ *First level*—the individual level. Personal self-interests are pursued by the individual. The political aspects of coalitions and networks are not obvious.

■ *Second level*—the coalition level. People with a common interest can become a political coalition

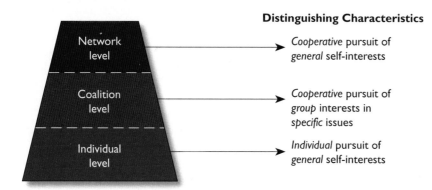

▶ FIGURE 9.2 Levels of Political Action in Organizations

Distinguishing Characteristics

Network level → *Cooperative* pursuit of *general* self-interests

Coalition level → *Cooperative* pursuit of *group* interests in *specific* issues

Individual level → *Individual* pursuit of *general* self-interests

SOURCE: A.T. Cobb, "Political Diagnosis: Aplications in Organizational Development," *Academy of Management Review,* July 1986, pp 482-96

■ *Third Level*—the network level. Political action involves networks.[32] In most major cities across the country, individuals can join a network of like-minded people (some refer to them as professional social clubs) who help each other achieve opportunities through word of mouth, and make broad connections and contacts that may serve them politically in the future. Unlike coalitions, which pivot on specific goals, networks are loose associations of individuals seeking social support for their general self-interests. Politically, networks are people-oriented, while coalitions are goal-oriented. Networks have broader and longer term agendas than do coalitions.

POLITICAL TACTICS

Anyone who has worked in an organization has firsthand knowledge of obvious politicking. Blaming someone else for your mistake is an obvious political ploy. But other political tactics are more subtle. Researchers have identified a range of political behaviour.

One landmark study, involving in-depth interviews with 87 people from 30 electronics companies, identified eight political tactics. According to the researchers, "Respondents were asked to describe organizational political tactics and personal characteristics of effective political actors based upon their accumulated experience in *all* organizations in which they had worked."[33]

Listed in descending order of occurrence, the eight political tactics that emerged were:

1. Attacking or blaming others
2. Using information as a political tool
3. Creating a favourable image (impression management)
4. Developing a base of support
5. Praising others (ingratiation)
6. Forming power coalitions with strong allies
7. Associating with influential people
8. Creating obligations (reciprocity)

Coalition

An informal group bound together by the active pursuit of a single goal.

by fitting the following definition. In an organizational context, a **coalition** is an informal group bound together by the active pursuit of a single goal. Coalitions may or may not coincide with formal group membership. For example, a group of employees could get together with a target goal of getting a sexual-harassing team leader fired. Once the problem is resolved and the goal reached, the coalition disbands. Experts note that political coalitions have "fuzzy boundaries," meaning they are fluid in membership, flexible in structure, and temporary in duration.[31]

"Stop whimpering and spin the wheel of blame, Lipton!"

SOURCE: *Harvard Business Review*, November 2003, p 86. ©Scott A Masear. Reprinted by permission of the author.

What is your attitude toward organizational politics? How often do you rely on the various tactics in Table 9.1? You can get a general indication of your political tendencies by comparing your behaviour with the characteristics in Table 9.1. Would you characterize yourself as politically naive, politically sensible, or a political shark? How do you think others view your political actions? What are the career, friendship, and ethical implications of your political tendencies?[34]

The Fundamentals of Decision Making

Now that you have some knowledge about power and politics, it is fitting to move on to the next discussion, understanding the decision-making process. Since power is about creating dependency or having influence to effect favourable outcomes, and politics is about creating outcomes that fulfill self-interest, then insight into the motives behind the decisions people make on a daily basis will enrich your understanding of this process; it's all about outcomes.

Decision making entails identifying and choosing alternative solutions that lead to a desired outcome. For example, you may be reading this book as part of an online course that you decided to take because you are working full time. Alternatively, you may be a full-time student reading this book as part of a course being taken on campus. Identifying and sorting out alternatives like when and how to take a course is the process of decision making.

Decision making

Identifying and choosing solutions that lead to a desired outcome.

Before we begin our discussion, you are encouraged to complete the Self-Assessment Exercise, "What Is Your Decision-Making Style?" Knowing your score may help you personalize the concepts discussed in the rest of this chapter.

THE RATIONAL MODEL

The *rational model* proposes that individuals use a rational six-step sequence when making decisions: (1) identify the problem or opportunity, (2) gather related information to make an informed decision, (3) formulate alternative solutions, (4) select the best alternative, (5) implement the solution, and (6) monitor and evaluate the solution. According to this model, individuals are completely objective and possess complete information to make a decision.[35] Despite criticism for being unrealistic, the rational model is helpful because it breaks down the decision-making process and serves as an anchor when designing future models.[36]

Rational model

A logical and sequential approach to decision making.

Identifying the Problem A problem exists when the actual situation and the desired situation differ. For example, a problem exists when you have to pay apartment rent at the end of the month and don't have enough money. Your problem is not that you have to pay rent. Your problem is obtaining the needed funds.

Gathering Related Information To make an informed decision, the decision maker has to consider related information. Sticking with our rent example, you have to consider all the variables that play into this problem, such as: Have you ever missed a payment in the past? Have you received a warning from the landlord about

TABLE 9.1	Are You Politically Naive, Politically Sensible, or a Political Shark?			
CHARACTERISTICS	NAIVE	SENSIBLE	SHARKS
Underlying attitude	Politics is unpleasant.	Politics is necessary.	Politics is an opportunity.
Intent	Avoid at all costs.	Further departmental goals.	Self-serving and predatory.
Techniques	Tell it like it is.	Network; expand connections; use system to give and receive favours.	Manipulate; use fraud and deceit when necessary.
Favourite tactics	None—the truth will win out.	Negotiate, bargain.	Bully, misuse information; cultivate and use "friends" and other contacts.

SOURCE: Reprinted from J.K. Pinto and O.P. Kharbanda, "Lessons for an Accidental Profession," *Business Horizons*, Vol. 38, No. 2, p 45, © 1995, with permission from Elsevier.

What Is Your Decision-Making Style?

INSTRUCTIONS: This survey consists of 20 questions, each with four responses. Consider each possible response for a question and then rank them according to how much you prefer each response. Because many of the questions are anchored to how individuals make decisions at work, feel free to use your student role as a frame of reference to answer the questions. For each question, use the space on the survey to rank the four responses with either 1, 2, 4, or 8. Use the number 8 for the responses that are **most** like you, a 4 for those that are **moderately** like you, a 2 for those that are **slightly** like you, and a 1 for the responses that are **least** like you. For example, a question might be answered [8], [4], [2], [1]. Do not repeat any number when answering a question, and put the numbers in the boxes next to each of the answers. Once you have all of the responses for the 20 questions, total the scores in each of the four columns. The total score for column one represents your directive style, column two your analytical style, column three your conceptual style, and column four your behavioural style. The column with the highest score is your decision-making style preference.

1. My prime objective in life is to:	☐ have a position with status	☐ be the best in whatever I do	☐ be recognized for my work	☐ feel secure in my job
2. I enjoy work that:	☐ is clear and well defined	☐ is varied and challenging	☐ lets me act independently	☐ involves people
3. I expect people to be:	☐ productive	☐ capable	☐ committed	☐ responsive
4. My work lets me:	☐ get things done	☐ find workable approaches	☐ apply new ideas	☐ be truly satisfied
5. I communicate best by:	☐ talking with others	☐ putting things in writing	☐ being open with others	☐ having a group meeting
6. My planning focuses on:	☐ current problems	☐ how best to meet goals	☐ future opportunities	☐ needs of people in the organization
7. I prefer to solve problems by:	☐ applying rules	☐ using careful analysis	☐ being creative	☐ relying on my feelings
8. I prefer information:	☐ that is simple and direct	☐ that is complete	☐ that is broad and informative	☐ that is easily understood
9. When I'm not sure what to do:	☐ I rely on my intuition	☐ I search for alternatives	☐ I try to find a compromise	☐ I avoid making a decision
10. Whenever possible, I avoid:	☐ long debates	☐ incomplete work	☐ technical problems	☐ conflict with others
11. I am really good at:	☐ remembering details	☐ finding answers	☐ seeing many options	☐ working with people
12. When time is important, I:	☐ decide and act quickly	☐ apply proven approaches	☐ look for what will work	☐ refuse to be pressured
13. In social settings, I:	☐ speak with many people	☐ observe what others are doing	☐ contribute to the conversation	☐ want to be part of the discussion
14. I always remember:	☐ people's names	☐ places I have been	☐ people's faces	☐ people's personalities
15. I prefer jobs where I:	☐ receive high rewards	☐ have challenging assignments	☐ can reach my personal goals	☐ am accepted by the group
16. I work best with people who:	☐ are energetic and ambitious	☐ are very competent	☐ are open-minded	☐ are polite and understanding
17. When I am under stress, I:	☐ speak quickly	☐ try to concentrate on the problem	☐ become frustrated	☐ worry about what I should do
18. Others consider me:	☐ aggressive	☐ disciplined	☐ imaginative	☐ supportive
19. My decisions are generally:	☐ realistic and direct	☐ systematic and logical	☐ broad and flexible	☐ sensitive to other's needs
20. I dislike:	☐ losing control	☐ boring work	☐ following rules	☐ being rejected

Column Totals	_____	_____	_____	_____
	Directive Style	Analytical Style	Conceptual Style	Behavioural Style

SOURCE: © Alan J Rowe, Professor Emeritus. Revised 12/18/98. Reprinted by permission.

missed payments in the past, and if so, what are the conditions of the warning? How much money is owed and how much do you actually have? When is the money due? Can it be paid in instalments over a few weeks? Is there a clause in the rental agreement that outlines the specifics if a payment is missed? Can you get access to a line of credit or take out a cash advance on a credit card until payday?

Generate Solutions   Now that you have considered all the related information, you remember that this will be your second warning for late rent payments, and if you miss again, the warning says that the landlord can kick you out. Furthermore, you are only missing $150 to pay the rent in full. So, the next logical step is generating alternative solutions with this context in mind. Since this is not a repetitive or routine decision, there aren't any hard and fast rules or policies that will help you solve this issue. You find yourself in a unique situation, and as a result, you need to create customized alternative solutions around your issue. You consider three possible alternative courses of action: (1) get a credit card cash advance, (2) ask your parents for a $150 short-term loan, or (3) pay the landlord as much as you currently have and then pay the balance once your paycheque comes in next week.

Selecting a Solution   According to the rational model, decision makers want to optimize the outcome by choosing the alternative with the greatest value, such as highest benefit, greatest profit, or lowest cost. This is no easy task. First, assigning values to alternatives is complicated and prone to error. Furthermore, evaluating alternatives assumes they can be judged according to some standards or criteria, such as benefit return, quality assessment, cost saving, or profit generated. Research demonstrates that people vary in their preferences for safety or risk when making decisions.[37] The Skills and Best Practices feature box discusses how Micheal Dell, chairman of Dell, and Kevin Rollins, Dell's CEO, attempt to overcome limitations associated with their personal preferences by collaborating with each other when making decisions. Evaluating alternatives assumes they can be judged according to some standards or criteria. This further assumes that (1) valid criteria exist, (2) each alternative can be compared against these criteria, and (3) the decision maker actually uses the criteria. As you know from making your own key life decisions, people frequently violate these assumptions. Finally, you should consider the ethics of the solution. In our rent example, you select to ask your parents for a $150 short-term loan. For you, this solution addresses your problem by providing the most benefit with the fewest disadvantages.

Skills & Best Practices

Michael Dell and Kevin Rollins Make Decisions Collaboratively

The following comments by Michael Dell and Kevin Rollins were obtained during an interview for the *Harvard Business Review*. The interview questions are shown in bold.

How do your decision-making styles differ?

Dell: We're pretty complementary. We've learned over time that each of us is right about 80 percent of the time, but if you put us together, our hit rate is much, much higher. We each think about a slightly different set of things, but there's a lot of overlap.

Rollins: We're both opinionated, but we also realize that listening to one another is a good thing. We have a lot of trust in each other's judgment.

You two have been a team for many years. Now Kevin is CEO and Michael is chairman—how does that relationship work?

Dell: We're very collaborative. We share all the issues and opportunities. It's not at all a typical hierarchy, and this transition was not at all a typical CEO-to-chairman transition . . . Ultimately, we make much better decisions because each of us comes up with ideas that aren't fully developed, we work through them together, and we end up with better decisions. For example, we both recognized the strategic importance of printers, but we debated the fine points between ourselves, and this led to a better decision process and rollout.

Rollins: From the beginning, Michael was enthusiastic about getting into printers, whereas I was a little risk averse (avoidance). With regard to our storage partnership with EMC, our positions were reversed. So it's not as though one of us always plays the optimist and one the pessimist. In both cases, we each talked a lot about the issues and our concerns and got the other comfortable. Then we proceeded as a team.

Implement the Solution Once you have chosen a solution, you need to implement it. This involves identifying and choosing key action items, giving responsibilities to those who will carry out the action items, and setting realistic timelines for planning purposes.

When in comes to implementing the solution, remember what you learned from our discussions about influencing people and politics. Before going home to talk to your parents tonight, you decide to wait until they've had their dinner (so they are more relaxed), you buy some flowers for your mother (because you know she loves receiving them), and you buy your father the latest car magazine (because you know he'll enjoy reading it)—and you also bring home your midterm mark of 89 percent to let them know how hard you are working at school.

Monitor and Evaluate the Solution After the solution is implemented, its effectiveness must be observed, monitored, and evaluated. If the solution is effective, it should reduce the difference between the actual and desired states that created the problem. If the gap is not closed, the implementation was not successful, and one of the following is true: the problem was incorrectly identified, or the solution was inappropriate.

Using our rent example, you consider: Did you get the money you needed from your parents? Were they receptive to your gifts and the request? Was your timing right when you asked them after dinner, or should you have considered a better time? If you need money again in the future, will they say yes?

Summarizing the Rational Model
The rational model is based on the premise that people optimize when they make decisions. *Optimizing* involves solving problems by producing the best possible solution that provides the highest return or greatest rewards.

As noted by decision theorist and Nobel Prize winner Herbert Simon, "The assumptions of perfect rationality are contrary to fact. It is not a question of approximation; they do not even remotely describe the processes that human beings use for making decisions in complex situations."[38] Since decision makers do not follow these rational procedures, Simon proposed a bounded rationality model of decision making.

Bounded rationality models

Decision strategy that takes into consideration constraints such as human limitations, time, problem complexity, and uncertainty.

Judgmental heuristics

Rules of thumb or shortcuts that people use to reduce information processing demands.

Optimizing

Choosing the solution that provides the highest return or rewards.

BOUNDED RATIONALITY MODEL OF DECISION MAKING

In contrast to the rational model's focus on how decisions *should* be made, **bounded rationality models** attempt to explain how decisions *actually* are made. They represent the notion that decision makers are bounded or restricted by a variety of constraints when making decisions, such as: limited capacity of the human mind, problem complexity and uncertainty, amount and timeliness of information at hand, criticality of the decision, and time demands.[39]

As opposed to the rational model, Herbert Simon's bounded rationality model suggests that decision making is characterized by (1) limited information processing, (2) judgmental heuristics, and (3) satisficing. We now explore each of these characteristics.

Limited Information Processing People are limited by how much information they process because of bounded rationality, which makes it difficult for them to identify all possible alternative solutions. In the long run, the constraints of bounded rationality cause decision makers to fail to evaluate all potential alternatives.

Judgmental Heuristics *Judgmental heuristics* represent rules of thumb or shortcuts that people use to reduce information processing demands.[40] We automatically use them without conscious awareness. Because these shortcuts represent knowledge gained from past experience, they can help decision makers evaluate current problems. But they also can lead to errors that erode the quality of decisions. There are two common categories of heuristics that are important to consider: the availability heuristic and the representativeness heuristic.

The *availability heuristic* represents a decision maker's tendency to base decisions on information that is readily available in memory.[41] Information is more accessible in memory when it involves an event that recently occurred, when it is most important (e.g., a plane crash), and when it evokes strong emotions (e.g., innocent people being killed). This heuristic is likely to cause people to overestimate the occurrence of unlikely events such as a plane crash or a high school shooting.

The *representativeness heuristic* is used when people estimate the probability of an event occurring. It

Availability heuristic

Tendency to base decisions on information readily available in memory.

reflects the tendency to assess the likelihood of an event occurring on the basis of one's impressions about similar occurrences. A team leader, for example, may hire a graduate from a particular college or university program because the past three people hired from that school were good performers. Unfortunately, this shortcut can result in a biased decision.

Satisficing   People do not always select the optimal solution because they do not have the time, information, or ability to handle the complexity associated with following a rational process. This is not necessarily undesirable. *Satisficing* consists of choosing a solution that meets some minimum qualifications, one that is good enough. Satisficing resolves problems by producing solutions that are satisfactory, as opposed to optimal.

Representativeness heuristic

Tendency to assess the likelihood of an event occurring on the basis of impressions about similar occurrences.

Satisficing

Choosing a solution that meets a minimum standard of acceptance.

This driver is satisficing with a temporary spare tire.

and tolerance for ambiguity.[42] Value orientation reflects the extent to which an individual focuses on either task and technical concerns versus people and social concerns when making decisions. The second dimension pertains to a person's tolerance for ambiguity, the extent to which people have a high need for structure or control in their life. When the dimensions of value orientation and tolerance for ambiguity are combined, they form four styles of decision making (see Figure 9.3): directive, analytical, conceptual, and behavioural.

1. **Directive**   People with a directive style have a low tolerance for ambiguity and are oriented toward task and technical concerns when making decisions. They are efficient, logical, practical, and systematic in their approach to solving problems. People with this style are action-oriented and decisive and like to focus on facts. In their pursuit of speed and results, however, these individuals tend to be autocratic (dominating), exercise power and control, and focus on the short run.

2. **Analytical**   This style has a much higher tolerance for ambiguity and is characterized by the tendency to over-analyze a situation. People with this style like to consider more information and alternatives than do directives. Analytic individuals are careful decision makers who take longer to make decisions, but who also respond well to new or uncertain situations. They can often be autocratic.

Dynamics of Decision Making

This section examines various dynamics of decision making—personal decision-making styles, the role of intuition (using your gut), decision trees, escalation of commitment, and the role for creativity. An understanding of these dynamics can help all employees make better decisions.

PERSONAL DECISION-MAKING STYLES

By now you have taken the Self-Assessment Exercise and know your own personal decision-making style, which can help you see preferences and patterns that you rely upon, rightly or wrongly. A personal decision-making style is based on the idea that styles vary along two different dimensions: value orientation

▶ **FIGURE** **9.3**   Decision-Making Styles

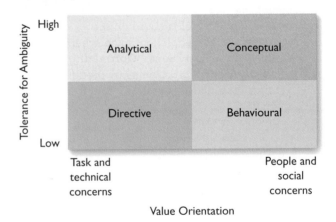

SOURCE: Based on discussion contained in A.J. Rowe and R.O. Mason, *Managing with Style: A Guide to Understanding, Assessing, and Improving Decision Making* (San Francisco: Jossey-Bass, 1987), pp 1–17.

3. **Conceptual** People with a conceptual style have a high tolerance for ambiguity and tend to focus on the people or social aspects of a work situation. They take a broad perspective to problem solving and like to consider many options and future possibilities. Conceptual types adopt a long-term perspective and rely on intuition and discussions with others to acquire information. They also are willing to take risks and are good at finding creative solutions to problems. On the downside, however, a conceptual style can foster an unrealistic and uncertain approach to decision making.

4. **Behavioural** People with this style work well with others and enjoy social interactions in which opinions are openly exchanged. Behavioural types are supportive, receptive to suggestions, show warmth, and prefer verbal to written information. Although they like to hold meetings, people with this style have a tendency to avoid conflict and to be too concerned about others. This can lead behavioural types to adopt a "wishy-washy" approach to decision making, to have a hard time saying no to others, and to have trouble making difficult decisions.

Research and Practical Implications Research shows that very few people have only one dominant decision-making style. Rather, most have characteristics that fall into two or three styles. Studies also show that decision-making styles vary across occupations, job levels, and countries.[43] You can use knowledge of decision-making styles in three ways. First, knowledge of styles can help you to understand yourself. Second, you can increase your ability to influence others by being aware of styles. For example, if you are dealing with an analytical person, you should provide as much information as possible to support your ideas. Finally, knowledge of styles gives you an awareness of how people can take the same information and yet arrive at different decisions by using a variety of decision-making strategies. It is important to conclude with the reminder that there is no best decision-making style that applies in all situations.

THE ROLE OF INTUITION

Have you ever had a hunch or gut feeling about something? If yes, then you have experienced the effects of intuition. *Intuition* "is a capacity for attaining direct knowledge or understanding without the apparent intrusion of rational thought or logical inference."[44] As a process, intuition is automatic and involuntary. There are two types of intuition and two sources for intuition.[45] We will discuss both briefly and then provide some pros and cons for using intuition for decision making.

There are two types of intuition:

- *A holistic hunch*—making a judgement that is based on a subconscious combination of information stored in your memory. For example: someone says, "It just feels right;" or "I can't explain it, but I just know this is not the right thing to do!"

- *Automated experience*—making a choice that is based on a familiar situation and a partially subconscious application of previously-learned information related to that situation. For example: driving a car or riding a bicycle.

There are two sources of intuition:

- *Expertise*—an individual's knowledge regarding an object, person, situation, or decision opportunity based on previous training, experience, and overall skills developed over time. For example: a well-seasoned employee who has been working at the same job for over 20 years.

- *Feelings*—an individual's emotive response when experiencing a situation, a person, an object, or decision opportunity. For example: an emotional response when a person cuts you off on the highway.

It is possible to combine the sources; considering the example of being cut off on the highway, your experience (intuitive expertise) would tell you that getting angry to the point of road rage (intuitive feelings) would not be rational nor safe, and so you make the decision to not make rude gestures back to the inconsiderate driver in the other car.

Pros and Cons of Using Intuition When Making Decisions
On the positive side, intuition can speed up the decision-making process.[46] Intuition thus can be valuable in our complex and ever-changing world. Intuition also is a good approach to use when people are faced with limited resources and tight deadlines. On the negative side, intuition is subject to the same type of biases associated with rational decision making. This means that intuition is particularly at risk to both types of heuristics mentioned earlier, as well as accusations from others that such a decision is bold

Intuition "is a capacity for attaining direct knowledge or understanding without (using) . . . rational thought or logical interference."

Intuition

Making a choice without the use of conscious thought or logical inference.

and biased.[47] A final limitation involves the difficulty in convincing others that a hunch makes sense. In the end, a good intuitive idea may be ignored because people do not understand the idea's underlying logic.

ROAD MAP TO ETHICAL DECISION MAKING: A DECISION TREE

In every chapter of this textbook, we have tried to emphasize the importance of ethics, especially as it relates to power and politics. Clearly, there is growing concern about the lack of ethical behaviour in business. This point is illustrated in a recent poll investigating the perception of corporate behaviour, which revealed that 72 percent of respondents perceived that corporate wrongdoing was rampant, and only 2 percent believed that leaders of large organizations were trustworthy.[48] While this trend partially explains the passage of laws to regulate ethical behaviour, we believe that ethical acts ultimately involve individual or group decisions (see Law & Ethics feature box). Harvard Professor Constance Bagley suggests that a decision tree can help people make more ethical decisions.[49] A **decision tree** is a graphical representation of the process underlying decisions, showing the resulting consequences of making various choices. Decision trees are used as an aid in decision making.

Ethical decision making frequently involves trade-offs, and a decision tree helps individuals to navigate through them. Individuals can apply the decision tree shown

Decision tree

Graphical representation of the process underlying decision making.

in Figure 9.4 to any type of decision or action they are contemplating. In this case, the decision tree is considering the action a public corporation is contemplating. Looking at the tree, the first question to ask is whether or not the proposed action is legal. If the action is illegal, do not do it. If the action is legal, then consider the impact of the action on shareholder value. A decision maximizes shareholder value when it results in a more favourable financial position (e.g., increased profits) for an organization. Whether or not an action maximizes shareholder value, the decision tree shows that employees still need to consider the ethical implications of the decision or action. For example, if an action maximizes shareholder value, the next question to consider is whether or not the action is ethical. The answer to this question is based on considering the positive effect of the action on an organization's other key constituents (e.g., customers, employees, the community, the environment, and suppliers) against the benefit to the shareholders. According to the decision tree framework, individuals should make the decision to engage in an action if the benefits to the shareholders exceed the benefits to the other key constituents. Individuals should not engage in the action if the other key constituents would benefit more from the action than shareholders.

It is important to keep in mind that the decision tree does not provide a quick formula that individuals can use to assess every ethical question. It does, however, provide

THE NEED TO FOSTER MORE ETHICS IN BUSINESS

Ethics involves the study of moral issues and choices. It is concerned with right versus wrong, good versus bad, and the many shades of grey in supposedly black-and-white issues. Moral implications spring from virtually every decision we make, both on and off the job. It is critical that decisions be ethical—entire organizations can disappear as a result of unethical decisions. The early part of the 21st century has been riddled with unprecedented accounting scandals, business fraud, and market debacles (disasters). The one factor consistent with all of these cases was that the CEOs reported to a higher moral compass called the board of directors. Further, each board answered to the

ultimate authority, their shareholders. When you then consider that each firm was held to operate within the guidelines of the Securities Exchange Commission (SEC) and/or Ontario Exchange Commission (OEC), not to mention the corporate protocols set by federal tax departments, it begs the following questions. How much more regulation is needed to prevent such situations from occurring again? Do we need more federal tax regulation? More stock market watchdogs? More involved shareholders? The ultimate response is that for every new law put into place, business will find a way around it; therefore, ethics must start with each of us—we are the shareholders, we are the regulators, so we must become the moral compass.

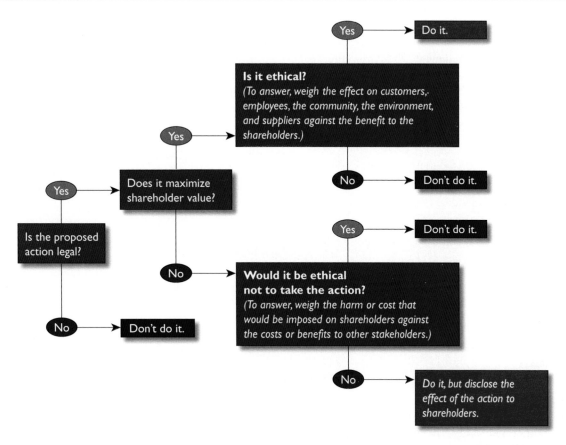

a framework for considering the trade-offs between individual, managerial, and corporate actions and ethics. Try using this decision tree the next time you are faced with a significant ethical question or problem.

LO 5 ESCALATION OF COMMITMENT

Escalation situations involve circumstances in which things have gone wrong, but where the situation can possibly be turned around by investing additional time, money, or effort. *Escalation of commitment* refers to the tendency to stick to an ineffective course of action when it is unlikely that the bad situation can be reversed; our opening chapter vignette illustrates this concept. Personal examples include investing more money into an old or broken car, waiting an extremely long time for a bus to take you somewhere that you could just as easily have walked to, or trying to save a disruptive interpersonal rela-

> **Escalation of commitment**
>
> Sticking to an ineffective course of action when it is unlikely that the bad situation can be reversed.

tionship that has lasted 10 years. Does this sound like any situations that you've been in?

Several reasons for escalation of commitment have been identified.[50] Research shows that individuals tend to (1) bias facts to support previous decisions and thus discourage change, (2) take more risks out of desperation when a decision is stated in negative terms (to recover losses) rather than positive ones (to achieve gains), and (3) get too ego-involved with the project. Because failure threatens an individual's self-esteem or ego, people tend to ignore negative signs and push forward. Also, peer pressure makes it difficult for individuals to drop a course of action when they publicly supported it in the past.

Breakdown in communication, workplace politics, and organizational inertia (momentum) cause organizations to maintain bad courses of action.

Project characteristics—the objective features of a project—have the greatest impact on escalation decisions. For example, because most projects do not reap benefits until some later time period, decision makers are motivated to stay with the project until the end.[51] Thus, there is a tendency to attribute setbacks to temporary causes that are correctable with additional expenditures.

Reducing Escalation of Commitment   It is important to reduce escalation of commitment because it leads to poor decision making for both individuals and groups. Recommended ways to reduce escalation of commitment include:

- Setting minimum targets for performance, and having decision makers compare their performance with these targets

- Having different individuals make the initial and subsequent decisions about a project

- Encouraging decision makers to become less ego-involved with a project

- Providing more frequent feedback about project completion and costs

- Reducing the risk or penalties of failure

- Making decision makers aware of the costs of persistence

THE ROLE OF CREATIVITY

You can identify a situation as either a problem or an opportunity. In addition, creative alternatives that you think of when trying to solve a problem can lead to an effective solution that no one has thought of. In light of today's need for sound, strategic, and yet fast-paced decisions, an organization's ability to stimulate its employees' creativity and innovation is becoming increasingly important. Although many definitions have been proposed, **creativity** is defined here as the process of using intelligence, imagination, and skill to develop a new or novel product, object, process, or thought.[52] It can be as simple as locating a new place to hang your car keys, or as complex as developing a pocket-sized microcomputer. There are three broad types of creativity: (1) create something new (creation), (2) combine or synthesize things (synthesis), or (3) improve or change things (modification).

Researchers are not absolutely certain how creativity takes place. Nonetheless, they know that creativity involves "making remote associations" between unconnected events, ideas, information stored in memory, or physical objects.

Improving Organizational Creativity and Innovation
Organizational creativity is directly influenced by individual characteristics, such as motivation (see Chapter 5).

Creativity

Process of using intelligence, imagination, and skill to develop a new or novel idea.

Individuals have to want to apply their knowledge and capabilities to create new ideas, things, or products.[53] In addition, creative people are dissatisfied with the status quo. They look for new and exciting solutions to problems, and because of this they can be perceived as disruptive and hard to get along with.

Organizational creativity is also affected by group and organizational characteristics. Group creativity is fuelled by a cohesive environment that supports open interactions, diverse viewpoints, and playful surroundings.[54] Finally, organizational characteristics such as resources for creativity, a commitment to creativity, and an organizational culture that encourages and rewards creative activity are important for generating organizational creativity.

Group Decision-Making   LO 6

Including groups in the decision-making process has both pros and cons (see Table 9.2). Before recommending that groups be included in the decision-making process, it is important to examine whether groups perform better or worse than individuals.

After reviewing 61 years of relevant research, a decision-making expert concluded, "Group performance was generally qualitatively and quantitatively superior to the performance of the average individual."[55] Although subsequent research of small-group decision making generally supported this conclusion, additional research suggests that team leaders, supervisors, and managers should use a contingency approach when determining whether to include others in the decision-making process. They can apply the following three guidelines to help decide whether groups should be included in the decision-making process:

1. If additional information would increase the quality of the decision, involve those people who can provide the needed information.

2. If acceptance is important, involve those individuals whose acceptance and commitment are important.

3. If people can be developed through their participation, involve those whose development is most important.[56]

Groupthink occurs when members of a cohesive group attempt to reach agreement to the extent that it overrides minority opinion (see Chapter 6). It is characterized by a deterioration of mental efficiency, reality testing, and moral judgment that results from group pressures to conform and agree.[57]

Advantages and Disadvantages of Group Decision-Making

ADVANTAGES	DISADVANTAGES
1. **Greater pool of knowledge.** A group can bring much more information and experience to bear on a decision or problem than can an individual acting alone.	1. **Social pressure.** Unwillingness to "rock the boat" and pressure to conform may combine to stifle the creativity of individual contributors.
2. **Different perspectives.** Individuals with varied experience and interests help the group see decision situations and problems from different angles.	2. **Domination by a vocal few.** Sometimes the quality of group action is reduced when the group gives in to those who talk the loudest and longest.
3. **Greater comprehension.** Those who personally experience the give-and-take of group discussion about alternative courses of action tend to understand the rationale behind the final decision.	3. **Logrolling.** Political wheeling and dealing can displace sound thinking when an individual's pet project or vested interest is at stake.
4. **Increased acceptance.** Those who play an active role in group decision-making and problem-solving tend to view the outcome as "ours" rather than "theirs."	4. **Goal displacement.** Sometimes secondary considerations such as winning an argument, making a point, or getting back at a rival displace the primary task of making a sound decision or solving a problem.
5. **Training ground.** Less experienced participants in group action learn how to cope with group dynamics by actually being involved.	5. **Groupthink.** Sometimes cohesive in-groups let the desire for unanimity (majority rule) override sound judgment when generating and evaluating alternative courses of action. (Groupthink was discussed in Chapter 6.)

SOURCE: R. Kreitner, *Management*, 8th ed (Boston: Houghton Mifflin, 2001), p 243. Copyright © 2001 by Houghton Mifflin Company. Used with permission.

GROUP PROBLEM-SOLVING TECHNIQUES

Groups can experience roadblocks when trying to arrive at a consensus decision. For one, groups may not generate all relevant alternatives to a problem because an individual dominates or intimidates other group members, because of shyness on the part of other members, or because of satisficing due to time and information constraints. To successfully achieve consensus, groups should use active listening skills, involve as many members as possible, seek out the reasons behind arguments, and dig for the facts. At the same time, groups should not horse-trade (I'll support you on this decision because you supported me on the last one), or agree just to avoid rocking the boat. Voting is not encouraged because it can split the group into winners and losers.[58]

To reduce such roadblocks, decision-making experts have developed three group problem-solving techniques: brainstorming, the nominal group technique, and the Delphi technique. Knowledge of these techniques can help employees to more effectively use group-aided decision making.

These ad agency employees are conducting a brainstorming session. Brainstorming can be fun and is used to generate multiple ideas and solutions for solving problems.

Brainstorming *Brainstorming* is defined as a process to generate a quantity of ideas within an open, creative, and non-judgmental context. It is used to help groups generate multiple ideas and alternatives for solving problems. This technique is effective because it helps reduce interference caused by critical and judgmental reactions to an individual's ideas by other group members.

Brainstorming

Process to generate a quantity of ideas within an open, creative, and non-judgmental context.

When brainstorming, a group is convened and the problem at hand is reviewed. Individual members are then asked to silently generate ideas/alternatives for solving the problem. Silent idea generation is recommended over the practice of having group members randomly shout out their ideas, because it leads to a greater number of unique ideas. Next, these ideas/alternatives are solicited and written on a board or flip chart. Finally, a second session is used to critique and evaluate the alternatives.

The Nominal Group Technique The *nominal group technique (NGT)* is defined as a face-to-face process to generate a variety of ideas, evaluate options using a combination of discussion/voting techniques, and finally select solutions through consensus. NGT helps groups generate ideas and evaluate and select solutions. NGT is a structured group meeting that follows a specific format.[59] A group is convened to discuss a particular problem or issue. After the problem is understood, individuals silently generate ideas in writing. Individuals, in round-robin fashion, then offer one idea from their list. The group leader records ideas on a board or flip chart; the group does not discuss the ideas at this stage of the process. Once all ideas are elicited, the group discusses them. Anyone may criticize or defend any item. During this step, clarification is provided, as well as general agreement or disagreement with the idea. Finally, group members anonymously vote for their top choices with a weighted voting procedure (e.g., 1st choice = 3 points; 2nd choice = 2 points; 3rd choice = 1 point). The group leader then adds the votes to determine the group's choice. Prior to making a final decision, the group may decide to discuss the top-ranked items and conduct a second round of voting.

The nominal group technique reduces the roadblocks to group decision making by (1) separating brainstorming from evaluation, (2) promoting balanced participation among group members, and (3) incorporating mathematical voting techniques to reach consensus.

The Delphi Technique The *Delphi technique* is a group process that anonymously generates ideas or judgments from physically dispersed experts.[60] Unlike the NGT, experts' ideas are obtained from questionnaires or via the Internet as opposed to face-to-face group discussions.

A group leader or manager begins the Delphi process by identifying the issue(s) to investigate. For example, a company might want to explore customers' future preferences, or the effect of locating a plant in a certain region of the country. Next, participants are identified and a questionnaire is developed. The questionnaire is sent to participants, often via email, and returned to the group leader or manager. The responses are summarized and feedback is sent back to the participants. At this stage, participants are asked to review the feedback, prioritize the issues being considered, and return their comments within a specified time period. This cycle repeats until the necessary information is obtained.

The Delphi technique is useful when face-to-face discussions are impractical, when disagreements and conflict are likely to impair communication, when certain individuals might severely dominate group discussion, and when groupthink is a probable outcome of the group process.[61]

> **Nominal group technique (NGT)**
>
> A face-to-face structured process to generate ideas using discussion and voting techniques.

> **Delphi technique**
>
> A computer-aided process to anonymously generate ideas or judgments from physically dispersed experts.

Summary of Learning Objectives

1. **Define *power*, *social power*, and *socialized power*.** Power is the ability to influence others to develop a dependent relationship. Social power is the ability to get things done with human, informational, and material resources. Socialized power is when power is directed to helping others.

2. **Identify and briefly describe French and Raven's five bases of power, relating factors to tactics used and work outcomes (e.g., job performance, job satisfaction, and turnover).** French and Raven's five bases of power are reward power (rewarding compliance), coercive power (punishing non-compliance), legitimate power (relying on formal authority), expert power (providing needed

information), and referent power (relying on personal attraction). Once individuals have power, they can use up to a possible eight types of influencing tactics to achieve the desired outcome. The eight tactics include: logic, emotional appeals, consultation, praise, personal appeals, exchange, coalition, threats, or reference to rules. Researchers have identified three relationship points between power bases and work outcomes: (1) expert and referent power have a generally positive impact on job performance, increasing job satisfaction and lowering turnover—using these types of power bases has a greater chance of getting commitment from others; (2) reward and positive legitimate power have only a slightly positive impact over the same variables—these power bases will likely result in getting others to be compliant with requests; (3) coercive power has a slightly negative impact on similar work outcomes, meaning you can expect compliance or even total resistance from others.

3. **Explain how uncertainty can trigger the production of organizational politics, which can lead to the use of personalized power tactics.** When a person feels uncertainty, it is typically a result of change where personal interests are at stake and power can be challenged. When faced with such uncertain threats, people will rely on personalized power tactics that will serve their own self-interests. As a result, the focus of energy turns away from serving the interests of the organization as a whole in a social way; instead, they employ political tactics to promote personal success.

4. **Compare and contrast the rational model of decision making to bounded rationality, decision trees, and intuition.** The rational decision-making model consists of identifying the problem, gathering related information, generating alternative solutions, evaluating and selecting a solution, and implementing, monitoring, and evaluating the solution. Research indicates that decision makers do not live in a perfect rational world and thus do not typically make decisions in such a manner. Rather, they use a bounded rationality model, which means that decision makers are bounded or restricted by a variety of constraints when making decisions, such as time constraints, ability, etc. There are three types of characteristics of the bounded rationality model: (1) limited information processing, (2) the use of judgmental heuristics, and (3) satisficing. Using intuition is another way of making choices, meaning a dependence on less rational thought or logic. There are two types of intuition: holistic hunch and automated experience. There are two sources of intuition: expertise and feelings. Intuition is helpful because it speeds up the decision-making process, but it can be biased and perceived as illogical. A decision tree helps make decisions, especially in ethical situations, because it is a graphical representation of the process. Through a series of trade-off choices, a person goes through a prescribed sequence until the logical solution emerges. A decision tree is helpful when considering tradeoffs between individual, managerial, or corporate actions.

5. **Infer what causes an escalation of commitment and predict what type of outcome can result.** There are three possible causes of an escalation of commitment: (1) individuals who bias facts to support previous decisions and thus discourage change, (2) individuals who are desperate and so they take more risks when a decision is stated in negative terms, and (3) individuals who have too much ego invested in a project. As individuals or organizations stick to an ineffective course of action when it is unlikely that the bad situation can be reversed, a situation can go from bad to worse.

6. **Summarize the pros and cons of involving groups in the decision-making process.** OB experts suggest using a contingency approach because there are both advantages and disadvantages to using teams in decision making. From a positive perspective, groups (1) collect a greater pool of knowledge, (2) provide

for different perspectives, (3) allow for greater comprehension, and (4) encourage greater acceptance. From a negative perspective, groups (1) can push pressure to conform to the point of stifling creativity, (2) can sometimes be dominated by one or a few members, (3) can experience wheeling and dealing in lots of political games, (4) can have misguided priorities and goal achievement, and (5) can experience groupthink.

 ## Discussion Questions

1. Of the nine generic influence tactics (see Experiential Exercise), which do you use the most when dealing with friends, parents, your boss, or your professors? Would other tactics be more effective?
2. In your opinion, is there such a thing as too much empowerment in the contemporary workplace?
3. What is it about organizational politics that can make individuals feel uneasy? Explain.
4. Why would decision-making styles be a source of interpersonal conflict when working in groups?
5. Describe a situation in which you exhibited escalation of commitment. Why did you escalate a losing situation?

Google Searches

1. **Google Search:** "Should Canada Bailout CBC?" and "Should Canada Bailout Nortel?" How much money did these companies ask the government for? Were the bailout requests successful? Was this a good decision on the governments' part and and an ethical use of taxpayer money?
2. **Google Search:** "International Olympic Committee – Site Selection" How does the NOC decide where the next Olympic games are going to be held? Based on what you have read, is their process equitable and free of prejudice? Where are the next series of games being held?
3. **Google Search:** "Canadian Sexual Harassment Laws" and "Canadian Anti-Harassment Laws" Write a short summary identifying what each of these laws is trying to achieve. Explain how organizational politics and office power games can interfere when it comes to an organization policing itself to ensure the workplace is free from such harassing behaviour.

 ## Experiential Exercise

Power Influencing Tactics Group Exercise
PURPOSE: This exercise is to help familiarize you with the nine influencing tactics used by individuals with power. Approx. Timing: 20 minutes.

ACTIVITY ASSIGNMENT
■ Work in small groups.
■ Think of workplace examples of each of the following list of tactics.
■ Share responses with the rest of the class to generate a rich list of examples.

The nine tactics, ranked in diminishing order of use in the workplace, are as follows:

1. Rational persuasion (reason, logic, or facts)
2. Inspirational appeals (appeal to others emotions, ideals, or values)
3. Consultation (get others involved in process)
4. Ingratiation (use praise or flattery to make the other person more open to listening)
5. Personal appeals (friendship)
6. Exchange (making promises or trading favours)
7. Coalition tactics (get a third party to agree with you and convince others)
8. Pressure (threats)
9. Legitimating tactics (rules, policies, or rights)

The **Presentation** Assistant

Here are possible topics and sources related to this chapter that can be further explored by student groups looking for ideas.

	THREE POSSIBLE OUTCOMES WHEN TRYING TO INFLUENCE PEOPLE—ITEMIZED, DEFINED, AND CASE EXAMPLES	WHO OR WHAT GIVES OFFICE POLITICS A BAD NAME? DEFINE, EXPLAIN, GIVE REASONS AND EXAMPLES	DECISION-MAKING MODELS FOR THE OFFICE —TYPES, APPLICATION, EXAMPLES; DECISIONS GONE BAD & GOOD
YouTube Videos	• Learn The Art of Selling Part 1 of 6 • MadTV—Cindy Delmont—Sexual Harassment at Work • Persecuted Teachers	• *Wall Street* (the movie) • *Survivor* (forming coalitions)	• Mac vs. PC TV Ads • The Paradox of Choice—Why More Is Less
TV Shows or Movies to Preview	• Any telethon or TV appeal asking for money • *The Office*—"Sexual Harassment Episode"	• *The Firm* (movie) • *Boiler Room* (the movie)	• *Enron* (the movie) • *The Queen*
Internet Searches	• *The 48 Laws of Power* (by R. Greene) • *Games People Play* (by E. Berne)	• Work Would Be Great If It Weren't For The People (*Office Politics* by R. Lichtenberg) • Office Politics and Power—Women Managers Know How To Use Them Wisely (web search)	• *Blink* (*Decision Making* by M. Gladwell) • *The Speed of Trust* (by S. Covey)
Ice Breaker Classroom Activity	• Ask students if anyone has ever succeeded in convincing someone at work to do something their way. Share responses. Has anyone been unsuccessful? If so, share responses.	• Ask students their opinion of office politics and if they have ever engaged in using it to their advantage. Share responses.	• Ask students what kinds of decisions they made just to get to class that day. Share responses.

OB In Action Case Study

What Should Margarita Deville Do?

Margarita Deville works as an account supervisor at a large advertising agency in downtown Edmonton. She has worked for this one firm for over five years, has earned a reputation of integrity, and has made many friends with trusted colleagues throughout the organization. In her current position, Margarita has four account executives and two support staff reporting to her, all of whom believe that some day Margarita will become a vice president and part owner of the agency because she is so well-liked. One day Margarita receives an unexpected phone call from a head-hunter, wondering if she is interested in interviewing for a job as a vice president of account services at an ad agency in Vancouver. The pay would be almost double what she is making now, and the opportunity would definitely advance her career to the next level in the industry. She agrees to an interview, takes a few personal days off work, and goes to B.C.

Three weeks after Margarita interviews for the Vancouver job, she receives a phone call stating that she has made the short list and they need to arrange for a second interview as soon as possible. Margarita is thrilled, but realizes that she must keep this secret from the rest of the firm, except Albert who is a friend and an account supervisor for a different group of clients in another part of the agency. Margarita leaves her office space to go ask Albert to be a professional reference for her on the new job, and he agrees. "Your secret is safe with me," says Albert.

That same afternoon, one of Margarita's support staff workers, Raya, comes into her office, asking if she has a minute to talk.

"Sure, what's up?" asks Margarita.

Raya informs Margarita that something is troubling her and she needs to talk about it with someone in authority at the firm.

"Yes of course Raya, come in," says Margarita.

Last week when Raya had to work late, she observed Albert walking into the supply room with a big empty box. "He was in there a long time, very very quiet, but I could still hear the cabinets opening and the boxes being torn apart. After about 10 minutes, Albert walked out with a box full of office supplies. I went in to the room after he left and double-checked the supplies myself—the place looked like it had been looted! And just today, again, I saw him walk out of the supply room with another box. Margarita, you are my boss, you are well respected around here, and I know you are also a friend of Albert's . . . what do you think we should do?" asked Raya.

Margarita has a real problem and some tough decisions to make, but she needs time to think this through. "Thank you for bringing this to my attention, Raya," Margarita says, "I'll take it from here, don't you worry." And with that, Raya leaves the office. Margarita turns her chair around to look out the office window to consider her options.

Discussion Questions

1. Who has power in this case and where does it come from?
2. What are some types of tactics being used to influence others?
3. What kinds of political behaviour is taking place in this case?
4. If you were Margarita, what would you do?
5. If you were Albert, what would you do?
6. What is the ethical thing to do in this case?

Ethical OB Dilemma

You Say You Never Lie? That's a Lie!

It can be hard to get people to face the truth sometimes. Especially about lying.

You don't want to hurt a colleague's feelings by being picky and negative (even though you can always see weaknesses), so when asked for your opinion of the PowerPoint presentation, you try and find at least one positive element to comment on ("good use of colour or graphics"), say that it looks like the colleague put in a lot of work, and wish the colleague all the best.

You don't feel like attending a workshop or conference downtown, so you tell your office colleagues that something important came up and you just can't get out of it.

You're overloaded with personal errands, so you call in sick to work.

Lies, all of them, but we don't really like calling them that. In an Associated Press-Ipsos poll, more than half of respondents said lying was never justified. Yet in the same poll, up to two-thirds said it was OK to lie in certain situations, like protecting someone's feelings. Apparently white lies are an acceptable, even necessary, part of many lives, even though we dislike the idea of lying. Among the groups more likely to say lying was sometimes OK are people ages 18–29, college and university graduates, and those with higher household incomes.

Q **Which of the following statements best describes how you feel about when, if ever, it is ethical for a person to lie?**

1. Never. A lie is a lie and it is immoral to deceive others, especially those for whom you are responsible.
2. Harmless white lies are okay when used to protect people's feelings (e.g., How do you like my new haircut? Do I look like I've gained some weight?).
3. True, it's wrong to lie. But life isn't perfect, so the truth needs to be bent a little bit sometimes.
4. Get real. Everyone lies one time or another. The trick is to do it skilfully and not overdo it.
5. A harmless white lie now and then is okay, but care needs to be taken because any sort of lying damages a manager's credibility.
6. I would respond differently. Explain.

Visit www.mcgrawhillconnect.ca to register.

McGraw-Hill Connect™ —Available 24/7 with instant feedback so you can study when you want, how you want, and where you want. Take advantage of the Study Plan—an innovative tool that helps you customize your learning experience. You can diagnose your knowledge with pre- and post-tests, identify the areas where you need help, search the entire learning package for content specific to the topic you're studying, and add these resources to your personalized study plan. Visit www.mcgrawhillconnect.ca to register—take practice quizzes, search the e-book, and much more.

10

Leader*ship*

Two Different Leadership Paths to the Top

Getting to the top is not always a direct route; it usually takes decades of hard work, long hours, and lots of networking with high-profile professionals in strategic positions. Take Stephen Wetmore, for example, the CEO of Canadian Tire Corporation Ltd., who started with a BA from Acadia University which lead to his CA designation. This was followed by seven years in public accounting, ten years in health care, two years in transportation, and another ten years in the telecommunications/IT industry. The accumulated skills and experience

Wetmore obtained at each job, covering decades of formal training and development, prepared him well; he was ready when offered the opportunity to sit on the Canadian Tire board of directors. After six years of being actively engaged in Canadian Tire issues, Wetmore felt more than qualified to accept the top position in this multi-billion dollar firm. As CEO, Wetmore manages an increasingly complex portfolio of businesses. Michael Sabia, Wetmore's former boss at Bell Aliant, said, "At Canadian Tire, he'll be very well suited to the leadership of that organization that involves work at both the corporate level and the very important work with the dealers and dealers' network. He's a master at being able to find his way through some pretty complex problems where there are a lot of differing and competing interests."

Isabelle Courville is another example of a leader who took an indirect route to the top. She started out with a degree in physics engineering from the Ecole Polytechnique de Montreal, and after graduation began working in technical positions with Bell Canada. She kept her hand in education by getting her law degree at McGill University. After a few years in management at Bell, Courville switched to the energy sector by landing a management position at Hydro-Quebec TransEnergie. Within a few years, at the age of 43, Courville was offered the position of president overseeing a massive $7-billion capital program with a division of 3,500 employees. With the switch from the telecommunication industry to the energy sector, "I had a big learning curve, and frankly I loved it. Managing is an art that consists of motivating and aligning our teams, but then freeing people to make decisions for themselves and act on those decisions," said Courville.

Think about the direction of your current academic career, and then stretch your mind beyond your wildest dreams. Based on the careers of Stephen Wetmore and Isabelle Courville, it's possible that someday you could become CEO of a billion dollar organization. By learning transferable skills at every job along the way, you can prepare yourself for the greatness that lies ahead. The question is: Do you want to be a leader?

SOURCES: M. Strauss, "Next Canadian Tire CEO new to retail," *The Globe and Mail – Report on Business*, November 7, 2008, pg B3; M. Gooderham, "Engineer, lawyer built career by breaking barriers," *The Globe and Mail – Report on Business*, November 25, 2008, pg E4.

Isabelle Courville, President Hydro-Quebec TransEnergie and Stephen Wetmore, CEO Canadian Tire Corporation, Ltd.

→ **LEARNING OBJECTIVES**

After reading this chapter, the student should be able to:

LO 1   **Define** *leadership.*

LO 2   **Differentiate** between being a leader versus a manager.

LO 3   **Explain** Fiedler's contingency theory.

LO 4   **Separate** the factors related to House's revised Path–Goal Theory from Hershey and Blanchard's Situational Leadership Theory.

LO 5   **Summarize** the key characteristics between transactional and transformational leadership.

H ave you ever thought about becoming a leader of an organization? Like the Self-Assessment Exercise on the next page asks, how ready are you to assume the leadership role? Your results may give you something to think about as you study this chapter on leadership. Someone once observed that a leader is a person who finds out which way the parade is going, jumps in front, and yells, follow me! The plain fact is that this approach to leadership has little chance of working in today's rapidly changing world. In short, successful leaders are those individuals who can step into a difficult situation and make a noticeable difference. As illustrated in the opening vignette of this chapter, both Stephen Wetmore and Isabelle Courville faced huge challenges when they assumed their leadership roles; Wetmore led Canadian Tire through one of the worse economic crisis since the Great Depression, and Courville was faced with overhauling a 50-year-old public-transport network that had to be replaced at almost triple the initial cost, which generated much resistance. But how much of a difference can leaders make in modern organizations?

OB researchers have discovered that leaders can make a difference. One study, for instance, revealed that leadership was positively associated with net profits for 167 companies over a time span of 20 years.[1] Research also showed that coaches' leadership skills affected the success of their team. Specifically, teams in Major League Baseball and college and university basketball won more games when players perceived the coach to be an effective leader.[2] Rest assured, leadership can make a difference!

How Ready Are You to Assume the Leadership Role?

INSTRUCTIONS: For each statement, indicate the extent to which you agree or disagree with it by circling one number from the scale provided. Remember, there are no right or wrong answers. After completing the survey, add your total score for the 20 items, and record it in the space provided.

1 = STRONGLY DISAGREE
2 = DISAGREE
3 = NEITHER AGREE NOR DISAGREE
4 = AGREE
5 = STRONGLY AGREE

1.	It is enjoyable having people count on me for ideas and suggestions.	1—2—3—4—5
2.	It would be accurate to say that I have inspired other people.	1—2—3—4—5
3.	It's a good practice to ask people provocative questions about their work.	1—2—3—4—5
4.	It's easy for me to compliment others.	1—2—3—4—5
5.	I like to cheer people up even when my own spirits are down.	1—2—3—4—5
6.	What my team accomplishes is more important than my personal glory.	1—2—3—4—5
7.	Many people imitate my ideas.	1—2—3—4—5
8.	Building team spirit is important to me.	1—2—3—4—5
9.	I would enjoy coaching other members of the team.	1—2—3—4—5
10.	It is important to me to recognize others for their accomplishments.	1—2—3—4—5
11.	I would enjoy entertaining visitors to my firm even if it interfered with my completing a report.	1—2—3—4—5
12.	It would be fun for me to represent my team at gatherings outside our department.	1—2—3—4—5
13.	The problems of my teammates are my problems too.	1—2—3—4—5
14.	Resolving conflict is an activity I enjoy.	1—2—3—4—5
15.	I would cooperate with another unit in the organization even if I disagreed with the position taken by its members.	1—2—3—4—5
16.	I am an idea generator on the job.	1—2—3—4—5
17.	It's fun for me to bargain whenever I have the opportunity.	1—2—3—4—5
18.	Team members listen to me when I speak.	1—2—3—4—5
19.	People have asked me to assume the leadership of an activity several times in my life.	1—2—3—4—5
20.	I've always been a convincing person.	1—2—3—4—5

Total Score = _____

Norms for Interpreting the Total Score

90–100 = High readiness for the leadership role

60–89 = Moderate readiness for the leadership role

40–59 = Some uneasiness with the leadership role

39 or less = Low readiness for the leadership role

SOURCE: Adapted from A.J. DuBrin, *Leadership: Research Findings, Practice, and Skills* (Boston: Houghton Mifflin in Company, 1995), pp 10–11.

When studying leadership principles, there are an unbelievable number of different theories; the number increases significantly if we count those proposed by managerial consultants. Rather than overwhelming you with all these theories of leadership, we have chosen to focus on the historical ones that have received the most research support.

LO 1 What Does Leadership Involve?

Disagreement about the definition of leadership stems from the fact that it involves a complex interaction among the leader, the followers, and the situation. For example, some researchers define leadership in terms of personality and physical traits, while others believe leadership is represented by a set of prescribed behaviours. In contrast, other researchers define leadership in terms of the power relationship between leaders and followers. According to this perspective, leaders use their power to influence followers' behaviour. Leadership also can be seen as an instrument of goal achievement. In other words, leaders are individuals who help others accomplish their goals. Still others view leadership from a skills perspective.

There are four commonalities among the many definitions of *leadership*: (1) leadership is a process between a leader and followers; (2) leadership involves social influence; (3) leadership occurs at multiple levels in an organization (at the individual level, for example, leadership involves mentoring, coaching, inspiring, and motivating; leaders also build teams, generate cohesion, and resolve conflicts at the group level; finally, leaders build culture and generate change at the organizational level);[3] and (4) leadership focuses on goal accomplishment.[4] Based on these commonalities, leadership is defined as a process that uses social influence to enable and seek the participation of subordinates in an effort to reach common organizational goals.[5]

Leadership

A process that uses social influence to enable and seek the participation of subordinates in an effort to reach common organizational goals.

APPROACHES TO LEADERSHIP

This chapter examines the different leadership approaches outlined in Table 10.1. OB researchers began studying leadership in the early part of the 20th century by focusing on the traits associated with leadership effectiveness. This perspective was followed by attempts in the 1950s and 1960s to examine the behaviours or styles exhibited by effective leaders. This research led to the realization that there is not one best style of leadership, which in turn spawned various contingency approaches to leadership in the 1960s and 1970s. Contingency approaches focused on identifying the types of leadership behaviours that are most effective in different settings. The transformational approach is the most popular perspective for studying leadership today. Research based on this approach began in the early 1980s and adheres to the idea that leaders transform employees to pursue organizational goals through a variety of leader behaviours.

LEADING VERSUS MANAGING   LO 2

It is important to appreciate the difference between leadership and management to fully understand what leadership is all about. Leaders inspire others, provide emotional support, and try to get employees to rally around a common goal. Leaders also play a key role in creating a vision and strategic plan for an organization. Managers, in turn, are charged with implementing the vision and strategic plan. Table 10.2 summarizes the key characteristics associated with being a leader and a manager.[6] There are several conclusions to be drawn from the information presented in Table 10.2. First, good leaders are not necessarily good managers, and good managers are not necessarily good leaders. Second, effective leadership requires effective managerial skills at some level. For example, good managerial skills turn a leader's vision into actionable items and successful implementation. This in turn leads to the realization that today's leaders need to be effective at both leading and managing. While this may seem like a huge task, the good news is that people can be taught to be more effective leaders and managers.[7]

Trait and Behavioural Approaches

This section examines the two earliest approaches used to explain leadership. Trait theories focused on identifying the personal traits that differentiated leaders from followers. Behavioural theorists examined leadership from a different perspective. They tried to uncover the different kinds of leader behaviours that resulted in higher work group performance. Both approaches to leadership can teach valuable lessons about leading.

Approaches to Studying Leadership

1. TRAIT APPROACHES

- Stogdill and Mann's five traits—intelligence, dominance, self-confidence, level of energy, and task-relevant knowledge
- Leadership prototypes—intelligence, masculinity, and dominance
- Kouzes and Posner's four traits—honesty, forward-looking, inspiring, and competent
- Goleman—emotional intelligence
- Judge and colleagues—two meta-analyses: importance of extraversion, conscientiousness, and openness; importance of personality over intelligence
- Kellerman's bad traits—incompetent, rigid, intemperate, callous, corrupt, insular, and evil

2. BEHAVIOURAL APPROACHES

- Ohio State Studies—two dimensions: initiating structure behaviour and consideration behaviour
- University of Michigan Studies—two leadership styles: job-centred and employee-centred

3. CONTINGENCY APPROACHES

- Fiedler's Contingency Theory—task-oriented style and relationship-oriented style; three dimensions of situational control: leader–member relations, task structure, and position power
- House's Revised Path–Goal Theory—eight leadership behaviours clarify paths for followers' goals; employee characteristics and environmental factors are contingency factors that influence the effectiveness of leadership behaviours; shared leadership that involves a mutual influence process in which people throughout organization share responsibility for leading
- Hersey and Blanchard's Situational Leadership Theory (SLT)—effective leadership behaviour depends on the readiness level of followers

4. TRANSFORMATIONAL APPROACH

- Leaders engage in four sets of leader behaviour—inspirational motivation, idealized influence, individualized consideration, and intellectual stimulation
- Full-Range Theory of Leadership—leadership varies along a continuum from laissez-faire leadership to transactional leadership to transformational leadership

SOURCE: Adapted from A. Kinicki and B. Williams, *Management: A Practical Introduction*, 3rd ed. (Burr Ridge, IL: McGraw-Hill/Irwin, 2008), p 453. Reprinted by permission of The McGraw-Hill Companies, Inc.

TRAIT THEORY

Trait Theory is the successor to what was called the "great man" theory of leadership. This approach was based on the assumption that leaders such as Pierre Trudeau, Frank Stronach, or David Suzuki were born with some inborn ability to lead. In contrast, trait theorists believed that leadership traits were not innate, but could be developed through experience and learning. A *leader trait* is a physical or personality characteristic that can be used to differentiate leaders from followers.

Before World War II, hundreds of studies were conducted to pinpoint the traits of successful leaders. Dozens of leadership traits were identified. During the postwar period, however, enthusiasm was replaced by widespread criticism. Researchers were simply unable to uncover a consistent set of traits that accurately predicted which individuals became leaders in organizations.

Leader trait

A physical trait or personality characteristic that can be used to differentiate leaders from followers.

Contemporary Trait Research Two OB researchers concluded in 1983 that past trait data may have been incorrectly analyzed. By applying modern statistical techniques to an old database, they demonstrated that the majority of a leader's behaviour could be attributed to stable underlying traits.[8] Unfortunately, their methodology did not single out specific traits.

Characteristics of Being a Leader and a Manager

TABLE 10.2

BEING A LEADER MEANS	BEING A MANAGER MEANS
Motivating, influencing, and changing behaviour	Practising stewardship, directing, and being held accountable for resources
Inspiring, setting the tone, and articulating a vision	Executing plans, implementing, and delivering the goods and services
Managing people	Managing resources
Being charismatic	Being conscientious
Being visionary	Planning, organizing, directing, and controlling
Understanding and using power and influence	Understanding and using authority and responsibility
Acting decisively	Acting responsibly
Putting people first; leaders know, respond to, and act for their followers	Putting customers first; managers know, respond to, and act for their customers
Leaders can make mistakes when 1. They choose the wrong goal, direction, or inspiration due to incompetence or bad intentions; or 2. They overlead; or 3. They are unable to deliver or implement the vision due to incompetence or a lack of follow-through commitment	Managers can make mistakes when 1. They fail to grasp the importance of people as the key resource; or 2. They underlead; they treat people like other resources, numbers; or 3. They are eager to direct and to control but are unwilling to accept accountability

SOURCE: Reprinted from P. Lorenzi, "Managing for the Common Good: Prosocial Leadership," *Organizational Dynamics*, vol. 33, no. 3, p 286, © 2004, with permission from Elsevier.

More recently, results from three separate meta-analyses shed light on important leadership traits. The first was conducted in 1986 by Robert Lord and his associates. Based on a re-analysis of past studies, Lord concluded that people have **leadership prototypes** that affect our perceptions of who is and who is not an effective leader. Your leadership prototype is a mental representation of the traits and behaviours that you believe are possessed by leaders. We thus tend to perceive that leaders exhibit traits or behaviours that are consistent with our prototypes.[9] Lord's research demonstrated that people are perceived as being leaders when they exhibit the traits associated with intelligence, masculinity, and dominance. Another study of 6,052 middle-level managers from 22 European countries revealed that leadership prototypes are culturally based. In other words, leadership prototypes are influenced by national cultural values.[10]

The next two meta-analyses were completed by Timothy Judge and his colleagues. The first examined the relationship among the Big Five personality traits (discussed in Chapter 3, Table 3.2) and leadership emergence and effectiveness in 94 studies. Results revealed that extraversion was most consistently and positively related to both leadership emergence and effectiveness. Conscientiousness and openness to experience were also positively correlated with leadership effectiveness.[11] Judge's second meta-analysis involved 151 samples and demonstrated that intelligence was modestly related to leadership effectiveness. Judge concluded that personality is more important than intelligence when selecting leaders.[12]

This conclusion is supported by research that examined emotional and political intelligence. Recall that emotional intelligence, which was discussed in Chapter 3, is the ability to manage oneself and one's relationships in mature and constructive ways. Given that leadership is an influence process, it should come as no surprise that emotional intelligence is associated with leadership effectiveness.[13]

Political intelligence is a recently proposed leadership trait and represents an offshoot of emotional intelligence. Politically intelligent leaders use power and intimidation to push followers in the pursuit of an inspiring vision and challenging goals. Although these leaders can be insensitive, hard to work with, and demanding,

Leadership prototype

A mental perception and representation of traits and behaviour that you believe are possessed by leaders.

they tend to be effective when faced with stagnant and change-resistant situations.[14] Martha Stewart and Disney's ex-CEO Michael Eisner are two such examples. Consider how colleagues described these leaders.

She [Stewart] had the most amazing, well-organized and disciplined mind I've ever known. She grasped things instantly, and she had the ability to direct your attention to the single most important thing you should be thinking about or doing at that particular moment. She could be incredibly impatient and brusque (rough) if you were slow on the uptake—but if you could keep up with her, and perform to her standard, it was tremendously satisfying.

What is lost in the stories about Mr. Eisner's arrogance, greed, and insensitivity is the more illuminating tale of how he transformed a faltering animation and amusement park company into one of the world's most successful entertainment companies. When he assumed command in 1984, Disney had a market value of $1.8 billion. Today its market value is $57.1 billion.[15]

Politically intelligent leaders seem to walk a fine line between using intimidation to achieve organizational goals, and humiliation and bullying to make themselves feel good. Future research is needed to examine the long-term effectiveness of leaders with political intelligence.

Culture and Leadership Cultural differences influence which traits are perceived to be positive or negative. As illustrated in the International OB feature box, research supports the claim that there is a significant variation around the world in the demonstration and perception of outstanding business leadership. What may work in one culture may actually impede leadership in another.

Gender and Leadership As illustrated in the Focus on Diversity feature box, women in leadership roles throughout corporate Canada still have a long way to go to reach the proportionate levels of their male counterparts. However, the increase of women in the workforce has generated much interest in understanding the similarities and differences in female and male leaders. Three separate meta-analyses and a series of studies conducted by consultants across the country uncovered

INTERNATIONAL OB

OVERVIEW OF GLOBE RESEARCH FINDINGS

GLOBE is the acronym for Global Leadership and Organizational Behaviour Effectiveness, a 62-nation, 11-year study involving 170 researchers worldwide. The GLOBE Project was introduced in 2004 and followed up the next year with specific findings about how leadership and leaders' styles vary among nations and cultures. Initially, the GLOBE team identified a significant list of attributes that are viewed around the world as being responsible, at least to some extent, for a leader's effectiveness or lack thereof. Eventually researchers created a short list of 22 attributes universally regarded as positive, (for example, trustworthy, motive arouser, and excellence-oriented). They did the same for eight negative attributes, such as irritable and dictatorial. Next, they identified 35 culturally-contingent leadership attributes, meaning that the response would vary depending on which country of the world you were asking for an opinion.

An outcome of the GLOBE Project was the set of six culturally-endorsed leadership theory dimensions, or CLTs, that summarize the characteristics, skills, and abilities culturally perceived to contribute to, or inhibit, outstanding leadership. The six CLTs are: charismatic/value-based, team-oriented, participative, humane-oriented, self-protective (against external corruption or fraud influences), and autonomous. For further details on the findings, go to www.Grovewell.com/GLOBE.

SOURCE: C. Grove, *Professional Knowledge Center 2005*, www.grovewell.com/pub-GLOBE-leadership.html; GROVEWELL LLC., www.Grovewell.com/GLOBE; R.J. House et al., *Culture, Leadership and Organizations: The GLOBE Study of 62 Societies*, Sage Publications, 2004.

FOCUS ON *Diversity*

IS CORPORATE LEADERSHIP IN CANADA A BIT OF A BOYS' CLUB?

The Globe and Mail reported the top equity-holding CEOs of the 100 largest companies (by market capitalization) in the S&P/TSX composite index. The chart is unique as it takes into account an accumulation of holdings related shares, share units, and stock options. Who made the list? There are well-seasoned executives who have been around corporate Canada for 36 years, like W. Galen Weston (#93); individuals who have assumed their leadership position within the last few years, like Edward Sampson (#6); there are French Canadians, like Jacques Lamarre (#23); as well as expatriates from China, like John Lau (#18). However, only one female made the list . . . near the bottom. The table below shows the wide gap between the first position and the only female on the list in the 80th position.

A recent study conducted by the Association for Psychological Science revealed that gender bias can occur when selecting leaders, especially in various group scenarios. For example, females are typically assigned to intragroups (groups housed within the company), and males were preferred to lead intergroups (groups outside of the company). Further, evidence pointed to gender bias when placing investment money behind a group fund lead by a female versus a male. For intergroup investments, more money was invested in the presence of a male leader. The authors of the study stated that findings suggest the bias might be prevalent because of the way our society has evolved: male leadership may be preferred because it is a tradition that has evolved over many years. How can you explain the gender differences when it comes to inter-group versus intra-group preferences?

RANK	NAME	COMPANY	ANNUAL SALARY ($)	BONUS ($)	OTHER BENEFITS ($)	STOCK OPTION GAINS ($)	TOTAL ($)
1	Michael Lazaridis	Research in Motion	625,101	0	0	78,537,743	79,162,844
80	Nancy Southern	Canadian Utilities Ltd.	900,000	1,080,000	13,500	0	1,993,500

SOURCES: J. McFarland, "Executive Compensation Annual Survey: Equity-Based Rewards Grow," *Report on Business*, October 6, 2008, p 1; "Gender Biases in Leadership Selection During Competitions Within And Between Groups. Eureka!," *Science News*, October 30, 2008, http://esciencenews.com/articles/2008/10/30/gender.biases.leadership.selection.during.competitions.within.and.between.groups.

the following differences: (1) men and women were seen as displaying more task and social leadership, respectively;[16] (2) women used a more democratic or participative style than men, and men used a more autocratic and directive style than women;[17] (3) men and women were equally assertive;[18] and (4) women executives, when rated by their peers, managers, and direct reports, scored higher than their male counterparts on a variety of effectiveness criteria.[19]

What Are the Takeaways from Trait Theory? We can no longer afford to ignore the implications of leadership traits. Traits play a central role in how we perceive leaders, and they ultimately impact leadership effectiveness. What can be learned from research on traits? Integrating results across past studies leads to the extended list of positive traits shown in Table 10.3. This list provides some guidance regarding the leadership traits you should attempt to cultivate if you want to assume a leadership role. Personality tests, discussed in Chapter 3, and other trait assessments can be considered, as they are continued efforts on the part of OB theorists to try and evaluate personal strengths and weaknesses. Some practitioners find it beneficial to consider the results from such assessments in preparation for a personal development plan.[20]

TABLE 10.3

Key Positive Leadership Traits

POSITIVE TRAITS	
Intelligence	Sociability
Self-confidence	Emotional intelligence
Determination	Extraversion
Honesty/integrity	Conscientiousness

There are two organizational applications of Trait Theory. First, organizations may want to include personality and trait assessments in their selection and promotion processes; not by themselves, but in combination with other selection tools. It is important to remember that this should only be done with valid measures of leadership traits. Second, management development programs can be enhanced to include identifying and exploring employees' leadership traits. Hasbro Inc., for example, sent a targeted group of managers to a program that included a combination of 360-degree feedback, trait assessments, executive coaching, classroom training, and problem-solving assignments on real-life projects. Hasbro is very excited and pleased with the results of their leadership development program.[21]

BEHAVIOURAL STYLES THEORY

This phase of leadership research began during World War II as part of an effort to develop better military leaders. It was an outgrowth of two events: the seeming inability of Trait Theory to explain leadership effectiveness, and the human relations movement (an outgrowth of the Hawthorne Studies). The thrust of early behavioural leadership theory was to focus on leader behaviour instead of on personality traits. It was believed that leader behaviour directly affected work group effectiveness. This led researchers to identify patterns of behaviour (called leadership styles) that enabled leaders to effectively influence others.

The Ohio State Studies Researchers at Ohio State University began by generating a list of behaviours exhibited by leaders. Ultimately, the Ohio State researchers concluded there were only two independent dimensions of leader behaviour: consideration and initiating structure. *Consideration* involves leader behaviour associated with creating mutual respect or trust and focuses on a concern

for group members' needs and desires. *Initiating structure* is leader behaviour that organizes and defines what group members should be doing to maximize output. These two dimensions of leader behaviour were oriented at right angles to yield four behavioural styles of leadership: low structure–high consideration, high structure–high consideration, low structure–low consideration, and high structure–low consideration.

It initially was hypothesized that a high structure–high consideration style would be the one best style of leadership. Through the years, the effectiveness of the high–high style has been tested many times. Overall, results have been mixed and there has been very little research about these leader behaviours until recently. Findings from a 2004 meta-analysis of 130 studies and more than 20,000 individuals demonstrated that consideration and initiating structure had a moderately strong, significant relationship with leadership outcomes. Results revealed that followers performed more effectively for structuring leaders, even though they preferred considerate leaders.[22] All told, results do not support the idea that there is one best style of leadership, but they do confirm the importance of considerate and structuring leader behaviours. Follower satisfaction, motivation, and performance are significantly associated with these two leader behaviours. Future research is needed to incorporate them into more contemporary leadership theories.

University of Michigan Studies As in the Ohio State Studies, this research sought to identify behavioural differences between effective and ineffective leaders. Researchers identified two different styles of leadership: one was employee-centred, the other was job-centred. These behavioural styles parallel the consideration and initiating-structure styles identified by the Ohio State group. In summarizing the results from these studies, one management expert concluded that effective leaders (1) tend to have supportive or employee-centred relationships with employees, (2) use group rather than individual methods of supervision, and (3) set high performance goals.[23]

What Are the Takeaways from Behavioural Styles Theory? By emphasizing leader behaviour, something that is learned, the behavioural style approach makes it clear that leaders are made, not born. Given

Initiating structure

A leader who organizes and defines what group members should be doing to maximize output.

Consideration

A leader with focused concern for group needs; practises creating mutual respect or trust with followers.

what we know about behaviour shaping and model-based training, leader behaviours can be systematically improved and developed.[24]

Behavioural styles research also revealed that there is no one best style of leadership. The effectiveness of a particular leadership style depends on the situation at hand. For instance, employees prefer structure over consideration when faced with role ambiguity.[25] Finally, research also revealed that it is important to consider the difference between how frequently and how effectively managers exhibit various leader behaviours. For example, a manager might ineffectively display a lot of considerate leader behaviours. Such a style is likely to frustrate employees, and possibly result in lowered job satisfaction and performance. Because the frequency of exhibiting leadership behaviours is secondary in importance to effectiveness, managers are encouraged to concentrate on improving the effective execution of their leader behaviours.[26]

Finally, Peter Drucker, an internationally renowned management expert and consultant, recommended a set of nine behaviours managers can focus on to improve their leadership effectiveness (see Skills & Best Practices feature box).

Contingency approaches

The effectiveness of a particular style of leader behaviour will depend on many variables.

Contingency Approaches

Contingency approaches grew out of an attempt to explain the inconsistent findings about traits and behavioural styles. The ability to predict successful leadership as a result of certain traits or behaviours fell short, and the search for other contributing variables needed to be considered. **Contingency approaches** propose that the effectiveness of a particular style of leader behaviour depends on the situation. As situations change, different styles become appropriate. This directly challenges the idea of one best style of leadership. Let us closely examine three alternative contingency approaches of leadership that reject the notion of one best leadership style: (1) Fiedler's Contingency Theory, (2) House's Path–Goal Theory, and (3) Hersey and Blanchard's Situational Leadership Theory.

FIEDLER'S CONTINGENCY THEORY

LO 3

Fred Fiedler, an OB scholar, developed a contingency model of leadership. It is the oldest and one of the most widely-known models of leadership. Fiedler's model is based on the following assumption:

The performance of a leader depends on two interrelated factors: (1) the degree to which the situation gives the leader control and influence—that

Skills & Best Practices

Peter Drucker's Tips for Improving Leadership Effectiveness

1 Determine what needs to be done.

2 Determine the right thing to do for the welfare of the entire enterprise or organization.

3 Develop action plans that specify desired results, probable restraints, future revisions, check-in points, and implications for how people should spend their time.

4 Take responsibility for decisions.

5 Take responsibility for communicating action plans and give people the information they need to get the job done.

6 Focus on opportunities rather than problems. Do not sweep problems under the rug. Treat change as an opportunity rather than a threat.

7 Run productive meetings. Different types of meetings require different forms of preparation and different results. Prepare accordingly.

8 Think and say "we" rather than "I." Consider the needs and opportunities of the organization before thinking of your own opportunities and needs.

9 Listen first, speak last.

is, the likelihood that [the leader] can success-fully accomplish the job; and (2) the leader's basic motivation—that is, whether [the leader's] self-esteem depends primarily on accomplishing the task or on having close supportive relations with others.[27]

With respect to a leader's basic motivation, Fiedler believes that leaders are either task-motivated or relationship-motivated. These basic motivations are similar to initiating structure/concern for production and consideration/concern for people.

Fiedler's theory is also based on the premise that leaders have one dominant or preferred leadership style that is resistant to change. He suggests that leaders must learn to manipulate or influence the situation to create a match between their leadership style and the amount of control within the situation at hand. After discussing the components of situational control and the leadership matching process, we review relevant research and managerial implications.[28]

Situational Control   Situational control refers to the amount of control and influence leaders have in their immediate work environment. Situational control ranges from high to low. High control implies that the leader's decisions will produce predictable results because the leader has the ability to influence work outcomes. Low control implies that the leader's decisions may not influence work outcomes because the leader has very little influence. There are three dimensions of situational control: leader–member relations, task structure, and position power. These dimensions vary independently, forming eight combinations of situational control (see Figure 10.1).

The three dimensions of situational control are defined as follows:

- Leader–member relations reflect the extent to which the leader has the support, loyalty, and trust of the work group.

- Task structure is concerned with the amount of structure contained within tasks performed by the work group.

- Position power refers to the degree to which the leader has formal power to reward, punish, or otherwise obtain compliance from employees.

Linking Leadership Motivation and Situational Control
Fiedler's complete contingency model is presented in Figure 10.1. The last row under the Situational Control column shows that there are eight different leadership situations. Each situation represents a unique combina-tion of leader–member relations, task structure, and position power. Situations I, II, and III represent high control situations. Figure 10.1 shows that task-motivated leaders are hypothesized to be most effective in situa-tions of high control. Under conditions of moderate control (situations IV, V, VI, and VII), relationship-motivated leaders are expected to be more effective. Finally, the results orientation of task-motivated leaders is predicted to be more effective under the condition of very low control (situation VIII).

Research and Managerial Implications   Research has provided mixed support for Fiedler's model, suggesting that the model needs theoretical refinement.[29] That said, the major contribution of Fiedler's model is that it prompted others to examine the contingency nature of leadership. This research, in turn, reinforced the notion that there is no one best style of leadership. Leaders are advised to take a mental audit of their own preferred task and relationship orientation, compare it to the one demanded by the situation, and then assess the gap or harmony between the two. If possible, find a different approach to the situation—remember that leaders have a preference for a style, not a limited ability.

Leaders should try and manipulate the situation to fit their style strengths, but as we've already mentioned, this isn't always possible. So, it's important for leaders to identify when a preferred leadership style is going to assist efforts or cause a barrier in achieving desired outcomes. If there is a gap, then consider how to compensate for it. This could include voluntarily step-ping down. It's not uncommon to find one type of leader during the building phase of an organization, and then a change in leadership during the reorganization of it at another time. For example, consider the different leader-ship styles of IBM's current CEO Sam Palmisano and former CEO Lou Gerstner:

His 'aw-schucks' nature, coupled with Palmisano's ability to chat up just about anyone he meets, makes him approachable for customers and employees . . . He's constantly on the phone, calling all over the world: "How's your quarter?" "Did we close this deal?" . . . Software chief Steve Mills calls Palmisano an "execution maniac" . . . This single-mindedness about results is a big reason Palmisano was selected by Gerstner to take over IBM. Says Merrill Lynch security analyst Steve Milunovich: "Sam is the right guy to run IBM right now. He's great externally and a hard-charging Marine internally."

Palmisano's style is a big departure from that of the gruff and intimidating Gerstner. But then

Situational Control	High Control Situations			Moderate Control Situations				Low Control Situations
Leader–member relations	Good	Good	Good	Good	Poor	Poor	Poor	Poor
Task structure	High	High	Low	Low	High	High	Low	Low
Position power	Strong	Weak	Strong	Weak	Strong	Weak	Strong	Weak
Situation	I	II	III	IV	V	VI	VII	VIII

Optimal Leadership Style	Task-Motivated Leadership	Relationship-Motivated Leadership	Task-Motivated Leadership

SOURCE: Adapted from F.E. Fiedler, "Situational Control and a Dynamic Theory of Leadership," in *Managerial Control and Organizational Democracy*, eds B. King, S. Streufert, and F.E. Fiedler (New York: John Wiley & Sons, 1978), p 114.

Gerstner's role wasn't to be nice; it was to keep IBM from disintegrating. He took over just as it was about to split itself up into 13 distinct, loosely affiliated entities.[30]

Sam Palmisano and Lou Gerstner had two different leadership styles, and each was successful at leading IBM employees, but at different times. As suggested by Fiedler, they both were effective because their respective leadership styles were appropriate for the situation at the time.

PATH–GOAL THEORY

Path–Goal Theory was originally proposed by Robert House in the 1970s.[31] He developed a model that describes how leadership effectiveness is influenced by the interaction between four leadership styles (directive, supportive, participative, and achievement-oriented) and a variety of contingency factors. **Contingency factors** are internal and external situational variables that cause one style of leadership to be more effective than another. Path–Goal Theory has two groups of contingency variables:

Contingency factors

Internal and external situational variables that influence the appropriateness of a leadership style.

employee characteristics and environmental factors. Five important employee characteristics include locus of control, task ability, need for achievement, experience, and need for clarity. Two relevant environmental factors include task structure (independent versus interdependent tasks) and work group dynamics. To gain a better understanding of how these contingency factors influence leadership effectiveness, we consider locus of control (discussed in Chapter 3), task ability and experience, and task structure.

Employees with an internal locus of control are more likely to prefer participative or achievement-oriented leadership because they believe they have control over the work environment. Such individuals are unlikely to be satisfied with directive leader behaviours that exert additional control over their activities. In contrast, employees with an external locus tend to view the environment as uncontrollable, thereby preferring the structure provided by supportive or directive leadership. Employees with high task ability and experience are less apt to need additional direction, and thus would respond negatively to directive leadership. These people are more likely to be motivated and satisfied by participative and achievement-oriented leadership. Oppositely, inexperienced employees would find achievement-oriented leadership overwhelming as they confront challenges associated with learning a new job. Supportive and directive leadership would be helpful in this situation. Finally, directive and supportive leadership should help employees experiencing role ambiguity. However, directive leadership is likely to frustrate employees working on routine and simple tasks. Supportive leadership is most useful in this context.

About 50 studies have tested various predictions derived from House's original model. Results have been mixed, with some studies supporting the theory and others not.[32] House thus proposed a new version of Path–Goal Theory in 1996 based on these results and the accumulation of new knowledge about OB.

A Reformulated Theory   The revised theory is presented in Figure 10.2.[33] There are three key changes in the new theory. First, House now believes that leadership is more complex and involves a greater variety of leader behaviour. He thus identifies eight categories of leadership styles or behaviour (see Table 10.4). Current research and descriptions of business leaders support the need for an expanded list of leader behaviours.[34] Consider the different leader behaviours exhibited by Jamie Dimon, CEO of J.P. Morgan Chase.

Jamie Dimon is not known for his subtlety ... He will lash out in meetings with trusted confidants— "That's the dumbest thing I've ever heard"—and expect them to come right back at him ... A huge operation "can get arrogant and full of hubris (excessive pride) and lose focus, like the Roman Empire," says Dimon. To prevent J.P. Morgan from falling into that trap, he has imposed rigorous pay-for-performance metrics (quantitative measurement tools) and requires managers to present exhaustive monthly reviews, then grills them on the data for hours at a time. "He jumps into the decision-making process," says Steve Black, co-head of investment banking ... While Dimon's rudeness can be offputting, the sheer force of his passion and intensity can be irresistible ... He yanked Bank One's sponsorship of the Masters golf tournament because the country club hosting the event doesn't accept women members.[35]

Jamie Dimon exhibits path–goal clarifying behaviours, achievement-oriented behaviours, group-oriented decision-making behaviours, and value-based behaviours. He also seems to rely on intimidation to get people to do what he wants.

The second key change involves the role of intrinsic motivation (discussed in Chapter 5) and empowerment (discussed in Chapter 9) in influencing leadership effectiveness. House places much more emphasis

---

▶ **FIGURE 10.2**   A General Representation of House's Revised Path–Goal Theory

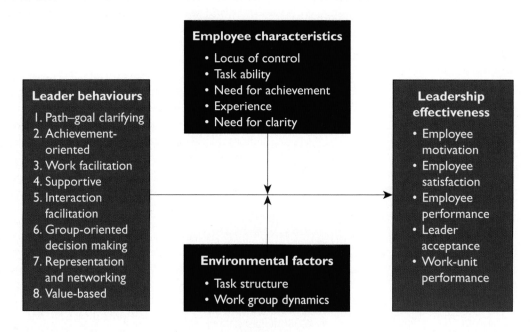

Categories of Leader Behaviour Within the Revised Path–Goal Theory

TABLE 10.4

CATEGORY OF LEADER BEHAVIOUR	DESCRIPTION OF LEADER BEHAVIOURS
Path–goal clarifying behaviours	Clarifying employees' performance goals; providing guidance on how employees can complete tasks; clarifying performance standards and expectations; use of positive and negative rewards contingent on performance
Achievement-oriented behaviours	Setting challenging goals; emphasizing excellence; demonstrating confidence in employees' abilities
Work facilitation behaviours	Planning, scheduling, organizing, and coordinating work; providing mentoring, coaching, counselling, and feedback to assist employees in developing their skills; eliminating roadblocks; providing resources; empowering employees to take actions and make decisions
Supportive behaviours	Showing concern for the well-being and needs of employees; being friendly and approachable; treating employees as equals
Interaction facilitation behaviours	Resolving disputes; facilitating communication; encouraging the sharing of minority opinions; emphasizing collaboration and teamwork; encouraging close relationships among employees
Group-oriented decision-making behaviours	Posing problems rather than solutions to the work group; encouraging group members to participate in decision making; providing necessary information to the group for analysis; involving knowledgeable employees in decision making
Representation and networking behaviours	Presenting the work group in a positive light to others; maintaining positive relationships with influential others; participating in organization-wide social functions and ceremonies; doing unconditional favours for others
Value-based behaviours	Establishing a vision, displaying passion for it, and supporting its accomplishment; demonstrating self-confidence; communicating high performance expectations and confidence in others' abilities to meet their goals; giving frequent positive feedback

SOURCE: Descriptions were adapted from R. J. House, "Path–Goal Theory of Leadership: Lessons, Legacy, and a Reformulated Theory," *Leadership Quarterly*, 1996, pp 323–52.

on the need for leaders to foster intrinsic motivation through empowerment. The final key change in the revised theory is called **shared leadership**. That is, Path-Goal Theory is based on the premise that an employee does not have to be a supervisor or manager to engage in leader behaviour. Rather, House believes that leadership is shared among all employees within an organization.

Shared Leadership A pair of OB scholars noted that "there is some speculation, and some preliminary evidence, to suggest that concentration of leadership in a single chain of command may be less optimal than shared leadership responsibility among two or more individuals in certain task environments."[36] This

Shared leadership

A simultaneous, ongoing, and mutually influencial process in which people throughout an organization share responsibility for leading.

perspective is quite different from traditional theories and models discussed thus far, which assume that leadership is a vertical, downward-flowing process. In contrast, the notion of shared leadership is based on the idea that people need to share information and collaborate to get things done at work. This, in turn, underscores the need for employees to adopt a horizontal process of influence or leadership.

Shared leadership entails a simultaneous, ongoing, mutual influence process in which individuals share responsibility for leading, regardless of formal roles and titles. An example of this occurred with Sarah Burghardt, who at the time was HR manager at A.D. Williams Engineering in Edmonton. She went through two tragic episodes at the company, when it lost five of its seven-member corporate leadership team in plane accidents in late 2007 and early 2008 (including the founder/CEO and his son).[37] This is how she explained it:

"The company was rocked. After that second crash we didn't have too many people left on the leadership team. We had mourning staff who were shocked it could happen again, we had the families looking for support and we of course had the public and media very interested in this story. But everyone banded together to figure out how to pull through and fill vacant roles. It was just amazing to see how good people are and how much they care."

During her acceptance speech for the TD Insurance Meloche Monnex Corporate Governance Award, Burghardt shed a few tears when she finally saw the submission, and said the award "should be for the whole company."

Shared leadership is most likely to be needed when people work in teams, when people are involved in complex projects, and when people are doing knowledge work— work that requires voluntary contributions of intellectual capital by skilled professionals.[38] Marv Levy, the former CFL football coach of the Montreal Alouettes and member of the NFL Hall of Fame, is a strong believer in shared leadership. He concluded that a head coach "must be willing and desirous of forming a relationship with others in the organization that results in their working together productively and even enjoyably. A head honcho who thinks he can do it all by himself is fooling no one but himself. Working in concert with the team owner, the general manager, the personnel department, etc., allows everyone the opportunity to maximize his talents."[39]

Researchers are just now beginning to explore the process of shared leadership, and results are promising. For example, shared leadership in teams was positively associated with group cohesion, group citizenship, and group effectiveness.[40] Table 10.5 contains a list of key questions and answers that managers should consider when determining how they can develop shared leadership.

TABLE 10.5

Key Questions and Answers to Consider When Developing Shared Leadership

KEY QUESTIONS	ANSWERS
What task characteristics call for shared leadership?	Tasks that are highly *interdependent*. Tasks that require a great deal of *creativity*. Tasks that are highly *complex*.
What is the role of the leader in developing shared leadership?	*Designing the team*, including clarifying purpose, securing resources, articulating vision, selecting members, and defining team processes. *Managing the boundaries* of the team.
How can organizational systems facilitate the development of shared leadership?	*Training and development systems* can be used to prepare both designated leaders and team members to engage in shared leadership. *Reward systems* can be used to promote and reward shared leadership. *Cultural systems* can be used to articulate and to demonstrate the value of shared leadership.
What vertical and shared leadership behaviours are important to team outcomes?	*Directive leadership* can provide task-focused directions. *Transactional leadership* can provide both personal and material rewards based on key performance metrics. *Transformational leadership* can stimulate commitment to a team vision, emotional engagement, and fulfillment of higher-order needs. *Empowering leadership* can reinforce the importance of self-motivation.
What are the ongoing responsibilities of the vertical leader?	The vertical leader needs to be able to step in and *fill* voids in the team. The vertical leader needs to continue to *emphasize the importance of the shared leadership approach*, given the task characteristics facing the team.

SOURCE: C.L. Pearce, "The Future of Leadership: Combining Vertical and Shared Leadership to Transform Knowledge Work," *Academy of Management Executive: The Thinking Manager's Source,* February 2004, p 48. Copyright 2004 by Academy of Management. Reproduced with permission of Academy of Management via Copyright Clearance Center.

Research and Managerial Implications There are not enough direct tests of House's revised Path–Goal Theory using appropriate research methods and statistical procedures to draw overall conclusions. Future research is clearly needed to assess the accuracy of this model. That said, there are still two important managerial implications. First, effective leaders possess and use more than one style of leadership. Managers are encouraged to familiarize themselves with the different categories of leader behaviour outlined in Path–Goal Theory and to try new behaviours when the situation calls for them. Second, a small set of employee characteristics (ability, experience, and need for independence) and environmental factors (task characteristics of autonomy, variety, and significance) are relevant contingency factors.[41]

LO 4 HERSEY AND BLANCHARD'S SITUATIONAL LEADERSHIP THEORY

Almost a decade after the Path–Goal Theory was introduced, another contingency approach was proposed by management writers Paul Hersey and Kenneth Blanchard.[42] Recall that Path–Goal Theory focuses on the leader, as well as a small set on the employees and the environment. In contrast, Situational Leadership Theory (SLT) takes a different approach, claiming that effective leader behaviour depends on the readiness level of a leader's followers.

Readiness is defined as the extent to which a follower possesses the ability and willingness to complete a task. Willingness is a combination of confidence, commitment, and motivation.

The SLT model is summarized in Figure 10.3. The appropriate leadership style is found by cross-referencing follower readiness, which varies from low to high, with one of four leadership styles. The four leadership styles represent combinations of task and relationship-oriented leader behaviours (S1 to S4). Leaders are encouraged to use a "telling style" for followers with low readiness. This style combines high task-oriented leader behaviours, such as providing instructions, with low relationship-oriented behaviours, such as close supervision. As follower readiness increases, leaders are advised to gradually move from a telling, to a selling, to a participating, and, ultimately, to a delegating style.[43]

Readiness

Follower's ability and willingness to complete a task as directed by a leader.

Transactional leadership

Leadership that focuses on clarifying employees' daily roles and providing rewards contingent on performance.

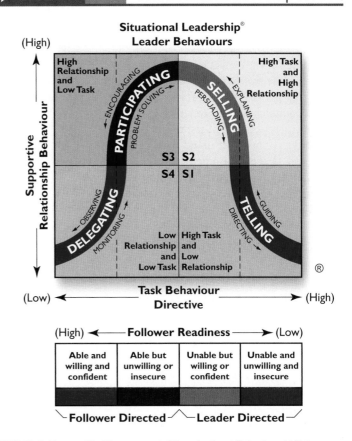

> **FIGURE 10.3** Situational Leadership Model

Although SLT is widely used as a training tool, it is not strongly supported by scientific research. Researchers have concluded that the self-assessment instrument used to measure SLT leadership style and follower readiness is inaccurate and should be used with caution.[44] In summary, managers should exercise discretion when using prescriptions from SLT.

Transformational Approach LO 5

Some of models we've discussed thus far in this chapter move leadership along a continuum toward an enlightened relationship between leader and employee. As we pursue these discussions, two types of leadership approaches surface that are worth exploring in greater detail. The first is called *transactional leadership,* which focuses on clarifying employees' daily roles and providing rewards contingent (dependent) on performance. Further, transactional leadership encompasses the fundamental managerial activities of setting goals, monitoring progress toward goal achievement, and rewarding and punishing people for their level of goal accomplishment.[45] You can see from this description that transactional leadership is based on using extrinsic motivation to increase employee productivity. Consider how Maple Leaf Foods CEO, Michael McCain, uses transactional leadership to improve organizational performance for Canada's largest meat company:

> Since the early 1990s the McCain family has created a food conglomerate out of the old Canada Packers. While Michael's dad can take the credit for the initial purchase of the firm, it's Michael that has modernized the company. As CEO since 1998, Michael has turned Maple Leaf into a giant food conglomerate; but it hasn't always been a smooth process. Take for example one of his earlier decisions to become competitive by restructuring the organization. According to a Maple Foods unionized member at the time, McCain decided to move machines from Edmonton to Hamilton where the company claimed it would control its costs by streamlining its supply chain; then came cutting wages by up to $9 per hour and benefits by 50 percent, eliminating seniority, making workers pay for each minute over 20 minutes spent going to the bathroom each week, introducing a flexible workweek to eliminate weekend overtime pay, and to force workers to give up a day's seniority for each day absent. Those were tough decisions that had to be made in order to get the business on track. Now, ten years later, the company has re-established a positive relationship with its union, created ongoing feedback loops with its employees, introduced performance reviews and state-of-the-art performance assessment and development programs for its management team, as well as recognition initiatives for outstanding performance.[46]

In contrast, transformational leaders "engender trust, seek to develop leadership in others, exhibit self-sacrifice and serve as moral agents, focusing themselves and followers on objectives that transcend the more immediate needs of the work group."[47] Transformational leaders can produce significant organizational change and results because this form of leadership fosters higher

Transformational leadership

Leadership with a vision that transforms the organization through role-modelling and inspiring behaviours, and encourages the pursuit toward achieving organizational goals.

levels of intrinsic motivation, trust, commitment, and loyalty from followers than does transactional leadership. That said, however, it is important to note that transactional leadership is an essential prerequisite to effective leadership, and that the best leaders learn to display both transactional and transformational leadership to various degrees. In support of this proposition, research reveals that transformational leadership leads to superior performance when it augments or adds to transactional leadership.[48] Let us return to our example of Maple Leaf Foods and Michael McCain, to see how he used **transformational leadership** to deal with the serious listeriosis outbreak that gripped his firm.

> In late August 2008, McCain had to direct all his attention toward a potentially debilitating situation that involved the presence of the infectious listeriosis bacteria. The bottom line: people were dying from food processed at its Toronto plant. McCain found himself in the middle of a crisis that every CEO dreads—having to publicly acknowledge corporate fault and lay claim to the undisputed fact of ultimate responsibility for a serious mishap. But as the person responsible for the interests of 23,000 employees, McCain accepted his role as CEO without hesitation. As the executive team battled the operational issues, McCain resolved to save the jobs of of those (300) employees at the Toronto processing plant.
>
> When faced with media doubt about the firm's ability to overcome this crisis, McCain responded with a determined belief that the organization would indeed survive thanks to the support of dedicated people; the quality, depth, and width of product offerings; the benefits received from customer loyalty; and strong brand recognition. In public appearances, McCain openly stated that the company would eventually recover and experience sales equal to pre-crisis levels.[49] McCain's leadership proved to be compelling, as Maple Leaf again began shipping meat from its Toronto plant within several months after the initial outbreak. Maple Leaf reported a 6.3 percent increase in sales over the previous year for the 2009 first quarter and second quarter earnings per share were adjusted to a positive 12 cents per share, rather than a loss of 1 cent per share the previous year. "While we have made good progress, there remains significant value creation opportunity with very positive effects on our future financial results," said McCain.[50]

We now turn our attention to examining the process by which transformational leadership influences followers.

HOW DOES TRANSFORMATIONAL LEADERSHIP TRANSFORM FOLLOWERS?

Transformational leaders transform followers by creating changes in their goals, values, needs, beliefs, and aspirations. Author and management professor Peter Senge would add sharing a vision to that list, as common mental models of what is to be achieved play a vital role in motivating followers. In his book, *The Fifth Discipline*, Senge refers to the movie *Spartacus* and the scene where the Romans trapped the leader and the thousands of former slaves who followed him to find their own freedom.[51] When the Roman legions asked Spartacus to surrender, no one from the group came forward. After continued prompts and eventual threats, Spartacus decided to give himself up to spare the lives of all his followers. Just as Spartacus was about to stand forward and surrender, one of his lieutenants stepped forward at the same time, verbally claiming to be Spartacus. Following the lead, other followers quickly stepped forward claiming to be Spartacus. Soon, the entire group of followers stood shouting out loud that they were Spartacus. Senge uses this story to demonstrate the effect a transformational leader can have on followers. It's their shared vision of freedom that kept them together and their shared mental models of what they wanted to accomplish (no more living as a slave) that motivated them to stay the course. Spartacus accomplished this transformation by appealing to followers' self-concepts—namely their values and personal identity. Figure 10.4 presents a model of how leaders accomplish this transformational process.

Figure 10.4 shows that transformational leader behaviour is first influenced by various individual and organizational characteristics. For example, research reveals that transformational leaders tend to have personalities that are more extraverted, agreeable, and proactive than non-transformational leaders, and female leaders use transformational leadership more than male leaders.[52] Organizational culture also influences the extent to which leaders are transformational. Cultures that are adaptive and flexible, rather than rigid and bureaucratic, are more likely to create environments that foster the opportunity for transformational leadership to be exhibited.

Transformational leaders engage in four key sets of leader behaviour (see Figure 10.4).[53] The first set, referred to as inspirational motivation, involves establishing an attractive vision of the future, the use of emotional arguments, and exhibition of optimism and

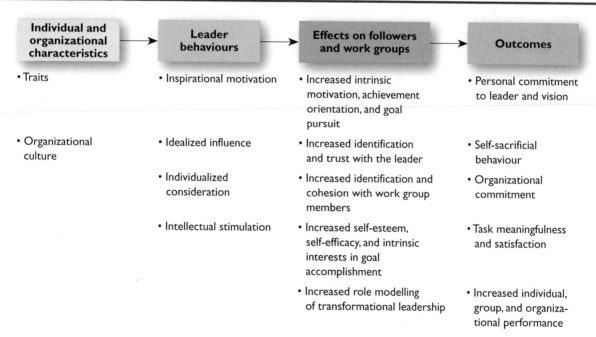

▶ **FIGURE 10.4** A Transformational Model of Leadership

Individual and organizational characteristics	Leader behaviours	Effects on followers and work groups	Outcomes
• Traits	• Inspirational motivation	• Increased intrinsic motivation, achievement orientation, and goal pursuit	• Personal commitment to leader and vision
• Organizational culture	• Idealized influence	• Increased identification and trust with the leader	• Self-sacrificial behaviour
	• Individualized consideration	• Increased identification and cohesion with work group members	• Organizational commitment
	• Intellectual stimulation	• Increased self-esteem, self-efficacy, and intrinsic interests in goal accomplishment	• Task meaningfulness and satisfaction
		• Increased role modelling of transformational leadership	• Increased individual, group, and organizational performance

SOURCE: Based in part on D.A. Waldman and F.J. Yammarino, "CEO Charismatic Leadership: Levels-of-Management and Levels-of-Analysis Effects," *Academy of Management Review*, April 1999, pp 266–85; and B. Shamir, R.J. House, and M.B. Arthur, "The Motivational Effects of Charismatic Leadership: A Self-Concept Based Theory," *Organization Science*, November 1993, pp 577–94.

enthusiasm. A vision is "a realistic, credible, attractive future for your organization."[54] According to Burt Nanus, a leadership expert, the "right" vision unleashes human potential because it serves as a beacon of hope and common purpose. It does this by attracting commitment, energizing workers, creating meaning in employees' lives, establishing a standard of excellence, promoting high ideals, and bridging the gap between an organization's present problems and its future goals and aspirations. Anne Mulcahy, Xerox's CEO, understands the importance of using a vision to energize the workforce. She used a vision, which was created by asking a group of her top management team to write a story about how various constituents would describe the company in five years, to gain employees' commitment to needed and difficult organizational change. This process resulted in increased buy in and support of a host of organizational changes that brought the company back from near bankruptcy.[55]

Idealized influence, the second set of leader behaviours, includes behaviours such as sacrificing for the good of the group, being a role model, and displaying high ethical standards. Through their actions, transformational leaders model the desired values, traits, beliefs, and behaviours needed to realize the vision. The third

> " . . . a realistic, credible, attractive future for your organization"

set, individualized consideration, entails behaviours associated with providing support, encouragement, empowerment, and coaching to employees. Intellectual stimulation, the fourth set of leadership behaviours, involves behaviours that encourage employees to question the status quo and to seek innovative and creative solutions to organizational problems.

RESEARCH AND MANAGERIAL IMPLICATIONS

Components of the transformational model of leadership have been the most widely researched leadership topic over the last decade. Overall, the relationships outlined in Figure 10.4 generally were supported by previous research. For example, transformational leader behaviours were positively associated with the extent to which employees identified with both their leaders and immediate work groups.[56] Followers of transformational leaders also were found to set goals that were consistent with those of the leader, to be more engaged in their work, to have higher levels of intrinsic motivation, and to have higher levels of group cohesion.[57] With respect to the direct relationship between transformational leadership and work outcomes, a meta-analysis of 49 studies indicated that transformational leadership was positively associated with measures of leadership effectiveness

LAW AND ETHICS *at Work*

SHOULD LEADERS GET PAID IF THEIR COMPANY FAILS?

The market disaster of 2009 left a wide gap between the haves and the have-nots. As their companies were losing billions of dollars the year before—resulting in job loss for hundreds of thousands of individuals around the world—the CEOs of those same firms held lucrative leadership positions, allowing them to enjoy tens of millions of dollars in salary. For example, Robert Prichard, the ex-CEO of Torstar Corp., received a $9.6 million (Cdn.) severance package amid layoffs, cutbacks, and a stock price that lost more than 80 percent from its peak. The gluttony was not as prevalent in Canada as in the U.S., where the bailout initiatives began to focus on the discrepancy between performance and

executive pay. For example, Richard Fuld, the CEO with global financial-services giant Lehman Brothers, was paid $22.1 million (U.S.) in salary, perks, bonuses, and stock options just months before the firm filed for bankruptcy protection, the largest in U.S. history at the time. Edward Liddy, the CEO of AIG, reported his executives were receiving death threats following $160 million dollars worth of bonus payouts after receiving taxpayer bailout money just a few months earlier. Up to this point, some of these same CEOs would have been held up as models of leaders who transformed the workplace and exhibited brilliant leadership. Do you think it's ethical for leaders to earn a salary when their firm is losing money?

SOURCE: J. McFarland, "U.S. Bailout Plan to Tackle CEO Pay," *The Globe & Mail—Report on Business*, September 25, 2008, p B1; G. Robertson, "Torstar CEO Grilled Over Severance Deal," *The Globe and Mail—Report on Business*, May 7, 2009, p B9.

and employees' job satisfaction.[58] At the organizational level, a second meta-analysis demonstrated that transformational leadership was positively correlated with organizational measures of effectiveness.[59]

These results underscore four important managerial implications. First, the best leaders are not just transformational; they are both transactional and transformational. Leaders should attempt to use these two types of leadership while avoiding a laissez-faire or wait-and-see style.

Second, transformational leadership not only affects individual-level outcomes like job satisfaction, organizational commitment, and performance, but it also influences group dynamics and group-level outcomes. Managers can thus use the four types of transformational leadership behaviours shown in Figure 10.4 as a vehicle to improve group dynamics and work-unit outcomes. This is important in today's organizations because most employees do not work in isolation. Rather, people tend to rely on the input and collaboration of others, and many organizations are structured around teams. The key point to remember is that transformational leadership transforms individuals as well as teams and work groups. We encourage you to use this to your advantage.

Third, employees at any level in an organization can be trained to be more transactional and transformational.[60] This reinforces the organizational value of developing and rolling out a combination of transactional and transformational leadership training for all employees.

Fourth, transformational leaders can be ethical or unethical. Whereas ethical transformational leaders enable employees to enhance their self-concepts, unethical ones select or produce obedient, dependent, and compliant followers. The Law and Ethics At Work feature box provides some interesting considerations about unethical leadership.

The following are suggestions for how top management can create and maintain ethical transformational leadership:

1. Create and enforce a clearly stated code of ethics.

2. Recruit, select, and promote people who display ethical behaviour.

3. Develop performance expectations around the treatment of employees—these expectations can then be assessed in the performance appraisal process.

4. Train employees to value diversity.

5 Identify, reward, and publicly praise employees who exemplify high moral conduct.[61]

Summary of Learning Objectives

1. **Define *leadership*.** Leadership is a social influence process in which the leader seeks the voluntary participation of subordinates in an effort to reach organizational goals.

2. **Differentiate between being a leader versus a manager.** Leaders play a key role in creating a vision and strategic plan for an organization. Leaders inspire others, provide emotional support, and try to get employees to rally around a common goal. Managers, in turn, are charged with implementing the vision and strategic plan. They look after the day-to-day activities, such as managing resources, executing plans, or controlling costs.

3. **Explain Fiedler's contingency theory.** Fiedler believed that leaders were either task motivated or relationship motivated. These basic motivations were similar to initiating structure/concern for production and consideration/concern for people. Fiedler's theory was also based on the premise that leaders had one dominant or preferred leadership style that was resistant to change. He suggested that leaders had to learn to manipulate or influence the leadership situation to create a match between their leadership style and the amount of control within the situation at hand.

4. **Separate the factors related to House's revised Path–Goal Theory from Hersey and Blanchard's Situational Leadership Theory.** There are three key changes in the revised Path–Goal Theory. Leaders now are viewed as exhibiting eight categories of leader behaviour (see Table 10.2) instead of four. In turn, the effectiveness of these styles depends on various employee characteristics and environmental factors. Second, leaders are expected to spend more effort fostering intrinsic motivation through empowerment. Third, leadership is not limited to people in managerial roles; rather, leadership is shared among all employees within an organization. Shared leadership involves a simultaneous, ongoing, mutual influence process in which individuals share responsibility for leading regardless of formal roles and titles. This type of leadership is most likely to be needed when people work in teams, when people are involved in complex projects, and when people are doing knowledge work. According to Situational Leadership Theory (SLT), effective leader behaviour depends on the readiness level of a leader's followers. As follower readiness increases, leaders are advised to gradually move from a telling, to a selling, to a participating, and finally, to a delegating style.

5. **Summarize the key characteristics between transactional and transformational leadership.** Transactional leaders focus on clarifying employees' daily roles and task requirements, and provide followers with positive and negative rewards contingent on performance. They are helpful to keep the organization on a schedule and on track. Transformational leaders motivate employees through inspiring modelling efforts, selling the vision, and pursuing organizational goals over their own self-interests. Both forms of leadership are important for organizational success. Individual characteristics and organizational culture are key forerunners of transformational leadership, which is comprised of four sets of leader behaviour. These leader behaviours, in turn, positively affect followers' and work groups' goals, values, beliefs, aspirations, and motivation. These positive effects are then associated with a host of preferred outcomes.

Discussion Questions

1. Is everyone destined to be a leader? Explain.

2. Have you ever worked for a transformational leader? Describe how this leader transformed followers.

3. "A leader makes a difference within a corporation." Do you agree with this statement? Explain.

4. Do you agree with the statement, "The best leaders are born, not taught in some classroom"? Explain your reasoning.

5. Think of the best leader you ever had in your life. Write five traits of that person on a piece of paper. Now think of the worst leader you ever had in your life. Write five traits of this person. Compare and contrast the two lists. What kind of leadership style did your best leader display?

 Google Searches

1. **Google Search:** "Canadian Business – Canada's Richest 100 201_" or "Top Canadian CEO Salaries 201_" or "CEO Scorecard 201_" or "William Doyle" Review the kind of compensation levels these people are earning. Find the person who makes the most salary annually. Now, compare the minimum wage in your province this year to the amount the top CEO makes in Canada. How many years would it take for a minimum wage earner to make the kind of money earned by the top CEO?

2. **Google Search:** "John Mackey CEO of Whole Foods Market"; "Jim Sinegal CEO of Costco"; "Susan Lyne CEO Martha Stewart Living Omnimedia" After reviewing their biographies and reading information about their leadership style, try and identify at least two characteristics or examples of behaviours that make these individuals so unique and transformational.

3. **Google Search:** Six corporate leadership scandals: "Bernard Ebbers CEO Worldcom Corporate Scandal"; "Conrad Black Hollinger International"; "Garth Drabinsky Livent Entertainment Group"; "Bernard Madoff New York Financier"; "Edward Liddy & AIG Bonus Payback"; "Kenneth Lay CEO Enron" Work in groups to research one of the corporate scandals lead by misguided leadership. Present a five-minute presentation to the class summarizing what happened, how it ended, and the lesson you learned from studying these corporate scandals.

Experiential Exercise

Leadership Group Exercise

PURPOSE: This exercise is meant to help you personalize the material from this leadership chapter by having you reflect on your own self-assessment scores. Expand your application knowledge by working in small groups to discuss how you can learn the behaviours that enable you to be a leader.

Approx. Timing: 30 minutes.

ACTIVITY ASSIGNMENT

- Complete the Self-Assessment Exercise found at the beginning of Chapter 10, *How Ready Are You to Assume the Leadership Role?*
- Work in small groups.
- Answer the questions below.
- Share responses to the questions and discuss each topic.

1. What do you think it means to practise self leadership? Give examples.

2. What do you think it means to practise informal leadership within the workplace? Who would display such behaviour? When?

3. As we move toward more on-line relationships, what does it mean to show virtual leadership? Explain and provide examples.

4. What can students do right now to practise leadership behaviour? (Think of specific examples of what, when, and where such behaviours can occur while at school.)

The **Presentation** Assistant

Here are possible topics and corresponding sources related to this chapter that can be further explored by student groups looking for ideas.

	THE GREAT LEADERS OF THE WORLD—CONTEMPORARY EXAMPLES OF TRUE LEADERSHIP	THE GREATEST LEADERS OF THE WORLD—HISTORICAL EXAMPLES OF TRUE LEADERSHIP	THE ROLES OF EMOTION AND SHARING A VISION TO SUCCESSFUL LEADERSHIP
YouTube Videos	• Desmond Tutu on Leadership • Lessons on Leadership (*Forbes* online) • Leadership in a Complex Technology Driven World	• Colin Powell's 13 Rules of Leadership • Leadership in an Age of Uncertainty	• Psychology of Leadership—Seth Klarman • Motivational Leadership Trainer—Employee Engagement and Emotional Intelligence
TV Shows or Movies to Preview	• *Blackhawk Down* (movie of failed leadership) • *Hoosiers* • *13 Days* (movie)	• *Gandhi* (movie) • *Spartacus* (movie) • *300* (movie)	• *Pay It Forward* (movie) • *The Queen* (movie)
Internet Searches	• Craig Kielburger—Free The Children • Candy Lightner—MADD founder • Nelson Mandella • John Kotter, researcher • Top 100 Living Geniuses • *The Leadership Challenge* (by J. Kouzes and B. Posner)	• Mahatma Gandi • Winston Churchill • Martin Luther King • *The Art of War* (by Sun Tzu) • Mother Teresa • *The 48 Laws of Power* (by R. Greene) • *Outliers: The Story of Success* (by M. Gladwell)	• *Fifth Discipline* (by P. Senge) • *Emotional Intelligence* (by D. Goldman) • *Executive Intelligence: What All Great Leaders Have* (by J. Menkes)
Ice Breaker Classroom Activity	• Consider a shorter version of the Google Search exercise #3 to get students thinking about leadership that has gone wrong and how they feel about it.	• Ask students to complete Discussion Question #5 found at the end of this chapter.	• Have students discuss how they feel when they see a leader who shows emotion, happiness or sadness. Does such behaviour imply incompetence and weakness?

OB In Action Case Study

Consolidated Products

Consolidated Products is a medium-sized manufacturer of consumer products with non-unionized production workers. Ben Samuels was a plant manager for Consolidated Products for 10 years, and he was very well-liked by the employees. They were grateful for the fitness centre he built for employees, and they enjoyed the social activities sponsored by the plant several times a year, including company picnics and holiday parties. He knew most of the workers by name, and he asked about their families or hobbies.

Ben believed it was important to treat employees properly so they would have a sense of loyalty to the company. He tried to avoid any layoffs when production demand was slack, figuring that the company could not afford to lose skilled workers who are so difficult to replace. When someone was injured but wanted to continue working, Ben found another job in the plant the person could do. He believed that if you treat people right, they will do a good job for you without close supervision or prodding. He mostly left his supervisors alone to run their departments as they saw fit. Ben did not set objectives and standards for the plant, and he never asked the supervisors to develop plans for improving productivity and product quality.

Under Ben, the plant had the lowest turnover among the company's five plants, but the second-worst record for costs and production levels. When the company was acquired by another firm, Ben was asked to take early retirement, and Phil Jones was brought in to replace him. Phil had a growing reputation as a manager who could get things done, and he quickly began making changes. Costs were cut by trimming a number of activities such as the plant fitness centre, company picnics, and parties, and the human relations training programs for the supervisors. Phil believed that training supervisors to be supportive was a waste of time. His motto was, "If employees don't want to do the work, get rid of them and find somebody else who does."

Supervisors were instructed to establish high performance standards for their departments and to insist that people achieve them. A computer monitoring system was introduced so that the output of each worker could be checked closely against the standards. Phil told his supervisors to give any worker who had substandard performance one warning; if performance did not improve within two weeks, fire the person. He believed that workers don't respect a supervisor who is weak and passive. When Phil observed a worker wasting time or making a mistake, he would reprimand the employee on the spot as an example to others. Phil also checked closely on the performance of his supervisors. He set demanding objectives for each department, and held weekly meetings to review department performance. Finally, Phil insisted that supervisors check with him before taking any significant actions that deviated from established plans and policies.

Phil reduced the frequency of equipment maintenance, which required machines to be idle when they could be productive. Because the machines had a good record of reliable operation, Phil believed that the current maintenance schedule was excessive and was cutting into production. Finally, when business was slow for one of the product lines, Phil laid workers off rather than find something else for them to do.

By the end of Phil's first year as plant manager, production costs were reduced by 20 percent and production output was up by 10 percent. However, three of his seven supervisors left to take other jobs, and turnover was also high among the machine operators. Some of the turnover was due to workers who had been fired, but competent machine operators were also quitting, and it was becoming increasingly difficult to find replacements for them. Finally, there was increasing talk of unionizing among the workers.

Questions for Discussion

1. Describe and compare the managerial behaviours of Ben and Phil. Which person uses shared leadership?

2. Who uses the transactional style of leadership and who uses transformational leadership?

3. Compare Ben and Phil in terms of their influence on employee attitudes, short-term performance, and long-term plant performance, and explain the reasons for the differences.

4. If you were selected to be the manager of this plant, what would you do to achieve both high employee satisfaction and performance?

SOURCE: G. Yukl, *Leadership in Organizations*, 5th ed. (Upper Saddle River, NJ: Prentice Hall, 2002), pp 76–78.

Ethical OB Dilemma

Call Centre Lay Offs

You are a manager at a call centre and are faced with the difficult task of having to lay off a friend who works for the company. This employee has performed wonderfully in the past and you would hate to see him go. Nonetheless, your company lost a contract with a major client and his position is obsolete. You are aware that this employee is buying a house and is 10 days from closing. He has sold his other home and now is living with his in-laws. The employee has come to you and is asking for a favour. He wants you to extend his employment for 10 more days so that he can qualify for the loan for his new home. Unfortunately, you do not have the authority to do so, and you told him you cannot grant this favour. He then told you that the mortgage company will be calling sometime soon to get a verbal confirmation of his employment. This confirmation is an essential prerequisite for your friend to obtain the loan for his new home. Because you can't extend his employment, he now is asking for another favour. He wants you to tell the mortgage company that he is still employed.

As a manager at this call centre, which of the following statements best describes how you would respond?

1. Tell the mortgage company he is still working for the company. Your friend needs a break and you are confident that he'll find a job in the near future.
2. Refuse to lie. It is unethical to falsify information regarding employment.
3. Simply avoid the mortgage company's phone call.
4. Explain how you would respond differently.

Visit www.mcgrawhillconnect.ca to register.

McGraw-Hill Connect™ —Available 24/7 with instant feedback so you can study when you want, how you want, and where you want. Take advantage of the Study Plan—an innovative tool that helps you customize your learning experience. You can diagnose your knowledge with pre- and post-tests, identify the areas where you need help, search the entire learning package for content specific to the topic you're studying, and add these resources to your personalized study plan. Visit www.mcgrawhillconnect.ca to register—take practice quizzes, search the e-book, and much more.

> *Everything affects everything else in one way or another. Whether you are aware of that or not does not change the fact that this is what is happening. That's why I say a business is a system. This system's perspective reminds us that this is what is going on. And when you see it this way, you can manage your business better."*
>
> John Woods (business author)

Organizational Culture, & Socialization, & Mentoring

The Starbucks Coffee (Canada) Culture

There's no doubt that developing and maintaining the right culture is a lot of work, but it can be done. Take Starbucks Coffee Canada. It does something that 65 percent of surveyed executives say their companies don't do: it regularly measures the status of its corporate culture. Every 18 months, the coffee chain asks its employees to spend 15 minutes filling out a Partner View Survey (every staff member is a partner, in Starbucks lingo). Among other topics, participants answer questions about their overall job satisfaction and commitment to the company, using a five-point scale from "very dissatisfied" to "very satisfied." These questions are designed to gauge Starbucks progress toward one of its core values, providing a great work environment where people treat each other with respect and dignity.

The Starbucks survey is voluntary, but the most recent assessment boasted a 90 percent-plus participation rate. The reason? The company makes it easy for staff members to fill out the questionnaire by allowing them to complete it online at the store, and Starbucks pays employees for their time. The senior management team also encourages employees to take part. But the biggest reason for the high participation rate is likely that the organization actually does something with the data. "People have seen tangible results from providing us feedback," says Colin Moore, president of Starbucks Coffee Canada. For example, the company recently learned its employees wanted to better understand career progression through the organization. Employees knew how a barista becomes a store manager, but they were less clear about how to land a job at the Toronto head office or one of the regional offices. "Our response was that we held career fairs in Vancouver, Calgary, and Toronto," says Moore, "where we rented halls and staffed them with our department heads and other people across our company who spoke about their roles and job opportunities within the organization."

The Partner View Survey also serves as a two-way communication tool. Employees provide feedback, and management reports the findings. During these discussions, the Canadian operation compares itself to operations in other countries and to the entire Starbucks organization. Since the business tracks the results over time, it can see if it's making improvements every 18 months. Stores, district managers, and functional departments of the company can also view the data and form workgroups to address specific issues and opportunities. "What the survey does," says Moore, "is give us another forum to talk to our people."

It seems to work. Even though one of Starbucks Coffee Canada's biggest challenges remains finding and keeping high-quality people, turnover is 40 percent to 60 percent lower than at many retail chains, says Moore. That's in spite of an aging population with fewer teenagers to take on junior positions. Make no mistake, part of what attracts people to work for the company is the culture. They know that Starbucks walks the talk: a pleasant upscale atmosphere of like-minded people who enjoy speaking the Starbucks language ("A Venti Chai Latte Skim, right?"); a generous package of perks, such as extending benefits to part-time employees and giving employees the option to buy company stock at a discount; and a commitment to give back through the Starbuck Foundation, which encourages socially responsible store initiatives to connect with the communities they serve. "The Partner View Survey is a quantitative way for us to continue to ensure we're doing things that are consistent with our guiding principles and what we say we're going to do," says Moore.[1]

SOURCE: Excerpted from C. Leung, "Culture Club," *Canadian Business*, October 9–12, 2006, pp 116–117.

LEARNING OBJECTIVES

After reading this chapter, you should be able to:

LO 1 **Define** o*rganizational culture,* *espoused values,* and *enacted values.*

LO 2 **Describe** the four functions of organizational culture.

LO 3 **Discuss** the four types of organizational culture associated with the competing values framework.

LO 4 **Summarize** the various methods used by organizations to change organizational culture.

LO 5 **Descibe** the three phases in Feldman's model of organizational socialization and explain how mentoring can assist the socialization process.

The opening vignette highlights three key things about organizational culture. First, an organization's culture can impact employee satisfaction and turnover. Starbucks Canada was able to lower its employee turnover below the industry average and increase employee satisfaction by creating a positive, employee-focused culture. Second, organizational culture can be a source of competitive advantage, just as Starbucks Canada differentiates itself on the basis of unique product offerings and an urban, sophisticated store atmosphere. Finally, managers can influence organizational culture. Starbucks Canada, for instance, actively influences or shapes its culture by using results from employee surveys.

This chapter will help you understand the important role of organizational culture within the contemporary workplace. After defining and discussing the context of organizational culture, we examine (1) the dynamics of organizational culture, (2) the process of culture change, (3) the organization socialization process, and (4) the embedding of organizational culture through mentoring.

LO 1 Organizational Culture: Definition and Context

Organizational culture is "the set of taken-for-granted implicit assumptions that a group holds and that determines how it perceives, thinks about, and reacts to its various environments."[2] In other words, it's the set of shared values and beliefs that underlie a company's identity. This definition highlights three important characteristics of organizational culture. First, organizational culture is passed on to new employees through the process of socialization, a topic discussed later in this chapter. Second, organizational culture influences our behaviour at work. Finally, organizational culture operates at different levels.

Figure 11.1 provides a conceptual framework for reviewing the widespread impact organizational culture has on organizational behaviour. It also shows the linkage between this chapter—culture, socialization, and mentoring—and other key topics in this book. To begin with, let's walk through the basics of Figure 11.1. As you can see, culture is created from four key sources: the founder's values, the industry and business environment, the national culture, and the senior leaders' vision and behaviour.[3] The fundamental philosophy and set of values that the company founders brought with them when they first created the company is paramount to setting the tone and is the driving force behind all strategy or future activity. It would be very difficult to separate the founder from the company, as they are so closely aligned. For example, Joseph-Armand Bombardier's vision as a youthful 16-year-old in 1924 of a functioning machine to use for transportation purposes lead to his invention of the first snowmobile made by the company that carries his name, Bombardier Inc. With the help of his family, Joseph-Armand used his passion and drive to propel the company into becoming a giant multi-national engineering and manufacturing business, far from its humble beginnings in Valcourt, Quebec. A review of Bombardier's corporate executive shows that several descendants of the Bombardier family continue to lead the company, using the guiding principles, core values, and appreciation for invention that helped create the company almost 100 years ago.

Organizational culture

The set of shared values and beliefs that underlie a company's identity.

In turn, organizational culture influences the type of organizational structure adopted by a company (we'll talk more about this in Chapter 12) and a host of practices, policies, and procedures implemented in pursuit of organizational goals. These organizational characteristics then affect a variety of group and social processes. This sequence ultimately affects employees' attitudes and behaviour and a variety of organizational outcomes. All told, Figure 11.1 reveals that organizational culture is a background variable influencing individual, group, and organizational behaviour.

There can be more than one dominant culture within an organization, along with subcultures that operate in a different location (building, department, or regional office). Because of a contrasting set of philosophical

▶ FIGURE 11.1 A Conceptual Framework for Understanding Organizational Culture

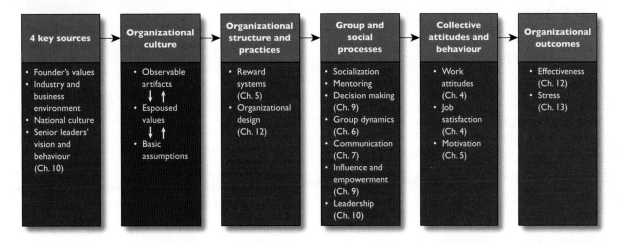

SOURCE: Adapted in part from C. Ostroff, A. Kinicki, and M. Tamkins, "Organizational Culture and Climate," in *Handbook of Psychology*, vol. 12, ed Weiner, pp 565–93, © 2003 John Wiley & Sons, Inc. Reprinted with permission of John Wiley & Sons, Inc.

values shared by management and employees working in this subculture area, it can operate almost like a separate company. Consider the many subcultures that may exist within your own school. While the institution itself may have one dominant public culture that it's known for, there may also be groups of people who may talk or dress differently, and even operate differently on a daily basis. For example, compare the students in the business area to those in the arts and creative design area. Such subcultures can be healthy alternative cultures that allow for creative expression, or, if left unchecked, they can become strong counter-cultures with competing values that work against the main organizational culture. This is what happened at Apple, when Steven Jobs was lured back to oversee the Macintosh Division that was housed physically away from the main head office building. When Jobs came back to Apple after being away for several years, his transformational leadership and infectious energy made the Macintosh Division "pirates" feel empowered and at the same time at odds with the "corporate shirts" as they competed over which product would be launched first to save Apple Inc.[4]

Dynamics of Organizational Culture

To gain a better understanding of how organizational culture is formed and used by employees, this section begins by discussing the layers of organizational culture. We then review the four functions of organizational culture, the types of organizational culture, and the outcomes associated with organizational culture.

LAYERS OF ORGANIZATIONAL CULTURE

Looking at Figure 11.1, you will notice the second box from the left shows the three fundamental layers of organizational culture: observable artifacts, espoused values, and basic assumptions. Each level varies in terms of outward visibility and resistance to change, and each level influences another level.

Observable Artifacts   At the more visible level, culture represents observable artifacts that consist of the physical manifestation (appearance) of an organization's culture. Here are some examples of what we mean by artifacts:

- **Legends and stories** Myths or truths handed down from employee to employee in informal or formal settings about how things came to be at the company. They can also include the historical past and how philosophy and values created the current policies and procedures. For example:

Ex-CEO of 3M, William L. McKnight, was a very influential leader from the past who created a series of guiding principles in 1948 that set the tone for delegating responsibility and encouraging men and women to exercise their initiative and innovation. These principles were formalized and to this day are still referred to in 3M workplace boardroom plaques and even printed onto employee computer mouse pads found in the London-based Canadian head office.

- **Language and acronyms** The words used to communicate create an atmosphere of club-like membership that only those who understand are included. This is common in highly tech-oriented work environments, where people talk about RAM, ISDN lines, JPEGS, etc. Unless you work in the field, these things can be very intimidating. For example:

The opening chapter vignette talks about Starbuck's coffee language, "I'll have a Tall Mocha Decaf Frappuccino."

- **Rituals and ceremonies** Observable behaviour exhibited by people and groups within the organization. For example:

Many companies hold lavish annual award celebrations acknowledging the achievements by individuals or groups. The awards could include office recognition plaques, posted photos and certificates for framing, company flags, buttons, T-shirts, and song. Mary Kay Cosmetics Ltd., McDonald's, and Walmart are known for their rituals and ceremonies.

- **Physical structure and office equipment** The physical look of the office can include furniture, decorations, equipment, design, colours, and layout. Collectively, they make a statement of the values held by the organization. For example:

Doctors' offices often include education degrees and framed certificates of credentials posted on the walls of the waiting area. They are there to show the patients that the doctors are qualified and serious about what they do. They help instil confidence in the doctors' abilities and demonstrate the doctors' values and commitment toward up-to-date medical training and ethical practice.

- **Dress code or uniform** The acceptable clothing to wear while engaged at work can be a clear indicator of the values of the organization. For example:

Observe if the office employees dress casually or formally. Are facial piercings and tattoos banned? A uniform sets up the expectations of some workplaces, such as a law firm, bank, accounting firm, high-end clothing store, certain restaurants, and hospital administrative offices. This would suggest a certain kind of respect for professional language, preference for traditional behaviours, and appreciation for deeply rooted processes that have been in place for many years.

Observable artifacts are easier to change because they are obvious and tangible in nature. However, not all culture is tangible, as we'll explore in this next section.

Espoused Values *Values* possess five key components. "Values (1) are concepts or beliefs, (2) pertain to desirable end-states or behaviours, (3) transcend situations, (4) guide selection or evaluation of behaviour and events, and (5) are ordered by relative importance."[5] It is important to distinguish between values that are espoused versus those that are enacted.

Values

Enduring belief in a mode of conduct or end-state.

Espoused values represent the explicitly stated values and norms that are preferred by an organization. They are generally established by the founder of a new or small company and by the top management team in a larger organization. At times the espoused

Espoused values

The stated values and norms that are preferred by an organization.

values of the organization are not congruent with the personal values of employees or the national values of their customer. When this happens, it can prove to be a disaster for the organization, as illustrated when Walmart tried to enter the German market in the late 1990s (see the International OB feature box).

On a positive note, more and more companies are espousing the value of sustainability. *Sustainability* represents the belief that organizations should meet "humanity's needs without harming future generations." A recent article in *Business Week* identified 24 companies committed to sustainability (e.g., Toyota, Nokia, Hewlett-Packard, ING, SONY, and Glaxo-SmithKline) and seven that were seriously lagging behind (e.g., Allegheny Energy, General Motors, Petrochina, and Walmart).[6] Unilever is a great example of a company committed to this important value.

Sustainability

Meeting humanity's needs without harming future generations.

The world is Unilever's laboratory. In Brazil, the company operates a free community laundry in a São Paulo slum, provides financing to help tomato growers convert to eco-friendly "drip" irrigation, and recycles 17 tons of waste annually at a

WHY THE WALMART CULTURE DIDN'T WORK IN GERMANY

The world's largest retailer, Walmart, tried operating in Germany several years ago, but after nine years of trying and taking a $1 billion hit to quit the market, you won't find any Walmart stores in Germany today. Why? Many put it down to Walmart exporting its North American value system and strong culture to a country that wasn't buying it. For example, the devout motivational cheer enthusiastically shouted by Walmart employees every morning became so annoying to German employees that some hid in the store bathrooms to avoid participating. Also in the mix of espoused values was the corporate policy discouraging inter-office romances, which many German employees found intrusive. One last example is Walmart's policy of bagging groceries, which many German consumers find

distasteful because they tend to not like strangers handling their food. Walmart's espoused values were created in the 1960s in the southern U.S. by its founder, Sam Walton, who believed in a certain retail and customer service philosophy. Even with the death of Walton in 1992, the corporation still adheres to these principles, as they are embodied in a strong organizational culture that sets the norms of business conduct and controls the kind of management intervention decisions administered at the store level. For example, can you imagine a store employee who didn't want to follow the dress code of wearing a vest? Or a manager who wanted to do away with the dozens of slogans posted around the store? Such initiatives would be neutralized by a culture that dictates what is acceptable and what is not.

INTERNATIONAL OB

SOURCES: P. Frost, W. Nord, L. Krefting, *Managerial and Organizational Reality—Stories of Life and Work*, (New Jersey: Pearson Prentice Hall, 2004), p 463; "Wal-Mart Around the World," *The Economist*, December 6, 2001; K. Norton, "Wal-Mart's German Retreat," *Business Week*, July 28, 2006, www.businessweek.com.

toothpaste factory. Unilever funds a floating hospital that offers free medical care in Bangladesh, a nation with just 20 doctors for every 10,000 people. In Ghana, it teaches palm oil producer's to reuse plant waste while providing potable water to deprived communities. In India, Unilever staff help thousands of women in remote villages start micro-enterprises. And responding to green activists, the company discloses how much carbon dioxide and hazardous waste its factories spew out around the world.[7]

Because espoused values represent aspirations that are explicitly communicated to employees, managers hope that those values will directly influence employee behaviour. Unfortunately, aspirations do not automatically produce the desired behaviours, because people do not always "walk the talk."

Enacted values

The values and norms that are exhibited by employees.

Enacted values, on the other hand, represent the values and norms that actually are exhibited or converted into employee behaviour. They represent the values that employees give credit to in an organization, based on their observations of what occurs on a daily basis. The following two examples are excellent representations of the difference between espoused and enacted values.

A major international corporation hung signs in its hallways proclaiming that trust was one of its driving principles. Yet that same company searched employees' belongings each time they entered or exited the building. In another case, a multinational corporation that claimed to be committed to work/life values drew up an excellent plan to help managers incorporate work/life balance into the business. The company gathered its top 80 officers to review the plan—but scheduled the meetings on a weekend.[8]

The first company espoused that it valued trust, and then behaved in an untrusting manner by checking employees' belongings. The second company similarly created a mismatch between espoused and enacted values by promoting work/life balance while simultaneously asking managers to attend weekend meetings.

It is important for managers to reduce gaps between espoused and enacted values because they can significantly influence employee attitudes and organizational performance.

Basic Assumptions Think of basic assumptions as the DNA of the organization: you cannot see them, but you know they are important and represent the very core of a human being. The same can be said for the basic assumptions found within organizational culture. They constitute organizational values that have become so taken for granted over time that they become assumptions that guide organizational behaviour. They are thus highly resistant to change. When basic assumptions are widely held among employees, people will find behaviour based on an inconsistent value inconceivable. For example, employees at WestJet Airlines would be shocked to see management act in ways that did not value employees' and customers' needs.

Practical Application of Research on Values
Organizations subscribe to a constellation of values rather than to only one, and can be profiled according to their values. Organizations are less likely to accomplish their corporate goals when employees perceive an inconsistency between espoused values (e.g., honesty) and the behaviours needed to accomplish the goals (e.g., shredding financial documents). Similarly, organizational change is unlikely to succeed if it is based on a set of values highly inconsistent with employees' individual values.

FOUR FUNCTIONS OF ORGANIZATIONAL CULTURE

LO 2

An organization's culture fulfills four functions. To help bring these four functions to life, let us consider how each of them has taken shape at WestJet Airlines. WestJet is a particularly instructive example because of its unique culture and phenomenal growth since it began operations out of Calgary in 1996. WestJet is the third-largest Canadian carrier, behind Air Canada and Jazz. It operates one of the most modern fleets in North America of any large commercial airline, and has been awarded the title of Most Admired Corporate Culture in Canada for 2006, 2007, and 2008 (by Waterstone Human Capital).[9]

1. **Organizational identity** WestJet Airlines helps their members have an organizational identity. It is known as a fun place to work that values employee satisfaction and customer loyalty over corporate profits. Sean Durfy, president and CEO, commented on this issue: "The caring and dedicated nature of our people is what makes WestJet a different kind of airline. We have seen a lot of changes . . . safety is a core value (at WestJet) and our exceptional guest service begins with the safety of our crews and our guests. Being successful in the airline industry is extremely difficult, but our culture and people are great constants and is what has helped us to achieve tremendous growth and success over the last (12) years and will continue to drive our success."[10]

    With the help of their employees, WestJet gets involved with event sponsorships and community partnerships as demonstrated by their involvement with Alpine Canada and each of Canada's Provincial Ski Organizations to support Canada's Men's, Ladies, and Para-Alpine Ski Teams through to 2010—just in time for the Olympics.[11]

2. **Collective commitment** An organization of employees that see themselves as part of a collective whole rather than a group of isolated individuals helps to bring more synergy to the workplace. The buy-in toward the belief that their collective efforts work in harmony to produce more than what they would produce if they had maintained an individualistic mindset is key to a strong organizational culture.

> "I have never been in an organization where people are more passionate about the job they do every day."

When WestJet was awarded their most recent title for Best Corporate Culture in Canada by an independent human resource firm, the company was quick to emphasize that the safe and cared-for feeling on every WestJet flight is created by the 6,700 fun and friendly WestJetters who care about each other and 'our' guests everyday. "This award belongs to each and every on one of them." In fact, when it came time for the award ceremony in Toronto, the company held an internal nomination contest to decide which of the WestJetters would attend on behalf of the company.[12] In other words, they didn't see the success and recognition of WestJet as being the resulting effort of just one person.

3. **Social system stability** Promoting social system stability reflects the extent to which the work environment is perceived as positive and reinforcing, and the extent to which conflict and change are effectively managed.

> *As Janice Webster, vice-president of talent management and retention stated, "I have never been in an organization where people are more passionate about the job they do every day." Webster joined WestJet a few years earlier and continues to marvel at WestJet's flat management structure and a long-standing culture that encourages employees to step forward with complaints and suggestions about daily operations.[13]*

4. **Sense-making device** Shaping behaviour by helping members make sense of their surroundings is a function of culture that helps employees understand

why the organization does what it does and how it intends to accomplish its long-term goals.

WestJetters clearly understand the airline's primary vision: "By 2016, WestJet will be one of the five most successful international airlines in the world, providing our guests with a friendly and caring experience that will change air travel forever." Employees understand their role in making that goal happen and that is why recruitment, training, and ongoing assessment of current employees are such important aspects of their operations. For example, to ensure that new recruits fit into the culture and buy into the values, front-line candidates for jobs must participate in games, team and individual tasks, and presentations in three-hour long group interview sessions. [14]

TYPES OF ORGANIZATIONAL CULTURE

Although organizational behaviour researchers have proposed three different frameworks to capture the various types of organizational culture,[15] this section will only discuss the most widely used approach for classifying organizational culture: the Competing Values Framework. It was named as one of the 40 most important frameworks in the study of organizations, and has been shown to be a valid approach for classifying organizational culture.[16]

The **Competing Values Framework** (CVF) provides a practical way to understand, measure, and change organizational culture. It was originally developed by a team of researchers who were trying to classify different ways to assess organizational effectiveness. This research showed that measures of organizational effectiveness vary along two fundamental dimensions or axes. One axis pertains to whether an organization focuses its attention and efforts on internal dynamics and employees or outward toward its external environment and its customers and shareholders. The second is concerned with an organization's preference for flexibility and discretion or control and stability. Combining these two axes creates four types of organizational culture that are based on different core values and different sets of criteria for accessing organizational effectiveness. The CVF is shown in Figure 11.2.[17]

LO 3

Competing Values Framework

A model for identifying, classifying, and categorizing organizational cultures based on effectiveness.

▶ FIGURE 11.2 Competing Values Framework

Flexibility and discretion

	Clan	**Adhocracy**	
	Thrust: Collaborate	**Thrust:** Create	
	Means: Cohesion, participation, communication, empowerment	**Means:** Adaptability, creativity, agility	
Internal focus and integration	**Ends:** Morale, people development, commitment	**Ends:** Innovation, Growth, cutting-edge output	**External focus and differentiation**
	Hierarchy	**Market**	
	Thrust: Control	**Thrust:** Compete	
	Means: Capable processes, consistency, process control, measurement	**Means:** Customer focus, productivity, enhancing competitiveness	
	Ends: Efficiency, timeliness, smooth functioning	**Ends:** Market share, profitability, goal achievement	

Stability and control

SOURCE: Adapted from K.S. Cameron, R.E. Quinn, J. Degraff, and A.V. Thakor, *Competing Values Leadership* (Northampton, MA: Edward Elgar, 2006), p 32.

Figure 11.2 shows each cultural type, along with the means used to accomplish the resulting ends or goals pursued by each cultural type. Before beginning our exploration of the CVF, it is important to note that organizations can possess characteristics associated with each culture type. That said, however, organizations tend to have one type of culture that is more dominant than the others. Let us begin our discussion of culture types by starting in the upper-left-hand quadrant of the CVF.

Clan culture

A culture that has an internal focus and values flexibility rather than stability and control.

Clan Culture A *clan culture* has an internal focus and values flexibility rather than stability and control. It resembles a family-type organization in which effectiveness is achieved by encouraging collaboration between employees. This type of culture is very employee-focused and strives to instil cohesion through consensus and job satisfaction and commitment through employee involvement. Clan organizations devote considerable resources to hiring and developing their employees, and they view customers as partners. WestJet Airlines represents a good example of a successful company with a clan culture.

Adhocracy Culture An *adhocracy culture* has an external focus and values flexibility. This type of culture fosters the creation of innovative products and services by being adaptable, creative, and fast to respond to changes in the marketplace. Adhocracy cultures do not rely on the type of centralized power and authority relationships that are part of market and hierarchical cultures. They also encourage employees to take risks, think outside the box, and experiment with new ways of getting things done. This type of culture is well suited for start-up companies, those in industries undergoing constant change, and those in mature industries that are in need of innovation to enhance growth. Two examples would be the Vancouver-based video game developer EA Canada, or the many dynamic members of the Aerospace Industries Association of Canada.

Adhocracy culture

A culture that has an external focus and values flexibility.

Market Culture A *market culture* has a strong external focus and values stability and control. Organizations with this culture are driven by competition and a strong desire to deliver results and

Market culture

A culture that has a strong external focus and values stability and control.

accomplish goals. Because this type of culture is focused on the external environment, customers and profits take precedence over employee development and satisfaction. The major goal of managers is to drive toward productivity, profits, and customer satisfaction. Employees are expected to react fast, work hard, and deliver quality work on time. Organizations with this culture tend to reward people who deliver results. Robert Nardelli, former CEO of Home Depot, decided that the company needed to eliminate some of its adhocracy characteristics and replace them with those associated with a market culture to grow its business.

He reduced store managers' autonomy and centralized the purchasing function. Nardelli also created common performance metrics (standard measurements that provide quantitative feedback) that were used during Monday morning conference calls with his top 15 executives. These meetings were used to reinforce accountability for results and to increase information sharing about operations, markets, and competitive conditions. He further reinforced the driving force of competition by conducting an annual eight-day planning session that was followed up with quarterly business reviews. He ultimately rewarded high performers and fired those who did not meet their goals. Although Home Depot's revenue climbed during Nardelli's tenure from $46 billion in 2000 to $80 billion in 2005, he resigned in January 2007. He was under pressure from stockholders who questioned his hefty pay package and the company's poor stock performance.[18]

Hierarchy Culture   Control is the driving force within a *hierarchical culture.* This culture has an internal focus, which produces a more formalized and structured work environment, and values stability and control over flexibility. This orientation leads to the development of reliable internal processes, extensive measurement, and the implementation of a variety of control mechanisms. For example, companies with a hierarchical culture are more likely to use a Total Quality Management (TQM) program. Effectiveness in a company with this type of culture is likely to be assessed with measures of efficiency, timeliness, and reliability of producing and delivering products and services. Dell is a good example of a company with a hierarchical culture, as it focuses on efficiency and cost-cutting to compete.[19]

Cultural Types Represent Competing Values   It is important to note that certain cultural types reflect opposing core values. These contradicting cultures are found along the two diagonals in Figure 11.2. For example, the clan culture—upper-left quadrant—is represented by values that emphasize an internal focus and flexibility, whereas the market culture—bottom-right quadrant—has an external focus and concern for stability and control. You can see the same conflict between an adhocracy culture that values flexibility and an external focus, and a hierarchical culture that endorses stability and control along with an internal focus. Why are these contradictions important?

They are important because an organization's success may depend on its ability to possess core values that are associated with competing cultural types. This is difficult to pull off, as demonstrated by the former IT giant Nortel Networks Corporation, a Canadian company, who at its peak in 2000 employed almost 90,000 people and accounted for more than a third of total valuation of all the companies listed on the TSX (Toronto Stock Exchange). In 2009, Nortel filed for bankruptcy protection, seeking to restructure itself to pay its financial obligations. However, it failed to achieve the kind of turnaround needed to stay afloat. Nortel is an example of a company that initially had a culture of adhocracy because of the nature of the products it made and the services it provided in the highly competitive telecommunications industry. However, it was unable to maintain consistent and tighter controls over its own processes, leading to its eventual sell-off.

Hierarchical culture

A culture that has an internal focus and values stability and control over flexibility.

OUTCOMES ASSOCIATED WITH ORGANIZATIONAL CULTURE

Academic researchers believe that organizational culture can drive employee attitudes and organizational effectiveness and performance. To test this possibility, various measures of organizational culture have been correlated with a variety of individual and organizational outcomes. So what have we learned? First, several studies demonstrated that organizational culture was significantly correlated with employee behaviour and attitudes. For example, a clan culture was positively associated with employees' job satisfaction, organizational commitment, intentions to stay at the company, and the quality of communication received from one's supervisor. Employees in clan cultures also reported having more positive relationships with their managers than employees working in organizations with an external focus, such as those with adhocracy or market cultures. Employees working in organizations with hierarchical or market-based cultures also reported lower job satisfaction and organizational commitment, and greater intentions to quit their jobs.[20] These results suggest that employees prefer to work in organizations that value flexibility over stability and control, and those that are more concerned with satisfying employees' needs than customer or shareholder desires.

Second, results from several studies revealed that the similarity between an individual's values and the organization's values was significantly associated with organizational commitment, job satisfaction, intention to quit, and turnover.[21]

Third, there is no clear pattern of relationships between organizational culture and outcomes such as service quality, customer satisfaction, and an organization's financial performance. For example, organizations with a market culture exhibit both higher and lower levels of financial performance.[22] While the aforementioned conclusion is supported by data obtained from employees' assessments of organizational culture, it must be tempered by results from two recent studies. A study of 200 companies in more than 40 industries showed that an organization's financial performance is significantly related to customer satisfaction.[23] These results imply that it is important for organizations to have an external focus on its customers if they want to make money. In contrast, a recent meta-analysis of 92 studies revealed that a firm's financial performance is positively associated with the extent to which it employs high performance work practices. High performance work practices reflect an internal cultural orientation and include such things as incentive compensation, employee involvement, employee training, and the use of flexible work schedules.[24] All told, these results suggest that it is important for managers to effectively accommodate the potential conflict between cultures that have both an internal and external focus.

This conclusion is consistent with findings from a study of 207 companies in 22 industries over an 11-year period. Results demonstrated that an organization's financial performance is higher among companies that have adaptive or flexible cultures.[25] Stated differently, successful companies modify their cultures over time so that they are appropriate or consistent with the market or business situation at hand.

Finally, studies of mergers indicated that they frequently fail due to incompatible cultures. Due to the increasing number of corporate mergers around the world, and the conclusion that 7 out of 10 mergers and acquisitions fail to meet their financial promise, managers within merged companies would be well-advised to consider the role of organizational culture in creating a new organization.[26]

In summary, research underscores the significance of organizational culture. It also reinforces the need to learn more about the process of cultivating and changing an organization's culture. An organization's culture is not determined by fate. It is formed and shaped by the combination and integration of everyone who works in the organization. A change-resistant culture, for instance, can undermine the effectiveness of any type of organizational change. Although it is not an easy task to change an organization's culture, the next section provides a preliminary overview of how this might be done.

The Process of Culture Change

LO 4

Before describing the specific ways in which organizational culture can be changed, let us review three factors related to culture change. First, it is possible to change an organization's culture, and the process essentially begins with targeting one of the three layers of organizational culture previously discussed—observable artefacts, espoused values, and basic assumptions for change. Ultimately, culture change involves changing people's minds and their behaviour.[27]

Second, it is important to consider the extent to which the current culture is aligned with the organization's vision and competitive business plan before attempting to change any aspect of organizational culture. A **vision** represents a long-term goal that describes "what" an organization wants to become.

Vision

Long-term goal describing "what" an organization wants to become.

A **strategic plan** outlines an organization's competitive business model, long-term goals, and the actions necessary to achieve these goals. Mark Fields, executive vice president of Ford Motor Company, firmly believes that culture, vision, and strategic plans should be aligned. According to Fields, "Culture eats strategy for breakfast. You can have the best plan in the world, and if the culture isn't going to let it happen, it's going to die on the vine."[28]

Strategic plan

A long-term plan outlining actions needed to achieve desired results.

Finally, it is important to use a structured approach when implementing culture change. Chapter 13 can help you in this regard, as it presents several models that provide specific steps to follow when implementing any type of organizational change. Let us now consider the specific methods or techniques that can be used to change an organization's culture.

Edgar Schein, a well-known OB scholar, notes that changing organizational culture involves a teaching process. That is, organizational members teach each other about the organization's preferred values, beliefs, norms, expectations, and behaviours. This is accomplished by using one or more of the following mechanisms:[29]

1. **Formal statements of organizational philosophy, mission, vision, values, and materials used for recruiting, selection, and socialization** Within the strategic plan are corporate mission and vision statements that often promote organizational values. Starbuck's core value of providing a great work environment for its employees was discussed at the beginning of this chapter in the opening vignette.

2. **The design of physical space, work environments, and buildings** There is something to be said for changing the workspace or context of where employees work. Consider how Acordia Inc., a diversified financial services company, attempted to create a more entrepreneurial culture by building a new one-floor facility:

   The new building facilitated interactive workflow procedures. Interactions among new-venture team members and among independent teams became grounded in forming and sharing tacit knowledge. Positive feelings surfacing from these interactions and the knowledge they fostered created positive morale in individuals and between employees and their vice president.[30]

3. **Slogans, language, acronyms, and sayings** For example, consider the look of Walmart, from the blue vests with slogans written on them, to the posters and slogans on the walls around the employee lunchrooms, the opening welcome message by the greeter, Sam's 10 foot rule and Sun Down Rule... all of these factors speak to the formalized Walmart culture. If Walmart ever decided to change its culture, these slogans and sayings would all have to change.

4. **Deliberate role modelling, training programs, teaching, and coaching by managers and supervisors** Boeing's CEO, Jim McNerney, leads by example.

   He wins praise from co-workers for paying attention to the small things like remembering people's names, listening closely to their presentations, and not embarrassing underlings in public.[31]

5. **Explicit rewards, status symbols (e.g., titles), and promotion criteria** Boeing is revising its reward system to reform its culture.

   In the old days, no points were awarded for collaborating with other units or following ethics rules. Now pay and bonuses are directly linked to how well executives embrace a set of six leadership attributes such as Living Boeing Values. That includes new criteria such as promoting integrity and avoiding abusive behaviour.[32]

LAW AND ETHICS *at Work*

HEWLETT-PACKARD HAD TO CHANGE THEIR CULTURE

Mark Hurd's response to a crisis underscores Hewlett-Packard's culture. To hear Hurd tell it, when HP's then board chairman Patricia C. Dunn authorized an investigation into press leaks from the board, he also trusted that she and the company's legal and security personnel would handle it properly. Hurd figured he had enough work resurrecting the company. However, red-eyed and clearly humbled, Hurd explained to *BusinessWeek*: "I'm a detail-oriented guy by trade. But when you have a place of this scale, you have to pick your spots where you're going to go dive. Compliance wasn't the first process I was going to go look at. I was going to go look at the performance of the company."

Even if Hurd is right about being mostly out of the loop, it's a decision he surely regrets. A few days after it became public, Hurd stood before a room of reporters and read a statement apologizing for the spying tactics that HP officials and security subcontractors used to track down the source of leaks. Hurd admitted that he was not paying close enough attention to spot some of the actions, which he called "very disturbing."

The scandal is filtering into Hurd's day-to-day management style in surprising ways. He says half-jokingly that he finds himself repeatedly telling employees in meetings that whatever they do has to be "legal and ethical." "We're going to have to regain the world's confidence one person at a time to prove that this is the company they thought it was." What cultural messages did Hurd show through his comments and behaviour?

SOURCE: Excerpted from P. Burrows, "Controlling the Damage at HP," *Business Week*, October 9, 2006, pp 38–39.

6. **Stories, legends, or myths about key people and events** To outsiders, such traditions and rituals may be perceived as odd. But to insiders, they are very important. If a company decides to take a new direction, they have to review old rituals to consider if they fit into the new culture.

7. **The organizational activities, processes, or outcomes that leaders pay attention to, measure, and control** Consider the behaviour of Jamie Dimon, CEO of J.P. Morgan Chase.

   He has imposed rigorous pay-for-performance metrics and requires managers to present exhaustive monthly reviews, then grills them on the data for hours at a time ... To be sure he's getting the real story, Dimon button holes staffers in the elevators and calls suppliers out of the blue like a hyperactive gumshoe (private investigator), collecting scraps of information he can throw back at executives ... He yanked Bank One's sponsorship of the Masters golf tournament because the country club hosting the event doesn't accept women members.[33]

8. **Leader reactions to critical incidents and organizational crises** Consider the cultural messages sent by Mark Hurd, CEO of Hewlett-Packard Co., when he responded to the crisis involving an investigation of press leaks from board members by then chairman, Patricia Dunn (see Law & Ethics feature box). His behaviour shows that he was more concerned about performance than ethics prior to this crisis. The charges against Ms. Dunn were dismissed in March, 2007.[34]

9. **The workflow and organizational structure** Hierarchical structures are more likely to embed an orientation toward control and authority than a flatter organization. Leaders from many organizations are increasingly reducing the number of organizational layers in an attempt to empower employees (restructuring is discussed in Chapter 12) and increase employee involvement.

10. **Organizational systems and procedures** An organization can promote achievement and competition through the use of sales contests.[35]

11. **Organizational goals and the associated criteria used for recruitment, selection, development, promotion, layoffs, and retirement of people** PepsiCo reinforces a high-performance culture by setting challenging goals.

The Organizational Socialization Process

Organizational socialization is defined as "the process by which a person learns the values, norms, and required behaviours which permit him to participate as a member of the organization."[36] Think about your own work experience; were you properly socialized when starting the job? To determine your own experience with the socialization process, you are invited to complete the Self-Assessment Exercise, "Were You Adequately Socialized?" This will help you understand the essence of what this section is discussing. As previously discussed, organization socialization is a key mechanism used by organizations to embed their organizational cultures. In short, organizational socialization turns outsiders into fully functioning insiders by promoting and reinforcing the organization's core values and beliefs. This section introduces a three-phase model of organizational socialization and examines the practical application of socialization research.

Organizational socialization

Process by which employees learn an organization's values, norms, and required behaviours.

FELDMAN'S MODEL OF ORGANIZATIONAL SOCIALIZATION

LO 5

The first year in a complex organization can be confusing for new employees. There is a constant swirl of new faces, strange jargon (language), conflicting expectations, and apparently unrelated events. Some organizations treat new members in a rather haphazard, sink-or-swim manner. More typically, though, the socialization process is characterized by a sequence of identifiable steps.

Organizational behaviour researcher Daniel Feldman has proposed a three-phase model of organizational socialization that promotes deeper understanding of this important process. The three phases are (1) anticipatory socialization, (2) encounter, and (3) change and acquisition. Each phase has its associated perceptual and social processes.[37]

Feldman's model also specifies behavioural and affective outcomes that can be used to judge how well an individual has been socialized. The entire three-phase sequence may take from a few weeks to a year to complete, depending on individual differences and the complexity of the situation.

Anticipatory socialization phase

Occurs before an individual joins an organization, and involves information people learn about different careers, occupations, professions, and organizations.

Phase 1: Anticipatory Socialization The ***anticipatory socialization phase*** occurs before an individual actually joins an organization. It is represented by the information

Were You Adequately Socialized?

INSTRUCTIONS: Complete the following survey items by considering either your current job or one you held in the past. If you have never worked, identify a friend who is working and ask that individual to complete the questionnaire for his or her organization. Read each item and circle your response by using the rating scale shown below. Compute your total score by adding up your responses and compare it to the scoring norms.

1 = STRONGLY DISAGREE
2 = DISAGREE
3 = NEITHER AGREE NOR DISAGREE
4 = AGREE
5 = STRONGLY AGREE

1. I have been through a set of training experiences that are specifically designed to give newcomers a thorough knowledge of job-related skills.   1—2—3—4—5

2. This organization puts all newcomers through the same set of learning experiences.   1—2—3—4—5

3. I did not perform any of my normal job responsibilities until I was thoroughly familiar with departmental procedures and work methods.   1—2—3—4—5

4. There is a clear pattern in the way one role leads to another, or one job assignment leads to another, in this organization.   1—2—3—4—5

5. I can predict my future career path in this organization by observing other people's experiences.   1—2—3—4—5

6. Almost all of my colleagues have been supportive of me personally.   1—2—3—4—5

7. My colleagues have gone out of their way to help me adjust to this organization.   1—2—3—4—5

8. I received much guidance from experienced organizational members as to how I should perform my job.   1—2—3—4—5

Total Score = _____

SCORING NORMS

8–18 = Low socialization

19–29 = Moderate socialization

30–40 = High socialization

SOURCE: Adapted from survey items excerpted from D. Cable and C. Parsons, "Socialization Tactics and Person-Organization Fit," *Personnel Psychology,* Spring 2001, pp 1–23.

people have learned about different careers, occupations, professions, and organizations. For example, anticipatory socialization partially explains the different perceptions you might have about working for the Canadian government versus a high-technology company like Microsoft. Anticipatory socialization information comes from many sources. For example, an organization's current employees are a powerful source of anticipatory socialization.

Unrealistic expectations about the nature of the work, pay, and promotions are often created during phase 1. Because employees with unrealistic expectations are more likely to quit their jobs in the future, organizations may want to use realistic job previews.[38] A *realistic job preview* (RJP) involves giving recruits a realistic idea of what lies ahead by presenting both positive and negative aspects of the job. RJPs may be verbal, in booklet form, audiovisual, or hands-on. Research supports the practical benefits of using RJPs. A meta-analysis of 40 studies revealed that RJPs were related to higher performance and to lower attrition from the recruitment process. Results also demonstrated that RJPs lowered job applicants' initial expectations and led to lower turnover among those applicants who were hired.[39]

Realistic job preview

Presents both positive and negative aspects of a job.

Phase 2: Encounter This second phase begins when the employment contract has been signed. During the *encounter phase* employees come to learn what the organization is really like. It is a time for recognizing unmet expectations and making sense of a new work environment. Many companies use a combination of orientation and training programs to socialize employees during the encounter phase. Onboarding is one such technique. *Onboarding* programs help employees to integrate, assimilate, and transition to new jobs by making them familiar with corporate policies, procedures, and culture, and by clarifying work role expectations and responsibilities.[40]

Phase 3: Change and Acquisition The *change and acquisition phase* requires employees to master important tasks and roles and to adjust to their work group's values and norms. Table 11.1 presents a list of socialization processes or tactics used by organizations to help employees through this adjustment process.

PRACTICAL APPLICATION OF SOCIALIZATION RESEARCH

Past research suggests six practical guidelines for managing organizational socialization.

Change and acquisition phase

Requires employees to master tasks and roles and to adjust to work group values and norms.

1. A recent survey of executives from 100 companies revealed that 65 percent did an average or poor job of socializing new hires.[41] This reinforces the conclusion that managers should avoid a haphazard, sink-or-swim approach to organizational socialization, because formalized socialization tactics positively affect new hires. Formalized or institutionalized socialization tactics were found to positively help employees in both domestic and international operations.[42]

2. Supervisors are encouraged to consider how they might best set expectations regarding ethical behaviour during all three phases of the socialization process.[43]

3. Supervisors play a key role during the encounter phase. Studies of newly hired accountants demonstrated that the frequency and type of information obtained during their first six months of employment significantly affected their job performance, their role clarity, and the extent to which they were socially integrated.[44] Supervisors need to help new hires integrate within the organizational culture. Consider the approach used by John Chambers, CEO of Cisco Systems: "He meets with groups of new hires to welcome them soon after they start, and at monthly breakfast meetings workers are encouraged to ask him tough questions."[45]

4. Support for stage models is mixed. Although there are different stages of socialization, they are not identical in order, length, or content for all people or jobs.[46] Supervisors are advised to use a contingency approach toward organizational socialization. In other words, different techniques are appropriate for different people at different times.

5. The organization can benefit by training new employees to use proactive socialization behaviours. Socialization tactics should encourage new employees to seek information as they proceed through the encounter, change, and acquisition phases of socialization. For example, a study of 140 co-op post-secondary students showed that the use of formalized socialization tactics was associated with newcomers' feedback-seeking and information-seeking behaviours.[47]

6. Supervisors should pay attention to the socialization of diverse employees. Research demonstrated that diverse employees, particularly those with disabilities, experienced different socialization activities than other newcomers. In turn, these different experiences affected their long-term success and job satisfaction.[48]

TACTIC	DESCRIPTION	EXAMPLE
Collective vs. individual	Collective socialization consists of grouping newcomers and exposing them to a common set of experiences, rather than treating newcomers individually and exposing them to more or less unique experiences.	New student orientation week is a common collective socialization activity organized at many post-secondary schools each fall.
Formal vs. informal	Formal socialization is the practice of segregating a newcomer from regular organization members during a defined socialization period, versus not clearly distinguishing a newcomer from more experienced members.	Military recruits are formally socialized by attending boot camp before they are allowed to work alongside established soldiers.
Sequential vs. random	Sequential socialization refers to a fixed progression of steps that culminate in the new role, compared to an ambiguous or dynamic progression.'	The socialization process of doctors involves a lock-step sequence from medical school, to internship, to residency before they are allowed to practise on their own. The same could be said for the trades, where years of training and apprenticeships must be earned prior to receiving journeyman certification.
Fixed vs. variable	Fixed socialization provides a timetable for the assumption of the role, whereas a variable process does not.	It's common for college and university students to spend one fixed year apiece as first-year students, then on to their second year of studies, and so on. It's more the exception than the rule to have students from various years co-mingled within the same classroom or even residency area.
Serial vs. disjunctive	A serial process is one in which the newcomer is socialized by an experienced member, whereas a disjunctive process does not use a role model.	A mentorship–protégé program is a serial socialization process that allows the experienced seasoned employee to help the newer employee adjust to the organization.
Investiture vs. divestiture	Investiture refers to the affirmation of a newcomer's incoming global and specific role identities and attributes. Divestiture is the denial and stripping away of the newcomer's existing sense of self, and the reconstruction of self in the organization's image.	During police training, cadets are socialized through investiture activities such as: requiring them to wear uniforms and maintain an immaculate appearance; addressing them as "officer"; and telling them they are no longer ordinary citizens, but are representatives of the police force. Divestiture processes are likened to fraternity hazing that typically involve denial and degrading techniques.

ADAPTATION: Descriptions were taken from B.E. Ashforth, *Role Transitions in Organizational Life: An Identity-Based Perspective* (Mahwah, NJ: Lawrence Erlbaum Associates, 2001), pp 149–83.

Embedding Organizational Culture through Mentoring

The modern word *mentor* derives from Mentor, the name of a wise and trusted counsellor in Greek mythology. Terms typically used in connection with mentoring are *teacher, coach, sponsor,* and *peer*. **Mentoring** is defined as the process of forming and maintaining intensive and lasting developmental relationships between a variety of developers (people who provide career and emotional support) and a junior person (the protégé).[49] There are two reasons why mentoring can serve to embed an organization's culture when developers and the protégé work in the same organization: first,

Mentoring

Process of forming and maintaining developmental relationships between a mentor and a junior person.

mentoring contributes to creating a sense of oneness by promoting acceptance of the organization's core values throughout the organization; and second, the socialization aspect of mentoring promotes a sense of membership.

Not only is mentoring important as a tactic for embedding organizational culture, but research suggests it can significantly influence the protégé's future career. For example, a meta-analysis revealed that mentored employees had higher compensation and more promotions than non-mentored employees. Mentored employees also reported higher job and career satisfaction and organizational commitment, and lower turnover.[50] This section focuses on how people can use mentoring to their advantage. We discuss the functions of mentoring, the developmental networks underlying mentoring, and the personal and organizational implications of mentoring.

FUNCTIONS OF MENTORING

Kathy Kram, a researcher, identified two general positive functions of the mentoring process. The first function was enhanced career development for protégés, where they gained legitimate sponsorship, exposure and visibility, coaching, protection, and challenging assignments. Mentors can help protégés gain exposure and visibility in the industry by inviting them to participate in local clubs and associations, such as attending a local Rotary International meeting. When faced with decisions that have overtones of organizational politics, the mentor can coach the protégé through the landmines to avoid career disasters. The career development aspect of mentoring is very beneficial for protégé success.

The second function Kram discovered was the psychological, emotional, and social support (called psycho-social) that mentoring provided for the protégé, such as role modelling, acceptance and confirmation, counselling, and friendship. The psycho-social functions clarified the participants' identities and enhanced their self-esteem needs.[51] Having a well-respected mentor on-side during uncertain times can help protégés feel more confident that they won't make a mistake. Further, protégés have someone cheering for them on the sidelines when things go well and congratulations are in order.

Diversity of developmental relationships

The variety of people in a network used by a protégé for developmental assistance.

> Mentors can assist protégés with coaching and career development assistance. They can also provide the needed psychological, emotional, and social support, which are key functions that help to embed an organization's culture.

DEVELOPMENTAL NETWORKS UNDERLYING MENTORING

Today, the changing nature of technology, organizational structures, and marketplace dynamics require that people seek career information and support from many sources. Contemporary mentoring programs go beyond a one-on-one relationship between the mentor and the protégé. Mentoring is evolving into a process in which protégés seek developmental guidance from a network of people, who are referred to as developers. Figure 11.3 presents a developmental network typology based on integrating the diversity and strength of developmental relationships.[52] To gain a better understanding of this model, let's spend some time exploring each quadrant; we'll begin by substituting the protégé with yourself and the kind of personal decisions you may be going through within the next year or two in preparation of graduation and getting your first post-grad job.

Along the side of Figure 11.3, we consider the *diversity of developmental relationships*, which reflects the variety of people within the network that a protégé uses for developmental assistance. For example, what kinds of contacts do you have—are they all students? Are they all business teachers? Do you participate in charity work on campus? Are you involved in community activities that allow you to network with industry professionals? Consider the two subparts associated with network diversity: (1) the number of different people the protégé is networked with, and (2) the various social systems from which the networked relationships stem (e.g., employer, school, family, community, professional associations, and religious affiliations). As shown in Figure 11.3, developmental relationship diversity ranges from low (few people or social systems) to high (multiple people or social systems).

Across the top of Figure 11.3 are measurements of

▶ FIGURE 11.3   Developmental Networks Associated with Mentoring

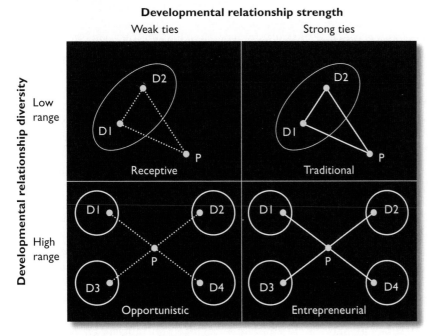

Developmental relationship strength

Weak ties   Strong ties

Developmental relationship diversity

Low range

Receptive   Traditional

High range

Opportunistic   Entrepreneurial

Key: D=developer; P=protégé

SOURCE: M. Higgins and K. Kram, "Reconceptualizing Mentoring at Work: A Developmental Network Perspective," *Academy of Management Review*, April 2001, p 270. Reprinted by permission of The Academy of Management via The Copyright Clearance Center.

developmental relationship strength that reflect the quality of relationships between protégés and those involved in their developmental network. For example, who at your school would you say you have *strong ties* to? This is a person with whom you have an ongoing relationship, based on frequent interactions and positive affect—it could be a professor, program advisor, or coach. Now think of the other relationships you have at school that would be considered as weak ties. In contrast, these contacts are based more on superficial relationships—this might be a fellow student who you've been in several classes with throughout the last few years, or a school administrator who you've had occasional contact with over the years. In other words, you know them, but it's not a deep relationship.

Bringing together diversity and strength of developmental relationships results in four quadrants, each representing a type of developmental network: (1) receptive, (2) traditional, (3) entrepreneurial, and (4) opportunistic.

> **Developmental relationship strength**
>
> The quality of relationships among protégés and those involved in their development networks.

A *receptive* developmental network is composed of a few weak ties from one social system, such as an employer or a professional association. The single oval around D1 and D2 indicates two developers who come from one social system. An example of this, continuing to use you as the protégé, could be one professor and one student, both from the same program, who you have casually spoken with over the years while in class together. They are weak ties because you only know them from being in class together; you've never spoken with them outside of class. In terms of variety, they are both superficial relationships, not based on any rich experiences that offer a variety of perspective or opinion. This is the weakest quadrant and the worst protégé position to be in.

A *traditional* network contains a few strong ties between a protégé and developers that all come from one social system. An example of this could be two well-respected professors, both from the same program, who work side-by-side as mentors. They are strong ties because they know you well and you feel comfortable with them. However, in terms of variety, they are too much alike and can't offer a variety of perspectives or opinions on your experience. This position is a bit better for the protégé, but it is still limiting in providing network assistance.

An *opportunistic* network is associated with having weak ties with multiple developers from different social systems. An example of this is joining a campus club during the first month of school that gives you the opportunity to interact with many different people from diverse program areas; the only problem is that you only joined to put it on your resume, you only attended two meetings, you never participated in any activities, and you never became engaged in the spirit of the club. The high degree of diversity this club offers is wonderful, but the relationships are almost non-existent as you don't know anyone well enough. Protégés who engage in this sort of development network are kidding themselves; it may look good on paper, but it is not any better than being in the *receptive* quadrant above.

Finally, an *entrepreneurial* network, which is the strongest type of developmental network, is made up of strong ties between several developers (D1–D4) who come from four different social systems. In this quadrant, you feel close to a variety of contacts. An example of this would be a professor who you know well; a supervisor who you have worked with for over one year who knows you well; a mentor from a club or organization who you have volunteered with over the last few years; and, finally, a former coach of a team on which you played for two years. This network shows diversity, as well as strong ties that you can benefit from. This quadrant should be the goal of every student reading this text.

PERSONAL AND ORGANIZATIONAL IMPLICATIONS

There are five key personal implications to consider. First, job and career satisfaction are likely to be influenced by the consistency between individuals' career goals and the type of developmental network at their disposal. For example, people with an entrepreneurial developmental network are more likely to experience change in their careers and to benefit from personal learning than people with receptive, traditional, and opportunistic networks. If this sounds attractive to you, try to increase the diversity and strength of your developmental relationships. In contrast, lower levels of job satisfaction are expected when employees have receptive developmental networks and they desire to experience career advancement in multiple organizations. Receptive developmental networks, however, can be satisfying to someone who does not wish to be promoted up the career ladder.[53]

Second, a developer's willingness to provide career and psycho-social assistance is a function of the protégé's ability, potential, and the quality of the interpersonal relationship.[54] This implies that you must take ownership for enhancing your skills, abilities, and developmental networks if you desire to experience career advancement throughout your life[55] (see Skills & Best Practices feature box).

Third, put effort into finding a mentor. A study of 4,559 leaders and 944 human resource professionals from 42 countries showed that 91 percent of those who used a mentor found the experience moderately or greatly beneficial to their career success.[56] That said, another recent study showed that the success of a mentoring relationship from a protégé's perspective is partly determined by the skills and abilities of the mentor.[57]

This leads to the fourth recommendation. If you believe that your mentor is ineffective or, worse yet, causing more harm than benefit, find a new mentor. Finally, although mentoring can help your career, and some mediocre people advance because of a strong mentor, don't be fooled into thinking that who you know is a replacement for talent, knowledge, and motivation.[58] We strongly encourage you to use your own passion, motivation, talents, and networking skills to accomplish your personal and professional goals.

Research also supports the organizational benefits of mentoring. For example, mentoring enhances the appropriateness and effectiveness of organizational communication (see Focus on Diversity feature box), it increases the amount of vertical communication both up and down an organization, and it provides a mechanism for modifying or reinforcing organizational culture.

Skills & Best Practices

Building an Effective Mentoring Network

1 **Become the perfect protégé.** It is important to invest ample time and energy to develop and maintain a network of developmental relationships. Trust and respect are needed among network members. Determine the right thing to do for the welfare of the entire enterprise or organization.

2 **Engage in 360-degree networking.** Share information and maintain good relationships with those above, below, and at the same status/responsibility level as yourself. Take responsibility for decisions.

3 **Commit to assessing, building, and adjusting the mentor network.** Begin by assessing the competencies you want to build. Next, find mentors who can assist in building your desired competencies. Finally, change network members commensurate with changes in your experience and knowledge.

4 **Realize that change is inevitable and that all good things come to an end.** Most mentoring relationships last an average of five years. When a relationship ceases to be beneficial, end the mentoring relationship.

SOURCE: Derived from S.C. de Janasz, S.E. Sullivan, and V. Whiting, "Mentor Networks and Career Success: Lessons for Turbulent Times," *Academy of Management Executive*, November 2003, pp 78–91.

HOW OLDER COHORTS CAN MENTOR THE MILLENNIAL GENERATION ON COMMUNICATION TECHNIQUES

"Why can't I just instant message a friend who works at a competitor?" "What is wrong with emailing colleagues about the change in budget and schedule?" "Why do I need to be trained on the corporate Code of Conduct?" Questions such as these can be expected from the new generation of employees entering the Canadian work world. According to Stanton Smith, National Director of Next Generation Initiatives, Deloitte Services LP, there are three major differences between millennials and older employees: Millennials (1) view electronic communications as an extension of how they live and interact with people, (2) can be cynical toward business, and (3) have a consumer mindset that expects easy-to-handle "microwavable" experiences. Seasoned employees can assist millennial protégés to understand the corporate culture nuances (factors) that guide employee behaviour, even though they have not been formalized in policy manuals. For example, a baby-boomer mentor can help the millennial understand the barriers or hierarchies that organizations have put into place to help coordinate workflow and ease daily operations. If an employee was wilfully communicating with a competitor employee on company time and using company resources to do so, then a mentor could catch such behaviour early enough to alert the protégé of the potential concern management would have (e.g., questioning motive and/or intent). Culture can guide employee behaviour, and seasoned mentors can educate the next generation of employee on appropriate conduct.

SOURCE: M. Bassett, "Ethics Don't Change with Age – But Millennials Need Tailored Training," The Conference Board of Canada Newsletter, *Inside Edge*, Summer 2008, p 11.

Summary of Learning Objectives

1. **Define *organizational culture, espoused values*, and *enacted values*.** Organizational culture represents the assumptions that a group holds. It influences employees' perceptions and behaviour at work. It is the shared values and beliefs held throughout the organization. Espoused values represent the explicitly-stated values and norms that are preferred by an organization. Enacted values, in contrast, reflect the values and norms that are actually exhibited or converted into employee behaviour. Employees become cynical when management espouses one set of values and norms and then behaves in an inconsistent fashion.

2. **Describe the four functions of organizational culture.** Four functions of organizational culture are organizational identity, collective commitment, social system stability, and sense-making device. See WestJet examples.

3. **Discuss the four types of organizational culture associated with the competing values framework.** The competing values framework identifies four different types of organizational culture. A clan culture has an internal focus and values flexibility rather than stability and control. An adhocracy culture has an external

focus and values flexibility. A market culture has a strong external focus and values stability and control. A hierarchy culture has an internal focus and values stability and control over flexibility.

4. **Summarize the various methods used by organizations to change organizational culture.** Changing culture amounts to teaching employees about the organization's new, enhanced, or preferred values, beliefs, expectations, and behaviours. This is accomplished by using one or more of the following 11 mechanisms: (1) formal statements of organizational philosophy, mission, vision, values, and materials used for recruiting, selection, and socialization; (2) the design of physical space, work environments, and buildings; (3) slogans, language, acronyms, and sayings; (4) deliberate role modelling, training programs, teaching, and coaching by managers and supervisors; (5) explicit rewards, status symbols, and promotion criteria; (6) stories, legends, and myths about key people and events; (7) the organizational activities, processes, or outcomes that leaders pay attention to, measure, and control; (8) leader reactions to critical incidents and organizational crises; (9) the workflow and organizational structure; (10) organizational systems and procedures; and (11) organizational goals and associated criteria used for recruitment, selection, development, promotion, layoffs, and retirement of people.

5. **Describe the three phases in Feldman's model of organizational socialization and explain how mentoring can assist the socialization process.** The three phases of Feldman's model are anticipatory socialization, encounter, and change and acquisition. Anticipatory socialization begins before an individual actually joins the organization. The encounter phase begins when the employment contract has been signed. The change and acquisition phase involves the period in which employees master important tasks and resolve any role conflicts. Mentorship programs can assist protégés to feel included in the organization, and increase understanding of the organization's values, norms, and required behaviours. The relationships that are developed between mentors and protégés provide the psycho-social functions necessary to help new employees establish their identity within the firm and enhance their feelings of competence.

⬇ Discussion Questions

1. Respond to the following statement: Organizational cultures are not important to an organization. Do you agree with it? Explain your response.

2. How would the culture of a unionized public sector workplace differ from a non-unionized private sector workplace? (For example, all government offices including police, hospital, and educational institutions versus Walmart, Toyota, and Google.)

3. Why is socialization essential to organizational success?

4. Have you ever had a mentor? Provide specific examples of how having a mentor assisted your socialization into the organizational culture.

5. How important are formal socialization and mentorship programs, especially in terms of a more diverse Canadian workplace? Explain.

Google Searches

1. **Google Search:** Mergers and acquisitions between organizations have become a common business phenomenon. Some work, some do not. Most often, a corporate takeover may look appealing on paper, yet after the ink dries, the corporate cultures clash. (1) Consider "Germany's DaimlerChrysler sell off" and "Fiat buys Chrysler" What happened in each of these situations and what role did culture play? (2) "Canada's TD Bank Financial Group Buys Commerce Bank New Jersey" or "RBC and CIBC" Considering the cultures of each, do you think these mergers will succeed?

2. **Google Search:** "Boston Pizza" OR "Four Season's Hotels and Resorts" Review the Web sites and try to identify the three layers of organizational culture for each: observable artefacts, espoused values, and/or enacted values.

3. **Google Search:** "Ontario Public Service Mentorship Program" In 2009, this program was recognized as one of Canada's Best Diversity Employers. Research the details of this award-winning program by reviewing the various Web sites cited. How has this unique program embraced the principles of diversity together with mentorship? How does this program effectively embed corporate culture?

www.mcgrawhill.ca/olc/kreitner

Experiential Exercise

Developing a Mentoring Network Group Exercise

PURPOSE: This exercise is to help familiarize you with the OB concept of developmental networks that underlie mentoring. Even as students, relationships can be formed at school that can help career development, as well as offer emotional support when needed. Approx. Timing: 20 minutes.

ACTIVITY ASSIGNMENT
- Review the section in this chapter that explains each quadrant in Figure 11.3. Fill in the table below.
- Work in small groups and share your network with others in your group.
- Help each other explore opportunities that exist on campus that may help to widen the diversity of your contacts.
- Identify how to strengthen relationships and offer suggestions on how others can accomplish this.

	WEAK TIES/RELATIONSHIPS	STRONG TIES/RELATIONSHIPS
Low Range of Diversity ▶		
High Range of Diversity ▶		

The **Presentation** Assistant

Here are possible topics and corresponding sources related to this chapter that can be further explored by student groups looking for ideas.

	HOW DO DIFFERENT GENERATIONS BRING THEIR VALUES TO THE WORKPLACE —WHAT EFFECT DOES THIS HAVE ON THE CURRENT ORGANIZATIONAL CULTURE?	THE SOCIALIZATION PROCESS: EXAMPLES OF TACTICS USED BY VARIOUS ORGANIZATIONS TO SOCIALIZE PEOPLE	THE MENTORING PROCESS—WHAT IS IT? HOW DOES IT WORK? WHAT ARE THE PROS AND CONS? DOES IT HELP WITH ORGANIZATIONAL CULTURE BUY-IN?
YouTube Videos	• Changing Culture with GM's Jack Smith • Google's Culture of Perks • The New World of Work (Managing Gen Y) • Organizational Culture— The Innovation Parking Lot (Second Life)	• New Employee Orientation Video • Louie Gravance Speech Preview (Disney Orientation) • Fraternity Hazing Rituals 1950 • UW Arts Orientation Week • The Socialization In Cults	• Eric Liu—Mentoring: The People Who Lead Us Toward Our Purpose In Life • Coaching and Business Mentor Training—Before It's Too Late
TV Shows or Movies to Preview	• *In Good Company* (movie) • *The Firm* (movie) • *Wall Street* (movie)	• *The Office: Season 3* "The Merger" Episode • *Old School* (movie)	• *Finding Forrester* (movie) • *Dead Poets Society* (movie)
Internet Searches	• *Unstuck* (by K. Yamashita) • *The Fish Culture* (the philosophy book) • *Now Discover Your Strengths* (by M. Buckingham) • *Who Says Elephants Can't Dance?* (by ex-IBM CEO L. Gerstner, Jr.)	• IBM Research— Knowledge Socialization (Web site) • *Understanding Canadian Military Culture* (by A. English)	• The Power of Mentorship (Web site) • Centre for coaching and mentoring (Web site) • *5 Questions Every Mentor Must Ask* (by Anthony Tjan—Harvard B. Review)
Ice Breaker Classroom Activity	• Ask students to identify the buildings around campus that were built by previous generations (i.e., by the Baby Boomers and earlier). Then ask them to identify the buildings on campus that were designed by Gen X or Y types. Identify the differences in artefacts between buildings.	• Ask students if anyone has ever been initiated into a club, or if they have ever belonged to an organization that had a socialization process. Share responses from the class.	• Ask students for their experiences with being a mentor or a protégé. Ask if they see any value in having a mentor at their current stage in life, or would it be more effective at an older age? Share responses from the class.

OB In Action Case Study

Google's Culture Is Truly Unique

At Google, it always comes back to the food. Whether it's at the main campus (headquaters) in Mountain View, California, or at any of their three Canadian offices in Waterloo, Toronto, or Montreal, Google offers free, healthy, gourmet (and often organic) meals with plenty of free snacks and munchies, including various sweetened or salted snacks and sodas, mineral waters, and fruit juices. These snacks are freely available for all Googlers in the kitchenettes. The cafés (almost a dozen at their Silicon Valley headquarters alone!) have a wide variety of food for breakfast, lunch, and dinner. All three Canadian offices have catered meals on-site.

Says co-founder Sergey Brin: "I mean, the cafés have always been pretty healthy, but the snacks are not, and the efforts to fix that have been remarkably challenging."

Though company lore has it that Brin and co-founder Larry Page believe no worker should be more than about 46 metres from a food source, clearly not all food is equal. "A lot of people like their M & Ms. But the easy access is actually what's bad for them," he says.

Of course, when it comes to working at the Best Workplace in Canada (2009) according to the Great Place To Work Institute, the food is, well, just the appetizer. The perks that make Google a great place to work certainly add up, but the one perk that stands out for most employees is that the company has created an environment that is more than just a bunch of offices where people punch in 9-to-5. Google incorporates healthy social environments where co-workers can collaborate and brainstorm in less formal and stressful workplaces. Here are some of the many perks offered at Google Canada:

- Employees are encouraged to take breaks and unwind by trying their skill at one of the many ping pong tables, foosball tables, video games, pinball machines, or pool tables around the office.
- Google provides 15–20 minute chair massages on site as a thank you for employees' hard work. If employees feel rejuvenated, they'll be more likely to want to work.
- Googlers are provided a monthly gym allowance toward membership at the gym of their choice. Exercise balls, office treadmills, and other exercise equipment are also available on-site.
- New-parents are given a $500 take-out meal reimbursement plan to use during the first three months after the baby's birth. Google wants to encourage employees to spend as much time as possible with their new baby, instead of spending time preparing meals and cleaning the kitchen. This way, they can enjoy food from their favourite restaurant on Google's dime. This benefit can be applied to grocery purchases, take-out meals, or home cooking provided by a catering service.
- Google provides a transport supplement that is paid with each employee's salary each month to put toward the expense of getting to work and back home. It can be used to help pay for bus tickets, train fares, or even to enable employees to buy fantastic shoes or roller blades so they can walk or skate to work. Whatever they choose to do, Google hopes they will use their allowance in a way that helps protect the environment.
- Google is committed to helping build a clean energy future. They are always working on ways to maintain employee health and reduce the carbon footprint of their operations at the same time. For example, in Toronto, the company focuses on using low energy supplies for the office by using green building materials, and encourages employees to ride their bikes to work and bring them into the bike room while at the office.
- The people at Google have many different opportunities to develop and enrich their professional skills. For example, they can sign up for numerous courses through the newly-established Google University, created specifically to offer Googlers a way to improve and learn in a variety of ways. Google University is comprised of four schools: Personal Growth, Google Life & Culture, Workplace Essentials, and Leadership & People Management. In addition to Google U, Google offers other programs and courses that focus on learning, including financial planning classes that discuss topics such as money management, investing, buying and selling a home, as well as strategies for retirement planning.

www.mcgrawhill.ca/olc/kreitner

Google's full-time employment roster is approximately 20,000 worldwide, with almost 100 employees in the Canadian offices. Hours are long—typical for this industry—and it's not unusual for engineers to be seen in the hallways at 3 a.m., debating some esoteric algorithmic conundrum. "Hardcore geeks are here because there's no place they'd rather be," says Dennis Hwang, a Google webmaster who doubles as the artist who draws all the fancifully dressed-up versions of Google's home-page logo, called Doodles.

Teamwork is the norm, especially for big projects. Google engineers are famously required to devote 20 percent of their time to pursuing projects they dream up that will help the company. The projects actually have a realistic chance of being adopted: Google Earth Outreach, Google News, Gmail, and the Google Finance site all sprouted from this 20 percent time. Non-tech ideas Googlers dream up have a shot at adoption as well.

Google's work culture is centred around promoting collaboration, the exchange of ideas, and offering employees challenging and exciting work. People transfer between projects, work closely with each other in small teams, and continuously learn from one another. The relationship Google has nurtured with its employees has made them the leader in search technology, and the culture continues to support their innovative spirit.

Perks and fun times aside, Google keeps its eye on the market, watching the changing environment and predicting how it will affect the company. "Google is a strong and healthy company, but we must still continue to increase efficiencies, reduce our costs, and manage risk," says Wendy Bairos Rozeluk, Global Communications and Public Affairs contact for Google Canada. "That just makes good business sense!"

SOURCE: W. Bairos Rozeluk interview, *Global Communications and Public Affairs*, Google Canada, 10 Dundas Street East, 6th Floor, Toronto, Ontario. April 1, 2009.

Discussion Questions:

1. In your opinion, what are the observable artefacts, espoused values, and basic assumptions associated with Google's culture? Explain.

2. Use the competing values framework to diagnose Google's culture. To what extent does it possess characteristics associated with a clan, adhocracy, adhocracy, market, and/or hierarchical cultures? Discuss.

3. Google's mission statement is to "organize the world's information and make it universally accessible and useful." Is the culture type you identified in #2 consistent with the accomplishment of this mission? Explain.

4. Would you like to work at Google? Explain your rationale.

Ethical OB Dilemma

Finding the Right Recruits for the RCMP

The post 9/11 era has caused the RCMP to introduce a rigorous polygraph test in which prospective Mounties are asked personal questions such as:

- Have you ever been involved in a domestic dispute?
- Do you associate with anyone who uses illegal drugs?
- What is the worst thing anyone is going to say you have done to them?
- Have you ever engaged in bestiality?
- Have you ever seriously considered committing suicide?

The reasons given for the candid questionnaire is that the force needs something to screen out people unfit to wear the red serge, identify those who have ulterior motives other than to serve and protect, and to find people with behaviours that are congruent with the espoused values of the RCMP.

Fitting into the RCMP culture is about understanding the principles and values. The Web site www.rcmp-grc.gc.ca lists the lengthy organizational mission, vision, core values, and commitment levels to various groups the RCMP serves. Over the last few years the RCMP has been plagued by internal problems, and as a result has worked hard to regain its unblemished reputation; recruiting the right people is a major part of restructuring and revitalizing the culture.

"It is just one tool, but that tool is helping us to ensure that we have the right people coming to our organization," said Supt. Glen Siegersma, director of the RCMP's national recruiting program. As terrorists and other serious criminals are trying to infiltrate the force, the RCMP is focusing attention on value-based questions such as those mentioned above.

SOURCE: J. Bronskill, "RCMP Grill Applicants On Bestiality, Drugs," The Canadian Press, *The Globe and Mail*, November 16, 2008, www.globeandmail.com.

Discussion Questions:

1. How do you feel about the candid questionnaire the RCMP is administering to potential applicants?
2. Why do you think the RCMP is focusing so much attention on personal value-laden questions during the screening process? Aren't the skills of shooting a gun straight or physical aptitude more important?
3. Considering the competing values framework, which of the four types would you say the RCMP fits?
4. Why do so many organizations place a large emphasis on (1) rigorous recruiting processes, (2) thorough screening of references, and (3) designing effective orientation processes for new hires?

McGraw-Hill Connect™ —Available 24/7 with instant feedback so you can study when you want, how you want, and where you want. Take advantage of the Study Plan—an innovative tool that helps you customize your learning experience. You can diagnose your knowledge with pre- and post-tests, identify the areas where you need help, search the entire learning package for content specific to the topic you're studying, and add these resources to your personalized study plan. Visit www.mcgrawhillconnect.ca to register—take practice quizzes, search the e-book, and much more.

Mc Graw Hill connect™

♦|OB

Visit www.mcgrawhillconnect.ca to register.

12

Organizational Structure & Design

The Ongoing Restructuring at Air Canada

In January 2001, Air Canada acquired Canada's second largest air carrier, Canadian Airlines. For the next two years, Air Canada tried to make it work, but there were more problems than it could handle: it owed creditors over $900 million, it was running a pension deficit of $1.8 billion, and the company began to consider bankruptcy protection. By April 2003, Air Canada had no choice; it filed for bankruptcy, and for the next eighteen months it looked for a buyer who could get it back on its feet. In the fall of 2004, the reorganized Air Canada was placed under a new parent company called ACE Aviation Holdings. As dictated by the financing package, the airline had to review its mission, overall operations, leadership

structure, product offerings, and strategic direction. By 2006, the firm was out of bankruptcy protection and celebrated its 70th anniversary. In 2008, Air Canada was reporting sound financial results as it moved closer to accomplishing higher revenues, planned fleet revamping, higher on-time arrival performance levels, strategic commercial alliances with other North American carriers, and improved fleet/operational efficiencies.

This may sound like good news for the company and its creditors, but restructuring had its painful human side. When Air Canada decided to cut costs, it meant closing flight attendant bases in Halifax and Winnipeg that resulted in 345 people losing their jobs. Soon after, another layoff announcement was made eliminating 300 more jobs in Vancouver, with plans to cut 2,000 additional positions across the country. "The loss of jobs is painful in view of our employees' hard work in bringing the airline back to profitability over the past four years," president and CEO at the time Montie Brewer said. "I regret having to take these actions but they are necessary to remain competitive going forward," he said. Some people disagreed with the downsizing effort. Joseph D'Cruz, a University of Toronto business professor and airline industry analyst said, "I'm really concerned Air Canada is going to get itself into a vicious cycle. As morale goes down, the treatment that frontline employees offer to passengers is bound to suffer. In the airline business, everything depends on how the frontline employees behave."

The journey has been a long and at times difficult process, but that is common when an organization considers how it needs to be structured and designed to operate effectively and efficiently to remain competitive. Air Canada has had to reinvent itself. Old strategies have been abandoned in favour of a new business template: for example, new brands like A.C. Jetz for sports-team travel and upscale corporate clients, and new subsidiaries like Jazz that appeals to the low-fare traveller. These changes seemed to be working. Or were they? In 2009, Air Canada announced that Calin Rovinescu was replacing Brewer as president and CEO. Rovinescu was involved in the 2003–04 round of restructuring and had a reputation for slashing costs and debts. Despite all the changes made, the weakening travel demand brought on by poor economic conditions caused mounting debt. Together with a growing pension deficit, expiring labour contracts, and stiff competition from WestJet, there were once again fears of bankruptcy for the carrier.

How many times will Air Canada have to restructure? During turbulent times, especially within such a volatile industry as the airline business, it's anyone's guess.

The opening vignette involving Air Canada illustrates the ups and downs that are possible with every organization. There will be times of feast, where sales revenue is strong as a result of healthy demand and organizations expand their operations; but there will also be times of famine during slow growth phases or poor economic cycles that result in layoffs. In today's competitive and uncertain marketplace, organizations find themselves under attack and have to be more flexible and fluid than ever before, especially related to their structure and operations. In this chapter, we begin our discussions about the fundamentals of organizations. In a manner of speaking, organizations are the chessboard upon which the game of organizational behaviour is played. Therefore, having a working knowledge of how organizations are created, how they grow, and why work is organized the way it is within a firm can help employees understand the big picture and how it can affect behaviour.

We'll explore the various structures in the business world and examine alternative organizational metaphors; then we'll move on to the criteria for assessing organizational effectiveness. Next, we'll discuss the contingency approach to designing organizations. This includes comparing mechanistic versus organic organizations, and new-style versus old-style organizations.

SOURCES: Transport Canada, *Airline Restructuring In Canada Final Report*, September 4, 2002; Air Canada Reports Third Quarter Results, *Corporate Website Financial Reports*, October 2008, www.aircanada.com; K. McArthur, Article abstracts ISSN: 0319-0714, "Air Canada Creditors Push For Larger Role In Restructuring"; "Air Canada's Pension Deficit Balloons," *The Globe & Mail, 2003; The Globe and Mail*, "CEO Resigns in Surprise Shake-up at Air Canada," March 31, 2009.

LEARNING OBJECTIVES

After reading this chapter, you should be able to:

LO 1 Define *organization, organizational structure*, and *unity of command*.

LO 2 Explain the process of how organizations grow and the effect growth has on span of control.

LO 3 Describe six possible departmentation structures with examples.

LO 4 Compare and contrast contemporary structures with bureaucratic and open systems.

LO 5 Summarize the criteria that can be used to assess organization effectiveness.

LO 6 Integrate the Burns and Stalker contingency design with old-style and new-style organizations.

Organizations: Definition and Dimensions

As a necessary springboard for this chapter, we need to formally define the term organization and clarify the meaning of organization charts.

LO 1 WHAT IS AN ORGANIZATION?

According to Chester I. Barnard's classic definition, an **organization** is "a system of consciously coordinated activities or forces of two or more persons."[1] Four common factors of how work is organized are found in the coordination aspect of this definition: (1) coordination of effort, (2) a common goal, (3) division of labour, and (4) a hierarchy of authority.[2] Organization theorists refer to these factors as **organizational structure**:

Organization

System of consciously coordinated activities of two or more people.

- **Coordination of effort** Achieved through creating and enforcing policies, rules, and regulations.

- **Common goal** An agreed-upon direction for the organization.

- **Division of labour** When the common goal is pursued by individuals performing different but related tasks.

- **Hierarchy of authority** Also called the chain of command, this control mechanism is dedicated to making sure the right people do the right things at the right time.[3]

Organizational structure

Four common factors of how work is organized: coordination of effort, common goal, division of labour, and hierarchy of authority.

This last factor is especially important in showing how contemporary organizations have moved away from having a traditional perspective of structure. In the historical model, OB experts insisted upon a **unity of command principle**, meaning that each employee should report to only one manager. It was believed that this was how an organization would remain efficient, how communication between employees and their supervisors would be accurate, and if necessary, how corrections to work behaviour could be administered. Can you imagine working at a job where each employee was given his or her own boss? It may sound good on paper, but today's empowered employee (we talked about empowerment in Chapter 9) would probably feel smothered by such constant attention.

Unity of command principle

A historical belief that each employee should report to a single manager.

When the four common structural factors work together—coordination of effort, a common goal, division of labour, and a hierarchy of authority—it enables an organization to come to life and function successfully.

HOW ORGANIZATIONS ARE CREATED LO 2

How do organizations come to life? Basically, this question is best addressed by the father of OB, Henry Mintzberg[4]: it starts with an entrepreneur type of person who has an idea. This person, as the owner/operator, forms the top manager who recognizes the need to hire employees to complete basic tasks for the organization to reach the goal, called the operating core of the business.

As the organization grows, the owner/operator takes on more line managers to oversee the coordination of effort within the operating core; hence the division of labour occurs. The organization may also find that it needs two kinds of staff personnel: (1) analysts who design systems concerned with planning and the control of work tasks, and (2) support staff who provide indirect services to the rest of the organization. As Mintzberg states:

. . . not all organizations need all of these parts. Some use few and are simple, others combine all in rather complex ways. The central purpose of structure is to coordinate the work divided in a variety of ways; how that co-ordination is achieved—by whom and with what—dictates what the organization will look like.[5]

THE GROWTH OF AN ORGANIZATION

The growth of an organization is best explained by way of an illustration called an **organization chart**, showing the formal authority and division of labour relationships. To the casual observer, the term organization chart means the family tree-like pattern of boxes and lines posted on workplace walls. The names and titles of current position holders are usually within each box. To organization theorists, however, organization charts reveal much more. The organization charts in Figure 12.1 show the progression of how an organization grows from the simplest structure to a more complex model. This progression reveals the four basic dimensions of organizational structure mentioned earlier. Mintzberg stated that almost all organizations begin their lives as simple structures, allowing their founding chief executive(s) considerable freedom to set them up the way they want. Just as simple structures

Organization chart

A box-and-line illustration showing the chain of formal authority and division of labour.

were prevalent in the pre-Industrial Revolution, the offspring of industrialization was bureaucracy, which is more complex and has many layers of middle managers. We'll expand on this idea later on in this chapter.

Hierarchy of Authority   As Figure 12.1 illustrates, when a new company is created, there is no hierarchy; but as it grows, adding more line managers and support staff to the chart, there becomes an unmistakable hierarchy of authority that shows who holds the most legitimate power in the company, in this case Pat Smith.[6] As the company acquires more layers of middle managers, it becomes taller and more narrow. We'll discuss this concept of hierarchy of authority a bit later in this chapter.

Division of Labour   As the organization grows, the chain of command of who oversees what area becomes more evident. Also, you can see application of division of labour as different managers oversee different functional areas. Further, different support staff support different areas. Working your way from top to bottom, jobs become more specialized at each successive level in the organization. Again, this concept will be discussed later in this chapter when we discuss bureaucracy structures.

Span of Control   *Span of control* refers to the number of people reporting directly to a given manager.[7] Spans of control can range from narrow (one manager:two employees or 1:2) to wide (1:10). For example, by the fourth year, Pat Smith in Figure 12.1 is widening the span of control to five. (Staff assistants usually are not included in a manager's span of control.) Raj Sunjie has a narrow span of three. Spans of control exceeding 30 can be found in assembly-line operations where machine-paced and repetitive work substitutes for close supervision. Historically, spans of five to six were considered best. Despite years of debate, organization theorists have not arrived at a consensus regarding the ideal span of control.

Generally, the narrower (smaller ratio) the span of control, the closer the supervision and the higher the administrative costs; this results in the organization becoming taller and pyramid-like. Recent emphasis on administrative efficiency dictates spans of control as wide as possible, but guarding against inadequate supervision and lack of coordination. Wider spans also complement the trend toward greater worker autonomy and empowerment. In this instance, the organization is shorter and wider.

> **Span of control**
>
> The number of direct reports stated as a ratio.

▶ **FIGURE 12.1 Organization Charts that Show Growth**

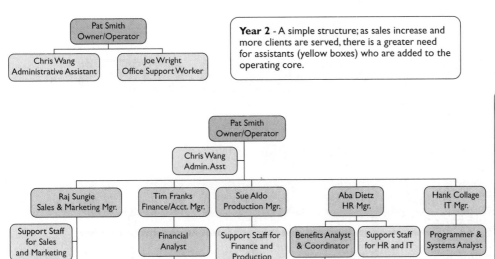

Line and Staff Positions The organization chart in Figure 12.1 also distinguishes between line and staff positions. Line managers such as the president and the five department managers occupy formal decision-making positions within the chain of command. Staff personnel such as the analysts and coordinators do background research and provide technical advice and recommendations to their line managers, who have the authority to make decisions. However, modern trends such as cross-functional teams and reengineering are blurring the distinction between line and staff, as employees are being empowered to make decisions on their own.

LO 3

DEPARTMENTATION

We've covered the fundamentals of what an organization is, how they are created, and how they grow; now let's take it a step further to try and understand how work is organized. When jobs are grouped together in an organization to gain greater efficiency and maintain effectiveness in customer service, it is called

Departmentation

The organizing of work by grouping jobs together to gain greater efficiency and maintain effectiveness in providing customer service.

departmentation. Departmentation assists in getting work completed through the creation of departments, units, sections, or divisions. While the names can vary from organization to organization, the purpose is the same: to organize and coordinate the flow of work. Figure 12.2 illustrates the basic types of departmentation listed below.

- **Functional** Work is separated using the major functional areas as guides. So, all marketing jobs are housed in the same department, all accounting and finance jobs are grouped in the accounting department, and so on. This is a very common way of organizing work. An example would be how Pat Smith organized the entrepreneurial company after 4 years, shown in Figure 12.1.[8]

- **Product** Work is grouped together that falls within the same product, product line, or service category. This is how Proctor & Gamble organizes their work, so that all House and Home products are found under this umbrella division that includes product lines such as

---

▶ **FIGURE 12.2** Different Departmentation Structures

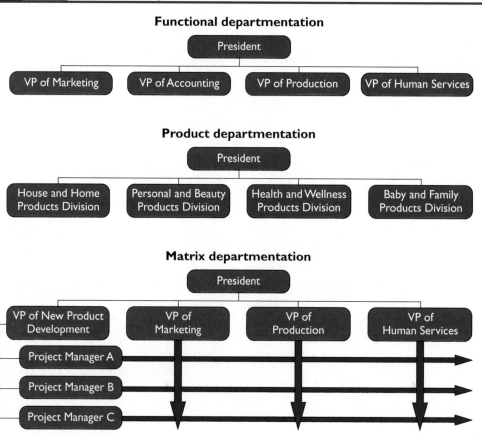

Functional departmentation

President
- VP of Marketing
- VP of Accounting
- VP of Production
- VP of Human Services

Product departmentation

President
- House and Home Products Division
- Personal and Beauty Products Division
- Health and Wellness Products Division
- Baby and Family Products Division

Matrix departmentation

President
- VP of New Product Development
  - Project Manager A
  - Project Manager B
  - Project Manager C
- VP of Marketing
- VP of Production
- VP of Human Services

Duracell, Swiffer, Tide, and Downy. The Personal and Beauty Division includes product lines such as Venus, Olay, Secret, and CoverGirl.

- **Matrix** In this model, workers remain in their functional areas, but are temporarily assigned to work on time-limited projects with other employees from across the organization. This is a highly cooperative design that requires a great amount of flexibility, since employees could in fact have more than one supervisor at one time, depending on the task they are working on. The project authority flows horizontally from project managers and works in cooperation with functional department managers on a vertical basis. An example of this could be a professor who teaches business classes to business students, but who is also assigned by the president to work on a special project with professors from other departments.[9]

> "... contemporary [organizational] structures ... include cross-funtional team structures, outsourcing structures, network organizations, and virtual organizational strictures"

- **Geographic** Workers and tasks are dispersed to the geographic territories where products or services are needed. An example of this is Toyota Motor Corporation, which includes Toyota Motor North America (Canada is in this area), Toyota Motor Philippines, Toyota Motor Thailand, Toyota Motor Europe, Toyota Ghana, Toyota Argentina, etc.[10]

- **Customer** Here, specific product groups are housed in almost self-contained environments to better serve each unique customer group. An example of this would be a company that distributes to both English-speaking Canada and French-speaking Quebec. Another example would be a firm that makes consumer products and has a division that just looks after that, but at the same time has large government contracts that require totally different service care. The company therefore sets up a separate division to serve just the government customer base.[11]

- **Hybrid** This is a combination of structures that may include any of the other departmentation structures mentioned so far. For example, the head office of a company may be structured using the functional model for things like centralized payroll and human resources, marketing, and accounting; but the regional offices may be set up by geographical locations to serve the different areas of Canada.[12]

CONTEMPORARY STRUCTURES

As the Industrial Age has given way to the Information Age, organizational structures have also changed. A few contemporary structures that have evolved include: cross-functional team structures, outsourcing structures, network organizations, and virtual organizational structures. Figure 12.3 provides various illustrations of each.

- **Cross-functional team structure** Similar to the matrix model, this wagon-wheel structure has individuals from various departments working together as a team (see Chapter 6). Typically, this group is together for a longer period of time compared to the shorter-lived projects under the matrix structure. An example of this is how Ford Motor Company designed the Mustang over a period of years, where over 30 cross-functional specialty teams worked together from day one to solve design problems and identify quality issues.[13]

- **Outsourcing structure** In this structure, one department within a structure is closed down and the work is redirected to an outside company to complete the task because of lower cost. An example of this would be hiring an outside agency to take care of payroll on a permanent basis because they can operate for less cost.

- **Network organization** In this structure, many departments are contracted out in a cooperative network of suppliers and distributors. The core organization remains structured according to either a functional or product way. However, rather than absorb all the costs from being a full-service company, it's less overhead and more effective to let those companies that do a task well for less money complete it. This leaves the core organization to take care of putting it all together, branding it, selling it, distributing it, etc. For example, an advertising agency may have in its core a president, account services personnel, accounting for billing purposes, one art director, and two copy writers, but contracts all other activities to various companies as needed (such as market research, media purchases, final art designs, and coordinating all direct mail promotions).[14]

- **Virtual Organization** A virtual organization is a type of network organization with core areas that broker out services over virtual networks that provide flexibility and adaptability for the firm. As

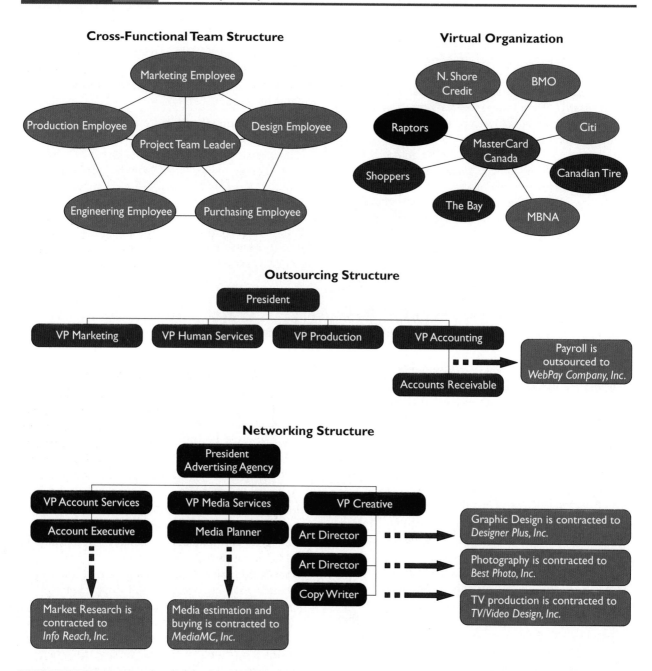

Cross-Functional Team Structure

Marketing Employee

Production Employee

Design Employee

Project Team Leader

Engineering Employee

Purchasing Employee

Virtual Organization

N. Shore Credit

BMO

Raptors

Citi

MasterCard Canada

Shoppers

Canadian Tire

The Bay

MBNA

Outsourcing Structure

President

VP Marketing

VP Human Services

VP Production

VP Accounting

Accounts Receivable

Payroll is outsourced to *WebPay Company, Inc.*

Networking Structure

President Advertising Agency

VP Account Services

VP Media Services

VP Creative

Account Executive

Media Planner

Art Director

Art Director

Copy Writer

Market Research is contracted to *Info Reach, Inc.*

Media estimation and buying is contracted to *MediaMC, Inc.*

Graphic Design is contracted to *Designer Plus, Inc.*

Photography is contracted to *Best Photo, Inc.*

TV production is contracted to *TV/Video Design, Inc.*

the Web provides more accessibility to specialists anywhere in the world, host firms can contract out more and more activity as they need to, resulting in a structure that grows and shrinks as needed, reacts to market demand in real time, and isn't saddled with countless bricks and mortar buildings to staff. The challenge is how to manage geographically dispersed employees who work within virtual organization structures; this is addressed in the Skills & Best Practices feature box. An example of a virtual organization could be MasterCard, which acts as the core organization with its own employee base, but is served by a network of thousands of financial institutions and retailers around the world. We'll talk more about virtual organizations when we discuss the globalization of organizations in Chapter 14.

Skills & Best Practices

Descriptions of Structures Using Organizational Metaphors

The complexity of modern organizations makes them somewhat difficult to describe. Consequently, organization theorists have resorted to the use of metaphors.[15] A *metaphor* is a figure of speech that characterizes one object in terms of another object. Good metaphors help us understand complicated things by describing them in everyday terms. For example, organizations are often likened to an orchestra. OB scholar Kim Cameron sums up the value of organizational metaphors as follows: "Each time a new metaphor is used, certain aspects of organizational phenomena are uncovered that were not evident with other metaphors. In fact, the usefulness of metaphors lies in their possession of some degree of falsehood so that new images and associations emerge."[16] With the orchestra metaphor, for instance, one could come away with an exaggerated picture of harmony in large and complex organizations. On the other hand, it realistically encourages us to view managers as facilitators rather than absolute dictators.

We will discuss two types of structures in this section using the metaphor method: (1) the bureaucracy, and (2) the open system. Early managers and management theorists used military units and machines as metaphors for organizations; we'll begin our discussion here.

STRUCTURE #1: ORGANIZATIONS AS MILITARY/MECHANICAL BUREAUCRACIES

A major by-product of the Industrial Revolution was the factory system of production. People left their farms and cottage industries to operate steam-powered machines in centralized factories. The social unit of production evolved from the family to formally-managed organizations encompassing hundreds or even thousands of people. Managers sought to maximize the economic efficiency of large factories and offices by structuring them according to military principles. At the turn of the 20th century, a German sociologist, Max Weber, formulated what he termed the most rationally efficient form of organization.[17] He patterned his ideal organization after the Prussian army and called it **bureaucracy.**

> *Bureaucracy*
>
> A tall organizational structure known for its division of labour, hierarchy of authority, formal framework of rules, and administrative impersonality.

Weber's Bureaucracy According to Weber's theory, the following four factors should make bureaucracies the essence of efficiency:

1. **Division of labour** People become better at what they do when they perform standardized tasks over and over again. Example: an assembly line worker who repeats the same task throughout the entire 8-hour day without any variety or change.

"You know, ever since I started working here, I've had this craving for cheese."

SOURCE: Reprinted by permission of Dave Carpenter from *Harvard Business Review*, April 2004.

2. **A hierarchy of authority** A formal chain of command ensures coordination and accountability. Example: If an employee can't fix a problem, then it is appropriate to take the concern to the next level in the structure to see if it can be solved there. To jump over several management levels to go directly to the top executive would be perceived as inappropriate and cause for discipline for not following chain of command.

3. **A framework of rules** Carefully formulated and strictly enforced rules ensure predictable behaviour. Example: Formal policies and procedures on how to get work done at the office so there aren't any questions or doubts about what to do. Everything is written down to the finest detail, like when a police officer makes an arrest on the street (i.e., they must follow formal policies and procedures so they don't make any legal mistakes).

Traditionally, the Canadian Department of Defence would be considered a bureaucratic system because of its formal chain of command and strict enforcement of procedure and rules.

4. **Administrative impersonality** Personnel decisions such as hiring and promoting should be based on competence, not favouritism.[18] Example: Long and lengthy postings to fill vacant jobs, meant to offer fairness to applicants, allow for proper screening of candidates and intense interviewing processes. It takes time to follow this process in the hopes of finding the best candidate for the job, instead of hiring the boss's relative.

How the Term Bureaucracy Became a Synonym for Inefficiency All organizations possess varying degrees of these characteristics. Thus, every organization is a bureaucracy to some extent. In terms of the ideal metaphor, a bureaucracy should run like a well-oiled machine, and its members should perform with the precision of a polished military unit. But practical problems can arise when bureaucratic characteristics become extreme. For example, consider the size of the school you are attending right now. Why did you decide to attend this particular school? Did the size of the campus and the potential for large class sizes play a role in the decision you made to apply to one school and not to another? Some students want to feel like they are important to the school and to the professor. Does this sound like you? When specialization, rule following, and impersonality cause a patron or client to feel like a number rather than a person, then the organization has become highly complex and bureaucratic.[19]

Another point to emphasize is the inefficiency of large bureaucracies. If you have studied micro-economics, then you've seen the cost-curves that clearly increase as an organization becomes larger and the diseconomies of scale that occur as it takes more resources just to

keep the big firm operating.[20] These organizations are tall/narrow in structure, tend to be fixed-cost heavy, and are slow to react to the environment. A classic example of this would be General Motors prior to their restructuring efforts.

Weber would probably be surprised and dismayed that his model of rational efficiency has become a synonym for inefficiency.[21] Today, bureaucracy stands for being put on hold, waiting in long lines, and getting shuffled from one office to the next. This irony can be explained largely by the fact that organizations with excessive or dysfunctional bureaucratic tendencies become rigid, inflexible, and resistant to environmental demands and influences.[22]

STRUCTURE #2: THE OPEN SYSTEM

The traditional military/mechanical metaphor, discussed earlier, is a **closed system** model because it is closed to surrounding environmental influences. It gives the impression that organizations are self-sufficient entities. In contrast, an **open system** depends on constant interaction with the environment for survival.

Closed system

A relatively self-sufficient structure that does not seek assistance from outside itself.

Open system

An interactive structure that must constantly interact with its environment to survive as it operates in a self-corrective, adaptable, and real time manner.

The distinction between closed and open systems is a matter of degree. Because every worldly system is partly closed and partly open, the key question is: How great a role does the environment play in the functioning of the system? For instance, a battery-powered clock is a relatively closed system. Once the battery is inserted, the clock performs its timekeeping function hour after hour until the battery goes dead. The human body, on the other hand, is a highly open system because it requires a constant supply of life-sustaining oxygen and nutrients from the environment. Open systems are capable of self-correction, adaptation, growth, are typically decentralized, and work in real time. Think of when you cut your finger—the body doesn't debate where to heal the wound. The problem is identified by the central nervous system and the brain registers the pain, but the solution takes place immediately at the point of injury. Referring to the human body both physically and mentally creates two types of open systems: the biological open system and the cognitive open system.

The Biological Open System Drawing upon the field of general systems theory that emerged during the 1950s,[23] organization theorists suggested a more dynamic model for modern organizations. This metaphor likens organizations to the human body; hence, it has been labelled the biological model. The biological open system emphasizes interaction between organizations and their environments. This newer model is based on open-system assumptions. It reveals helpful insights about organizations and how they work. In his often-cited organization theory text, *Organizations in Action*, James D. Thompson explained the biological model of organizations in the following terms:

> *Approached as a natural system, the complex organization is a set of interdependent parts which together make up a whole because each contributes something and receives something from the whole, which in turn is interdependent with some larger environment. Survival of the system is taken to be the goal, and the parts and their relationships presumably are determined through evolutionary processes . . .*
>
> *Central to the natural-system approach is the concept of self-stabilization, which spontaneously, or naturally, governs the necessary relationships among parts and activities and thereby keeps the system viable in the face of disturbances stemming from the environment.[24]*

Unlike the traditional military/mechanical theorists who downplayed the environment, advocates of the biological model characterize the organization as an open system that transforms inputs into various outputs. The outer boundary of the organization is permeable (porous). People, information, capital, and goods and services move back and forth across this boundary. Moreover, each of the five organizational subsystems—goals and values, technical, psycho-social, structural, and managerial—is dependent on the others. Feedback about such things as sales and customer satisfaction or dissatisfaction enables the organization to self-adjust and survive, despite uncertainty and change.[25] In effect, the organization is alive.

The Cognitive Open System A more recent metaphor characterizes organizations in terms of thinking functions. According to respected organization theorists Richard Daft and Karl Weick,

> *This perspective represents a move away from mechanical and biological metaphors of organizations. Organizations are more than transformation processes or control systems. To survive, organizations must have mechanisms to interpret ambiguous events and to provide meaning and direction for participants. Organizations are meaning systems, and this distinguishes them from lower-level systems . . .*

Almost all outcomes in terms of organization structure and design, whether caused by the environment, technology, or size, depend on the interpretation of problems or opportunities by key decision makers. Once interpretation occurs, the organization can formulate a response.[26]

As it migrates throughout the organization, this interpretation process leads to organizational learning and adaptation.[27] In fact, the concept of the learning organization[28] is currently popular in management circles. It takes a cooperative culture, mutual trust, and lots of internal cross-communication to fully exploit the organization as a cognitive (thinking) system, or *learning organization*. This is illustrated by the reaction from Maple Leaf Foods during the crisis of 2008 in which people were dying across Canada due to an outbreak of listeriosis originating from one of its meat packing facilities. Maple Leaf credits its vertical coordination strategy in monitoring the quality and safety of product produced.[29] Here is how they explain it:

Learning organization

A type of open system that compares itself to the cognitive abilities of the human body, able to adapt and change according to environmental needs.

> *By fostering greater cooperation between independent operating companies at various stages of meat production, Maple Leaf is able to review all possible aspects of a problem and narrow possible causes. The vertical coordination model enhances food safety by allowing management to see the entire chain of operations . . . from animal feed, right through to end processing and packaging. Maple Leaf can offer greater quality and health assurances because they know how and where the animal was raised.*[30]

Striving for Organizational Effectiveness

The opening chapter vignette described how Air Canada merged with another company in hopes of making it a more successful company. But did it? Soon after the merger, Air Canada was faced with tremendous problems, which begs the question: Did the merger between Air Canada and Canadian Airlines make Air Canada a more effective organization? In this next section we provide the tools to assess such a situation. Assessing organizational effectiveness is an important topic for many people, including managers, stockholders, government agencies, and OB specialists.

GENERIC EFFECTIVENESS CRITERIA

LO 5

To better understand this complex subject, consider four generic approaches to assessing an organization's effectiveness (see Figure 12.4). These effectiveness criteria apply equally well to large or small and profit or not-for-profit organizations. Notice how the circles in Figure 12.4 overlap; that's because the four effectiveness criteria can be used in various combinations. The key thing to remember is "no single approach to the evaluation of effectiveness is appropriate in all circumstances or for all organization types."[31] Because a multidimensional approach is required, we need to look more closely at each of the four generic effectiveness criteria.

Goal Accomplishment   Goal accomplishment is the most widely used effectiveness criterion for organizations. Key organizational results or outputs are compared with previously-stated goals or objectives. Deviations, either plus or minus, require corrective action. This is simply an organizational variation of the personal goal-setting process discussed in Chapter 5.[32] Effectiveness, relative to the criterion of goal accomplishment, is gauged by how well the organization meets or exceeds its goals.[33]

Productivity improvement, involving the relationship between inputs and outputs, is a common organization-level goal.[34] Goals also may be set for organizational efforts such as minority recruiting, pollution prevention, and quality improvement. Given today's competitive pressures and e-commerce revolution, innovation and speed are very important organizational goals worthy of measurement and monitoring.[35] Toyota gave a powerful indicator of where things are going in this regard. The Japanese automaker announced in 2008 that it could custom-build a car in just five days! That meant a customer's new Toyota would roll off the Woodstock, Ontario assembly line just five days after the order was placed—quite a difference compared to the 30-day industry standard.[36]

Toyota is an effective organization that continues to accomplish many strategic goals, including the opening of the $1.1 billion Woodstock, Ontario assembly plant, able to produce a car five days after it's ordered . . . compared to 30 days it takes competitors.

▶ FIGURE 12.4 Four Dimensions of Organizational Effectiveness

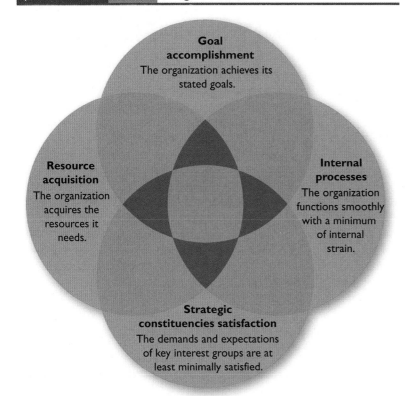

Goal accomplishment
The organization achieves its stated goals.

Resource acquisition
The organization acquires the resources it needs.

Internal processes
The organization functions smoothly with a minimum of internal strain.

Strategic constituencies satisfaction
The demands and expectations of key interest groups are at least minimally satisfied.

SOURCES: Adapted from discussion in K. Cameron, "Critical Questions in Assessing Organizational Effectiveness," *Organizational Dynamics*, Autumn 1980, pp 66–80; and K.S. Cameron, "Effectiveness as Paradox: Consensus andConflict in Conceptions of Organizational Effectiveness," *Management Science*, May 1986, pp 539–53.

A healthy organization, Peck says, is one that has a genuine sense of community: It's a place where people are emotionally present with one another, and aren't afraid to talk about fears and disappointments—because that's what allows us to care for one another. It's a place where there is authentic communication, a willingness to be vulnerable, a commitment to speaking frankly and respectfully—and a commitment not to walk away when the going gets tough.[37]

Organizations with healthy internal processes tend to be incubators for creativity and innovation, both of which are very important.[38]

Strategic Constituencies' Satisfaction Organizations both depend on people and affect the lives of people. Consequently, many consider the satisfaction of key interested parties to be an important criterion of organizational effectiveness.

> *A **strategic constituency** is any group of individuals who have some stake in the organization—for example, resource providers, users of the organization's products or services, producers of the organization's output, groups whose cooperation is essential for the organization's survival, or those whose lives are significantly affected by the organization.*[39]

Strategic constituencies (or stakeholders) generally have competing or conflicting interests.[40] This forces executives to do some strategic juggling to achieve workable balances. In a recent *BusinessWeek* interview, Microsoft's CEO, Steve Ballmer, offered this perspective:

Resource Acquisition This second criterion relates to inputs rather than outputs. An organization is deemed effective in this regard if it acquires necessary factors of production such as raw materials, labour, capital, and managerial and technical expertise. Charitable organizations such as Habitat for Humanity judge their effectiveness in terms of how much money they raise from private and corporate donations.

> **Strategic constituency**
>
> Any group of people with a stake in the organization's operation or success.

Internal Processes Some refer to this third effectiveness criterion as the "healthy systems" approach. An organization is said to be a healthy system if information flows smoothly and if employee loyalty, commitment, job satisfaction, and trust prevail. Goals may be set for any of these internal processes. Healthy systems, from a behavioural standpoint, tend to have minimal dysfunctional conflict and destructive political manoeuvring. M. Scott Peck, the physician who wrote the highly regarded book, *The Road Less Traveled*, characterizes healthy organizations in ethical terms:

> *When you have gone through the kind of experience that we went through with government authorities (accusations of being a monopoly), it really does cause you to step back and reflect: Who are we, what are we doing? The expectation bar, be it from government, be it from customers, be it from industry partners, is different, and the bar is higher. How do you hit the balance between being forceful and aggressive and still [having the] right level of cooperation [with our industry and] with government? We have worked hard on that theme of responsible leadership.*[41]

INTERNAL PROCESSES IN A FAMILY BUSINESS

A few years ago, an article in *The Globe and Mail's Report on Business* posed the question to its readers regarding the appointment of Edward S. Rogers III to the position of president of Rogers Cable: Was he ready to take the lead? After all, he was only 33 years old at the time, shy but pleasant. More importantly, critics wondered if he had what it took to stand up to the high profile CEO of Rogers Communication Inc., who also just happened to be his father, Ted Rogers, the fourth richest person in Canada. Just after Edwards's promotion, Ted said he would not treat his son with kid gloves. "The biggest risk of placing Edward ... is that he will do a less than competent job. He knows that too ... and I've told him, "Look, if you don't produce, I've got to take you out." Years later, the evidence speaks for itself, as it appears that Edward was ready to face the many challenges of his demanding position, including working with his "hands-everywhere" father, holding the same last name as the CEO as well as the company. Perhaps it was a secret parental dream or just part of his own succession planning, but within five years of making the announcement about his son's promotion, Ted passed away, leaving his son in an advantageous position to take the lead, when ready. For Edward, this would prove to be a pivotal point, for at the age of 38 he would now be without his father's strong presence and looming shadow.

You decide: Is it ethical to hand family businesses down to family members? Is this fair to other stakeholders, including employees, shareholders, customers, suppliers, etc.? Does your opinion change if the organization is a multi-billion dollar publicly-traded firm?

SOURCE: Adapted from G. MacDonald, "Jr.," *Report on Business*, March 2003, pp 40-48; *Rogers Communication Inc.*, "Senior Leadership," www.rogers.com.

In another example, consider how stakeholders felt when Ted Rogers appointed his son as president of Rogers Cable (see Law & Ethics at Work feature box). At the outset, were the interests of the stakeholders being considered? In the long run, did Ted Rogers achieve a workable balance for all concerned?

MIXING EFFECTIVENESS CRITERIA: PRACTICAL GUIDELINES

Referring back to our earlier question, how will the new CEO of Air Canada know if the company is effective or whether it's time for restructuring? Experts on the subject recommend a multidimensional approach to assess the effectiveness of modern organizations. This means no single criterion is appropriate for all stages of the organization's life cycle. Nor will a single criterion satisfy competing stakeholders. For example, if goal accomplishment is the only criteria we use to measure effectiveness, then profit maximization takes priority over all other factors. This is like saying that as a student, you have only benefited from a class or shown evidence of learning where a grade of 95 percent or more was earned ... and that is probably not true. So, reaching a goal or number alone doesn't equal knowledge learned or a standard of effectiveness.

Well-managed organizations mix and match effectiveness criteria to fit the unique requirements of the situation.[42] Managers need to identify and seek input from strategic constituencies. This information, when merged with the organization's stated mission and philosophy, enables management to derive an appropriate combination of effectiveness criteria. The following guidelines are helpful in this regard:

■ *The goal accomplishment approach* is appropriate when "goals are clear, mutually agreed upon, time-bounded, measurable."[43]

■ *The resource acquisition approach* is appropriate when inputs have a traceable effect on results or output. For example, the amount of money the Red Cross receives through donations dictates the level of services provided.

■ *The internal processes approach* is appropriate when organizational performance is strongly influenced by specific processes (e.g., cross-functional teamwork).

■ *The strategic constituencies approach* is appropriate when powerful stakeholders can significantly benefit or harm the organization.[44]

It's worth stressing that applying all four criteria at once is unrealistic, as organizations don't operate in a perfect world with perfect information and unlimited resources. So, when evaluating an organizations' effectiveness, it's better to prioritize and fit the criteria to a strategic plan.

The Contingency Approach to Designing Organizations

According to the **contingency approach to organization design**, organizations tend to be more effective when they are structured to fit the demands of the situation.[45] The purpose of this section is to introduce you to the contingency approach to organization design by reviewing a landmark study, showing the differences between centralized and decentralized decision making, and comparing new-style and old-style organizations.

MECHANISTIC VERSUS ORGANIC ORGANIZATIONS

A landmark contingency design study was reported by a pair of British behavioural scientists, Tom Burns and G.M. Stalker. In the course of their research, they drew a very useful difference between what they called mechanistic and organic organizations. **Mechanistic organizations** are bureaucracies with strict rules, narrowly defined tasks, and top-down communication. They are typically rigid, formalized in terms of following policy and procedure, and comparable to a closed system that operates in a self-sufficient manner. Ironically, it is at the cutting edge of technology that this seemingly out-of-date approach has found a home. In the highly competitive business of Web hosting—running clients' Web sites in high-security facilities humming with Internet servers—speed and reliability are everything. Enter military-style managers who require strict discipline, faithful observance to policies and rules, and flawless execution. But, as *BusinessWeek* observed, "The strictly controlled atmosphere and military themes . . . may be tough to stomach for skilled workers used to a more free-spirited

atmosphere."[46] A few examples of mechanistic organizations are Scouts Canada, Girl Guides Canada, RCMP, Tim Horton's, McDonald's and Walmart. The operations are highly regimented, dependent on large policy manuals for guidance, with strict rules on how to run the business. In the case of fast food chains, much is regimented: recipes, promotions, price-points, uniforms, and how to greet a customer correctly.

In comparison, **organic organizations** are fluid and flexible networks, similar to the open systems mentioned earlier. These kinds of firms rely less on formalized policies and procedures to provide direction, problem solving guidelines, and directions. Typically, you'll find multitalented individuals working for these firms who are expected to perform a variety of tasks.[47] Examples of organic organizations are Laurentide Controls in Quebec (the largest supplier of automation solutions in eastern Canada), Arcis Corp. in Calgary (offers information on earth tremors and seismic solutions to energy industry), Bitheads Inc. in Ottawa (software development partner), and Vivendi Games Canada, Ltd. in Vancouver (interactive video game maker). All of these organizations are small enough (Vivendi has the most employees at 220+) that it's easy to flex what they do, how they operate, and the level of service given a specific customer request. The amount of inter-dependence and inter-communication that takes place on a daily basis is necessary and desired. The type of industry they are in, as well as the context of their work environment are still fluid enough to keep rigid policies, rules, and fixed thinking away.

A Matter of Degree Importantly, as illustrated in the Self-Assessment Exercise, each of the mechanistic-organic characteristics is a matter of degree. Organizations tend to be relatively mechanistic or relatively organic. Pure types are rare because divisions, departments, or units in the same organization may be more or less mechanistic or organic. From an employee's standpoint, which organization structure would you prefer? What kind of firms have you worked for in the past?

Different Approaches to Decision Making Decision making tends to be centralized in mechanistic organizations and decentralized in organic organizations. **Centralized decision making** occurs when key decisions are made by top management.

Contingency approach to organization design

Creating an effective organization that is a good fit with its environment and the customer it serves.

Organic organizations

A fluid and flexible open systems network structure that relies less on policies and procedures for problem solving and direction.

Mechanistic organizations

Rigid, closed system of command-and-control bureaucracies that follow formal policies and procedures.

Centralized decision making

All key decisions are formally made only by top managers who advise others on what to do.

Mechanistic or Organic?

INSTRUCTIONS: Think of your present (or a past) place of employment and rate it on the following eight factors. Calculate a total score and compare it to the scale.

CHARACTERISTICS

1. Task definition and knowledge required

    NARROW, TECHNICAL   1   2   3   4   5   6   7   BROAD, GENERAL

2. Linkage between individual's contribution and organization's purpose

    VAGUE OR INDIRECT   1   2   3   4   5   6   7   CLEAR OR DIRECT

3. Task flexibility

    RIGID, ROUTINE   1   2   3   4   5   6   7   FLEXIBLE, VARIED

4. Specification of techniques, obligations, and rights

    SPECIFIC   1   2   3   4   5   6   7   GENERAL

5. Degree of hierarchical control

    HIGH   1   2   3   4   5   6   7   LOW (SELF-CONTROL EMPHASIZED)

6. Primary communication pattern

    TOP-DOWN   1   2   3   4   5   6   7   LATERAL (BETWEEN PEERS)

7. Primary decision-making style

    AUTHORITARIAN   1   2   3   4   5   6   7   DEMOCRATIC, PARTICIPATIVE

8. Emphasis on obedience and loyalty

    HIGH   1   2   3   4   5   6   7   LOW

Total score = _____

SCALE

8–24 = Relatively mechanistic
25–39 = Mixed
40–56 = Relatively organic

SOURCE: Adapted from discussion in T. Burns and G.M. Stalker, *The Management of Innovation* (London: Tavistock, 1961), pp 119–25.

Decentralized decision making occurs when important decisions are made by middle- and lower-level managers and empowered non-managerial employees. Generally, centralized organizations are more tightly controlled, while decentralized organizations are more adaptive to changing situations.[48] Each has its appropriate use. For example, both Hudson's Bay Company and WestJet are very respected and successful companies, yet the former prefers centralization and the latter prefers decentralization decision making (see the International OB feature box for another application of centralized and decentralized decision making).

Experts on the subject warn against extremes of centralization or decentralization. The challenge is to achieve a workable balance between the two extremes. A management consultant put it this way:

> The modern organization in transition will recognize the pull of two polarities: a need for greater centralization to create low-cost shared resources; and, a need to improve market responsiveness with greater decentralization. Today's winning organizations are the ones that can handle the paradox and tensions of both pulls. These are the firms that analyze the optimum organizational solution in each particular circumstance, without prejudice for one type of organization over another. The result is, almost invariably, a messy mixture of decentralized units sharing cost-effective centralized resources.[49]

Decentralized decision making

Mid-managers and staff employees are empowered to make important decisions without seeking top management permission or input.

Centralization and decentralization are not an either–or proposition; they are more of a balancing act.

Practical Research Insights When they classified a sample of actual companies as either mechanistic or organic, Burns and Stalker discovered one type was not superior to the other. Each type had its appropriate place, depending on the environment. When the environment was relatively stable and certain, the successful organizations tended to be mechanistic. Organic organizations tended to be the successful ones when the environment was unstable and uncertain.[50]

In a more recent study of 103 department managers from eight manufacturing firms and two aerospace organizations, managerial skill was found to have a greater impact on a global measure of department effectiveness in organic departments than in mechanistic departments. This led the researchers to recommend the following contingencies for management staffing and training:

> If we have two units, one organic and one mechanistic, and two potential applicants differing in overall managerial ability, we might want to assign the more competent to the organic unit since in that situation there are few structural aids available to the manager in performing required responsibilities. It is also possible that managerial training is especially needed by managers being groomed to take over units that are more organic in structure.[51]

LO 6

LESSONS LEARNED FROM DECENTRALIZED INTEGRATED COASTAL MANAGEMENT

INTERNATIONAL OB

The centralized and decentralized decision making processes discussed in this chapter are applicable to organizations in the public and not-for-profit sectors. A case in point comes from noting the different styles between China's and Canada's approach to the integrated coastal management (ICM) process in deciding how coastal areas will be used and what activities can take place in them. While many ICM Programs are national government initiatives, some ICM Programs are decentralized, managed by community groups or local governments. Canada's Atlantic Coastal Action Program (ACAP) is a community-based program that uses a multi-stakeholder approach and consensus decision making. China's Xiamen ICM Program is managed by a centralized coordinating office within a local government. Which is the most effective organizational approach? After comparing the two programs, some general lessons learned are that the appropriate use of either model for ICM depends on the cultural, economic, and political environment of the program. However, stakeholder involvement, scientific consultation, and the use of a detailed management plan are important components of any decentralized ICM program.

ADAPTED: Gardner Pinfold Consulting Economists Ltd., "An Update of the Economic Impact of the ACAP," prepared for Environment Canada, March 31, 2008, p 1; "Lessons Learned from 'decentralized' ICM," *Ocean & Coastal Management*, ISSN 0964-5691, 2003, vol 46, pp 59-76.

Another interesting finding comes from a study of 42 voluntary church organizations. As the organizations became more mechanistic (more bureaucratic), the intrinsic motivation (see Chapter 5) of their members decreased. Mechanistic organizations apparently undermined the volunteers' sense of freedom and self-determination. Additionally, the researchers believe their findings help explain why bureaucracy tends to feed on itself: "A mechanistic organizational structure may breed the need for a more extremely mechanistic system because of the reduction in intrinsically motivated behaviour."[52] Thus, bureaucracy creates greater bureaucracy.

Most recently, field research in two factories, one mechanistic and the other organic, found expected communication patterns. Command-and-control (downward) communication characterized the mechanistic factory. Consultative or participative (two-way) communication prevailed in the organic factory.[53]

Both Mechanistic and Organic Structures Have their Places Although achievement-oriented students of OB typically express a distaste for mechanistic organizations, not all organizations or subunits can or should be organic. For example, McDonald's could not achieve its admired quality and service standards without extremely mechanistic restaurant operations. Imagine the food and service you would get if McDonald's employees used their own favourite ways of doing things and worked at their own

pace! On the other hand, mechanistic structure alienates some employees because they believe it erodes their sense of self-control. Some mechanistic organizations are trying to change. For example, consider Hydro One, the energy firm wholly owned by the province of Ontario. It represents a classic mechanistic organization because of its large size, the nature of the service it provides, and the rigid standards by which it must adhere to. But Hydro One has made some impressive changes worth noting, debunking the myth that working at a mechanistic organization erodes employees' sense of self-control (see Focus on Diversity feature box).

NEW-STYLE VERSUS OLD-STYLE ORGANIZATIONS

Organization theorists Jay R. Galbraith and Edward E. Lawler III have called for a "new logic of organizing."[54] They recommend a whole new set of adjectives to describe organizations (see Table 12.1). Traditional pyramid-shaped organizations, conforming to the old-style pattern, tend to be too slow and inflexible. This was the case in our example at Hydro One, a definite old-style organization. However, under the leadership of a new executive team and a more forward thinking board, it is slowly changing. Mind you, it still has a way to go before it can be termed new-style, but nonetheless it is moving in the right direction. And that is the challenge for all old-style organizations who succeeded in the old paradigm but are fighting for their life in the new global economy.

Diversity

FOCUS ON

HYDRO ONE IS A MECHANISTIC ORGANIZATION—BUT IT'S CHANGING

With revenues exceeding $1 billion, Hydro One is wholly owned by the province of Ontario, has a unionized workplace of over 5,500 employees, and in the past would easily have fallen under the mechanistic category due to its market monopoly. But times are changing and so is Hydro One. Over the last several years, it has had to restructure itself, downsize by laying off 500 employees to coincide with market segments, gain greater understanding of competitive forces, and slowly flex under social pressure. Hydro One had to start looking at the environment and considering factors that it had once ignored. That's a big step for this firm.

Over the last few years, Hydro One has reached out to recruit men and women in skilled trades and other professions in their industry. Hydro

One's new Aboriginal outreach program has also been successful in drawing interest in careers with the firm. The company has put in place a five-year plan to further increase the diversity of its workplace and to attract new employees to jobs in the electricity sector. Hydro One has been recognized two years in a row by *Corporate Knights* magazine for being in the top ten in terms of leadership diversity. The magazine considered Hydro One's great visible minority and female representation, in both the boardroom and the executive offices, as well the workplace challenges of recent immigrants, Aboriginals, and disabled persons.

SOURCES: M. Shin, "Best 50 Corporate Citizens," *Corporate Knights*, Issue 2008, pg 20; Nationtalk website: www.nationtalk.ca/modules/news/article.

Leaner, more open system and organic organizations are increasingly needed to accommodate a strategic balancing act between cost, quality, and speed. These new-style organizations are customer-focused, dedicated to continuous improvement and learning, and structured around teams. These qualities, along with computerized information technology, will hopefully enable big organizations to mimic the speed and flexibility of small organizations.

New-Style Versus Old-Style Organizations

NEW	OLD
Dynamic, learning	Stable
Information rich	Information is scarce
Global	Local
Small and large	Large
Product/customer oriented	Functional
Team oriented	Job oriented
Skills oriented	Individual oriented
Command/control oriented	Involvement oriented
Lateral/networked	Hierarchical
Customer oriented	Job requirements oriented

SOURCE: From J.R. Galbraith and E.E. Lawler III, "Effective Organizations: Using the New Logic of Organizing," in *Organizing for the Future: The New Logic for Managing Complex Organizations*, eds J.R. Galbraith, E.E. Lawler III, and Associates, 1993, p 298. Copyright © 1993 John Wiley & Sons, Inc. Reprinted with permission of John Wiley & Sons, Inc.

TABLE 12.1

Summary of Learning Objectives

1. **Define *organization*, *organizational structure*, and *unity of command*.** An organization is a system of coordinated activities of two or more people. Organizational structure is a reference made to four factors: (1) coordination of effort (achieved through policies and rules), (2) a common goal (a collective purpose), (3) division of labour (people performing different but related tasks), and (4) a hierarchy of authority (the chain of command). Unity of command principle is a historical belief that each employee should report to a single manager. This is significant to appreciate because this belief lead to taller and narrower organizational structures.

2. **Explain the process of how organizations grow and the effect growth has on span of control.** Mintzberg states that organizations come to life as a result of an entrepreneur who has an idea. That idea gives way to an owner/operator who recognizes the need to hire employees to complete basic tasks for the organization to reach the goal; they are called the operating core of the business. As the organization grows, the owner/operator takes on more line managers to oversee the coordination of effort within the operating core, hence

division of labour occurs. The organization may also find that it needs two kinds of staff personnel: (1) analysts who design systems concerned with planning and the control of work tasks, and (2) support staff who provide indirect services to the rest of the organization. Span of control is typically stated as a ratio and refers to the number of people reporting directly to a given manager. In the past, as organizations grew, the span of control was kept very narrow because of the unity of command principle; hence the organizations were tall and narrow. The more contemporary model is to have a wider span of control (higher ratio), as emphasis has shifted to leanness and efficiency. This trend also complements greater worker autonomy and empowerment; as a result this has created shorter and wider organizational structures.

3. **Describe six possible departmentation structures with examples.**
Departmentation is organizing work by grouping jobs together to gain greater efficiency and maintain effectiveness in providing customer service. The six types of structures discussed include: (1) functional—work separated using functional areas as guides (marketing, accounting/finance, human services, production); (2) product—work grouped together based on product, product line, or service category (car division, truck division, tank division); (3) matrix—workers remain in their functional areas but are temporarily assigned to work on time-limited projects with other employees found throughout the organization (cross-functional teams); (4) geographic—workers and tasks are dispersed to the geographic territories where products or services are needed (Western Region, Atlantic Regions, Quebec); (5) customer—specific product groups are housed in almost self-contained environments to better serve each unique customer group (opening a separate office to serve the needs of just one dominant customer, like Walmart or the Canadian Government); and (6) hybrid—a combination of structures that may include any of the other departmentation structures mentioned above (head offices that are functionally structured but regional offices that are structured in specific geographic areas to serve specific customer needs).

4. **Compare and contrast contemporary structures with bureaucratic and open systems.** The text discussed four contemporary structures: cross-functional team structures, outsourcing, network, and virtual organizations. All of the contemporary structures can be considered to be more open than closed systems. This means that each of these structures considers the necessity of the organization to remain in somewhat constant interaction with its environment to survive, so their structures can flex as needed because they are shorter/wider. Open system organizations tend to operate in a self-corrective, adaptable, and real-time manner. In comparison, a bureaucracy tends to be a closed system, as it is slow to respond to the outside environment because it is so big and consuming of its own resources; typically they are tall/narrow structures that are slow to change and fixed-cost heavy. Although Weber identified a bureaucracy as the most efficient of all structures, the study of micro-economics provides strong evidence that large structures are especially inefficient.

5. **Summarize the criteria that can be used to assess organization effectiveness.**
Experts on the subject of organizational effectiveness recommend a multi-dimensional approach. This means no single criterion is appropriate for all stages of the organization's life cycle. Nor will a single criterion satisfy competing stakeholders. Well-managed organizations mix and match effectiveness criteria to fit the unique requirements of the situation; they are (1) goal accomplishment (satisfying stated objectives), (2) resource acquisition (gathering the necessary productive inputs), (3) internal processes (building and maintaining healthy organizational systems), and (4) strategic constituencies satisfaction (achieving at least minimal satisfaction for all key stakeholders).

6. **Integrate the Burns and Stalker contingency design with old-style and new-style organizations.** British researchers Burns and Stalker found that mechanistic (bureaucratic, centralized) organizations tended to be effective in stable situations. In unstable situations, organic (flexible, decentralized) organizations were more effective. These findings underscored the need for a contingency approach to organization design. New-style organizations are characterized as being more organic as they are dynamic and learning, information rich, global, small and large, product/customer oriented, skills oriented, team oriented, involvement oriented, lateral networked, and customer oriented. Old-style organizations are characterized as being more mechanistic as they tend to be more stable, larger, functional, command/control oriented, hierarchical, and job-requirements oriented.

Discussion Questions

1. Draw an example of an organization chart for your current (or last) place of employment. Does your chart reveal the hierarchy (chain of command), division of labour, span of control, and line-staff distinctions? Does it reveal anything else? Explain.

2. Why is it appropriate to view modern organizations as open systems?

3. Combining topics from Chapters 11 and 12, consider the following statement: *It's been said that organizational culture can be considered the unofficial structure of the organization; it can also supplement the formal structure or it can substitute for it.* Do you agree with this statement? Why or why not?

4. If organic organizations are popular with most employees, why can't all organizations be structured in an organic fashion?

5. In your opinion, which of the organizational structures discussed in this chapter will be most common 20 years from now? Explain your response.

Google Searches

1. **Google Search:** "_____ college" or "_____ university" Find the organizational structure of your own institution. See if you can determine where your professor is located on the organizational chart.

2. **Google Search:** "Fisheries and Oceans Canada Organizational Structure" or "French National Center for Scientific Research—CNRS" Double click on *About CNRS* and then again on *Organizational Chart*. Review the chart posted on the Web site and determine the average span of control, the amount of hierarchy of authority in the department, whether labour is divided, and the number of line managers and staff personnel in the department.

3. **Google Search:** "Canadian Virtual University" Consider the various types of programs and courses available on this CVU site. Review the type of educational institutions that is affiliated with CVU. Would you consider taking a course at the CVU? Explain your response.

Experiential Exercise

Strengths and Weaknesses of Departmentation Type Group Exercise

PURPOSE   This exercise is meant to help familiarize you with the various departmentation structures discussed in this chapter. By participating in this group activity, you should gain a greater understanding of the concepts and the differences between various departmentation types. Approx. Timing: 30 minutes.

ACTIVITY ASSIGNMENT
- If necessary, review Figure 12.2 before beginning the exercise.
- Work in small groups. Fill in the chart to describe the strengths and weaknesses of each type of departmentation.
- After approximately 15 minutes, share your group's responses with the rest of the class.

TYPE OF DEPARTMENTATION	STRENGTHS	WEAKNESSES
Functional		
Product		
Matrix		
Geographic		
Customer		
Hybrid		

 # The Presentation Assistant

Here are possible topics and corresponding sources related to this chapter that can be further explored by student groups looking for ideas.

	TALL/NARROW VS. SHORT/WIDE STRUCTURES—IN TERMS OF HIERARCHY OF AUTHORITY & SPAN OF CONTROL, WHICH MODEL IS LESS EXPENSIVE AND MORE EFFICIENT TO OPERATE AND WHY? PROVIDE EXAMPLES.	WHY MOST BUREAUCRATIC STRUCTURES TEND TO BE UNIONIZED—WHAT IS THE STRUCTURE OF MOST UNIONS? IS THERE A CONNECTION?	DEPARTMENTATION HELPS TO KEEP ORGANIZED AND REMAIN EFFICIENT—EXAMPLES OF THE VARIOUS TYPES OF WAYS COMPANIES ORGANIZE THEIR WORK AND HOW IT BENEFITS THEM.
YouTube Videos	• Big Organization Acting Small—The Mayo Clinic • Management Lessons from *Star Wars* or *Star Trek*	• *Bureaucracy* (movie) • *Seinfeld*—"Newman and the Post Office" • Fighting Walmartization	• Proctor & Gamble Products • Work At Home Business—Learn How To Organize Your Business
TV Shows or Movies to Preview	• *Star Wars* (Movie) • *Star Trek* (TV Show)	• *The Corporation* (movie)	• *Office Space* (movie)

Internet Searches	• *The World Is Flat* (by T.L. Friedman) • Best Buy vs. Sears Web sites • Toyota vs. GM Web sites • Fed Ex. vs. Canada Post • "Bureaucracy" (the board game)	• CUPE & CAW Web sites • The effort to unionize Walmart In Canada • Yahoo—Canadian Labour Listing • Canada Post Web site— Management Team and Fast Facts • Ontario Hydro Web site	• Colgate Palmolive Products Web site (product) • H & M clothing (outsourcing) • How Black & Decker and Xerox Corporations Used Functional Teams (cross-functional teams) • SME—Cavendish Management Resources (virtual) • Coca Cola or Google (geographic) • Coca Cola Virtual Vender Web site
Ice Breaker Classroom Activity	• Draw a tall/narrow pyramid structure on the board and next to it draw a short/wide pyramid. Ask students the following question: "If both organizations have 3,000 employees, which structure would be less expensive to operate? Why?"	• Ask students to identify at least five bureaucratic old-style kinds of companies. Write them on the board. Then ask how many of the organizations listed are unionized. Is there a connection?	• Have students go to www. PG.com, the Web site for Proctor & Gamble. Pick one division listed on the left-hand side of the menu box. Before opening, ask students to identify all the products made by P&G that fall under that division. After a short while, show students the answers.

OB In Action Case Study

The Woody Manufacturing Company

Mr. Woody, the owner/operator of a small furniture company specializing in the manufacture of high-quality bar stools, has experienced tremendous growth in demand for his products. He has standing orders of $750,000. Consequently, Mr. Woody has decided to expand his organization and aggressively attack the market. His stated mission is "to manufacture world-class products that are competitive in the world market in quality, reliability, performance, and profitability." He would like to create a culture where "pride, ownership, employment security, and trust" are a way of life. He just finished a set of interviews, and he has hired 32 new workers with the following skills:

■ Four skilled craftspeople
■ Ten people with some woodworking experience
■ Twelve people with no previous woodworking experience or other skills
■ One nurse
■ One schoolteacher
■ One bookkeeper
■ Three people with some managerial experience in non-manufacturing settings

Mr. Woody (with your help) must now decide how to design his new organization. This design will include the management structure, pay system, and the allocation of work to individuals and groups.

The bar stool-making process has 15 steps:

1. Select wood.
2. Cut wood to size.
3. Remove defects.
4. Plane wood to exact specifications.
5. Cut joints.
6. Glue and assemble tops.
7. Prepare legs/bases.
8. Attach legs/bases to tops.
9. Sand bar stools.
10. Apply stain.
11. Apply varnish.
12. Sand bar stools.
13. Reapply varnish.
14. Package bar stools.
15. Deliver bar stools to the customer.

Mr. Woody currently manufactures three kinds of bar stools: pedestal, four-legged corner, and four-legged recessed. There is no difference in the difficulty of making each of the three types. Major cost variations have been associated with defective wood, imprecise cuts, and late deliveries to customers. Mr. Woody must decide how to organize his company to maintain high quality and profits.

He has considered several options. He might have some individuals perform the first step for all types of stools; he might have an individual perform several steps for one type; or he might have a team perform some combination of steps for one or more stools. He wonders if the way he organizes the company will affect the quality or costs. He is also aware that, while the demand for all types of stools has been roughly equal over the long run, there are short periods in which one type is in greater demand than the others. Because Mr. Woody wants to use his people effectively, he has commissioned an expert in work design to help him set up an optimal organization.

SOURCE: "Case Study: The Woody Manufacturing Company," in A.B. Shami and J.B. Lau, *Behaviour in Organizations: An Experiential Approach*, 8th ed (New York: McGraw Hill, 2005), pp 370–371.

Discussion Questions

1. How would you describe Woody Manufacturing using the open systems biological model of organizations?
2. What are important effectiveness criteria for Woody Manufacturing?
3. Should the organization be mechanistic or organic? Explain.
4. Should decision making be centralized or decentralized at the company? Explain.
5. On the basis of your answers to the above questions, draw an organization chart for Woody Manufacturing. Explain your reasons for the division of labour, the spans of control, and line versus staff positions that you have chosen.

Ethical OB Dilemma

Life in a Virtual Organization—Close Supervision or "Snoopervision"?

Virtual organizations are contemporary open systems of networked people who communicate and get work completed using the World Wide Web. The concern is how to manage employee behaviour if they aren't sitting at a desk in the office;

how can work performance be observed? Or, if a cross-functional team leader is trying to meet a deadline, how is that possible when employees aren't working right beside each other?

The days when managers and team leaders could check up on employees by looking out over rows of desks are over. More and more workers are toiling far away from the head office—at home, in hotel rooms, or in other remote locations. So, how is a supervisor or team leader to know whether employees are really labouring at the monthly report and not shopping on eBay or watching Oprah?

Many organizations may find comfort in the fact that the very technology that allows employees to work anywhere also enables companies to monitor their actions. In fact, a wealth of high-tech tools makes it possible to keep a closer eye on employees than ever before. Some software, like *IMonitor Employee Activity Monitor 4.8*, can monitor whether employees are logged on to their computers or working in particular applications. Other programs, like *360 Monitor for Corporate Networks* and *Keylogger*, can track each keystroke or block access to undesirable Web sites. Web-connected video cameras can even watch workers at their desks.

SOURCE: Excerpted from R. Richmond, "It's 10am: Do You Know Where Your Workers Are?" *The Wall Street Journal*, Eastern Edition, January 12, 2004, PPRI, R4. Copyright@ 2006 by Dow Jones & Co. Inc. Reproduced with permission of Dow Jones & Co. Inc. via Copyright Clearance Center.

How much supervision in the workplace is too much? Consider the following statements. Which one best describes how you would respond?

1. "This is so bureaucratic! The use of electronic surveillance software is a signal of distrust in employees' minds; if used, it will erode morale, and ultimately hamper productivity." Explain your rationale.
2. "Control over assets is important. Employers sign the paycheques and own the equipment, so they have the right to make sure they are getting their money's worth and their equipment is being used properly." Explain.
3. "This sort of 'snoopervision' creates a cat-and-mouse game in which beating the system becomes more important than productivity." Explain.
4. "Electronic surveillance is old-style command and control thinking; it isn't necessary if properly trained and equipped employees are held accountable for meeting challenging but fair performance goals." Explain your rationale.
5. "No amount of electronic performance monitoring can make up for poor hiring decisions, inadequate training, a weak performance-reward system, and inept supervision." Explain.
6. "I would respond differently." Explain.

13

{ *"A corporation is a living organism; it has to continue to shed its skin. Methods have to change. Focus has to change. Values have to change. The sum total of these changes is transformation."*
—Andrew Grove (Intel Founder)

Managing Change *&* Stress

Rio Tinto Cuts 14,000 Globally— The Canadian Mining Industry Undergoes More Changes

The British-Australian company Rio Tinto Group is one of the world's largest mining organizations, with offices in 40 countries, including Canada. As a result of external factors and internal strategic direction, the mining company found itself with nearly $38 billion (Cdn) in net debt and had to act quickly to shore up the gap. "Given the difficult and uncertain economic conditions, and the unprecedented rate of deterioration of our markets, our imperative is to maximize cash generation and pay down debt," chief executive Tom Albanese said. He continued, "We have undertaken a thorough review of all our operations and are executing a range of actions."

In 2008, the Rio Tinto Group was no different from any other business hit hard with sharp declines in both the building and manufacturing sectors worldwide; demand was down and so was sales revenue. But external factors alone weren't the company's only concerns. Internally, wages and salaries for a global workforce of approximately 110,000, in addition to capital financing costs, were starting to become a significant burden on cash flow. At a time when they needed money fast, the executive team made a decision to shed 12.5 percent of its global workforce, which translated into 14,000 jobs. By doing so, Rio Tinto calculated a savings of $1.6 billion per year by 2010. Further operating-cost reductions would add to that total in hopes of reaching its goal to trim $8.25 billion (Cdn) by the start of 2010.

From Montreal, the Canadian spokesperson and president of the aluminium division, Dick Evans, was able to confirm that while the $800 million expansion of its iron ore operations in Labrador and another $6 billion worth of projects were being slowed down, Canadian employment level commitments at this time were expected to be maintained as promised.

Rio is only the latest in a string of international mining powerhouses forced to cut operations in Canada. Anglo-Swiss miner Xstrata PLC announced the closing of two nickel mines in Sudbury that were once owned by Canadian miner Falconbridge, and asked 250 workers to accept early retirement packages. Brazil's Companhia Vale do Rio Doce (Vale) announced that it was closing the Copper Cliff South mine in Sudbury, which was once owned by Canada's Inco.

As you can see, changes due to various factors can occur within an organization, and that often translates into job loss for many. Perhaps this is why it has become common for members of the workforce to develop stress responses during times of corporate adjustment. They see their jobs as being potentially threatened, and that creates great uncertainty. In addition, the survivors left behind to deal with the heavy work demands are experiencing added stress as well. One thing is certain: change and related stress will continue to influence Canadian organizational life for many years to come.

SOURCES: A. Hoffman, "Rio Tinto targets $7-billion in spending," *The Globe & Mail—Report on Business*, December 11, 2008, p B1.

Tom Albanese, CEO of Rio Tinto Group, has guided the organization through very turbulent times that have forced it to change often.

External environmental factors like increased global competition, startling breakthroughs in information technology, changes in social values, shifting consumer preferences, and calls for greater corporate ethics are forcing companies to change the way they do business. In addition, matters related to internal corporate factors, such as employees wanting empowerment and respect for who they are and demanding safe work environments, customers demanding greater value, and investors wanting more integrity in financial disclosures are also affecting many organizations. The rate of organizational and societal change is clearly accelerating.

As a result, organizations must change to satisfy employees, customers, and shareholders. However, change is also likely to encounter resistance, even when it represents an appropriate course of action. Therefore, it is critical that employees understand the forces of change that are influencing the organizations they work for, and just as important for current and future managers to learn how they can successfully implement and navigate the journey of organizational change.

Specifically, we open this chapter discussion with the forces that create the need for organization change, models of planned change, resistance to change, and how people can better manage the stress associated with organizational change.

➡️ **LEARNING OBJECTIVES**

After reading this chapter, you should be able to:

LO 1 **Discuss** the external and internal forces that create the need for organizational change.

LO 2 **Describe** Lewin's change model and the systems model of change.

LO 3 **Explain** Kotter's eight steps for leading organizational change.

LO 4 **Summarize and explain** the 11 reasons why employees resist change.

LO 5 **Compare and contrast** the three moderators of occupational stress and identify various kinds of stress-reduction techniques.

LO 1 Forces of Change

How do organizations know when they should change? Although there is no clear-cut answer to this question, organizations will find the cues that signal the need for change by monitoring the forces for change.

Organizations encounter many different forces for change, both from external sources and from internal sources. This section examines these forces that create the need for change. Awareness of the forces of change can help employees understand the responses from their organization. In addition, it can help managers determine when they should consider implementing organizational change in response. The external and internal forces for change are presented in Figure 13.1.[1]

External forces for change

Those forces of change that originate outside the organization.

EXTERNAL FORCES

External forces for change originate outside the organization. Because these forces have global effects, they may cause an organization to question the essence of its business and the process by which products and services are produced. There are four key external forces for change: (1) demographic characteristics, (2) technological advancements, (3) market changes, and (4) social and political pressures. We will now discuss each of these external forces.

Demographic Characteristics Canada is a pluralistic society, meaning that it has a high degree of multiculturalism, ranging from ethnic to religious diversity. This is something that is going to continue into Canada's future, and it will be a driving external force for organizations looking to hire new employees. According to Statistics Canada, the visible minority population is growing quickly, particularly in large urban areas. Over 50 percent of Toronto's and Vancouver's populations are expected to be visible minorities by 2017.[2] Consider, as well, that the number of new Canadian immigrants from Asia, the Middle East, and India is increasing, and they hold a variety of religious beliefs (e.g., Sikh, Muslim, Buddhist, Hindu).

Add to this an aging Baby Boom generation (born after WWII) that has dominated the workforce and is retiring at a steady rate. Behind them, filling their old positions, are Generation X, Y, and Digitals. Why is an aging population so significant? First, because it emphasizes our earlier point: Statistics Canada reports that by 2020, the only population growth in Canada will be due to immigration, (as natural growth declines because of our aging population.)[3] Secondly, consider the implications associated with hiring the 80 million Digitals (dubbed the Net or Echo-Boom Generation born between 1977 and 1997). Employers will have to face the new realities of the Digital Generation's culture and values and what they want from work, if they expect to attract and retain those talents and align them with corporate goals. The young members

FIGURE 13.1 The External and Internal Forces for Change

External Forces

Demographic Characteristics
- Age
- Education
- Skill level
- Gender
- Immigration

Technological Advancements
- Manufacturing automation
- Information technology

Customer and Market Changes
- Changing customer preferences
- Domestic and international competition
- Mergers and acquisitions

Social and Political Pressures
- War
- Values
- Leadership

The need for change

Internal Forces

Human Resource Problems/Prospects
- Unmet needs
- Job dissatisfaction
- Absenteeism and turnover
- Productivity
- Participation/suggestions

Managerial Behaviour/Decisions
- Conflict
- Leadership
- Reward systems
- Structural reorganization

of the labour market entering the workforce during the next 20 years are technologically equipped, and therefore armed with the most powerful tools for business.[4]

The organizational challenge will be to motivate and use this talented pool of diverse employees to its maximum potential.

Technological Advancements   The labour–capital debate is basic to business—do we increase productivity and output by hiring more labour? Or, do we invest in more capital assets (machines) instead and let the technology increase output? It is important for students of OB to see that, in Canada, there is no economic advantage to hiring more people if machines can do the work for less. We acknowledge the difficulty some readers may have with this statement, but there is no denying the reality. Both manufacturing and service organizations are increasingly using technology as a means to improve productivity, competitiveness, and customer service, while also cutting costs.

Microsoft is a good example. Microsoft hired Ray Ozzie, a renowned software expert who designed Lotus Notes, to "webify" all of Microsoft's products. To do this, "Microsoft must build a global network of server farms that will cost staggering amounts of money," says Ozzie.[5] Microsoft is pursuing this change strategy in response to technological changes occurring within the global software industry.

Customer and Market Changes   Customers are simply demanding more than they did in the past. Moreover, customers are likely to shop elsewhere if they do not get what they want because of lower customer switching costs. Walmart, for example, stays abreast of customer preferences by conducting consumer surveys and focus groups. This has enabled Walmart to customize the product mix in its stores to local tastes.[6]

With respect to market changes, service companies are experiencing increased pressure to obtain more productivity because competition is fierce and prices have remained relatively stable.[7] Further, the emergence of a global economy is forcing companies to change the way they do business.[8] Canadian companies have been forging new partnerships and alliances with their suppliers and potential competitors to gain advantages in the global marketplace.[9]

Social and Political Pressures   These forces are created by social and political events, such as social pressure and political pressure (e.g., an increase in demand for green products; or pressure to ban the sale of chemical lawn products in certain communities).

In general, social and political pressure is exerted through legislative bodies that represent the Canadian population.[10] Political events can also create substantial change. For example, the war in Iraq created tremendous opportunities for defence contractors and organizations like General Dynamics in Ontario. Although it is difficult for organizations to predict changes in political forces, many organizations hire consultants to help them detect and respond to social and political changes.

Organizational Crises   An organizational crisis may result from an accident, ignored problems that build over time, acts of nature, or criminal acts. For example, recall the traumatic 2004 SARS outbreak that brought the Canadian health care industry to its knees. This crisis caused Canadian hospitals and health care professionals in general to change many things, including some of their policies, to upgrade their communications systems, and to train more people in controlling and preventing the spread of deadly diseases. Time has shown that changes made in response to SARS were positive over the long term, as hospitals, schools, and public health officials were well prepared for the H1N1 Swine Flu pandemic (virus) that surfaced in 2009.

In each of these situations, an organizational crisis forced significant change upon the firm and its stakeholders. There was no hiding from the forces; they had to be dealt with.

INTERNAL FORCES

Internal forces for change come from inside the organization. These forces can be subtle, such as low job satisfaction, or can manifest in outward signs, such as low productivity or high turnover and conflict. Internal forces for change come from a variety of sources, such as: human resource problems; managerial preferences or decisions; organizational processes, systems, structure, or culture; or insufficient resources in general.

Internal forces for change

Forces of change that originate from inside the organization.

Human Resource Problems or Prospects   These problems stem from employee perceptions about how they are treated at work, and the match between individual and organization needs and desires. In earlier chapters, we discussed the relationship between an employee's unmet needs and job dissatisfaction. Dissatisfaction is a symptom of an underlying employee problem that should be addressed. Dell, for example, instituted a process of semi-annual employee surveys to determine employees' job satisfaction and to assess the quality of managers' leadership skills. A manager's effectiveness ratings are tied to compensation, promotions, and attendance at management training.[11] Unusual or high levels of absenteeism and turnover also represent forces for change.

Managerial Preferences or Decisions   Preferences for certain policies, procedures, and directions can be strong internal forces, as the ideology and philosophy of key executives becomes old-style and perhaps counter to external forces. For example, the desire by one set of executives and employees to merge with another firm may be met by opposition from an opposing set of executives and employees that are against the merger. When this sort of force occurs, dialogue is very important. If not, the result can be excessive interpersonal conflict, which can be a sign that change is needed. If conflict becomes more prevalent than dialogue, then both managers and employees may need assistance from a training consultant through interpersonal skills workshops, coaching, and/or mentoring. Inappropriate management behaviours such as inadequate direction or support may result in human resource problems requiring change.

Organizational Processes, Systems, Structure, or Culture
The way an organization is structured, as well as the systems or processes that are in place, may be inadequate to accomplish desired goals and new strategies. For example, just because a cross-functional team comes up with a new strategy in response to market demand doesn't mean the structure is in place to make it happen. In fact, these internal forces can collectively resist new ideas or prevent new strategies from being successful because of their inability to flex and adapt.

Insufficient Resources   The lack of resources is a very common problem for corporations. We've already identified human capital as an internal resource that can force change, but an organization is dependent upon other resources as well. Insufficient land, labour, and capital place tremendous pressure on the organization, because it brings into question whether the organization's goals and objectives can be achieved. Resources go beyond the traditional definition, and include having an entrepreneurial mindset as well as access to knowledge. In the age of information, knowledge is a key resource that must remain as current and relevant as possible. During times of economic uncertainty, of course, the lack of capital assets is at a premium. The unprecedented number of requests for government bailouts in 2009, as well as the increasing number of bankruptcies over previous year levels, support this claim.[12]

Models and Dynamics of Planned Change

Researchers have tried to identify effective ways to manage the change process within organizations. This section reviews three models of planned change: (1) Lewin's change model, (2) a systems model of change, and (3) Kotter's eight steps for leading organizational change and organizational development.

TYPES OF CHANGE

There are three types of change: adaptive, innovative, and radically innovative. Adaptive change is lowest in complexity, cost, and uncertainty. It involves reimplementation of a change in the same organizational unit at a later time, or imitation of a similar change by a different unit. For example, an adaptive change for a department store would be to rely on 12-hour days during the annual inventory week. The store's accounting department could imitate the same change in work hours during tax preparation time. Adaptive changes are not particularly threatening to employees because they are familiar.

Innovative changes fall somewhere in the middle in terms of complexity, cost, and uncertainty. An experiment with flexible work schedules by a farm supply warehouse company qualifies as an innovative change if it entails modifying the way other firms in the industry already use it. Unfamiliarity, and hence greater uncertainty, makes fear of change a problem with innovative changes.

Radically innovative changes are typically complex and costly, and create high degrees of uncertainty. Changes of this sort are the most difficult to implement and tend to be the most threatening to managerial confidence and employee job security. Radical changes must be supported by an organization's culture. Organizational change is more likely to fail if it is inconsistent with any of the three levels of organizational culture: observable artefacts, espoused values, and basic assumptions (see the discussion in Chapter 11). General Motors Corporation is a good example of a company that has undergone

> "General Motors Corporation is a good example of a company that has undergone radical changes in the last few years . . . (it) will have to introduce some new and radically innovative practices and products, unlike any currently in the industry, if it is ever to compete successfully."

radical changes in the last few years. General Motors will have to introduce some new and radically innovative practices and products, unlike any currently in the industry, if it is ever to compete successfully.

LO 2 ## LEWIN'S CHANGE MODEL

Most theories of organizational change originate from the landmark work of social psychologist Kurt Lewin. He developed a three-stage model of planned change that explained how to initiate, manage, and stabilize the change process.[13] The three stages are unfreezing, changing, and refreezing, as shown in Figure 13.2.

Unfreezing The focus of this stage is to create the motivation to change. In so doing, individuals are encouraged to replace old behaviours and attitudes with those desired by management. Managers can begin the unfreezing process by disconfirming the usefulness of employees' present behaviours or attitudes. For example, Mark Hurd, CEO of Hewlett-Packard (HP), unfroze the organization about the need to restructure by using information he obtained from corporate customers and HP employees. Customers told Hurd that HP's structure was so confusing that they did not know who to call for help. HP salespeople complained that they spent only 33 percent of their time with customers because they were required to complete so much administrative paperwork.[14]

Benchmarking is another technique that can be used to unfreeze an organization. **Benchmarking** "describes the overall process by which a company compares its performance with that of other companies, then learns how the strongest-performing companies achieve their results."[15] For example, one company discovered through benchmarking that their costs to develop software were twice as high as the best companies in the industry, and the time it took to get a new product to market was four times longer than the benchmarked organizations. These data were ultimately used to unfreeze employees' attitudes and motivate people to change the organization's internal processes to remain competitive.

Benchmarking

Process by which a company compares its performance with that of high-performing organizations.

Changing Organizational change, whether large or small, is undertaken to improve some process, procedure, product, service, or outcome of interest to management. Because change involves learning and doing things differently, this stage entails providing employees with new information, new behavioural models, new processes or procedures, new equipment, new technology, or new ways of getting the job done.

Organizational change can be aimed at improvement or growth, or it can focus on solving a problem such as poor customer service or low productivity. Change also can be targeted at different levels in an organization. For example, sending managers to leadership training programs can improve individuals' job satisfaction and productivity. In contrast, installing new information technology may be the change required to increase work group productivity and overall corporate profits. The point to keep in mind is that change should be targeted at some type of desired end-result.

Refreezing Change is stabilized during refreezing by helping employees integrate the changed behaviour or attitude into their normal way of doing things. This is accomplished by first giving employees the chance to exhibit the new behaviours or attitudes. Once exhibited, positive reinforcement is used to reinforce the desired change. Additional coaching and modelling are also used at this point to reinforce the stability of the change. Extrinsic rewards, particularly monetary incentives (recall our discussion in Chapter 5), are frequently used

▶ FIGURE **13.2** Lewin's Three-Step Change Model

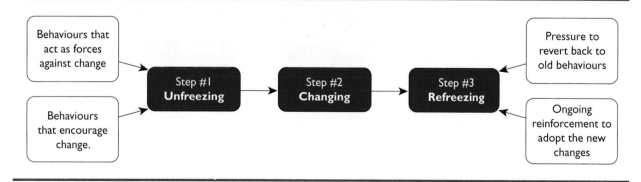

to reinforce behavioural change. Reinforcement is important otherwise behaviour may revert back, as the same forces that were initially present to resist the change wait to resist again.

A SYSTEMS MODEL OF CHANGE

A systems approach takes a big picture perspective of organizational change. It is based on the notion that any change, no matter how large or small, has a spill-over effect throughout an organization.[16]

A systems model of change offers a framework or model to use for diagnosing what to change and for determining how to evaluate the success of a change effort. To

Mission statement

A statement that summarizes the essence, or reason why, an organization exists.

further your understanding about this model, we first describe its components and then discuss a brief application. The four main components of a systems model of change are inputs, strategic plans, target elements of change, and outputs (see Figure 13.3).

Inputs All organizational changes should be consistent with an organization's mission, vision, and resulting strategic plan. A *mission statement* represents the reason why an organization exists, and an organization's vision is a long-term goal that describes what an organization wants to become. Consider how the difference between mission and vision affects

▶ **FIGURE 13.3** A Systems Model of Change

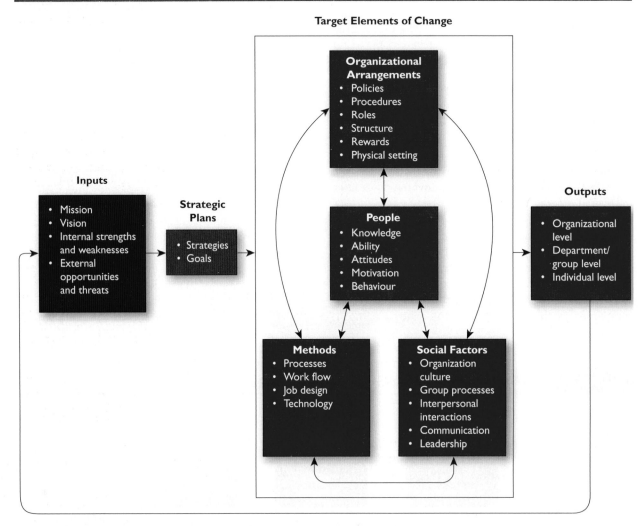

SOURCES: Adapted from D.R. Fuqua and D.J. Kurpius, "Conceptual Models in Organizational Consultation," *Journal of Counselling & Development*, July/August 1993, pp 602–18; and D.A. Nadler and M.L. Tushman, "Organizational Frame Bending: Principles for Managing Reorientation," *Academy of Management Executive*, August 1989, pp 194–203.

organizational change. Your college or university probably has a mission to educate people. This mission does not necessarily imply anything about change; it simply defines the institution's overall purpose. In contrast, the college or university may have a vision to be recognized as the best in the country. This vision requires the organization to benchmark itself against other world-class higher education institutions and to create plans for achieving the vision. For example, the vision of Languages Canada is to be internationally recognized as the symbol of excellence, representing Canada as the number one destination for quality English and French language training. An assessment of an organization's internal strengths and weaknesses against its environmental opportunities and threats (SWOT) is another key input within the systems model. This SWOT analysis is a key component of the strategic planning process.

Strategic Plans   When we talked about strategic plans in Chapter 11, you will recall that we outlined an organization's long-term direction and the actions necessary to achieve planned results. Among other things, strategic plans are based on results from a SWOT analysis. This analysis helps to develop an organizational strategy to attain desired goals such as profits, customer satisfaction, quality, adequate return on investment, acceptable levels of turnover, and employee satisfaction and commitment. When completing a SWOT analysis, the strengths and weaknesses of the internal resources are evaluated against the external market factors that can either be opportunities or threats to the company. We discussed these earlier when we looked at internal and external forces of change.

Target elements of change

Components of an organization that may be changed.

Target Elements of Change   *Target elements of change* are the components of an organization that may be changed. As shown in Figure 13.3, there are four targeted elements of change: organizational arrangements, social factors, methods, and people.[17] Each target element of change contains a subset of more detailed organizational features. For instance, the social factors component includes consideration of an organization's culture, group processes, interpersonal interactions, communication, and leadership. There are two final issues to keep in mind about the target elements of change shown in Figure 13.3. First, the double-headed arrows connecting each target element of change convey the message that change ripples across an organization. Second, the people component is placed in the centre of the target elements of change box because all organizational change ultimately impacts employees.

Outputs   Outputs represent the desired end-results of a change. Once again, these end-results should be consistent with an organization's strategic plan. Figure 13.3 indicates that change may be directed at the organizational level, department/group level, or individual level. Change efforts are more complicated and difficult to manage when they are targeted at the organizational level. This occurs because organizational-level changes are more likely to affect multiple target elements of change shown in the model.

Applying the Systems Model of Change   There are two different ways to apply the systems model of change. The first is as an aid during the strategic planning process. Once a group of managers has determined its vision and strategic goals, the target elements of change can be considered when developing action plans to support the accomplishment of goals. The second application involves using the model as a diagnostic framework to determine the causes of an organizational problem and to propose solutions.

KOTTER'S EIGHT STEPS FOR LEADING ORGANIZATIONAL CHANGE   LO 3

John Kotter, an expert in leadership and change management, believes that organizational change typically fails because senior management makes a host of implementation errors. Based on these errors, Kotter proposes an eight-step process for leading change.[18] Unlike the systems model of change, this model is more like Lewin's model of change in that it prescribes how managers should sequence or lead the change process.

Kotter's eight steps, shown in Table 13.1, take Lewin's model of change into account. The first four steps represent Lewin's "unfreezing" stage. Steps 5, 6, and 7 represent "changing," and step 8 corresponds to "refreezing." The value of Kotter's steps is that they provide specific recommendations about behaviours that managers need to exhibit to successfully lead organizational change. It is important to remember that Kotter's research reveals that it is ineffective to skip steps, and that successful organizational change is 70 percent to 90 percent leadership, and only 10 percent to 30 percent management. Senior managers are thus advised to focus on leading rather than managing change.[19]

CREATING CHANGE THROUGH ORGANIZATION DEVELOPMENT

Organization development (OD) is much broader in orientation than any of the previously discussed models. OD constitutes a set of techniques or interventions that are used to implement planned organizational

Organization development

A set of techniques or tools used to implement organizational change.

TABLE 13.1

Steps to Leading Organizational Change

STEP	DESCRIPTION
1. Establish a sense of urgency	Unfreeze the organization by creating a compelling reason for why change is needed.
2. Create the guiding coalition	Create a cross-functional, cross-level group of people with enough power to lead the change.
3. Develop a vision and strategy	Create a vision and strategic plan to guide the change process.
4. Communicate the change vision	Create and implement a communication strategy that consistently communicates the new vision and strategic plan.
5. Empower broad-based action	Eliminate barriers to change, and use target elements of change to transform the organization. Encourage risk taking and creative problem solving.
6. Generate short-term wins	Plan for and create short-term "wins" or improvements. Recognize and reward people who contribute to the wins.
7. Consolidate gains and produce more change	The guiding coalition uses credibility from short-term wins to create more change. Additional people are brought into the change process as change cascades throughout the organization. Attempts are made to reinvigorate the change process.
8. Anchor new approaches in the culture	Reinforce the changes by highlighting connections between new behaviours and processes and organizational success. Develop methods to ensure leadership development and succession.

SOURCE: The steps were developed by J.P. Kotter, *Leading Change* (Boston: Harvard Business School Press, 1996).

change aimed at increasing "an organization's ability to improve itself as a humane and effective system."[20] OD techniques or interventions apply to each of the change models discussed in this section. For example, OD is used during Lewin's "changing" stage. It is also used to identify and implement targeted elements of change within the systems model of change. Finally, OD might be used during Kotter's steps 1, 3, 5, 6, and 7. In this section, we briefly review the four identifying characteristics of OD and associated research and practical implications.[21]

OD Involves Profound Change   Change agents using OD generally desire deep and long-lasting improvement. OD consultant Warner Burke, for example, who strives for fundamental cultural change, wrote: "By fundamental change, as opposed to fixing a problem or improving a procedure, I mean that some significant aspect of an organization's culture will never be the same."[22]

OD Is Value Loaded   Owing to the fact that OD is rooted partially in humanistic psychology, many OD consultants carry certain values or biases into the client organization. They prefer cooperation over conflict, self-control over institutional control, and democratic and participative management over dictatorial management. In addition to OD being driven by a consultant's values, OD

practitioners now believe that there is a broader value perspective that should underlie any organizational change. Specifically, OD should always be customer focused and it should help an organization achieve its vision and strategic goals. This approach implies that organizational interventions should be aimed at helping to satisfy customers' needs and thereby provide enhanced value of an organization's products and services.[23]

OD Is a Diagnosis/Prescription Cycle   OD theorists and practitioners have long adhered to a medical model of organization. Like medical doctors, internal and external OD consultants approach the "sick" organization, "diagnose" its ills, "prescribe" and implement an intervention, and "monitor" progress. Consider this list of different OD interventions that can be used to change individual, group, or organizational behaviour as a whole:

- **Survey feedback**   A questionnaire is distributed to employees to ascertain their perceptions and attitudes. The results are then shared with them.

- **Process consultation**   An OD consultant observes the communication process (interpersonal-relations, decision-making, and conflict-handling patterns) occurring in work groups, and provides feedback to the members involved.

- **Team building** Work groups are made more effective by helping members learn to function as a team.

- **Techno-structural activities** These interventions are concerned with improving the work technology or organizational design with people on the job. An intervention involving a work-technology change might be the introduction of email to improve employee communication.[24]

OD Is Process Oriented Ideally, OD consultants focus on the form and not the content of behavioural and administrative dealings. For example, product design engineers and market researchers might be coached on how to communicate more effectively with one another, without the consultant knowing the technical details of their conversations. In addition to communication, OD specialists focus on other processes, including problem solving, decision making, conflict handling, trust, power sharing, and career development.

OD Research and Practical Implications Before discussing OD research, it is important to note that many of the topics contained in this OB textbook are used during OD interventions. Team building, for example, is commonly used as an OD technique. It is used to improve the functioning of work groups. The point is that OD research has practical implications for a variety of OB applications previously discussed. OD-related interventions have produced the following insights:

- A meta-analysis of 18 studies indicated that employee satisfaction with change was higher when top management was highly committed to the change effort.[25]

- A meta-analysis of 52 studies provided support for the systems model of organizational change. Specifically, varying one target element of change created changes in other target elements. Also, there was a positive relationship between individual behaviour change and organizational-level change.[26]

- A meta-analysis of 126 studies demonstrated that comprehensive interventions using more than one OD technique were more effective in changing job attitudes and work attitudes than interventions that relied on only one human-process or techno-structural approach.[27]

- A survey of 1,700 firms from China, Japan, and Europe revealed that (1) European firms used OD interventions more frequently than firms from China and Japan, and (2) some OD interventions are culture-free and some are not.[28]

There are four practical implications derived from this research. First, planned organizational change works. However, management and change agents are advised to rely on multifaceted interventions. As indicated elsewhere in this book, goal setting, feedback, recognition and rewards, training, participation, and challenging job design have good track records relative to improving performance and satisfaction. Second, change programs are more successful when they are geared toward meeting both short-term and long-term results. Managers should not engage in organizational change for the sake of change; change efforts should produce positive results. Third, organizational change is more likely to succeed when top management is truly committed to the change process and the desired goals of the change program. This is particularly true when organizations pursue large-scale transformation. Finally, the effectiveness of OD interventions is affected by cross-cultural considerations. Managers and OD consultants should not blindly apply an OD intervention that worked in one country to a similar situation in another country.

Understanding and Managing Resistance to Change

It is important for managers, supervisors, and team-leaders to learn to manage resistance because failed change efforts are costly. Costs include decreased employee loyalty, lowered probability of achieving corporate goals, waste of money and resources, and difficulty in fixing the failed change effort. This section examines resistance to change and practical ways of dealing with the problem.

WHY PEOPLE RESIST CHANGE IN THE WORKPLACE

LO 4

No matter how technically or administratively perfect a proposed change may be, people make or break it (see International OB feature box). Individual and group behaviour following an organizational change can take many forms. The extremes range from acceptance to active resistance. **Resistance to change** is an emotional/behavioural response to real or imagined threats to an established work routine; it acts as barriers. Resistance can be as subtle as passive acceptance and as obvious as deliberate sabotage. Let us now consider the reasons employees resist change in the first place. Eleven of the leading reasons are listed below.[29]

Resistance to change

Emotional/behavioural response to real or imagined work changes that act as barriers.

ASHOK KHENY ENCOUNTERS EXTREME RESISTANCE WHEN TRYING TO BUILD A HIGHWAY IN INDIA

To understand why it's so hard to get things built in India, consider Ashok Kheny's idealistic quest. For 12 years he has sought to create a vision of modern India. Along the way he has become entangled in India's unique blend of politics, bureaucracy, and corruption.

Kheny started off with high hopes. A native of Bangalore, he got his master's degree in engineering in North America, then stayed on to work as a transportation contractor. In 1995 he returned to Bangalore with a bold proposal: to build a limited-access toll highway between Bangalore and neighbouring Mysore, a ring road around half of Bangalore, and a handful of new townships nearby. The Karnataka state government approved the plan, so Kheny moved back—never suspecting that dynamiting the rocky terrain would turn out to be a snap compared with breaking through India's stubborn bureaucracy.

Officially, Kheny and his Nandi Infrastructure Corridor Enterprise Ltd. have been held up by land disputes and government reviews and approvals. But he claims the real problem is that he refuses to go along with the traditional way of getting things done in Karnataka. He won't pay bribes, and he won't buy off landowners or redraw his maps to accommodate them. Land-owners and state agencies have filed more than 300 lawsuits against the project, and so far all have gone in Kheny's favour, including an appeal to the country's Supreme Court. But the battle isn't over. "I get letters and phone calls threatening to kill me and my family," he says.

With such strong resistance, do you think Ashok Kheny will be able to accomplish his goals without doing business the traditional way? Explain.

SOURCE: Excerpted from S. Hamm, "Change Agents: A Long and Winding Road," *BusinessWeek*, March 19, 2007, p 56.

1. **An individual's predisposition toward change** While some people are distrustful and suspicious of change, others see change as a situation requiring flexibility, patience, and understanding.[30]

2. **Surprise and fear of the unknown** When innovative or radically different changes are introduced without warning, affected employees become fearful of the implications.

3. **Climate of mistrust** Trust involves reciprocal faith in others' intentions. Mutual mistrust can doom an otherwise well-conceived change to failure. Mistrust encourages secrecy, which creates deeper mistrust.

4. **Fear of failure** Intimidating changes on the job can cause employees to doubt their capabilities. Self-doubt works against self-confidence and cripples personal growth and development.

5. **Loss of status and/or job security** Changes that threaten to alter power bases or eliminate jobs generally trigger strong resistance.

6. **Peer pressure** People who are not directly affected by a change may actively resist it to protect the interest of their friends and co-workers.

7. **Disruption of cultural traditions and/or group relationships** Whenever individuals are transferred, promoted, or reassigned, cultural and group dynamics are thrown into confusion.

8. **Personality conflicts** The personalities of change agents can breed resistance as they engage in political power games that help themselves rather than the organization.

9. **Lack of tact and/or poor timing** Undue resistance can occur because changes are introduced in an insensitive manner or at an awkward time.

10. **Non-reinforcing reward systems** Individuals resist when they do not foresee positive rewards for changing. For example, employees are unlikely to support change that they think requires them to work longer with more pressure.

11. **Past success** Success can breed smugness. It also can foster a stubbornness to change because people come to believe that what worked in the past will work in the future. Who could have predicted the bankruptcy of the Chrysler Corporation and its ownership by Italian auto maker Fiat?[31]

RESEARCH ON RESISTANCE TO CHANGE

The classic study of resistance to change was reported in 1948 by Lester Coch and John R.P. French. They observed the introduction of a new work procedure in a garment factory, where one set of workers was given no explanation for proposed changes, while another set of workers was given full explanations. The first group faltered, but the latter group experienced an increase in output, no grievances, and no turnover.[32] Since the Coch and French study, participation has been the recommended approach for overcoming resistance to change.

Empirical (evidence of data) research uncovered additional personal characteristics related to resistance to change:

Commitment to change

A mind-set of doing whatever it takes to effectively implement change.

1. **Commitment to change** is defined as a mind-set "that binds an individual to a course of action deemed necessary for the successful implementation of a change initiative."[33] A series of studies showed that an employee's commitment to change was a significant and positive predictor of behavioural support for a change initiative.[34]

2. **Resilience to change** is a composite characteristic reflecting high self-esteem, optimism, and an internal locus of control (self-esteem and locus of control were discussed in Chapter 3). People with high resilience are expected to be more open and adaptable toward change.[35]

Resilience to change

Composite personal characteristic reflecting high self-esteem, optimism, and an internal locus of control.

3. Positive self-concept and tolerance for risk were positively related to coping with change. That is, people with a positive self-concept and a tolerance for risk handled organizational change better than those without these dispositions.[36]

4. High levels of self-efficacy (discussed in Chapter 3) were negatively associated with resistance to change.[37]

The preceding research is based on the assumption that individuals directly or consciously resist change. Some experts contend that this is not the case. Rather, there is a growing belief that resistance to change really represents employees' responses to obstacles in the organization that prevent them from changing.[38] For example, John Kotter, the researcher who developed the eight steps for leading organizational change that were discussed earlier in this chapter, studied more than 100 companies and concluded that employees generally wanted to change, but were unable to do so because of obstacles that prevented implementation.

He noted that obstacles in the organization's structure or in a "performance appraisal system [that] makes people choose between the new vision and their own self-interests" prevented change more than an individual's direct resistance.[39] This new perspective implies that a systems model, such as the one shown in Figure 13.3, should be used to determine the causes of failed change. Such an approach would likely reveal that ineffective organizational change is due to faulty organizational processes and systems, as opposed to employees' direct resistance. For example, employees frequently resist change because management has not effectively communicated the rationale to support the change.[40] In conclusion, a systems perspective suggests that people do not resist change, per se, but rather that individuals' anti-change attitudes and behaviours are caused by obstacles within the work environment.

ALTERNATIVE STRATEGIES FOR OVERCOMING RESISTANCE TO CHANGE

We noted previously that participation has historically been the recommended approach for overcoming resistance to change. More recently, however, organizational change experts have criticized the tendency to treat participation as a cure-all for resistance to change. They prefer a contingency approach because resistance can take many forms and, furthermore, because situational factors vary. Participation + involvement does have its place, but it takes time that is not always available. There are other methods to consider, such as:

- **Education+communication** This method is used in situations when there is a lack of information or inaccurate information and analysis. These actions are illustrated by TD Canada Trust in the Skills & Best Practices feature box.

- **Participation+involvement** This is helpful when the initiators do not have all the information they need to design the change and when others have considerable power to resist.

- **Facilitation+support** This method is commonly used when people are resisting change because of adjustment problems.

- **Negotiation+agreement** Use this method when someone or some group will clearly lose out in a change and when that group has considerable power to resist.

- **Manipulation+co-optation** This method is helpful when other tactics will not work or are too expensive.

Skills &Best Practices

Communication Is Key During Change

To achieve TD Canada Trust's long-term goal to be the leading Canadian-based North American financial institution, continued growth is important, and that means mergers and lots of change. Fred Tomczyk, Vice-Chair of the Bank Financial Group, said in a speech, "I've learned from previous mergers that the first word in merger is 'me.' And so we had to create certainty as soon as possible by answering those 'me' questions quickly and honestly. How will all this affect me? Do I have a job? Who do I report to? How does this impact my pay and benefits? What do you want me to do?

Our senior executive team knew and communicated the answer to these questions to all our titled officers within 30 days of the close of the transaction. We sent out lots of written communication to employees, but face-to-face was the preferred method. We learned that people don't necessarily read things you send them, but they sure listen up during a session with their manager or the CEO. I must admit it got tiresome to live on an airplane, and day after day say the same things a hundred times. But it's what people needed. And when it's important enough, they speak up too."

SOURCE: Excerpted from Executive Speech by F. Tomczyk, Vice-Chair, TD Bank Financial Group, June 12, 2002. Corporate information: www.tdcanadatrust.com.

- **Explicit+implicit coercion** This method is used when speed is essential and when the change initiators possess considerable power.[41]

In short, each method has its situational niche, advantages, and drawbacks; there is no universal strategy for overcoming resistance to change.

Change Causing Occupational Stress

In our hectic urbanized and industrialized society, change is causing people stress, meaning physical, psychological, or behavioural responses that may trigger negative side effects, including headaches, ulcers, insomnia, heart attacks, high blood pressure, and strokes. Sources of stress can include tight deadlines, role conflict and ambiguity, increasing amounts of financial responsibilities, information overload, too much complexity with technology and systems, traffic congestion, noise and air pollution, family problems, and work overload. Formally defined, **stress** is "an adaptive response, mediated by individual characteristics and/or psychological processes, that is a consequence of any external action, situation, or event that places special physical and/or psychological demands upon a person."[42]

This definition is not as difficult as it seems when we reduce it to three inter-related dimensions of stress: (1) environmental demands, referred to as stressors, that produce (2) an adaptive response, that is influenced by (3) individual differences. We'll talk more about stressors shortly.

For now, however, consider that there is good and bad stress. McGill University professor Dr. Hans Selye, known to many as the father of the modern concept of stress, completed research that emphasized that both positive and negative events can trigger an identical stress response that can be beneficial or harmful. He referred to stress that is positive or produces a positive outcome as **eustress.** An example of eustress would be receiving an award in front of a large crowd that would scare a lot of people, or successfully completing a difficult work assignment that you didn't like but feel a sense of pride and accomplishment once completed. Selye also noted the following:

- Stress is not merely nervous tension.

- Stress can have positive consequences.

- Stress is not something to be avoided. The complete absence of stress is death.[43]

These points make it clear that stress is inevitable. Efforts need to be directed at managing stress, not at somehow escaping it altogether. Because stress and its consequences are manageable, it is important for all employees to learn as much as they can about occupational stress.

A MODEL OF OCCUPATIONAL STRESS

We all experience stress on a daily basis. To an orchestra violinist, stress may stem from giving a solo performance before a big audience. While heat, smoke, and

Eustress

Stress that is good or produces a positive outcome.

Stress

Behavioural, physical, or psychological response to stressors.

flames may represent stress to a firefighter, delivering a semester presentation or speaking in front of classmates may be stressful for those who are shy. In short, stress means different things to different people. In this section we'll review a thorough model of occupational stress, define stressors, and then apply it to the contemporary workplace.

Figure 13.4 presents an instructive model of occupational stress. The model shows that an individual initially appraises four types of stressors. This appraisal then motivates an individual to choose a coping strategy aimed at managing stressors, which, in turn, produces a variety of outcomes. The model also specifies several individual differences that moderate the stress process. A moderator is a variable that causes the relationship between two variables—such as

Stressors

Environmental factors that produce stress.

stressors and cognitive appraisal—to be stronger for some people and weaker for others. This definition is important to note: a moderator doesn't mean decreasing stress; it refers to the relationship between the two variables. Three key moderators are discussed in the next section. Let us now consider the remaining components of this model in detail.

Stressors *Stressors* are environmental factors that produce stress. Figure 13.4 shows the four major types of stressors: individual, group, organizational, and extra-organizational. Individual-level stressors are those directly associated with a person's job duties. The most common examples of individual stressors are job demands, work overload, role conflict, job characteristics, and work/family conflict.[44]

> **FIGURE 13.4** A Model of Occupational Stress

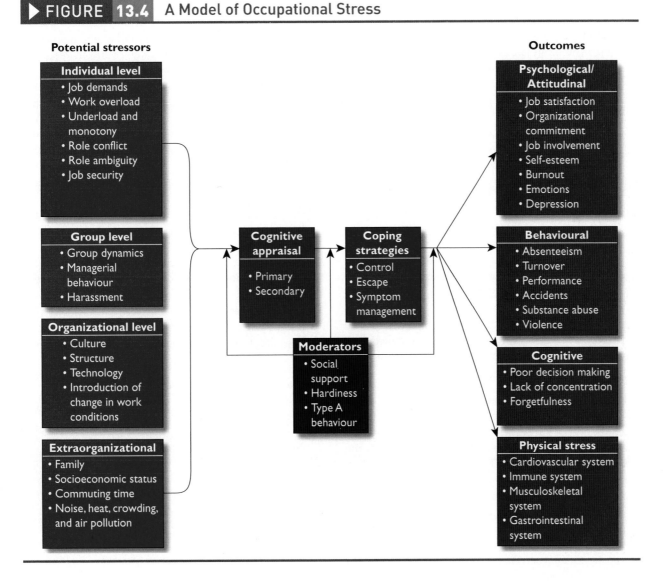

Losing one's job is another important individual-level stressor that is associated with decreased psychological and physical well-being[45] (see the opening chapter vignette). Finally, sleep-related issues are important stressors. Research shows that most people need about seven hours of sleep per night and that alertness, energy, performance, creativity, and thinking are related to how much we sleep.[46]

Group-level stressors are caused by group dynamics (recall our discussion in Chapter 6) and managerial behaviour. Managers create stress for employees by (1) exhibiting inconsistent behaviours, (2) failing to provide support, (3) showing lack of concern, (4) providing inadequate direction, (5) creating a high-productivity environment, and (6) focusing on negatives while ignoring good performance. Sexual harassment experiences represent another group-level stressor. A recent meta-analysis of 90 studies involving over 19,000 people demonstrated that harassing experiences were negatively associated with self-esteem, life and job satisfaction, and organizational commitment, and positively associated with intentions to quit, absenteeism, anxiety, depression, and physical symptoms of stress.[47]

Organizational stressors affect many employees. Organizational culture, which was discussed in Chapter 11, is a prime example. For instance, a high-pressure environment that fuels employee fear about performing up to standard increases the stress response.[48] The increased use of information technology is another source of organizational stress, as is the air quality and ventilation found throughout the organization.

Extra-organizational stressors are those caused by factors outside the organization. For example, trying to balance career and family life is stressful. Socioeconomic status is another extra-organizational stressor. Stress is higher for people with lower socioeconomic status, which represents a combination of (1) economic status, as measured by income, (2) social status, assessed by education level, and (3) work status, as indexed by occupation. These stressors are likely to become more important in the future.

Cognitive Appraisal of Stressors Cognitive appraisal reflects an individual's overall perception or evaluation of a situation or stressor. It is an important component within the stress process, because people interpret the same stressors differently. For example, some individuals perceive unemployment as a positive liberating experience, whereas others perceive it as a negative debilitating (weakening) one.

Figure 13.4 shows that people make two types of appraisals when evaluating the potential impact of stressors on their lives: primary and secondary appraisals.[49] A **primary appraisal** is an initial response and results in categorizing a situation or stressor as irrelevant, positive, or stressful. Stress appraisals are obviously the most important in terms of our current discussion, because they imply that a situation or stressor is perceived as harmful, threatening, or challenging. Think of your own situation and your decision to pursue a higher education. You knew it was going to be difficult at times and even stressful. Your initial primary appraisal of your first days on campus, sitting in classrooms hearing about all the work that was going to be accomplished in the forthcoming months, probably caused you to have some sort of response. Try and recall what that response was. Did you panic, or did you feel challenged in a healthy way? Your response dictated whether you continued on with your decision to go to school, or whether to quit. Obviously you decided to stick with it, and here you sit learning OB! Now, let's move on to what you did next.

A **secondary appraisal** only occurs in response to a stressful primary appraisal. It entails an assessment of what might and can be done to reduce the level of perceived stress. During this evaluation, a person considers which coping strategies are available and which ones are most likely to help resolve the situation at hand. For you and your education, you probably decided to take good notes, buy a laptop and get organized, make some friends in the class to share notes with, and whatever other coping mechanisms you designed. Ultimately, the combination of an individual's primary and secondary appraisal influences the choice of coping strategies used to reduce stress.

Coping Strategies Coping strategies are characterized by the specific behaviours and cognitions used to cope with a situation. People use a combination of three approaches to cope with stressors and stress.

1. **Control Strategy** A **control strategy** consists of using behaviours and cognitions to directly anticipate or solve problems. A control strategy has a take-charge tone. Examples include talking to your boss about workload if you feel overwhelmed with your responsibilities. Results from a meta-analysis of 34 studies and more than 4,000 people indicated that control coping was positively related to overall health outcomes.[50]

Primary appraisal

An initial response to stress to determine whether a stressor is irrelevant, positive, or stressful.

Secondary appraisal

A reassessment of a stressor in terms of what might and can be done to reduce stress.

Control strategy

Coping strategy that directly confronts or solves problems.

2. **Escape Strategy** An *escape strategy* onsists of behaviours and cognitions used to avoid or escape situations. Individuals use this strategy when they passively accept stressful situations or avoid them by failing to confront the cause of stress (an obnoxious co-worker, for instance).

Escape strategy

Coping strategy that avoids or ignores stressors and problems.

3. **Symptom Management Strategy** A *symptom management strategy* consists of using methods such as relaxation, meditation, medication, or exercise to manage the symptoms of occupational stress. A vacation, for example, can reduce the symptoms of stress.[51]

Symptom management strategy

Coping strategy that focuses on reducing the symptoms of stress.

Stress Outcomes Theorists contend that stress has psychological/attitudinal, behavioural, cognitive, and physical health outcomes. As discussed earlier, Dr. Selye from Montreal's McGill University has identified the positive effects of certain kinds of stress. However, there is also a large body of research that supports the negative effects of perceived stress on many aspects of our lives. Workplace stress is negatively related to job satisfaction, organizational commitment, organizational citizenship behaviour, positive emotions, performance, and turnover.[52] Research also shows that stress is associated with negative behaviours such as yelling, verbal abuse, and violence toward others. Finally, sufficient evidence supports the conclusion that stress negatively affects our physical health. Stress contributes to the following health problems: lessened ability to ward off illness and infection, high blood pressure, coronary artery disease, tension headaches, back pain, diarrhea, and constipation.[53]

LO 5 **MODERATORS OF OCCUPATIONAL STRESS**

Moderators, once again, are variables that cause the relationships between stressors, perceived stress, and outcomes to be weaker for some people and stronger for others. We will now examine three important moderators: social support, hardiness, and Type A behaviour. Recall the definition of moderator: a variable that causes the relationship between two variables—such as stressors and cognitive appraisal—to be stronger for some people and weaker for others.

Social support

Amount of helpfulness derived from social relationships.

Social Support Talking with a friend can be comforting during times of fear, stress, or loneliness. For a variety of reasons, meaningful social relationships help people do a better job of handling stress. *Social support* is the amount of perceived helpfulness derived from social relationships.

Research shows that people with low social support tend to have poorer cardiovascular and immune system functioning than those with strong social support networks. Further, social support protects against the perception of stress, depression, psychological problems, anxiety, and a variety of other ailments. In contrast, negative social support, which amounts to someone undermining (destabilizing) another person, negatively affects one's mental health.[54] We are well-advised to avoid people who try to undermine us.

Social support research highlights two practical recommendations. First, employees need to be kept informed about external and internal social support systems. Second, participative management programs and company-sponsored activities that make employees feel they are an important part of an extended family can be rich sources of social support.

Hardiness

Personality characteristic that neutralizes stress.

Hardiness Suzanne Kobasa, a behavioural scientist, identified a collection of personality characteristics that neutralize occupational stress. This collection of characteristics, referred to as *hardiness*, includes the ability to perceptually or behaviourally transform negative stressors into positive challenges. Hardiness embraces the personality dimensions of commitment, locus of control, and challenge.[55]

Commitment reflects the extent to which individuals are involved in whatever they are doing. Committed people have a sense of purpose and do not give up under pressure because they tend to invest themselves in the situation. As discussed in Chapter 3, individuals with an *internal locus of control* believe they can influence the events that affect their lives. People possessing this trait are more likely to foresee stressful events, thereby reducing their exposure to anxiety-producing situations. Moreover, their perception of being in control leads "internals" to use proactive coping strategies. *Challenge* is represented by the belief that change is a normal part of life. Hence, change is seen as an opportunity for growth and development, rather than as a threat to security.

Type A Behaviour Pattern According to Meyer Friedman and Ray Rosenman (the cardiologists who isolated the Type A syndrome in the 1950s):

Type A behaviour pattern is an action-emotion complex that can be observed in any person who

Type A behaviour pattern

Aggressively involved in a chronic, determined struggle to accomplish more in less time.

is aggressively involved in a chronic, incessant struggle to achieve more and more in less and less time, and if required to do so, against the opposing efforts of other things or persons.[56]

While labelling Type A behaviour as "hurry sickness," Friedman and Rosenman noted that Type A individuals frequently tend to exhibit most of the behaviours listed below:

- Hurried speech

- Tendency to walk, move, and eat rapidly

- Constant impatience with the rate at which most events take place

- Multi-tasking

- Tendency to interrupt others

- Feel guilty during periods of relaxation

- Tendency to schedule more and more in less and less time[57]

> "Type A behaviour pattern . . . can be observed in any person who is aggressively involved in a chronic, incessant struggle to achieve more and more in less and less time . . ."

Complete the Self-Assessment Exercise, *Where Are You on the Type A–B Behaviour Continuum?*, to determine if you have tendencies toward being a Type A or B personality. Because Type A behaviour is a matter of degree, it is measured on a continuum (scale). This continuum has the hurried, competitive Type A behaviour pattern at one end, and the more relaxed Type B behaviour pattern at the other. Let us now consider the pros and cons of being Type A.

OB research has demonstrated that Type A employees tend to be more productive than their Type B co-workers. For instance, Type A behaviour yielded a significant and positive correlation with 766 students' grade point averages, the quantity and quality of 278 university professors' performance, and sales performance of 222 life insurance brokers.[58]

On the other hand, Type A behaviour is associated with some negative consequences. A meta-analysis of 99 studies revealed that Type A individuals had higher heart rates and blood pressure than Type B people. Type A people also showed greater cardiovascular activity when they encountered the following situations: receipt of positive or negative feedback, receipt of verbal harassment or criticism, and/or tasks requiring mental as opposed to physical work.[59] Unfortunately for Type A individuals, these situations are frequently experienced at work. A second meta-analysis of 83 studies further demonstrated that the hard-driving and competitive aspects of Type A are related to coronary heart disease, but the speed and impatience and job involvement aspects are not. This meta-analysis also showed that feelings of anger, hostility, and aggression were more strongly related to heart disease than was Type A behaviour.[60]

Do these results signal the need for Type A individuals to quit working so hard? Not necessarily. First off, the research indicated that feelings of anger, hostility, and aggression were more detrimental to our health than being Type A. We should all attempt to reduce these negative emotions. Second, researchers have developed stress-reduction techniques to help Type A

LAW AND ETHICS *at Work*

MANAGEMENT CANNOT MANDATE COUNSELLING

How should management deal with an employee who is facing a great deal of stress and is failing to achieve a healthy work–life balance? It's important to remember that management cannot mandate that an employee go to counselling. A manager who notices work is not getting completed is obligated to discuss concerns and expectations with employees, but cannot force them to get help. Further, management may elect to review with employees the various benefits of employment that may include cognitive assistance from a trained therapist. It's important that the employee not feel picked on, isolated, or be identified publicly, as this may cause feelings of prejudice since others are not receiving the same treatment. Failure by management to be sensitive to an employee's rights may cause the employee to claim discrimination or harassment during a vulnerable time. The solution? Clearly provide literature and resources to all employees, not just one. Under the Canadian Human Rights Act–3.1 Anti Harassment Policy Statement, employees have the right to work in a non-harassing work environment.

SOURCE: Canadian Human Rights Commission: www.chrc-ccdp.ca/publications/anti_harassment_part3-en.asp#33

Where Are You on the Type A–B Behaviour Continuum?

INSTRUCTIONS: For each question, indicate the extent to which each statement is true of you.

1 = NOT AT ALL TRUE OF ME
2
3 = NEITHER VERY TRUE NOR VERY UNTRUE OF ME
4
5 = VERY TRUE OF ME

1.	I hate giving up before I'm absolutely sure that I'm licked.	1—2—3—4—5
2.	Sometimes I feel that I shouldn't be working so hard, but something drives me on.	1—2—3—4—5
3.	I thrive on challenging situations. The more challenges I have, the better.	1—2—3—4—5
4.	In comparison to most people I know, I'm very involved in my work.	1—2—3—4—5
5.	It seems as if I need 30 hours a day to finish all the things I'm faced with.	1—2—3—4—5
6.	In general, I approach my work more seriously than most people I know.	1—2—3—4—5
7.	I guess there are some people who can be nonchalant about their work, but I'm not one of them.	1—2—3—4—5
8.	My achievements are considered to be significantly higher than those of most people I know.	1—2—3—4—5
9.	I've often been asked to be an officer of some group or groups.	1—2—3—4—5

Total Score = _____

ARBITRARY NORMS

9–22 = Type B

23–35 = Balanced Type A and Type B

36–45 = Type A

SOURCE: Taken from R.D. Caplan, S. Cobb, J.R.P. French, Jr., R. Van Harrison, and S.R. Pinneau, Jr., *Job Demands and Worker Health* (HEW Publication No. [NIOSH] 75-160) (Washington, DC: US Department of Health, Education, and Welfare, 1975), pp 253–54.

people pace themselves more realistically and achieve better balance in their lives (these are discussed in the next section). Management and team leaders can help Type A people, however, by not overloading them with work despite their apparent eagerness to take an ever increasing workload. Managers and team leaders need to help rather than exploit Type A individuals.

STRESS-REDUCTION TECHNIQUES

How can organizations help stressed employees? Experts recommend that organizations use employee assistance programs, and that individuals use a holistic wellness approach. Let us now consider each of these approaches to stress reduction.[61]

> **Employee assistance programs**
>
> Help employees to resolve personal problems that affect their productivity.

Employee Assistance Programs (EAPs) *Employee assistance programs* consist of a broad array of programs aimed at helping employees to deal with personal problems such as substance abuse, health-related problems, family and marital issues, and other problems that negatively affect their job performance. EAPs are typically provided by employers or in combination with unions. EAPs typically fall under employee benefits, which some employees may not fully understand or feel comfortable engaging in (see Law & Ethics at Work feature box). Alternatively, referral-only EAPs simply provide managers with telephone numbers that they can distribute to employees in need of help.

Employees then pay for these services themselves. It's worth emphasizing here that since not all employees will embrace the EAP concept for various reasons (see Focus on Diversity feature box), managers will need to be sensitive to such resistance by finding an alternative to diffuse employee stress.

Holistic Wellness Approach A *holistic wellness approach* encompasses and goes beyond stress reduction by advocating that individuals strive for "a harmonious and productive balance of physical, mental, and social well-being brought about by the acceptance of one's personal responsibility for developing and adhering to a health promotion program."[62] Five dimensions of a holistic wellness approach are as follows:

> **Holistic wellness approach**
>
> Advocates personal responsibility for healthy living.

1. **Self-responsibility** Take personal responsibility for your wellness (e.g., quit smoking).

2. **Nutritional awareness** Become aware of what you take into your system.

3. **Stress reduction and relaxation** Use techniques to relax and reduce the symptoms of stress.

4. **Physical fitness** Exercise regularly to maintain strength, flexibility, endurance, and a healthy body weight. A review of employee fitness programs indicated that they were positively linked with job performance and job satisfaction.[63]

5. **Environmental sensitivity** Try to identify and eliminate the stressors that are causing your stress.

FOCUS ON Diversity

SOME EMPLOYEES WON'T SEEK COUNSELLING WILLINGLY

As the Canadian workplace continues to see an increase in new Canadian immigrants as well as more integration from Canadian Aboriginal people, it is important for managers to remember that not all cultures will welcome stress reduction efforts from the organization. To some, counselling or therapy is for the sick and it has negative connotations. They would rather find their own way to cope than have it publicly identified by strangers at their workplace. In the case of Aboriginal employees, it was reported in the *Journal of Aboriginal Health* that community and culture are foundations for resiliency when stressed—not talking to someone in HR. In the case of new

Canadians of Chinese descent who have begun working in Canadian organizations, they can find the stress overwhelming just like the rest of us, but may have some resistance to accepting stress reduction techniques. In the Chinese culture, psychological therapy has long been disliked. Admitting you need help is just not done in a face-saving culture. Here in North America, it is becoming more common for firms to offer their employees counselling benefits to help with professional and personal issues.

SOURCES: *Journal of Aboriginal Health*, September 2006, pp 4–7. R. Kreitner and A. Kinicki, *Organizational Behaviour 8th US Edition*, Chapter 18, p 531.

---

1. **Discuss the external and internal forces that create the need for organizational change.** Organizations encounter both external and internal forces for change. There are five key external forces for change: (1) demographic characteristics, (2) technological advancements, (3) customer and market changes, (4) social and political pressures, and (5) organizational crises. Internal forces for change come from human resource problems; managerial preferences, behaviours, or decisions; poorly designed organizational processes or structures; and insufficient resources.

2. **Describe Lewin's change model and the systems model of change.** Lewin developed a three-stage model of planned change that explained how to initiate, manage, and stabilize the change process. The three stages were unfreezing (creating the motivation to change), changing, and stabilizing change through refreezing. A systems model of change takes a big picture perspective of change. It focuses on the interaction among the key components of change. The three main components of change are inputs, target elements of change, and outputs. The target elements of change represent the components of an organization that may be changed. They include organizational arrangements, social factors, methods, and people.

3. **Explain Kotter's eight steps for leading organizational change.** John Kotter believes that organizational change fails for one or more of eight common errors. He proposed eight steps that organizations should follow to overcome these errors. The eight steps are (1) establish a sense of urgency, (2) create the guiding coalition, (3) develop a vision and strategy, (4) communicate the change vision, (5) empower broad-based action, (6) generate short-term wins, (7) consolidate gains and produce more change, and (8) anchor new approaches in the culture.

4. **Summarize and explain the 11 reasons why employees resist change.** Resistance to change is an emotional/behavioural response to real or imagined threats to an established work routine. Eleven reasons why employees resist change are (1) an individual's predisposition toward change, (2) surprise and fear of the unknown, (3) climate of mistrust, (4) fear of failure, (5) loss of status or job security, (6) peer pressure, (7) disruption of cultural traditions or group relationships, (8) personality conflicts, (9) lack of tact or poor timing, (10) non-reinforcing reward systems, and (11) past success.

5. **Compare and contrast the three moderators of occupational stress and identify various kinds of stress-reduction techniques.** Recall that a moderator is a variable that causes the relationship between two variables—such as stressors and cognitive appraisal—to be stronger for some people and weaker for others. People use social support, hardiness, and Type A behaviour to help reduce the impact of stressors that are appraised as harmful, threatening, or challenging. Social support represents the amount of perceived helpfulness derived from social relationships. Hardiness is a collection of personality characteristics that neutralize stress. It includes the characteristics of commitment, locus of control, and challenge. The Type A behaviour pattern is characterized by someone who is aggressively involved in a chronic, determined struggle to accomplish more and more in less and less time. Management can help Type A individuals by not overloading them with work despite their apparent eagerness to take on an ever-increasing workload. Stress-reduced techniques include EAP programs, as well as holistic wellness programs.

Discussion Questions

1. How would you respond to a manager who made the following statement? "Unfreezing is not important; employees will follow my directives."

2. Have you ever gone through a major organizational change at work? If yes, what type of organizational development intervention was used? Was it effective? Explain.

3. Which of the eleven sources of resistance to change mentioned in this chapter do you think is the most common? Which is the most difficult for management to deal with?

4. Why would certain people resist EAP counselling when trying to cope with change?

5. It was mentioned in the chapter that *stress is higher for people with lower socioeconomic status, which represents a combination of income, education level, and occupation*, and that these stressors would become more important in the future. What kinds of reasons can you provide to explain this statement?

Google Searches

1. **Google Search:** "Job Stress In Canada 20____" or "French Workers Release 3M Manager Held Hostage During Labour Dispute" After reading about a few events, determine if stress on the job is real or just imagined in the global workforce. In your opinion, how does added stress impact job performance and job satisfaction?

2. **Google Search:** "Priszm Canadian Income Fund" Which organizations does Priszm represent? According to *Canadian Business Magazine*, profit for Priszm decreased by nearly 50 percent between 2006 and 2007. To hold on to their market share, some experts believe that Priszm should just cut their prices and their sales will increase. In your opinion, is such cost cutting a sustainable business strategy for these companies? What sort of external forces of change are affecting Priszm's profit?

3. **Google Search:** "Loblaw changes name—Walmart watch" or "London Free Press Loblaw changes name 2008" To compete against other companies, Loblaw stores have undergone numerous changes for the last several years. Who is Loblaw's greatest competitor? What sort of changes did Loblaw make? When the initial announcement came from Loblaw about their plans, some stores experienced having almost 50 percent of their current employees hand in their resignation. Why would so many people leave Loblaw prior to the changes taking place?

Experiential Exercise

Why People Resist Change Group Exercise

PURPOSE This exercise is meant to help you to reflect upon those variables that cause employees to become stressed from workplace changes, and as a result experience stress on the job. Approx. Timing: 15 minutes.

ACTIVITY ASSIGNMENT
- Work in small groups.
- Discuss the questions below.

- After 7 minutes of discussion, share your responses with the rest of the class in an open dialogue.

1. Identify at least five possible reasons why employees resist workplace change. Be sure to explain each reason. For example: *Employees don't like change because they are afraid of the unknown. This causes stress because the unknown causes fear—fear of failure, fear of possible loss of a job, fear of added pressure, etc.*

2. Think of at least four possible ways in which employees can show their resistance toward change. For example: *Employees may show force against the change by calling in sick more often. An increase in absenteeism may occur.*

3. List at least three possible techniques that the organization can use through its management, supervisory, and/or team leadership group to help move employees along to accepting the new changes in the workplace. For example: *Management can call a meeting with all employees and show them the financials—nothing like a few pages of actual accounting numbers to present a sobering picture.*

The **Presentation** Assistant

Here are possible topics and corresponding sources related to this chapter that can be further explored by student groups looking for ideas.

	DEFINE STRESS. IS IT BAD FOR THE ORGANIZATION? HOW CAN THE ORGANIZATION HELP REDUCE STRESS?	INTERNAL FORCES OF CHANGE: WHAT FACTORS CAN MAKE AN ORGANIZATION CHANGE? PROVIDE EXAMPLES.	EXTERNAL FORCES OF CHANGE: WHAT FACTORS CAN MAKE AN ORGANIZATION CHANGE? PROVIDE EXAMPLES.
YouTube Videos	• On The Job Stress (vids.myspace.com) • Duke stress expert Dr. Redford Williams on job stress • Stress and job, Gooo out • Work Life Balance—Dr. Dixon	• Workplace Angst On The Job • BBC news—Half of UK forces ready to quit • Should Canada Bailout The Auto Industry?	• Emerging Market Business Trends—for Aditya Birla by Dr. Patrick Dixon • Climate Change and Business: The ROI for Going Green • Canadian Unemployment Rate 200
TV Shows or Movies to Preview	• *The Island* (movie—job satisfaction) • *Pushing Tin* (movie—stress)	• *In Good Company* • *Wall Street* • *Gung Ho*	• *The Corporation* • *An Inconvenient Truth* (movie—Al Gore) • *Monsters, Inc.* (animated movie)
Internet Searches	• The Anxiety Disorders Association of Ontario • www.Canadastudentdebt.ca (student stress) • Canadian Centre for Occupational Health & Safety • www.shepellfgi.com (help for the stressed) • *Don't Sweat The Small Stuff* (by K. & R. Carlson)	• *Finding Flow—The Psychology of Engagement With Everyday Life* (by M. Csikszent-mihalyi) • *Who Moved My Cheese* (by S. Johnson) • Nortel and Air Canada retirees facing pension cuts	• Reinventing the business (Web sites) • Reengineering the organization (Web sites) • Canadian bankruptcy rate 20__ (facts) • *Our Iceberg Is Melting* (by J. Kotter)

Ice Breaker Classroom Activity	• Ask students what sorts of things they worry about on a daily basis that in the long run really don't matter. List them on the board or on an overhead.	• Ask students how they feel about companies like GM, Chrysler, or Nortel that mishandle their own finances and then ask the government for a bailout.	• Ask students to identify what world-changing events have occurred in the business world over the last 18 months.

OB In Action Case Study

Eastman Kodak

Background

If you look on the corporate Web site for Eastman Kodak, they explain the history of their company in the following statement: *With the slogan "you press the button, we do the rest," George Eastman put the first simple camera into the hands of a world of consumers in 1888. In so doing, he made a cumbersome and complicated process easy to use and accessible to nearly everyone.* There was a time when the word Kodak was synonymous with cameras—its respected long history made it a well-known brand name.

But times change and even 100+ years of being in business isn't enough to keep the forces of change away from the Kodak Corporation.

External Forces of Change

Eastman Kodak Company was a very strong market leader in the 1970s. Kodak used the export strategy of designing and producing products in several plants for the U.S. market, and shipping them to domestic and foreign customers, including Canada. However, Kodak began losing its strong leadership position as competition increased from the Japanese.

One of its problem areas of business, for which it was best known to the public, was its photographic products. The Japanese came out with the 35-millimetre camera, while Kodak ignored the market for too long and gave the first mover advantage to the Japanese companies. Kodak also unsuccessfully spent years and millions of dollars to develop an instant camera to compete with Polaroid, and got sued in the process for patent infringements. In the film area, it was losing market share to Fuji and other companies.

On top of the heavy competition, the price of silver rose dramatically. Kodak was in a crisis, because silver was a critical raw material in its photographic products. In the age of the digital camera, Kodak's change was designed to keep the company competitive in the future.

Internal Forces of Change

Top managers identified three major factors contributing to problems at Kodak. First, internal operating costs were too high. Second, information at the bottom of the operation was not being shared throughout the company, and managers were not being held accountable for performance. Third, strategic planning was developed by staff specialists but not implemented by the line managers. In other words, the planning process was not working. On the basis of these factors, the company decided to restructure itself from a functional departmentation to a divisional departmentation, which it believed would be more responsive to the global environment. The next decision was how to plan and implement the departmental change. Managers, concerned about making the reorganization a success, decided to use participative management to implement the change.

Fourteen months of intensive preparation and planning took place as teams of managers throughout the layers of the organization were brought in to take part in the process so that the new design became their plan, rather than someone else's. The next step was to appoint people to the top jobs in the new organization. Appointments were based first on assessment of talent, and only then on seniority. Most of the top 150 managers involved in the process had new jobs. But most importantly, the large majority of managers supported the reorganization regardless of their new jobs.

Implementing Change

Kodak's reorganization began with a 12 percent reduction of employees over a two-year period. Most left voluntarily for other jobs or retired. Over time, the number of managers was reduced by about 25 percent, and Kodak stopped its habit of promoting managers from within. Over a five-year period, nearly 70 percent of the key managers were new to their jobs.

Next, nearly 30 independent business units were created with the responsibility for developing and implementing their own strategy and worldwide profit performance. The export strategy changed, depending on the business unit, all the way to the direct investment level. The business units were grouped into traditional imaging business, image-intensive information technology, and plastic polymers. Kodak acquired Sterling Drug and expanded into pharmaceuticals as an additional business group.

Manufacturing and R&D were split up and distributed in the business units to achieve better focus on customers, markets, and technology. The relationship between the business units and the different geographic areas where Kodak conducted its business was articulated: in simple terms, each business unit was responsible for developing the strategic thrust of the business, while the geographic unit was responsible for implementing the thrust.

Each business unit was subject to periodic evaluation of its earnings and value. Each was required to generate a return that exceeded an internally established cost of equity, reflecting its own level of risk and market conditions. Businesses unable to attain the required rate of return were put on probation, and if they did not reach the goal, they were taken apart or separated from the rest of the company.

Kodak's reorganization was successful by most measures. It improved its financial, productivity, and market share performance. Kodak's performance improved at a rate four times the U.S. average for several years in a row.

Case Update

Toward the end of the fourth quarter in 2008, the 128-year-old photography company saw its stock fall to its lowest price in at least 34 years, after cutting its yearly sales and profit projections twice. All salary increases planned for 2009 were suspended. The cuts kindled doubt about the success of current CEO Antonio Perez's four-year restructuring that saw 28,000 jobs eliminated and money invested more in digital products as demand waned for traditional film. In early 2009, Kodak continued to bash on with plans by merging with Bowe Bell + Howell; their stocks decreased 5.9 percent after the merger was announced.

SOURCE: R.N. Lussier, *Human Relations in Organizations: Applications and Skill Building* (New York: McGraw-Hill Ryerson, 2005), pp 503–4.

Discussion Questions

1. What kind of forces led to the changes made by Kodak?
2. Which of the methods for overcoming resistance to change did Kodak focus on throughout its change?
3. Why didn't Kodak just dictate change from the top CEO position? Didn't they waste 14 precious months?

4. Did Kodak follow the steps in Lewin's change model?

5. There is no evidence in the case that Kodak included non-managerial personnel in their planning—do you see this as a strength or weakness? Explain.

⬇ Ethical OB Dilemma

I Think My Boss Is Sick—What Should I Do?

Paul Holkin was a 40-something rising star in the publishing world, sought after for top positions at major book publishers in Montreal. In meetings with authors, business associates, and employees, he was a take-charge executive. No one realized that sometimes at the end of the day, Mr Holkin would sit at his desk, exhausted, and think about jumping out the window . . .

Coping with employee depression is increasingly on the minds of workplace managers. But what happens when the boss is the one who is stressed and/or suffering from depression? The repercussions on a business, its employees, and stockholders can be enormous if the illness interferes with a leader's performance.

Securities laws require public companies to disclose anything that materially affects the company, and that can theoretically include serious health problems of key executives. Case in point: the mysterious illness of Steven Jobs in January 2009 caused him to leave Apple for six months. In 2004, Jobs battled pancreatic cancer. Every time Jobs leaves Apple, stocks fall.

SOURCE: J. Golson, "Apple Stocks Drop 52 Week Low," *Industry Standard*, January 14, 2009, http://www.thestandard.com/news/2009/01/14/apple-stock-rocked-steve-jobs-medical-leave.

Assume that your boss had a nervous breakdown and is now suffering from depression. Your boss is trying to withhold this information from others. Consider the following statements. Which one best describes how you would respond?

1. "Nothing. The boss's emotional or mental condition is none of my business."
2. "I would not say a word because I could be punished for saying anything."
3. "I would discuss the issue only with my boss and encourage my boss to get help through the EAP program." Explain your rationale.
4. "I would discuss the issue with someone from the human resources department and how it is stressing me out." Explain your rationale.
5. "I would respond differently." Explain.

Visit www.mcgrawhillconnect.ca to register.

McGraw-Hill Connect™—Available 24/7 with instant feedback so you can study when you want, how you want, and where you want. Take advantage of the Study Plan—an innovative tool that helps you customize your learning experience. You can diagnose your knowledge with pre- and post-tests, identify the areas where you need help, search the entire learning package for content specific to the topic you're studying, and add these resources to your personalized study plan. Visit www.mcgrawhillconnect.ca to register—take practice quizzes, search the e-book, and much more.

CHAPTER 14

Developing a
Global Organization

*Visa Woes?
Immigration Quotas?
No Problem in
Canada—Bring Your
Company (and Jobs)
to Us!*

Foreign companies experiencing immigration quotas and visa bans in their own country are finding that Canada may be the answer to their problems. It has been reported that every year, over 90,000 foreign workers enter Canada temporarily to help Canadian employers address skill shortages in this country, and to also assist firms to get around immigration quotas in their own country. According to Lowe and Company, a Vancouver-based law firm specializing in Canadian immigration and work visas, foreign-trained workers are supported by Citizenship and Immigration Canada and

Human Resources Development Canada to ensure these workers enhance economic growth in Canada and help create more opportunities for all Canadian job seekers. This strategy must be attractive, because it has already lured Microsoft beyond its Redmond, Washington head office to open up a prestigious software development office in the Vancouver area.

Back in 2007, Microsoft Corp. tried pushing for an expanded H-1B visa program that would have let the company hire more foreign programmers at its U.S. office, but the immigration reform bill was rejected by Washington, DC. H-1B visas let foreigners work in the U.S. for several years and are capped at 65,000 per year for the entire U.S. In comparison, Canada doesn't specify the number of skilled foreign workers allowed into the country under work permits, and makes it easier for foreign workers to gain status as permanent residents and possibly become Canadian citizens, according to lawyer David Cohen of Montreal-based Campbell Cohen.

The result? Microsoft Canada Co. opened their first development centre in early 2008. According to company spokesperson Lou Gellos, Microsoft Canada is forecasting that the 900 people currently employed by the company will double in years to come. When asked why Microsoft considered Canada for this centre, the company cited three reasons: Vancouver's close proximity to Redmond (only three hours by car), its status as "a global gateway with a diverse population," and a Canadian office allows the company to recruit and retain highly skilled people from around the world affected by immigration issues in the U.S.

The centre is indeed a multi-cultural experience, with engineers representing 45 different countries and speaking 15 distinct languages. With this model of operation, Microsoft is able to recruit the best employees from around the world. Microsoft believes that having a diverse workforce enriches the company and allows it to serve its globally diverse customer base more effectively.

Sharif Khan, Vice-President of Human Resources, spent a number of years outside of Canada as Senior HR Manager on the Global Leadership team for Europe, the Middle East, and Africa. Being a visible minority member allows Sharif to have a personal sensitivity for Microsoft's ongoing diversity development needs, as well as its efforts to evolve into a truly global organization.

SOURCES: Microsoft website: http://www.microsoft.com/presspass/press/2007/jul07/07-05MSExpandVancouverPR.mspx; U.S. Citizen and Immigration services website: http://www.edmontonsun.com/News/Canada/2008/09/10/pf-6725156.html

"We have long advocated that Canada would be a wonderful place to locate Microsoft development," says Phil Sorgen, president of Microsoft Canada.

LEARNING OBJECTIVES

After reading this chapter, you should be able to:

LO 1 Define *ethnocentrism*.

LO 2 **Explain** what Hofstede concluded about applying Canadian management theories in other countries.

LO 3 **Differentiate** between five cultural perspectives relevant to individuals becoming cross-culturally competent.

LO 4 **Summarize** what the GLOBE project has taught us about leadership.

LO 5 **Synthesize** the four stages of the foreign assignment cycle by identifying an OB trouble spot for each stage.

We often hear comments about the global economy. On one level, it seems so grand, so vague, and so distant; but on another level, it is here, it is now, and it is very personal. For example, put yourself into this scenario:

It's Saturday morning and your alarm clock (made in China) buzzes—it's time to get up. After driving your Japanese Toyota RAV (made in Woodstock Ontario) to TD Canada Trust (that has offices around the world) to deposit your paycheque from London Life (owned by Power Financial Group, a trans-national global organization), you decide to go to Tim Horton's to get a double-double (once co-owned by Wendy's International) before shopping at the Hudson's Bay/Zeller stores (now owned by NRDC, the same company that owns Lord & Taylor's in the U.S.). You notice that your Nokia cell phone (made in Finland) is ringing. It's your girlfriend calling from India. She's using her Blackberry (made in Canada) while trekking through the Himalayas. Finally, it's time to have lunch at your favourite local pub and you order a Labatt Blue beer (now co-owned by Belgium-based Interbrew and Brazil's AmBev). After lunch, it's time to finish shopping for your apartment furnishings at IKEA (from Sweden). It's late and you have to hurry home to begin e-learning for a strategic management exam (from the University of Manchester, England) with your new classmate, Aadon (who is Australian).

Yes, welcome to the global economy! And you are a big part of it—just check the labels on the products you buy and the clothes you wear. Goods, money, and talent are crossing international borders at an accelerating pace. To illustrate the point, consider the persistent labour shortages in certain industries throughout Canada over the last few decades and how Canadian employers have had to recruit potential candidates from India, the United Kingdom, and South Africa. Alberta, whose booming oil economy was especially strapped for skilled workers in 2008, attended the first ever Opportunities Canada Expo held in the United Kingdom. According to Canadian participants at the Expo, which included the City of Calgary, Calgary Economic Development, and Alberta Employment and Immigration department, it was a great success and yielded a large pool of qualified candidates.[1] For better or for worse, even more economic globalization lies ahead.

From an OB standpoint, continued globalization means an exponential increase in both cross-cultural interactions and the demand for managers, supervisors, and employees who are comfortable and effective working with people from other countries and cultures. Competition for businesses and those seeking well-paying jobs in the global economy promises to be very tough. The purpose of this chapter is to help you meet the challenge.

SOURCE: Courtesy of Vahan Shirvanian

Developing a Global Mind-Set

Managing in a global economy is as much about patterns of thinking and behaviour as it is about trade agreements, goods and services, and currency exchange rates. Extended periods in a single dominant culture establish assumptions about how things are and should be. Global employees, whether they work at home for a foreign-owned company or actually work in a foreign country, need to develop a global mind-set (involving open-mindedness, adaptability, and a strong desire to learn).[2]

This section encourages a global mind-set by defining societal culture and contrasting it with organizational culture, discussing ethnocentrism, exploring ways to become a global employee, and examining the applicability of Canadian management theories in other cultures.

A MODEL OF SOCIETAL AND ORGANIZATIONAL CULTURES

Societal culture involves shared meanings that we are generally not consciously aware of because they involve *taken-for-granted assumptions* about how we should perceive, think, act, and feel.[3] Cultural anthropologist Edward T. Hall put it this way:

Societal culture

Socially derived shared meanings that are taken-for-granted assumptions about how to perceive, act, think, and feel.

Since much of culture operates outside our awareness, frequently we don't even know what we know. We pick . . . [expectations and assumptions] up in the cradle. We unconsciously learn what to notice and what not to notice, how to divide time and space, how to walk and talk and use our bodies, how to behave as men or women, how to relate to other people, how to handle responsibility, whether experience is seen as whole or fragmented. This applies to all people. The Chinese or the Japanese or the Arabs are as unaware of their assumptions as we are of our own. We each assume that they're part of human nature. What we think of as "mind" is really internalized culture.[4]

Peeling the Cultural Onion Culture is difficult to grasp because it is multi-layered. International management experts Fons Trompenaars (from the Netherlands) and Charles Hampden-Turner (from Britain) offer this instructive analogy in their landmark book, *Riding the Waves of Culture*:

Culture comes in layers, like an onion. To understand it you have to unpeel it layer by layer. On the outer layer are the products of culture, like the soaring skyscrapers of Toronto, pillars of private power, with congested public streets between them. These are expressions of deeper values and norms in a society that are not directly visible (values such as upward mobility, "the more-the-better," status, material success). The layers of values and norms are deeper within the "onion," and are more difficult to identify.[5]

Merging Societal and Organizational Cultures   As illustrated in Figure 14.1, culture influences organizational behaviour in two ways. First, employees bring their societal culture to work with them in the form of customs and language. Organizational culture, a by-product of societal culture, in turn affects the individual's values, ethics, attitudes, assumptions, and expectations.[6] The term societal culture is used here instead of national culture because the boundaries of many modern nation-states were not drawn along cultural lines. The former Soviet Union, for example, included 15 republics and more than 100 ethnic nationalities, many with their own distinct language.[7] Meanwhile, English-speaking Canadians in Vancouver are culturally closer to Americans in Seattle than to their French-speaking compatriots in Quebec. Societal culture is shaped by the various environmental factors listed in the left-hand side of Figure 14.1.

Once inside the organization's sphere of influence, the individual is further affected by the *organization's* culture. Mixing of societal and organizational cultures can produce interesting dynamics in multinational companies. When Proctor & Gamble Canada Inc. was selected as one of Canada's Best Diversity Employers, it had 387 full-time employees, of which only 14 percent were visible minorities. However, it introduced one of the most dedicated diversity programs in the country, including: (1) requiring all employees to complete mandatory diversity training, (2) operating a special diversity training program for managers, (3) attending post-secondary educational events to recruit visible minority students, and (4) hosting several employee network teams for Asian, French, lesbian/gay/bisexual/transgender, Black, and Latino groups.[8] Trinh Lam, a P&G employee, talks about her experience:

The ALC (Asian Learning Conference—an in-house training forum for Asian employees) was a great opportunity to network with my Asian co-workers and learn from their unique experiences.

Even though Trinh is from an Asian culture, it was still helpful to network with other Asian employees at P&G, since they are all products of different societal cultures within the large Asian continent, but working in the same organizational culture.

When managing people at work, the individual's societal culture, the organizational culture, and any interaction between the two need to be taken into consideration.[9] For example, Itsuo Naniwa was once a banker in Canada. He returned to his native Japan in 1990 to take over the family business when his father, the founder, fell ill. Mr. Naniwa assumed the role of president of Sparta Co. Ltd., the small garment-making company, but faced the difficulty of running it during one of the worst economic times in modern Japan. He struggled to keep it open. Unlike the western culture, where corporate bankruptcies are dealt with swiftly during troubled times, the idea of letting a company go under, even if it is grossly inefficient, runs against the grain in the Japanese culture and against what his father would have wanted. So Mr. Naniwa had to put aside the western business values he was trained on and consider the effects that going out of business would have on his ten Japanese employees (whose average age was 65, while one was 80). Mr. Naniwa's waited until they reached retirement age and then replaced them with younger people.[10]

▶ FIGURE 14.1   Cultural Influences on Organizational Behaviour

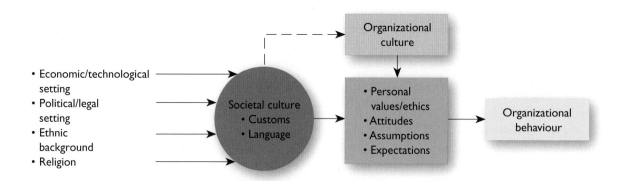

SOURCES: Adapted from D.R. Fuqua and D.J. Kurpius, "Conceptual Models in Organizational Consultation," *Journal of Counselling & Development,* July/August 1993, pp 602–18; and D.A. Nadler and M.L. Tushman, "Organizational Frame Bending: Principles for Managing Reorientation," *Academy of Management Executive,* August 1989, pp 194–203.

LO 1 ETHNOCENTRISM: REMOVING A CULTURAL ROADBLOCK IN THE GLOBAL ECONOMY

Ethnocentrism, the belief that one's native country, culture, language, and modes of behaviour are superior to all others, has its roots in the dawn of civilization. First identified as a behavioural science concept in 1906, involving the tendency of groups to reject outsiders,[11] the term *ethnocentrism* generally has a more encompassing (national or societal) meaning today. Worldwide evidence of ethnocentrism is plentiful. For example, ethnocentrism led to deadly ethnic cleansing in Bosnia and Kosovo and genocide in the African nations of Rwanda, Burundi, and Sudan.

Ethnocentrism

Belief that one's native country, culture, language, and behaviour are superior.

Less dramatic, but still troublesome, is ethnocentrism within organizational contexts. Experts on the subject have framed the problem this way:

[Ethnocentric managers have] a preference for putting home-country people in key positions everywhere in the world and rewarding them more handsomely for work, along with a tendency to feel that this group is more intelligent, more capable, or more reliable . . . Ethnocentrism is often not attributable to prejudice as much as to inexperience or lack of knowledge about foreign persons and situations. This is not too surprising, since most executives know far more about employees in their home environments. As one executive put it, "At least I understand why our own managers make mistakes. With our foreigners, I never know. The foreign managers may be better. But if I can't trust a person, should I hire him or her just to prove we're multinational?"[12]

Research Insight Research suggests ethnocentrism is bad for business. A survey of 918 companies with home offices in Japan (309), Europe (337), and the United States (272), found ethnocentric staffing and human resource policies to be associated with increased personnel problems. Those problems included recruiting difficulties, high turnover rates, and lawsuits over personnel policies. Among the three regional samples, Japanese companies had the most ethnocentric human resource practices and the most international human resource problems.[13] Current and future employees can effectively deal with ethnocentrism through education, greater cross-cultural awareness, international experience, and a conscious effort to value cultural diversity.[14] Take a moment and complete the Self-Assessment Exercise to identify whether you have tendencies toward ethnocentric behaviour.

BECOMING A GLOBAL EMPLOYEE

On any given day in our global economy, a Canadian employee can interact with colleagues from several different countries or cultures, and never leave the office. For instance, at PolyGram, the British music company, the top 33 managers are from 15 different countries.[15] As we discussed in the opening chapter vignette, Microsoft Canada has hired a person to head up the HR department that oversees the culturally diverse Vancouver development office, whose workforce comes from 45 different countries and speaks 15 different languages. At both PolyGram and Microsoft, developing a global mind-set and sensitivity toward cross-cultural skills is critical for these individuals to find success (see Skills & Best Practices feature box).

Skills & Best Practices

Geekcorps Volunteers Gain Valuable International Experience

Matt Berg spent his first few post-college years like any other geek: coding software under the glow of fluorescent lights. But today the 28-year-old rigs makeshift radio towers near the sands of Tombouctou in Africa. As a volunteer for Geekcorps, he's part of an IT-savvy army that's bringing technology infrastructure to developing nations around the world. "I have always been interested in how technology can make people's lives better," he says.

Since it was launched in 2000, . . . Geekcorps has become a sort of Peace Corps for young tech workers. A division of the International Executive Service Corps, the non-profit organization has deployed more than 80 volunteers to develop software in Vietnam, assemble computer networks in Romania, and help the Lebanese IT industry increase international exports. Volunteers typically take four-month sabbaticals from their jobs, and Geekcorps provides housing, airfare, and a stipend for meals and incidental expenses.

SOURCE: Excerpted from D. Kushner, "A Peace Corps for the Tech Set," *Business 2.0*, March 2006; http://money.cnn.com/magazines/business2/business2_

How Strong Is Your Potential For Ethnocentrism?

INSTRUCTIONS: If you were born and raised or have spent most of your life in *Canada*, select one number from the following scale for each item. If you are from a different country or culture, substitute the country/language you most closely identify with for the terms *Canadian* and *English* or *French*, and then rate each item.

1 = STRONGLY DISAGREE
2 = DISAGREE
3 = NEUTRAL
4 = AGREE
5 = STRONGLY AGREE

1.	I was raised in a way that was [truly] Canadian.	1—2—3—4—5
2.	Compared to how much I criticize other cultures, I criticize Canadian culture less.	1—2—3—4—5
3.	I am proud of Canadian culture.	1—2—3—4—5
4.	Canadian culture has had a positive effect on my life.	1—2—3—4—5
5.	I believe that my children should read, write, and speak [only] English or French.	1—2—3—4—5
6.	I go to places where people are Canadian.	1—2—3—4—5
7.	I admire people who are Canadian.	1—2—3—4—5
8.	I would prefer to live in a Canadian community.	1—2—3—4—5
9.	At home, I eat [only] Canadian food.	1—2—3—4—5
10.	Overall, I am Canadian.	1—2—3—4—5

SCORING

10–23 = Low potential for ethnocentrism

24–36 = Moderate potential for ethnocentrism

37–50 = High potential for ethnocentrism

SOURCE: Adapted from and survey items excerpted from J.L. Tsai, Y-W Ying, and P.A. Lee, "The Meaning of 'Being Chinese' and 'Being American': Variation among Chinese American Young Adults," *Journal of Cross-Cultural Psychology*, May 2000, pp 302–32.

Even during times of economic slowdown, Canadian employees have gone abroad in record numbers, with more than 60,000 reporting a place of employment outside Canada, says Statistics Canada in its 2006 census. According to the *Canadian HR Reporter,* it is predicted that "once the economy recovers, so too will the demand for Canadian expertise in the areas of infrastructure engineering, mining, transportation, and IT—industries that are expected to do remarkably well in the coming year as global economic stimulus packages begin to gain traction."[16] Developing skilled employees who move comfortably from culture to culture takes time. Consider, for example, this comment by the head of Gillette, who wants twice as many global managers on the payroll. "We could try to hire the best and the brightest, but it's the experience with Gillette that we need. About half of our [expatriates] are now on their fourth country—[gaining] that kind of experience. It takes 10 years to make the kind of Gillette manager I'm talking about."[17]

Importantly, these global skills will help employees in a culturally diverse country such as Canada do a more effective job on a day-to-day basis.

LO 2

THE HOFSTEDE STUDY: HOW WELL DO CANADIAN MANAGEMENT THEORIES APPLY IN OTHER COUNTRIES?

The short answer to this important question is: *not very well*. This answer derives from a landmark study conducted nearly 30 years ago by Dutch researcher Geert Hofstede. His unique cross-cultural comparison of 116,000 IBM employees from 53 countries worldwide focused on four cultural dimensions:

- **Power distance** How much inequality does someone expect in social situations?[18]

- **Individualism-collectivism** How loosely or closely is the person socially bonded?

- **Masculinity-femininity** Does the person embrace stereotypically competitive, performance-oriented masculine traits, or nurturing, relationship-oriented feminine traits?

- **Uncertainty avoidance** How strongly does the person desire highly structured situations?

Jackie Fouse is CFO of Alcon, one of the world's biggest producers of eye-care products. Before taking the job at the $4.4 billion global manufacturer, she had spent nine years working abroad, adding subtle skills like cultural sensitivity to her management expertise. Of her global experience at Nestlé and Swissair, Fouse, who is fluent in French and German, says, "Everything else being equal—educational background, years of experience—that was the thing more than any other that set me apart from other people."

The Canadian sample ranked at a moderate level on power distance and uncertainty avoidance, and at a high level on individualism and masculinity.[19]

The high degree of variation among cultures led Hofstede to two major conclusions:

1. Management theories and practices need to be adapted to local cultures. This is particularly true for made-in-Canada management theories, such as Mintzberg's organizational structure, and Japanese team management practices. *There is no one best way to manage across cultures.*[20]

2. Cultural arrogance is a luxury individuals, companies, and nations can no longer afford in a global economy.

Becoming Cross-Culturally Competent

LO 3

Cultural anthropologists believe we can learn interesting and valuable lessons by comparing one culture with another. Over the years, researchers have suggested many dimensions to help contrast and compare the world's rich variety of cultures. We discuss five cultural perspectives in this section, which are especially relevant to present and aspiring global employees: (1) basic cultural dimensions and cultural intelligence, (2) individualism versus collectivism, (3) high-context and low-context cultures, (4) monochronic and polychronic time orientation, and (5) cross-cultural leadership. Separately or together, these cultural distinctions can become huge stumbling blocks when doing business across cultures.

BASIC CULTURAL DIMENSIONS—CULTURAL INTELLIGENCE NEEDED

An important qualification needs to be made at this time. All of the cultural differences in this chapter and elsewhere need to be viewed as tendencies and patterns rather than as absolutes. As soon as one falls into the trap of assuming all Italians are this, and all Koreans will do that, and so on, potentially useful generalizations become mindless stereotypes. It is possible, for example, for different cultures to have a similar viewpoint on a topic. This is illustrated by the number of countries that are embracing corporate social responsibility, especially in Europe (see Law & Ethics at Work feature box).

Avoiding stereotype thinking and other possible errors in judgment can be minimized through greater awareness gained by having a global mindset. For example, a pair of professors with extensive foreign work experience advise, "As teachers, researchers, and managers in cross-cultural contexts, we need to recognize that our original characterizations of other cultures are best guesses that we need to modify as we gain more experience."[21] Consequently, they argue, we will be better prepared to deal with foreseeable cultural paradoxes. By paradox, they mean there are always exceptions to the rule: individuals who do not fit the expected cultural pattern. A good example is the head of Canon.

Cultural intelligence

The ability to make a decision, enact change, and accurately interpret ambiguous cross-cultural situations that are consistent with cultural expectations.

"By Japanese CEO standards, Canon, Inc.'s Fujio Mitarai is something of an anomaly (variation). For starters, he's fast and decisive—a far cry from the consensus builders who typically run Japan, Inc."[22]

When we talk about a global mindset, what do we mean? Basically, we are referring to the ability to look at a situation from multiple perspectives. For business to succeed on a global basis, we need employees who are able to have relationships with people who are different from themselves. From a management perspective, it becomes necessary to train business leaders to influence people who are very different from themselves. In a diverse country such as Canada, it encompasses having the intellectual ability to understand how motivation varies among people, the psychological ability to appreciate diversity, and the social capacity to build trusting relationships with people who are different from oneself.[23] Bottom line: the Canadian workforce needs to have cultural intelligence.

Cultural intelligence can be defined as the ability to make a decision, enact (ratify) change, and accurately interpret ambiguous cross-cultural situations that are consistent with cultural expectations. Those interested in developing their cultural intelligence need to first develop their emotional intelligence (EI), discussed in Chapter 3. Briefly, this is when a person

LAW AND ETHICS *at Work*

CORPORATE SOCIAL RESPONSIBILITY BECOMING MAINSTREAM CONCEPT

Although values and attitudes can differ from culture to culture, there is a global movement reshaping business conduct that relates to corporate social responsibility (CSR). CSR has been a priority in the United Kingdom and the rest of Europe for over twenty years, while North American businesses have been trying to catch up ever since the early mega-accounting scandals of Enron and Worldcom. The idea that organizations have an obligation to consider the interests of customers, employees, shareholders, communities, and the environment is being attributed in part to greater public awareness of climate change, product safety issues, and rapid industrialization. CSR is a sweeping trend affecting organizations around the globe as various countries adopt CSR legislation. Canadian organizations looking to do business in Europe, Great Britain, or the U.S. need to be aware of the different laws and their responsibilities to comply. For example, this would be reflected in supporting fundamental human rights legislation abroad, subscribing to emission controls under the Kyoto Protocol, or adhering to the Sarbanes-Oxley Act that holds corporate officers criminally responsible for their company's financial reporting errors.

SOURCE: B. Kniss, "Corporate Social Responsibility Becoming Mainstream Concept," *Canadian HR Reporter – Global HR*, December 15, 2008, p 20.

has empathy for others and holds the capacity to understand and manage one's own emotions. It includes self awareness, social awareness, and relationship management. These EI characteristics fit nicely into the kind of mind-set needed to have cultural intelligence. People who have high EI have the flexibility to effectively deal with different people, perspectives, and personalities. Managers with high cultural intelligence have the capacity to understand cultural distinctions and thus lead in a culturally appropriate fashion. Cultural intelligence enables the globally-minded employee to transfer emotional intelligence to different cultural contexts.[24]

Nine Basic Cultural Dimensions from the GLOBE Project Project GLOBE (Global Leadership and Organizational Behaviour Effectiveness) is a massive and ongoing attempt to "develop an empirically based theory to describe, understand, and predict the impact of specific cultural variables on leadership and organizational processes and the effectiveness of these processes."[25] You will recall our brief discussion of this research in Chapter 10; in this section and further on in this chapter, we provide a more in-depth review of the research results.

Since the project was launched in Calgary, Alberta, in 1994, GLOBE has evolved into a network of more than 160 scholars from 62 societies. Most of the researchers are native to the particular cultures they study, thus greatly enhancing the credibility of the results. During the first two phases of the GLOBE project, a list of nine basic cultural dimensions was developed and statistically validated. Translated questionnaires based on the nine dimensions were administered to thousands of managers in the banking, food, and telecommunications industries around the world to build a database. Results are being published on a regular basis.[26] Much work and many more years are needed to attain the project's goal, as stated above. In the meantime, we have been given a comprehensive, valid, and up-to-date tool for better understanding cross-cultural similarities and differences.

The nine cultural dimensions from the GLOBE project are:

1. **Power distance** How much unequal distribution of power should there be in organizations and society?

2. **Uncertainty avoidance** How much should people rely on social norms and rules to avoid uncertainty and limit unpredictability?

3. **Institutional collectivism** How much should leaders encourage and reward loyalty to the social unit, as opposed to the pursuit of individual goals?

4. **In-group collectivism** How much pride and loyalty should individuals have for their family or organization?

5. **Gender egalitarianism** How much effort should be put into minimizing gender discrimination and role inequalities?

6. **Assertiveness** How confrontational and dominant should individuals be in social relationships?

7. **Future orientation** How much should people delay gratification by planning and saving for the future?

8. **Performance orientation** How much should individuals be rewarded for improvement and excellence?

9. **Humane orientation** How much should society encourage and reward people for being kind, fair, friendly, and generous?[27]

Notice how the two forms of collectivism, along with the dimensions of power distance and uncertainty avoidance, correspond to the similarly-labelled variables in Hofstede's classic study discussed earlier. It is important to understand how Hofsteded and the GLOBE findings are related.

Where did Canada rank on these dimensions?

- **High:** performance, future orientation, and individualism

- **Moderately High:** assertiveness, uncertainty avoidance, and humane orientation

- **Moderately Low:** power distance

- **Low:** in-group collectivism and gender differentiation[28]

Remember, the GLOBE project is an attempt to try and understand, as well as predict, cultural behaviours as they exist within organizations as a whole. Therefore, the broad profile mentioned above for Canada is for its organizations—not to be confused with the characteristics and values of the many subcultures of people that live within Canada. A case in point would be the potentially contrasting values of Canadian Aboriginal people, Francophone people, and newly landed immigrants to Canada. We explore this in more detail over the next few sections.

Bringing the GLOBE Cultural Dimensions to Life A fun and worthwhile exercise is to reflect on your own cultural roots, family traditions, and belief system and develop a personal cultural profile, using as many of the GLOBE dimensions as possible. For example, which of the GLOBE cultural dimensions relates to the following biographical sketch?

Matthew is a 21-year-old student who has put his 4th year of studies on hold to volunteer as a classroom teacher in an elementary school located in

Inuvik, Northwest Territories. Like many his age, he has no money saved for a rainy day; in fact, he's in debt from his first three years at school. Matthew says, "I'm not sure what I want to do with my life. I've spent three years studying theory, but how is that helping me? Listen, I'm still young, so I think I'll travel for one year and see the world. I'll figure it out while I'm gone. For now I might as well enjoy travelling, see the world, and be happy. I can worry about paying off my debt later."

If you said "future orientation," you're right! Indeed, his behaviour is counter to Canadians who are notorious when it comes to saving (see Table 14.1). Matthew scores low on future orientation and thus has inadequate savings for the future.

Let's take another example, except this time we'll relate it to an organization. Which of the GLOBE cultural dimensions relate to the following scenario?

Sergio is a citizen of Spain working in Canada on a contract basis for two years as a software engineer for ABC Inc. He is the team leader for a cross-functional self-managed team. Sergio is having difficulty with a decision that was made prior to his arrival. Currently, the office asks the team for production paperwork to be completed prior to starting a project . . . but he would prefer to file the paperwork after the project is started, once the specifics of the job are known and details are assigned. Sergio hesitates to disagree with the current process. He doesn't want to take problems to his boss for fear of looking incompetent, and instead decides to not file the paperwork as requested. He begins experiencing interpersonal conflict from members of the team who believe he isn't doing his job; as a result he is stressed. "I don't know what to do!" says Sergio.

In this case, Sergio comes from a high-power distance culture like Spain, but is working in a moderately low-power distance culture like Canada. He doesn't want to offend his boss or be perceived as violating chain of command by not following formal process, so instead he is stressed and paralyzed to act. In Spain, he would be expected to take problems to his boss and follow the chain of command of formal authority; that is what he is used to. In Canada, he has been given the position and authority of being a team member, and management expects him to be empowered and lead the cross-functional team. Sergio would benefit from a face-to-face meeting with the department manager to review the concept of shared decision making and empowerment, and re-examine the functions of being a team leader.

TABLE 14.1 Countries Ranking Highest and Lowest on the GLOBE Cultural Dimensions

DIMENSION	HIGHEST	LOWEST
Power distance	Morocco, Argentina, Thailand, Spain, Russia	Denmark, Netherlands, South Africa—Black sample, Israel, Costa Rica
Uncertainty avoidance	Switzerland, Sweden, German—former West, Denmark, Austria	Russia, Hungary, Bolivia, Greece, Venezuela
Institutional collectivism	Sweden, South Korea, Japan, Singapore, Denmark	Greece, Hungary, Germany—former East, Argentina, Italy
In-group collectivism	Iran, India, Morocco, China, Egypt	Denmark, Sweden, New Zealand, Netherlands, Finland
Gender egalitarianism	Hungary, Poland, Slovenia, Denmark, Sweden	South Korea, Egypt, Morocco, India, China
Assertiveness	Germany—former East, Austria, Greece, U.S., Spain	Sweden, New Zealand, Switzerland, Japan, Kuwait
Future orientation	Singapore, Switzerland, Netherlands Canada—English speaking, Denmark	Russia, Argentina, Poland, Italy, Kuwait
Performance orientation	Singapore, Hong Kong, New Zealand, Taiwan, U.S.	Russia, Argentina, Greece, Venezuela, Italy
Humane orientation	Philippines, Ireland, Malaysia, Egypt, Indonesia	Germany—former West, Spain, France, Singapore, Brazil

SOURCE: Adapted from M. Javidan and R.J. House, "Cultural Acumen for the Global Manager: Lessons from Project GLOBE," *Organizational Dynamics*, Spring 2001, pp 289–305.

Country Profiles and Practical Implications How do different countries score on the GLOBE cultural dimensions? Data from 18,000 managers yielded the profiles in Table 14.1. A quick overview shows a great deal of cultural diversity around the world. But thanks to the nine GLOBE dimensions, we have a more precise understanding of *how* cultures vary. Closer study reveals telling cultural *patterns*, or cultural fingerprints, for nations. Australia's moderate scores on gender egalitarianism explain why there is still evidence of gender bias in that country (see Focus on Diversity feature box). Switzerland's high scores on uncertainty avoidance and future orientation help explain its centuries of political neutrality and world-renowned banking industry. Singapore is known as a great place to do business because it is clean and safe, and its people are well-educated and hardworking. This is no surprise, considering Singapore's high scores on institutional collectivism, future orientation, and performance orientation. In contrast, Russia's low scores on future orientation and performance orientation could foreshadow a slower-than-hoped-for transition from a centrally planned economy to free enterprise capitalism. These illustrations bring us to an important practical lesson: *Knowing the cultural tendencies of foreign business partners and competitors can give you a strategic competitive advantage.*

In 2007, professor Mansour Javidan spoke about the GLOBE study to a group of business and HR professionals. Javidan suggested that the next step for developing business leaders who can succeed in multiple cultures is to teach people how to manage others who are culturally different from themselves.[29] Global organizations can use tools such as executive coaching, 360 degree evaluations, professional development courses, and role-playing simulations to help participants become more culturally sensitive. In addition, contemporary business schools have to invest in more courses related to cultural intelligence, heighten awareness of different cultures through class trips or guest speakers, initiate more internships and co-op opportunities outside of Canada, and facilitate cross-cultural student work teams for projects related to the topic.

INDIVIDUALISM VERSUS COLLECTIVISM: A CLOSER LOOK

Have you ever been torn between what you personally wanted and what the group, organization, or society expected of you? If so, you have firsthand experience with a fundamental and important cultural distinction in both the Hofstede and GLOBE studies: individualism versus collectivism. Awareness of this distinction, as we will soon see, can spell the difference between success and failure in cross-cultural business dealings.

Individualistic culture

Primary emphasis on personal freedom and choice.

Collectivist culture

Personal goals are less important than community goals and interests.

Individualistic and Collectivist Cultures Characterized as "I" and "me" cultures, *individualistic cultures* give priority to individual freedom and choice. *Collectivist cultures*, oppositely called "we" and "us" cultures, rank shared goals higher than individual desires and goals. People in collectivist cultures are expected to lower their own wishes and goals to those of the relevant social unit. A worldwide survey

GENDER EGALITARIANISM IN AUSTRALIA

A recently-commissioned study by the Australian government's Equal Opportunity for Women in the Workplace Agency (EOWA) found many Aussie women felt that they weren't being treated equally in the workplace. Further, almost one half of all men in the study admitted that their workplace was a "bit of a boys' club," but only 20 percent subscribed to the notion that women aren't being treated equally in the workplace. When it came to handing out promotions, nearly half of all women and men in the survey agreed that merit was not always the basis for advancement.

As a result, female respondents felt they had to "work a lot harder to prove themselves" than their male counterparts, and were often promoted at a much slower rate as well. Anna McPhee, director of EOWA said, "Gender biases and old-school attitudes are preventing women aged 16 to 65 from fully participating in the workforce." The findings of this study are consistent with the moderate GLOBE scoring for Australia's gender egalitarianism.

SOURCE: "Australian workplace a 'bit of a boys' club': Study," *Canadian HR Reporter*, November 20, 2008, www.hrreporter.com.

FOCUS ON *Diversity*

of 30,000 managers by Trompenaars and Hampden-Turner, who prefer the term *communitarianism* to collectivism, found the highest degree of individualism in Israel, Romania, Nigeria, Canada, and the United States. Countries ranking lowest in individualism—thus qualifying as collectivist cultures—were Egypt, Nepal, Mexico, India, and Japan. Brazil, China, and France also ended up toward the collectivist end of the scale.[30]

Dualistic Cultures One can expect to encounter both individualists and collectivists in culturally diverse countries such as Canada. As economist Walter Block, PhD, debated in an article that appeared in the *Edmonton Journal*:

> *Because of (Canadian) Aboriginals' so-called collectivist approach to governance, individuals are forbidden from owning property on reserves, most federal monies are paid to the band rather than to individuals (so the chief and council get to decide who gets paid and how much), too many women who have married non-natives are denied their rights by their own bands and there is little accountability among far too many leaders . . . any change to federal law that weakens the collectivist mindset is helpful" (in his opinion, to create a more individualistic mindset).*

Whether you agree or disagree with Dr. Block is not the point; the fact that two different cultural orientations can exist within the same country illustrates the need for organizations that service the Canadian Aboriginal community to be sensitive and respectful of their collectivist values. Conversely, Dr. Block would argue that those in the Aboriginal communities need to be sensitive and respectful toward Federal laws, such as the Canadian Human Rights Act.

Allegiance to Whom? The Aboriginal example brings up an important question about collectivist cultures. Specifically, which unit of society predominates? For Canadian Aboriginals, the band is the key reference group. But, as Trompenaars and Hampden-Turner observe, important differences exist among collectivist (or communitarian) cultures:

> *For each single society, it is necessary to determine the group with which individuals have the closest identification. They could be keen to identify with their trade union, their family, their corporation, their religion, their profession, their nation, or the state apparatus. The French tend to identify with la France, la famille, le cadre; the Japanese with the corporation; the former eastern bloc*

with the Communist Party; and Ireland with the Roman Catholic Church. Communitarian goals may be good or bad for industry depending on the community concerned, its attitude, and relevance to business development.[31]

HIGH-CONTEXT AND LOW-CONTEXT CULTURES

High-context cultures

Primary meaning derived from various non-verbal situational cues.

People from **high-context cultures** are those who look at a broader, more holistic approach to understanding each other. This means that more than words are taken into consideration; things such as the strength of a relationship, time approximation, relative space allowance, and/or communication all work together to give meaning to behaviour. Countries with high-context cultures include China, Korea, Japan, Vietnam, Mexico, and Arab cultures—they rely heavily on situational cues for meaning when interacting with others.[32] Non-verbal cues, such as official position, status, or family connections, convey messages more powerfully than do spoken words. Thus, we come to better understand the ritual of exchanging *and reading* business cards in Japan. Japanese culture is relatively high context. Business cards, listing employer and official position, convey vital silent messages about status to members of Japan's homogeneous society. Also, people from high-context cultures who are not especially talkative during a first encounter with a stranger are not necessarily being unfriendly; they are simply taking time to collect contextual information.

Reading the Fine Print in Low-Context Cultures
In **low-context cultures**, written and spoken words carry the burden of shared meanings. Low-context cultures include those found in Canada, Germany, Switzerland, Scandinavia, the United States, and Great Britain. True to form, Germany has precise written rules for even the smallest details of daily life. In high-context cultures, agreements tend to be made on the basis of someone's word or a handshake, after a rather prolonged get-acquainted and trust-building period. Low-context Canadians, who have cultural roots in Northern Europe, see the handshake as a signal to get a signature on a detailed, lawyer-approved, iron-clad contract.

Low-context cultures

Primary meaning derived from written and spoken words.

Avoiding Cultural Collisions Misunderstanding and miscommunication often cause problems in international business dealings when the parties are from high- versus low-context cultures. A Mexican business professor made this instructive observation:

Over the years, I have noticed that across cultures there are different opinions on what is expected from a business report. (North American) managers, for instance, take a pragmatic, get-to-the-point approach, and expect reports to be concise and action-oriented. They don't have time to read long explanations: "Just the facts, ma'am." Latin American managers will usually provide long explanations that go beyond simple facts . . . I have a friend who is the Latin America representative for a (North American) firm and has been asked by his boss to provide regular reports on sales activities. His reports are long, including detailed explanations on the context in which the events he is reporting on occur and the possible interpretations that they might have. His boss regularly answers these reports with very brief messages, telling him to "cut the crap and get to the point!"[33]

Awkward situations such as this can be avoided when those on both sides of the context divide make good-faith attempts to understand and accommodate their counterparts.

MONOCHRONIC AND POLYCHRONIC TIME ORIENTATION—DIFFERENT CULTURAL PERCEPTIONS

In the Canadian culture, time seems to be a simple matter. It is linear, relentlessly marching forward, never backward, in standardized chunks. When working across cultures, however, time becomes a very complex matter. For example, consider this example of a Canadian company that established a joint venture partnership with a Mexican company:

The joint venture company manufactured a Canadian-designed product in Mexico, basing its production numbers on estimates from the Mexican company of how much its employees could sell in the Mexican market. The Canadian company soon noticed its Mexican partner had not made several payments for goods manufactured by the joint venture, and was surprised to find that the Mexicans had been stock-piling the product in inventory because they were not selling nearly the amount they forecasted. Instead of lowering the forecast over time to be consistent with the Mexican demand, the Mexicans continued to order the same amount each quarter so as not to disappoint the Canadians. To reduce inventory, the Canadian company was forced to flog old product in the Mexican market for two years.[34]

Monochronic time

Preference for doing one thing at a time because time is limited, precisely segmented, and schedule driven.

Notice how the time implication of the inventory depreciating and losing value was not a priority to the Mexican partner; but became an unfortunate long-term concern for the Canadian company. The need for patience in cross-cultural business deals where perceptions of time vary can be explained in part by the distinction between **monochronic time** (Canada) and **polychronic time** (Mexico):

The former is revealed in the ordered, precise, schedule-driven use of public time that typifies and even caricatures efficient Northern Europeans and North Americans. The latter is seen in the multiple and cyclical activities and concurrent involvement with different people in Mediterranean, Latin American, and especially Arab cultures.[35]

Polychronic time

Preference for doing more than one thing at a time because time is flexible and multidimensional.

A Matter of Degree Monochronic and polychronic are relative rather than absolute concepts. Generally, the more things a person tends to do at once, the more polychronic that person is.[36] Thanks to computers and advanced telecommunications systems, highly polychronic employees can engage in multi-tasking.[37] For instance, it is possible to talk on the telephone, read and respond to email messages, print a report, check a cell phone message, and eat a stale sandwich all at the same time. Unfortunately, this extreme polychronic behaviour too often is not as efficient as hoped, and can be very stressful.[38] Monochronic people prefer to do one thing at a time. What is your attitude toward time?

Practical Implications Low-context cultures, such as that of Canada, tend to run on monochronic time, while high-context cultures, such as that of Mexico, tend to run on polychronic time. People in polychronic cultures view time as flexible, fluid, and multidimensional, so the sequence of what task they prefer to complete first is varied. The Germans and Swiss have made an exact science of monochronic time. In fact, a radio-controlled watch made by a German company, Junghans, is "guaranteed to lose no more than one second in one million years."[39] Time is more elastic in polychronic cultures. During the Islamic holy month of Ramadan in Middle Eastern nations, for example, the faithful fast during daylight hours, and the general pace of things markedly slows.[40] Employees need to reset their mental clocks when doing business across cultures, as many are polychronic.

CROSS-CULTURAL LEADERSHIP—LESSONS FROM THE GLOBE PROJECT

Earlier in the chapter we discussed the GLOBE Project in general. Here we link the research results directly to international leadership. In phase 2 of the GLOBE Project, researchers set out to discover which, if any, attributes of leadership were universally liked or disliked. They surveyed 17,000 middle managers working for 951 organizations across 62 countries. Their results, summarized in Table 14.2, have important implications for trainers and global managers today, as well as in the future. Visionary and inspirational charismatic leaders who are good team builders generally do the best. On the other hand, self-centred leaders, seen as loners or face-savers, generally receive a poor reception worldwide (see Chapter 10 for a comprehensive treatment of leadership). Local and foreign managers who heed these results are still advised to use a contingency approach to leadership, using their cultural intelligence to read the local people and culture.[41] David Whitwam, the long-time CEO of appliance maker Whirlpool, recently framed the challenge this way:

Leading a company today is different from the 1980s and '90s, especially in a global company. It requires a new set of competencies. Bureaucratic structures don't work anymore. You have to take the command-and-control types out of the system. You need to allow and encourage broad-based involvement in the company. Especially in consumer kinds of companies, we need a diverse workforce with diverse leadership. You need strong regional leadership that lives in the culture. We have a North American running the North American business, and a Latin American running the Latin American business.[42]

Preparing for a Foreign Assignment

As the reach of global companies continues to grow, many opportunities for living and working in foreign countries will arise. Imagine, for example, the opportunities for foreign duty and cross-cultural experiences at Siemens, the German electronics giant. While Siemens' corporate headquarters is near Munich, the vast majority of the firm's business is international. Worldwide, the company has 427,000 employees: 31 percent are located in Germany, 23 percent in the Americas, and 8 percent in China.[43] Siemens and other global players need a vibrant and growing pool of employees who are willing and able to do business across cultures. Thus, the purpose of this final section is to help you prepare yourself and others to work successfully in foreign countries.

TABLE 14.2 Leadership Attributes Universally Liked and Disliked Across 62 Nations

UNIVERSALLY POSITIVE LEADER ATTRIBUTES	UNIVERSALLY NEGATIVE LEADER ATTRIBUTES
Trustworthy	Loner
Just	Asocial
Honest	Non-cooperative
Foresight	Irritable
Plans ahead	Non-explicit
Encouraging	Egocentric
Positive	Ruthless
Dynamic	Dictatorial
Motive arouser	
Confidence builder	
Motivational	
Dependable	
Intelligent	
Decisive	
Effective bargainer	
Win–win problem solver	
Administrative skilled	
Communicative	
Informed	
Coordinator	
Team builder	
Excellence oriented	
Involvement oriented	

SOURCE: Excerpted and adapted from P.W. Dorfman, P.J. Hanges, and F.C. Brodbeck, "Leadership and Cultural Variation: The Identification of Culturally Endorsed Leadership Profiles," in *Culture, Leadership, and Organizations: The GLOBE Study of 62 Societies*, eds R.J. House, P.J. Hanges, M. Javidan, P.W. Dorfman, and V. Gupta (Thousand Oaks, CA: Sage, 2004), Tables 21.2 and 21.3, pp 677–78.

TRACKING CANADIAN FOREIGN ASSIGNMENTS

As we use the term here, ***expatriate*** refers to anyone living and/or working outside their home country. Hence, they are said to be *expatriated* when transferred to another country and *repatriated* when transferred back home. Canadian

Expatriate

Anyone living or working in a foreign country.

employees assigned overseas have been tracked ever since the 1996 census. As mentioned earlier, Statistics Canada has been able to confirm that foreign assignments are increasing, along with employee resistance. The Canadian Employee Relocation Council conducts surveys related to corporate relocation policies and found over the years that the three major concerns about relocation are: family issues (uprooting school-aged children as well as affecting the career of the spouse), career planning ("How long will I be gone and what will happen upon my return?"), and international security (political hot spots of Columbia, Bolivia, and Afghanistan rank near the top).[44]

One survey conducted by a Canadian consulting firm found that despite economic uncertainty and corporate cost-cutting, more than 46 percent of multi-national Canadian firms surveyed said they expected to expand their expatriate workforces over the next five years. Most of the 72 companies surveyed believed they were doing an adequate job preparing employees for their foreign positions, but nearly 40 percent of respondents admitted they saw room for improvement. About half of the people being sent abroad have never worked outside of Canada before, the study found. Most are sent to manage foreign operations or sales forces, to expand into a new market, or to do jobs the local work force lacks the skills to perform. The investment cost of sending professionals to foreign assignments can be costly. The survey results show Canadian firms typically make an investment in excess of $1 million (Cdn) to keep an employee overseas for three years.[45]

SOME GOOD NEWS: CANADIAN WOMEN ON FOREIGN ASSIGNMENTS

Historically, women from Canada on a foreign assignment were a rarity. Things are changing, albeit slowly. A review of research evidence and anecdotal accounts uncovered these insights:

- Statistics Canada reported a 40 percent increase in the number of female managers taking foreign assignments between 1990 and 2004.[46]

- Self-disqualification and management's assumption that women would not be welcome in foreign cultures—not foreign prejudice itself—are the primary barriers for potential female expatriates.

- Expatriate North American women are viewed first and foremost by their hosts as being foreigners, and only secondarily as being female.

- Women trained and educated in the west have a very high success rate on foreign assignments.[47]

Considering the rapidly growing demand for global employees, self-disqualification and management's prejudicial policies are counterproductive. Our advice to women who have their heart set on a foreign assignment: Go for it!

AVOIDING OB TROUBLE SPOTS IN THE FOREIGN ASSIGNMENT CYCLE **LO 5**

Finding the right person (often along with a supportive and adventurous family) for a foreign position is a complex, time-consuming, and costly process.[48] For our purposes, it is sufficient to narrow the focus to common OB trouble spots in the foreign assignment cycle. According to Professor Lorna Wright, Ph.d., from the Schulich School of Business at York University, there are many factors that need to be considered when accepting a foreign assignment. We will blend her fifteen years of experience working with governments and private companies with Figure 14.2. There are four stages in the foreign assignment cycle, each with related OB trouble spots.

1. **Selection and training** This stage takes place in the home country prior to leaving. At this point, unrealistic expectations are identified and corrected. A growing trend is for companies to assign outside mentors or consultants who specialize in preparing professionals for their foreign assignment. They can provide a complete package, including advice

▶ **FIGURE 14.2** The Foreign Assignment Cycle (With OB Trouble Spots)

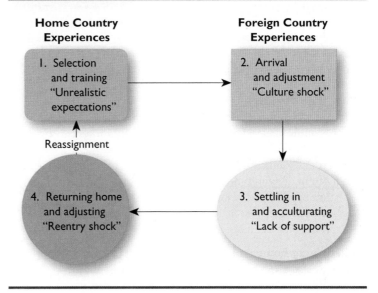

on housing, schools, and tax implications. According to an earlier study, Canadian companies that saw room for improvement during this phase often cited the urgency to get a position filled as a reason why employees didn't get enough preparation before starting their assignment. "You should opt in and not be co-opted into a foreign assignment," says Wright.[49]

"In a globalized world, you may be limiting your chances of advancement if you turn down a foreign posting. But you have to think about how you are going to parlay the experience in the next step of your career plan," says consultant Lorna Wright, who currently directs the International MBA program for York University, Schulich School of Business.

2. **Arrival and adjustment** This stage takes place in the foreign country, where the professional can typically experience culture shock. If possible, candidates should be given a chance to go to the country, have a look around, and see whether this is something they want to do. Due to the high expense, this option is generally reserved for large companies. Wright recalls the first time she went to a store to buy groceries on her first posting in Tokyo: "Everything was in Kanji, the Japanese pictograms, no English. I was holding a package of white crystals in my hand and wondering whether it was salt or sugar and there was no one in the store who could help me." Language barriers can turn simple decisions into major frustrations and challenges.[50]

3. **Settling in and acculturating** This stage also takes place in the foreign country, where the professional feels somewhat without corporate support. An earlier study found only 54 percent of expatriates felt their company did a good job of keeping in touch, and half of the companies surveyed reported they communicated differently with foreign workers than with employees in Canada, often relying on email and dedicated Web sites. The "out of sight, out of mind" syndrome can be overcome by constant communication between the head office and foreign placement using such technology as Skype, WebEx, MSN video calls, etc.[51]

4. **Returning home and adjusting** This stage takes place back home, where the professional experiences re-entry shock. Resistance from others and feeling

that they don't fit in become the biggest concerns for repatriated professionals. "On their return to the Canadian office, many employees who go overseas feel out of place, as though they no longer fit into the organization," says Wright. That's partly because employers don't capitalize on the valuable experience the employee has gained working independently in the foreign posting.[52]

In this next section we'll explore each of these stages in greater detail. It's important to anticipate trouble spots and neutralize the effects; otherwise, the bill for another failed foreign assignment will grow.[53]

STAGE #1: Avoiding Unrealistic Expectations with Cross-Cultural Training Realistic job previews (RJPs) have proven effective at bringing people's unrealistic expectations about a pending job assignment down to earth, by providing a realistic balance of good and bad news. People with realistic expectations tend to quit less often and be more satisfied than those with unrealistic expectations. RJPs are a must for future expatriates. In addition, cross-cultural training is required.

Cross-cultural training is any type of structured experience designed to help departing employees adjust to a foreign culture. The trend is toward more of this type of training. Although costly, companies believe cross-cultural training is less expensive than failed foreign assignments. Programs vary widely in type and also in rigour.[54] Of course, the greater the difficulty, the greater the time and expense:

Cross-cultural training

Structured training experiences to help people adjust to a new culture/country.

- **Easiest** Pre-departure training is limited to informational materials, including books, lectures, films, videos, and Internet searches.

- **Moderately difficult** Experiential training is conducted through case studies, role playing, assimilators (simulated intercultural incidents), and introductory language instruction.

- **Most difficult** Departing employees are given some combination of the preceding methods, plus comprehensive language instruction and field experience in the target culture. As an example of the latter, PepsiCo Inc. transfers "about 25 young foreign managers a year to the U.S. for one-year assignments in bottling plants."[55]

Which approach is the best? Research to date does not offer a final answer. As a general rule of thumb, the more rigorous the cross-cultural training, the better. The nine competencies detailed in Table 14.3 should be the core of any comprehensive cross-cultural training program.

STAGE #2: Avoiding Culture Shock Have you ever been in a totally unfamiliar situation and felt disoriented and perhaps a bit frightened? If so, you already know something about *culture shock*. According to anthropologists, culture shock involves anxiety and doubt caused by an overload of unfamiliar expectations and social cues.[56] Consider your first year as a student at your current school—remember experiencing a variation of culture shock after leaving high school? An expatriate employee, or family member, may be thrown off-balance by an avalanche of strange sights, sounds, and behaviours. Among them may be unreadable road signs, strange-tasting food, inability to use your left hand for social activities (in Islamic countries, the left hand is the toilet hand), or failure to get a laugh with your sure-fire joke. For the expatriate employee trying to concentrate on the fine details of a business negotiation, culture shock is more than an embarrassing inconvenience: It is a disaster! Like the confused first year post-secondary student who quits and goes home, culture-shocked employees often panic and go home early.

The best defence against culture shock is comprehensive cross-cultural training, including intensive language study. This type of program reduces culture shock by taking the anxiety-producing mystery out of an unfamiliar culture.

STAGE #3: Support During the Foreign Assignment A support system needs to be in place, especially during the first six months when everything is so new to the expatriate.[57] *Host-country sponsors*, assigned to individual employees or families, are recommended because they serve as cultural seeing-eye dogs. In a foreign country, where even the smallest errand can turn into an utterly exhausting production, sponsors can get things done quickly because they know the cultural and geographical territory. Another way to support expatriates during the transition phase of a new foreign assignment is to maintain an active dialogue with established mentors from back home. This can be accomplished via email, telephone, and, when possible, an occasional face-to-face meeting.[58]

Culture shock

Anxiety and doubt caused by an overload of new expectations and cues.

> "The best defence against culture shock is comprehensive cross-cultural training, including intensive language study."

Key Cross-Cultural Competencies

CROSS-CULTURAL COMPETENCY CLUSTER	KNOWLEDGE OR SKILL REQUIRED
Building relationships	Ability to gain access to and maintain relationships with members of host culture
Valuing people of different cultures	Empathy for difference; sensitivity to diversity
Listening and observation	Knows cultural history and reasons for certain cultural actions and customs
Coping with ambiguity	Recognizes and interprets implicit behaviour, especially non-verbal cues
Translating complex information	Knowledge of local language, symbols or other forms of verbal language, and written language
Taking action and initiative	Understands intended and potentially unintended consequences of actions
Managing others	Ability to manage details of a job, including maintaining cohesion in a group
Adaptability and flexibility	Views change from multiple perspectives
Managing stress	Understands own and other's mood, emotions, and personality

▲ TABLE 14.3

SOURCE: Excerpted from Y. Yamazaki and D.C. Kayes, "An Experiential Approach to Cross-Cultural Learning: A Review and Integration of Competencies for Successful Expatriate Adaptation," *Academy of Management Learning and Education*, December 2004, Table 2, p 372.

THE REVERSE BRAIN DRAIN OCCURRING AS EXPATRIATES GO BACK HOME

In the mid-2000s, thousands of skilled professionals flocked to the fast-growing city of Dubai, the expanding metropolis of Madrid, and the world-class city of London—a knowledge and skills brain drain that took the best of the best from around the world and placed them in high paying jobs. But then the unexpected happened: global markets tanked in 2008–09 leaving job futures uncertain. Expatriates who got caught up in the assignment forgot that such placements are best looked upon as part of a career path, not an isolated experience. As a result, they lost their jobs and were given few options. For those who kept their focus, going back to their homeland seems opportunistic. Reverse migration has become a major phenomenon in a number of countries. The financial sectors in India and China are being bolstered by a reverse exodus of highly-trained but suddenly jobless bankers and analysts. Brazil, Israel, Australia, and Turkey have observed the same effect. The Higher-Education Minister of Malaysia recently announced an international program "to identify Malaysian professionals who lost their jobs abroad to return and work."

SOURCE: D. Saunders, "The Reverse Brain Drain," *The Globe and Mail – Report on Business*, December 11, 2008, p 1B.

STAGE #4: Avoiding Re-entry Shock Strange as it may seem, many otherwise successful expatriate employees encounter their first major difficulty only after their foreign assignment is over. Why? Returning to one's native culture is taken for granted because it seems so routine and ordinary. But having adjusted to another country's way of doing things for an extended period of time can put one's own culture and surroundings in a strange new light. Three areas for potential re-entry shock are work, social activities, and general environment (e.g., politics, climate, transportation, food).

Work-related adjustments were found to be a major problem for samples of repatriated Finnish and Japanese employees.[59] Upon being repatriated, a 12-year veteran of one company said: "Our organizational culture was turned upside down. We now have a different strategic focus, different 'tools' to get the job done, and different buzzwords to make it happen. I had to learn a whole new corporate language."[60] Re-entry shock can be reduced through employee career counselling and home-country mentors and sponsors. Simply being forewarned about the problem of re-entry shock is a big step toward effectively dealing with it.[61]

Overall, the key to a successful foreign assignment is making it a well-integrated link in a career chain, rather than treating it as an isolated adventure (see International OB feature box).

Summary of Learning Objectives

1. **Define *ethnocentrism*.** Ethnocentrism is a prejudicial belief that one's native country, culture, language, behaviour, and traditions are better than all others.

2. **Explain what Hofstede concluded about applying Canadian management theories in other countries.** Due to the wide variations in key dimensions Hofstede found among cultures, he warned against directly applying North American-made management theories to other cultures without adapting them first. He said there is no one best way to manage across cultures.

3. **Differentiate between five cultural perspectives relevant to individuals becoming cross-culturally competent.** (1) Individuals wishing to become more cross-culturally competent need to understand basic cultural dimensions that exist between people from different countries, as well as develop cultural intelligence about others. (2) People in individualistic cultures think primarily in terms of "I" and "me" and place a high value on freedom and personal choice. Collectivist cultures teach people to be "we" and "us" oriented and to subordinate personal wishes and goals to the interests of the relevant social unit (such as family, group, organization, or society). (3) People in high-context cultures (such as China, Japan, and Mexico) derive great meaning from a broad spectrum of situational cues, above and beyond written and spoken words. Low-context cultures (including Canada, Germany, and the United States) derive key information from precise, written and/or spoken messages. (4) In monochronic cultures (e.g., Canada and Germany), time is precise and rigidly measured. Polychronic cultures (such as those found in Latin America and the Middle East), view time as multidimensional, fluid, and flexible. Monochronic people prefer to do one thing at a time, while polychronic people like to tackle multiple tasks at the same time. Polychronic people are not necessarily more efficient, but rather they have no particular preference of sequence for completing tasks. (5) Developing the kind of cross-cultural leadership traits that are universally liked can enhance success.

4. **Summarize what the GLOBE project has taught us about leadership.** Across 62 cultures, the researchers identified leader attributes that are universally liked and universally disliked. The universally liked leader attributes, including trustworthy, dynamic, motive arouser, decisive, and intelligent, are associated with the charismatic/transformational leadership style that is widely applicable. Universally disliked leader attributes, such as non-cooperative, irritable, egocentric, and dictatorial, should be avoided in all cultures.

5. **Synthesize the four stages of the foreign assignment cycle by identifying an OB trouble spot for each stage.** The four stages of the foreign assignment cycle (and OB trouble spots) are (1) selection and training (unrealistic expectations), (2) arrival and adjustment (culture shock), (3) settling in and acculturating (lack of support), and (4) returning home and adjusting (re-entry shock).

Discussion Questions

1. How many of the cultural dimensions discussed in this chapter can you identify in the chapter-opening vignette? Explain.

2. How would you describe the prevailing culture in your country to a stranger from another land, in terms of the nine GLOBE project dimensions?

3. Why are people from high-context cultures such as China and Japan likely to be misunderstood by low-context Westerners?

4. How strong is your desire for a foreign assignment? Why? If it is strong, where would you like to work? Why? How prepared are you for a foreign assignment? What would you need to do to be better prepared?

5. What is your personal experience with culture shock? Which of the OB trouble spots in Figure 14.2 do you believe is the greatest threat to expatriate employee success? Explain.

Google Searches

1. **Google Search:** "The Department of Foreign Affairs and International Trade" or "Export Development Canada" or "The Canadian Employee Relocation Council" Working in groups, choose one of the search sites and review what the organization/department can do for expatriates or Canadian repatriates. Report the findings to the rest of the class.

2. **Google Search:** "Citizenship and Immigration Canada" Go to the home site. Find the Media Centre on the right hand side of the site. Scroll down to "Success Stories." Double click on this to go to the site of "Newcomers to Canada – Success Stories." Work in small groups to analyze some of the latest postings. Share some of the stories with the rest of the class, relating cultural dimensions learned from this chapter to the personal stories selected.

3. **Google Search:** "International Monetary Fund – Nominal GDP by country" or "CIA World Fact Book – Nominal GDP by country" and "Walmart Gross Global Sales Revenue" Compare Walmart's revenue to the GDP of the top 25 countries in the world. How much larger is Walmart compared to global countries and their wealth? In your opinion, is Walmart a global company? How can an organization like Walmart prepare its expatriate managers and employees for overseas assignments? How can Walmart better integrate newly-landed Canadians into the current Canadian workforce?

Experiential Exercise

The Globalized Classroom Exercise

PURPOSE: This exercise will show you how international your own classroom is by having you survey the cultural dimensions of all the students, including the professor. This exercise will heighten your cultural awareness. Approx. Timing: 25 minutes.

ACTIVITY ASSIGNMENT
- Work in small groups of five or six students.
- *Predict* the following: How many countries are represented by the students in your class? How many different languages are spoken? How many different religions are represented? How many international students in your class are studying on educational visas? —5 minutes
- Determine the demographic, mother-tongue languages, cultural and religious backgrounds of the students in your small group. Summarize the results and hand it in. —5 minutes
- Collectively place all group submissions onto a board. —5 minutes
- Review the collective profile of the class. —5 minutes
- Discuss the questions below.

1. How accurate was your initial prediction of the diversity in your classroom?
2. If you were close, try and find reasons for your cultural intelligence. How and where did you develop it?
3. If your prediction was way off, find reasons for your lack of cultural intelligence. How and where could you further develop it?

The **Presentation** Assistant

Here are possible topics and sources related to this chapter that can be further explored by student groups looking for ideas.

	OVERSEAS JOB OPPORTUNITIES—WHERE ARE THEY, WHAT ARE THEY, AND HOW TO FIND THEM?	CULTURAL INTELLIGENCE & EMOTIONAL INTELLIGENCE—BRIDGING THE GAP TO GREATER AWARENESS	CULTURAL DIVERSITY 101—FOOD, FAITH, AND FOLLY
YouTube Videos	• Beijing Job Fair—Graduates looking for job (world competition for jobs) • Canadian Foreign Workers	• Ethnocentrism • White supremacy groups and Xenophobia • Don Cherry is crazy • *Emotional Intelligence*—movie • Cultural Intelligence—IMD Leading with . . . Prof. Maznevski • Authors @ Google: Dan Ariely (irrational practices vs. rational behaviour: people know it's not right to be against others but they still are—why?)	• *Borat* on ABC News on Australian Television or *Ali G Show*—(Folly) • Cultural Differences Ordering Beer—Dan Ariely (collectivist Asians vs. Western individualists) • Cultural Differences at Work
TV Shows or Movies to Preview	• *All The Right Moves* (movie) • *Manufactured Landscapes* (documentary) • *The Island* (movie)	• *The Terminal* (movie) • *Star Trek* (movie—Data the Android who wants to feel human emotions)	• *The Office, Season 1*—"Diversity Training" • *Gattaca* (movie)
Internet Searches	• NAPP Canada (Web site) • Opportunities Expo Canada • www.Monster.ca—international search • www.workopolis.com—international locations • http://www.canadaimmigrants.com/forum_2.asp (Canadian immigration blog site) • www.Canadajobs.com (overseas jobs for Canadian govt.)	• www.diversityinc.com (magazine) • http://diversity.monster.ca/section2976.asp (issues related to cultural diversity) • *Cultural Intelligence*—People Skills for Global Intelligence (by D. Thomas and K. Inkson, 2004) • *Emotional Intelligence* (by D. Goleman)	• www.multiculturalcanada.ca (different ethnic cultures in Canada) • www.religioustolerance.org (comparing different religions) • www.interfaithcalendar.org/Foodsofreligions.htm (foods, practices of religions) • www.interfaithcalendar.org (interfaith calendar)
Ice Breaker Classroom Activity	• Ask students if any of them have ever worked outside of Canada. Share comments and experiences. Ask if any students have an interest in working outside of Canada. Share comments and experiences.	• Find three photographs of successful visible minority individuals, one photo of a successful female, and one photo of a white male who is a house husband. Show the pictures to the students one at a time with no narration. Ask students: Which person is the successful business person? Who doesn't speak English? Who is paid the most? Who is paid the least? Share the correct answers.	• Bring in at least 10 samples of different food from various cultures and share them with the students. Relate the culture to the religion and to the country where they are found.

OB In Action Case Study

It Takes A Village—and a Consultant

[In the summer of 2004], accounting-and-consulting giant Pricewaterhouse-Coopers (PwC) tapped partner Tahir Ayub for a consulting gig unlike anything he had done before. His job: helping village leaders in the Namibian outback grapple with their community's growing AIDS crisis. Faced with language barriers, cultural differences, and scant access to electricity, Ayub, 39, and two colleagues had to scrap their PowerPoint presentations in favour of a more low-tech approach: face-to-face discussion. The village chiefs learned that they needed to garner community support for programs to combat the disease, and Ayub learned an important lesson as well: Technology isn't always the answer. "You better put your beliefs and biases to one side and figure out new ways to look at things," he said.

Ayub may never encounter as extreme a cultural disconnect as he did in Namibia. But for the next generation of partners, overcoming barriers and forging a connection with clients the world over will be a crucial part of their jobs. PwC hopes to foster these skills in partners who participate in the Ulysses Program, which sends top mid-career talent to the developing world for eight-week service projects. For a fairly modest investment—$15,000 per person, plus salaries—Ulysses both tests the talent and expands the worldview of the accounting firm's future leaders. Since the company started the program four years ago, it has attracted the attention of Johnson & Johnson, Cisco Systems, and other big companies considering their own programs.

While results are hard to quantify, PwC is convinced that the program works. All two dozen graduates are still working at the company. Half of them have been promoted, and most have new responsibilities. Just as important, all 24 people say they have a stronger commitment to PwC—in part because of the commitment the firm made to them, and in part because of their new vision of the firm's values. Says Global Managing Partner Willem Bröcker, "We get better partners from this exercise."

The Ulysses Program is PwC's answer to one of the biggest challenges confronting professional services companies: identifying and training up-and-coming leaders who can find unconventional answers to intractable problems. By tradition and necessity, new PwC leaders are nurtured from within. But with 8,000 partners, identifying those with the necessary business savvy and relationship-building skills isn't easy. Just as the program gives partners a new view of PwC, it also gives PwC a new view of them, particularly their ability to hold up under pressure.

For mid-career partners who were weaned on email and the Blackberry, this was no walk in the park. They had become accustomed to a world of wireless phones, sleek offices, and Chinese take-out—so the rigours of the developing world came as quite a shock. Brian P. McCann, 37, a mergers and acquisitions expert from PwC's Boston office, had never been to a Third World country before his stint in Belize, where he encountered dirt-floored houses, sick children, and grinding poverty.

Ayub, having been born in Africa, considered himself worldly. Even so, long days spent among Africa's exploding HIV-positive population took their psychological toll. With his work confined to daylight hours—there was often no electricity—Dinu Bumbacea, a 37-year-old partner in PwC's Romanian office who spent time in Zambia working with an agricultural centre, had plenty of time to dwell on the misery all around him. "Africa is poor, and we all know that," says Bumbacea. "But until you go there, you don't understand how poor it is. We take so much for granted."

For more than 15 years, companies have used social-responsibility initiatives to develop leaders. But PwC takes the concept to a new level. Participants spend eight weeks in developing countries, lending their business skills to local aid groups—from an ecotourism collective in Belize, to small organic farmers in Zambia, to AIDS groups in Namibia. Ulysses also presents participants with the challenge of collaborating across cultures with local clients, as well as with PwC colleagues from other global regions. Ayub, for example, was paired with partners from Mexico and the Netherlands.

Beyond Accounting

PWC says the program, now in its third cycle, gives participants a broad, international perspective that's crucial for a company that does business around the world. Traditional executive education programs turn out men and women who have specific job skills, but little familiarity with issues outside their narrow specialty, according to Douglas Ready, director of the International Consortium for Executive Development Research. PwC says Ulysses helps prepare participants for challenges that go beyond the strict confines of accounting or consulting, and instils values such as community involvement that are fundamental to its corporate culture.

Ulysses is also a chance for partners to learn what they can accomplish without their usual resources to lean on. The program forces them to take on projects well outside their expertise. In the summer of 2003, for example, McCann developed a business plan for an ecotourism group in Belize. The experience was an eye-opener. McCann's most lasting memory is a dinner he shared in the home of a Mayan farmer after they spent a day discussing their plan. "He didn't even have electricity," McCann recalls, "but he made do."

PwC partners say they've already adapted their experiences to the task of managing people and clients. Malaysian partner Jennifer Chang says her team noticed a shift in her managerial style after the Belize trip. She listened more and became more flexible. "Once you see how slowly decisions are made in other places, you gain patience for the people you work with," she says. Ayub, who was promoted in June, now manages 20 partners. He says he favours face-to-face conversations over email because the low-tech approach builds trust. "It made the difference in Namibia," he says.

If insights like those ripple out across the firm, Ulysses will be more than a voyage of personal discovery for a handful of partners. It could help build leaders capable of confronting the challenges of an increasingly global business. And that, says PwC, is the whole point.

SOURCE: J. Hempel, "It Takes a Village—and a Consultant," *Business Week*, September. 6, 2004, pp 76–77.

Discussion Questions

1. If you were the CEO of PricewaterhouseCoopers, how would you defend the Ulysses Program to shareholders concerned about spending?

2. What benefit would the Ulysses Program be to PwC employees who do not seek or take a foreign assignment?

3. How do the facts of this case confirm the GLOBE Project's research findings about leadership? Explain.

4. Using Table 14.3 as a guide, what cross-cultural competencies were developed among the people featured in this case study? Explain.

5. Would you like to participate in this type of leadership development program? Why or why not?

Ethical OB Dilemma

3M Tries to Make a Difference in Russia

Russian managers aren't inclined to reward people for improved performance. They spurn (reject) making investments for the future in favour of realizing immediate gains. They avoid establishing consistent business practices that can reduce uncertainty. Add in the country's high political risk and level of corruption, and it's no wonder that many multinationals have all but given up on Russia.

The Russian business environment can be corrupt and dangerous; bribes and protection money are facts of life. But unlike many international companies that try to distance themselves from such practices by simply banning them, 3M Russia actively promotes not only ethical behaviour, but also the personal security of its employees.

3M Russia also strives to differentiate itself from competitors by being an ethical leader. For example, it holds training courses in business ethics for its customers.

SOURCE: Excerpted from M.V. Gratchev, "Making the Most of Cultural Differences," *Harvard Business Review*, October 2001, pp 28, 30.

Should 3M Export its North American Ethical Standards to Russia? Consider the following statements. Which one best describes how you would respond?

1. "If 3M doesn't like the way things are done in Russia, it shouldn't do business there." Explain your rationale.
2. "3M should do business in Russia but not meddle in Russian culture. When in Russia, do things the Russian way." Explain your rationale.
3. "3M has a basic moral responsibility to improve the ethical climate in foreign countries where it does business." Explain your rationale.
4. "3M should find a practical middle ground between the North American and Russian ways of doing business." Explain how that should happen.
5. "I would respond differently." Explain.

Visit www.mcgrawhillconnect.ca to register.

McGraw-Hill Connect™ —Available 24/7 with instant feedback so you can study when you want, how you want, and where you want. Take advantage of the Study Plan—an innovative tool that helps you customize your learning experience. You can diagnose your knowledge with pre- and post-tests, identify the areas where you need help, search the entire learning package for content specific to the topic you're studying, and add these resources to your personalized study plan. Visit www.mcgrawhillconnect.ca to register—take practice quizzes, search the e-book, and much more.

APPENDIX

A1 OB Research

A2 Case Study Analysis—A Framework

A1 OB Research

FIVE SOURCES OF OB RESEARCH INSIGHTS

OB gains its credibility as an academic discipline by being research-driven. Scientific rigour pushes aside speculation, prejudice, and untested assumptions about workplace behaviour. We systematically cite evidence from five different categories by drawing upon the following priority of research methodologies:

- **Meta-analyses** A meta-analysis is a statistical pooling technique that permits behavioural scientists to draw general conclusions about certain variables from many different studies. It typically encompasses a vast number of subjects, often reaching the thousands. Meta-analyses are instructive (helpful) because they focus on general patterns of research evidence, not fragmented bits and pieces or isolated studies.

- **Field studies** In OB, a field study probes individual or group processes in an organizational setting. Because field studies involve real-life situations, their results often have immediate and practical relevance for supervisors.

- **Laboratory studies** In a laboratory study, variables are manipulated (changed) and measured in contrived (artificial) situations. College students are commonly used as subjects. The highly controlled nature of laboratory studies enhances research precision, but generalizing the results to organizational management requires caution.

- **Sample surveys** In a sample survey, samples of people from specified populations respond to questionnaires. The researchers then draw conclusions about the relevant population. Generalizability of the results depends on the quality of the sampling and questioning techniques.

- **Case studies** A case study is an in-depth analysis of a single individual, group, or organization. Because of their limited scope, case studies yield realistic but not very generalizable results.

A2 Case Study Analysis—A Framework

NINE STEPS TO CASE STUDY ANALYSIS

To be an effective manager or supervisor, individuals need to develop a variety of skill sets related to all facets of the organization, such as being able to: assess current conditions of a situation; anticipate potential problems; assess or identify the skills and abilities of direct reports; and accurately gauge on-the-job interdependence with colleagues/peers.

Some individuals are placed in jobs and are expected to 'hit the ground running' with very little knowledge or training in how to manage people or systems. Case analysis puts students in the role of the 'person-in-charge' who may or may not be directly referred to in the case; however, that is the perspective to take when analyzing a case. Cases intentionally have limited amounts of information; this encourages students to make inferences (conclusions) and assumptions about situations. Below is a simple model for analyzing OB cases:

STEP #1: SIZE UP   This step is sometimes referred to as the situation analysis. To begin, read the case thoroughly and identify any necessary data/information that appears key and relevant. In this step, try to identify critical issues and draw logical inferences (conclusions) from the data. Most students tend to do a good job at collecting and summarizing the data; where they do poorly is in the drawing of inferences (e.g., What does such data imply? What does it mean?). Be sure to include the key aspects of the organization (e.g., name, market competitors, industry/sector, product type, key characters of the case and their title). Remember to stick to the facts mentioned in the case and identify all the problematic symptoms taking place in the case.

STEP #2: ASSUMPTIONS   What assumptions are you making as you read this case? After making a statement, ask yourself how you know something to be a fact. Was it stated in the case? If so, where? If not, did you infer it from what was written? In any event, it is helpful to list your assumptions to focus your awareness that such knowledge is more of an opinion than a fact and can be easily argued against. This can weaken your position.

STEP #3: PROBLEM STATEMENT   Keep this statement broad and simple. The subhead suggests a problem, not problems. To help this process, try writing the problem statement as a question (e.g., What should ABC Inc. do to restore productivity?). Eventually you'll have to link this step to your final recommendation; if they don't address one another, then there is a gap that needs to be addressed. Try not to solve the problem in this step by placing your solution within your problem statement. If the problem is solved, then most or all of those symptoms mentioned in the size-up should disappear.

STEP #4: ENVIRONMENTAL SCANNING (SWOT)   The purpose of this step is to identify strategic factors from an internal and external perspective. SWOT is the simplest way to conduct environmental scanning. SWOT is the acronym used to describe those particular S = Strengths, W = Weaknesses, O = Opportunities, and T = Threats of the situation. Gauge the internal resources of the firm from the perspective of S and W only. Gauge the external market factors facing the industry in total using O and T only. Here is a guideline of what types of items can be considered in which areas:

- **S/W Gauge Internal Resources:** Review the organizational structure, culture, employee skills/knowledge, HR (Human Resources) training and motivational initiatives, R & D (Research and Development), IT (Information Technology), employee attitude, morale of workplace, job satisfaction, ethical management practices, pricing strategy, product, place, and promotional position.

- **O/T Gauge External Market Factors:** Consider the external economic conditions that this industry could possibly be facing that could pose a threat or an opportunity to it. Consider the demographic trends of the market threatening the industry: political pressures, global economic conditions, market shifts, legal changes, social trends changing that will help or harm the industry, environmental restrictions, changes to the amount or type of competition and impact from technological changes.

STEP #5: ORGANIZING A FIRM   When possible, you should review the current organizational structure as it could be creating the OB related problems in the case. Create a diagram to show the reporting relationships in the case, identifying key departments, people/titles. How would you classify this structure? If this is not an issue, then you may ask your instructor to leave it out. But, if structure is a possible problem, it must be analyzed here.

STEP #6: ALTERNATIVE COURSES OF ACTION   Based on past experience, this area is the one where most students do a minimal job at best. Inevitably, they want to go from analysis to recommendations. They forget that one of their roles is to identify and present the various alternative courses of action that are available. The reason for presenting this step is that others may disagree with your final recommendation and dismiss your thinking. If you have several choices that you considered and analyzed, you'll be able to defend your final decision with more confidence. Each alternative presented should include at least three advantages and three disadvantages listed as part of the analysis. Your instructor will let you know if "Do Nothing" is an option worth mentioning as a viable alternative; some prefer analyzing the status quo because it gives purpose to the need for immediate change.

STEP #7: RECOMMENDATION   Having presented the decision-maker with the range of options available, it is now time for you to move to the action stage. At this point, it is important that you consider the following points:

- Develop and present decision-making criteria. Tell why this alternative was selected over the others. How will this alternative choice address the problem statement?

- No "rabbits out of magic hat," meaning you can't recommend something that was never analyzed. For example, if you want to say, "We recommend a combination of alternative #1 and #2," unless a 'combo' solution was analyzed back in step #6, it can not be selected as a recommendation. You can first offer it up as an alternative, analyzing it just like you would any other alternative with advantages and disadvantages. Then, once you have it included as one of your possible choices in step #6, you can select it as your recommendation in step #7.

- Try to prioritize your recommendations—what action needs to be taken immediately?

- Be sure to write in the actual recommendation you are selecting. Repeat the alternative here word for word from step #6 before explaining why you picked it.

- Go back and double-check by reading your problem statement in Step 2. Does your recommendation solve the problem? If not, then either your problem is too narrow or too broad and needs to be rewritten OR your recommendation is addressing a different problem and needs to be rewritten with more focus.

STEP #8: IMPLEMENTATION   This is a timeline of your recommendation. State the action, who is responsible for it, and when it should be implemented. You may wish to organize this step in a table or Excel spreadsheet. Three possible timelines are recommended: immediate action (0–6 months), short term (6–12 months), and long term (12 months+).

STEP #9: CONCLUDING REMARKS   This final section should satisfy several important functions:

- Summarize the major issues and problems discussed in the report.

- Summarize the recommendation.

- Point out to the reader the ultimate impact of acting on the recommendation. It should end on a positive note, and, if possible, provide a compelling call to action.

Checklist Chart

	BRIEF DESCRIPTION	COMPLETED (X)
Step #1 SIZE UP	Summarize key points: Name of firm, key characters/title, industry/sector, size of firm, various symptoms occurring in the case.	
Step #2 ASSUMPTIONS	Include statements that are not found in the case but you infer (conclude) them to be true.	
Step #3 PROBLEM STATEMENT	Describe the main problem causing all/most of the symptoms mentioned in the size up; if this problem is solved, then those symptoms should disappear.	
Step #4 ENVIRONMENTAL SCAN	S & W—Comment on internal company resources only, referring to the firm by name. O & T—Comment on external market factors affecting the industry only; do not make any reference to the firm specifically as these items pertain to all members of the industry.	
Step #5 ORGANIZING FIRM	If applicable, draw the organization chart for this firm as it currently exists, and then analyze its strengths/weaknesses, if applicable.	
Step #6 ALTERNATIVES	List possible alternative courses of action that can be taken to solve the problem statement.	
Step #7 RECOMMENDATION	Provide the final solution to resolve the main problem.	
Step #8 IMPLEMENTATION	Create a timeline to implement the recommendation using a table insert.	
Step #9 CLOSING REMARKS	Write summary statements that close the report nicely.	

→ DEALING WITH BABIES TO HORSES – Unit 1 Case Study

The Veterinary Teaching Hospital at the University of Saskatchewan is the only place in Western Canada that provides training for veterinary students. Its new director, Lana Clark, is a former nurse who worked in the Saskatoon Health Service for many years as a senior administrator. Lana is not a veterinarian and has never worked in a veterinary hospital. But the university recognized her skills as highly transferable and she obviously has an interest in animals (since she operates a horse farm and cattle business).

Lana is responsible for running the hospital as a business. This means ensuring that students have a sufficient caseload, that all staffing and equipment needs are met, and that appropriate funding is secured for the hospital. Five unit supervisors report to Lana, ranging from human resources to materials management. And, like anyone moving into a new supervisory position, Lana must also build credibility with her new staff. "People will look at how I make decisions and how I react to things. They'll make up their mind about me based on what I do." Lana also has to get to know the staff and understand their work. To accomplish this, Lana has spent much time in her first month on the job on the work units, helping out wherever she could, watching and asking questions. "If I understand the work, then I can explain it better to others and this is especially important when I go to lobby and get funds for the hospital."

As Lana does her best to fulfill the expectations and hopes of her new colleagues and subordinates, her actions will reflect the experience and skills she gains working in a health services focused on humans rather than on animals. This posed many challenges for Lana, One challenge involved merging obstetrical services from two locations into one. Although it was not her decision, nor that of her subordinates, they were responsible for executing it. "I told the staff that there was no choice about what the future would be, but we could help shape the future." The merger affected 150 staff and, in line with her decision-making philosophy, they were involved as much as possible in the change. Committees were formed to deal with the renovations and the actual movement of people, among other things. Lana believes that the "worst you can do is make a decision on your own without involving the people that work in the area affected. If you let them participate, then they know what they're getting into and they share a common vision." To learn whether the merger negatively affected service quality and access to obstetrical services, an outcome evaluation was planned. A baseline survey was conducted before the merger, followed up two and a half years later by another survey. This second survey indicated that results were as good as or better than the results before the merger. Lana felt it was important for all the staff to know how well they had managed the merger.

Another challenge Lana has had to deal with in her administrative past is laying off employees. She has been through several downsizings and has had to lay off people—from individuals on a one-on-one basis to sitting down with a group of up to 50 people to inform them of the bad news. "I try to help them understand the rationale of why it is happening, why their area is affected, that it has nothing to do with their performance, nothing to do with them personally. It's much harder to lay off people due to a reorganization, not a downsizing because the decision seems so much more subjective. I listen to them, hear them out, and offer whatever assistance I can to help them move forward."

What challenges will Lana face on this new job? "One major one is the fact that many of our employees are very long-term - more than 20 years. They are very specialized and very experienced with knowledge of the equipment and the building that others don't have. We have to make sure people are developed and ready to fill in their shoes when those long-term people leave. A second challenge is financial. We have major equipment capital needs. We can't make enough money ourselves to pay for the expensive equipment so we need ongoing funcing for replacing the equipment as needed. Planning can also be a challenge. We can basically plan what we should need in future but, if something breaks down unexpectedly or if there's a big medical advancement, we can't predict that and the equipment can be very expensive. So the department heads, the vets, and I need to keep up with research advances so we can budget for them. "This veterinary hospital, like the health services before, is challenging in that both places deliver a 24-hour-a-day service. Running the business but still giving people their needed time off can be tough. Being flexible with time off can be important in satisfying employees (who can't always plan exactly when they will need time off). But the hospital still needs to be staffed.

"Another organizational challenge is looking at the new ways to do work. Money doesn't always solve the problem. For example, sometimes you need changes to the physical environment or the schedule so that the activity peaks are handled more smoothly and people feel less overloaded.

"What have I liked about being in management positions? Lots of challenges. I'm never bored—never sure what my day will be like. I like the challenge of solving a problem, getting everyone to buy in. And I love working with people."

➡ COUNTRYSIDE ENVIRONMENTAL SERVICES – Unit 2 Case Study

John straightened his tie as he walked down the hallway to the conference room. Vincent paced eagerly at his side. "You've told Andy and Gwen exactly what my role in this project is, haven't you?" Vincent muttered nervously to John. He was quite sure he knew the answer, but wanted to be sure he was going into this meeting in tune with John. Vincent had met with John on many occasions during the preceding month to negotiate his joining Countryside Environmental Services (CES). Once the contract had been negotiated, John had provided Vincent with a general orientation and overview of the company's operations. Now, Vincent was to meet the rest of the team.

"Oh don't worry, I'll make it clear in this meeting this morning" replied John. "As we've already discussed you're to be the guiding authority in this project, I'll be overseeing your progress however you will be responsible for the team's success or failure. We both know that you are more familiar than I with the procedures and politics involved in getting a landfill approved. We can benefit tremendously from your input. Yes, there's no doubting it, you'll be the key play Vincent." John hurried through this last sentence as they reached the meeting room and pushed open the door. He was pleased that Andy and Gwen were already seated and awaiting his arrival.

"We've been given the green light with the new name, so Countryside Environmental Services it is" John said with pride as he entered the small meeting room. This was an exciting moment in the history of Countryside Construction. It was the beginning of another venture for John and his company. Currently, Countryside employs eighty-five people and grosses more than $15 million. John attributed much of the company's success to his own management philosophy of diversity and perseverance.

John Hopkins established Countryside Construction some thirty years ago. The company started business as a small aggregate producer, excavating and selling sand and gravel from a local gravel pit. Today the company supplies aggregate to most of the region's sand blasting and construction businesses. Countryside also has a dominant presence in the local waste management industry. It ventured into waste management a decade ago after being awarded the City of Blensford's contract for the curb side pickup of household waste.

In response to this success, John created a new division of the company to handle waste management. It had been a successful venture for Countryside and John remained close to the action, personally managing the division. During the past five years the division acquired two additional contracts for the operation and management of two other County landfills.

Countryside Environmental Services (CES) had just been established as a spin off company from Countryside Construction to develop a new landfill on a parcel of land centered around one of the company's old gravel pits.

John had visualized owning his own landfill ever since Countryside first became involved in waste management. He believed that the owners of the landfills (in most cases the Government) pocketed all the profits. John was aware of the crippling environmental problems of the existing waste management system and knew that current landfill capacity was rapidly diminishing. He believed the economic potential for opening a new large scale landfill was promising.

Vincent Woodman had just been hired as the environmental consultant and manager of Countryside Environmental Services. Recently Vincent had vacated his seat on County Council, where he had been the County Warden and Reeve of the Town of Innsport for nine years. In this role, he had chaired the County Waste Management Committee and had represented the County on the Provincial Waste Management Steering Committee.

John was very pleased to have recruited Vincent. Vincent had developed an impressive reputation for effective input into waste management planning during his terms in County politics. He eventually became frustrated with the lack of vision with which the County approached its worsening waste management problems. Vincent, like John could see that the increasing public outcry for environmentally safe landfills combined with a strong push towards the three R's (Reduce, Recycle and Re-use) was an opportunity for private enterprise. The best way to handle the Country's waste was for the County to enter into a joint venture with the private sector. The County simply did not have the necessary funds and pressure was mounting both from the public and provincial government officials for change. Vincent knew this better than anyone.

Once Andy and Gwen had joined Vincent and John in the boardroom, John pulled a few papers from his briefcase and shuffled them on the table. "Well I know you've met Andy and Gwen prior to today albeit for a brief moment. I've talked to Andy and Gwen about you joining CES and I am sure they are as enthusiastic as I am. However I should perhaps fill you in on my aspirations for this team and what I would like to see happen. As you know, Andy has been with us now for nearly three years in the capacity of Projects Engineer. Gwen is the Office Manager and joined us about six months prior to Andy." John was speaking quickly, his excitement evident. "Gwen is responsible for the day to day running of the office. She has been involved with the bookkeeping of some of our accounts. However I know that you are well acquainted with accounting Vincent. Andy will be in charge of all the technical/engineering work and Vincent, you will handle the political end of the plans as well as managing the project. I believe we have the basis for a solid and valuable group and I look forward to seeing progress. Vincent has briefed me on what we will need to concentrate on and he will be directing us through the environmental approval process. He has a wealth of knowledge and experience to share with us, so let's work together, be productive and have some fun at the same time." "Perhaps now is a good time, Vincent, for you to brief us on what you consider our plan of attack should be." John leaned back in his chair keen to listen to Vincent's remarks to this newly established team.

"Thank you John. I feel you have provided us with a very exciting opportunity here and I am honoured to be a part of this team. I believe we all have very valuable and relevant skills to utilize in this project and I can't stress enough the importance of working as a team. I truly believe we can make this vision of yours a reality."

"Just as I thought. A long winded politician." Gwen muttered for Andy's benefit. He heard her comment but decided to ignore it.

Vincent continued. "John, you have provided me with an overview of the situation here at Countryside. I would appreciate a day or so to settle in and become familiar with the environment. Then we could get together and go over some specific task assignments. For now you could all help me by answering a few questions. First of all have any business cards or letterhead been printed yet?" Vincent turned and faced Gwen.

"No, I haven't!" Gwen was quick to respond. "I thought we should wait until we can come up with a company logo, perhaps a tree or a dove of something like that would be fitting. I'll organize that tomorrow."

"I think it is important to get that taken care of quickly. I have a meeting next week with the County Waste Management Committee and I would like to have some cards to hand out. Andy, it might be worthwhile for you to come along to the meeting." Vincent paused to consider his next remark.

Gwen interjected. "John, I think I should be a part of that County meeting as well. We know that County is cash strapped at the moment. I think I should give them some figures regarding the cost savings they could benefit from if they adopt our landfill proposal."

Vincent looked to John, a little startled by the authority in Gwen's voice. John turned and looked out the window. Vincent continued. "I don't think that will be necessary for this meeting Gwen. They are not really interested in the costs right now, they just want a brief as to what approach we will be taking. It is encouraging to hear that you have already collected some cost data, perhaps you should pass it on to me. I'll combine it with the work I have already done. John had not informed me that any costings had been tabled yet. What figures have you put together?" Vincent enquired.

"Well I ummm . . ." Gwen stammered. "Well you know it's just preliminary figures. However I could get up and talk about costs just as well as any one else here and it sure would be a darn sight cheaper to have me there than you, Vincent."

Vincent again turned to John, hoping he would offer some comment to ease the situation. John continued to stare out the window. Vincent was concerned that he had not been forewarned of this conflict. He sat back carefully considering his next remarks, still hopeful that John would break the silence; "Gwen, I have been placed in charge of this project and I will not be requiring your presence at this meeting. I know the people on the Waste Management Committee well and I know what they are wanting to hear at this early stage. I respect your eager attitude, however must insist that I go alone or with Andy." Vincent paused, feeling satisfied that he had handled the situation well. He continued. "With John's approval I have drafted up a structural layout for the team, defining each individual's tasks and who they are responsible to. I shall bring you all a copy in the next day or so. If you have any comments or suggestions regarding the content then please feel free to come and see me." Vince thought hard about this last comment, perhaps he would have to revise Gwen's task description. "Well I feel that is all we need to cover today, so perhaps we could meet again in a couple of days. Does anyone have anything else which they feel needs to be discussed?" Vincent searched for somebody to take the conversation away from him.

Andy cleared his throat and addressed Vincent. "Perhaps we could sit down together after you have settled in and go over the current status of our landfill application in detail. We really have just touched the surface of what is required, but nonetheless there are several key site-specific facts that I can brief you on."

Andy was a no nonsense, hard working individual who had been involved in a wide variety of projects in his time with the company. He looked forward to the work ahead of him. Vincent turned to face Andy, acknowledging the value of his suggestions with a smile.

John considered it was time to put an end to the meeting. "O.K. then. I think you have given us all a taste of what lies ahead. Perhaps next Tuesday we could meet again. Is that suitable?" John glanced around the room, noting everyone's agreement. "Let's wrap it up for now. Thank you all for your time. Gwen, could you stay behind for a minute? I want to go over a few things with you."

Vincent packed his suitcase and quickly left the room. "Wait up Andy," Vincent called to the young engineer as he closed the meeting room door and hurried down the hallway after him.

John gazed out the window, watching the passing traffic and waited till he could no longer hear Vincent and Andy as they continued down to the hallway, locked in serious conversation. "Well, what in the hell was that all about? Do you realize the position you're putting me in here?" John turned to face Gwen, and waited for her response. "Well?"

"I'm sorry, but I just can't understand why Vincent has to exclude me. Why does he have to get paid so much? It's a joke. How could you pay him so much more than me? I tell you now, I am not going to sit around here and have him tell me what to do. As office manager, I assume I'm in charge of everyone in the office and that includes Vincent. O.K.!!" Gwen exclaimed. "Please understand me John. We've worked hard to build this company and I've played a key role in building client relationship and been at the table in the earlier deals we've developed. I want us all to be happy here but that isn't going to happen if we let this guy come in and start calling the shots."

"Listen Gwen, there is no doubting that you're an efficient and dependable worker. Everyone here recognizes and appreciates that, but I have to warn you, don't push it this time. Vincent seems to be a very nice and reasonable fellow and by all accounts he can add a great deal to this team. I don't believe your attack on him was necessary."

"Well John, you know I have been on edge with all that I am going through at home and perhaps I am overreacting somewhat, but I would like you to talk to Vincent and get him to include me in this waste management meeting at the County. I think it is very important that I attend. For what it's worth I could even take Andy's place, I know a little about the engineering of a landfill. I just think you need to have me there to keep an eye on things." Gwen was unrelenting.

John knew of the turmoil in Gwen's family life and felt a real sense of pain every time he thought about it. Gwen seemed to take every opportunity to fill John in on the current traumas with her husband. John had been divorced less than two years ago, he knew of the pain and the sense of rejection. He could not bring himself to look at Gwen, he just quietly said, "Just leave it with me, I'll have a word to Vincent about it, O.K.? Don't worry, we'll work something out."

Gwen smiled and got to her feet, feeling like she had salvaged some grace from this morning's meeting. She liked John. She patted him on the shoulder and walked out the door. John remained in the meeting room by himself for some time, contemplating the morning's events. He felt hopeful.

Vincent returned to his office after a lengthy conversation with Andy, who had filled him in on the internal workings of the company. Andy warned Vincent to tread lightly if he was going to confront John about Gwen's behaviour. He told him that it was a well-circulated rumour (and one that he did not believe) that John and Gwen were having an affair and that Gwen had been experiencing difficulties with her husband. Even though it was Vincent's first full day with the company, it was not a surprise when Andy mentioned that John was very supportive of Gwen and was allowing her tremendous flexibility at work. Gwen's behaviour of late apparently had many other people in the company on edge. Andy reported that two secretaries had just resigned and that he knew of another staff member who was currently looking for a new job. It was, according to Andy, no coincidence that this was occurring just as Gwen was becoming more difficult. John was not offering any assistance or advice to anyone apart from Gwen.

Vincent was interested to hear that John had asked for Andy's input in the selection of a secretary for Countryside Environmental. John, however, had made it clear at the time that he wanted Gwen to be transferred. Andy knew his objections would be in vain and so decided that he would have to learn to deal with the situation as best he could. Andy did however think highly of Gwen's work, but had pointed out that over the past six months her performance had suffered and her attitude to fellow employees had changed for the worse. He had lost a great deal of respect for her and now felt that working with her would be a very testing experience.

Vincent was surprised by and appreciative of Andy's openness. He considered Andy to be believable and knew that John saw Andy as talented and credible. Vincent was all too familiar with situations like this and considered that the time to act was now, before the situation was allowed to get out of hand. He sat down at his desk and picked up the documents he had prepared for Gwen, defining her tasks and position. It was only now that he remembered that John had studied Gwen's job definition very closely and had made Vincent make several changes before approving it. Each alteration tended to make her job description vague and her position somewhat unclear. He decided that it was imperative to define exactly what she would and would not be required to do and who she would be accountable to. Vincent read through the documents again, making note of any changes he would like to make. In the light of the morning's events he knew he would have to discuss this further with John.

Vincent felt unsettled about the conflict that existed at Countryside and remembered all the petty squabbles, power struggles and internal politics he had to deal with in his term as County Warden. He was disgusted at the lack of maturity exhibited by some of his former colleagues and certainly did not want to be put in the same situation again. Vincent pushed his papers aside and reclined in his chair trying to relax. He considered the possibility that he was overreacting, but quickly dismissed this thought. He found himself wondering why he had chosen to accept John's offer to work for Countryside. Everything had seemed so promising and full of hope when he had met with John. One particular comment that John had made stuck in his mind. "If you have any troubles, then feel free to come and see me, my door is always open. I don't imagine however that you will encounter any major problems, the waste management division has been very successful in the past. I am excited to have you with us Vincent." Vincent had been very impressed with John; he had seemed very warm and sincere and had been a key factor in Vincent's final decision to accept the position. ". . . my door is always open."" Vincent pondered over this comment for a minute before rising to his feet and heading down to John's office. He knocked lightly on the door and walked in. "Yes Vincent, what can I do for you?" John looked tired and worn out.

"I want to discuss with you Gwen's performance in the meeting this morning. I fail to see a need for the comments she made regarding her ability to outperform me at the County meeting. I'd appreciate it if you could provide me with some insight here." Vincent's statement was just what John had feared.

"Well you see Vincent, Gwen has always been an excellent performer here. She is just having a tough time with her personal life at the moment. I don't think there is any cause for alarm, she'll get over her problems soon and I know that she will bounce back to her former cheerful self. I ask you not to be overly critical of Gwen for now and that you give me a little time to work things out. We can't be too tough on her." John glanced up at Vincent, hoping he would understand.

"I would rather deal early with anything I see as potentially harmful to our progress, and this concerns me. If you consider that we should go easy, then I will respect your judgment. I just want you to know where I am coming from. Perhaps it would be advisable for one of us to sit down with her and go over just where she fits in here."

"No I don't think that is necessary. Don't let it get you down, it will clear itself up in time. Oh by the way, I was pleased with the way you handled the meeting this morning." John turned back to his desk and began sorting through some papers. Vincent took the hint and decided to hold off discussing the issue further. He returned to his office to concentrate his efforts on becoming familiar with company protocol and making his office a more workable environment.

The next Monday morning, Vincent approached Andy and handed him a copy of his job description which included an itemization of both individual and group goals. Andy quickly glanced through the listed points but offered no immediate objections. Vincent suggested he take his time and thoroughly study the papers and come to him with any other comments.

Vincent looked around the cluttered office noting how claustrophobic it felt. Andy's desk was in one corner of the square room, desks belonging to secretaries were in two of the other corners and at the far end was Gwen's desk. Vincent was glad he had his own office. Since Gwen was away from her desk. Vincent pulled out her job description and scribbled on it:

"INTER-OFFICE MEMO
To: Gwen
From: Vincent
Subject: Job Description"

He placed the document on her desk and returned to his office.

About a minute after Gwen returned to her desk, Vincent heard her march boisterously past his office down the hall way in the direction of John's office. He suspected what the commotion was about and expected that he would soon be summoned into John's office. Much to his surprise he was not. Half an hour later John's office door was opened and Vincent heard John say "just leave it with me, I'll have a word with Vincent and straighten this out." Gwen glared at Vincent as she walked past him back to her own desk. John left the office and Vincent did not see him again at all that day. Neither John nor Gwen approached him regarding the job description report.

One morning, a week later, Vincent was the first to arrive at work. He noticed that a package had arrived over-

> ". . . my door is always open." Vincent pondered over this comment for a minute before rising to his feet and heading down to John's office.

night addressed to Countryside Environmental Services. It was from Hasty Print. He opened up the package and discovered that the company letterhead and business cards had arrived. He retrieved his own cards, and as he lifted them out of the box he uncovered Gwen's. He was shocked to see the title that appeared on them "MANAGER—FINANCE AND ACCOUNTS." His eyes nearly popped out of their sockets. He now understood why he had not heard the slightest mention of letterhead or business cards since their first meeting.

Vincent felt very frustrated and believed the team was going nowhere. Any efforts he made were being thwarted by Gwen. He considered that the time for letting things settle out had well passed and as soon as John arrived in his office, he cornered him.

"Can I have a word with you John." John swiveled in his chair to see Vincent standing at his office door. Vincent's concern was noticeable both in his appearance and the serious tone of his voice.

"Sure, come on in." John replied.

Vincent closed the door behind him. "I am of the understanding that Gwen is the office manager. Is that correct?" Vincent paused and waited for John's response.

"Yes that is right." John said with some hesitation.

Vincent's voice increased in volume. "I have just this morning received our business cards. Are you aware of the title she has put down for herself?"

"Yes, she actually came to me last week to complain about the job description document you had given her. She was in quite a rage when she came storming in here. She figured she would be in charge of managing the finances of this project. You see she has just started going to night school for her Certified General Accountants certificate and I think she's pretty keen to practice what she is learning. I explained to her that you were responsible for deciding who did what and suggested that she sit down and discuss the matter with you. I figured that if she wanted to call herself the financial manager or anything else then so be it. You and I both know where she is at." John's face turned a pale shade of red. He could not bring himself to look up at Vincent. "Vincent I firmly believe that we should not intervene here. We need to give her some room and a bit more time to sort out her problems."

"Well John I'm no more for hitting someone when they're down than you are, but can you not see that she is the sole cause of the terrible atmosphere in this place? I'm not the only one that is affected here. I think we're in danger of losing some valuable players if you allow this kind of behaviour to continue. I have already been approached by a couple of the staff in this office who have voiced their objections. They believe she has changed dramatically over the past six months although certain individuals commented that she has always been somewhat bossy and power hungry. I gather my presence here has caused

an escalation of the problem. I don't believe this is something we can just turn away from and hope that it will go away. It needs to be dealt with. When I first met with you I shared some concerns about the small size of this office and the necessity for a close knit team effort. I feel I can't perform effectively if this is allowed to continue." Vincent waited for John to respond to his comments, but was not surprised to receive nothing but silence. John slowly got up from his chair and left the room. Vincent could see that he was very troubled. He desperately hoped that John could see the ramifications of his action.

A couple of days following Vincent's discussions with John, Gwen was away sick for two days. She returned to work one morning and began quizzing Andy as to what Vincent had been working on while she had been away. "Well I believe he was reading through the Environmental Assessment Act and making some notes. Perhaps you should ask him when he comes in." Andy was young and had become somewhat intimidated by her, a fact that she was well aware of.

"I thought you had already made some notes from the Act. You did, didn't you?" Gwen continued, determined to create a scene.

Andy reluctantly replied "Well yes I did look at part of it, but that was some time ago."

Just as Andy finished these last comments, John walked into the office. Gwen was quick off the mark. "John, I think we need to do something about Vincent. Andy says Vincent has been duplicating work. That's a waste of time and with the money we pay him it's something we cannot afford."

"Well you're right, we don't need anyone to duplicate another person's work. I'll have to have a word with Vincent about that." John reached the coffee machine and filled his cup. He wanted to change the subject, but Gwen continued before he had a chance.

"And another thing," Gwen was winding up, "How is it that he can just come and go as he pleases, he is never in here before 8:30 a.m. Who gave him special rights?"

John ignored this last question and walked into his own office, hoping to escape the outburst. Andy had followed him and startled John when he spoke. "John I feel I should clarify what Gwen was referring to in there about Vincent duplicating my work. I think that was a very unfair comment to make. She is taking what I said completely out of context. You see Vincent and I can read the same article, looking for different facts. That is exactly what happened here. I was looking for the engineering data, while Vincent was looking at the same papers with a political slant, extracting different material. I do not appreciate someone taking something I say out of context and blowing it up, especially in front of you. I ask you to consider this before you approach Vincent." Andy was rarely one to speak his mind, but felt a great sense of satisfaction with his remarks.

"Don't get your dander up Andy, I wasn't even going to mention it to Vincent. I was pretty sure that Vincent would not duplicate any work. Thanks for your comments though." John picked up his coffee and nervously smiled at Andy before taking a sip. Andy turned and left John's office, almost knocking over Gwen who was standing just around the corner, apparently listening in on what had been said.

Two months passed by. Vincent had been working for Countryside Environmental Services now for nearly three months. He was still feeling the frustrations of working with Gwen. Her behaviour continued to be erratic and her performance as a team member left a great deal to be desired. Vincent had approached John many times and on three specific occasions asked him to resolve the problems. Each time John had expressed his concern but asked Vincent to put up with the situation for a little longer. Vincent's personal secretary had resigned, stating that she required more time with her family. Vincent was well aware that the true reasons for her departure were not aired. In addition to this, Andy had confided with Vincent that he had been given a temporary offer of employment with a large mining company in the north of the province and would probably be accepting the offer when it is finalized. Vincent was very disturbed and troubled as to what he should do.

THE CASE OF THE UNSEEN CUSTOMERS (A) – Unit 3 Case Study

"I've had it!" exclaimed Chris to the other managers as she closed the boardroom door.

Chris was Committee Secretary and one of four supervisors of the Licensing and City Clerk Sections of the City of Townsville. Yet again, one of the younger clerks had complained to her that, although she felt like she was doing more work than anyone else, she was being continually picked on by one of the more experienced clerks, or "mother" as she vocally referred to her. The two clerks constantly bickered with each other, even in front of customers. All the arguments were essentially the same: "I end up dealing with customers when they needed licensing service and I don't get help." Or "When someone finally does help me, they do so reluctantly." Or "I always have to answer the phone even though it is seldom for me – I can't get my committee minutes done as a result."

Mark and Rob, Assistant City Clerks, agreed that they too were getting fed up with the constant complaining. "Our Deputy always used the principle 'If I don't hear about it, I don't care'. We have certainly heard about it now. I'm not getting my own work done!," said Mark. "I've tried asking some of the other clerks what the issue is, but they never seem to give me any direct feedback," stated Rob.

"Well," said Chris, "Something has to be done. This has finally reached a point where I need to do something about it. I know we managers don't usually work together, but maybe this time we need too. I think this last emotional outburst has pushed all of us over the edge. So what should we do?"

CITY OF TOWNSVILLE

Townsville was a city of 167,500 people or 62,780 households located in the Region of Binhampton in the heart of Southwestern Ontario, less than one hour's drive from Toronto. Townsville was a vibrant, confident and cosmopolitan community that had a strong industrial and business base. Its industrial base and growth rate it an attractive community to live in.

The City was the local, municipal governing body of Townsville and employed approximately 1000 people. City Council was chaired by the Mayor and consisted of a local councilor for each of the nine wards within Townsville. The Chief Administrative Officer was the senior administrator of the City and was responsible to City Council for the effective and efficient operation of the City. All City Departments reported to Council through the Chief Administrator who served as Chairman of the Senior Management Committee. The Corporate Services and Clerks Division included both the Licensing Section and the City Clerk Section, the location of the conflict. (See Exhibit 1 for a partial organization chart.)

Just prior to the events of the case, the employees of the City of Townsville had moved to a new, modernly designed building located in the downtown. The building was designed in a u-shape, around a large atrium that reached from ground to the roof and was used for various community exhibits and activities throughout the year. Winding stairs and a bank of elevators led to the second floor offices; some of the parking entrances also entered onto the second floor. On the North side of the second floor were the Mayor's Office and the City Council Chamber. On the South side, there were the Chief Administrative Officer's Office and the City Clerk and Licensing Sections.

THE CITY CLERK AND LICENSING SECTIONS

The elevators and stairs on the second floor led immediately into a wide hallway leading to the office space that housed the City Clerk Section and Licensing Sections. This wide, narrow room was dominated by a with a 60-foot counter where a resident could get service. While these two sections were in the same Division, they had distinct operational responsibilities. They shared the same office space and had joint responsibility to serve the public at the front counter. The four managers within these sections also had distinct responsibilities and operated relatively independently. (See Exhibit 2 for a physical layout of the office.)

"I've had it!" exclaimed Chris to the other managers as she closed the boardroom door.

Chris was Committee Secretary and one of four supervisors of the Licensing and City Clerk Sections of the City of Townsville. Yet again, one of the younger clerks had complained to her that, although she felt like she was doing more work than anyone else, she was being continually picked on by one of the more experienced clerks, or "mother" as she vocally referred to her. The two clerks constantly bickered with each other, even in front of customers. All the arguments were essentially the same: "I end up dealing with customers when they needed licensing service and I don't get help." Or "When someone finally does help me, they do so reluctantly." Or "I always have to answer the phone even though it is seldom for me — I can't get my committee minutes done as a result."

Mark and Rob, Assistant City Clerks, agreed that they too were getting fed up with the constant complaining. "Our Deputy always used the principle 'If I don't hear about it, I don't care'. We have certainly heard about it now. I'm not getting my own work done!," said Mark. "I've tried asking some of the other clerks what the issue is, but they never seem to give me any direct feedback," stated Rob.

"Well," said Chris, "Something has to be done. This has finally reached a point where I need to do something about it. I know we managers don't usually work together, but maybe this time we need too. I think this last emotional outburst has pushed all of us over the edge. So what should we do?"

CITY OF TOWNSVILLE

Townsville was a city of 167,500 people or 62,780 households located in the Region of Binhampton in the heart of Southwestern Ontario, less than one hour's drive from Toronto. Townsville was a vibrant, confident and cosmopolitan community that had a strong industrial and business base. Its industrial base and growth rate it an attractive community to live in.

The City was the local, municipal governing body of Townsville and employed approximately 1000 people. City Council was chaired by the Mayor and consisted of a local councilor for each of the nine wards within

▶ EXHIBIT 1 Partial Organization Chart: Corporate Services and Clerks

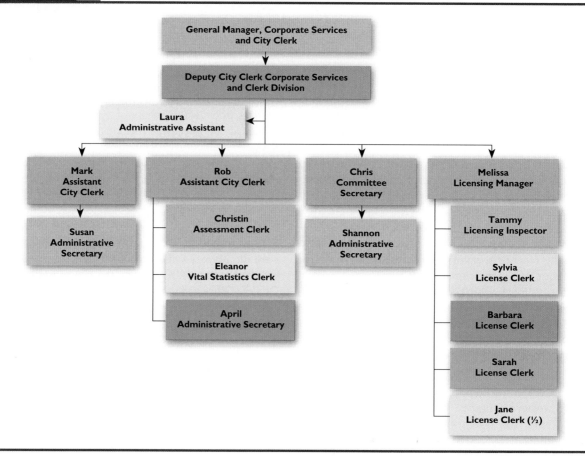

Townsville. The Chief Administrative Officer was the senior administrator of the City and was responsible to City Council for the effective and efficient operation of the City. All City Departments reported to Council through the Chief Administrator who served as Chairman of the Senior Management Committee. The Corporate Services and Clerks Division included both the Licensing Section and the City Clerk Section, the location of the conflict. (See Exhibit 1 for a partial organization chart.)

Just prior to the events of the case, the employees of the City of Townsville had moved to a new, modernly designed building located in the downtown. The building was designed in a u-shape, around a large atrium that reached from ground to the roof and was used for various community exhibits and activities throughout the year. Winding stairs and a bank of elevators led to the second floor offices; some of the parking entrances also entered onto the second floor. On the North side of the second floor were the Mayor's Office and the City Council Chamber. On the South side, there were the Chief Administrative Officer's Office and the City Clerk and Licensing Sections.

THE CITY CLERK AND LICENSING SECTIONS

The elevators and stairs on the second floor led immediately into a wide hallway leading to the office space that housed the City Clerk Section and Licensing Sections. This wide, narrow room was dominated by a with a 60-foot counter where a resident could get service. While these two sections were in the same Division, they had distinct operational responsibilities. They shared the same office space and had joint responsibility to serve the public at the front counter. The four managers within these sections also had distinct responsibilities and operated relatively independently. (See Exhibit 2 for a physical layout of the office.)

LICENSING SECTION

The Licensing Section was responsible for issuing City of Townsville business, marriage and lottery licenses (in accordance with provincial requirements), auditing lottery activities, and producing related reports.

Melissa, the Licensing Manager, was overall supervisor. Tammy as the License Inspector spent much of her time on-the-road checking for licenses and auditing bingo groups, bazaars, Monte Carlos, and raffles. Sylvia, Barbara and Sarah, were License Clerks. Jane worked as a half time License Clerk. They issued licenses, handled customers who came into the office, dealt with customer phone requests and inquiries, and conducted computer-based administration activities. They also performed other administrative duties: photocopying, sorting and filing. Although the workload was fairly evenly distributed throughout the year, it did become hectic every

two months when bingo licenses had to be renewed. All License Clerks plus Tammy, when she was in, were expected to respond to customers at the front counter when needed. As well, each person's phone rang when a call came in to the department. Clerks who were free were expected to pick up the calls.

Most of the Licensing Clerks had been in their jobs for several years. Their salary grades were between 9-16.

CLERK SECTION

The Clerk Section ensured that the responsibilities of the City Clerk were carried out in accordance with the statutes of Ontario and City by-laws. It provided assist-

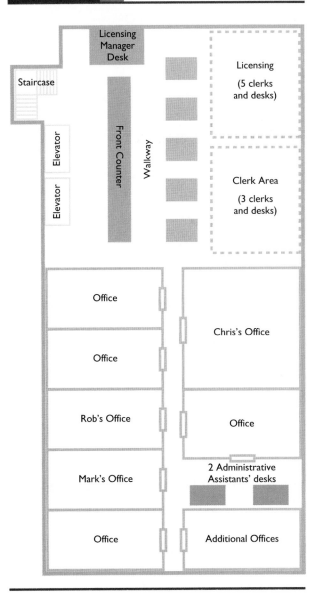

▶ **EXHIBIT 2** — **Physical Layout of the Operation**

ance for municipal elections, issued marriage licenses and burial permits and registered births. The section also had the responsibility for providing corporate support services to City Council. It was also responsible for taking and managing council/committee minutes and agendas, managing corporate records, and handling unanswered calls to the Chief Administrative Officer's office, Mayor's office, Licensing Section, and Records Centre.

Rob, an Assistant City Clerk, managed the clerks' activities and had three clerks reporting directly to him. Christin was the Assessment Clerk who handled property ownership questions and lot rezoning, severing and adjustments. Eleanor was the Vital Statistics Clerk who handled birth and death registration and marriage licenses. April operated primarily as Rob's administrative secretary and occasionally assisted with customer requests and counter traffic when others were busy. Another clerk/administrative assistant, Susan, was an administrative secretary for Mark, the other Assistant City Clerk. Chris was Committee Secretary and had Shannon reporting to her as an Administrative Secretary.

Similar to Licensing Clerks, City Clerks were to respond to customers when they came to the counter. As well, phone calls to the Clerk's Section and unanswered calls to the Chief Administrative Officer's Office rang to all five clerk's phones. Clerk positions had job grades ranging between 7-10. The section was typically seen as providing entry positions for employment with the City; despite recent vacancies in the Clerk's Section, few employees within the City of Townsville had applied for these positions.

THE PHYSICAL LAYOUT

Upon entering the office, either from the stairs or the elevators, customers were faced with a 60-foot-long front counter. A five foot walkway was directly behind the counter. (See Exhibit 2 for Physical Layout of Operation.) On the left side of the counter, was the Licensing Section where Melissa and the five licensing employees' desks were located. On the right side of the counter was the City Clerk Section, which was occupied by the three front-line clerks and their desks. The walkway led to a long hallway where other managers' offices (including Mark's and Rob's offices) were located. April's and Susan's desks were located directly outside of Mark and Rob's offices.

THE NATURE OF THE COMPLAINTS FROM THE CITY CLERK SECTION

As they wondered what to do, each of the managers reflected on what they had recently heard from their staff.

"One of the most common complaints that I remember" said Rob is "'You're not pulling your weight, dear; you didn't answer the phone enough today.' And

answered by, 'Yes, mother!' That ends up coming to us as a complaint, 'Why does she always pick on me? I'm working as hard as anyone else here!'"

"That's where the key issue is located," Chris reflected. "I always hear 'My desk is right at the front counter, so I'm the first person the customers see. I'm getting tired of always being the one who has to stop work to help a customer! It means that I am late with my own work.' And then there is the 'Why can't she help out? She never goes to the counter or answers phones! And she was so miserable today, I can guarantee that she'll call in sick tomorrow.' If only there was no truth in what was said.' And then, if confronted the other clerk just says, 'I'm sorry! I didn't see that there was a customer waiting! I sit behind this pillar, and it makes it difficult to see.'"

As they talked the three managers were surprised at the volume of complaints they could recall, including:

- "I'm the only one answering phones here! No one else is helping out!"

- "Why don't Mark and Rob's Assistants have to help out at the front counter or with the phones! They're being paid the same as the rest of us clerks but they sure seem to get preferential treatment!"

- "When a customer calls, all our phones ring—but Mark and Rob's Assistants never pick up the phone."

It was also apparent that the interpersonal and workload issues were being aggravated by the overlap in assigned duties between the Licensing Section and the Clerk Section. As Rob recalled, one person had commented, "Licensing is not helping out enough! Why can't they pick up our phones like we do for them? And why do they get paid more than me, just because they are in Licensing? What do the License clerks do anyway that makes them so great?"

Mark, Rob and Chris knew that everyone was busy with their own work. Doing "joint work" was an issue. As one clerk had reported, "I knew that customer was here for Licensing—why should I get up? Customers see one counter and assume anyone can help them. I was busy with my work and they clearly were not here to see me. Yesterday, Licensing ignored this customer so I got up and, of course, I just had to send them to the other end of the counter."

Other issues resulted from the location of the office. As one clerk stated, "I feel like we're the reception for the full City! It seems like half of the customers who come here are just looking for directions!"

The phone system had created other issues. Chris talked about how one customer was on hold, while the clerk ran around finding the right person. Not only did this block a line, it took up the clerk's time as well. Other clerks handled things differently. As one had said, "If I can't answer the customer's question on the phone, I just take a message; I don't get involved in what other's do."

"You know," said Rob, "when we have tried to do something, perhaps we haven't followed through as we should have. I overheard two people griping: 'How can management not notice her poor performance? That's just unacceptable!' Maybe we should be thinking more about performance management?"

Other comments were more general but related to the overall performance of the Section:

- "Why should I talk to management—they don't listen to what I have to say anyway!"

- "I'm getting tired of having to walk to the other end of hall to drop off photocopying and mail."

- "All anyone thinks I can do is type! I can handle harder work than that!"

- "We still need new dictaphones! These are really wearing out."

- "I still haven't received training on WordPerfect."

- "I feel bad asking for help from Susan and April during lunch; I feel like I'm imposing on them or disturbing their work."

THE NATURE OF COMPLAINTS FROM THE LICENSING SECTION

Later on that day, Chris asked Melissa how things were going in the Licensing Section.

Melissa sighed. "I'm getting really tired of hearing their constant complaining and arguing — I have to sit right in the middle of it all day long! But quite frankly, I have no idea what I should do with these types of issues! 'How am I supposed to get my work done if I have to constantly answer the phone?'; 'I don't understand what the Clerks are so busy with! Why does it take so long for them to answer the phones?'; 'I knew that customer was the funeral director and thus not my client; why should I get up?'; 'I was busy concentrating on my computer work when suddenly a customer showed up beside me out of no where! He had walked right past the counter to my desk!'; 'Why does management constantly interfere? I'll ask for help if I need it!'; 'Management doesn't give a rip one way or the other! They never do anything if we raise issues anyway! I've given up trying to give them ideas.' The complaints seem endless. 'I can't believe we still don't have a legal-sized tray for the front computer! And what about those new fonts we asked for?' 'I'm really tired of always having to wait for the photocopier!' 'How are we supposed to issue all of these licenses with three people. There's just too much work.'"

"And to add one of my own complaints", continued Melissa, "I have a clear view of the full counter from where I sit, but I really don't need to! Lately I end up waiting on the customer when really I should be back up to back up! The clerks don't seem to understand that I have too much to do . . ."

THE DECISION

At the end of the day, Rob dropped by Chris's office. "Well, we all know what the Deputy's response to this would be!" said Rob. "He'd say, 'This is just how it is given the nature of the people and the nature of the task. Don't worry about it; just get people to do their jobs. If they are not doing their jobs then begin discipline proceedings. In other words, we're paying them for their job, so just get them to do it!'"

"Which is exactly what we've all been doing so far!" exclaimed Chris. "What concerns me most is that this has gotten severe enough to start affecting our level of service. To date, we managers have been operating independently and minding our own business. We probably all have different perspectives on what's going on here and on how we should handle this situation, but we are all responsible for maintaining an acceptable level of service to the Deputy. Where do we go from here?"

 # NORTHWELL INC. – Unit 4 Case Study

When Northwell's Senior Management and Board first gave Claudia the leadership role in the development of a virtual medical product and service mall with Medichek, a year and a half ago, she was delighted. She and Nathan Daniels (V-P Marketing) had uncovered the opportunity, Medichek was an excellent organization, and it had been clear that this was a venture well worth embracing. Claudia Leung, CFO of Northwell, had an excellent working relationship with senior management at Medichek. Since Northwell's major contribution in the shorter term would be cash ($7.5 million as of now), she was the ideal candidate for the assignment. The development of this initiative would increase her entrepreneurial skill set and profile and looked to be a manageable addition to her portfolio of responsibilities.

Claudia was beginning to wonder if this dream assignment was about to become a nightmare. The project had run into technical problems, was 4 to 5 months behind schedule, and the Board and Senior Management at Northwell were frustrated and putting pressure on Claudia to get things moving. Executives at

Medichek were pushing back, in response to their own frustration, stating that Claudia's interventions were hindering progress. In addition, she'd been hearing growing rumblings of concern and unhappiness in the sales and marketing areas, evidenced in the recent resignation of three staff members and the loss of a good distributor from the mid-west U.S.

Northwell's Senior Management and Board Chair had asked Claudia to recommend a course of action that would rectify problems with this undertaking. They were expecting this advice to be tabled within the next two weeks.

HISTORY OF THE FIRM

Northwell Medical was founded 25 years ago, as the result of a merger between a Canadian and US firm. Northern Medical, the Canadian partner, had specialized in durable hospital/medical products, while Wellness Medical had focused on consumable hospital products. Both had distributed their products in Canada and the U.S. for a decade prior to the merger, and had shared marketing and distribution services for five years.

The actual merger announcement was anticipated and welcomed by most shareholders and managers. There were some initial difficulties as structures, systems, processes, roles, and reporting relationships were sorted out during the first year. By year three the merger was viewed by both insiders and outsiders as a success. Market penetration and sales accelerated while average costs declined (after accounting for one-time restructuring costs). Growth rates averaged 20% (discounting for inflation) throughout the first 15 years in what was a fairly mature market. Northwell made aggressive investments in technology and product development during this period. Profitability grew at rates 10% above industry norms, with the return on equity averaging 18% during this period. This growth was partially stimulated by the addition of new and/or improved products, but it was largely due to Northwell's spreading reputation for value, service and support. They won market share from competitors, even though their price structure was typically 2% to 10% higher.

As consolidation occurred in the hospital and nursing care delivery systems, it was clear that Northwell was well positioned to solidify its position as a preferred supplier amongst purchasing agents, administrators and hospital user groups. In U.S. industry surveys of hospital suppliers, Northwell regularly placed in the top 5 for quality, service, support, and overall customer satisfaction during the two decades that followed.

Northwell Medical produced a wide range of medical products for institutional usage. Products ranged from consumable patient supplies such as wound dressings, bandages, and disposable surgical supplies to more durable products (e.g., IV units, walkers, canes). In addition to the products it produced, Northwell used its sales network to distribute high quality, higher margin products, sourced largely from European and smaller North American specialty manufacturers. Ten years ago these accounted for 10% of the products listed, 15% of sales and 6% of the profits, and by the most recent year end they represented 10% of products listed, 15% of sales and 25% of profits. These products included hospital beds, wheel chairs, and orthopedic supports (braces for limbs and neck). The intent was to provide purchasing agents and their therapeutic committees with one stop shopping for their medical product needs in particular product categories.

Northwell's production facilities were located in the US, Canada, and Mexico. The Canadian plant specialized in products that involve metal fabrication (approximately 20% of total manufactured products, 25% of sales and 30% of profits in the most recent year end), while the two US plants manufactured both plastic and fabric related product (40% of manufactured products, 30% of sales, and 15% of profits). The Mexican plant also produced plastic and fabric related products (20% of manufactured products listed, 15% of sales, and 10% of profits). In addition, Northwell sourced manufacturing services for some of its products in the Asia-Pacific area (10% of manufactured products listed, 10% of sales, 15% of profits).

In North America, Northwell marketed and sold its products primarily through its own sales force. In addition, a number of medical product distribution companies carried some or all of the Northwell line. They were prequalified by Northwell and tended to service smaller hospitals and nursing homes, medical and dental offices, and regional medical product retail supply outlets. The prequalification checks included financial stability, reputation, and service quality. Those selected, committed to agreed-to minimum sales volumes. Distributors were not given exclusive territories, but over the years they had sorted themselves out in ways that meant that most American markets were well serviced. These independent distributors accounted for 25% of sales and approximately 30% of the profits. Wholesale prices allowed for dealer margins that varied from 15% to 30%, depending upon the type of product and the complexity involved in selling and servicing the product (e.g., in-service hospital staff training in product use).

Over the years certain managers and board members had expressed interest in extending their activities into foreign markets (Europe and Japan were the ones most frequently mentioned). However, Northwell had shied away from these opportunities, due to concerns over their ability to compete and the belief that there were more profitable growth opportunities available in North America. Throughout the years, at the request of specific

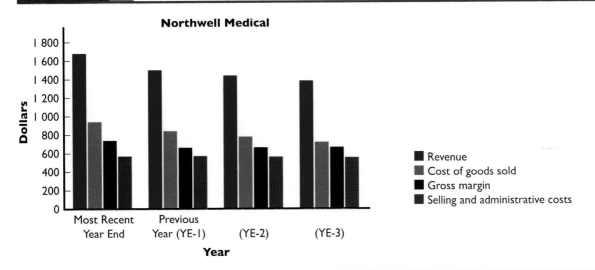

Northwell Medical

Legend:
- Revenue
- Cost of goods sold
- Gross margin
- Selling and administrative costs

X-axis (Year): Most Recent Year End, Previous Year (YE-1), (YE-2), (YE-3)
Y-axis (Dollars): 0 to 1 800

European firms they trusted, Northwell had engaged in the export of a limited range of relatively unique products. For the most recent year end, these accounted for approximately 5% of sales and 5% of the profits.

Growth and profitability slowed at Northwell nine years ago and flattened thereafter. A year ago, sales growth was 4%, profitability had fallen to 6% of sales and the return on equity was 6.5%. Their reputation as a benchmark to be emulated in the medical products sector was now a memory.

Two notable new product failures about a decade ago had resulted in staff changes and a new Director of New Product Development. Since Sales and Marketing were seen as the primary clients of New Product Development, funding responsibility for R&D shifted to Sales and Marketing eight years ago. The changes succeeded in reducing costs in this area by 33% through more careful screening and approval processes and tighter budget controls. However, within two years of the change, most of the output from New Product Development was in the form of incremental product improvements, and there was limited work underway in the area of significant product innovations. In an effort to increase their productivity, new product development personnel restricted their direct field involvement with sales personnel and clients. The problem/opportunity finding role was delegated to marketing and sales personnel, who were expected to forwarded project and product suggestions to the Product Development Approval Team. The Director of New Product Development chaired this committee, with representation from Sales, Marketing, and Finance/Accounting.

The percentage of sales coming from products introduced in the previous four years declined from 25% a decade ago to 8% a year ago. Finger pointing had become the order of the day, as frustration surfaced over the slow pace of innovation. New Product Development staff complained about a lack of resources, equipment, and bureaucracy, while Sales and Marketing personnel grumbled that Northwell's reputation as a problem solver and innovator was being eroded due to the inability of R&D to deliver the right products at the right time and price.

Profitability was negatively affected during the past eight years by competitive pressures on price and customer servicing costs. Northwell was still a preferred supplier, but the emergence of health care cost containment pressures and powerful buying groups had reduced Northwell's capacity to command a price premium. More importantly, key competitors caught up with Northwell in the areas of sales, support, and solutions, but were able to do so in innovative ways that reduced their sales costs (e.g., call centers, logistical streamlining, and electronically distributed training support). Sales and servicing costs at Northwell were now approximately 15% higher than their key competitors. However, customers did not perceive significant differences in the levels of support and responsiveness.

THE MEDICHEK OPPORTUNITY

Two years ago Northwell's Senior Management Team received clear feedback that stockholders were very dissatisfied with cost containment and market expansion activities. At that time, the Board replaced the Vice Presidents of Sales and Manufacturing (the President was replaced a year earlier). All 3 appointments were from outside the organization — something unheard of in the past. In addition, the Board instituted performance contracts with members of the Senior Management Team. These performance contracts required the following improvements to be achieved within a four year period: sales growth of 30% over levels in the most recent year; a return on equity of 18%; a return to gross profitability levels that exceeded industry averages by 10%; 15% of sales coming from products introduced in the previous 4 years; and a return of customer satisfaction levels to those achieved a decade earlier.

Nathan Daniels, the V-P Marketing and Claudia Leung, the CFO, had grown up in Northwell and both had the trust and respect of the new CEO and the Board Chair. Both were appointed to their senior roles three years ago, following the early retirement of their predecessors. Approximately 2 years ago the CEO gave them joint responsibility for identifying growth opportunities. Nathan and Claudia had bumped heads in the past over the value of marketing expenditures, but they recognized the assignment's importance and decided to set aside past difficulties. Both possessed a strong interest in emerging information technologies and this quickly led them to investigate Web-based marketing, distribution, and E-commerce opportunities for Northwell.

Research conducted three years ago told Northwell that their primary customers were either currently able to order and receive information over the Internet or soon would be Internet-enabled. Sales personnel reported that an increasing amount of their customer communications was being conducted over the Internet and that Northwell's capacities in this area were lagging behind their key competitors, as they were in other areas of technologically enabled customer support. Further, many of these primary customers seemed quite interested in exploiting this technology to enhance efficiency, speed, communications, and the efficacy of training and development. These interests seemed to fit well with the ideas that Nathan and Claudia were pursuing.

Shortly after being assigned responsibility for identifying growth opportunities, Nathan and Claudia decided to meet with the senior management of Medichek. Medichek was an emerging net-based U.S. firm, specializing in health care. They had been founded eight years ago, were located in Dallas, were growing very quickly (200+% per year) and had 275 employees.

Medichek's primary business was the design and management of Web sites for a number of leading health care organizations (hospitals, nursing homes, pharmaceutical manufacturers and distributors, medical product manufacturers), including Northwell's (as of approximately 2 years ago). In addition, three years ago, Medichek launched a subscription service that provided on-line access to medical information to health care professionals and researchers. This was an expensive service to develop and maintain, but subscriber growth over the first 18 months exceeded Medichek's expectations by a factor of 2. Medichek had a reputation for innovation, honesty, responsiveness, quality, candidness, and trustworthiness. They were very selective in terms of whom they chose to do business with. It was said that Medichek picked its clients and those who were selected were the lucky ones.

Medichek was 75% owned by the five individuals who had founded the company (all were in their 30's and directly involved in the business). They had resisted take-over and IPO opportunities, preferring to develop and control their own organization. Nathan first met the Medichek's owners 3 years ago, when he was looking for a Website designer for Northwell. True to form, it was Medichek who, after careful deliberation, selected Northwell as a client. While initially "put off" by Medichek's approach, Nathan and Claudia quickly became fans, and this enthusiasm extended to other members of senior management. Their work was fairly priced by industry standards, but more importantly, their strategic approach to site design and management resulted in customer accolades and industry awards in recent years. Sales and marketing personnel responded favourably to Northwell's new Website, when it went live, reporting positive customer reactions to its layout, content, and functionality. Though they still felt that technology enabled customer support was lagging (e.g., electronic access to technical training support materials), they viewed this as an important step in the right direction.

Medichek's owners and employees often commented about how comfortable they felt working with Northwell. They particularly appreciated Northwell's commitment to dealing with its clients in ways that emphasized customer knowledge, value, and informed decision-making. Medichek officials complained that Northwell's decision-making sometimes took too long, that Northwell over-attended to cost rather than value, and that Northwell had difficulty keeping its "fingers out of the pot" once decisions were made. However, they discounted these frustrations, chalking them up to Northwell's concern for quality and competitiveness.

During the development of Nothwell's Website, it became apparent to Claudia and Nathan that there might be good reason to get closer to Medichek concerning another venture they were pursuing. Medichek had

> They particularly appreciated Northwell's commitment to dealing with its clients in ways that emphasized customer knowledge, value, and informed decision-making.

been exploring the development of a virtual health service mall, for use by the health care industry. The idea was that professional end users (hospitals, nursing homes, physicians, pharmacists) could access this site in order to electronically shop for the products they needed. Products and services supplying firms would be carefully screened to ensure that they met quality, value and customer service standards. Quotes could be solicited, orders placed, and payments received electronically. Further, the mall would serve as a primary source of product information, product warnings and recalls, educational on-line health care forums, health care news, and distributed web-based training in health care matters (e.g., product use education).

From the initial meeting on the virtual mall approximately two years ago, Medichek was clear that it wanted to partner with Northwell in the development of this undertaking. They proposed that the mall be established as an independent business unit and that Northwell and Medichek own it equally. Northwell would commit to becoming a prime occupant in the mall and would supply the needed development funds (estimated at $5 to $10 million). Medichek would develop the necessary technology platforms, structure the services and pricing arrangements with mall occupants, structure the entry criteria, and market the mall service. Medichek's reputation would prove very helpful here. They estimated that it would take a year to make this project a reality.

Nathan and Claudia were excited by this opportunity. It had the potential to significantly reduce costs for both customers and suppliers and provide Northwell with opportunity to dramatically extend its reach into foreign markets. Though quality competitor products would also be listed at the mall, these were already readily available in the marketplace. More importantly, the mall would be selective concerning who was allowed to be listed and exhibit. When combined with the quality of the information, news and other services available, it was anticipated that there would be a very positive halo cast on firms allowed to market their goods and services at the site.

When Nathan and Claudia talked to Northwell's IT group and the CEO about this opportunity, interest and excitement spread. Sales and marketing personnel also expressed interested, but were concerned with the implications on existing channels of distribution and customer contact. This was a company that had built its reputation on its personal relationships with its distributors and customer (i.e., responsiveness and support), and they were concerned with how things would be affected by this new venture. Nathan and Claudia asked them to relax and give the new venture time to develop. They told staff that the new venture would increase the exposure and reach of Northwell, thereby opening up new opportunities. Channels would not change overnight, and staff

was advised that Northwell would monitor things closely and help employees adapt and transition into new roles, as needed. They were told that this was new territory for everyone, so the keys were to be patient and open-minded, communicating information, questions, and concerns in a timely fashion.

Claudia worked with the Medichek's CFO to develop the business plan, projections and a Letter of Understanding during April a year ago. Northwell's Board was first informed of the possible opportunity in January a year ago. In May, Northwell's senior management team recommended the partnership (as set out in the Letter of Understanding), to its Board. Medichek and Northwell jointly signed the Letter of Understanding in June a year ago, with the first $2 million installment of development support issued in June. Northwell's managers were shocked (pleasantly) by the speed of the approval process. Primary responsibility for managing the relationship with Medichek was assigned to Claudia.

During the latter half of the previous year Medichek hired additional staff and proceeded with the development work. By February of the current year Northwell had advanced $4.5 million in development support. During this period Northwell had focused on shoring up it internal operations and improving its profitability. By December of the previous year, products introduced within the past 4 years had grown to 9% of sales, and growth had increased 12% over previous year. Profitability had improved to 10% of sales and an 8% return on equity, and customer satisfaction results had improved marginally. Both the Board and the Senior Management Team were pleased to see progress, but felt there was still a long way to go. Discussion amongst these groups clearly indicated that they saw the virtual mall as the initiative with the greatest potential, as well as the greatest risks.

Personnel in sales and marketing expressed increasing concern over how their functions and roles would be affected by the new venture and what would be the impact on their customers. Nathan continued to tell them to relax while they were waiting to see how roles and functions would need to adapt in the wake of the virtual mall. Though he couldn't guarantee there would be no job losses, he truly believed this new venture would open up significant new opportunities and more meaningful customer relationships for many. In spite of these words of reassurance, the number of voluntary resignations in these areas rose by 15% and there were rumours that others were looking as well. Many of these resignations involved individuals viewed as high performers. In addition, some distributors were also expressing concern and looking for alternative lines of business to represent, in the event that they became redundant to Northwell.

Human resources advised the executive to slow its recruiting initiatives for departing personnel until the effects of the new venture were better understood. Nathan and other senior managers in sales and marketing saw the wisdom in this advice, but they were also concerned about sending the wrong message to staff, customers and distributors. As a result, recruitment was slowed, positions were left unfilled for longer than in the past (150 days on average vs 60), and contract employees were brought in to help, where needed. The consideration of a new call center was also put on the back burner until the ramifications for Nothwell of the virtual mall were better understood.

By April the Senior Management Team was placing increasing pressure on Claudia to get the mall up and running. Marketing of the mall was going extremely well. Product and service suppliers had been solicited and screened and a critical mass of these organizations was signed and ready to go (i.e., their initial product information, visual material, and related systems and supports were developed). The news and related information services and site features had been developed, staffed and beta tested by those who would be using the mall. Primary customers were anxiously awaiting access to the new service. However, Medichek reported that the development of the technological platform and related supports (in particular, the E-commerce and security components) were proving more difficult than originally anticipated and that the complete Mall's formal launch was about 4 months behind schedule.

Claudia began to spend more time monitoring the pace of developments at Medichek. Monthly visits became weekly. In May she requested bi-weekly reports on progress achieved, funds expended, and the time allocations of the various project teams. These were very similar to the reporting Northwell required from its own operations.

Relations with Medichek chilled in response to the increased frequency of site visits and the request for more detailed reporting. At first they resisted complying with the reporting request, but after a month of mounting pressure they acquiesced. Medichek's senior management wrote that such information would be furnished under duress, because it would serve no useful purpose, be expensive and time consuming to develop, and divert attention from where it was most needed.

The resignation of three more capable staff members from the sales and marketing area and the loss of a valued distributor from the mid-west U.S. in the late spring elevated Nathan's anxiety over progress and he wanted to know just how much longer it would be before "Virtual Northwell" would be fully operational. Nathan continued to believe that it would be unwise to make major changes in sales and marketing until they really knew how customers would react to the new channel. He felt that it was difficult to predict, with any degree of certainty, what the ideal approach to sales and marketing should be, and he preferred to adopt an approach that reacted to what evolved as a result of the new channel. However, he was also aware of the need to address employee and distributor uncertainty as quickly as possible, recognizing that the "be patient until we have a better understanding" strategy was not working well. Since Claudia was in change of the new venture and since there would be organizational design, budget and control implications, he wanted Claudia's advice on how best to handle the matter.

When Medichek reported continuing development problems in July, Senior Management at Northwell voiced increasing dissatisfaction with the progress to date and asked Claudia to recommend a course of action that would rectify matters.

➡ JESSICA CASSERRA'S TASK FORCE: HOSPITAL INTEGRATION IN THE REGION OF ERIE – Unit 5 Case Study

Jessica Casserra stretched back from the monitor and rubbed her eyes. Technology had made it possible to be home in the evenings with her family, but as they pointed out, that didn't mean they saw much of her. For the past two months, most evenings and weekends had been spent pouring over internal reports, briefs, governmental documents, spreadsheets, and consulting studies concerning the integration of hospital services in the Region of Erie.

The taxpayers of the Region had received far more than their fair share of her time, but she wasn't sure that was translating into added value. Budgeting, control, program integration, human resource and organization design issues had not been resolved—they had only festered as senior hospital management, board members and key stakeholders groups squabbled and continued to avoid making difficult decisions.

Nonetheless, the formal organizational integration of Metropolitan with five smaller hospitals and ancillary services (e.g., laundry, food services) was required to be agreed to and set in motion within ten months. The Ministry of Health had fixed the timing. It was extremely unlikely the provincial governing party would back down from the start date, given the political heat they had taken throughout the review process that resulted in their decision to regionalize hospital services. Jessica knew they would not want to give integration opponents additional opportunities to mobilize resistance or any hope that decisions might be reversed. They would also want this matter long past prior to the next provincial election.

HOSPITAL SERVICES IN THE REGION AND THEIR RESPONSE TO INTEGRATION

The combined hospital services in the southeast region of the Province responded to the needs of 250,000 people in their catchment area of approximately 30 kilometres by 60 kilometres. Metropolitan Hospital was, by far, the largest facility, with 150 beds and 700 employees or 493 full-time equivalents. Metropolitan specialized in primary care and offered a fairly full range of hospital services, from emergency to surgical, basic cancer care and dialysis. The specific services offered varied depending upon the medical specialists they were able to attract to their area at any particular point in time. However specialized needs in such areas as neonatal, advanced trauma, MRI and more complex cardiac and cancer care interventions were transferred to a larger hospital.

Metropolitan was located in the major urban area (population = 90,000) in the region. It was surrounded by agricultural and tourist areas and a number of smaller municipalities. Five of these towns hosted 20 to 50 bed hospitals, offering limited services to residents in the immediate area.

Each of the hospitals in the region had strong local support and good reputations for the quality of care and services they provided. In recent years this support had been tested as waiting periods for medical procedures increased, and emergency care lineups lengthened. Shortages of funds and health care workers (nurses, specialists and general practitioners) were stressing the system and there was a growing concern over the future of public health care in the region.

For several years the Province had been involved in efforts directed towards reining in escalating healthcare costs through initiatives aimed at improving the efficiency and effectiveness of the hospital health care delivery system. This had led to provincially initiated studies of how best to rationalize and deploy services. In the southeast region of the Province, this had translated into the provincially mandated integration of Metropolitan with the five rural hospitals and related ancillary services in the area.

The specific terms and conditions of the merger were yet to be determined, but the default position was clear. If the parties were unable to come to an agreement, the Province would appoint an administrator who would impose the terms and conditions of the merger. In addition, de-facto penalties would be imposed upon the hospitals in the region, because they would be responsible for all integration costs and would lose access to provincial transitional funding support – sums that could run to $10-20 million over the next two to five years.

The prospects of the forced integration had not been met with open arms. While the Metropolitan Board was largely supportive of the idea, the boards of the other five hospitals had all opposed the move. They saw it as usurping local control and as code language for the maintenance and enhancement of urban services at the expense of local services. They believed it would lead to service degradation in rural areas, culminating in the closure of some of the facilities they had worked so hard to develop and sustain. In addition, four of the five rural hospitals perceived this to be a blatant cash grab on the part of the Province and Metropolitan hospital. These four had all managed to save significant funds over the years, due to fundraising and fiscal prudence. Metropolitan, however, found itself with a modest operating deficit ($250,000 on a $42 million operating budget). It also had an accumulated debt of $3.3 million. The smaller hospitals were free of debt.

Board members of the four hospitals with significant surpluses saw the budgetary situation as an example of urban mismanagement, where-as Metropolitan board members saw it as the result of years of over-funding of rural hospitals, combined with the fact that Metropolitan inherited the more expensive and difficult to manage patients.

JESSICA CASSERRA'S APPOINTMENT

Following the decision of the Ministry of Health to require the realignment of hospital service in the southeast region, Jessica Casserra was approached to lead the initiative by the chief administrative officers of three of the hospitals involved (including Metropolitan). Jessica was a former nurse with a Masters in Health Administration and she was a Certified Management Accountant. She was the head of Finance, Administration, and Ancillary Services at Metropolitan. She was 47 years old and had a stellar reputation as an honest and creative hospital administrator who understood the health care issues of the region. When approached privately, most senior administrators at all six hospitals admitted that Jessica had, by far, the best chance of any administrator in the area of managing the integration successfully. In addition to her technical and managerial talent, she was politically astute and in possession of excellent facilitation skills.

At first Jessica had rejected the overtures. She knew this would be a very difficult assignment, she worried about the level of local support she could expect from medical and hospital staff in region, and she doubted whether the Province had the will to see it through to its conclusion. Moreover, Jessica wondered whether she had the organization skills to take on this task. Once Jessica became convinced there would be no provincial backsliding, her professional sense of responsibility, combined with her commitment to the quality of health care in the region moved her to agree to head the hospital integration taskforce.

To maintain her legitimacy in the region, she retained her responsibilities at Metropolitan. Additional help was recruited at both the hospital and taskforce levels to assist her with her new responsibilities, but Jessica soon found herself working 55 to 65 hours per week. This was not unexpected, but it was tiring and stressful. She was now two months into this assignment, with ten months to go to the deadline. If agreements could be achieved by that point, she recognized that she would likely retain significant responsibilities for integration activities that would run for at least the next two to three years. If agreements could not be reached, Jessica would step down from her taskforce role and a provincial administrator would be appointed. What would happen then was far from clear.

THE TASKFORCE DESIGN

When Jessica agreed to chair the taskforce, the Ministry of Health had already decided upon its membership structure. In addition to the chair (formally appointed by the Ministry of Health), each hospital nominated three members, the local physician's association nominated 3 members, the nurses' association nominated 2 members, and the member communities each nominated 1 member of the public. Further, the Ministry of Health appointed 2 non-voting, ex-officio members to represent its interests. In addition to the chair, the task force had 29 voting members and two non-voting members. The taskforce was expected to seek consensus and act in an advisory role to the involved hospitals and the Province. In addition to those from health care professions, about a third of the taskforce members came from other walks of life (e.g., 2 farmers, 1 engineer, 2 lawyers, 1 pastor, 2 business owners, 2 accountants). Jessica remembered when members had been told by the Province at the first meeting that service on the taskforce would not unduly impair their capacity to meet their regular responsibilities. Jessica reckoned that since that first meeting, task force duties had taken 20 to 30 hours per week of her time and about 10 hours per week of the time of other members.

The taskforce had adequate funds to hire professional staff, consultants, and support personnel to help them in their deliberations. They had a full-time staff of 8 including two hospital planners, an information systems specialist, a human resource specialist, a financial specialist, and 3 staff supports. These employees were hired directly by the task force through the efforts of Jessica and her staff subcommittee. In addition, consultants had received contracts from the task force to assist in the needed background work and analysis. They included two well-respected retired hospital CEO's who were contracted to investigate service structure and delivery options. Once implementation of the plan became the focus, an implementation taskforce would be formed. It was anticipated that most implementation taskforce members would be drawn from the existing hospital staff, but it had yet to be designed.

The staff of the task force was housed in office space supplied by the Region of Erie and the task force used Erie's council chamber for its meetings. In addition, there was temporary office space and a board room available to task force members, and Jessica had permanent office space available to her there.

Following the initial task force meeting a month ago and a half ago (a session hosted by the Ministry of Health), the taskforce had been meeting one day per week and working fairly well on exploratory matters, but they had not yet had to face difficult questions. Once the more contentious strategic and operational questions came to the table, Jessica was concerned that they might simply defer to the public positions of the various groups that had selected them for membership. This was not a recipe for success. If they were going to really add value, she believed that they had to seize this unique opportunity to reinvent hospital service delivery in the region—a tough concept to sell. Board members and representatives of other stakeholders were quick to point fingers at who needed to improve. To this point most task force members were not prepared to publicly argue that the current system was in crisis. The preference of members seemed to be for targeted analysis and solutions that intervened in ways that preserved and enhanced the position of the stakeholder group that was recommending the tinkering.

Jessica wondered what she should do to increase the chances of taskforce success. How should the taskforce be managed and what things should she be doing outside of the formal taskforce meetings? Jessica had developed a good working knowledge of the medical and managerial talent available in the hospital system in the southeast region and she had fairly good knowledge of the various stakeholders involved. She was

> She was also a respected administrator who had developed a reputation for being a fair minded and independent thinker who understood and cared about health care.

also a respected administrator who had developed a reputation for being a fair minded and independent thinker who understood and cared about health care. She knew her capacities in these areas would be taxed to the utmost.

THE STRATEGIC QUESTIONS

From a strategic perspective, Jessica continued to ponder what would be the best way to integrate hospital services and configure their management and governance structures, systems, and supports. There were a range of options, but all came with strings attached.

When thinking about the integration challenge, Jessica was very aware of the fact that Metropolitan had a well-developed strategic plan that had already contemplated some of these questions. However, she also believed these documents would likely be more of an impediment than an aid at this time. Two of the smaller hospitals had made some attempt at developing a strategic plan for themselves while the other three had spent little time engaged in such activity. However, virtually all the hospital CEO's and their senior managers seemed to believe that they were skilled strategists who knew what the region needed. If the services offered by a newly constructed regional hospital delivery system were to be as effective and efficient as possible, Jessica knew that the hospitals would have to depart dramatically from the way they had organized themselves in the past. At present, Jessica did not have a strong sense of the strategic focus or skill set of most taskforce members, but it was her belief that many would be tempted to defer to the various groups that had nominated them.

INTEGRATION OPTIONS

Option A From the perspective of the Board and CEO of Metropolitan, full integration was the preferred way to approach hospital integration. This approach would rationalize services and lead to higher levels of resource use. This would mean moving to a single board and CEO, a consolidated budget and governance structure, a complete realignment of services and roles, control over all ancillary services, access to accumulated surpluses and contingency funds, and the possible consolidation of all hospital foundations into one for the entire region. This approach was seen to minimize organization risk in the sense that all major management functions would be centralized. The fundraising foundations were supposedly independent but most were effectively controlled by the hospital that they were focused on. The smaller hospital foundations had combined savings of $17 million. Metropolitan's foundation controlled $15 million. In addition, the accumulated reserves and contingency funds held by the smaller hospitals themselves totaled $16 million.

The Metropolitan Board salivated at the thought of what they could do with this money, but Jessica knew that any integration that was viewed by the smaller hospitals as a frontal attack would lead protracted court battles, particularly over the control of the assets managed by the fundraising foundations. She was told that there was a 60% chance Metropolitan would be successful, but it could take up to five years to conclude the legal wrangling and the financial and organizational costs would be substantial.

She also knew that it could have a profoundly negative effect on future fundraising activities in these communities and she anticipated that most staff and volunteers in the smaller hospitals would view the approach very negatively. Staff resistance would likely come in the form of absenteeism, less willingness to work overtime and extra shifts, and resignations by nurses and physicians. Only the staff at Metropolitan, most of the medical specialists and some of the GP's would be likely to view this option positively, due to their beliefs concerning the need for the infusion of funds to shore up their ability to supply new and higher quality leading edge medical care to citizens in the region.

Option B: At the other end of the integration continuum was a model that would allow all hospitals to retain their independent structures and boards, with member hospitals each nominating representatives to a supra Board that would act as a planning and coordinating body. This was the option that was favoured by the smaller hospitals and towns, because it allowed continued local access and control of the institutions that the smaller communities had been instrumental in developing and supporting. Neither Metropolitan not the Province viewed this model favourably, because it seemed likely to perpetuate fairly siloed operations and did not seem likely to result in significant savings from consolidation and increased efficiency. These potential savings were thought to be in the order of at least $4 to $6 million per year. Given the position of the Province, this would leave Metropolitan scrambling to find ways to fund an operating deficit likely to grow by $100,000 to $350,000 per year over the next few years as the population aged and the smaller hospitals continued downloading their more difficult and expensive cases.

Between these two extremes there were many other possibilities and Jessica knew that these needed to be narrowed, developed and assessed. In addition, there was the wild card issue of how to best handle chronic, long-term care in the region, but task force members and the Province seemed prepared to set this issue aside for the present.

COMPETITION

Competition was becoming more intense—somewhat surprising because this was not supposed to happen in a publicly funded system. Competition came from several sources. Private clinics had opened in or near the southeast region and were offering a number of services that had previously been supplied by Metropolitan.

Hospitals had found that these specific services were financially attractive to supply because they were relatively easy to perform, in many cases patients (or insurers) paid for the service themselves, and in other cases the provincial reimbursement rate greatly exceeded the costs of supplying the services. Cosmetic surgery, routine hernia treatment, rehabilitation services, CT services, and diet and lifestyle counseling were the types of services that were coming under increased competitive pressure.

In addition, residents in the area could easily access private medical facilities by crossing into the United States. A number of these facilities were actively marketing their services to Canadians and it was not unusual to find Canadian physicians affiliated in some way, with these U.S. facilities. Jessica noted that the Provincial government was willing to pay U.S. suppliers the provincially mandated rates for insured services. Individual patients were responsible for any differences, but for procedures such as CT's and MRI's, the provincial payments covered the majority of the bill.

> Competition was becoming more intense—somewhat surprising because this was not supposed to happen in a publicly funded system.

ANCILLARY SERVICES

Ancillary services represented both a competitive opportunity and threat. Metropolitan Hospital, in particular, was in the catering, vehicle repair, fundraising, payroll services, security, housekeeping/cleaning, hazardous material handling, homecare and laundry businesses, to name just a few. These were services that they could potentially commercialize and/or privatize and spin off. While Jessica had only begun inspecting these opportunities, she already knew that some were fairly efficient and effective operations—laundry, payroll services, and food services, in particular. Others (custodial/cleaning services and homecare) were less efficient and cost effective than private sector competitors at the present. It was not clear how she should go about structuring and evaluating these opportunities and risks. Several Board members looked at such initiatives very favourably, because they saw them as a way to address deficit problems and provide funding for mainstream medical care delivery. However, a minority continued to have serious concerns about the commercialization of hospital services.

Equipment and physical plant were, on the whole, in a fairly good state of repair in the region. Equipment was never as modern or as abundant as staff would like, but overall the hospitals had managed maintenance programs well.

Jessica recognized that some of the commercialization opportunities would require significant investments in order to realize their potential. For example, the laundry facility required an investment of $13 million to allow it to take advantage of the commercialization opportunities in the area (supplying hospitals, nursing homes, the University and Community College, and others in need in institutional laundry services). While the laundry, in particular, seemed to have solid economic potential, she recognized that some would argue that the resources were needed to fund hospital plant and equipment needs that more directly served the delivery of medical services.

CONTROL AND INFORMATION SYSTEMS

With the exceptions of Metropolitan's computerized accounting and payroll systems, computer information systems represented a serious point of concern. Each hospital had its own system or systems and the systems did not communicate with each another. Some of these were clearly antiquated and even within Metropolitan there was duplication of information entry, difficulties with information flow, and far too much reliance on paper.

Jessica knew that the issues in the areas of control system design extended well beyond software and computer concerns. Ministry of Health and Ministry of Finance requirements drove much of the activity in this area, but Jessica felt that this would be an ideal time to sort through and establish the management control information that could really benefit managers and the organization. For example, there was little to no consistency in the boundary, belief, diagnostic or interactive control systems in operation in the various hospitals. Metropolitan's system was the most developed, but even here Jessica believed improvement was needed with both its design and use. She believed the new organization would be well served if it approached the design of the control system with an open mind and then insured that their managers were literate in the effective use of the information emanating from it.

The critical questions concerning the control system were what should the system be designed to do and how should its implementation be approached? Jessica believed these would be impossible to determine in a definitive way until the fundamental strategy questions had been answered. She knew that gaining interest and approval for control system initiatives (other than those required by statute) would be a challenge. However, building the business case for control processes that went beyond historical reporting requirements would get progressively more difficult as time passed and resources tightened.

PEOPLE

Managing hospital employees during the transition represented a key point of risk. Hospitals in the region were already short of nurses and the area had been classified as under-serviced by general practitioners and specialists. Little in the way of strategy had guided hospital activities, with the exception of Metropolitan that had a fairly well developed strategic plan. For example, three years earlier Metropolitan had developed detailed and sophisticated initiatives aimed at attracting and retaining general practitioners and specialists. They had also developed initiatives to improve management practices and employee satisfaction and performance by moving to team-based management. Their efforts had met with some limited success in the areas of attraction, retention, and satisfaction, but Jessica still believed they relied far too much on hierarchy and traditional management practices. Team members still deferred to managers and physicians and engaged in few of the self-management behaviours Jessica had hoped to see.

Once integration was undertaken, the human resource challenges would escalate. Each hospital and ancillary service had their own bargaining units and each represented a unique culture, with its own approach to financial, physical plant and human resource management. For example, two of the smaller hospitals had served as exemplars for Metropolitan when they had begun investigating team management. They had achieved high degrees of success with the approach and were viewed as extremely well managed.

At the other end of the continuum was one small hospital that was believed to be in fairly serious difficulty with respect to their management practices. Turnover and absenteeism were high, satisfaction was reported to be low, and efficiency and effectiveness were both well below national norms. None-the-less, the Board of that hospital was highly supportive of its practices and the performance of its senior managers. They attributed observed shortfalls to unique issues in their catchment area, but Jessica felt that this assessment didn't stand up to closer scrutiny. The fact that the hospital CEO and the head of nursing were respectively 62 and 60 years old might make change easier to manage at this site, if they should chose to retire early.

Jessica knew that integration activities would occasion job insecurity, with its magnitude dependent upon what integration approach was adopted. At present, this fear was most pronounced in middle and senior management levels, but unions had already voiced concerns about possible job losses caused by service rationalization, contracting out, and/or privatization. Until the post integration roles of the various hospitals were clarified, staff uncertainty and anxiety were bound to escalate.

NEXT STEPS

Jessica mulled over her options but then stopped and laughed. For many years she had been a vocal advocate of strategic thinking, accompanied by action, execution, supportive management, measurement and learning. Here she was, three months into her taskforce assignment, bogged down by tactical and operational concerns. Maybe it was time to step back and do some strategic planning for herself, but she was unclear about how best to proceed.

▶ UNIT 1

Introduction to Organizational Behaviour

A RUNNING SUCCESS (CEOTV.COM) ⏱ 3:38

This video is an interview with John Stanton, President of Running Room, Inc., an enthusiastic entrepreneur who started this successful Canadian business back in 1984 in the living room of an old renovated Edmonton home. As a veteran runner, Stanton wasn't satisfied with the kind of service he received nor the quality of equipment typically found in sporting goods stores. He wanted to start a business to provide top quality athletic running wear sold by knowledgeable sales personnel. Today Stanton oversees a growing enterprise that has become North America's largest chain of specialty stores for walkers and runners, with over 90 stores in both Canada and the U.S. John Stanton's philosophy and personal commitment drive this organization. As stated on their Web site: "We are not just selling shoes and equipment, we are selling a commitment to active living."

Questions for Discussion

1. How do John Stanton's values and philosophy guide the daily operations of 90+ Running Room stores? (Note: refer to the last line of the summary " . . . we are selling a commitment to active living.")
2. What kind of employees should Running Room management look for when interviewing potential candidates?

THE RECIPE FOR SUCCESS (CEOTV.COM) ⏱ 5:10

In May 1987, Cora Mussely Tsouflidou bought a defunct snack bar in the Ville Saint-Laurent district of Montreal and embarked on a venture that would take her further than she'd ever dreamed. In the business world, Cora is the best example of a "self-made business woman." In 2003, she won the Governor General's Award. She has also won several other awards, including the Ernst & Young Entrepreneur of the Year Award in the Manufacturing/Consumer Products Category, the Pinnacle Award, and the Tops in Hospitality Award from Food Service and Hospitality magazine. The Cora Franchise Group Inc. network has annual sales of over $100 million. The "Chez Cora" banner is recognized as the leader in the breakfast industry in Quebec, and Cora's Breakfast & Lunch is well on its way to becoming a pre-eminent leader across Canada. This organization was built on the hard work and vision of Cora Mussely Tsouflidou; her employees know what is important to her and strive to live up to the expectations she has set for them.

Questions for Discussion

1. What role does Cora play in the success of her corporation? In other words, do you think franchise operations would be as successful if Cora was not the CEO?
2. What kind of work ethic do you think Cora would expect from her employees? Explain.

IS FLEXTIME THE WAY OF THE FUTURE (CEOTV.COM) ⏱ 3:01

The contemporary workplace is changing, and one of the variables employees are interested in exploring is the option of flextime and the compressed work week. Employers who want to offer a motivating work environment may be interested in introducing this time-shift schedule to their employees. But what exactly does flextime mean? This video explores the concept of how the world of work is changing, and that it's worth considering alternative schedules if productivity is enhanced along with increased job satisfaction.

Questions for Discussion

1. Does working flextime and/or a compressed work week motivate you? If so, why? If not, why not?
2. How can an organization determine if seasoned employees who have always worked 9 to 5 are open to flextime and/or a compressed work week? What about new candidates applying for a job?
3. Do you think such scheduling can be introduced overnight as part of a restructuring initiative, or is this something that must be phased in over time on a voluntary basis at first? Explain your reasoning.

▶ UNIT 2

Managing Individual Behaviour

PATAGONIA ⏱ 11:37

Yvon Chouinard began climbing as a 14-year-old member of the Southern California Falconry Club. At the time, the only available pitons (spikes used in mountain climbing) were made of soft iron, used once, and left in the rock. In 1957, Chouinard bought a used coal-fired forge to make reusable iron pitons; the word spread and soon he was in business.[1] From climbing equipment to apparel, his company, Patagonia, has evolved into a highly successful private firm with annual revenues of $250 million. Chouinard has kept it private so that he can continue to pursue his mission: earth first, profits second.[2]

According to CEO Michael Crooke, Patagonia is a very special company with core values that are more than the bottom line. Because of these basic values, employees come to work every day with the attitude that they are making a difference. For each new hire, Patagonia receives 900 resumés. To understand the firm's success in satisfying employees, one needs only to look at a catalogue. Not many companies place such significance on environmental and social issues. From the start, Yvon Chouinard advocated a purer, equipment-light approach to making climbing hardware to preserve the environment.[3] The philosophy has continued. A recent catalogue featured an essay entitled, "Do You Need This Product?" The message? If you don't need another shirt or jacket, don't buy it. Patagonia's management believes that this honest approach, while rare, creates loyal customers and dedicated employees.

To many environmentalists, corporations are the enemy. Patagonia takes a different approach. The company's goal is to make a difference, using its power to work from within the system. Patagonia is a successful company socially, environmentally, and financially. The success starts with great products and great people. Product quality and guarantees assure that the products meet high expectations at any store, no matter its location in the world. In choosing employees, Patagonia looks for people passionate about an interest or cause. Over the years, many workers with similar causes and values have joined the company. The culture is based on commitment to environmental, moral, ethical, and philosophical causes.

Patagonia employees derive true meaning from work, family, and health, rather than money and status. The goal is psychological success, achieved through a varied career. Patagonia spends little on recruiting. The firm experiences very low turnover, about 4 percent annually. Each year, Fortune magazine rates the company as one of the best to work for. Why have workers found so much satisfaction with their jobs at Patagonia? Four reasons:

- **Let My People Surf**   The philosophy of Yvon Chouinard, an accomplished climber and also a passionate surfer, is that you have to surf when the surf's up. At Patagonia, workers set their own schedules; when they need to work, they get their jobs finished. To develop great products, you need to be users of the products. You can't develop great surfboards if you don't surf.

- **Enviro Internships**   After employees have completed a year, the company pays up to 60 days' salary for each individual to intern for an environmental group. The only requirement is that employees present a slide show when they return. Some employees have left Patagonia after the internships to become full-time activists. That's fine with the firm. Patagonia recently joined with several other apparel companies and six leading anti-sweatshop groups to devise a single set of labour standards with a common factory inspection system.[4]

- **Child Development Centre**   Started in 1985, the firm's child care facility is one of the first of its kind and an integral component of the company. Children are part of the campus all day, every day. The connection between work and family increases job satisfaction. Knowing their children are being well cared for onsite helps employees become fully committed.

- **One Percent for the Planet**   In 1985, Patagonia started an "earth tax" and donates 1 percent of sales to grassroots environmental activists worldwide. Each group has its own budget for local activism. Patagonia employees serve on grant committees that fund proposals. Because of employee involvement, this program also contributes to worker satisfaction.

Questions for Discussion

1. What values are important at Patagonia? How do values play an important role in attracting and retaining top employees?
2. How does Patagonia foster organizational commitment?
3. How does the firm influence the work attitudes of job involvement and job satisfaction?

[1] www.patagonia.com/culture/patagonia_history.shtml.
[2] Abraham Lustgarten et al., "14 Innovators," Fortune, November 15, 2004, p 193.
[3] www.patagonia.com/culture/clean_climb.shtml.
[4] Aaron Bernstein, "A Major Swipe at Sweatshops," BusinessWeek, May 23, 2005, p 98.

▶ UNIT 3

Managing Group and Team Behaviour

FALL FROM GRACE (CEOTV.COM)   ⏱ 4:45

By early 2002, Eleanor (Ellie) Clitheroe was one of the highest paid females in Canada, appearing on the cover of some of the most prominent business publications in the country. By the summer of that same year, she was fired from her job, one of the most high-profile jobs in corporate Canada: CEO of Hydro One, Ontario's transmission-grid operator.

In 2002, a new government at Queen's Park was intent on privatizing the utility, which would have netted Ontario an estimated $5.5 billion. With Clitheroe in charge of the changeover, things seemed to be on track until controversy erupted over her $2.2 million-a-year salary, benefits, and expenses. When the cabinet brought in legislation to curb the utility's executive salaries, the board resigned en masse over what it saw as government interference. In response, Queen's Park appointed a new board of directors who hastily terminated Clitheroe's contract.

How does a highly educated, experienced leader cope with being fired very publicly and very politically from a high position? In Clitheroe's case, she tapped into her spirituality and it changed her life. "When I lost my job, I sometimes felt overwhelmed and full of emotion," she said. "There were many days when I felt God was carrying me; that He was there by my side."

Clitheroe is now President and CEO of Prison Fellowship Canada. Born in Montreal, Quebec, she obtained a Bachelor of Common Law (LL.B.) and a Master in Business Administration (MBA) from the University of Western Ontario in London, and a Bachelor of Civil Law (B.C.L.) from McGill University. She is currently a candidate for Doctor of Philosophy in Theology, at Wycliffe College, Toronto School of Theology, University of Toronto. She holds an Honourary Doctorate of Laws from Trinity Western University (LL D). She is Chancellor Emerita of the University of Western Ontario, and is a director of Canadian Friends of the Ecole Biblique, Opportunity International Canada, Sanctuary, Media Voice Generation, and Canadian Green Power. She has been a director of Alcan, TD Canada Trust, Dofasco, Suncor, and Inco, with responsibility on sub-committees of audit, governance, human resources, and safety and environment at different times.

She speaks widely on matters of sailing, ethics, women, and her faith. She has taught ethics courses at the university and community level. She was a director of King Bay Chaplaincy, and both spoke and taught there. She was a founding member of the Centre for Ethics and Corporate Policy, and the MBA Women's Association. As a young person, she was involved in mission work (Bolivia) and church camp with the Baptist church, volunteered at Maimonides Hospital, and led Girl Scouts. She has spoken at the Ontario Prayer Breakfast, Oakville Prayer Breakfast, Women's Executive Network, Missionfest, Women's Christian Leadership, International Women's Forum, and Federation of Christian Farmers. She has appeared on Vision 360, Listen Up TV, and CTV, and has taught and preached at St. Patrick's and St. Cuthbert's Anglican Churches as an intern. She has also taught advanced sailing and navigation for Humber College and the Canadian Yachting Association, and scuba diving under National Association of Underwater Instructors.

Questions for Discussion

1. Do you see Clitheroe as a victim of unfortunate but common business behaviour (Don't take it personally, it's just business!) or a model of transformational leadership? What sorts of power struggles and political games occurred in the Clitheroe situation while she was CEO of Hydro One?

2. Given her background, would you see Clitheroe as having the kind of credibility and expertise needed to motivate others within an organization during the strategic management effort of achieving corporate goal(s)? Explain your response.

3. How much of a difference is there between Clitheroe's decision to change careers from being CEO of Hydro One to one of Rev. Clitheroe at Oakville's St. Cuthbert's Anglican Church, as well as providing pastoral care for area prisoners?

TOYING WITH SUCCESS: THE MCFARLANE TOY COMPANY

Todd McFarlane, president and CEO of the McFarlane Companies, is an entrepreneur who understands the importance of product development. Comics, sports, toys, and rock-and-roll have all benefited from his creativity. When McFarlane's dream to play major league baseball didn't happen, he fell back on another interest he developed as a teenager—drawing superheroes. He faced the same question faced by all entrepreneurs: Could he make money pursuing his dream? He sent his sketches to prospective employers, and after 300 rejection letters McFarlane got a job freelancing for Marvel Comics. Working many hours for low pay, he made a name for himself and by 1990 was the highest-paid comic book artist in the industry.

Frustrated over creative differences and his desire to own the rights to his characters, McFarlane quit, took six other artists with him, and started his own company. He went from artist to entrepreneur overnight. While industry experts predicted he would last less than a year, McFarlane didn't even think about the future. Spawn, his first comic, sold 1.7 million copies.

Entrepreneurship rewards individuals willing to take risks. In Todd McFarlane's case, the need to control his destiny drove his aspirations. His path is similar to that taken by many: receiving training at a large company, and then leaving when he decided he could provide a better product on his own.

Today's dynamic business environment has a tremendous effect on the success or failure of entrepreneurs like Todd McFarlane. Economics plays a key role at the McFarlane Companies. The firm must protect the many intellectual properties it creates and licenses. The business uses technology to support and spark creativity in developing new products. The competitive environment drives quality at McFarlane, which produces high-quality products even if they cost more, and thus gains an edge over competitors. The CEO uses the Web to interact with his key demographic, or as he puts it, the freaks with long hair and cool tattoos. Spawn.com provides a place where fans can interact with each other and with the company. Finally, the global influence on business impacts all the other environments. Knowing he can't control the global environment, McFarlane focuses on managing what he can control.

Todd McFarlane's purchase of Mark McGwire's 70th home run ball for $3 million illustrates his willingness to take a risk and focus on what he controls. While many thought he was crazy, McFarlane saw an opportunity. He combined the ball with several others hit by McGwire and Sammy Sosa to create the McFarlane Collection, which was displayed in every major league stadium and garnered enormous publicity. A portion of the proceeds was donated to the Lou Gehrig Foundation. Most significantly, McFarlane began a relationship with professional sports that led to his obtaining the exclusive rights to nearly every professional sports team toy license.

Questions for Discussion

1. What personality traits do entrepreneurs like Todd McFarlane possess that distinguish them from other individuals? Do you think McFarlane has an internal or external locus of control?
2. What cognitive abilities do you think contributed most to McFarlane's success?
3. Do you think Todd would be a team player? What evidence of his behaviour leads you to such a conclusion?

HAVING A BALL (CEOTV.COM) ⊙ 5:31

This video is about one of the all-time greatest winter athletes, Johann Koss of Norway. In 1992 he made his Olympic debut, and over the next several years earned four gold medals, broke 11 world records, earned three all-time records, and was nominated as *Sports Illustrated's* Athlete of the Year in 1994. You would think that being a successful world athlete, appearing on the cover of *Time Magazine*, and being the best speed skater in the world would be enough for a person who accomplished so much in his young life, but Koss wanted to do more. Marriage brought him to Canada where he brought his vision to life—an organization dedicated to bringing gifted Olympic athletes together with needy children from the world's poorest countries. Koss named the international humanitarian organization "Right to Play" because he felt a calling to use sport and play as tools for the development of children and youth wherever they could be of service. Today, athletes who believe in the cause approach Koss to volunteer their time and themselves to the *Right to Play* cause.

Questions for Discussion

1. Speed skating is a solo sport, yet today Koss shows the ability to motivate others in ways far different from his past experiences. In your opinion, is Johann Koss a transformational leader? Explain your response.
2. Is there a place for organizations to be socially responsible and look beyond the bottom line?

LIVING THE GOODLIFE (CEOTV.COM) ⊘ 3:25

In 1979, David Patchell-Evans, opened his first fitness studio in London, Ontario and called it "The Goodlife Fitness Club." Since then the business has grown significantly, and now Patch, as he prefers to be called, is the CEO of the largest group of fitness clubs in Canada (currently 158 and counting!), employing over 6,000 associates and serving 400,000+ members. Goodlife has a reputation for having an unequalled level of educated fitness professionals using the highest-quality equipment benchmarked against the highest standards of operation. But being a successful business person wasn't enough for Patch; he wanted to offer more of himself, use the expertise from the clubs, and make a difference in the world. He authored the book, *Living The Goodlife—Your Guide To Health and Success,* where he shares his personal journey that brought him to the fitness industry. He talks about the basics of fitness, balanced health, and the equilibrium between body, mind, and spirit.

When his daughter was diagnosed with autism, Patch turned his attention to helping medical experts conduct more research to find the cause and cure. With the proceeds from his book and other charitable initiatives, Patch donated over $1.5 million of his own personal resources in 2006 alone. Since then, he has founded the Kilee Patchell-Evans Autism Research Group that continues to assist clinical and basic neuroscientists conduct the needed research to unlock the mystery of this debilitating affliction. In addition to serving as president of the Autism Canada Foundation, Patch has found a way to give back and make a difference—a true testament to his dynamic leadership style.

Questions for Discussion

1. How important is credibility to leadership? In your opinion, would Patch have credibility and respect from his employees? Explain your response.
2. What kind of power would Patch have as CEO of Goodlife Fitness Clubs?

TEAMWORK: TEAM ACTIVITIES FOR COWORKERS ⊘ 2:17

Corporations are using new and somewhat unorthodox methods of teambuilding and skills training activities. Many organizations are using activities such as ranching type experiences, games (like playing with hoola-hoops or playing Chinese Checkers on oversized boards that use workers as playing pieces), and cooking together to help instil a team atmosphere and learn communication skills for use back in the workplace. The activities are designed not only for the employees to have some fun, but also to teach them how to communicate, effectively manage and coordinate their activities, and work together—skills that will pay off back at work. According to one participant, games are the best way to learn. Rather than concentrating on the fact that they are learning a new skill, the trainees are able to take in the knowledge while having fun playing a game.

Companies spend upwards of $100 million per year to train employees with these new and entertaining programs. For example, bank employees training in a cooking class learn about communication, goal setting, coordination, and consensus building. To be successful in their cooking tasks, the employees must plan and coordinate their efforts, as well as communicate their ideas succinctly to each other and execute a harmonious strategy. These skills can translate into being able to work better back in the office. Informal and fun methods of training have grown tremendously in popularity. The company that provides cooking training says that their programs have grown as much as 75 percent in the past year—and everyone seems to benefit. Not only are the employees having fun and gaining skills, but the training providers are benefiting by increased business, and the companies that send their employees see improvements in their bottom line.

Questions for Discussion

1. How do things like playing games or cooking together help employees work together back in the office?
2. Is there justification for the expenses companies incur for these training programs? Would you be willing to authorize the expenses for your employees to attend these types of training?

▶ UNIT 4

Managing Systems that Affect Behaviour

HOT TOPIC: EMPLOYEES WITH PASSION ⏱ 11:38

Hot Topic Incorporated, located in City of Industry, California is a retailer that licenses various products such as t-shirts, clothes, and accessories geared toward alternative and pop culture and modern music trends. The average age of the employees at Hot Topic is 25 years old. Hot Topic Incorporated reaches its customers through its two retail store lines—Hot Topic, and its sister store, Torrid. Hot Topic offers a myriad of cultural items as well as accessories, clothing, and t-shirts aimed at a younger market segment. Torrid is a fashion store offering modern trendy clothing catering to plus- size women. This organization has been on the "Best Small Companies" and "Best Companies to Work For" lists many times over its twenty year history.

Betsy McLaughlin is the CEO of Hot Topic Incorporated. McLaughlin believes that the culture at Hot Topic is based on a passion for a concept. For Hot Topic, that passion is music, and for Torrid, it is a passion for fashion. McLaughlin says that this passion for the products and the inspiration behind them is what makes her company different from many others, and the passion that drives their culture is shared across all levels and positions of the organization. In fact, McLaughlin claims that music not only inspires the products they sell, but also store design and even the people they hire.

Hot Topic has a unique corporate culture, but structurally it does not differ tremendously from other organizations. Employees are fiercely loyal to the firm due to a great working environment where they feel they fit in and are appreciated for what they contribute to the organization. One example of how Hot Topic encourages this culture is through their concert reimbursement program. Employees can attend a concert and bring someone with them, fill out an expense report, and be reimbursed for the cost of their tickets. The only requirement for this benefit is to submit a fashion report. But fitting in is not all. The culture also values collaboration, open communication, and empowerment, and is perpetuated by a lack of walls and doors in the corporate headquarters. Everyone works in one big room and shares space, taking the emphasis off of hierarchy and promoting collaboration and open communication. The employees are supported (within reason) in risk-taking decisions when taking care of the needs of customers. This gives employees a feeling of inclusion and empowerment to make decisions.

Hot Topic has grown from fifteen stores just fifteen years ago to nearly 800 stores today. This provides for a ready applicant pool to allow them to hire for corporate jobs from within—a practice that has workers bring their sense of the corporate culture with them to their new job. Employees are kept satisfied through such perks as cell phone discounts, on-site massages, health fairs, scholarship reimbursement, and Employee of the Month programs. Another interesting and no-cost perk offered to employees is their 9/80 program. This program allows employees to work eighty hours over nine days—giving them a three day weekend every other weekend. McLaughlin talks to her employees and customers to learn what direction they want Hot Topic to go in. This, along with all of the innovative ideas and programs, provide Hot Topic with a unique culture that helps keep their employees and customers satisfied and loyal.

Questions for Discussion

1. What makes Hot Topic so successful as a retailer? What makes them so popular with their employees? How can they keep their success going?
2. How does the idea of no walls and no doors in the corporate headquarters encourage the culture Hot Topic is trying to perpetuate? Do you think you would like to work in such an atmosphere?

ONE SMOOTH STONE ⏱ 9:19

One Smooth Stone is a competitor in the corporate event planning industry. They offer their clients practically every type of event service, from live theatre productions, celebrity appearances, and pre-produced video footage, to rock band performances and live action presentations. Organizations use the services of One Smooth Stone for sales or client meetings, as well as new product launches. Mark Ledogar is the vice-president of Smooth Stone Productions. He explains that each time they provide a service to a client, they only get one chance to do it right—it is often a live production with millions of dollars at stake. This type of environment calls for good organizing as well as efficient and effective organizational processes.

The organization not only produces the events, but also helps in the entire planning and execution process to ensure their clients get a return on their investment. They start by listening to what the client wants or needs and then assist in writing the strategy for delivering the message or event. These events can take place literally anywhere, and companies such as Motorola, International Truck and Engine, and Kos Pharmaceuticals use their services. The productions provide not only an educational component for the audience, but are entertaining as well. In an environment such as this, with well-educated knowledge-based workers, an organization must be able to adapt and respond quickly to changes in market conditions. The principles and styles of organization as professed by some of the original theorists of organization, such as Fayol and Weber, simply won't allow an organization the flexibility necessary to react to market conditions and the needs of workers today. One Smooth Stone hires highly skilled and empowered workers to work in teams on customized client projects. These employees work in a decentralized and relatively flat organizational structure. This is necessary to fulfill the frequently changing and adapting needs of their clients.

Solutions that One Smooth Stone cannot provide in-house are outsourced, but they are very selective in who they hire, ensuring their vendors also embody the same principles and values as One Smooth Stone. They look at three categories when considering a vendor: knowledge of the services One Smooth Stone provides;

an understanding of the culture at One Smooth Stone and how they deliver the services; and the match between the vendor's personal skills and personality with the client. One Smooth Stone devised the concept of "strategic improvising" to counter the effects of rapidly changing strategic initiatives. Strategic improvising involves devising ground rules and creating a template for the future without constraining themselves to rigid strategic plans that quickly become obsolete. This type of strategizing allows the company to be successful in a very dynamic industry. At the end of the day, however, One Smooth Stone believes it is their values that make them successful. The company embraces the values of being smart, fast, and kind, and believes that if they deliver their services to their clients based on those three values, the clients will keep coming back.

Questions for Discussion

1. How much of a part can values truly play in the success of a company like One Smooth Stone?
2. What characteristics of One Smooth Stone make it necessary to have a flat and decentralized structure as opposed to a rigid command-and-control hierarchical structure?

▶ UNIT 5

Managing Change and Change Agents that Affect Behaviour

WORKING ABROAD CAN ADD TO YOUR SUCCESS (CEOTV.COM) ⏱ 4:03

Bayer Inc., Canada has a motto "Bayer: Science for a Better Life." The company believes that they are making a positive difference to the overall health of the world and because of their success, many are benefiting. The success of Bayer can be attributed to many factors, including the leadership of Phil Blake, President and CEO. A scientist himself, Blake began his career in medical research working with kidney transplant tissue. From there, Blake began working more closely with pharmaceuticals in his native Britain, but quickly moved on to the global market scene where he was assigned to duties in Japan, the United States, and eventually Canada.

Bayer Inc. has been recognized in the past as one of Canada's Top 100 Employers. The company prides itself in its high performing, 'love winning' culture, a place where employees come to work each day with a sense of adventure. Blake states that he enjoys having meetings with hospital workers and scientists where he is able to dialogue about research protocol, hospital processes, funding, and publishing—a surprise to those who don't expect a CEO to have such hands-on knowledge of the research process. He champions more home-grown science in the area of Canadian health care, and believes that more knowledge would empower a sense of competition within the country.

Blake attributes his success in part to his international experience, and encourages other leaders to broaden their career horizons by looking outside of their comfort zone and enjoying the benefit of taking an overseas route to reach their desired professional goals.

Questions for Discussion

1. How has Blake's international experience helped his leadership at Bayer Inc., Canada?
2. Have you ever considered a job working overseas?
3. In the future, it will be to the benefit of a company to have employees with international experience? Explain.

DISNEY IMAGINEERING ⏱ 10:15

A man named Walt Disney was searching for vacation options his two young daughters would enjoy and that he could enjoy with them. He realized that there were no good options that would fulfill his goal, so he set out to create one. In 1955, Disneyland opened its doors in Anaheim, California. The theme park was quickly dubbed "the happiest place on earth." Disney formed a company called Disney Imagineering, staffed with artists and craftspeople. Their charge was to create and design the themed venues that would make up the park(s). Jim Thomas of Disney Imagineering says that the company has three strategic priorities: creativity and innovation, application of technology, and global expansion. After a relatively short time, a second park called Disney World opened its doors (1971) in Orlando, Florida. Epcot Center soon opened on the same campus, offering visitors to the park exposure to cultures from across the world. The theme of Epcot was perhaps foretelling of Disney's future global expansion.

Joe Lanzisero of Disney Imagineering says that at its core, the Disney brand is about "human traits that cross cultural boundaries" and transcend "the human experience." The themes of the stories told by the Disney brand touch on issues such as family, humour, and fears. Thomas adds that by fulfilling the company's strategic priorities, they provide their guests with unique and memorable experiences that provide a lifetime of memories. Disney is a global company in all respects, and every visitor to their European and Asian locations is contributing to global trade. With the U.S. making up only 5 percent of the world's population, strategically there is no question why Disney chose to expand globally. This expansion not only benefits Disney; the parks have significant financial and cultural impacts on the areas where they are located. This type of global expansion requires Disney to overcome barriers such as language, cultural difference, political issues, and dealing with fluctuating foreign currencies.

When creating a new global location, Disney has to be careful about making assumptions about the local culture, as these assumptions may be erroneous and could create significant issues. One way in which Disney proactively avoided problems is illustrated in the opening of the Hong Kong location. When designing Tomorrowland for the Hong Kong location (an attraction that highlights what the future might bring), the Imagineers realized that Hong Kong was a city that was in many ways already living in "tomorrowland." They decided to redesign this feature of the park and based it on a different planet far away in the galaxy. Disney also hired a feng shui consultant to assist in the placement and orientation of the park, the buildings, and even the interiors of the buildings and attractions.

With such vast global expansion, Disney has to be mindful of maintaining their own cultural integrity, while simultaneously respecting and acknowledging local cultures. They also have to pay attention to the lessons and insights they have learned through their previous growth to help anticipate challenges in future expansions. One way they learn is by collecting feedback after a new location opens, often by using the Internet. This data is used to make "software" adjustments—adjustments to the "programming" within the parks. Overall, the Disney organization is an excellent example of a truly global company that provides tremendous benefit to the local cultures they expand into.

Questions for Discussion

1. Should Disney accommodate local cultures so much? Wouldn't the parks provide a better experience by bringing consistency across all of the locations?
2. What benefits does a theme park the magnitude of a Disney location bring to the local area? Would your city/province be able to support such a park?

CIRQUE DU SOLEIL ⏱ 9:58

In 1984, Guy Laliberté left his home in Canada to make his way across Europe as a circus performer. There, he and other artists entertained in the street. The troupe was called Cirque du Soleil—circus of the sun. It started with a simple dream: a group of young artists getting together to entertain audiences, see the world, and have fun doing it.[1] Laliberté and company quickly found that their entertainment form without words—stilt-walking, juggling, music, and fire breathing—transcended all barriers of language and culture. Though he understood that an entertainer could bring the exotic to every corner of the world, Laliberté did not envision the scope to which his Cirque du Soleil would succeed.

Today, Cirque has five permanent shows—four in Las Vegas and one in Walt Disney World—and five travelling shows. Combined, they gross about $500 million annually.[2] In 20-plus years of live performances, 44 million people have seen a Cirque show.[3] Despite a long-term decline in the circus industry, Cirque has increased revenue 22-fold over the last 10 years.[4] Growth plans include additional tours in Asia and permanent shows in New York, Tokyo, and London.[5] Cirque du Soleil is a family of more than 3,000 individuals—700 of whom are the shows' artists—from 40 different countries.[6] Each of Cirque's employees is encouraged to contribute to the group. This input has resulted in rich, deep performances and expansion into alternative media outlets such as music, books, television, film, Web sites, and merchandising. The company's diversity assures that every show reflects many different cultural influences.

Different markets will have an exotic experience at a Cirque show, regardless of which show is playing where. Cirque does target specific markets with products designed to engage a particular audience. However, Cirque has little need to adapt its product to new markets; the product is already a blend of global influences. The result is a presentation of acrobatic arts and traditional, live circus with an almost indescribable freshness and beauty. Cirque du Soleil's commitment to excellence and innovation transcends cultural differences and the limits of many modern media.

Its intense popularity has made Cirque both the global standard of live entertainment and the place for talented individuals from around the world to perfect their talents. The extent of the diversity, however, does pose a host of unique challenges. Every employee must be well-versed in various forms and styles. To foster cultural enrichment, Cirque purchases and shares a large collection of art with employees and gives them tickets to different events and shows. The performers work in the most gruelling and intimate situations, with their lives depending on one another. The astounding spectacles they achieve on stage result from hours of planning, practice, and painstaking attention to detail among artists from diverse cultures who speak 25 different languages. Sensitivity, compromise, and hunger for new experiences are prerequisites for success at Cirque. The organization has learned the art of sensitivity and compromise in its recruiting. Cirque du Soleil has also had a presence in the Olympics for a decade. It works closely with coaches and teams to help athletes consider a career with Cirque after their competitive years are over, rather than luring talent away from countries that have made huge investments in athletes. This practice has given Cirque a huge advantage in the athletic community, a source of great talent from all over the globe.

Guy Laliberté has not forgotten his humble beginnings as a Canadian street performer. Now that Cirque du Soleil has achieved an international presence and incredible success—the group expected to be doing $1 billion in annual gross revenue by 2007—it has chosen to help at-risk youth, especially street kids. Cirque allocates 1 percent of its revenues to outreach programs targeting youth in difficulty, regardless of location in the world.[7] Laliberté understands that to be successful in a world market, one must be a committed and sensitive neighbour. Cirque's Montreal headquarters is the centre of an urban revitalization project that the company sponsors. Community participation and outreach bring international goodwill and help Cirque du Soleil prevent many of the difficulties global brands often face when spanning cultures.

Questions for Discussion

1. Why is Cirque du Soleil successful throughout the world? Why does the product transcend culture differences between countries?
2. How do the cultural influences discussed in Figure 14.1 influence organizational behaviour at Cirque du Soleil?
3. Why is it important for Cirque du Soleil to be a good corporate citizen? How does ethnocentrism relate to fulfilling this role?

[1] "Founder's Message," www.cirquedusoleil.com.
[2] Richard Corliss, "Bigger than Vegas," *Time*, February 14, 2005, p 52.
[3] Mario D'Amico and Vincent Gagné, "Big Top Television," *Marketing 109*, no. 26 (August 9–16, 2004), p 20.
[4] W. Chan Kim and Renée Mauborgne, "Blue Ocean Strategy," *Harvard Business Review*, October 2004, p 77.
[5] "Business: Lord of the Rings," *The Economist*, February 5, 2005, p 66.
[6] Cindy Waxer, "Life's a Balancing Act for Cirque du Soleil's Human Resources Troupe," *Workforce Management*, January 2005, p 52.
[7] "Social Action," www.cirquedusoleil.com.

JOHNSON & JOHNSON: CREATING A GLOBAL LEARNING ORGANIZATION ⊚ 9:07

Johnson & Johnson is a health and personal care products company with 115,000 workers globally distributed among 200 operating units. The company supplies commonly-used products such as band-aids, diapers, baby oil and powder, and Tylenol, and less visible brands such as Neutrogena, Aveno, and Roc. They also produce pharmaceuticals and medical products that are subject to federal regulation and control. The corporate culture at Johnson & Johnson is one of service and social responsibility. They are consistently ranked as one of the top 10 places to work and financially outperform many rival companies. This is handled through a highly decentralized structure that, according to Director of Johnson & Johnson eUniversity, Kee Mang Yeo, allows each business and functional unit to "do their own thing."

The culture of this decentralized global competitor is the glue that keeps them together, and is perpetuated through its rich history as a family company with family values. Founded by Robert Johnson, the company expanded globally and through acquisition under the leadership of his grandson, Robert Wood-Johnson. Wood-Johnson, affectionately known as "The General," brought professional management to the company and authored a set of value statements known as "The Credo." This document, after nearly 70 years, remains largely the same as when it was originally written, and guides the decision-making process for the managers of the organization.

Some of the text of the credo reads "We believe our first responsibility is to doctors, nurses, and patients . . . to the mothers and fathers and all who use our products and services. In meeting their needs everything we do must be of high quality . . . We are responsible to our employees . . . We must be respectful of their dignity and recognize their merit." According to Charles Corace, Director of Johnson & Johnson Credo Survey, the credo is the corporate culture—it is in essence the very glue that holds them together. All Johnson & Johnson employees, regardless of level, go through credo training in their first six months of employment. The training allows the employees to do more than just espouse the values expressed in the credo; it teaches them how to demonstrate it. In addition to being the foundation of initial employee credo training, the credo also serves as the basis for all of Johnson & Johnson's leadership training programs.

The credo allows employees to view the company and their decisions in the context of their jobs from a long-term perspective. According to one manager, the credo applies equally "whether you are in New Jersey or in India." The credo becomes personalized for each of the employees and becomes the underpinning of their entire experience at work. The Johnson & Johnson Credo is an excellent example of organizational values that transcend boundaries and truly serve as a guide and moral compass for members of the Johnson & Johnson family.

Questions for Discussion

1. In what ways are the values described in The Credo expressed in the actions of the employees of Johnson & Johnson? Should The Credo be changed after all these years?

2. Why would Johnson & Johnson's Credo translate into financial performance for the company? In other words, why would people positively respond to these values for this company in particular?

3. How does The Credo assist Johnson & Johnson in incorporating sustainable business practices throughout the global community?

ENDNOTES

CHAPTER 1

[1] H L Tosi, Jr and J W Slocum, Jr, "Contingency Theory: Some Suggested Directions," *Journal of Management*, Spring 1984, p 9.

[2] H Mintzberg, "The Manager's Job: Folklore and Fact," *Harvard Business Review*, July–August 1975, p 61. Also see M M Clark, "NLRB General Counsel's Office Issues Liberal Criteria for Defining 'Supervisor,'" *HR Magazine*, February 2004, p 30.

[3] See T J Tentenbaum, "Shifting Paradigms: From Newton to Chaos", *Organizational Dynamics*, Spring 1998, pp 21-32; and R W Oliver, *The Shape of Things to Come* (New York: McGrawHill, 1999).

[4] Essential sources on reengineering are M Hammer and J Champy, *Reengineering the Corporation: A Manifesto for Business Revolution* (New York: HarperCollins, 1993); and J Champy, *Reengineering Management: The Mandate for New Leadership* (New York: HarperCollins, 1995). Also see "Anything Worth Doing Is Worth Doing from Scratch," *Inc.*, May 18, 1999 (20th Anniversary Issue),

[5] For thoughtful discussion, see G G Dess, A M A Rasheed, K J McLaughlin, and R L Priem, "The New Corporate Architecture," *Academy of Management Executive*, August 1995, pp 7-20.

[6] Frederick Winslow Taylor, The Principles of Scientific Management, (1911). The Modern History Sourcebook: Fordham University website: http://www.fordham.edu/halsall/mod/1911taylor.html.

[7] ibid.

[8] ibid.

[9] See M Parker Follett, *Freedom and Coordination* (London: Management Publications Trust, 1949).

[10] As quoted in P LaBarre, "The Industrialized Revolution," *Fast Company*, November 2003, pp 116, 118.

[11] See J M Ivancevich, T N Duening, and W Lidwell, 'Bridging the Manager-Organizational Scientist Collaboration Gap,' *Organizational Dynamics*, no. 2, 2005, pp 103-17; E W Ford, W J Duncan, A G Bedeian, P M Ginter, M D Rousculp, and A M Adams, 'Mitigating Risks, Visible Hands, Inevitable Disasters, and Soft Variables: Management Research That Matters to Managers,' *Academy of Management Executive*, November 2005, pp 24-38; and J M Bartunek, S L Rynes, and R D Ireland, 'What Makes Management Research Interesting, and Why Does It Matter?' *Academy of Management Journal*, February 2006, pp 9-15.

[12] This discussion is based on material in R R Thomas, Jr, *Redefining Diversity* (New York: AMACOM, 1996), pp 4-9.

[13] This distinction is made by M Loden, *Implementing Diversity* (Chicago: Irwin, 1996).

[14] "The 50 Best Companies to Work For in Canada," *Report on Business Magazine*, January 2002, pp 41-52.

[15] A Tomlinson, "Concrete Ceiling Harder to Break Than Glass for Women of Colour," *Canadian HR Reporter*, December 17, 2001, pp 7, 13.

[16] Morrison, *The New Leaders: Guidelines on Leadership Diversity in America*.

[17] Empirical support is provided by H Ibarra, "Race, Opportunity and Diversity of Social Circles in Managerial Networks," *Academy of Management Journal*, June 1995, pp 673-703; and P J Ohlott, M N Ruderman, and C D McCauley, "Gender Differences in Managers' Developmental Job Experiences," *Academy of Management Journal*, February 1994, pp 46-67.

[18] Academy of Management Review by A J Dabaub. Copyright 1995 by Academy of Management (NY). Reproduced with permission of Academy of Management (NY) in the format Textbook via Copyright Clearance Centre (See 8th US edition page 22 – Figure 1.4)

[19] As quoted in D Jones, "Military a Model for Execs", *USA Today*, June 9, 2004, p 4B.

[20] For a good discussion of values, see S D Steiner and M A Watson, "The Service Learning Componentin Business Education: The Values Linkage Void," *Academy of Management Learning and Education*, December 2006, pp 422-34. For more on courage, see J McCain, "In Search of Courage," *Fast Company*, September 2004, pp 53-56; D Lidsky, "How Do You Rate? Take the Courage Quiz," *Fast Company*, September 2004, pp 107-09; and K K Reardon, "Courage," *Harvard Business Review* , Special Issue: The Tests of a Leader, January 2007, pp 58-64.

[21] See S Baker, "Wiser About the Web," *BusinessWeek*, March 27, 2006, pp 54-58; S Levy and B Stone, "The New Wisdom of the Web," *Newsweek*, April 3, 2006, pp 46-53; and A Lashinsky, "The Boom Is Back," *Fortune*, May 1, 2006, pp 70-87.

[22] M J Mandel and R D Hof, "Rethinking the Internet," *BusinessWeek*, March 26, 2001, p 118. Also see G T Lumpkin and G G Dess, "E-Business Strategies and Internet Business Models: How the Internet Adds Value," *Organizational Dynamics*, no. 2, 2004, pp 161-73; and T J Mullaney, "E-Biz Strikes Again!" *BusinessWeek*, May 10, 2004, pp 80-82.

[23] A Bernasek, "Buried in Tech," *Fortune*, April 16, 2001, p. 52.

[24] See M A Tucker, "E-Learning Evolves," *HR Magazine*, October 2005, pp 74-78; S Boehle, "Putting the 'Learning' Back in E-Learning," *Training*, January 2006, pp 30-34; B West, "Online, It's All About Design," *Training*, March 2006, p 76; and J Gordon, "Seven Revelations About E-Learning," *Training*, April 2006, pp 28-31.

CHAPTER 2

[1] C Palmeri, *BusinessWeek*, February 6, 2006, p 53.

[2] Examples can be found in T Lowry, "A McKinsey of Pop Culture'?" *BusinessWeek*, March 26, 2007, pp 104-08; and "Virtual Marketing Makes a False Impression," *BizEd*, March/April 2007, pp 54, 56.

[3] Object perception is discussed by L J Rips, S Blok, and G Newman, "Tracing the Identity of Objects," *Psychological Bulletin*, January 2006, pp 1-30.

[4] ST Fiske and S E Taylor, *Social Cognition*, 2nd ed (Reading, MA: Addison-Wesley Publishing, 1991), pp 1-2.

[5] The negative bias was examined by N Kyle Smith, J T Larsen, T L Chartrand, J T Cacioppo, H A Katafiasz, and K E Moran, "Being Bad Isn't Always Good: Affective Context Moderates the Attention Bias Toward Negative Information," *Journal of Personality and Social Psychology*, February 2006, pp 210-220.

[6] E Rosch, C B Mervis, W D Gray, D M Johnson, and P BoyesBraem, "Basic Objects in Natural Categories," *Cognitive Psychology*, July 1976, p 383.

[7] Results can be found in M Rotundo, D-H Nguyen, and P R Sackett, "A Meta-Analytic Review of Gender Differences in Perceptions of Sexual Harassment," *Journal of Applied Psychology*, October 2001, pp 914-22. Also see J L Berdahl, "The Sexual Harassment of Uppity Women," *Journal of Applied Psychology*, March 2007, pp 425-37.

[8] See J Halberstadt, "Featural Shift in Explanation-Biased Memory for Emotional Faces," *Journal of Personality and Social Psychology*, January 2005, pp 38-49.

[9] See A J Kinicki, P W Hom, M R Trost, and K J Wade, "Effects of Category Prototypes on Performance-Rating Accuracy," *Journal of Applied Psychology*, June 1995, pp 354-70.

[10] For a thorough discussion about the structure and organization of memory, see L R Squire, B Knowlton, and G Musen, "The Structure

and Organization of Memory," in *Annual Review of Psychology*, eds L W Porter and M R Rosenzweig (Palo Alto, CA: Annual Reviews Inc., 1993), vol. 44, pp 453–95.

[11] Implicit cognition is discussed by Y Dunham, A S Baron, and M R Banaji, "From American City to Japanese Village: A Cross-Cultural Investigation of Implicit Race Attitudes," *Child Development*, September 2006, pp 1268–81; and A G Greenwald and M R Banaji, "Implicit Social Cognition: Attitudes, Self-Esteem, and Stereotypes," *Psychological Review*, January 1995, pp 4–27.

[12] See M Orey, "White Men Can't Help It," *BusinessWeek*, May 15, 2006, pp 54, 57; and P Babcock, "Detecting Hidden Bias," *HR Magazine*, February 2006, pp 51–55.

[13] Details of this study can be found in C K Stevens, "Antecedents of Interview Interactions, Interviewers' Ratings, and Applicants' Reactions," *Personnel Psychology*, Spring 1998, pp 55–85.

[14] The effectiveness of rater training was supported by D V Day and L M Sulsky, "Effects of Frame-of-Reference Training and Information Configuration on Memory Organization and Rating Accuracy," *Journal of Applied Psychology*, February 1995, pp 158–67.

[15] Results can be found in J S Phillips and R G Lord, "Schematic Information Processing and Perceptions of Leadership in Problem-Solving Groups," *Journal of Applied Psychology*, August 1982, pp 486–92.

[16] Results can be found in M Sandy Hershcovis, N Turner, J Barling, K A Arnold, K e Dupré, M Inness, M M Le Blanc, and N Sivanathan, "Predicting Workplace Aggression: A Meta-Analysis," *Journal of Applied Psychology*, January 2007, pp 228–38; and S Thau, K Aquino, and R Wittek, "An Extension of Uncertainty Management Theory to the Self: The Relationship between Justice, Social Comparison Orientation, and Antisocial Work Behaviours," *Journal of Applied Psychology*, January 2007, pp 250–58.

[17] See S Begley, "All In Your Head? Yes, and Scientists Are Figuring Out Why," *The Wall Street Journal*, March 17, 2006, p B1.

[18] S Power, "Mickey Mouse, Nike Give Advice on Air Security," *The Wall Street Journal*, January 24, 2002, p B4.

[19] C M Judd and B Park, "Definition and Assessment of Accuracy in Social Stereotypes," *Psychological Review*, January 1993, p 110.

[20] For a thorough discussion of stereotype accuracy, see M C Ashton and V M Esses, "Stereotype Accuracy: Estimating the Academic Performance of Ethnic Groups," *Personality and Social Psychology Bulletin*, February 1999, pp 225–36.

[21] Stereotype formation and maintenance is discussed by J V Petrocelli, Z L Tormala, and D D Rucker, "Unpacking Attitude Certainty: Attitude Clarity and Attitude Correctness," *Journal of Personality and Social Psychology*, January 2006, pp 30–41.

[22] See S Madon, M Guyll, S J Hilbert, E Kyriakatos, and D L Vogel, "Stereotyping the Stereotypic: When Individuals Match Social Stereotypes," *Journal of Applied Social Psychology*, January 2006, pp 178–205.

[23] Results are presented in E Tahmincioglu, "Men Rule-At Least in Workplace Attitudes," *MSNBC*, http://www.msnbc.msn.com/id/17345308/, accessed March 6, 2007.

[24] See M E Heilman and T G Okimoto, "Why Are Women Penalized for Success at Male Tasks?: The Implied Communality Deficit," *Journal of Applied Psychology*, January 2007, pp 81–92.

[25] See J D Olian, D P Schwab, and Y Haberfeld, "The Impact of Applicant Gender Compared to Qualifications on Hiring Recommendations: A Meta-Analysis of Experimental Studies," *Organizational Behaviour and Human Decision Processes*, April 1988, pp 180–95.

[26] Results from the meta-analyses are discussed in K P Carson, C L Sutton, and P D Corner, "Gender Bias in Performance Appraisals: A Meta-Analysis," paper presented at the 49th Annual Academy of Management Meeting, Washington, DC: 1989. Results from the field study can be found in T J Maurer and M A Taylor, "Is Sex by Itself Enough? An Exploration of Gender Bias Issues in

Performance Appraisal," *Organizational Behaviour and Human Decision Processes*, November 1994, pp 231–51.

[27] See J Landau, "The Relationship of Race and Gender to Managers' Ratings of Promotion Potential," *Journal of Organizational Behaviour*, July 1995, pp 391–400.

[28] Results can be found in K S Lyness and M E Heilman, "When Fit Is Fundamental: Performance Evaluations and Promotions of Upper-Level Female and Male Managers," *Journal of Applied Psychology*, July 2006, pp 777–85.

[29] K Helliker, "The Doctor Is Still in: Secrets of Health from a Famed 96-Year-Old Physician," *The Wall Street Journal*, March 8, 2005, p D1.

[30] For a complete review, see S R Rhodes, "Age-Related Differences in Work Attitudes and Behaviour: A Review and Conceptual Analysis," *Psychological Bulletin*, March 1983, pp 328–67. Also see S DeArmond, M Tye, P Y Chen, A Krauss, D A Rogers, and E Sintek, "Age and Gender Stereotypes: New Challenges in a Changing Workplace and Workforce," *Journal of Applied Social Psychology*, September 2006, pp 2184–214.

[31] See G M McEvoy, "Cumulative Evidence of the Relationship between Employee Age and Job Performance," *Journal of Applied Psychology*, February 1989, pp 11–17.

[32] A thorough discussion of the relationship between age and performance is contained in D A Waldman and B J Avolio, "Aging and Work Performance in Perspective: Contextual and Developmental Considerations," in *Research in Personnel and Human Resources Management*, ed G R Ferris (Greenwich, CT: JAI Press, 1993), vol. 11, pp 133–62.

[33] For details, see B J Avolio, D A Waldman, and M A McDaniel, "Age and Work Performance in Nonmanagerial Jobs: The Effects of Experience and Occupational Type," *Academy of Management Journal*, June 1990, pp 407–22.

[34] D H Powell, "Aging Baby Boomers: Stretching Your Workforce Options," *HR Magazine*, July 1998, p 83.

[35] Results can be found in R W Griffeth, P W Hom, and S Gaertner, "A Meta-Analysis of Antecedents and Correlates of Employee Turnover: Update, Moderator Tests, and Research Implications for the Next Millennium," *Journal of Management*, 2000, pp 463–88.

[36] See J J Martocchio, "Age-Related Differences in Employee Absenteeism: A Meta-Analysis," *Psychology and Aging*, December 1989, pp 409–14.

[37] Racial stereotypes are studied and discussed by J K Maner, D T Kenrick, V D Becker, T E Robertson, B Hofer, and S Neuberg, "Functional Projection: How Fundamental Social Motives Can Bias Interpersonal Perception," *Journal of Personality and Social Psychology*, January 2005, pp 63–78; and N London-Vargas, *Faces of Diversity* (New York: Vantage Press, 1999).

[38] See J L Eberhardt, "Imaging Race," *American Psychologist*, February 2005, pp 181–90.

[39] Summaries of this research can be found in M Greer, "Automatic Racial Stereotyping Appears Based on Facial Features in Addition to Race," *Monitor on Psychology*, January 2005, p 14; and L Winerman, "Racial Stereotypes Can Speed Visual Processing," *Monitor on Psychology*, January 2005, p 15.

[40] This information was obtained from the official Web site of Tiger Woods, www.tigerwoods.com/defaultflash.spc, accessed April 1, 2007.

[41] C. Barkley, Who's Afraid of a Large Black Man? (New York: Penguin Press, 2005) p.7.

[42] Statistics Canada – Visible Minorities and Victimization Report. Samuel Perreault, Executive Summary http://www.statcan.gc.ca/pub/85f0033m/85f0033m2008015-eng.pdf

[43] *Muslim Women Settle Discrimination Suit With UPS*, by J. Stewart. The Mississauga News, Nov. 19, 2008.

[44] *Racism, Poverty, Aboriginal Issues cited in UN Report On Canada* by Peter O'Neil, CanWest News Service, Feb. 5, 09

[45] Ibid.

[46] Visible Minorities In Canada's Workplaces—A perspective on the 2017 Projection by Krishna Pendakur, 2005, pg. 9 http://www.sfu.ca/~pendakur/

[47] These statistics were reported in C Komp, "Unemployment, Poverty Higher for People with Disabilities," *The New Standard*, October 4, 2006, http://newstandardnews.net/content/index.cfm/items/3727

[48] Kelley's model is discussed in detail in H H Kelley, "The Processes of Causal Attribution," *American Psychologist*, February 1973, pp 107–28.

[49] For examples, see J Susskind, K Maurer, V Thakkar, D L Hamilton, and J W Sherman, "Perceiving Individuals and Groups: Expectancies, Dispositional Inferences, and Causal Attributions," *Journal of Personality and Social Psychology*, February 1999, pp 181–91; and J McClure, "Discounting Causes of Behaviour: Are Two Reasons Better than One?" *Journal of Personality and Social Psychology*, January 1998, pp 7–20.

[50] The effect of the self-serving bias was tested and supported by P E De Michele, B Gansneder, and G B Solomon, "Success and Failure Attributions of Wrestlers: Further Evidence of the Self-Serving Bias," *Journal of Sport Behaviour*, August 1998, pp 242–55; and C Sedikides, W K Campbell, G D Reeder, and A J Elliot, "The Self-Serving Bias in Relational Context," *Journal of Personality and Social Psychology*, February 1998, pp 378–86.

[51] Details may be found in S E Moss and M J Martinko, "The Effects of Performance Attributions and Outcome Dependence on Leader Feedback Behaviour Following Poor Subordinate Performance," *Journal of Organizational Behaviour*, May 1998, pp 259–74; and E C Pence, W C Pendelton, G H Dobbins, and J A Sgro, "Effects of Causal Explanations and Sex Variables on Recommendations for Corrective Actions Following Employee Failure," *Organizational Behaviour and Human Performance*, April 1982, pp 227–40.

[52] See D Konst, R Vonk, and R V D Vlist, "Inferences about Causes and Consequences of Behaviour of Leaders and Subordinates," *Journal of Organizational Behaviour*, March 1999, pp 261–71.

[53] See J Silvester, F Patterson, E Ferguson, "Comparing Two Attributional Models of Job Performance in Retail Sales: A Field Study," *Journal of Occupational and Organizational Psychology*, March 2003, pp 115–32.

CHAPTER 3

[1] D Seligman, "The Trouble with Buyouts," *Fortune*, November 30, 1992, p 125. For related reading, see P Falcone, "Preserving Restless Top Performers," *HR Magazine*, March 2006, pp 117–22.

[2] See G A Odums, "A New Year's Resolution: Optimize Older Workers," *Training and Development*, January 2006, pp 34–36; P Babcock, "Detecting Hidden Bias," *HR Magazine*, February 2006, pp 50–55; J A Segal, "Time Is on Their Side," *HR Magazine*, February 2006, pp 129–33; A Fisher, "The Sky's the Limit," *Fortune*, May 1, 2006, pp 124B–124H; S Kehrli and T Sopp, "Managing Generation Y," *HR Magazine*, May 2006, pp 113–19; and M Orey, "White Men Can't Help It: Courts Have Been Buying the Idea That They Have Innate Biases," *BusinessWeek*, May 15, 2006, pp 54, 57.

[3] Data from "If We Could Do It Over Again," *USA Today*, February 19, 2001, p 4D.

[4] See D S Vogt and C R Colvin, "Assessment of Accurate Self-Knowledge," *Journal of Personality Assessment*, June 2005, pp 239–51; L M Roberts, J E Dutton, G M Spreitzer, E D Heaphy, and R E Quinn, "Composing the Reflected Best-Self Portrait: Building Pathways for Becoming Extraordinary in Work Organizations," *Academy of Management Review*, October 2005, pp 712–36; S Srivastava and J S Beer, "How Self-Evaluations Relate to Being Liked by Others: Integrating Sociometer and Attachment Perspectives," *Journal of Personality and Social Psychology*, December 2005, pp 966–77; N Haslam, P Bain, L Douge, M Lee, and B Bastian, "More Human Than You: Attributing Humanness to Self and Others," *Journal of Personality and Social Psychology*, December 2005, pp 937–50; G D Bromgard, D Trafimow, and I K Bromgard, "Valence of Self-Cognitions: The Positivity of Individual Self-Statements," *The Journal of Social Psychology*, no. 1, 2006, pp 85–94; and S P Forrest III and T O Peterson, "It's Called Andragogy," *Academy of Management Learning and Education*, March 2006, pp 113–22.

[5] V Gecas, "The Self-Concept," in *Annual Review of Sociology*, eds R H Turner and J F Short, Jr. (Palo Alto, CA: Annual Reviews Inc., 1982), vol. 8, p 3.

[6] L Festinger, *A Theory of Cognitive Dissonance* (Stanford, CA: Stanford University Press, 1957), p 3. Also see T Lombardo, "Thinking Ahead: The Value of Future Consciousness," *The Futurist*, January/February 2006, pp 45–50.

[7] A Canadian versus Japanese comparison of self-concept can be found in J D Campbell, P D Trapnell, S J Heine, I M Katz, L F Lavallee, and D R Lehman, "Self-Concept Clarity: Measurement, Personality Correlates, and Cultural Boundaries," *Journal of Personality and Social Psychology*, January 1996, pp 141–56. Also see R W Tafarodi, C Lo, S Yamaguchi, W W S Lee, and H Katsura, "The Inner Self in Three Countries," *Journal of Cross-Cultural Psychology*, January 2004, pp 97–117.

[8] Based in part on a definition found in Gecas, "The Self-Concept." Also see N Branden, *Self-Esteem at Work: How Confident People Make Powerful Companies* (San Francisco: Jossey-Bass, 1998).

[9] H W Marsh, "Positive and Negative Global Self-Esteem: A Substantively Meaningful Distinction or Artifacts?" *Journal of Personality and Social Psychology*, April 1996, p 819.

[10] Ibid.

[11] See P Borghesi, "I Was Out of a Job—And an Identity," *Newsweek*, January 30, 2006, p 13.

[12] See D G Gardner, L Van Dyne, and J L Pierce, "The Effects of Pay Level on Organization-Based Self-Esteem and Performance: A Field Study," *Journal of Occupational and Organizational Psychology*, September 2004, pp 307–22.

[13] A J Fiacco, "Over 50? Keep Foot in Door," *Arizona Republic*, June 20, 2004, p D4.

[14] Ibid.

[15] E Diener and M Diener, "Cross-Cultural Correlates of Life Satisfaction and Self-Esteem," *Journal of Personality and Social Psychology*, April 1995, p 662. For cross-cultural evidence of a similar psychological process for self-esteem, see T M Singelis, M H Bond, W F Sharkey, and C S Y Lai, "Unpackaging Culture's Influence on Self-Esteem and Embarrassability," *Journal of Cross-Cultural Psychology*, May 1999, pp 315–41. Also see Z Stambor, "People Rate Their Self-Esteem High across Cultures," *Monitor on Psychology*, December 2005, p 13.

[16] See C Kobayashi and J D Brown, "Self-Esteem and Self-Enhancement in Japan and America," *Journal of Cross-Cultural Psychology*, September 2003, pp 567–80.

[17] Based on data in F L Smoll, R E Smith, N P Barnett, and J J Everett, "Enhancement of Children's Self-Esteem through Social Support Training for Youth Sports Coaches," *Journal of Applied Psychology*, August 1993, pp 602–10.

[18] W J McGuire and C V McGuire, "Enhancing Self-Esteem by Directed-Thinking Tasks: Cognitive and Affective Positivity Asymmetries," *Journal of Personality and Social Psychology*, June 1996, p 1124.

[19] S Begley, "Real Self-Esteem Builds on Achievement, Not Praise for Slackers," *The Wall Street Journal*, April 18, 2003, p B1. Also see A Dijksterhuis, "I Like Myself But I Don't Know Why: Enhancing Implicit Self-Esteem by Subliminal Evaluative Conditioning," *Journal of Personality and Social Psychology*, February 2004, pp 345–55; and J V Wood, S A Heimpel, I R Newby-Clark, and M Ross, "Snatching Defeat from the Jaws of Victory: Self-Esteem Differences in the Experience and Anticipation of Success," *Journal of Personality and Social Psychology*, November 2005, pp 764–80.

20 M E Gist, "Self-Efficacy: Implications for Organizational Behaviour and Human Resource Management," *Academy of Management Review*, July 1987, p 472. Also see A Bandura, "Self-Efficacy: Toward a Unifying Theory of Behavioural Change," *Psychological Review*, March 1977, pp 191–215; M E Gist and T R Mitchell, "Self-Efficacy: A Theoretical Analysis of Its Determinants and Malleability," *Academy of Management Review*, April 1992, pp 183–211; and T J Maurer and K D Andrews, "Traditional, Likert, and Simplified Measures of Self-Efficacy," *Educational and Psychological Measurement*, December 2000, pp 965–73.

21 C Brennan, "Tiger Loses Favorite Driver," *USA Today*, May 4, 2006, p 3C.

22 Based on D H Lindsley, D A Brass, and J B Thomas, "Efficacy-Performance Spirals: A Multilevel Perspective," *Academy of Management Review*, July 1995, pp 645–78.

23 See, for example, V Gecas, "The Social Psychology of Self-Efficacy," in *Annual Review of Sociology* eds W R Scott and J Blake (Palo Alto, CA: Annual Reviews, Inc., 1989), vol. 15, pp 291–316; C K Stevens, A G Bavetta, and M E Gist, "Gender Differences in the Acquisition of Salary Negotiation Skills: The Role of Goals, Self-Efficacy, and Perceived Control," *Journal of Applied Psychology*, October 1993, pp 723–35; and D Eden and Y Zuk, "Seasickness as a Self-Fulfilling Prophecy: Raising Self-Efficacy to Boost Performance at Sea," *Journal of Applied Psychology*, October 1995, pp 628–35.

24 For more on learned helplessness, see Gecas, "The Social Psychology of Self-Efficacy"; M J Martinko and W L Gardner, "Learned Helplessness: An Alternative Explanation for Performance Deficits," *Academy of Management Review*, April 1982, pp 195–204; and C R Campbell and M J Martinko, "An Integrative Attributional Perspective of Empowerment and Learned Helplessness: A Multimethod Field Study," *Journal of Management*, no. 2, 1998, pp 173–200. Also see A Dickerson and M A Taylor, "Self-Limiting Behaviour in Women: Self-Esteem and Self-Efficacy as Predictors," *Group & Organization Management*, June 2000, pp 191–210.

25 For an update on Bandura, see D Smith, "The Theory Heard 'Round the World," *Monitor on Psychology*, October 2002, pp 30–32.

26 Research on this connection is reported in R B Rubin, M M Martin, S S Bruning, and D E Powers, "Test of a Self-Efficacy Model of Interpersonal Communication Competence," *Communication Quarterly*, Spring 1993, pp 210–20.

27 Excerpted from T Petzinger Jr, "Bob Schmonsees Has a Tool for Better Sales, and It Ignores Excuses," *The Wall Street Journal*, March 26, 1999, p B1. Also see H Zhao, S E Seibert, and G E Hills, "The Mediating Role of Self-Efficacy in the Development of Entrepreneurial Intentions," *Journal of Applied Psychology*, November 2005, pp 1265–272.

28 Data from A D Stajkovic and F Luthans, "Self-Efficacy and Work-Related Performance: A Meta-Analysis," *Psychological Bulletin*, September 1998, pp 240–61.

29 Based in part on discussion in Gecas, "The Social Psychology of Self-Efficacy."

30 See S K Parker, "Enhancing Role Breadth Self-Efficacy: The Roles of Job Enrichment and Other Organizational Interventions," *Journal of Applied Psychology*, December 1998, pp 835–52.

31 The positive relationship between self-efficacy and readiness for retraining is documented in L A Hill and J Elias, "Retraining Midcareer Managers: Career History and Self-Efficacy Beliefs," *Human Resource Management*, Summer 1990, pp 197–217. Also see A M Saks, "Longitudinal Field Investigation of the Moderating and Mediating Effects of Self-Efficacy on the Relationship between Training and Newcomer Adjustment," *Journal of Applied Psychology*, April 1995, pp 211–25.

32 See A D Stajkovic and Fred Luthans, "Social Cognitive Theory and Self-Efficacy: Going beyond Traditional Motivational and Behavioural Approaches," *Organizational Dynamics*, Spring 1998, pp 62–74.

33 See P C Earley and T R Lituchy, "Delineating Goal and Efficacy Effects: A Test of Three Models," *Journal of Applied Psychology*, February 1991, pp 81–98.

34 See P Tierney and S M Farmer, "Creative Self-Efficacy: Its Potential Antecedents and Relationship to Creative Performance," *Academy of Management Journal*, December 2002, pp 1137–48.

35 See W S Silver, T R Mitchell, and M E Gist, "Response to Successful and Unsuccessful Performance: The Moderating Effect of Self-Efficacy on the Relationship between Performance and Attributions," *Organizational Behaviour and Human Decision Processes*, June 1995, pp 286–99; R Zemke, "The Corporate Coach," *Training*, December 1996, pp 24–28; and J P Masciarelli, "Less Lonely at the Top," *Management Review*, April 1999, pp 58–61.

36 For a comprehensive update, see S W Gangestad and M Snyder, "Self-Monitoring: Appraisal and Reappraisal," *Psychological Bulletin*, July 2000, pp 530–55.

37 M Snyder and S Gangestad, "On the Nature of Self-Monitoring: Matters of Assessment, Matters of Validity," *Journal of Personality and Social Psychology*, July 1986, p 125.

38 Data from M Kilduff and D V Day, "Do Chameleons Get Ahead? The Effects of Self-Monitoring on Managerial Careers," *Academy of Management Journal*, August 1994, pp 1047–60.

39 Data from D B Turban and T W Dougherty, "Role of Protege Personality in Receipt of Mentoring and Career Success," *Academy of Management Journal*, June 1994, pp 688–702.

40 See F Luthans, "Successful vs. Effective Managers," *Academy of Management Executive*, May 1988, pp 127–32. Also see I M Jawahar and J Mattsson, "Sexism and Beautyism Effects in Selection as a Function of Self-Monitoring Level of Decision Maker," *Journal of Applied Psychology*, May 2005, pp 563–73; M R Barrick, L Parks, and M K Mount, "Self-Monitoring as a Moderator of the Relationships between Personality Traits and Performance," *Personnel Psychology*, Autumn 2005, pp 745–67; and K G DeMarree, S C Wheeler, and R E Petty, "Priming a New Identity: Self-Monitoring Moderates the Effects of Nonself Primes on Self-Judgments and Behaviour," *Journal of Personality and Social Psychology*, November 2005, pp 657–71.

41 See A Bandura, *Social Learning Theory* (Englewood Cliffs, NJ: Prentice Hall, 1977). A further refinement is reported in A D Stajkovic and F Luthans, "Social Cognitive Theory and Self-Efficacy: Going Beyond Traditional Motivational and Behavioural Approaches," *Organizational Dynamics*, Spring 1998, pp 62–74. Also see M Uhl-Bien and G B Graen, "Individual Self-Management: Analysis of Professionals' Self-Managing Activities in Functional and Cross-Functional Work Teams," Academy of Management Journal, June 1998, pp 340–50.

42 Bandura, *Social Learning Theory*, p 13.

43 For related research, see M Castaneda, T A Kolenko, and R J Aldag, "Self-Management Perceptions and Practices: A Structural Equations Analysis," Journal of Organizational Behaviour, January 1999, pp 101–20. An alternative model is discussed in K M Sheldon, D B Turban, K G Brown, M R Barrick, and T M Judge, "Applying Self-Determination Theory to Organizational Research," in Research in Personnel and Human Resources Management, vol 22, eds J J Martocchio and G R Ferris (New York: Elsevier, 2003), pp 357–93.

44 "Career Self-Management," Industry Week, September 5, 1994, p 36.

45 See L Nash and H Stevenson, "Success That Lasts," Harvard Business Review, February 2004, pp 102–9.

46 S R Covey, The 7 Habits of Highly Effective People (New York: Simon & Schuster, 1989), p 42. Also see S R Covey, The 8th Habit: From Effectiveness to Greatness (NY: Free Press, 2004); and S Covey, "Power to the People," Training, April 2006, p 64.

47 "Labor Letter: A Special News Report on People and Their Jobs in Offices, Fields, and Factories," *The Wall Street Journal*, October 15, 1985, p 1.

48 R McGarvey, "Rehearsing for Success," *Executive Female*, January/February 1990, p 36.

49. See W P Anthony, R H Bennett, III, E N Maddox, and W J Wheatley, "Picturing the Future: Using Mental Imagery to Enrich Strategic Environmental Assessment," *Academy of Management Executive*, May 1993, pp 43–56.

50. D S Looney, "Mental Toughness Wins Out," *The Christian Science Monitor*, July 31, 1998, p B4.

51. For excellent tips on self-management, see C P Neck, "Managing Your Mind," *Internal Auditor*, June 1996, pp 60–63.

52. C Zastrow, *Talk to Yourself: Using the Power of Self-Talk* (Englewood Cliffs, NJ: Prentice Hall, 1979), p 60. Also see C C Manz and C P Neck, "Inner Leadership: Creating Productive Thought Patterns," *Academy of Management Executive*, August 1991, pp 87–95; C P Neck and R F Ashcraft, "Inner Leadership: Mental Strategies for Nonprofit Staff Members," *Nonprofit World*, May–June 2000, pp 27–30; and T C Brown, "The Effect of Verbal Self-Guidance Training on Collective Efficacy and Team Performance," *Personnel Psychology*, Winter 2003, pp 935–64.

53. E Franz, "Private Pep Talk," *Selling Power*, May 1996, p 81. Also see B Blades, "7 Strategies to Successful Selling," *Training*, April 2006, p 17; J Mandell, "Saying No Can Be a Positive," *USA Today*, April 24, 2006, p 9D; and A Danigelis, "Like, Um, You Know: Verbal Tics May Be Holding You Back. How to Identify Them and Overcome Them. Totally," *Fast Company*, May 2006, p 99.

54. Drawn from discussion in A Bandura, "Self-Reinforcement: Theoretical and Methodological Considerations," *Behaviourism*, Fall 1976, pp 135–55.

55. R Kreitner and F Luthans, "A Social Learning Approach to Behavioural Management: Radical Behaviourists 'Mellowing Out,' " *Organizational Dynamics*, Autumn 1984, p 63.

56. See K Painter, "We Are Who We Are, or Are We?" *USA Today*, October 3, 2002, p 9; S Begley, "In the Brave Guppy and Hyper Octopus, Clues to Personality," *The Wall Street Journal*, October 10, 2003, p B1; and S Kuchinskas, "A Match Made in Hormones," *Business 2.0*, January/February 2006, p 24.

57. For more on personality measurement and assessment, see C H Van Iddekinge, P H Raymark, and P L Roth, "Assessing Personality with a Structured Employment Interview: Construct-Related Validity and Susceptibility to Response Inflation," *Journal of Applied Psychology*, May 2005, pp 536–52; P Barrett, "What If There Were No Psychometrics? Constructs, Complexity, and Measurement," *Journal of Personality Assessment*, October 2005, pp 134–40; E D Heggestad, M Morrison, C L Reeve, and R A McCloy, "Forced-Choice Assessments of Personality for Selection: Evaluating Issues of Normative Assessment and Faking Resistance," *Journal of Applied Psychology*, January 2006, pp 9–24; S Stark, O S Chernyshenko, F Drasgow, and B A Williams, "Examining Assumptions about Item Responding in Personality Assessment: Should Ideal Point Methods Be Considered for Scale Development and Scoring?" *Journal of Applied Psychology*, January 2006, pp 25–39; and J R Matthews and L H Matthews, "Personality Assessment Training: View from a Licensing Board," *Journal of Personality Assessment*, February 2006, pp 46–50.

58. Data from S V Paunonen et al., "The Structure of Personality in Six Cultures," *Journal of Cross-Cultural Psychology*, May 1996, pp 339–53. Also see C Ward, C Leong, and M Low, "Personality and Sojourner Adjustment: An Exploration of the Big Five and the Cultural Fit Proposition," *Journal of Cross-Cultural Psychology*, March 2004, pp 137–51.

59. See M R Barrick and M K Mount, "The Big Five Personality Dimensions and Job Performance: A Meta-Analysis," *Personnel Psychology*, Spring 1991, pp 1–26. Also see R P Tett, D N Jackson, and M Rothstein, "Personality Measures as Predictors of Job Performance: A Meta-Analytic Review," *Personnel Psychology*, Winter 1991, pp 703–42; and S E Seibert and M L Kraimer, "The Five-Factor Model of Personality and Career Success," *Journal of Vocational Behaviour*, February 2001, pp 1–21.

60. Barrick and Mount, "The Big Five Personality Dimensions and Job Performance: A Meta-Analysis," p 18. Also see J E Kurtz and S B Tiegreen, "Matters of Conscience and Conscientiousness: The Place of Ego Development in the Five-Factor Model," *Journal of Personality Assessment*, December 2005, pp 312–17; and N M Dudley, K A Orvis, J E Lebiecki, and J M Cortina, "A Meta-Analytic Investigation of Conscientiousness in the Prediction of Job Performance: Examining the Intercorrelations and the Incremental Validity of Narrow Traits" *Journal of Applied Psychology*, January 2006, pp 40–57.

61. For details, see S Clarke and I T Robertson, "A Meta-Analytic Review of the Big Five Personality Factors and Accident Involvement in Occupational and Non-Occupational Settings," *Journal of Occupational and Organizational Psychology*, September 2005, pp 355–76.

62. Barrick and Mount, "The Big Five Personality Dimensions and Job Performance: A Meta-Analysis," p 21. Also see D M Tokar, A R Fischer, and L M Subich, "Personality and Vocational Behaviour: A Selective Review of the Literature, 1993–1997," *Journal of Vocational Behaviour*, October 1998, pp 115–53; and K C Wooten, T A Timmerman, and R Folger, "The Use of Personality and the Five-Factor Model to Predict New Business Ventures: From Outplacement to Start-up," *Journal of Vocational Behaviour*, February 1999, pp 82–101.

63. For details, see L A Witt and G R Ferris, "Social Skill as Moderator of the Conscientiousness-Performance Relationship: Convergent Results across Four Studies," *Journal of Applied Psychology*, October 2003, pp 809–20. Also see H Liao and A Chuang, "A Multilevel Investigation of Factors Influencing Employee Service Performance and Customer Outcomes," *Academy of Management Journal*, February 2004, pp 41–58.

64. Lead researcher William Fleeson, as quoted in M Dittmann, "Acting Extraverted Spurs Positive Feelings, Study Finds," *Monitor on Psychology*, April 2003, p 17. Also see L D Smillie, G B Yeo, A F Furnham, and C J Jackson, "Benefits of All Work and No Play: The Relationship between Neuroticism and Performance as a Function of Resource Allocation," *Journal of Applied Psychology*, January 2006, pp 139–55.

65. J M Crant, "Proactive Behaviour in Organizations," *Journal of Management*, no. 3, 2000, p 439.

66. Ibid., pp 439–41. Also see J A Thompson, "Proactive Personality and Job Performance: A Social Capital Perspective," *Journal of Applied Psychology*, September 2005, pp 1011–017; and B Erdogan and T N Bauer, "Enhancing Career Benefits of Employee Proactive Personality: The Role of Fit with Jobs and Organizations," *Personnel Psychology*, Winter 2005, pp 859–91.

67. For inspiration, see P Burrows, "HP's Ultimate Team Player," *BusinessWeek*, January 30, 2006, pp 76–78; B Hagenbaugh and S Kirchhoff, "From BET to Hotels to Banking, Johnson Keeps Moving Forward," *USA Today*, April 12, 2006, pp 1B–2B; and P B Gray, "Business Class," *Fortune*, April 17, 2006, pp 336B–336H.

68. D.S. Summer, The Formation of Entrepreneurial Intentions, Routledge 2000, preface pg. Ix.

69. See S B Gustafson and M D Mumford, "Personal Style and Person-Environment Fit: A Pattern Approach," *Journal of Vocational Behaviour*, April 1995, pp 163–88; and T M Glomb and E T Walsh, "Can Opposites Attract? Personality Heterogeneity in Supervisor-Subordinate Dyads as a Predictor of Subordinate Outcomes," *Journal of Applied Psychology*, July 2005, pp 749–57.

70. For an instructive update, see J B Rotter, "Internal versus External Control of Reinforcement: A Case History of a Variable," *American Psychologist*, April 1990, pp 489–93. A critical review of locus of control and a call for a meta-analysis can be found in R W Renn and R J Vandenberg, "Differences in Employee Attitudes and Behaviours Based on Rotter's (1966) Internal-External Locus of Control: Are They All Valid?" *Human Relations*, November 1991, pp 1161–77.

71 For an overall review of research on locus of control, see P E Spector, "Behaviour in Organizations as a Function of Employee's Locus of Control," *Psychological Bulletin*, May 1982, pp 482–97; the relationship between locus of control and performance and satisfaction is examined in D R Norris and R E Niebuhr, "Attributional Influences on the Job Performance–Job Satisfaction Relationship," *Academy of Management Journal*, June 1984, pp 424–31; salary differences between internals and externals were examined by P C Nystrom, "Managers' Salaries and Their Beliefs about Reinforcement Control," *Journal of Social Psychology*, August 1983, pp 291–92. Also see S S K Lam and J Schaubroeck, "The Role of Locus of Control in Reactions to Being Promoted and to Being Passed Over: A Quasi Experiment," *Academy of Management Journal*, February 2000, pp 66–78.

72 Robert Solomon, as quoted in D Vera and A Rodriguez-Lopez, "Strategic Virtues: Humility as a Source of Competitive Advantage," *Organizational Dynamics*, no. 4, 2004, pp 394–95.

73 Ibid., p 395.

74 For interesting reading on intelligence, see J R Flynn, 'Searching for Justice: The Discovery of IQ Gains over Time,' *American Psychologist*, January 1999, pp 5–20; and E Benson, 'Intelligent Intelligence Testing,' *Monitor on Psychology*, February 2003, pp 48–54.

75 For an excellent update on intelligence, including definitional distinctions and a historical perspective of the IQ controversy, see R A Weinberg, 'Intelligence and IQ,' *American Psychologist*, February 1989, pp 98–104. Genetics and intelligence are discussed in R Plomin and F M Spinath, 'Intelligence: Genetics, Genes, and Genomics,' *Journal of Personality and Social Psychology*, January 2004, pp 112–29.

76 Ibid. Also see M Elias, "Mom's IQ, Not Family Size, Key to Kids' Smarts," *USA Today*, June 12, 2000, p 1D; and R Sapolsky, "Score One for Nature—or Is It Nurture?" *USA Today*, June 21, 2000, p 17A.

77 S L Wilk, L Burris Desmarais, and P R Sackett, "Gravitation to Jobs Commensurate with Ability: Longitudinal and Cross-Sectional Tests," *Journal of Applied Psychology*, February 1995, p 79. Also see J Menkes, "Hiring for Smarts," *Harvard Business Review*, November 2005, pp 100–09.

78 B Azar, "People Are Becoming Smarter—Why?" *APA Monitor*, June 1996, p 20. Also see " 'Average' Intelligence Higher than It Used to Be," *USA Today*, February 18, 1997, p 6D.

79 See D Lubinski, "Introduction to the Special Section on Cognitive Abilities: 100 Years after Spearman's (1904) 'General Intelligence,' Objectively Determined and Measured," *Journal of Personality and Social Psychology*, January 2004, pp 96–111.

80 See F L Schmidt and J E Hunter, "Employment Testing: Old Theories and New Research Findings," *American Psychologist*, October 1981, p 1128; and N R Kuncel, S A Hezlett, and D S Ones, "Academic Performance, Career Potential, Creativity, and Job Performance: Can One Construct Predict Them All?" *Journal of Personality and Social Psychology*, January 2004, pp 148–61. A brief overview of the foregoing study can be found in M Greer, "General Cognition Also Makes the Difference on the Job, Study Finds," *Monitor on Psychology*, April 2004, p 12. Also see F L Schmidt and J Hunter, "General Mental Ability in the World of Work: Occupational Attainment and Job Performance," *Journal of Personality and Social Psychology*, January 2004, pp 162–73; and R L Cardy and T T Selvarajan, "Competencies: Alternative Frameworks for Competitive Advantage," *Business Horizons*, May/June 2006, pp 235–45.

81 See H Gardner, *Frames of Mind: The Theory of Multiple Intelligences*, 10th anniversary ed (New York: Basic Books, 1993); and H Gardner, *Intelligence Reframed: Multiple Intelligences for the 21st Century* (New York: Basic Books, 2000).

82 For a good overview of Gardner's life and work, see M K Smith, "Howard Gardner and Multiple Intelligences," *Encyclopedia of Informal Education*, 2002, www.infed.org/ thinkers/gardner.htm. Also see B Fryer, "The Ethical Mind: A Conversation with Psychologist Howard Gardner," *Harvard Business Review*, March 2007, pp 51–56.

83 R J Sternberg, "WICS: A Model of Leadership in Organizations," *Academy of Management Learning and Education*, December 2003, p 388. "Executive intelligence" is discussed in J Menkes, "Hiring for Smarts," *Harvard Business Review*, November 2005, pp 100–09 and "political intelligence" is discussed in R M Kramer, "The Great Intimidators," *Harvard Business Review*, February 2006, pp 88–96.

84 See K Albrecht, "Social Intelligence: Beyond IQ," *Training*, December 2004, pp 26–31; and AA Loort, "Multiple Intelligences: A Comparative Study Between the Preferences

85 S Hamm, "Bill's Co-Pilot," *BusinessWeek*, September 14, 1998, pp 85, 87.

86 G Anders, "John Chambers after the Deluge," *Fast Company*, July 2001, p 108.

87 R S Lazarus, *Emotion and Adaptation* (New York: Oxford University Press, 1991), p 6. Also see, J A Russell and L F Barrett, "Core Affect, Prototypical Emotional Episodes, and Other Things Called Emotion: Dissecting the Elephant," *Journal of Personality and Social Psychology*, May 1999, pp 805–19; S Fineman, *Understanding Emotion at Work* (Thousand Oaks, CA: Sage, 2003); D DeSteno, R E Petty, D D Rucker, D T Wegener, and J Braverman, "Discrete Emotions and Persuasion: The Role of Emotion-Induced Expectancies," *Journal of Personality and Social Psychology*, January 2004, pp 43–56; L A King, J A Hicks, J L Krull, and A K Del Gaiso, "Positive Affect and the Experience of Meaning in Life," *Journal of Personality and Social Psychology*, January 2006, pp 179–96; and G Morse, "Decisions and Desire," *Harvard Business Review*, January 2006, pp 42–51

88 Based on discussion in R D Arvey, G L Renz, and T W Watson, 'Emotionality and Job Performance: Implications for Personnel Selection,' in *Research in Personnel and Human Resources Management*, vol. 16, ed G R Ferris (Stamford, CT: JAI Press, 1998), pp 103–47. Also see L A King, 'Ambivalence over Emotional Expression and Reading Emotions,' *Journal of Personality and Social Psychology*, March 1998, pp 753–62; and J L Tsai and Y Chentsova-Dutton, 'Variation among European Americans in Emotional Facial Expression,' *Journal of Cross-Cultural Psychology*, November 2003, pp 650–57.

89 Data from S D Pugh, "Service with a Smile: Emotional Contagion in the Service Encounter," *Academy of Management Journal*, October 2001, pp 1018–27.

90 Drawn from P Totterdell, S Kellett, K Teuchmann, and R B Briner, "Evidence of Mood Linkage in Work Groups," *Journal of Personality and Social Psychology*, June 1998, pp 1504–15. Also see C D Fisher, "Mood and Emotions while Working: Missing Pieces of Job Satisfaction," *Journal of Organizational Behaviour*, March 2000, pp 185–202; K M Lewis, "When Leaders Display Emotion: How Followers Respond to Negative Emotional Expression of Male and Female Leaders," *Journal of Organizational Behaviour*, March 2000, pp 221–34; and A Singh-Manoux and C Finkenauer, "Cultural Variations in Social Sharing of Emotions: An Intercultural Perspective," *Journal of Cross-Cultural Psychology*, November 2001, pp 647–61.

91 As quoted in D Jones, "Music Director Works to Blend Strengths," *USA Today*, October 27, 2003, p 6B.

92 Hochschild, A.R. (1983), The Managed Heart – Commercialization of Human Feeling, Berkley, CA: University of California Press.

93 N M Ashkanasy and C S Daus "Emotion in the Workplace: The New Challenge for Managers," *Academy of Management Executive*, February 2002, p 79. Also see A A Grandey, "When 'The Show Must Go On': Surface Acting and Deep Acting as Determinants of Emotional Exhaustion and Peer-Rated Service Delivery," *Academy of Management Journal*, February 2003, pp 86–96; C M Brotheridge and R T Lee, "Development and Validation of the Emotional Labour Scale," *Journal of Occupational and Organizational Psychology*, September 2003, pp 365–79; Y Guerrier and A Adib, "Work at Leisure and Leisure at Work: A Study of the Emotional Labour of Tour Reps," *Human Relations*, November 2003, pp 1399–417; A A Grandey, G M Fisk, and

D D Steiner, "Must 'Service With a Smile' Be Stressful? The Moderating Role of Personal Control for American and French Employees," *Journal of Applied Psychology*, September 2005, pp 893–904; R H Gosserand and J M Diefendorff, "Emotional Display Rules and Emotional Labor: The Moderating Role of Commitment," *Journal of Applied Psychology*, November 2005, pp 1256–264; S Burling, "Stress Study Shows Ills of Call-Center Workers," *The Arizona Republic*, December 10, 2005, p D3; and P O'Connell, "Taking the Measure of Mood," *Harvard Business Review*, March 2006, pp 25–26.

94 Data from A M Kring and A H Gordon, "Sex Differences in Emotions: Expression, Experience, and Physiology," *Journal of Personality and Social Psychology*, March 1998, pp 686–703.

95 D Goleman, *Emotional Intelligence* (New York: Bantam Books, 1995), p 34. For more, see M Dittmann, "How 'Emotional Intelligence' Emerged," *Monitor on Psychology*, October 2003, p 64; M M Tugade and B L Fredrickson, "Resilient Individuals Use Positive Emotions to Bounce Back from Negative Emotional Experiences," *Journal of Personality and Social Psychology*, February 2004, pp 320–33; I Goldenberg, K Matheson, and J Mantler, "The Assessment of Emotional Intelligence: A Comparison of Performance-Based and Self-Report Methodologies," *Journal of Personality Assessment*, February 2006, pp 33–45; and J E Barbuto Jr. and M E Burbach, "The Emotional Intelligence of Transformational Leaders: A Field Study of Elected Officials," *The Journal of Social Psychology*, February 2006, pp 51–64.

96 See the box titled "Get Happy Carefully" on p 49 of D Goleman, R Boyatzis, and A McKee, "Primal Leadership: The Hidden Driver of Great Performance," *Harvard Business Review*, Special Issue: Breakthrough Leadership, December 2001, pp 43–51.

97 J S Lublin, "Surviving the Pressure with a Ready Plan or, Literally, a Script," *The Wall Street Journal*, March 2, 2004, p B1.

98 M N Martinez, "The Smarts That Count," *HR Magazine*, November 1997, pp 72–78.

99 "What's Your EQ at Work?" *Fortune*, October 26, 1998, p 298.

100 Based on M Davies, L Stankov, and R D Roberts, "Emotional Intelligence: In Search of an Elusive Construct," *Journal of Personality and Social Psychology*, October 1998, pp 989–1015; and K A Barchard, "Does Emotional Intelligence Assist in the Prediction of Academic Success?" *Educational and Psychological Measurement*, October 2003, pp 840–58. Also see B P Chapman and B Hayslip, Jr., "Incremental Validity of a Measure of Emotional Intelligence," *Journal of Personality Assessment*, October 2005, pp 154–69.

101 A Fisher, "Success Secret: A High Emotional IQ," *Fortune*, October 26, 1998, p 294. Also see Daniel Goleman, "Never Stop Learning," *Harvard Business Review*, Special Issue: Inside the Mind of the Leader, January 2004, pp 28–29.

CHAPTER 4

1 Research on turnover is summarized by P W Hom and R W Griffeth, *Employee Turnover* (Cincinnati, OH: Southwestern, 1995).

2 Examples are provided in R Levering and M Moskowitz, "The 100 Best Companies to Work For," *Fortune*, January 22, 2007, pp 94–114.

3 M Rokeach, *The Nature of Values* (New York: Free Press, 1973), p 5.

4 See S H Schwartz and T Rubel, "Sex Differences in Value Priorities: Cross-Cultural and Multimethod Studies," *Journal of Personality and Social Psychology*, December 2005, pp 1010–28.

5 See M Rokeach, *Beliefs, Attitudes, and Values* (San Francisco: Jossey-Bass, 1968).

6 M. Rokeach and S.J. Ball-Rokeach, "Stability and Change in American Value Priorities, 1968–1981," American Psychologist, May 1989, pp 775–784.)

7 P B Brown, "What I Know Now," *Fast Company*, February 2005, p 96.

8 This example was derived from D Lieberman, "L.A. Times' Publisher Forced Out Over Refusal to Cut Staff," *USA Today*, October 6, 2006, p 1B.

9 For a thorough discussion of person-culture fit, see A L Kristof-Brown, R D Zimmerman, and E C Johnson, "Consequences of Individuals' Fit at Work: A Meta-Analysis of Person-Job, Person-Organization, Person-Group, and Person-Supervisor Fit," *Personnel Psychology*, Summer 2005, pp 281–342.

10 Supportive results can be found in H A Elfenbein and C A O'Reilly III, "Fitting In: The Effects of Relational Demography and Person-Culture Fit on Group Process and Performance," *Group & Organization Management*, February 2007, pp 109–42; and C Ostroff, Y Shin, and A Kinicki, "Multiple Perspectives of Congruence: Relationships between Value Congruence and Employee Attitudes," *Journal of Organizational Behaviour*, September 2005, pp 591–624.

11 B Moses, "The Busyness Trap," *Training*, November 1998.

12 See P Sellers, "A Kinder, Gentler Lehman Brothers," *Fortune*, January 22, 2007, pp 36–38; K Gurchiek, "Give Us Your Sick," *HR Magazine*, January 2007, pp 91–93; and M J Frase, "International Commuters," *HR Magazine*, March 2007, pp 91–95.

13 P L Perrewé and W A Hochwarter, "Can We Really Have It All? The Attainment of Work and Family Values," *Current Directions in Psychological Science*, February 2001, p 31.

14 Results can be found in D Brady, "Hopping Aboard the Daddy Track," *BusinessWeek*, November 8, 2004, p 101.

15 See L M Graves, P J Ohlott, and M N Ruderman, "Commitment to Family Roles: Effects on Managers' Attitudes and Performance," *Journal of Applied Psychology*, January 2007, pp 44–56.

16 Examples can be found in S Shellenbarger, "Employers Step Up Efforts to Lure Stay-at-Home Mothers Back to Work," *The Wall Street Journal*, February 9, 2006, p D1.

17 The need for flexibility is discussed by S Shellenbarger, "Reasons to Hold Out Hope for Balancing Work and Home," *The Wall Street Journal*, January 11, 2007, p D1; and S Shellenbarger, "Time on Your Side: Rating Your Boss's Flexible Scheduling," *The Wall Street Journal*, January 25, 2007, p D1.

18 T R Nielson, D S Carlson, and M J Lankau, "The Supportive Mentor as a Means of Reducing Work-Family Conflict," *Journal of Vocational Behaviour*, December 2001, pp 374–75.

19 Results can be found in M T Ford, B A Heinen, and K L Langkamer, "Work and Family Satisfaction and Conflict: A Meta-Analysis of Cross-Domain Relations," Journal of Applied Psychology, January 2007, pp 57–80; and W J Casper, L T Eby, C Cordeaux, A Lockwood, and D Lambert, "A Review of Research Methods in IO/OB Work-Family Research," Journal of Applied Psychology, January 2007, pp 28–43.

20 Based on S Parasuraman and C A Simmers, "Type of Employment, Work-Family Conflict and Well-Being: A Comparative Study," *Journal of Organizational Behaviour*, August 2001, pp 551–68.

21 R Rapoport, L Bailyn, J K Fletcher, and B H Pruitt, *Beyond Work-Family Balance: Advancing Gender Equity and Workplace Performance* (San Francisco: Jossey-Bass, 2002), p 36.

22 Fanshawe College 2nd Floor of Student Centre Building—London, Ont. And the University of Western Ontario, University College Bulding 2nd Floor location—London, Ontario.

23 These results are discussed in L Winerman, "A Healthy Mind, a Longer Life," *Monitor on Psychology*, November 2006, pp 42–44.

24 See D A Harrison, D A Newman, and P L Roth, "How Important Are Job Attitudes? Meta-Analytic Comparisons of Integrative Behavioural Outcomes and Time Sequences," *Academy of Management Journal*, April 2006, pp 305–25.

25 M Fishbein and I Ajzen, *Belief, Attitude, Intention and Behaviour: An Introduction to Theory and Research* (Reading, MA: Addison-Wesley Publishing, 1975), p 6.

26 The components or structure of attitudes is thoroughly discussed by A P Brief, *Attitudes in and around Organizations* (Thousand Oaks, CA: Sage, 1998), pp 49–84.

27 For details about this theory, see L Festinger, *A Theory of Cognitive Dissonance* (Stanford, CA: Stanford University Press, 1957). Also see J V

Petrocelli, Z L Tormala, and D D Rucker, "Unpacking Attitude Certainty: Attitude Clarity and Attitude Correctness," *Journal of Personality and Social Psychology*, January 2007, pp 30–41; and S C Wheeler, P Brinol and A D Hermann, "Resistance to Persuasion As Self-Regulation: Ego-depletion and Its Effects on Attitude Change Processes," *Journal of Experimental Social Psychology*, January 2007, pp 150–56.

[28] See B M Staw and J Ross, "Stability in the Midst of Change: A Dispositional Approach to Job Attitudes," *Journal of Applied Psychology*, August 1985, pp 469–80. Also see J Schaubroeck, D C Ganster, and B Kemmerer, "Does Trait Affect Promote Job Attitude Stability?" *Journal of Organizational Behaviour*, March 1996, pp 191–96.

[29] Data from P S Visser and J A Krosnick, "Development of Attitude Strength over the Life Cycle: Surge and Decline," *Journal of Personality and Social Psychology*, December 1998, pp 389–410.

[30] I Ajzen, "The Theory of Planned Behaviour," *Organizational Behaviour and Human Decision Processes*, vol. 50 (1991), p 188.

[31] See R P Steel and N K Ovalle II, "A Review and Meta-Analysis of Research on the Relationship between Behavioural Intentions and Employee Turnover," *Journal of Applied Psychology*, November 1984, pp 673–86.

[32] Results can be found in M R Barrick and R D Zimmerman, "Reducing Voluntary Turnover through Selection," *Journal of Applied Psychology*, January 2005, pp 159–66.

[33] Drawn from I Ajzen and M Fishbein, *Understanding Attitudes and Predicting Social Behaviour* (Englewood Cliffs, NJ: Prentice Hall, 1980); and C-S Lu, K-H Lai, and T C E Cheng, "Application of Structural Equation Modeling to Evaluate the Intention of Shippers to Use Internet Services in Liner Shipping," *European Journal of Operational Research*, July 2007, pp 845–67; A McKinlay and S Cowan, " 'If You're Frail You've Had It': A Theory of Planned Behaviour Study of Nurses' Attitudes Towards Working with Older Patients," *Journal of Applied Social Psychology*, April 2006, pp 900–17; J G Pesek, R D Raehsler, and R S Balough, "Future Professionals and Managers: Their Attitudes Toward Unions, Organizational Beliefs, and Work Ethic," *Journal of Applied Social Psychology*, June 2006, pp 1569–94; D Albarracín, B T Johnson, M Fishbein, and P A Muellerleile, "Theories of Reasoned Action and Planned Behaviour as Models of Condom Use: A Meta Analysis," *Psychological Bulletin*, January 2001, pp 142–61; and P W Hom and C L Hulin, "A Competitive Test of the Prediction of Reenlistment by Several Models," *Journal of Applied Psychology*, February 1981, pp 23–39.

[34] Results can be found in E A J Hooft, M P Born, T W Taris, and H V D Flier, "The Cross-Cultural Generalizability of the Theory of Planned Behaviour," *Journal of Cross-Cultural Psychology*, March 2006, pp 127–35.

[35] Supportive research is presented in T L Webb and P Sheeran, "Does Changing Behavioural Intentions Engender Behaviour Change: A Meta-Analysis of the Experimental Evidence," *Psychological Bulletin*, March 2006, pp 249–68.

[36] Results can be found in M L Kraimer, S J Wayne, R C Liden, and R T Sparrowe, "The Role of Job Security in Understanding the Relationship between Employees' Perceptions of Temporary Workers and Employees' Performance," *Journal of Applied Psychology*, March 2005, pp 389–98.

[37] The concept of commitment and its relationship to motivated Behaviour is thoroughly discussed by J P Meyer, T E Becker, and C Vandenberghe, "Employee Commitment and Motivation: A Conceptual Analysis and Integrative Model," *Journal of Applied Psychology*, December 2004, pp 991–1007.

[38] J P Meyer and L Herscovitch, "Commitment in the Workplace: Toward a General Model," *Human Resource Management Review*, Autumn 2001, p 301.

[39] J P Meyer and N J Allen, "A Three-Component Conceptualization of Organizational Commitment," *Human Resource Management Review*, Spring 1991, p 67.

[40] See R E Johnson and C-H Chang, " 'I' Is to Continuance as 'We' Is to Affective: The Relevance of the Self-Concept For Organizational Commitment," *Journal of Organizational Behaviour*, August 2006, pp 549–70; and J P Meyer, T E Becker, and R Van Dick, "Social Identities and Commitments at Work: Toward an Integrative Model," *Journal of Organizational Behaviour*, August 2006, pp 665–83.

[41] This definition was provided by D M Rousseau, "Psychological and Implied Contracts in Organizations," *Employee Responsibilities and Rights Journal*, June 1989, 121–39.

[42] Results can be found in N P Podsakoff, J A LePine, M A LePine, "Differential Challenge Stressor-Hindrance Stressor Relationships with Job Attitudes, Turnover Intentions, Turnover, and Withdrawal Behaviour: A Meta-Analysis," *Journal of Applied Psychology*, March 2007, pp 438–54.

[43] Results can be found in M Riketta, "Attitudinal Organizational Commitment and Job Performance: A Meta-Analysis," *Journal of Organizational Behaviour*, March 2002, pp 257–66.

[44] Results can be found in R W Griffeth, P W Hom, and S Gaertner, "A Meta-Analysis of Antecedents and Correlates of Employee Turnover: Update, Moderator Tests, and Research Implications for the Next Millennium," *Journal of Management*, 2000, pp 463–88. Also see P F McKay, D R Avery, S Tonidandel, M A Morris, M Hernandez, and M R Hebl, "Racial Differences in Employee Retention: Are Diversity Climate Perceptions the Key?" *Personnel Psychology*, Spring 2007, pp 35–62.

[45] These examples were discussed in R Levering and M Moskowitz, "The 100 Best Companies to Work For," *Fortune*, January 22, 2007, p 94.

[46] R Levering and M Moskowitz, "The 100 Best Companies to Work For," *Fortune*, January 24, 2005, p 84.

[47] Ibid, pp 80, 82. Also see M A S Al-Emadi and M J Marquardt, "Relationship between Employees' Beliefs Regarding Training Benefits and Employees' Organizational Commitment in a Petroleum Company in the State of Qatar," *International Journal of Training and Development*, March 2007, pp 49–70.

[48] I M Paullay, G M Alliger, and E F Stone-Romero, "Construct Validation of Two Instruments Designed to Measure Job Involvement and Work Centrality," *Journal of Applied Psychology*, April 1994, p 224.

[49] Yerkes, *Fun Works*, p 126.

[50] Ibid.

[51] Results can be found in S P Brown, "A Meta-Analysis and Review of Organizational Research on Job Involvement," *Psychological Bulletin*, September 1996, pp 235–55.

[52] Results can be found in J M Diefendorff, D J Brown, A M Kamin, and R G Lord, "Examining the Roles of Job Involvement and Work Centrality in Predicting Organizational Citizenship Behaviours and Job Performance," *Journal of Organizational Behaviour*, February 2002, pp 93–108.

[53] Results can be found in N A Bowling, T A Beehr, and L R Lepisto, "Beyond Job Satisfaction: A Five-Year Prospective Analysis of the Dispositional Approach to Work Attitudes," *Journal of Vocational Behaviour*, October 2006, pp 315–30.

[54] See S Sonnentag and U Kruel, "Psychological Detachment from Work During Off-Job Time: The Role of Job Stressor, Job Involvement, and Recovery-Related Self-Efficacy," *European Journal of Work and Organizational Pscyhology*, June 2006, pp 197–17.

[55] See J Wegge, K-H Schmidt, C Parkes, and R van Dick, "Taking a Sickie: Job Satisfaction and Job Involvement as Interactive Predictors of Absenteeism in a Public Organization," *Journal of Occupational and Organizational Psychology*, March 2007, pp 77–90.

[56] Supportive results can be found in "Job Satisfaction Palls Quickly for Most Workers," *HR Magazine*, March 2007, p 16; S Miller, "Satisfaction with Pay, Benefits Falling," *HR Magazine*, January 2007, pp 38–39; and "Middle Managers Unhappy," *HR Magazine*, July 2006, p 16.

57 For a review of these models, see Brief, *Attitudes in and around Organizations.*

58 The survey was conducted by Hewitt and Associates, and results were presented in J Saranow, "Anybody Want to Take a Nap?" *The Wall Street Journal*, January 24, 2005, p R5.

59 For a review of need satisfaction models, see E F Stone, "A Critical Analysis of Social Information Processing Models of Job Perceptions and Job Attitudes," *Job Satisfaction: How People Feel about Their Jobs and How It Affects Their Performance,* eds C J Cranny, P Cain Smith, and E F Stone (New York: Lexington Books, 1992), pp 21–52.

60 See J P Wanous, T D Poland, S L Premack, and K S Davis, "The Effects of Met Expectations on Newcomer Attitudes and Behaviours: A Review and Meta-Analysis," *Journal of Applied Psychology*, June 1992, pp 288–97.

61 A complete description of this model is provided by E A Locke, "Job Satisfaction," in *Social Psychology and Organizational Behaviour,* eds M Gruneberg and T Wall (New York: John Wiley & Sons, 1984).

62 The results and recommendations can be found in J Chatzky, "Making Time for Time Off," *Money,* April 2005, pp 48, 50.

63 Results can be found in J Cohen-Charash and P E Spector, "The Role of Justice in Organizations: A Meta-Analysis," *Organizational Behaviour and Human Decision Processes,* November 2001, pp 278–321.

64 A thorough discussion of this model is provided by C L Hulin, and T A Judge, "Job Attitudes," in *Handbook of Psychology,* vol. 12, eds W C Borman, D R Ilgen, and R J Klimoski (Hoboken, NJ: John Wiley & Sons, Inc., 2003), pp 255–76.

65 A summary and interpretation of this research is provided by B M Staw and Y Choen-Charash, "The Dispositional Approach to Job Satisfaction: More than a Mirage, but Not Yet an Oasis," Journal of Organizational Behaviour, February 2005, pp 59–78.

66 See R D Arvey, T J Bouchard Jr, N L Segal, and L M Abraham, "Job Satisfaction: Environmental and Genetic Components," *Journal of Applied Psychology,* April 1989, pp 187–92. Also see S E Hammpson, L R Goldberg, T M Vogt, and J P Dubanoski, "Mechanisms by Which Childhood Personality Traits Influence Adult Health Status: Educational Attainment and Healthy Behaviours," *Health Psychology,* January 2007, pp 121–25.

67 See C Dormann and D Zapf, "Job Satisfaction: A Meta-Analysis of Stabilities," *Journal of Organizational Behaviour,* August 2001, pp 483–504.

68 P Wakeman, "The Good Life and How to Get It," *Inc.,* February 2001, p 50.

69 See A J Kinicki, F M McKee-Ryan, C A Schriesheim, and K P Carson, "Assessing the Construct Validity of the Job Descriptive Index: A Review and Meta-Analysis," *Journal of Applied Psychology,* February 2002, pp 14–32.

70 See Brown, "A Meta-Analysis and Review of Organizational Research on Job Involvement."

71 D W Organ, "The Motivational Basis of Organizational Citizenship Behaviour," in *Research in Organizational Behaviour,* eds B M Staw and L L Cummings (Greenwich, CT: JAI Press, 1990), p 46.

72 Results can be found in B J Hoffman, C A Blair, J P Meriac, and D J Woehr, "Expanding the Criterion Domain? A Quantitative Review of the OCB Literature," *Journal of Applied Psychology,* March 2007, pp 555–66.

73 Supportive results can be found in D Kamdar, D J McAllister, and D B Turban, " 'All in a Day's Work': How Follower Individual Differences and Justice Perceptions Predict OCB Role Definitions and Behaviour," *Journal of Applied Psychology,* July 2006, pp 841–55; and B J Tepper, M K Duffy, J Hoobler, and M D Ensley, "Moderators of the Relationship between Coworkers' Organizational Citizenship Behaviour and Fellow Employees' Attitudes," *Journal of Applied Psychology,* June 2004, pp 455–65.

74 Supportive findings are presented in T D Allen, "Rewarding Good Citizens: The Relationship Between Citizenship Behaviour, Gender, and Organizational Rewards," *Journal of Applied Social Psychology,*

January 2006, pp 120–43; and T W Lee, T R Mitchell, C J Sablynski, J P Burton, and B C Holtom, "The Effects of Job Embeddedness on Organizational Citizenship, Job Performance, Volitional Absences, and Voluntary Turnover," *Academy of Management Journal,* October 2004, pp 711–22.

75 Results can be found in D J Koys, "The Effects of Employee Satisfaction, Organizational Citizenship Behaviour, and Turnover on Organizational Effectiveness: A Unit-Level, Longitudinal Study," *Personnel Psychology,* Spring 2001, pp 101–14.

76 These results can be found in K Gurchiek, " 'I Can't Make It to Work Today, Boss ... Gotta Round Up My Ostriches,' " *HR Magazine,* March 2005, p 30.

77 These cost estimates are provided in E Robertson Demby, "Do Your Family-Friendly Programs Make Cents?" *HR Magazine,* January 2004, pp 74–78.

78 See R D Hackett, "Work Attitudes and Employee Absenteeism: A Synthesis of the Literature," *Journal of Occupational Psychology,* 1989, pp 235–48.

79 A thorough review of the cognitive process associated with quitting is provided in C P Maertz Jr and M A Campion, "Profiles in Quitting: Integrating Process and Content Turnover Theory," *Academy of Management Journal,* August 2004, pp 566–82.

80 Results can be found in P W Hom and A J Kinicki, "Toward a Greater Understanding of How Dissatisfaction Drives Employee Turnover," *Academy of Management Journal,* October 2001, pp 975–87.

81 Statistics are presented in A Fisher, "Playing For Keeps," *Fortune,* January 22, 2007, p 85; and "CFO: All Pain, No Gain," *Fortune ,* February 5, 2007, pp 18.

82 Y Lermusiaux, "Calculating the High Cost of Employee Turnover," www.ilogos.com/en/expertviews/articles/strategic/ 200331007_YL.html, accessed April 15, 2005, p 1. The various costs of employee turnover are also discussed by W G Bliss, "Cost of Employee Turnover," www.isquare.com/turnover.cfm, accessed April 15, 2005.

83 See Lermusiaux, "Calculating the High Cost of Employee Turnover." An automated program for calculating the cost of turnover can be found at "Calculate Your Turnover Costs," www.keepemployees.com/turnovercalc.htm, accessed April 15, 2005.

84 Techniques for reducing employee turnover are discussed by K Gurchiek, "Execs Take Exit Interview Seriously," *HR Magazine,* January 2007, p 34; and J Brandon, "Rethinking the Time Clock," *Business 2.0 ,* March 2007, p 24.

85 Results can be found in Griffeth, Hom, and Gaertner, "A Meta-Analysis of Antecedents and Correlates of Employee Turnover."

86 Results can be found in Podsakoff, LePine, and LePine, "Differential Challenge Stressor-Hindrance Stressor Relationships with Job Attitudes, Turnover Intentions, Turnover, and Withdrawal Behaviour: A Meta-Analysis."

87 The various models are discussed in T A Judge, C J Thoresen, J E Bono, and G K Patton, "The Job Satisfaction– Job Performance Relationship: A Qualitative and Quantitative Review," *Psychological Bulletin,* May 2001, pp 376–407.

88 Results can be found in ibid.

89 One example is provided by D J Schleicher, J D Watt, and G J Greguras, "Reexamining the Job Satisfaction–Performance Relationship: The Complexity of Attitudes," *Journal of Applied Psychology,* February 2004, pp 165–77.

90 Results can be found in J K Harter, F L Schmidt, and T L Hayes, "Business-Unit-Level Relationship between Employee Satisfaction, Employee Engagement, and Business Outcomes: A Meta-Analysis," *Journal of Applied Psychology,* April 2002, pp 268–79.

CHAPTER 5

1 T R Mitchell, "Motivation: New Direction for Theory, Research, and Practice," *Academy of Management Review,* January 1982, p 81.

[2] A review of content and process theories of motivation is provided by R M Steers, R T Mowday, and D L Shapiro, "The Future of Work Motivation Theory," *Academy of Management Review*, July 2004, pp 379–87.

[3] For a complete description of Maslow's theory, see A H Maslow, "A Theory of Human Motivation," *Psychological Review*, July 1943, pp 370–96.

[4] See W B Swann Jr., C Chang-Schneider, and K L McClarty, "Do People's Self-Views Matter?" *American Pscyhologist*, February–March 2007, pp 84–94.

[5] See "Comp and Hiring Landscape: Still Rocky in 2007, *HR Magazine*, February 2007, p 14; R Wiles, "Tips Aimed to Help Debt-Ridden Workers, Boost Productivity," *The Arizona Republic*, March 3, 2007, p D1; and A Johnson, "4 Generations Can Challenge Management," *The Arizona Republic*, September 21, 2006, pp D1, D5.

[6] A sample is provided by L Bassi and D McMurrer, "Maximizing Your Return on People," *Harvard Business Review*, March 2007, pp 115–24.

[7] For a complete review of ERG theory, see C P Alderfer, *Existence, Relatedness, and Growth: Human Needs in Organizational Settings* (New York: Free Press, 1972)

[8] See ibid., and J P Wanous and A Zwany, "A Cross-Sectional Test of Need Hierarchy Theory," *Organizational Behaviour and Human Performance*, February 1977, pp 78–97.

[9] L Buchanan, "Managing One-to-One," *Inc.*, October 2001, p 87.

[10] H A Murray, *Explorations in Personality* (New York: John Wiley & Sons, 1938), p 164.

[11] See the discussion in "Can't We All Just Get Along?" *HR Magazine*, April 2005, p 16.

[12] See G D Parsons and R T Pascale, "Crisis at the Summit," *Harvard Business Review*, March 2007, pp 80–89; and D K McNeese-Smith, "The Relationship between Managerial Motivation, Leadership, Nurse Outcomes and Patient Satisfaction," *Journal of Organizational Behaviour*, March 1999, pp 243–59; A M Harrell and M J Stahl, "A Behavioural Decision Theory Approach for Measuring McClelland's Trichotomy of Needs," *Journal of Applied Psychology*, April 1981, pp 242–47.

[13] Evidence for the validity of motivation training can be found in H Heckhausen and S Krug, "Motive Modification," in *Motivation and Society*, ed A J Stewart (San Francisco: Jossey-Bass, 1982).

[14] Results can be found in D B Turban and T L Keon, "Organizational Attractiveness: An Interactionist Perspective," *Journal of Applied Psychology*, April 1993, pp 184–93.

[15] See T W H Ng, K L Sorensen, and D C Feldman, "Dimensions, Antecedents, and Consequences of Workaholism: A Conceptual Integration and Extension," *Journal of Organizational Behaviour*, January 2007, pp 111–36.

[16] See F Herzberg, B Mausner, and B B Snyderman, *The Motivation to Work* (New York: John Wiley & Sons, 1959).

[17] Excerpted from J Mero, "Gumologist," *Fortune*, April 3, 2006, p 33.

[18] Excerpted from M Conlin and A Bernstein, "Working . . . and Poor," *BusinessWeek*, May 31, 2004, p 60.

[19] F Herzberg, "One More Time: How Do You Motivate Employees?" *Harvard Business Review*, January–February 1968, p 56.

[20] For a thorough review of research on Herzberg's theory, see C C Pinder, *Work Motivation: Theory, Issues, and Applications* (Glenview, IL: Scott, Foresman, 1984).

[21] Supportive results can be found in N R Lockwood, "Leveraging Employee Engagement for Competitive Advantage," *2007 SHRM Quarterly*, 2007, pp 1–11; and "Respect: Find Out What It Means to Employees," *Training*, June 2006, p 12.

[22] The generalizability of the equity norm was investigated by T M Begley, C Lee, and C Hui, "Organizational Level as a Moderator of the Relationship between Justice Perceptions and Work-Related Reactions," *Journal of Organizational Behaviour*, September 2006, pp 705–21; and R Loi, N Hang-Yue, and S Foley, "Linking Employees' Justice Perceptions to Organizational Commitment and Intention to Leave: The Mediating Role of Perceived Organizational Support," *Journal of Occupational and Organizational Psychology*, March 2006, pp 101–20.

[23] Hugh Mackenzie, *The Great CEO Pay Race: Over Before It Begins*, Canadian Centre for Policy Alternatives, Dec. 2007, pg. 3)

[24] Ibid

[25] M N Bing and S M Burroughs, "The Predictive and Interactive Effects of Equity Sensitivity in Teamwork-Oriented Organizations," *Journal of Organizational Behaviour*, May 2001, p 271.

[26] Types of equity sensitivity are discussed by ibid., pp 271–90.

[27] For a complete discussion of Vroom's theory, see V H Vroom, *"Work and Motivation* (New York: John Wiley & Sons, 1964).

[28] E E Lawler III, *Motivation in Work Organizations* (Belmont, CA: Wadsworth, 1973), p 45.

[29] "Federal Express's Fred Smith," *Inc.*, October 1986, p 38.

[30] Results can be found in W van Eerde and H Thierry, "Vroom's Expectancy Models and Work-Related Criteria: A Meta-Analysis," *Journal of Applied Psychology*, October 1996, pp 575–86.

[31] See J P Wanous, T L Keon, and J C Latack, "Expectancy Theory and Occupational/Organizational Choices: A Review and Test," *Organizational Behaviour and Human Performance*, August 1983, pp 66–86.

[32] See the discussion in T R Mitchell and D Daniels, "Motivation," in *Handbook of Psychology*, vol. 12, eds W C Borman, D R Ilgen, and R J Klimoski (Hoboken, NJ: John Wiley & Sons, Inc., 2003), pp 225–54.

[33] See "Insights on Maximizing the Value of Employee Awards," *The Power of Incentives*, 2006, pp 103–10; J Useem, "What's That Spell? Teamwork," *Fortune*, June 12, 2006, pp 65–66; and S J Dubner, "The Freaky Side of Business," *Training*, February 2006, pp 8–10.

[34] E A Locke, K N Shaw, L M Saari, and G P Latham, "Goal Setting and Task Performance: 1969–1980," *Psychological Bulletin*, July 1981, p 126.

[35] Annika Sorenstam's biography can be found at www.lpga. com/ player-career.aspx?id= 29, accessed April 5, 2007.

[36] J Davis, "For Now, Sorenstam Feels She Still Has Peaks to Scale," *Arizona Republic*, March 18, 2004, p C14.

[37] See G P Latham and E A Locke, "Enhancing the Benefits and Overcoming the Pitfalls of Goal Setting," *Organizational Dynamics*, November 2006, pp 332–40.

[38] Supportive results can be found in K L Langeland, C M Johnson, and T C Mawhinney, "Improving Staff Performance in a Community Mental Health Setting: Job Analysis, Training, Goal Setting, Feedback, and Years of Data," *Journal of Organizational Behaviour Management*, 1998, pp 21–43.

[39] See E A Locke and G P Latham, *A Theory of Goal Setting and Task Performance* (Englewood Cliffs, NJ: Prentice Hall, 1990).

[40] See J J Donovan and D J Radosevich, "The Moderating Role of Goal Commitment on the Goal Difficulty-Performance Relationship: A Meta-Analytic Review and Critical Reanalysis," *Journal of Applied Psychology*, April 1998, pp 308–15.

[41] See Latham and Locke, "Enhancing the Benefits and Overcoming the Pitfalls of Goal Setting."

[42] J L Bowditch and A F Buono, *A Primer on Organizational Behaviour* (New York: John Wiley & Sons, 1985), p 210.

[43] This framework was proposed by M A Campion and P W Thayer, "Development and Field Evaluation of an Interdisciplinary Measure of Job Design," *Journal of Applied Psychology*, February 1985, pp 29–43.

[44] See the related discussion in S Wagner-Tsukamoto, "An Institutional Economic Reconstruction of Scientific Management: On the Lost Theoretical Logic of Taylorism," *Academy of Management Review*, January 2007, pp 105–17.

[45] This type of program was developed and tested by M A Campion and C L McClelland, "Follow-Up and Extension of the Interdisciplinary Costs and Benefits of Enlarged Jobs," *Journal of Applied Psychology*, June 1993, pp 339–51.

46 T R Shea, "Quick-Decision Hiring," *HR Magazine*, September 2006, pp 123–24.

47 J R Hackman, G R Oldham, R Janson, and K Purdy, "A New Strategy for Job Enrichment," *California Management Review*, Summer 1975, p 58.

48 Definitions of the job characteristics were adapted from J R Hackman and G R Oldham, "Motivation through the Design of Work: Test of a Theory," *Organizational Behaviour and Human Performance*, August 1976, pp 250–79.

49 See F P Morgeson and S E Humphrey, "The Work Design Questionnaire (WDQ): Developing and Validating a Comprehensive Measure for Assessing Job Design and the Nature of Work," *Journal of Applied Psychology*, November 2006, pp 1321–339.

50 These examples were taken from R Levering and M Moskowitz, "The 100 Best Companies to Work for 2007," *Fortune*, January 22, 2007, p 94; and R Levering and M Moskowitz, "The 100 Best Companies to Work For," *Fortune*, January 24, 2005, p 76.

51 Supportive results were found by S K Parker, H M Williams, and N Turner, "Modeling the Antecedents of Proactive Behaviour at Work," *Journal of Applied Psychology*, May 2006, pp 636–52; and J B Fuller, L E Marler, and K Hester, "Promoting Felt Responsibility for Constructive Change and Proactive Behaviour: Exploring Aspects of an Elaborated Model of Work Design," *Journal of Organizational Behaviour*, December 2006, pp 1089–120.

52 See R F Piccolo and J A Colquitt, "Transformational Leadership and Job Behaviours: The Mediating Role of Core Job Characteristics," *Academy of Management Journal*, April 2006, pp 327–40; and S Ohly, S Sonnentag, and F Pluntke, "Routinization, Work Characteristics and Their Relationship with Creative and Proactive Behaviours," *Journal of Organizational Behaviour*, May 2006, pp 257–79.

53 The turnover meta-analysis was conducted by R W Griffeth, P W Hom, and S Gaertner, "A Meta-Analysis of Antecedents and Correlates of Employee Turnover: Update, Moderator Tests, and Research Implications for the Next Millennium," *Journal of Management*, 2000, pp 463–88. Absenteeism results are discussed in Y Fried and G R Ferris, "The Validity of the Job Characteristics Model: A Review and Meta-Analysis," *Personnel Psychology*, Summer 1987, pp 287–322.

54 Results can be found in M R Kelley, "New Process Technology, Job Design, and Work Organization: A Contingency Model," *American Sociological Review*, April 1990, pp 191–208.

55 Productivity studies are reviewed in R E Kopelman, *Managing Productivity in Organizations* (New York: McGraw-Hill, 1986).

56 See A Athavaley, "The Ball's in Your Cubicle," *The Wall Street Journal*, February 27, 2007, pp D1, D3.

57 See R Malkin, S D Hudock, C Hayden, T J Lentz, J Topmiller, and R W Niemeier, "An Assessment of Occupational Safety and Health in Selected Small Business Manufacturing Wood Pallets—Part 1. Noise and Physical Hazards," Journal of Occupational and Environmental Hygiene, April 2005, pp D18–D21.

58 These descriptions were excerpted from J Prichard, "Reinventing the Office," Arizona Republic, January 16, 2002, p D1.

59 "NINDA Repetitive Motor Disorders Information Page," http://www.ninds.nih.gov/disorders/repetitive_motion/repetitive_motion.htm, last updated March 30, 2005.

60 Canadian Centre for Occupational Health and Safety – government website: HYPERLINK "http://www.ccohs.ca/oshanswers/diseases/rmirsi.html" www.ccohs.ca/oshanswers/diseases/rmirsi.html Work-related Musculoskeletal Disorders (WMSDs), 2005; page 1.

CHAPTER 6

1 See R Mirchandani, "Postmodernism and Sociology: From the Epistemological to the Empirical," *Sociological Theory*, March 2005, pp 86–115.

2 This definition is based in part on one found in D Horton Smith, "A Parsimonious Definition of 'Group': Toward Conceptual Clarity and Scientific Utility," *Sociological Inquiry*, Spring 1967, pp 141–67. Also see W B Swann, Jr; J T Polzer; D C Seyle; and S J Ko, "Finding Value in Diversity: Verification of Personal and Social Self-Views in Diverse Groups," *Academy of Management Review*, January 2004, pp 9–27.

3 E H Schein, *Organizational Psychology*, 3rd ed (Englewood Cliffs, NJ: Prentice Hall, 1980), p 145. For more, see L R Weingart, "How Did They Do That? The Ways and Means of Studying Group Process," in *Research in Organizational Behaviour*, vol. 19, eds L L Cummings and B M Staw (Greenwich, CT: JAI Press, 1997), pp 189–239.

4 See R Cross, N Nohria, and A Parker, "Six Myths about Informal Networks—and How to Overcome Them," *MIT Sloan Management Review*, Spring 2002, pp 67–75; C Shirky, "Watching the Patterns Emerge," *Harvard Business Review*, February 2004, pp 34–35; P Chattopadhyay, M Tluchowska, and E George, "Identifying the Ingroup: A Closer Look at theInfluence of Demographic Dissimilarity on Employee Social Identity," *Academy of Management Review*, April 2004, pp 180–202; S Allen, "Water Cooler Wisdom," *Training*, August 2005, pp 30–34; and E Watters, "The Organization Woman," *Business 2.0*, April 2006, pp 106–10.

5 Data from "Co-workers Support Each Other," *USA Today*, May 28, 2003, p 1B.

6 Excerpted from S Armour, "Company 'Alumni' Groups Keep Word Out after Workers Go," *USA Today*, August 30, 2005, p 4B.

7 See J Janove, "FOB: Friend of Boss," *HR Magazine*, June 2005, pp 153–56.

8 See Schein, *Organizational Psychology*, pp 149–53.

9 For an instructive overview of five different theories of group development, see J P Wanous, A E Reichers, and S D Malik. "Organizational Socialization and Group Development: Toward an Integrative Perspective," *Academy of Management Review*, October 1984, pp 670–83. Also see L R Offermann and R K Spiros, "The Science and Practice of Team Development: Improving the Link," *Academy of Management Journal*, April 2001, pp 376–92; and A Chang, P Bordia, and J Duck, "Punctuated Equilibrium and Linear Progression: Toward a New Understanding of Group Development," *Academy of Management Journal*, February 2003, pp 106–17.

10 See B W Tuckman, "Developmental Sequence in Small Groups", *Psychological Bulletin*, June 1965, pp 384–99; and B W Tuckman and M A C Jensen, "Stages of Small-Group Development Revisited", *Group and Organization Studies*, December 1977, pp 419–27. An instructive adaption of the Tuckman model can be found in L Holpp, "If Empowerment Is So Good, Why Does It Hurt?" *Training*, March 1995, p. 56.

11 See T Postmes, R Spears, A T Lee, and R J Novak, "Individuality and Social Influence in Groups: Inductive and Deductive Routes to Group Identity," *Journal of Personality and Social Psychology*, November 2005, pp 747–63.

12 A useful resource book is T Ursiny, *The Coward's Guide to Conflict: Empowering Solutions for Those Who Would Rather Run than Fight* (Naperville, IL: Sourcebooks, 2003). Also see J Li and D C Hambrick, "Factional Groups: A New Vantage on Demographic Faultlines, Conflict, and Disintegration in Work Teams," *Academy of Management Journal*, October 2005, pp 794–813; and M D Johnson, J R Hollenbeck, S E Humphrey, D R Ilgen, D Jundt, and C J Meyer, "Cutthroat Cooperation: Asymmetrical Adaptation to Changes in Team Reward Structures," *Academy of Management Journal*, February 2006, pp 103–19.

13 For related research, see M Van Vugt and C M Hart, "Social Identity as Social Glue: The Origins of Group Loyalty," *Journal of Personality and Social Psychology*, April 2004, pp 585–98.

14 See C M Mason and M A Griffin, "Group Task Satisfaction: The Group's Shared Attitude to Its Task and Work Environment," *Group and Organization Management*, December 2005, pp 625–52.

[15] Connie Gersick, *Times and Transition in Work Teams: Toward A New Model of Group Development*, Academy of Management Journal, vol. 31, no 1 (March 1988) pp 9–41.

[16] J. Richard Hackman, *Why Teams Don't Work*, Theory and Research on Small Groups, Vol. 4, 1998, pages 245 – 267.

[17] G Graen, "Role-Making Processes within Complex Organizations," in *Handbook of Industrial and Organizational Psychology*, ed M D Dunnette (Chicago: Rand McNally, 1976), p 1201. Also see S D Dobrev and W P Barnett, "Organizational Roles and Transition to Entrepreneurship," *Academy of Management Journal*, June 2005, pp 433–49; M A Eys, A V Carron, M R Beauchamp, and S R Brays, "Athletes' Perceptions of the Sources of Role Ambiguity," *Small Group Research*, August 2005, pp 383–403; and T Schellens, H Van Keer, and M Valcke, "The Impact of Role Assignment on Knowledge Construction in Asynchronous Discussion Groups: A Multilevel Analysis," *Small Group Research*, December 2005, pp 704–45.

[18] See K D Benne and P Sheats, "Functional Roles of Group Members," *Journal of Social Issues*, Spring 1948, pp 41–49.

[19] See H J Klein and P W Mulvey, "Two Investigations of the Relationships among Group Goals, Goal Commitment, Cohesion, and Performance," *Organizational Behaviour and Human Decision Processes*, January 1995, pp 44–53; D F Crown and J G Rosse, "Yours, Mine, and Ours: Facilitating Group Productivity through the Integration of Individual and Group Goals," *Organizational Behaviour and Human Decision Processes*, November 1995, pp 138–50; and D Knight, C C Durham, and E A Locke, "The Relationship of Team Goals, Incentives, and Efficacy to Strategic Risk, Tactical Implementation, and Performance," *Academy of Management Journal*, April 2001, pp 326–38.

[20] A Zander, "The Value of Belonging to a Group in Japan," *Small Group Behaviour*, February 1983, pp 7–8. Also see E Gundling, *Working GlobeSmart: 12 People Skills for Doing Business across Borders* (Palo Alto, CA: Davies-Black Publishing, 2003).

[21] R R Blake and J Srygley Mouton, "Don't Let Group Norms Stifle Creativity," *Personnel*, August 1985, p 28.

[22] See D Kahneman, "Reference Points, Anchors, Norms, and Mixed Feelings," *Organizational Behavior and Human Decision Processes*, March 1992, pp 296–312; and J M Marques, D Abrams, D Paez, and C Martinez-Taboada, "The Role of Categorization and In-Group Norms in Judgments of Groups and Their Members," *Journal of Personality and Social Psychology*, October 1998, pp 976–88.

[23] Maclean's Magazine Special Report – Canada's Top 100 Employers. October 1, 2008. Story from Macleans.ca: http://www.macleans.ca/business/companies/article.jsp?content=20081001_105916_105916

[24] See J Pfeffer, "Bring Back Shame," *Business 2.0*, September 2003, p 80.

[25] P Sellers, "Gap's New Guy Upstairs," *Fortune*, April 14, 2003, p 112.

[26] D C Feldman, "The Development and Enforcement of Group Norms," *Academy of Management Review*, January 1984, pp 50–52.

[27] Ibid.

[28] "Top 10 Leadership Tips from Jeff Immelt," *Fast Company*, April 2004, p 96.

[29] See N Enbar, "What Do Women Want? Ask 'Em," *Business Week*, March 29, 1999, p 8; and M Hickins, "Duh! Gen Xers Are Cool with Teamwork," *Management Review*, March 1999, p 7. For related reading, see L Gerdes, "Why Put Real Work Off Till Tomorrow?" *BusinessWeek*, May 8, 2006, p 92.

[30] Quote and data from D Jones, "Optimism Puts Rose-Colored Tint in Glasses of Top Execs," *USA Today*, December 16, 2005, p 2B.

[31] J R Katzenbach and D K Smith, The Wisdom of Teams: Creating the High-Performance Organization (New York: HarperBusiness, 1999), p 45. J E Mathieu, L L Gibson, and T M Ruddy, "Empowerment and Team Effectiveness: An Empirical Test of an Integrated Model," *Journal of Applied Psychology*, January 2006, pp 97–108; P Balkundi and W A Harrison, "Ties, Leaders, and Time in Teams: Strong Inference about Network Structure's Effects on Team Viability and Performance," *Academy of Management Journal*, February 2006, pp 49–68; and J M Howell and C M Shea, "Effects of Champion Behaviour, Team Potency, and External Communication Activities on Predicting Team Performance," *Group and Organization Management*, April 2006, pp 180–211.

[32] Condensed and adapted from ibid., p 214. Also see B Beersma, J R Hollenbeck, S E Humphrey, H Moon, D Conlon, and D R Ilgen, "Cooperation, Competition, and Team Performance: Toward a Contingency Approach," *Academy of Management Journal*, October 2003, pp 572–90; L L Gilson, J E Mathieu, C E Shalley, and T M Ruddy, "Creativity and Standardization: Complementary or Conflicting Drivers of Team Effectiveness?" *Academy of Management Journal*, June 2005, pp 521–31; B Fischer and A Boynton, "Virtuoso Teams," *Harvard Business Review*, July/August 2005, pp 116–23; R D Hof, "Teamwork Supercharged," *BusinessWeek*, November 21, 2005, pp 90–94; J E Mathieu, L L Gibson , and T M Ruddy, "Empowerment and Team Effectiveness: An Empirical Test of an Integrated Model," *Journal of Applied Psychology*, January 2006, pp 97–108; P Balkundi and W A Harrison, "Ties, Leaders, and Time in Teams: Strong Inference about Network Structure's Effects on Team Viability and Performance," *Academy of Management Journal*, February 2006, pp 49–68; and J M Howell and C M Shea, "Effects of Champion Behaviour, Team Potency, and External Communication Activities on Predicting Team Performance," *Group and Organization Management*, April 2006, pp 180–211.

[33] See M P Hillmann, P Dongier, R P Murgallis, M Khosh, E K Allen, and R Evernham, "When Failure Isn't an Option," *Harvard Business Review*, July/August 2005, pp 41–50.

[34] J R Katzenbach and D K Smith, "The Discipline of Teams," *Harvard Business Review*, March/April 1993, p 112.

[35] "A Team's-Eye View of Teams," *Training*, November 1995, p 16.

[36] G. Chen, L M Donahue, and R I Klimoski, "Training Undergraduates to work in Organizational Teams," Academy of Management Learning and Education, March 2004, Appendix A, p. 40. (See 3rd US Edition for Kreitner, page 233, chpt. 9).

[37] P Burrows, "Cisco's Comeback," *BusinessWeek*, November 24, 2003, p 124. For material related to teamwork skills, see F P Morgenson, M H Reider, and M A Campion, "Selecting Individuals in Team Settings: The Importance of Social Skills, Personality Characteristics, and Teamwork Knowledge," *Personnel Psychology*, Autumn 2005, pp 583–611; A P J Ellis, B S Bell, R E Ployhart, J R Hollenbeck, and D R Ilgen, "An Evaluation of Generic Teamwork Skills Training with Action Teams: Effects on Cognitive and Skills-Based Outcomes," *Personnel Psychology*, Autumn 2005, pp 641–72; L Conley, "Credit Where Credit Is Due," *Fast Company*, November 2005, pp 99–101; B Erdogan, R C Liden, and M L Kraimer, "Justice and Leader-Member Exchange: The Moderating Role of Organizational Culture," *Academy of Management Journal*, April 2006, pp 395–406; and P Kaihla, "Office Graffiti," *Business 2.0*, April 2006, p 90.

[38] Data from C Joinson, "Teams at Work," *HR Magazine*, May 1999, pp 30–36.

[39] B Dumaine, "Who Needs a Boss?" *Fortune*, May 7, 1990, p 52. Also see D Vredenburgh and I Y He, "Leadership Lessons from a Conductorless Orchestra," *Business Horizons*, September/October 2003, pp 19–24; and C A O'Reilly III and M L Tushman, "The Ambidextrous Organization," *Harvard Business Review*, April 2004, pp 74–81.

[40] Adapted from Table 1 in V U Druskat and J V Wheeler, "Managing from the Boundary: The Effective Leadership of Self-Managing Work Teams," *Academy of Management Journal*, August 2003, pp 435–57.

[41] See A E Randal and K S Jaussi, "Functional Background Identity, Diversity, and Individual Performance in Cross-Functional Teams," *Academy of Management Journal*, December 2003, pp 763–74; and G S Van Der Vegt and J S Bunderson, "Learning and Performance in Multidisciplinary Teams: The Importance of Collective Team

Identification," *Academy of Management Journal,* June 2005, pp 532–47.

[42] Excerpted from "Fast Talk," *Fast Company,* February 2004, p 50. For cross-functional teams in action, see B Nussbaum, "How to Build Innovative Companies: Get Creative!" *BusinessWeek,* August 1, 2005, pp 61–68; C Edwards, "Inside Intel," *BusinessWeek,* January 9, 2006, pp 46 –54; "How to Break Out of Commodity Hell," *BusinessWeek,* March 27, 2006, p 76; and B Finn, "Outside-In R&D," *Business 2.0,* April 2006, p 85.

[43] For example, see J Merritt, "How to Rebuild a B-School," *BusinessWeek,* March 29, 2004, pp 90–91.

[44] See "1996 Industry Report: What Self-Managing Teams Manage," *Training,* October 1996, p 69.

[45] See L L Thompson, *Making the Team: A Guide for Managers* (Upper Saddle River, NJ: Prentice Hall, 2000).

[46] See P S Goodman, R Devadas, and T L Griffith Hughson, "Groups and Productivity: Analyzing the Effectiveness of Self-Managing Teams," in *Productivity in Organizations,* eds J P Campbell, R J Campbell and Associates (San Francisco: Jossey-Bass, 1988), pp 295–327. Also see R C Liden, S J Wayne, and M L Kraimer "Managing Individual Performance in Work Groups," *Human Resource Management,* Spring 2001, pp 63–72; R Batt, "Who Benefits from Teams? Comparing Workers, Supervisors, and Managers," *Industrial Relations,* January 2004, pp 183–209; F P Morgeson, "The External Leadership of Self-Managing Teams: Intervening in the Context of Novel and Disruptive Events," *Journal of Applied Psychology,* May 2005, pp 497–508; and S Kauffeld, "Self-Directed Work Groups and Team Competence," *Journal of Occupational and Organizational Psychology,* March 2006, pp 1–21.

[47] Drawn from H van Mierlo, C G Rutte, M A Kompier, and H A C M Doorewaard, "Self-Managing Teamwork and Psychological Well-Being: Review of a Multilevel Research Domain," *Group and Organization Management,* April 2005, pp 211–35.

[48] For more, see W F Cascio, "Managing a Virtual Workplace," *Academy of Management Executive,* August 2000, pp 81–90; and the collection of articles on E-leadership and virtual teams in *Organizational Dynamics,* no 4, 2003.

[49] Excerpted from M Conlin, "The Easiest Commute of All," *BusinessWeek,* December 12, 2005, pp 78–79. Also see J T Arnold, "Making the Leap," *HR Magazine,* May 2006, pp 80–86.

[50] See A M Townsend, S M DeMarie, and A R Hendrickson, "Virtual Teams: Technology and the Workplace of the Future," *Academy of Management Executive,* August 1998, pp 17–29.

[51] See C Saunders, C Van Slyke, and D R Vogel, "My Time or Yours? Managing Time Visions in Global Virtual Teams," *Academy of Management Executive,* February 2004, pp 19–31.

[52] Based on P Bordia, N DiFonzo, and A Chang, "Rumor as Group Problem Solving: Development Patterns in Informal Computer-Mediated Groups," *Small Group Research,* February 1999, pp 8–28.

[53] See K A Graetz, E S Boyle, C E Kimble, P Thompson, and J L Garloch, "Information Sharing in Face-to-Face, Teleconferencing, and Electronic Chat Groups," *Small Group Research,* December 1998, pp 714–43.

[54] Based on F Niederman and R J Volkema, "The Effects of Facilitator Characteristics on Meeting Preparation, Set Up, and Implementation," *Small Group Research,* June 1999, pp 330–60.

[55] Based on J J Sosik, B J Avolio, and S S Kahai, "Inspiring Group Creativity: Comparing Anonymous and Identified Electronic Brainstorming," *Small Group Research,* February 1998, pp 3–31. For practical advice on brainstorming, see C Caggiano, "The Right Way to Brainstorm," *Inc.,* July 1999, p 94. Also see A M Hardin, M A Fuller, and J S Valacich, "Measuring Group Efficacy in Virtual Teams: New Questions in an Old Debate," *Small Group Research,* February 2006, pp 65–85.

[56] See B L Kirkman, B Rosen, C B Gibson, P E Tesluk, and S O McPherson, "Five Challenges to Virtual Team Success: Lessons from Sabre, Inc.," *Academy of Management Executive,* August 2002,

pp 67–79; P J Hinds and D E Bailey, "Out of Sight, Out of Sync: Understanding Conflict in Distributed Teams," *Organization Science,* November– December 2003, pp 615–32; and Y Shin, "Conflict Resolution in Virtual Teams," *Organizational Dynamics,* November 2005, pp 331–45.

[57] See E Kelley, "Keys to Effective Virtual Global Teams," *Academy of Management Executive,* May 2001, pp 132–33.

[58] Practical perspectives are offered in "Virtual Teams that Work," *HR Magazine,* July 2003, p 121; D D Davis, "The Tao of Leadership in Virtual Teams," *Organizational Dynamics,* no 1, 2004, pp 47–62; A Majchrzak, A Malhotra, J Stamps, and J Lipnack, "Can Absence Make a Team Grow Stronger?" *Harvard Business Review,* May 2004, pp 131–37; and J Gordon, "Do Your Virtual Teams Deliver Only Virtual Performance?" *Training,* June 2005, pp 20–26.

[59] See, for example, P Suciu, "Listen Up, Soldiers," *Newsweek,* July 11, 2005, p 70; J Alsever, "Hello Muddah, Hello Faddah ... What Executives Learn at Summer Camp," *Fast Company,* September 2005, p 30; and S Datta, "Cooking Up a Better Team," *Business 2.0,* May 2006, p 143.

[60] Excerpted from S Max, "Seagate's Morale-athon," *BusinessWeek,* April 3, 2006, p 110–12.

[61] See D McDonald, "Why We All Hate Offsites," *Business 2.0,* May 2006, pp 79–80.

[62] Excerpted from R Underwood, "The Art of the Off-site," *Fast Company,* September 2005, p 30. See 3rd US edition of Kreitner page 235, chpt 9).

[63] Graham Lowe *Best Workplaces 2006: Trust is tops – building a better workplace culture.* Canadian Business Magazine online April 10-23,2006. http://www.canadianbusiness.com/shared/print.jsp?Content=20060410_76260_76260&adzone=managing/

[64] IBID

[65] See D M Rousseau, S B Sitkin, R S Burt, and C Camerer, "Not So Different After All: A Cross-Discipline View of Trust," *Academy of Management Review,* July 1998, pp 393–404; and A C Wicks, S L Berman, and T M Jones, "The Structure of Optimal Trust: Moral and Strategic Implications," *Academy of Management Review,* January 1999, pp 99–116.

[66] J D Lewis and A Weigert, "Trust as a Social Reality," *Social Forces,* June 1985, p 971. Trust is examined as an *indirect* factor in K T Dirks, "The Effects of Interpersonal Trust on Work Group Performance," *Journal of Applied Psychology,* June 1999, pp 445–55. Also see J B Cunningham and J MacGregor, "Trust and the Design of Work: Complementary Constructs in Satisfaction and Performance," *Human Relations,* December 2000, pp 1575–88.

[67] Adapted from C Johnson-George and W C Swap, "Measurement of Specific Interpersonal Trust: Construction and Validation of a Scale to Assess Trust in a Specific Other," *Journal of Personality and Social Psychology,* December 1982, pp 1306–17; and D J McAllister, "Affectand Cognition-Based Trust as Foundations for Interpersonal Cooperation in Organizations," *Academy of Management Journal,* February 1995, pp 24–59.

[68] See R Zemke, "Little Lies," *Training,* February 2004, p 8.

[69] For support, see G M Spreitzer and A K Mishra, "Giving Up Control without Losing Control: Trust and Its Substitutes' Effects on Managers' Involving Employees in Decision Making," *Group & Organization Management,* June 1999, pp 155–87. Also see G Johnson, "11 Keys to Leadership," *Training,* January 2004, p 18.

[70] Adapted from F Bartolomé, "Nobody Trusts the Boss Completely—Now What?" *Harvard Business Review,* March/April 1989, pp 135–42. For more on building trust, see R Galford and A S Drapeau, "The Enemies of Trust," *Harvard Business Review,* February 2003, pp 88–95; L C Abrams, R Cross, E Lesser, and D Z Levin, "Nurturing Interpersonal Trust in Knowledge-Sharing Networks," *Academy of Management Executive,* November 2003, pp 64–77; C Huxham and S Vangen, "Doing Things Collaboratively: Realizing the Advantage or Succumbing to Inertia?" *Organizational Dynamics,* no 2, 2004,

pp 190–201; S A Joni, "The Geography of Trust," *Harvard Business Review,* March 2004, pp 82–88; P Evans and B Wolf, "Collaboration Rules," *Harvard Business Review,* July/August 2005, pp 96–104; and R Goffee and G Jones, "Managing Authenticity: The Paradox of Great Leadership," *Harvard Business Review,* December 2005, pp 86–94.

[71] I L Janis, *Groupthink,* 2nd ed (Boston: Houghton Mifflin, 1982), p 9. Alternative models are discussed in K Granstrom and D Stiwne, "A Bipolar Model of Groupthink: An Expansion of Janis's Concept," *Small Group Research,* February 1998, pp 32–56; A R Flippen, "Understanding Groupthink from a Self-Regulatory Perspective," *Small Group Research,* April 1999, pp 139–65; and M Harvey, M M Novicevic, M R Buckley, and J R B Halbesleben, "The Abilene Paradox after Thirty Years: A Global Perspective," *Organizational Dynamics,* no 2, 2004, pp 215–26.

[72] Ibid. For an alternative model, see R J Aldag and S Riggs Fuller, "Beyond Fiasco: A Reappraisal of the Groupthink Phenomenon and a New Model of Group Decision Processes," *Psychological Bulletin,* May 1993, pp 533–52. Also see A A Mohamed and F A Wiebe, "Toward a Process Theory of Groupthink," *Small Group Research,* August 1996, pp 416–30.

[73] Adapted from Janis, *Groupthink,* pp 174–75. Also see J M Wellen and M Neale, "Deviance, Self-Typicality, and Group Cohesion: The Corrosive Effects of the Bad Apples on the Barrel," *Small Group Research,* April 2006, pp 165–86.

[74] D D Henningsen, M L M Henningsen, J Eden, and M G Cruz, "Examining the Symptoms of Groupthink and Retrospective Sensemaking," *Small Group Research,* February 2006, pp 36–64.

[75] Based on discussion in B Latane, K Williams, and S Harkins, "Many Hands Make Light the Work: The Causes and Consequences of Social Loafing," *Journal of Personality and Social Psychology,* June 1979, pp 822–32; and D A Kravitz and B Martin, "Ringelmann Rediscovered: The Original Article," *Journal of Personality and Social Psychology,* May 1986, pp 936–41.

[76] See S J Karau and K D Williams, "Social Loafing: Meta-Analytic Review and Theoretical Integration," *Journal of Personality and Social Psychology,* October 1993, pp 681–706; and L Thompson, "Improving the Creativity of Organizational Work Groups," *Academy of Management Executive,* February 2003, pp 96–109.

[77] See S J Zaccaro, "Social Loafing: The Role of Task Attractiveness," *Personality and Social Psychology Bulletin,* March 1984, pp 99–106; J M Jackson and K D Williams, "Social Loafing on Difficult Tasks: Working Collectively Can Improve Performance," *Journal of Personality and Social Psychology,* October 1985, pp 937–42; and J M George, "Extrinsic and Intrinsic Origins of Perceived Social Loafing in Organizations," *Academy of Management Journal,* March 1992, pp 191–202.

[78] For complete details, see K Williams, S Harkins, and B Latane, "Identifiability as a Deterrent to Social Loafing: Two Cheering Experiments," *Journal of Personality and Social Psychology,* February 1981, pp 303–11.

[79] See J M Jackson and S G Harkins, "Equity in Effort: An Explanation of the Social Loafing Effect," *Journal of Personality and Social Psychology,* November 1985, pp 1199–1206.

[80] Both studies are reported in S G Harkins and K Szymanski, "Social Loafing and Group Evaluation," *Journal of Personality and Social Psychology,* June 1989, pp 934–41. Also see R Hoigaard, R Safvenbom, and F E Tonnessen, "The Relationship between Group Cohesion, Group Norms, and Perceived Social Loafing in Soccer Teams," *Small Group Research,* June 2006, pp 217–32.

[81] Data from J A Wagner III, "Studies of Individualism-Collectivism: Effects on Cooperation in Groups," *Academy of Management Journal,* February 1995, pp 152–72. Also see P W Mulvey and H J Klein, "The Impact of Perceived Loafing and Collective Efficacy on Group Goal Processes and Group Performance," *Organizational Behaviour and Human Decision Processes,* April 1998, pp 62–87; P W Mulvey, L Bowes-Sperry, and H J Klein, "The Effects of Perceived Loafing and Defensive Impression Management on Group Effectiveness," *Small Group Research,* June 1998, pp 394–415; and H Goren, R Kurzban, and A Rapoport, "Social Loafing vs. Social Enhancement: Public Goods Provisioning in Real-Time with Irrevocable Commitments," *Organizational Behaviour and Human Decision Processes,* March 2003, pp 277–90.

[82] See S G Scott and W O Einstein, "Strategic Performance Appraisal in Team-Based Organizations: One Size Does Not Fit All," *Academy of Management Executive,* May 2001, pp 107–16.

CHAPTER 7

[1] C Hymowitz, "In the Lead: What Adecco Can Do to Improve Its Image after Bad News Bungle," *The Wall Street Journal,* January 20, 2004, p B1.

[2] Results are summarized in "Why Am I Here," *Training,* April 2006, p 13. Also see J Robison, "An HCA Hospital's Miracle Workers," *Gallup Management Journal,* January 12, 2006, http://gmj.gallup.com/content/default.asp?ci=20707.

[3] J L Bowditch and A F Buono, *A Primer on Organizational Behaviour,* 4th ed (New York: John Wiley & Sons, 1997), p 120.

[4] M Orey, "Lawyer's Firing Signals Turmoil in Legal Circles," *The Wall Street Journal,* May 21, 2001, p B1. Also see "The Good News About Bad News," *Training,* April 2006, pp 10–11.

[5] For a detailed discussion about selecting an appropriate medium, see B Barry and I Smithey-Fulmer, "The Medium and the Message: The Adaptive Use of Communication Media in Dyadic Influence," *Academy of Management Review,* April 2004, pp 272–92.

[6] C Hymowitz, "Diebold's New Chief Shows How to Lead After a Sudden Rise," *The Wall Street Journal,* May 8, 2006, p B1.

[7] Excerpted from J Sandberg, "Cookies, Gossip, Cubes: It's a Wonder Any Work Gets Done at the Office," *The Wall Street Journal,* April 28, 2004, p B1.

[8] Communication noise is discussed by J Sandberg, "Office Minstrels Drive the Rest of Us Nuts but Are Hard to Silence," *The Wall Street Journal,* February 14, 2006, p B1.

[9] Ideas for improving personal communication skills are discussed by J S Lublin, "Improv Troupe Teaches Managers How to Give Better Presentations," *The Wall Street Journal,* February 6, 2007, p B1; and R Tucker, "Four Key Skills to Master Now," *Fortune,* October 30, 2006, p 123.

[10] See "Interpersonal Effectiveness Training: Beyond the Water Cooler," *Training,* April 2006, p 10.

[11] For a thorough discussion of these barriers, see C R Rogers and F J Roethlisberger, "Barriers and Gateways to Communication," *Harvard Business Review,* July–August 1952, pp 46–52.

[12] Ibid., p 47.

[13] The use of jargon and acronyms is discussed by C Hymowitz, "Mind Your Language: To Do Business Today, Consider Delayering," *The Wall Street Journal,* March 27, 2006, p B1.

[14] J Sandberg, "'It Says Press Any Key. Where's the Any Key?'" *The Wall Street Journal,* February 20, 2007, p B1.

[15] J Sandberg, "In the Workplace, Every Bleeping Word Can Show Your Rank," *The Wall Street Journal,* March 21, 2006, p B1.

[16] A C Poe, "Don't Touch That 'Send' Button!" *HR Magazine,* July 2001, pp 74–75.

[17] R L Daft and R H Lengel, "Information Richness: A New Approach to Managerial Behaviour and Organizational Design," in *Research in Organizational Behaviour,* eds B M Staw and L L Cummings (Greenwich, CT: JAI Press, 1984), p 196.

[18] Details of this example are provided in L Grensing-Pophal, "Spread the Word—Correctly," *HR Magazine,* March 2005, pp 83–88.

[19] See E Binney, "Is E-Mail the New Pink Slip?" *HR Magazine,*

November 2006, pp 32, 38; and D M Cable and K Y T Yu, "Managing Job Seekers' Organizational Image Beliefs: The Role of Media Richness and Media Credibility," *Journal of Applied Psychology,* July 2006, pp 828–40.

[20] See B Barry and I S Fulmer, "The Medium and the Message: The Adaptive Use of Communication Media in Dyadic Influence," *Academy of Management Review,* April 2004, pp 272–92; and A F Simon, "Computer-Mediated Communication: Task Performance and Satisfaction," *The Journal of Social Psychology,* June 2006, pp 349–79.

[21] See R E Rice and D E Shook, "Relationships of Job Categories and Organizational Levels to Use of Communication Channels, Including Electronic Mail: A Meta-Analysis and Extension," *Journal of Management Studies,* March 1990, pp 195–229.

[22] Results can be found in J D Johnson, W A Donohue, C K Atkin, and S Johnson, "Communication, Involvement, and Perceived Innovativeness," *Group & Organization Management,* March 2001, pp 24–52; and B Davenport Sypher and T E Zorn Jr, "Communication-Related Abilities and Upward Mobility: A Longitudinal Investigation," *Human Communication Research,* Spring 1986, pp 420–31.

[23] See F Timmins and C McCabe, "How Assertive Are Nurses in the Workplace? A Preliminary Pilot Study," *Journal of Nursing Management,* January 2005, pp 61–67.

[24] J A Waters, "Managerial Assertiveness," *Business Horizons,* September/October 1982, p 25.

[25] Ibid., p 27.

[26] This statistic was provided by A Fisher, "How Can I Survive a Phone Interview?" *Fortune,* April 19, 2004, p 54.

[27] Problems with body language analysis are discussed by A Pihulyk, "Communicate with Clarity: The Key to Understanding and Influencing Others," *The Canadian Manager,* Summer 2003, pp 12–13.

[28] Related research is summarized by J A Hall, "Male and Female Nonverbal Behaviour," in *Multichannel Integrations of Nonverbal Behaviour,* eds A W Siegman and S Feldstein (Hillsdale, NJ: Lawrence Erlbaum, 1985), pp 195–226.

[29] See R E Axtell, *Gestures: The Do's and Taboos of Body Language around the World* (New York: John Wiley & Sons, 1991).

[30] See J A Russell, "Facial Expressions of Emotion: What Lies Beyond Minimal Universality?" *Psychological Bulletin,* November 1995, pp 379–91.

[31] Norms for cross-cultural eye contact are discussed by C Engholm, *When Business East Meets Business West: The Guide to Practice and Protocol in the Pacific Rim* (New York: John Wiley & Sons, 1991).

[32] See R D Ramsey, "Ten Things That Never Change for Supervisors," *SuperVision,* April 2007, pp 16–18; "CEOs Emphasize Listening to Employees," *HR Magazine,* January 2007, p 14; and M Marchetti, "Listen to Me!" *Sales and Marketing Management,* April 2007, p 12.

[33] See D Knight, "Perks Keeping Workers out of Revolving Door," *The Wall Street Journal,* April 30, 2005, p D3; and G Rooper, "Managing Employee Relations," *HR Magazine,* May 2005, pp 101–104.

[34] The discussion of listening styles is based on "5 Listening Styles," http://www.crossroadsinstitute.org/listyle.html, June 19, 2004; and "Listening and Thinking: What's Your Style," http://www.pediatricservices.com/prof/prof-10.htm, last modified August 10, 2002.

[35] See the related discussion in J Condrill, "What Is Your Listening Style?" *AuthorsDen,* July 7, 2005, http://www.authorsden.com/visit/viewarticle.asp?id=18707; and D A Nadler, "Confessions of a Trusted Counselor," *Harvard Business Review,* September 2005, pp 68–77.

[36] These recommendations were excerpted from J Jay, "On Communicating Well," *HR Magazine,* January 2005, pp 87–88.

[37] See H Green, "Twitter: All Trivia, All the Time," *Business Week,* April 2, 2007, p 40; and "Word-of-Mouth: Heard It Through the Grapevine," *MarketingWeek,* September 28, 2006, p 42.

[38] H B Vickery III, "Tapping into the Employee Grapevine," *Association Management,* January 1984, pp 59–60.

[39] The most recent research is discussed by S M Crampton, J W Hodge, and J M Mishra, "The Informal Communication Network: Factors Influencing Grapevine Activity," *Public Personnel Management,* Winter 1998, pp 569–84, "Pruning the Company Grapevine," *Supervision,* September 1986, p 11; and R Half, "Managing Your Career: 'How Can I Stop the Gossip?' " *Management Accounting,* September 1987, p 27.

[40] B Gates, "How I Work: 'Paper Isn't a Big Part of My Day'," *Fortune,* April 17, 2006, pp 45–46.

[41] These statistics were obtained from "Kids' Lives 'Saturated' by Media, Study Says," *Arizona Republic,* March 10, 2005, p A7.

[42] These statistics were obtained from "Internet World Statistics—The Big Picture: World Internet Users and Population Stats," March 31, 2006, http://www.internetworldstats.com/stats.htm, accessed June 1, 2006. Also see R O Crockett, "Why the Web Is Hitting a Wall," *Business Week,* March 20, 2006, pp 90–92.

[43] This result was presented in "On Any Given Day, About 40 Millon Internet Users Go Online Just For Fun," *The Pew Charitable Trusts,* February 2006, http:www.pewtrusts.org/ideas/ideas_item.cfm?content_item_id=3254&content_type_id=8.

[44] See B Hemphill, "File, Act, or Toss?" *Training & Development,* February 2001, pp 38–41.

[45] Results can be found in L Winerman, "E-Mails and Egos," *Monitor on Psychology,* February 2006, pp 16–17; and J Kruger, N Epley, J Parker, and Z-W Ng, "Egocentrism Over E-Mail: Can We Communicate As Well As We Think?" *Journal of Applied Psychology,* December 2005, pp 925–36.

[46.] This statistic was reported in E Chambers, 'Web Watch: The Lid on Spam Is Still Loose,' *Business Week,* February 7, 2005, p 10.

[47] Results can be found in M S Thompson and M S Feldman, "Electronic Mail and Organizational Communication: Does Saying 'Hi' Really Matter?" *Organization Science,* November/December 1998, pp 685–98.

[48] See the related discussion in A Pomeroy, "Business 'Fast and Loose' with E-Mail, IMs—Study," *HR Magazine,* November 2004, pp 32, 34.

[49] See descriptions in "Labor Notes: The Boss Is Watching—So Watch Your iPod," *Business Week,* April 24, 2006, p 16; and "Podcast Popularity Grows," *Training,* April 2006, p 14.

[50] Excerpted from J Spencer, "The BlackBerry Squint: Growing PDA Use Hurts Eyes," *The Wall Street Journal,* April 25, 2006, p D1.

[51] See Conlin, "Take a Vacation from Your BlackBerry."

[52] These statistics were reported in J M Alterio, "IBM Taps into Blogosphere," *The Arizona Republic,* January 21, 2006, p D3.

[53] Fanshawe College Website—www.fanshawec.on.ca 'President's Blog'—Dr. Howard Rundle, President.

[54] See Alterio, "IBM Taps Into Blogosphere."

[55] This example is discussed in "Firms Taking Action against Worker Blogs," *MSNBC News,* posted March 7, 2005, www.msnbc.msn.com/id/7116338, accessed March 7, 2005.

[56] See J Gordon, "Straight Talk: Wasting Time on the Company Dime," *Training,* May 2006, p 6.

[57] *Sharing Information,* by Luann LaSalle of the Canadian Press, London Free Press, March 12, 2009, p A2.

[58] Ibid.

[59] Blogger Jason Cox June 13, 2007 http://www.articlesbase.com/video-conferencing-articles/video-conferencing-a-pros-and-cons-decision-164238.html

[60] See M Naylor, "There's No Workforce Like Home," *Business Week Online,* May 2, 2006, http://www.businessweek.com/print/technology/content/may2006/tc20060502_763202.htm.

[61] These statistics are reported in S Shellenbarger, "Outsourcing Jobs to the Den: Call Centers Tap People Who Want to Work at Home," *The Wall Street Journal,* January 12, 2006, p D1.

[62] See A Donoghue, "2010: The Year of the Techie," ZDNet *UK News,* May 13, 2006, http://news.zdnet.co.uk/business/0,39020645,39269493,00.htm.

63 Supporting evidence can be found in B Hemphill, "Telecommuting Productively," *Occupational Health & Safety*, March 2004, pp 16, 18; R Konrad, "Sun's 'iWork' Shuns Desks for Flexibility," *Arizona Republic*, May 28, 2003, p D4; and C Hymowitz, "Remote Managers Find Ways to Narrow the Distance Gap," *The Wall Street Journal*, April 6, 1999, p B1·

CHAPTER 8

1 D Tjosvold, Learning to Manage Conflict: Getting People to Work Together Productively (New York: Lexington Books, 1993), p xi.
2 Ibid., pp xi–xii. High-tech change is discussed in B Stone, "Big Bucks, Big Thinker," Newsweek, May 22, 2006, p 46.
3 See M Conlin, "Good Divorce, Good Business," BusinessWeek, October 31, 2005, pp 90–91.
4 J A Wall Jr and R Robert Callister, "Conflict and Its Management," *Journal of Management*, no. 3 (1995), p 517.
5 Ibid., p 544.
6 D Stead, "The Big Picture," *BusinessWeek* , January 8, 2007, p 11.
7 See M A von Glinow, D L Shapiro, and J M Brett, "Can We *Talk*, and Should We? Managing Emotional Conflict in Multicultural Teams," *Academy of Management Review*, October 2004, pp 578–92; C Palmeri, "Hair-Pulling in the Dollhouse," *BusinessWeek*, May 2, 2005, pp 76–77; and G Colvin, "CEO Knockdown," *Fortune*, April 4, 2005, pp 19–20.
8 K Cloke and J Goldsmith, *Resolving Conflicts at Work: A Complete Guide for Everyone on the Job* (San Francisco: Jossey-Bass, 2000), pp 25, 27, 29.
9 D Brady, "It's All Donald, All the Time," *BusinessWeek* , January 22, 2007, p 51.
10 See P J Sauer, "Are You Ready for Some Football Clichés?" *Inc.*, October 2003, pp 97–100; and V P Rindova, M Becerra, and I Contardo, "Enacting Competitive Wars: Competitive Activity, Language Games, and Market Consequences," *Academy of Management Review*, October 2004, pp 670–86.
11 Cloke and Goldsmith, *Resolving Conflicts at Work*, pp 31–32. Also see K Fackelmann, "Arguing Hurts the Heart in More Ways Than One," *USA Today* , March 6, 2006, p 10D; D Meyer, "The Saltshaker Theory," *Inc* ., October 2006, pp 69–70; J Welch and S Welch, "The Blame Game—Forget It," *BusinessWeek* , March 5, 2007, p 92; and J Welch and S Welch, "The Right Way to Say Goodbye," *BusinessWeek*, March 26, 2006, p 144.
12 See M J Martinko, S C Douglas, and P Harvey, "Understanding and Managing Workplace Aggression," *Organizational Dynamics*, no. 2, 2006, pp 117–130; Z Stambor, "Bullying Stems From Fear, Apathy," *Monitor on Psychology* , July-August 2006, pp 72–78; T J Brown and K E Sumner, "Perceptions and Punishments of Workplace Aggression: The Role of Aggression Content, Context, and Perceiver Variables," *Journal of Applied Social Psychology* , October 2006, pp 2509–2531; and J Deschenaux, "Bills Prohibit Employer Bans on Firearms," *HR Magazine*, February 2007, pp 34, 39.
13 See S Alper, D Tjosvold, and K S Law, "Interdependence and Controversy in Group Decision Making: Antecedents to Effective Self-Managing Teams," *Organizational Behaviour and Human Decision Processes*, April 1998, pp 33–52; and T Simons and R S Peterson, "When to Let Them Duke It Out," *Harvard Business Review*, June 2006, pp 23–24.
14 S P Robbins, "'Conflict Management' and 'Conflict Resolution' Are Not Synonymous Terms," *California Management Review*, Winter 1978, p 70. For examples of functional and dysfunctional conflict, see D Dahl, "Case Study: Michael Kalinsky Was Sick of Fighting with His Vice President, Who Was Also His Ex-Brother-in-Law. Was Firing Him Too Drastic?" *Inc* ., October 2006, pp 51–54; J S Lublin and E White, "Drama in the Boardroom," *The Wall Street Journal* , October 2, 2006, pp B1, B3; and S Clifford, "The Worst Case Scenario," *Inc* ., November 2006, p 111.

15 Cooperative conflict is discussed in Tjosvold, Learning to Manage Conflict: Getting People to Work Together Productively. Also see A C Amason, "Distinguishing the Effects of Functional and Dysfunctional Conflict on Strategic Decision Making: Resolving a Paradox for Top Management Teams," Academy of Management Journal, February 1996, pp 123–48.
16 Adapted in part from discussion in A C Filley, *Interpersonal Conflict Resolution* (Glenview, IL: Scott, Foresman, 1975), pp 9–12; and B Fortado, "The Accumulation of Grievance Conflict," *Journal of Management Inquiry*, December 1992, pp 288–303.
17 Adapted from discussion in Tjosvold, *Learning to Manage Conflict*, pp 12–13. A Bizman and Y Yinon, "Intergroup Conflict Management Strategies as Related to Perceptions of Dual Identity and Separate Groups," *Journal of Social Psychology*, April 2004, pp 115–26; and R J Crisp and J K Nicel, "Disconfirming Intergroup Evaluations: Asymmetric Effects for In-Groups and Out-Groups," *Journal of Social Psychology*, June 2004, pp 247–71.
18 L Gardenswartz and A Rowe, *Diverse Teams at Work: Capitalizing on the Power of Diversity* (New York: McGraw-Hill, 1994), p 32.
19 S Armour, "Music Hath Charms for Some Workers—Others It Really Annoys," *USA Today*, March 24, 2006, p 1B.
20 See O Barker, "Whatever Happened to Thank-You Notes?" *USA Today*, December 27, 2005, pp 1A–2A; and S Jayson, "Are Social Norms Steadily Unraveling?" *USA Today*, April 13, 2006, p 4D.
21 See D L Coutu, "In Praise of Boundaries: A Conversation with Miss Manners," *Harvard Business Review*, December 2003, pp 41–45; R Kurtz, "Is Etiquette a Core Value?" *Inc.*, May 2004, p 22; and K Gurchiek, "Office Etiquette Breaches: Dial It Down," *HR Magazine*, May 2006, p 36.
22 P Falcone, "Days of Contemplation," *HR Magazine* , February 2007, p 107.
23 See L M Andersson and C M Pearson, "Tit for Tat? The Spiraling Effect of Incivility in the Workplace," *Academy of Management Review*, July 1999, pp 452–71; J Pfeffer, "How to Turn On the Charm," *Business 2.0*, June 2004, p 76; and S Lim and L M Cortina, "Interpersonal Mistreatment in the Workplace: The Interface and Impact of General Incivility and Sexual Harassment," *Journal of Applied Psychology*, May 2005, pp 483–96.
24 Chris Morris, Canadian Press, *Workplace Bullying Worldwide Drain*, London Free Press, October 15, 2008, p C9.
25 Ibid
26 Ibid
27 Ontario Considers Workplace Violence Legislation, Canadian HR Reporter, Sept. 27, 2008, http://www.hrreporter.com/ArticleView.aspx?l=1&articleid=6367
28 For practical advice, see N Nicholson, "How to Motivate Your Problem People," *Harvard Business Review*, Special Issue: Motivating People, January 2003, pp 56–65; and M Archer, "How to Work With Annoying People," *USA Today*, March 20, 2006, p 4B.
29 Based on discussion in G Labianca, D J Brass, and B Gray, "Social Networks and Perceptions of Intergroup Conflict: The Role of Negative Relationships and Third Parties," *Academy of Management Journal*, February 1998, pp 55–67. Also see A Bizman and Y Yinon, "Intergroup Conflict Management Strategies as Related to Perceptions of Dual Identity and Separate Groups," *Journal of Social Psychology*, April 2004, pp 115–26; and R J Crisp and J K Nicel, "Disconfirming Intergroup Evaluations: Asymmetric Effects for In-Groups and Out-Groups," *Journal of Social Psychology*, June 2004, pp 247–71.
30 See L A Rudman and S A Goodwin, "Gender Differences in Automatic In-Group Bias: Why Do Women Like Women More than Men Like Men?" *Journal of Personality and Social Psychology*, October 2004, pp 494–509; G Cowan, "Interracial Interactions at Racially Diverse University Campuses," *Journal of Social Psychology*, February 2005, pp 49–63; and G B Cunningham, "The Influence of

Group Diversity on Intergroup Bias Following Recategorization," *The Journal of Social Psychology* , October 2006, pp 533–47.

[31] See C D Batson, M P Polycarpou, E Harmon-Jones, H J Imhoff, E C Mitchener, L L Bednar, T R Klein, and L Highberger, "Empathy and Attitudes: Can Feeling for a Member of a Stigmatized Group Improve Feelings toward the Group?" *Journal of Personality and Social Psychology*, January 1997, pp 105–18.

[32] For more, see N J Adler, International Dimensions of Organizational Behavior, 4th ed (Cincinnati: South-Western, 2002); P Engardio, "The Future of Outsourcing," *BusinessWeek*, January 30, 2006, pp 50–58; F Balfour, "One Foot in China," *BusinessWeek*, May 1, 2006, pp 44–45; E Iwata, "Immigrants Courted as Good Customers," USA Today, May 11, 2006, p 3B; L Buchanan, "The Thinking Man's Outsourcing," *Inc.*, May 2006, pp 31–33; B Helm, "Life on the Web's Factory Floor," *BusinessWeek*, May 22, 2006, pp 70–71; B Einhorn, "The Hunt for Chinese Talent," *BusinessWeek*, May 22, 2006, p 104; and R Buderi, "The Talent Magnet," *Fast Company*, June 2006, pp 80–84.

[33] Reprinted from A Rosenbaum, "Testing Cultural Waters," *Management Review,* July/August 1999, p 43. Copyright 1999 American Management Association. Reproduced with permission of American Management Association via Copyright Clearance Center.

[34] See R L Tung, "American Expatriates Abroad: From Neophytes to Cosmopolitans," *Journal of World Business*, Summer 1998, pp 125–44.

[35] See H M Guttman, "Conflict Management as a Core Leadership Competency," *Training*, November 2005, pp 34–39.

[36] A statistical validation for this model can be found in M A Rahim and N R Magner, "Confirmatory Factor Analysis of the Styles of Handling Interpersonal Conflict: First-Order Factor Model and Its Invariance across Groups," *Journal of Applied Psychology*, February 1995, pp 122–32.

[37] M A Rahim, "A Strategy for Managing Conflict in Complex Organizations," *Human Relations*, January 1985, p 84.

[38] See R Rubin, "Study: Bullies and Their Victims Tend to Be More Violent," *USA Today*, April 15, 2003, p 9D; D Salin, "Ways of Explaining Workplace Bullying: A Review of Enabling, Motivating and Precipitating Structures and Processes in the Work Environment," *Human Relations*, October 2003, pp 1213–32; K Gurchiek, "Bullying: It's Not Just on the Playground," *HR Magazine*, June 2005, p 40; L W Andrews, "When It's Time For Anger Management," *HR Magazine*, June 2005, pp 131–35; and K Hannon, "You Can Take That Bully Down, Gently," *USA Today*, July 5, 2005, p 4B.

[39] For more on managing conflict, see G Roper, "Managing Employee Relations," *HR Magazine*, May 2005, pp 101–04; Y Shin, "Conflict Resolution in Virtual Teams," *Organizational Dynamics*, no. 4, 2005, pp 331–45; and M DuPraw, "Cut the Conflict with Consensus Building," *Training*, May 2006, p 8.

[40] See J Rasley, "The Revolution You Won't See on TV," *Newsweek*, November 25, 2002, p 13; and C Bendersky, "Organizational Dispute Resolution Systems: A Complementarities Model," *Academy of Management Review*, October 2003, pp 643–56.

[41] B Morrow and L M Bernardi, "Resolving Workplace Disputes," *Canadian Manager*, Spring 1999, p 17.

[42] Adapted from discussion in K O Wilburn, "Employment Disputes: Solving Them Out of Court," *Management Review*, March 1998, pp 17–21; and Morrow and Bernardi, "Resolving Workplace Disputes," pp 17–19, 27. Also see L Ioannou, "Can't We Get Along?" *Fortune,* December 7, 1998, p 244[E]; and D Weimer and S A Forest, "Forced into Arbitration? Not Any More," *BusinessWeek*, March 16, 1998, pp 66–68.

[43] For more, see M M Clark, "A Jury of Their Peers," *HR Magazine,* January 2004, pp 54–59.

[44] Wilburn, "Employment Disputes: Solving Them Out of Court," p 19.

[45] See R E Jones and B H Melcher, "Personality and the Preference for Modes of Conflict Resolution," *Human Relations*, August 1982, pp 649–58.

[46] See R A Baron, "Reducing Organizational Conflict: An Incompatible Response Approach," *Journal of Applied Psychology*, May 1984, pp 272–79.

[47] See G A Youngs Jr, "Patterns of Threat and Punishment Reciprocity in a Conflict Setting," *Journal of Personality and Social Psychology*, September 1986, pp 541–46.

[48] For more details, see V D Wall Jr and L L Nolan, "Small Group Conflict: A Look at Equity, Satisfaction, and Styles of Conflict Management," *Small Group Behaviour*, May 1987, pp 188–211. Also see S M Farmer and J Roth, "Conflict-Handling Behaviour in Work Groups: Effects of Group Structure, Decision Processes, and Time," *Small Group Research,* December 1998, pp 669–713.

[49] Based on B Richey, H J Bernardin, C L Tyler, and N McKinney, "The Effects of Arbitration Program Characteristics on Applicants' Intentions toward Potential Employers," *Journal of Applied Psychology,* October 2001, pp 1006–13.

[50] See M E Schnake and D S Cochran, "Effect of Two Goal-Setting Dimensions on Perceived Intraorganizational Conflict," *Group & Organization Studies,* June 1985, pp 168–83. Also see O Janssen, E Van De Vliert, and C Veenstra, "How Task and Person Conflict Shape the Role of Positive Interdependence in Management Teams," *Journal of Management*, no. 2, 1999, pp 117–42.

[51] See K K Smith, "The Movement of Conflict in Organizations: The Joint Dynamics of Splitting and Triangulation," *Administrative Science Quarterly,* March 1989, pp 1–20. Also see J B Olson-Buchanan, F Drasgow, P J Moberg, A D Mead, P A Keenan, and M A Donovan, "Interactive Video Assessment of Conflict Resolution Skills." *Personnel Psychology,* Spring 1998, pp 1–24; and D E Conlon and D P Sullivan, "Examining the Actions of Organizations in Conflict: Evidence from the Delaware Court of Chancery," *Academy of Management Journal,* June 1999, pp 319–29.

[52] Based on C Tinsley, "Models of Conflict Resolution in Japanese, German, and American Cultures," *Journal of Applied Psychology,* April 1998, pp 316–23; and S M Adams, "Settling Cross-Cultural Disagreements Begins with 'Where' Not 'How,' " *Academy of Management Executive,* February 1999, pp 109–10. Also see K Ohbuchi, O Fukushima, and J T Tedeschi, "Cultural Values in Conflict Management: Goal Orientation, Goal Attainment, and Tactical Decision," *Journal of Cross-Cultural Psychology,* January 1999, pp 51–71; and R Cropanzano, H Aguinis, M Schminke, and D L Denham, "Disputant Reactions to Managerial Conflict Resolution Tactics: A Comparison among Argentina, the Dominican Republic, Mexico, and the United States," *Group & Organization Management,* June 1999, pp 124–54.

[53] Based on a definition in M A Neale and M H Bazerman, "Negotiating Rationally: The Power and Impact of the Negotiator's Frame," *Academy of Management Executive,* August 1992, pp 42–51.

[54] See K Tyler, "Good-Faith Bargaining," *HR Magazine,* January 2005, pp 48–53; S Clifford, "Something for Nothing," *Inc.,* May 2005, pp 54, 56; L Stern, "Getting Your Slice," *Newsweek* , October 9, 2006, pp 66–67; P Bathurst, "Once Offered the Job, It Can Pay to Negotiate," *The Arizona Republic* , December 10, 2006, p EC 1; E Pooley, "Get a Killer Raise in 2007," Canadian Business, January 14, 2007, pp 61–62.

[55] M H Bazerman and M A Neale, *Negotiating Rationally* (New York: Free Press, 1992), p 16. Also see G Cullinan, J Le Roux, and R Weddigen, "When to Walk Away from a Deal," *Harvard Business Review,* April 2004, pp 96–104; P B Stark and J Flaherty, "How to Negotiate," *Training & Development,* June 2004, pp 52–54; K Tyler, "The Art of Give-and-Take," *HR Magazine,* November 2004, pp 107–16; D Ertel, "Getting Past Yes: Negotiating as if Implementation Mattered," *Harvard Business Review,* November 2004, pp 60–68; and M Kaplan, "How to Negotiate Anything," *Money,* May 2005, pp 117–19.

[56] Good win–win negotiation strategies can be found in R R Reck and B G Long, *The Win–Win Negotiator: How to Negotiate Favorable Agreements That Last* (New York: Pocket Books, 1987);

R Fisher and W Ury, *Getting to YES: Negotiating Agreement without Giving In* (Boston: Houghton Mifflin, 1981); and R Fisher and D Ertel, *Getting Ready to Negotiate: The Getting to YES Workbook* (New York: Penguin Books, 1995). Also see B Spector, "An Interview with Roger Fisher and William Ury," *Academy of Management Executive*, August 2004, pp 101–8; B Booth and M McCredie, "Taking Steps toward 'Getting to Yes' at Blue Cross and Blue Shield of Florida," *Academy of Management Executive*, August 2004, pp 109–12; C Woodyard, "Working Hand-in-Hand," *USA Today* , February 6, 2007, pp 1B–2B; E A Grant, "Playing Hard to Get," *Inc* ., March 2007, pp 104–9; and N Brodsky, "The Paranoia Moment. Are They Stalling? Is This Deal About to Fall Apart?" *Inc* ., April 2007, pp 67–68.

[57] See L R Weingart, E B Hyder, and M J Prietula, "Knowledge Matters: The Effect of Tactical Descriptions on Negotiation Behaviour and Outcome." *Journal of Personality and Social Psychology,* June 1996, pp 1205–17.

[58] For more, see A Valenzuela, J Srivastava, and S Lee, "The Role of Cultural Orientation in Bargaining under Incomplete Information: Differences in Causal Attributions," *Organizational Behaviour and Human Decision Processes,* January 2005, pp 72–88; K Lee, G Yang, and J L Graham, "Tension and Trust in International Business Negotiations: American Executives Negotiating with Chinese Executives," *Journal of International Business Studies* , September 2006, pp 623–41; and L E Metcalf, A Bird, M Shankarmahesh, Z Aycan, J Larimo, and D D Valdelamar, "Cultural Tendencies in Negotiation: A Comparison of Finland, India, Mexico, Turkey, and the United States," *Journal of World Business* , December 2006, pp 382–94.

[59] For supporting evidence, see J K Butler Jr, "Trust Expectations, Information Sharing, Climate of Trust, and Negotiation Effectiveness and Efficiency," *Group & Organization Management,* June 1999, pp 217–38.

[60] See H J Reitz, J A Wall Jr, and M S Love, "Ethics in Negotiation: Oil and Water or Good Lubrication?" *Business Horizons,* May–June 1998, pp 5–14; M E Schweitzer and Jeffrey L Kerr, "Bargaining under the Influence: The Role of Alcohol in Negotiations," *Academy of Management Executive,* May 2000, pp 47–57; and A M Burr, "Ethics in Negotiation: Does Getting to Yes Require Candor?" *Dispute Resolution Journal,* May–July 2001, pp 8–15.

[61] For related research, see A E Tenbrunsel, "Misrepresentation and Expectations of Misrepresentation in an Ethical Dilemma: The Role of Incentives and Temptation," *Academy of Management Journal,* June 1998, pp 330–39.

[62] Based on R L Pinkley, T L Griffith, and G B Northcraft, " 'Fixed Pie' a la Mode: Information Availability, Information Processing, and the Negotiation of Suboptimal Agreements," *Organizational Behaviour and Human Decision Processes,* April 1995, pp 101–12.

[63] Based on B Barry and R A Friedman, "Bargainer Characteristics in Distributive and Integrative Negotiation," *Journal of Personality and Social Psychology,* February 1998, pp 345–59. Also see K J Sulkowicz, "The Psychology of the Deal," *BusinessWeek* , April 9, 2007, p 14.

[64] For more, see J P Forgas, "On Feeling Good and Getting Your Way: Mood Effects on Negotiator Cognition and Bargaining Strategies," *Journal of Personality and Social Psychology,* March 1998, pp 565–77. Also see G A van Kleef, C K W De Dreu, and A S R Manstead, "The Interpersonal Effects of Anger and Happiness in Negotiations," *Journal of Personality and Social Psychology,* January 2004, pp 57–76; and G A van Kleef, C K W De Dreu, and A S R Manstead, "The Interpersonal Effects of Emotions in Negotiations: A Motivated Information Processing Approach," *Journal of Personality and Social Psychology,* October 2004, pp 510–28.

[65] Data from B Campbell and M M Marx, "Toward More Effective Stakeholder Dialogue: Applying Theories of Negotiation to Policy and Program Evaluation," *Journal of Applied Social Psychology* , December 2006, pp 2834–63.

[66] Drawn from L H Chusmir and J Mills, "Gender Differences in Conflict Resolution Styles of Managers: At Work and at Home," *Sex Roles,* February 1989, pp 149–63.

[67] Based on A E Walters, A F Stuhlmacher, and L L Meyer, "Gender and Negotiator Competitiveness: A Meta-Analysis," *Organizational Behaviour and Human Decision Processes,* October 1998, pp 1–29.

[68] L Babcock, S Laschever, M Gelfand, and D Small, "Nice Girls Don't Ask," *Harvard Business Review,* October 2003, p 14. Also see L A Barron, "Ask and You Shall Receive? Gender Differences in Negotiators' Beliefs about Requests for a Higher Salary," *Human Relations,* June 2003, pp 635–62; L D Tyson, "New Clues to the Pay and Leadership Gap," *BusinessWeek,* October 27, 2003, p 36; D Kersten, "Women Need to Learn the Art of the Deal," *USA Today,* November 17, 2003, p 7B; A Fels, "Do Women Lack Ambition?" *Harvard Business Review,* April 2004, pp 50–60; B Brophy, "Bargaining for Bigger Bucks: A Step-by-Step Guide to Negotiating Your Salary," *Business 2.0,* May 2004, p 107; and H R Bowles, L Babcock, and K L McGinn, "Constraints and Triggers: Situational Mechanics of Gender in Negotiation," *Journal of Personality and Social Psychology,* December 2005, pp 951–65.

CHAPTER 9

[1] For example, see K Gurchiek, "How To Defuse an Unreasonable Boss," *HR Magazine,* August 2006, pp 28, 30; S Berfield, "Don't Get Mad. Get Even," *BusinessWeek,* August 21–28, 2006, pp 64–65; and G Colvin, "Undercutting CEO Power," *Fortune,* March 5, 2007, p. 42.

[2] M W McCall, Jr, Power, Influence, and Authority: The Hazards of Carrying a Sword, Technical Report No. 10 (Greensboro, NC: Center for Creative Leadership, 1978), p 5. For an excellent discussion, see J O Hagberg, Real Power: Stages of Personal Power in Organizations, 3rd ed (Salem, WI: Sheffield Publishing, 2003).

[3] D W Cantor and T Bernay, *Women in Power: The Secrets of Leadership* (Boston: Houghton Mifflin, 1992), p 40; and K Morris, "Trouble in Toyland," *BusinessWeek,* March 15, 1999, p 40.

[4] See J R P French and B Raven, "The Bases of Social Power," in *Studies in Social Power,* ed D Cartwright (Ann Arbor: University of Michigan Press, 1959), pp 150–67. Also see S M Farmer and H Aguinis, "Accounting for Subordinate Perceptions of Supervisor Power: An Identity-Dependence Model," *Journal of Applied Psychology,* November 2005, pp 1069–83.

[5] G Edmondson, "Power Play at VW," *BusinessWeek,* December 4, 2006, p 45. Also see M Weinstein, "Alpha Male on Your Hands: Here's How to Deal," *Training,* October 2006, p 16.

[6] See M Maccoby, "Why People Follow the Leader: The Power of Transference," *Harvard Business Review,* September 2004, pp 76–85; and G R Weaver, L K Trevino, and B Agle, " 'Somebody I Look Up To:' Ethical Role Models in Organizations," *Organizational Dynamics,* no. 4, 2005, pp 313–30.

[7] See D Kipnis, S M Schmidt, and I Wilkinson, "Intraorganizational Influence Tactics: Explorations in Getting One's Way," *Journal of Applied Psychology,* August 1980, pp 440–52. Also see C A Schriesheim and T R Hinkin, "Influence Tactics Used by Subordinates: A Theoretical and Empirical Analysis and Refinement of the Kipnis, Schmidt, and Wilkinson Subscales," *Journal of Applied Psychology,* June 1990, pp 246–57; G Yukl and C M Falbe, "Influence Tactics and Objectives in Upward, Downward, and Lateral Influence Attempts," *Journal of Applied Psychology,* April 1990, pp 132–40; and G Yukl and B Tracey, "Consequences of Influence Tactics Used with Subordinates, Peers, and the Boss," in *Organizational Influence Processes,* eds L W Porter, H L Angle, and R W Allen (Armonk, NY: M E Sharpe, 2003), 2nd ed, pp 96–116.

[8] Based on Table 1 in G Yukl, C M Falbe, and J Y Youn, "Patterns of Influence Behaviour for Managers," *Group & Organization Management,* March 1993, pp 5–28. An additional influence tactic is

presented in B P Davis and E S Knowles, "A Disrupt-then-Reframe Technique of Social Influence," *Journal of Personality and Social Psychology,* February 1999, pp 192–99. For more on ingratiation, see D B Yoffie and M Kwak, "With Friends Like These: The Art of Managing Complementors," *Harvard Business Review,* September 2006, pp 88–98.

[9] P M Podsakoff and C A Schriesheim, "Field Studies of French and Raven's Bases of Power: Critique, Reanalysis, and Suggestions for Future Research," *Psychological Bulletin,* May 1985, p 388. Also see M A Rahim and G F Buntzman, "Supervisory Power Bases, Styles of Handling Conflict with Subordinates, and Subordinate Compliance and Satisfaction," *Journal of Psychology,* March 1989, pp 195–210; D Tjosvold, "Power and Social Context in Superior-Subordinate Interaction," *Organizational Behaviour and Human Decision Processes,* June 1985, pp 281–93; and C A Schriesheim, T R Hinkin, and P M Podsakoff, "Can Ipsative and Single-Item Measures Produce Erroneous Results in Field Studies of French and Raven's (1950) Five Bases of Power? An Empirical Investigation," *Journal of Applied Psychology,* February 1991, pp 106–14.

[10] Based on discussion in G Yukl, H Kim and C M Falbe, "Antecedents of Influence Outcomes," *Journal of Applied Psychology,* June 1996, pp 309–17.

[11] For related research, see L G Pelletier and R J Vallerand, "Supervisors' Beliefs and Subordinates' Intrinsic Motivation: A Behavioural Confirmation Analysis," *Journal of Personality and Social Psychology,* August 1996, pp 331–40.

[12] See T R Hinkin and C A Schriesheim, "Relationships between Subordinate Perceptions and Supervisor Influence Tactics and Attributed Bases of Supervisory Power," *Human Relations,* March 1990, pp 221–37. Also see D J Brass and M E Burkhardt, "Potential Power and Power Use: An Investigation of Structure and Behaviour," *Academy of Management Journal,* June 1993, pp 441–70; K W Mossholder, N Bennett, E R Kemery, and M A Wesolowski, "Relationships between Bases of Power and Work Reactions: The Mediational Role of Procedural Justice," *Journal of Management,* no. 4, 1998, pp 533–52; and J Sell, M J Lovaglia, E A Mannix, C D Samuelson, and R K Wilson, "Investigating Conflict, Power, and Status within and among Groups," *Small Group Research,* February 2004, pp 44–72.

[13] See J Scelfo, "10 Power Tips," *Newsweek,* September 25, 2006, p 78; and A Carter, "Curiously Strong Teamwork," *BusinessWeek,* February 26, 2007, pp 90, 92.

[14] As quoted in M Bartiromo, "What to Expect at Davos," *Business Week,* January 29, 2007, p 100. Also see G Mangurian, "Responsibility Junkie," *Harvard Business Review,* October 2006, p 30.

[15] As quoted in W A Randolph and M Sashkin, "Can Organizational Empowerment Work in Multinational Settings?" *Academy of Management Executive,* February 2002, p 104. (Emphasis added.) Also see J S Harrison and R E Freeman, "Special Topic: Democracy in and around Organizations: Is Organizational Democracy Worth the Effort?" *Academy of Management Executive,* August 2004, pp 49–53; J L Kerr, "The Limits of Organizational Democracy," *Academy of Management Executive,* August 2004, pp 81–97; and N R Lockwood, "Leveraging Employee Engagement for Competitive Advantage: HR's Strategic Role," 2007 SHRM Research Quarterly, *HR Magazine,* March 2007, pp 1–12.

[16] R M Hodgetts, "A Conversation with Steve Kerr," *Organizational Dynamics,* Spring 1996, p 71. For example, see B De Lollis, "Hotels Train Employees to Think Fast," *USAToday,* November 29, 2006, pp 1B–2B.

[17] L Shaper Walters, "A Leader Redefines Management," *Christian Science Monitor,* September 22, 1992, p 14. Also see B George, P Sims, A N McLean, and D Mayer, "Discovering Your Authentic Leadership," *Harvard Business Review,* February 2007, pp 129–38.

[18] For a 15-item empowerment scale, see Table 1 on p 103 of B P Niehoff, R H Moorman, G Blakely, and J Fuller, "The Influence of Empowerment and Job Enrichment on Employee Loyalty in a Downsizing Environment," *Group & Organization Management,* March 2001, pp 93–113.

[19] F Vogelstein, "Star Power: Greg Brown, Motorola," *Fortune,* February 6, 2006, p 57.

[20] H Malcolm and C Sokoloff, "Values, Human Relations, and Organization Development," in *The Emerging Practice of Organizational Development,* eds W Sikes, A Drexler, and J Gant (San Diego: University Associates, 1989), p 64.

[21] R W Allen, D L Madison, L W Porter, P A Renwick, and B T Mayes, "Organizational Politics: Tactics and Characteristics of Its Actors," *California Management Review,* Fall 1979, p 77. A comprehensive update can be found in K M Kacmar and R A Baron, "Organizational Politics: The State of the Field, Links to Related Processes, and an Agenda for Future Research," in *Research in Personnel and Human Resources Management,* vol. 17, ed G R Ferris (Stamford, CT: JAI Press, 1999), pp 1–39. Also see K A Ahearn, G R Ferris, W A Hochwarter, C Douglas, and A P Ammeter, "Leader Political Skill and Team Performance," *Journal of Management,* no. 3, 2004, pp 309–27; P L Perrewé and D L Nelson, "Gender and Career Success: The Facilitative Role of Political Skill," *Organizational Dynamics,* no. 4, 2004, pp 366–78; G R Ferris, D C Treadway, R W Kolodinsky, W A Hochwarter, C J Kacmar, C Douglas, and D D Frink, "Development and Validation of the Political Skill Inventory," *Journal of Management,* no. 1, 2005, pp 126–52; and T B Lawrence, M K Mauws, B Dyck, and R F Kleysen, "The Politics of Organizational Learning: Integrating Power into the 4I Framework," *Academy of Management Review,* January 2005, pp 180–91.

[22] See P M Fandt and G R Ferris, "The Management of Information and Impressions: When Employees Behave Opportunistically," *Organizational Behaviour and Human Decision Processes,* February 1990, pp 140–58.

[23] D J Burrough, "Office Politics Mirror Popular TV Program," *Arizona Republic,* February 4, 2001, p EC1.

[24] L B MacGregor Serven, *The End of Office Politics as Usual* (New York: American Management Association, 2002), p 5. Also see K J McGregor, "Sweet Revenge: The Power of Retribution, Spite, and Loathing in the World of Business," *BusinessWeek,* January 22, 2007, pp 64–70; D A Kaplan, "Suspicions and Spies in Silicon Valley," *Newsweek,* September 18, 2006, pp 40–47; J Fox, "Board Games," *Fortune,* October 2, 2006, pp 23–24, 26; G Anders and A Murray, "Behind H-P Chairman's Fall, Clash With a Powerful Director," *The Wall Street Journal,* October 9, 2006, pp A1, A14; and P Burrows, "Controlling the Damage at HP," *BusinessWeek,* October 9, 2006, pp 36–44.

[25] R Bhasin, "On Playing Corporate Politics," *Pulp & Paper,* October 1985, p 175. Also see G R Ferris, P L Perrewé, W P Anthony, and D C Gilmore, "Political Skill at Work," *Organizational Dynamics,* Spring 2000, pp 25–37; R M Kramer, "When Paranoia Makes Sense," *Harvard Business Review,* July 2002, pp 62–69; J Barbian, "Office Politics: Swinging with the Sharks," *Training,* July 2002, p 16; L P Frankel, *Nice Girls Don't Get the Corner Office: Unconscious Mistakes Women Make That Sabotage Their Career* (New York: Warner, 2004); T Estep, "Winning the Rat Race," *Training & Development,* January 2005, pp 71–72; and S B Bacharach, "Politically *Proactive,*" *Fast Company,* May 2005, p 93; and R M Kramer, "The Great Intimidators," *Harvard Business Review,* February 2006, pp 88–96.

[26] Data from M Weinstein, "Training Today: Q&A," *Training,* January–February 2007, p 7. Also see A Pomeroy, "Politics 101 for Women," *HR Magazine,* June 2006, pp 24, 26; and C Wilbert, "You Schmooze, You Win," *Fast Company,* July–August 2006, p 109.

[27] First four based on discussion in D R Beeman and T W Sharkey, "The Use and Abuse of Corporate Politics," *Business Horizons,* March–April 1987, pp 26–30. For supportive evidence, see C C Rosen, P E Levy, and R J Hall, "Placing Perceptions of Politics in the Context of the Feedback Environment, Employee Attitudes, and Job Performance," *Journal of Applied Psychology,* January 2006, pp 211–20.

[28] A Raia, "Power, Politics, and the Human Resource Professional," *Human Resource Planning,* no. 4, 1985, p 203.

29 A J DuBrin, "Career Maturity, Organizational Rank, and Political Behavioural Tendencies: A Correlational Analysis of Organizational Politics and Career Experience," *Psychological Reports,* October 1988, p 535.

30 This three-level distinction comes from A T Cobb, "Political Diagnosis: Applications in Organizational Development," *Academy of Management Review,* July 1986, pp 482–96.

31 An excellent historical and theoretical perspective of coalitions can be found in W B Stevenson, J L Pearce, and L W Porter, "The Concept of 'Coalition' in Organization Theory and Research," *Academy of Management Review,* April 1985, pp 256–68.

32 See H Ibarra and M Hunter, "How Leaders Create and Use Networks," *Harvard Business Review,* January 2007, pp 40–47; and N Anand and J A Conger, "Capabilities of the Consummate Networker," *Organizational Dynamics,* no. 1, 2007, pp 13–27.

33 Allen et al., "Organizational Politics," p 77. Also see D C Treadway, W A Hochwarter, C J Kacmar, and G R Ferris, "Political Will, Political Skill, and Political Behaviour," *Journal of Organizational Behaviour,* May 2005, pp 229–45.

34 See the second Q&A in J Welch and S Welch, "Avoiding Strikes—and Unions," *BusinessWeek,* January 15, 2007, p 92; S Berfield, "Mentoring Can Be Messy," *BusinessWeek,* January 29, 2007, pp 80–81; and the second Q&A in J Welch and S Welch, "The Succession Opportunity," *BusinessWeek,* February 5, 2007, p 106.

35 For a review of research on rational decision making, see K E Stanovich, *Who Is Rational?* (Mahwah, NJ: Lawrence Erlbaum, 1999), pp 1–31.

36 Strengths and weaknesses of the rational model are discussed by M H Bazerman, *Judgment in Managerial Decision Making* (Hoboken, NJ: John Wiley & Sons, Inc., 2006).

37 Results can be found in J P Bymes, D C Miller and W D Schafer, "Gender Differences in Risk Taking: A MetaAnalysis," *Psychological Bulletin,* May 1999, pp 367–83.

38 H A Simon, "Rational Decision Making in Business Organizations," *American Economic Review,* September 1979, p 510.

39 For a complete discussion of bounded rationality, see H A Simon, *Administrative Behaviour,* 2nd ed (New York: Free Press, 1957).

40 Biases associated with using shortcuts in decision making are discussed by A Tversky and D Kahneman, "Judgment under Uncertainty: Heuristics and Biases," *Science,* September 1974, pp 1124–31.

41 For a study of the availability heuristic, see L A Vaughn, "Effects of Uncertainty on Use of the Availability of Heuristic for Self-Effi cacy Judgments," *European Journal of Social Psychology,* March/May 1999, pp 407–10.

42 The discussion of styles was based on A J Rowe and R O Mason, *Managing with Style: A Guide to Understanding, Assessing, and Improving Decision Making* (San Francisco: Jossey-Bass, 1987).

43 See ibid, and M J Dollinger and W Danis, "Preferred Decision-Making Styles: A Cross-Cultural Comparison," *Psychological Reports,* 1998, pp 755–61.

44 E Sadler-Smith and E Shefy, "The Intuitive Executive: Understanding and Applying 'Gut Feel' in Decision-Making," *Academy of Management Executive,* November 2004, p 77.

45 Based in part on E. Sadler-Smith and E Shefy, "The Intuitive Executive: Understanding and Applying "Gut Feel" in Decision Making." Academy of Management Executive, November 2004, pp 76–91; and C C Miller and R D Ireland, "Intuition in Strategic Decision Making: Friend or Foe in the Fast-Paced 21st Century," Academy of Management Executive, Februrary 2005, pp 19–30.

46 See E Dane and M G Pratt, "Exploring Intuition and Its Role in Managerial Decision Making," *Academy of Management Review,* January 2007, pp 33–54.

47 See D Begley, "You Might Help a Teen Avoid Dumb Behaviour By Nurturing Intuition," *The Wall Street Journal,* November 3, 2006, p B1.

48 Results were reported in "The Ethical Mind," *Harvard Business Review,* March 2007, pp 51–56.

49 The decision tree and resulting discussion is based on C E Bagley, "The Ethical Leader's Decision Tree," *Harvard Business Review,* February 2003, pp 18–19.

50 The details of this case are discussed in J Ross and B M Staw, "Organizational Escalation and Exit: Lessons from the Shoreham Nuclear Power Plant," *Academy of Management Journal,* August 1993, pp 701–32.

51 Supportive results can be found in H Moon, "Looking Forward and Looking Back: Integrating Completion and Sunk-Cost Effects within an Escalation-of-Commitment Progress Decision," *Journal of Applied Psychology,* February 2001, pp 104–13.

52 This definition was based on R J Sternberg, "What Is the Common Thread of Creativity?" *American Psychologist,* April 2001, pp 360–62.

53 P Magnusson, "Small Biz vs. the Terrorists," *Business Week,* March 4, 2002, p 68.

54 See the related discussion in T M Amabile, "How to Kill Creativity," *Harvard Business Review,* September/October 1998, pp 77–87.

55 G W Hill, "Group versus Individual Performance: Are N + 1 Heads Better Than One?" *Psychological Bulletin,* May 1982, p 535.

56 These guidelines were derived from G P Huber, *Managerial Decision Making* (Glenview, IL: Scott, Foresman, 1980), p 149.

57 I L Janis, *Groupthink,* 2nd ed (Boston: Houghton Mifﬂ in, 1982). For an alternative model, see R J Aldag and S Riggs Fuller, "Beyond Fiasco: A Reappraisal of the Groupthink Phenomenon and a New Model of Group Decision Processes," *Psychological Bulletin,* May 1993, pp 533–52. Also see A A Mohamed and F A Wiebe, "Toward a Process Theory of Groupthink," *Small Group Research,* August 1996, pp 416–30.

58 These recommendations were obtained from Parker, *Team Players and Teamwork: The New Competitive Business Strategy.*

59 See J G Lloyd, S Fowell, and J G Bligh, "The Use of the Nominal Group Technique as an Evaluative Tool in Medical Undergraduate Education," *Medical Education,* January 1999, pp 8–13; and A L Delbecq, A H Van de Ven, and D H Gustafson, *Group Techniques for Program Planning: A Guide to Nominal Group and Delphi Processes* (Glenview, IL: Scott, Foresman, 1975).

60 See N C Dalkey, D L Rourke, R Lewis, and D Snyder, *Studies in the Quality of Life: Delphi and Decision Making* (Lexington, MA: Lexington Books: D C Heath and Co, 1972).

61 Benefits of the Delphi technique are discussed by N I Whitman, "The Committee Meeting Alternative: Using the Delphi Technique," *Journal of Nursing Administration,* July/August 1990, pp 30–36.

CHAPTER 10

1 See S Lieberson and J F O'Connor, 'Leadership and Organizational Performance: A Study of Large Corporations,' *American Sociological Review,* April 1972, pp 117–30.

2 Results can be found in K T Dirks, "Trust in Leadership and Team Performance: Evidence from NCAA Basketball," *Journal of Applied Psychology,* December 2000, pp 1004–12; and D Jacobs and L Singell, "Leadership and Organizational Performance: Isolating Links between Managers and Collective Success," *Social Science Research,* June 1993, pp 165–89.

3 The multiple levels of leadership are discussed by F J Yammarino, F Dansereau, and C J Kennedy, "A Multiple-Level Multidimensional Approach to Leadership: Viewing Leadership through an Elephant's Eye," *Organizational Dynamics,* 2001, pp 149–63.

4 The four commonalities were identified by P G Northouse, *Leadership: Theory and Practice,* 4th ed (Thousand Oaks, CA: Sage Publications, 2007), p 3.

5 Ibid.

6 For a discussion about the differences between leading and managing, see L A Hill, "Becoming the Boss," *Harvard Business*

Review, January 2007, pp 49–56; and G Colvin, "Catch a Rising Star," Fortune, February 6, 2006, pp 46–50.

[7] Leadership development is discussed by H Dolezalek, "Got High Potentials?" Training, January–February 2007, pp 18–22; "Best Practices and Outstanding Training Initiatives," Training, March 2007, pp 84–86; and J Weber, "The Accidental CEO," BusinessWeek, April 23, 2007, pp 64–72.

[8] See D A Kenny and S J Zaccaro, "An Estimate of Variance Due to Traits in Leadership," Journal of Applied Psychology, November 1983, pp 678–85.

[9] See J S Phillips and R G Lord, "Schematic Information Processing and Perceptions of Leadership in Problem-Solving Groups," Journal of Applied Psychology, August 1982, pp 486–92.

[10] Results from this study can be found in F C Brodbeck et al., "Cultural Variation of Leadership Prototypes across 22 European Countries," Journal of Occupational and Organizational Psychology, March 2000, pp 1–29. Also see M Javidan, P W Dorfman, M S de Lugue, and R J House, "In the Eye of the Beholder: Cross Cultural Lesson in Leadership from Project Globe," Academy of Management Perspectives, February 2006, pp 67–90.

[11] Results can be found in T A Judge, J E Bono, R Ilies, & M W Gerhardt, "Personality and Leadership: A Qualitative and Quantitative Review," Journal of Applied Psychology, August 2002, pp 765–80.

[12] See T A Judge, A E Colbert, and R Ilies, "Intelligence and Leadership: A Quantitative Review and Test of Theoretical Propositions," Journal of Applied Psychology, June 2004, pp 542–52.

[13] Supportive results can be found in S Xavier, "Are You at the Top of Your Game? Checklist for Effective Leaders," Journal of Business Strategy, 2005, pp 35–42.

[14] Political intelligence is discussed by R M Kramer, "The Great Intimidators," Harvard Business Review, February 2006, pp 88–96. An example can be found in J Ball, "The New Act at Exxon," The Wall Street Journal, March 8, 2006, pp B1, B2.

[15] Kramer, "The Great Intimidators," pp 95–96.

[16] Gender and the emergence of leaders was examined by A H Eagly and S J Karau, "Gender and the Emergence of Leaders: A Meta-Analysis," Journal of Personality and Social Psychology, May 1991, pp 685–710; and R K Shelly and P T Munroe, "Do Women Engage in Less Task Behavior than Men?" Sociological Perspectives, Spring 1999, pp 49–67.

[17] See A H Eagly, S J Karau, and B T Johnson, "Gender and Leadership Style among School Principals: A Meta-Analysis," Educational Administration Quarterly, February 1992, pp 76–102.

[18] Supportive findings are contained in J M Twenge, "Changes in Women's Assertiveness in Response to Status and Roles: A Cross-Temporal Meta-Analysis, 1931–1993," Journal of Personality and Social Psychology, July 2001, pp 133–45.

[19] For a summary of this research, see R Sharpe, "As Leaders, Women Rule," BusinessWeek, November 20, 2000, pp 74–84. Also see C Casaburi, "Avon, the New, and Glass Ceilings," BusinessWeek, February 6, 2006, p 104.

[20] The process of preparing a development plan is discussed by L Morgan, G Spreitzer, J Dutton, R Quinn, E Heaphy, and B Barker, "How to Play to Your Strengths," Harvard Business Review, January 2005, pp 75–80.

[21] Details on Hasbro's program can be found in A Pomeroy, "Head of the Class," HR Magazine, January 2005, pp 54–58. Leadership development is also discussed by J Durett, "GE Hones Its Leaders at Crotonville," Training, May 2006, pp 25–27; and K Lamoureux, "Wanted: Better Leaders," Training, May 2006, p 16.

[22] Results can be found in T A Judge, R F Piccolo, and R Ilies, "The Forgotten Ones? The Validity of Consideration and Initiating Structure in Leadership Research," Journal of Applied Psychology, February 2004, pp 36–51.

[23] See V H Vroom, "Leadership," in Handbook of Industrial and Organizational Psychology, ed M D Dunnette (Chicago: Rand McNally, 1976).

[24] For corporate examples of leadership development see J Sandberg, "Tyring to Tease Out My Leadership Talent in One Easy Seminar," The Wall Street Journal, March 28, 2006, p B1; J Sandberg, "The Sensitive Me Won't Be Leading Corporate America," The Wall Street Journal, April 11, 2006, p B1; and S Max, "Seagate's Morale-athon," BusinessWeek, April 3, 2006, p 110–12.

[25] See B M Bass, Bass & Stogdill's Handbook of Leadership: Theory, Research, and Managerial Applications, 3rd ed (New York: The Free Press, 1990), chs 20–25.

[26] The relationships between the frequency and mastery of leader behavior and various outcomes were investigated by F Shipper and C S White, "Mastery, Frequency, and Interaction of Managerial Behaviors Relative to Subunit Effectiveness," Human Relations, January 1999, pp 49–66.

[27] F E Fiedler, "Job Engineering for Effective Leadership: A New Approach," Management Review, September 1977, p 29.

[28] For more on this theory, see F E Fiedler, "A Contingency Model of Leadership Effectiveness," in Advances in Experimental Social Psychology, vol. 1, ed L Berkowitz (New York: Academic Press, 1964); F E Fiedler, A Theory of Leadership Effectiveness (New York: McGraw-Hill, 1967).

[29] See L H Peters, D D Hartke, and J T Pohlmann, "Fiedler's Contingency Theory of Leadership: An Application of the Meta-Analyses Procedures of Schmidt and Hunter," Psychological Bulletin, March 1985, pp 274–85; and C A Schriesheim, B J Tepper, and L A Tetrault, "Least Preferred Co-Worker Score, Situational Control, and Leadership Effectiveness: A Meta-Analysis of Contingency Model Performance Predictions," Journal of Applied Psychology, August 1994, pp 561–73.

[30] Excerpted from D Kirkpatrick, "Inside Sam's $100 Billion Growth Machine," Fortune, June 14, 2004, pp 86, 88. Also see B Groyberg, A N McLean, and N Nohria, "Are Leaders Portable?" Harvard Business Review, May 2006, pp 92–100.

[31] For more detail on this theory, see R J House, "A Path–Goal Theory of Leader Effectiveness," Administrative Science Quarterly, September 1971, pp 321–38.

[32] This research is summarized by R J House, "Path–Goal Theory of Leadership: Lessons, Legacy, and a Reformulated Theory," Leadership Quarterly, Autumn 1996, pp 323–52.

[33] See ibid.

[34] Examples can be found in K Brokker, "The Pepsi Machine," Fortune, February 6, 2006, pp 68–72; B Morris, "Star Power: Ursula Burns," Fortune, February 6, 2006, p 57; and P Burrows, "HP's Ultimate Team Player," BusinessWeek, January 30, 2006, pp 76–78.

[35] Excerpted from S Tully, "The Contender in This Corner: Jamie Dimon," Fortune, April 3, 2006, pp 56, 58.

[36] R J House and R N Aditya, "The Social Scientific Study of Leadership: Quo Vadis?" Journal of Management, 1997, p 457.

[37] Tragedy inspires Leadership & Co operation—Summit Awards—Canadian HR Reporter Feb 28/09 p6.

[38] A thorough discussion of shared leadership is provided by C L Pearce, "The Future of Leadership: Combining Vertical and Shared Leadership to Transform Knowledge Work," Academy of Management Executive, February 2004, pp 47–57.

[39] M Levy, 'Coaching Success Boils Down to Three Traits,' USA Today, November 2, 2005, p 6C. This research is summarized in B J Avolio, J J Soskik, D I Jung, and Y Berson, 'Leadership Models, Methods, and Applications,' in Handbook of Psychology, eds W C Borman, D R Ilgen, R J Klimoski (Hobohen, NJ: John Wiley & Sons, 2003), vol 12, pp 277–307.

[40] This research is summarized in B J Avolio, J J Soskik, D I Jung, and Y Berson, "Leadership Models, Methods, and Applications," in

Handbook of Psychology, eds W C Borman, D R Ilgen, R J Klimoski (Hobohen, NJ: John Wiley & Sons, 2003), vol 12, pp 277–307.
[41] Results can be found in P M Podsakoff, S B MacKenzie, M Ahearne, and W H Bommer, 'Searching for a Needle in a Haystack: Trying to Identify the Illusive Moderators of Leadership Behaviors,' *Journal of Management*, 1995, pp 422–70. Also see S Yun, S Faraj, and H P Sims Jr, 'Contingent Leadership and Effectiveness of Trauma Resuscitation Teams,' *Journal of Applied Psychology*, November 2005, pp 1288–296.
[42] A thorough discussion of this theory is provided by P Hersey and K H Blanchard, *Management of Organizational Behavior: Utilizing Human Resources*, 5th ed (Englewood Cliffs, NJ: Prentice Hall, 1988).
[43] A comparison of the original theory and its latent version is provided by P Hersey and K H Blanchard, "Great Ideas Revisited," *Training & Development*, January 1996, pp 42–47.
[44] See D C Lueder, "Don't Be Misled by LEAD," *Journal of Applied Behavioral Science*, May 1985, pp 143–54; and C L Graeff, "The Situational Leadership Theory: A Critical View," *Academy of Management Review*, April 1983, pp 285–91.
[45] A definition and description of transactional leadership is provided by J Antonakis and R J House, 'The Full-Range Leadership Theory: The Way Forward,' in *Transformational and Charismatic Leadership: The Road Ahead*, eds B J Avolio and F J Yammarino (New York: JAI Press, 2002), pp 3–34.
[46] Susan Berman, *Maple Leaf Strikers Fight Attempt To Move Out Machinery*. The Militant, Vol.62/No.5, Feb. 9/98. (at the time of writing the article, Berman was a member of United Steelworkers of America Local 5338 in Toronto.)
[47] U R Dumdum, K B Lowe, and B J Avolio, "A Meta-Analysis of Transformational and Transactional Leadership Correlates of Effectiveness and Satisfaction: An Update and Extension," in *Transformational and Charismatic Leadership: The Road Ahead*, eds B J Avolio and F J Yammarino (New York: JAI Press, 2002), p 38.
[48] Supportive research is summarized by J Antonakis and R J House, "The Full-Range Leadership Theory: The Way Forward."
[49] Gordon Pitts, *The Testing of Michael McCain*, Report on Business Magazine Dec. 2008, pg. 62–66.
[50] Ibid.
[51] *The Fifth Discipline*, Peter Senge, Random House, Inc. NY, NY 1994.
[52] Supportive results can be found in R S Rubin, D C Munz, and W H Bommer, "Leading from Within: The Effects of Emotion Recognition and Personality on Transformational Leadership Behavior," *Academy of Management Journal*, October 2005, pp 845–58; and T A Judge and J E Bono, "Five-Factor Model of Personality and Transformational Leadership," *Journal of Applied Psychology*, October 2000, pp 751–65.
[53] These definitions are derived from R Kark, B Shamir, and C Chen, "The Two Faces of Transformational Leadership: Empowerment and Dependency," *Journal of Applied Psychology*, April 2003, pp 246–55. Also see A E Rafferty and M A Griffin, "Refining Individualized Consideration: Distinguishing Developmental Leadership and Supportive Leadership," *Journal of Occupational and Organizational Psychology*, March 2006, pp 37–61.
[54] B Nanus, *Visionary Leadership* (San Francisco: Jossey-Bass, 1992), p 8.
[55] W H Bulkeley, "Back from the Brink: Mulcahy Leads a Renaissance at Xerox by Emphasizing Color, Customers, and Costs," *The Wall Street Journal*, April 24, 2006, pp B1, B3.
[56] See R Kark, B Shamir, and G Chen, "The Two Faces of Transformational Leadership," *Journal of Applied Psychology*, April 2003, pp 246–55.
[57] Supportive results can be found in W H Bommer, G A Rich, and R S Rubin, "Changing Attitudes about Change: Longitudinal Effects of Transformational Leader Behavior on Employee Cynicism about Organizational Change," *Journal of Organizational Behavior*, November 2005, pp 733–53; B M Bass, B J Avolio, D I Jung, and

Y Berson, "Predicting Unit Performance by Assessing Transformational and Transactional Leadership," *Journal of Applied Psychology*, April 2003, pp 207–18; and J E Bono and T A Judge, "Self-Concordance at Work: Toward Understanding the Motivational Effects of Transformational Leaders," *Academy of Management Journal*, October 2003, pp 554–71.
[58] Results can be found in U R Dumdum, K B Lowe, and B J Avolio, "A Meta-Analysis of Transformational and Transactional Leadership Correlates of Effectiveness and Satisfaction: An Update and Extension." Also see R T Keller, "Transformational Leadership, Initiating Structure, and Substitutes for Leadership: A Longitudinal Study of Research and Development Project Team Performance," *Journal of Applied Psychology*, January 2006, pp 202–10.
[59] See K B Lowe, K G Kroeck, and N Sivasubramaniam, 'Effectiveness Correlates of Transformational and Transactional Leadership: A Meta-Analytic Review of the MLQ Literature,' *Leadership Quarterly*, 1996, pp 385–425. Also see B R Agle, N J Nagarajan, J A Sonnenfeld, and D Srinivasan, 'Does CEO Charisma Matter? An Empirical Analysis of the Relationship among Organizational Performance, Environmental Uncertainty, and Top Management Team Perceptions of CEO Charisma,' *Academy of Management Journal*, February 2006, pp 161–74.
[60] See A J Towler, "Effects of Charismatic Influence Training on Attitudes, Behavior, and Performance," *Personnel Psychology*, Summer 2003, pp 363–81; and L A DeChurch and M A Marks, "Leadership in Multiteam Systems," *Journal of Applied Psychology*, March 2006, pp 311–29.
[61] These recommendations were derived from J M Howell and B J Avolio, "The Ethics of Charismatic Leadership: Submission or Liberation," *The Executive*, May 1992, pp 43–54.

CHAPTER 11

[1] Excerpted from C Leung, "Culture Club," *Canadian Business*, October 9–22, 2006, pp 116–17.
[2] E H Schein, "Culture: The Missing Concept in Organization Studies," *Administrative Science Quarterly*, June 1996, p 236.
[3] See the related discussion in L Buchanan, "The Office," *Inc. Magazine*, February 2007, p 120; and R Berner, "My Year at Wal-Mart," *BusinessWeek*, February 12, 2007, pp 70–74.
[4] Hormby, Thomas, A History of Apples Lisa, 1979–1986, Low End Mac, 2005-10-06 Retrieved on 2007-03-02. (cached—Apple—A knol by Rogerio Coelho)
[5] S H Schwartz, "Universals in the Content and Structure of Values: Theoretical Advances and Empirical Tests in 20 Countries," in *Advances in Experimental Social Psychology*, ed M P Zanna (New York: Academic Press, 1992), p 4.
[6] See P Engardio, "Beyond The Green Corporation," *BusinessWeek*, January 29, 2007, pp 50–64.
[7] Ibid, p 50–51.
[8] P Babcock, "Is Your Company Two-Faced?" *HR Magazine*, January 2004, p 43.
[9] WestJet corporate website: www.westjet.ca "Message from Sean" Durfy, President/CEO & Profile and History—Our Fleet tabs.
[10] Ibid.
[11] Ibid—WestJet News Releases, Community Investment & Sponsorship request tabs.
[12] Ibid—WestJet Great jobs tab
[13] Paul Brent, *WestJet Culture Gets Employees On-board*, Nov. 28, 2007 www.workopolis.ca – article
[14] WestJet corporate website: www.westjet.ca—WestJet Culture tab & article: *WestJet Tops List of Canadian's 10 Most Admired Corporate Cultures* Canadian Business– Jan 16, 2008 www.canadianbusiness.com
[15] See C Ostroff, A Kinicki, and M Tamkins, "Organizational Culture and Climate," in *Handbook of Psychology*, vol. 12, eds W C Borman, D R Ilgen, and R J Klimoski (New York: Wiley and Sons, 2003), pp 565–93.

[16] See the related discussion in S Ten Have, W Ten Have, A F Stevens, M Vander Elst, and F Pol-Coyne, *Key Management Models: The Management Tools and Practices that will Improve Your Business* (San Francisco: Jossey-Bass, 2003); and P Kwan and A Walker, "Validating the Competing Values Model as a Representation of Organizational Culture Through Inter-Institutional Comparisons," *Organizational Analysis*, 2004, pp 21–37.

[17] A thorough description of the CVF is provided in K S Cameron, R E Quinn, J Degraff, and A V Thakor, *Creating Values Leadership* (Northampton, MA: Edward Elgar, 2006); and K S Cameron and R E Quinn, *Diagnosing and Changing Organizational Culture* (New York: Addison-Wesley, 1999).

[18] The Home Depot example was based on R Charan, "Home Depot's Blueprint for Culture Change," *Harvard Business Review*, April 2006, pp 61–71; B Grow, "Renovating Home Depot," *BusinessWeek*, March 6, 2006, pp 50–58; and "Nardelli Out at Home Depot," *BusinessWeek.com*, January 3, 2007; http: www.businessweek.com/bwdaily/dnflash/ccontent/jan2007/ db20070103_534405.htm.

[19] See C Daniels, "Meet Mr. Nuke," *Fortune*, May 15, 2006, pp 140–46; and L Lee, "It's Dell vs. The Dell Way," *BusinessWeek*, March 6, 2006, pp 61–62.

[20] Results can be found in E A Goodman, R F Zammuto, and B D Gifford, "The Competing Values Framework: Understanding the Impact of Organizational Culture on the Quality of Work Life," *Organization Development Journal*, Fall 2001, 58–68; P A Balthazard, R A Cooke, and R E Potter, "Dysfunctional Culture, Dysfunctional Organization," *Journal of Managerial Psychology*, 2006, pp 709–32; and B Erdogan, R C Liden, and M L Kraimer, "Justice and Leader-Member Exchange: The Moderating Role of Organizational Culture," *Academy of Management Journal*, April 2006, pp 395–406.

[21] Supportive results can be found in C Ostroff, Y Shin, and A Kinicki, "Multiple Perspectives of Congruence: Relationships between Value Congruence and Employee Attitudes," *Journal of Organizational Behaviour*, September 2005, pp 591–624; and W Arthur Jr, S T Bell, A J Villado, and D Doverspike, "The Use of Person-Organization Fit in Employment Decision Making: An Assessment of Its Criterion-Related Validity," *Journal of Applied Psychology*, July 2006, pp 786–801.

[22] Culture and performance was examined by M Škerlavaj, M I Štemberger, R Škrinjar, and V Dimovski, "Organizational Learning Culture—The Missing Link between Business Process Change and Organizational Learning," *International Journal of Production Economics*, April 2007, pp 346–67; A Xenikou and M Simosi, "Organizational Culture and Transformational Leadership as Predictors of Business Unit Performance," *Journal of Managerial Performance*, 2006, pp 566–79; T Igo and M Skitmore, "Diagnosing the Organizational Culture of an Australian Engineering Consultancy Using the Competing Values Framework," *Construction Innovation*, June 2006, pp 1221–139; and R Hauser and R Paul, "IS Service Quality and Culture: An Empirical Investigation," *Journal of Computer Information Systems*, Fall 2006, pp 15–22.

[23] Results are reported in C W Hart, "Beating the Market with Customer Satisfaction," *Harvard Business Review*, March 2007, pp 30–31.

[24] Results can be found in J Combs, Y Liu, A Hall, and D Ketchen, "How Much Do High-Performance Work Practices Matter? A Meta-Analysis of Their Effects on Organizational Performance," *Personnel Psychology*, Autumn 2006, pp 501–28.

[25] Results can be found in J P Kotter and J L Heskett, *Corporate Culture and Performance* (New York: Free Press, 1992).

[26] The success rate of mergers is discussed in M J Epstein, "The Drivers of Success in Post-Merger Integration," *Organizational Dynamics*, May 2004, pp 174–89. Also see "Dealing with Cultural Misfits," *HR Magazine*, March 2007, pp 14, 16; and "Focus on the People During a Merger," *HR Magazine*, March 2007, p 16.

[27] See the related discussion in V Sathe and E J Davidson, "Toward a New Conceptualization of Culture Change," in *Handbook of Organizational Culture & Climate*, eds N M Ashkanasay, C P M Wilderom, and M F Peterson (Thousand Oaks, CA: Sage Publications, 2000), pp 279–96; and M Nunno, "The Effects of the ARC Organizational Intervention on Caseworker Turnover, Climate, and Culture in Children's Services Systems," *Child Abuse & Neglect*, August 2006, pp 849–54.

[28] D-A Durbin, "Ford Cuts Part of Culture Shift," *The Arizona Republic*, January 24, 2006, p D3.

[29] The mechanisms were based on material contained in E H Schein, "The Role of the Founder in Creating Organizational Culture," *Organizational Dynamics*, Summer 1983, pp 13–28.

[30] Excerpted from D F Kuratko, R D Ireland, and J S Hornsby, "Improving Firm Performance through Entrepreneurial Actions: Acordia's Corporate Entrepreneurship Strategy," *Academy of Management Executive*, November 2001, p 67.

[31] S Holmes, "Cleaning Up Boeing," *BusinessWeek*, March 13, 2006, p 66.

[32] Ibid, p 68.

[33] S Tully, "Taking a Shot at the Title of World's Most Important Banker," *Fortune*, April 3, 2006, p 58.

[34] See "Calif. Charges Are Resolved in HP Spying Case," *The Arizona Republic*, March 15, 2007, p D1, D2; and P Burrows, "Controlling the Damage at HP," *BusinessWeek*, October 9, 2006, pp 36–44.

[35] Practical examples can be found in P Dvorak, "A Firm's Culture Can Get Lost in Translation," *The Wall Street Journal*, April 3, 2006, pp B1, B3; and B E Litzky, K A Eddleston, and D L Kidder, "The Good, the Bad, and the Misguided: How Managers Inadvertently Encourage Deviant Behaviors," *Academy of Management Perspectives*, February 2006, pp 91–102.

[36] J Van Maanen, "Breaking In: Socialization to Work," in *Handbook of Work, Organization, and Society*, ed R Dubin (Chicago: Rand-McNally, 1976), p 67.

[37] Adapted from material in D C Feldman, "The Multiple Socialization of Organization Members," Academy of Management Review, April 1981, pp 309–18. Reprinted by permission of The Academy of Management via The Copyright Clearance Center.

[38] Supportive evidence is provided by R W Griffeth and P W Hom, *Retaining Valued Employees* (Thousand Oaks, CA: Sage Publications, 2001), pp 46–65.

[39] See J M Phillips, "Effects of Realistic Job Previews on Multiple Organizational Outcomes: A Meta-Analysis," *Academy of Management Journal*, December 1998, pp 673–90.

[40] Onboarding programs are discussed by J McGregor, "How to Take the Reins at Top Speed," *BusinessWeek*, February 5, 2007, pp 55–56; and J M Brodie, "Getting Managers On Board," *HR Magazine*, November 2006, pp 105–108.

[41] These results are presented in "Outsider Longer," *Training*, March 2007, p 6.

[42] See J P Slattery, T T Selvarajan, and J E Anderson, "Influences of New Employee Development Practices on Temporary Employee Work-Related Attitudes," *Human Resource Development Quarterly*, 2006, pp 279–303.

[43] See E H Offstein and R L Dufresne, "Building Strong Ethics and Promoting Positve Character Development: The Influence of HRM at the United States Military Academy at West Point," *Human Resource Management*, Spring 2007, pp 95–114.

[44] See D Cable and C Parsons, "Socialization Tactics and Person-Organization Fit," *Personnel Psychology*, Spring 2001, pp 1–23.

[45] R Levering and M Moskowitz, "The 100 Best Companies to Work For: And the Winners Are . . . " *Fortune*, January 23, 2006, p 94.

[46] A review of stage model research can be found in B E Ashforth, *Role Transitions in Organizational Life: An Identity-Based Perspective* (Mahwah, NJ: Lawrence Erlbaum Associates, 2001).

[47] See J A Gruman, A M Saks, and D I Zweig, "Organizational Socialization Tactics and Newcomer Proactive Behaviours: An Integrative Study," *Journal of Vocational Behaviour*, August 2006,

pp 90–104; and H D Cooper-Thomas and N Anderson, "Organizational Socialization," *Journal of Managerial Psychology*, 2006, pp 492–516.

48 For a thorough review of research on the socialization of diverse employees with disabilities, see A Colella, "Organizational Socialization of Newcomers with Disabilities: A Framework for Future Research," in *Research in Personnel and Human Resources Management*, ed G R Ferris (Greenwich, CT: JAI Press, 1996), pp 351–417.

49 This definition is based on the network perspective of mentoring proposed by M Higgins and K Kram, "Reconceptualizing Mentoring at Work: A Developmental Network Perspective," *Academy of Management Review*, April 2001, pp 264–88.

50 Results can be found in T D Allen, L T Eby, M L Poteet, and E Lentz, "Career Benefits Associated with Mentoring for Protégés: A Meta-Analysis," *Journal of Applied Psychology*, February 2004, pp 127–36; and T D Allen, L T Eby, and E Lentz, "Mentorship Behaviours and Mentorship Quality Associated with Formal Mentoring Programs: Closing the Gap Between Research and Practice," *Journal of Applied Psychology*, May 2006, pp 567–78.

51 Career functions are discussed in detail in K Kram, *Mentoring of Work: Developmental Relationships in Organizational Life* (Glenview, IL: Scott, Foresman, 1985).

52 This discussion is based on Higgins and Kram, "Reconceptualizing Mentoring at Work."

53 Ibid.

54 Supportive results can be found in T Allen, M Poteet, and J Russell, "Protégé Selection by Mentors: What Makes the Difference?" *Journal of Organizational Behaviour*, May 2000, pp 271–82.

55 Recommendations for improving your networking skills can be found in S Berfield, "Mentoring Can Be Messy," *BusinessWeek*, January 29, 2007, pp 80–81.

56 Results can be found in "Leadership Needs Development," *Training*, February 2006, p 7.

57 See S Tonidandel, D R Avery, and M G Phillips, "Maximizing Returns on Mentoring: Factors Affecting Subsequent Protégé Performance," *Journal of Organizational Behaviour*, January 2007, pp 89–110.

58 This recommendation was derived from J Welch and S Welch, "Ideas the WelchWay: Avoiding Strikes—and Unions," *BusinessWeek*, January 15, 2007, p 92.

CHAPTER 12

1 C I Barnard, *The Functions of the Executive* (Cambridge, MA: Harvard University Press, 1938), p 73.

2 Drawn from E H Schein, *Organizational Psychology*, 3rd ed (Englewood Cliffs, NJ: Prentice Hall, 1980), pp 12–15.

3 For related reading, see N Bennett and S A Miles, "Second in Command: The Misunderstood Role of the Chief Operating Officer," *Harvard Business Review*, May 2006, pp 71–78.

4 Organization Design: fashion or fit? Henry Mintzberg. Harvard Business Review, Jan 1, 1981.

5 Ibid

6 For an interesting historical perspective of hierarchy, see P Miller and T O'Leary, "Hierarchies and American Ideals, 1900–1940," *Academy of Management Review*, April 1989, pp 250–65. Also see H J Leavitt, "Why Hierarchies Thrive," *Harvard Business Review*, March 2003, pp 96–102.

7 For an excellent overview of the span of control concept, see D D Van Fleet and A G Bedeian, "A History of the Span of Management," *Academy of Management Review*, July 1977, pp 356–72. Also see E E Lawler III and J R Galbraith, "New Roles for the Staff: Strategic Support and Service," in *Organizing for the Future: The New Logic for Managing Complex Organizations*, eds J R Galbraith, E E Lawler III, and Associates (San Francisco: Jossey-Bass, 1993), pp 65–83.

8 For a comparison of functional and product departmentation, see McCann & Galbraith, 1981; Walker, A.H., & Lorsch, J.W. (1968,

November—December). Organizational choice: Product vs. function. Harvard Business Review, 129–138.

9 See Davis, S.M., & Lawrence, P.M. (1977). Matrix. Reading, MA: Addison-Wesley.

10 Treatment of these forms of departmentation can be found in Daft, R.L. (2007). Organization theory and design (9th ed.). Cincinnati, OH: Thompson South-Western; Robey, D. (1991). Designing organizations (3rd ed.). Homewood, IL: Irwin.

11 Ibid.

12 Ibid.

13 Waterman, R.H., Jr. (1987). The renewal factor. New York: Bantam Books; McElroy, J. (1985, April). Ford's new way to build cars. Road & Track, 156–158.

14 From R. E. Miles and C. C. Snow. "Causes of failure in network organizations." California Management Review, Vol. 34, No. 4.

15 For an illustrative management-related metaphor, see J E Beatty, "Grades as Money and the Role of the Market Metaphor in Management Education," *Academy of Management Learning and Education*, June 2004, pp 187–96. Also see C Oswick and P Jones, "Beyond Correspondence? Metaphor in Organization Theory," *Academy of Management Review*, April 2006, pp 483–85; and J Cornelissen, "Metaphor in Organization Theory: Progress and the Past," *Academy of Management Review*, April 2006, pp 485–88.

16 K S Cameron, "Effectiveness as Paradox: Consensus and Conflict in Conceptions of Organizational Effectiveness," *Management Science*, May 1986, pp 540–41. Also see S Sackmann, "The Role of Metaphors in Organization Transformation," *Human Relations*, June 1989, pp 463–84; and H Tsoukas, "The Missing Link: A Transformational View of Metaphors in Organizational Science," *Academy of Management Review*, July 1991, pp 566–85.

17 See W R Scott, "The Mandate Is Still Being Honored: In Defense of Weber's Disciples," *Administrative Science Quarterly*, March 1996, pp 163–71. Also see D Jones, "Military a Model for Execs," *USA Today*, June 9, 2004, p 4B.

18 Based on M Weber, *The Theory of Social and Economic Organization*, translated by A M Henderson and T Parsons (New York: Oxford University Press, 1947). An instructive analysis of the mistranslation of Weber's work may be found in R M Weiss, "Weber on Bureaucracy: Management Consultant or Political Theorist?" *Academy of Management Review*, April 1983, pp 242–48.

19 For a critical appraisal of bureaucracy, see R P Hummel, *The Bureaucratic Experience*, 3rd ed (New York: St. Martin's Press, 1987). The positive side of bureaucracy is presented in C T Goodsell, *The Case for Bureaucracy: A Public Administration Polemic* (Chatham, NJ: Chatham House Publishers, 1983).

20 *Managerial Economics*, 4th ed., by Paul Keat & Philip Young, Pearson Education Inc., Upper Saddle River, New Jersey, 2003, pp 384–395. See reference to evaluate the efficiency of the alternative methods of allocating scare resources.

21 See G Pinchot and E Pinchot, "Beyond Bureaucracy," *Business Ethics*, March–April 1994, pp 26–29; and O Harari, "Let the Computers Be the Bureaucrats," *Management Review*, September 1996, pp 57–60.

22 For examples of what managers are doing to counteract bureaucratic tendencies, see B Dumaine, "The Bureaucracy Busters," *Fortune*, June 17, 1991, pp 36–50; and C J Cantoni, "Eliminating Bureaucracy—Roots and All," *Management Review*, December 1993, pp 30–33.

23 A management-oriented discussion of general systems theory—an interdisciplinary attempt to integrate the various fragmented sciences—may be found in K E Boulding, "General Systems Theory—The Skeleton of Science," *Management Science*, April 1956, pp 197–208.

24 J D Thompson, *Organizations in Action* (New York: McGraw-Hill, 1967), pp 6–7. Also see A C Bluedorn, "The Thompson Interdependence Demonstration," *Journal of Management Education*, November 1993, pp 505–9.

[25] For interesting updates on the biological systems metaphor, see A M Webber, "How Business Is a Lot Like Life," *Fast Company*, April 2001, pp 130–36; E Bonabeau and C Meyer, "Swarm Intelligence: A Whole New Way to Think about Business," *Harvard Business Review*, May 2001, pp 106–14; and R Adner, "Match Your Innovation Strategy to Your Innovation Ecosystem," *Harvard Business Review*, April 2006, pp 98–107.

[26] R L Daft and K E Weick, "Toward a Model of Organizations as Interpretation Systems," *Academy of Management Review*, April 1984, p 293. Also see J Reingold, "My (Long) Day at the Top," *Fast Company*, June 2006, pp 64–66.

[27] See M Crossan, "Altering Theories of Learning and Action: An Interview with Chris Argyris," *Academy of Management Executive*, May 2003, pp 40–46; D Gray, "Wanted: Chief Ignorance Officer," *Harvard Business Review*, November 2003, pp 22, 24; and G T M Hult, D J Ketchen, Jr, and S F Slater, "Information Processing, Knowledge Development, and Strategic Supply Chain Performance," *Academy of Management Journal*, April 2004, pp 241–253.

[28] For good background reading, see the entire Autumn 1998 issue of *Organizational Dynamics*; D Lei, J W Slocum, and R A Pitts, "Designing Organizations for Competitive Advantage: The Power of Unlearning and Learning," *Organizational Dynamics*, Winter 1999, pp 24–38; L Baird, P Holland, and S Deacon, "Learning from Action: Imbedding More Learning into the Performance Fast Enough to Make a Difference," *Organizational Dynamics*, Spring 1999, pp 19–32; "Leading-Edge Learning: Two Views," *Training & Development*, March 1999, pp 40–42; and A M Webber, "Learning for a Change," *Fast Company*, May 1999, pp 178–88.

[29] Maple Leaf Foods website – tab "We Take Care" Maple Leaf's Vertical Coordination Strategy: A Key to Enhanced Safety—www.mapleleaf.com

[30] "Top Forty Under 40," *Report on Business Magazine*, May 2002, p 73.

[31] K Cameron, "Critical Questions in Assessing Organizational Effectiveness," *Organizational Dynamics*, Autumn 1980, p 70. Also see T D Wall, J Michie, M Patterson, S J Wood, M Sheehan, C W Clegg, and M West, "On the Validity of Subjective Measures of Company Performance," *Personnel Psychology*, Spring 2004, pp 95–118; W F Joyce, "What Really Works: Building the 4 2 Organization," *Organizational Dynamics*, no. 2, 2005, pp 118–29; and J Kirby, "Toward a Theory of High Performance," *Harvard Business Review*, July–August 2005, pp 30–39.

[32] See G H Seijts, G P Latham, K Tasa, and B W Latham, "Goal Setting and Goal Orientation: An Integration of Two Different yet Related Literatures," *Academy of Management Journal*, April 2004, pp 227–39.

[33] For discussion of a very goal-oriented company, see "What Makes GE Great?" *Fortune*, March 6, 2006, pp 90–96.

[34] See, for example, R O Brinkerhoff and D E Dressler, *Productivity Measurement: A Guide for Managers and Evaluators* (Newbury Park, CA: Sage Publications, 1990); and D Jones and B Hansen, "Productivity Gains Roll at Their Fastest Clip in 31 Years," *USA Today*, June 14, 2004, pp 1B–2B.

[35] See S Baker, "Wiser about the Web," *BusinessWeek*, March 27, 2006, pp 54–58; S Levy and B Stone, "The New Wisdom of the Web," *Newsweek*, April 3, 2006, pp 46–53; and A Lashinsky, "The Boom Is Back," *Fortune*, May 1, 2006, pp 70–87.

[36] Data from M Maynard, "Toyota Promises Custom Order in 5 Days," *USA Today*, August 6, 1999, p 1B.

[37] "Interview: M Scott Peck," *Business Ethics*, March/April 1994, p 17. Also see C B Gibson and J Birkinshaw, "The Antecedents, Consequences, and Mediating Role of Organizational Ambidexterity," *Academy of Management Journal*, April 2004, pp 209–26.

[38] See P Puranam, H Singh, and M Zollo, "Organizing for Innovation: Managing the Coordination-Autonomy Dilemma in Technology Acquisitions," *Academy of Management Journal*, April 2006, pp 263–80; R E Herzlinger, "Why Innovation in Health Care Is So Hard," *Harvard Business Review*, May 2006, pp 58–66; and D L Laurie, Y L Doz, and C P Sheer, "Creating New Growth Platforms," *Harvard Business Review*, May 2006, pp 80–90.

[39] Cameron, "Critical Questions in Assessing Organizational Effectiveness," p 67. Also see W Buxton, "Growth from Top to Bottom," *Management Review*, July/August 1999, p 11.

[40] See R K Mitchell, B R Agle, and D J Wood, "Toward a Theory of Stakeholder Identification and Salience: Defining the Principle of Who and What Really Counts," *Academy of Management Review*, October 1997, pp 853–96; T J Rowley and M Moldoveanu, "When Will Stakeholder Groups Act? An Interest- and Identity-Based Model of Stakeholder Group Mobilization," *Academy of Management Review*, April 2003, pp 204–19; G Kassinis and N Vafeas, "Stakeholder Pressures and Environmental Performance," *Academy of Management Journal*, February 2006, pp 145–59; and N A Gardberg and C J Fombrun, "Corporate Citizenship: Creating Intangible Assets across Institutional Environments," *Academy of Management Review*, April 2006, pp 329–46.

[41] S B Shepard, "Steve Ballmer on Microsoft's Future," *BusinessWeek*, December 1, 2003, p 72. See J Greene, "A Rendezvous with Microsoft's Deep Throat," *BusinessWeek*, September 26, 2005, p 104; and D Kirkpatrick, "Microsoft's New Brain," *Fortune*, May 1, 2006, pp 56–68.

[42] See J Welch and S Welch, "How Healthy Is Your Company?" *BusinessWeek*, May 8, 2006, p 126.

[43] K S Cameron, "Effectiveness as Paradox: Consensus and Conflict in Conceptions of Organizational Effectiveness," *Management Science*, May 1986, p 542.

[44] Alternative effectiveness criteria are discussed in ibid.; A G Bedeian, "Organization Theory: Current Controversies, Issues, and Directions," in *International Review of Industrial and Organizational Psychology*, eds C L Cooper and I T Robertson (New York: John Wiley & Sons, 1987), pp 1–33; and M Keeley, "Impartiality and Participant-Interest Theories of Organizational Effectiveness," *Administrative Science Quarterly*, March 1984, pp 1–25.

[45] For updates, see M Goold and A Campbell, "Do You Have a Well-Designed Organization?" *Harvard Business Review*, March 2002, pp 117–24; and J A A Sillince, "A Contingency Theory of Rhetorical Congruence," *Academy of Management Review*, July 2005, pp 608–21.

[46] B Elgin, "Running the Tightest Ships on the Net," *BusinessWeek*, January 29, 2001, p 126.

[47] See D A Morand, "The Role of Behavioural Formality and Informality in the Enactment of Bureaucratic versus Organic Organizations," *Academy of Management Review*, October 1995, pp 831–72.

[48] See G P Huber, C C Miller, and W H Glick, "Developing More Encompassing Theories about Organizations: The Centralization-Effectiveness Relationship as an Example," *Organization Science*, no. 1, 1990, pp 11–40; and C Handy, "Balancing Corporate Power: A New Federalist Paper," *Harvard Business Review*, November/December 1992, pp 59–72. Also see A Slywotzky and D Nadler, "The Strategy Is the Structure," *Harvard Business Review*, February 2004, p 16; and N Gull, "Managing on the Front Lines," *Inc.*, May 2004, p 24.

[49] P Kaestle, "A New Rationale for Organizational Structure," *Planning Review*, July/August 1990, p 22. For examples, see N McKinstry, "Changing Direction," *Fortune*, November 14, 2005, p 153; A A King, M J Lenox, and A Terlaak, "The Strategic Use of Decentralized Institutions: Exploring Certification with the ISO 14001 Management Standard," *Academy of Management Journal*, December 2005, pp 1091–1106; and A Barrett, "J&J: Reinventing How It Invents," *BusinessWeek*, April 17, 2006, pp 60–61.

[50] Details of this study can be found in T Burns and G M Stalker, *The Management of Innovation* (London: Tavistock, 1961). Also see W D Sine, H Mitsuhashi, and D A Kirsch, "Revisiting Burns and Stalker: Formal Structure and New Venture Performance in Emerging Economic Sectors," *Academy of Management Journal*, February 2006, pp 121–32; and N Nohria, "Survival of the Adaptive," *Harvard Business Review*, May 2006, p 23.

51 D J Gillen and S J Carroll, "Relationship of Managerial Ability to Unit Effectiveness in More Organic versus More Mechanistic Departments," *Journal of Management Studies*, November 1985, pp 674–75.

52 J D Sherman and H L Smith, "The Influence of Organizational Structure on Intrinsic versus Extrinsic Motivation," *Academy of Management Journal*, December 1984, p 883.

53 See J A Courtright, G T Fairhurst, and L E Rogers, "Interaction Patterns in Organic and Mechanistic Systems," *Academy of Management Journal*, December 1989, pp 773–802.

54 See J R Galbraith and E E Lawler III, "Effective Organizations: Using the New Logic of Organizing," in J R Galbraith, E E Lawler III, and Associates, eds, *Organizing for the Future: The New Logic for Managing Complex Organizations* (San Francisco: Jossey-Bass, 1993), pp 285–99.

CHAPTER 13

1 Forces for change are thoroughly discussed by L R Beach, *Leadership and the Art of Change* (Thousand Oaks, CA: Sage, 2006).

2 Alain Belanger, Co ordiantor of research and analysis in Statics Canada's demography division who co authored a report on cultural shifts—The Vancouver Sun, March 23, 2005 by Joel Baglole and Krisendra Bisetty "Cultural shift takes aim at British Columbia".

3 Ibid.

4 M L Alch, "Get Ready for the Net Generation," *Training & Development*, February 2000, pp 32, 34.

5 D Kirkpatrick, "Microsoft's New Brain," *Fortune*, May 1, 2006, p 59.

6 See J Mero and M Boyle, 'Star Power: Eduardo Castro-Wright,' *Fortune*, February 6, 2006, p 58.

7 Productivity in the service industry is discussed by S Hamm, S E Ante, A Reinhardt, and M Kripalani, 'Services,' *BusinessWeek*, June 21, 2004, pp 82–83

8 Examples are provided by G Edmondson, "The Race to Build Really Cheap Cars," *BusinessWeek*, April 23, 2007, pp 44–48; D Welch, "Why Toyota Is Afraid of Being Number One," *BusinessWeek*, March 5, 2007, pp 42–50.

9 See the related discussion in J W Upson, D J Ketchen, Jr., and R D Ireland, "Managing Employee Stress: A Key to the Effectiveness of Strategic Supply Chain Management," *Organizational Dynamics*, 2007, pp 78–92.

10 Examples are provided in J Lublin and P Dvorak, "How Five New Players Aid Movement to Limit CEO Pay," *The Wall Street Journal*, March 13, 2007, pp A1, A20; and A Tomisawa, "Matsushita Aims to Boost Quality, Guard Image with Suppliers Rules," *The Wall Street Journal*, March 30, 2007, p A12.

11 This example was discussed A Pomeroy, "Agent of Change," *HR Magazine*, May 2005, pp 52–56.

12 Industry Canada Report 'Insolvency Statistics and Economic Analysis' January 2009 http://strategis.ic.gc.ca/eic/site/bsf-osb.nsf/eng/h_br01011.html

13 For a thorough discussion of the model, see K Lewin, *Field Theory in Social Science* (New York: Harper & Row, 1951).

14 This example was derived from P-W Tam, "System Reboot: Hurd's Big Challenge at HP: Overhauling Corporate Sales," *The Wall Street Journal*, April 3, 2006, pp A1, A3; and A Lashinsky, "The Hurd Way," *Fortune*, April 17, 2006, pp 92–102.

15 C Goldwasser, "Benchmarking: People Make the Process," *Management Review*, June 1995, p 40.

16 See T A Stewart, "Architects of Change," *Harvard Business Review*, April 2006, p 10.

17 A thorough discussion of the target elements of change can be found in M Beer and B Spector, "Organizational Diagnosis: Its Role in Organizational Learning," *Journal of Counseling and Development*, July–August 1993, pp 642–50; and M Hammer, "The Process Audit," *Harvard Business Review*, April 2007, pp 111–23.

18 These errors are discussed in J P Kotter, "Leading Change: When Transformation Efforts Fail," *Harvard Business Review*, January 2007, pp 96–103.

19 See F Ostroff, "Change Management in Government," *Harvard Business Review*, May 2006, pp 141–47

20 Different stage-based models of OD are discussed by R A Gallagher, "What Is OD?" www.orgdct.com/what_is_od.htm, accessed May 12, 2005.

21 Over 60 different OD techniques are discussed by P Holman, T Devane, and S Cady, *The Change Handbook*, 2nd ed (San Francisco: Berrett-Kohler, 2007).

22 W W Burke, *Organization Development: A Normative View* (Reading, MA: Addison-Wesley Publishing, 1987), p 9.

23 See R Gulati, "Silo Busting: How to Execute on the Promise of Customer Focus," *Harvard Business Review*, May 2007, pp 98–108.

24 A Kinicki and B Williams, *Management: A Practical Introduction*, 2nd ed. (Burr Ridge: IL: McGraw-Hill/Irwin, 2006), p 329.

25 See R Rodgers, J E Hunter, and D L Rogers, "Influence of Top Management Commitment on Management Program Success," *Journal of Applied Psychology*, February 1993, pp 151–55.

26 Results can be found in P J Robertson, D R Roberts, and J I Porras, "Dynamics of Planned Organizational Change: Assessing Empirical Support for a Theoretical Model," *Academy of Management Journal*, June 1993, pp 619–34. Also see J M Hiatt, *ADKAR: A Model for Change in Business, Government and Our Community* (Loveland, CO: Prosci Learning Center Publications, 2006).

27 Results from the meta-analysis can be found in G A Neuman, J E Edwards, and N S Raju, "Organizational Development Interventions: A Meta-Analysis of Their Effects on Satisfaction and Other Attitudes," *Personnel Psychology*, Autumn 1989, pp 461–90.

28 Results can be found in C-M Lau and H-Y Ngo, "Organization Development and Firm Performance: A Comparison of Multinational and Local Firms," *Journal of International Business Studies*, First Quarter 2001, pp 95–114.

29 Adapted from R J Marshak, *Covert Processes at Work* (San Francisco: Berrett-Koehler Publishers, 2006); and A S Judson, *Changing Behaviour in Organizations: Minimizing Resistance to Change* (Cambridge, MA: Blackwell, Inc., 1991).

30 An individual's predisposition to change was investigated by C R Wanberg and J T Banas, "Predictors and Outcomes of Openness to Changes in a Reorganizing Workplace," *Journal of Applied Psychology*, February 2000, pp 132–42.

31 Nick Carey, "Can Chrysler Come Back?"—*Globe&Mail Report on Business*, May 1, 2009 http://business.theglobeandmail.com/servlet/story/RTGAM.20090501.wchryslerwireanalysis0501/BNStory/Business/home?cid=al_gam_mostview

32 See L Coch and J R P French Jr, "Overcoming Resistance to Change," *Human Relations*, 1948, pp 512–32.

33 L Herscovitch and J P Meyer, "Commitment to Organizational Change: Extension of a Three-Component Model," *Journal of Applied Psychology*, June 2002, p 475.

34 Ibid., pp 474–87.

35 Research regarding resilience is discussed by K Kersting, "Resilience: The Mental Muscle Everyone Has," *Monitor on Psychology*, April 2005, pp 32–33; Also see G E Mangurian, "Realizing What You're Made Of," *Harvard Business Review*, March 2007, pp 125–130.

36 Results from this study can be found in T A Judge, C J Thoresen, V Pucik, and T W Welbourne, "Managerial Coping with Organizational Change: A Dispositional Perspective," *Journal of Applied Psychology*, February 1999, pp 107–22.

37 See Wanberg and Banas, "Predictors and Outcomes of Openness to Changes in a Reorganizing Workplace," pp 132–42.

38 See the related discussion in E B Dent and S G Goldberg, "Challenging 'Resistance to Change,'" *Journal of Applied Behavioural Science*, March 1999, pp 25–41.

[39] J P Kotter, "Leading Change: Why Transformation Efforts Fail," *Harvard Business Review*, 1995, p 64.

[40] Communicating about organizational change is discussed in Z Ruimin, "Raising Haier," *Harvard Business Review*, February 2007, pp 141–46; and C M Christensen, M Marx, and H H Stevenson, "The Tools of Cooperation and Change," *Harvard Business Review*, October 2006, pp 73–81.

[41] Reprinted by permission of Harvard Business School Press. Exhibit from J P Kotter and L A Schlesinger, "Choosing Strategies for Change," March/April 1979. Copyright © 1979 by the Harvard Business School of Publishing Corporation; all rights reserved.

[42] J M Ivancevich and M T Matteson, *Stress and Work: A Managerial Perspective* (Glenview, IL: Scott, Foresman, 1980), pp 8–9.

[43] See Selye, *Stress without Distress*.

[44] See C Liu, P E Spector, and L Shi, "Cross-National Job Stress: A Quantitative and Qualitative Study," *Journal of Organizational Behaviour*, January 2007, pp 209–239; T Deangelis, "American: A Toxic Lifestyle?" *Monitor on Psychology*, April 2007, pp 50–52; and C Hymowitz, "Executive Adopts Motto for Job Stress: Work Hard, Be Nice," *The Wall Street Journal*, April 16, 2007, p B1.

[45] Supportive results can be found in F M McKee-Ryan, Z Song, C R Wanberg, and A J Kinicki, "Psychological and Physical Well-Being during Unemployment: A Meta-Analytic Study," *Journal of Applied Psychology*, January 2005, pp 53–76.

[46] Sleep deprivation is discussed by C A Czeisler, "Sleep Deficit: The Performance Killer," *Harvard Business Review*, October 2006, pp 53–59.

[47] Results are reported in N A Bowling and T A Beehr, "Workplace Harassment from the Victim's Perspective: A Theoretical Model and Meta-Analysis," *Journal of Applied Psychology*, September 2006, pp 998–1012

[48] See the related discussion in E M Hallowell, "Smart People Underperform," *Harvard Business Review*, January 2005, pp 55–62.

[49] The discussion of appraisal is based on R S Lazarus and S Folkman, *Stress, Appraisal, and Coping* (New York: Springer Publishing, 1984).

[50] Results are presented in J A Penley, J Tomaka, and J S Wiebe, "The Association of Coping to Physical and Psychological Health Outcomes: A Meta-Analytic Review," *Journal of Behavioural Medicine*, December 2002, pp 551–609; Also see M Fugate, A Kinicki, and G Prussia, "Employee Coping with Organizational Change: An Examination of Alternative Theoretical Perspectives and Models," 2007, manuscript under review.

[51] The impact of vacations are discussed by E White, "For Young Workers, Taking Time Off Can be Stressful," *The Wall Street Journal*, March 27, 2007, p B10; and C Fritz and S Sonnentag, "Recovery, Well-Being, and Performance-Related Outcomes: The Role of Workload and Vacation Experiences," *Journal of Applied Psychology*, July 2006, pp 936–45.

[52] Supportive results can be found in J R B Halbesleben and W M Bowler, "Emotional Exhaustion and Job Performance: The Mediating Role of Motivation," *Journal of Applied Psychology*, January 2007, pp 93–106; and J D Jonge and C Dormann, "Stressors, Resources, and Strain at Work: A Longitudinal Test of the Triple-Match Principle," *Journal of Applied Psychology*, November 2006, pp 1359–74.

[53] Supportive results can be found in G E Miller, E Chen, and E S Zhou, "If It Goes Up, Must It Come Down? Chronic Stress and the Hypothalamic-Pituitary-Adrenocortical Axis in Humans," *Psychological Bulletin*, January 2007, pp 25–45; and L Meyers, "Building a Stronger Heart," *Monitor on Psychology*, January 2007, pp 52–53.

[54] R A Clay, "One Heart-Many Threats," *Monitor on Psychology*, January 2007, pp 46–54; J-P Neveu, "Jailed Resources: Conservation of Resources Theory as Applied to Burnout Among Prison Guards," *Journal of Organizational Behaviour*, January 2007, pp 21–42; and J R B Halbesleben, "Sources of Social Support and Burnout: A Meta-Analytic Test of the Conservation of Resources Model," *Journal of Applied Psychology*, September 2006, pp 1134–45.

[55] This pioneering research is presented in S C Kobasa, "Stressful Life Events, Personality, and Health: An Inquiry into Hardiness," *Journal of Personality and Social Psychology*, January 1979, pp 1–11.

[56] M Friedman and R H Rosenman, *Type A Behaviour and Your Heart* (Greenwich, CT: Fawcett Publications, 1974), p 84.

[57] Adapted from M Friedman and R H Rosenman, Type A Behaviour and Your Heart (Greenwich, CT: Fawcett Publications, 1974), pp 100–2.

[58] See C Lee, L F Jamieson, and P C Earley, "Beliefs and Fears and Type A Behaviour: Implications for Academic Performance and Psychiatric Health Disorder Symptoms," *Journal of Organizational Behaviour*, March 1996, pp 151–77; S D Bluen, J Barling, and W Burns, "Predicting Sales Performance, Job Satisfaction, and Depression by Using the Achievement Strivings and Impatience–Irritability Dimensions of Type A Behaviour," *Journal of Applied Psychology*, April 1990, pp 212–16; and M S Taylor, E A Locke, C Lee and M E Gist, "Type A Behaviour and Faculty Research Productivity: What Are the Mechanisms?" *Organizational Behaviour and Human Performance*, December 1984, pp 402–18.

[59] Results from the meta-analysis are contained in S A Lyness, "Predictors of Differences between Type A and B Individuals in Heart Rate and Blood Pressure Reactivity," *Psychological Bulletin*, September 1993, pp 266–95.

[60] See T Q Miller, T W Smith, C W Turner, M L Guijarro, A J Hallet, "A Meta-Analytic Review of Research on Hostility and Physical Health," *Psychological Bulletin*, March 1996, pp 322–48; and N Geipert, "Don't Be Mad," *Monitor on Psychology*, January 2007, pp 50–51.

[61] An evaluation of stress-reduction programs is conducted by P A Landsbergis and E Vivona-Vaughan, "Evaluation of an Occupational Stress Intervention in a Public Agency," *Journal of Organizational Behaviour*, January 1996, pp 29–48; and D C Ganster, B T Mayes, W E Sime, and G D Tharp, "Managing Organizational Stress: A Field Experiment," *Journal of Applied Psychology*, October 1982, pp 533–42.

[62] R Kreitner, "Personal Wellness: It's Just Good Business," *Business Horizons*, May–June 1982, p 28.

[63] See T Parker-Pope, "Doctor's Orders: Ways to Work Exercise Into a Busy Day," *The Wall Street Journal*, January 9, 2007, p D1; and M P McQueen, "Wellness Plans Reach Out to the Healthy," *The Wall Street Journal*, March 28, 2007, pp D1, D3.

CHAPTER 14

[1] Canadian Companies Actively Recruiting Overseas August 6, 2008 www.canadavisa.com

[2] Also see D Nilsen, B Kowske, and K Anthony, "Managing Globally," *HR Magazine*, August 2005, pp 111–115; and A Taylor III, "How I Work," *Fortune*, March 20, 2006, pp 66, 68.

[3] See Y Kashima, "Conceptions of Culture and Person for Psychology," *Journal of Cross-Cultural Psychology*, January 2000, pp 14–32; and the cultural dimensions in Table 1 of G T Chao and H Moon, "The Cultural Mosaic: A Metatheory for Understanding the Complexity of Culture," *Journal of Applied Psychology*, November 2005, pp 1128–140.

[4] "How Cultures Collide," *Psychology Today*, July 1976, p 69. Also see E T Hall, *The Hidden Dimension* (Garden City, NY: Doubleday, 1966).

[5] F Trompenaars and C Hampden-Turner, *Riding the Waves of Culture: Understanding Cultural Diversity in Global Business*, 2nd ed (New York: McGraw-Hill, 1998), pp 6–7.

[6] See M Mendenhall, "A Painless Approach to Integrating 'International' into OB, HRM, and Management Courses," *Organizational Behavior Teaching Review*, no. 3 (1988-89), pp 23–27.

[7] See C L Sharma, "Ethnicity, National Integration, and Education in the Union of Soviet Socialist Republics," *The Journal of East and*

West Studies, October 1989, pp 75–93; and R Brady and P Galuszka, "Shattered Dreams," *BusinessWeek*, February 11, 1991, pp 38–42.
[8] Canada's Top 100 Employers http://www.canadastop100.com/diversity/Proctor & Gamble Inc.
[9] See M R Testa, S L Mueller, and A S Thomas, "Cultural Fit and Job Satisfaction in a Global Service Environment," *Management International Review*, April 2003, pp 129–148; R E Nelson and S Gopalan, "Do Organizational Cultures Replicate National Cultures? Isomorphism, Rejection and Reciprocal Opposition in the Corporate Values of Three Countries," *Organization Studies*, September 2003, pp 1115–51; P B Smith, "Nations, Cultures, and Individuals," *Journal of Cross-Cultural Psychology*, January 2004, pp 6–12; and G P Zachary, "Plugging into Africa," Business 2.0, November 2005, pp 134–44.
[10] Marcus Gee *Hanging on by a thread*, Globe and Mail ROB pg. B1—Dec. 12, 2008.
[11] See G A Sumner, *Folkways* (New York: Ginn, 1906). Also see J G Weber, "The Nature of Ethnocentric Attribution Bias: Ingroup Protection or Enhancement?" *Journal of Experimental Social Psychology*, September 1994, pp 482–504.
[12] D A Heenan and H V Perlmutter, *Multinational Organization Development* (Reading, MA: Addison-Wesley, 1979), p 17
[13] Data from R Kopp, "International Human Resource Policies and Practices in Japanese, European, and United States Multinationals," *Human Resource Management*, Winter 1994, pp 581–99.
[14] See D Doke, "Shipping Diversity Abroad," *HR Magazine*, November 2003, pp 58–64; M B Marklein, "Foreign Student Enrollment on the Decline, Study Finds," *USA Today*, November 14, 2005, p 7D; M B Marklein, "USA Losing Its Advantage Drawing Foreign Students," *USA Today*, January 6, 2006, p 10A; and "Foreigners Returning to U.S. Grad Schools," USA Today, March 23, 2006, p 6D.
[15] Data from B Hagerty, "Trainers Help Expatriate Employees Build Bridges to Different Cultures," *The Wall Street Journal*, June 14, 1993, pp B1, B3.
[16] Canadian HR Reporter—*Homeward Bound* by Stephen Cryne, March 9/09 page 14.
[17] C M Farkas and P De Backer, "There Are Only Five Ways to Lead," *Fortune*, January 15, 1996, p 111.
[18] For related research, see G S Van Der Vegt, E Van De Vliert, and X Huang, "Location-Level Links Between Diversity and Innovative Climate Depend on National Power Distance," *Academy of Management Journal*, December 2005, pp 1171–182.
[19] Adapted from G. Hofstede, "Cultural Constraints in Management Theories," Academy of Management Executive, February 1993, pg. 91; G. Hofstede, "The Cultural Relativity of Organizational Practices and Theories, "Journal of International Business Studies, 14, 1983, pp. 75–89.
[20] A similar conclusion is presented in the following replication of Hofstede's work: A Merritt, "Culture in the Cockpit: Do Hofstede's Dimensions Replicate?" Journal of Cross-Cultural Psychology, May 2000, pp 283–301. Another extension of Hofstede's work can be found in S M Lee and S J Peterson, "Culture, Entrepreneurial Orientation, and Global Competitiveness," *Journal of World Business*, Winter 2000, pp 401–16.
[21] J S Osland and A Bird, "Beyond Sophisticated Stereotyping: Cultural Sensemaking in Context," *Academy of Management Executive*, February 2000, p 67.
[22] "Fujio Mitarai: Canon," *BusinessWeek*, January 14, 2002, p 55.
[23] 2008 International Leadership Association Conference—Nov 15, 2008—Presentation: Global Business Leadership: The Need for Emotional and Cultural Intelligence—Presented by: Prof. F Ngunjiri, Dr. L. LSchumacher and professor K. Bowman.
[24] Ilan Alon; Higgins, James M. (2005). Global leadership success through emotional and cultural intelligences. Business Horizons, Vol 48 (6), p501.

[25] R House, M Javidan, P Hanges, and P Dorfman, "Understanding Cultures and Implicit Leadership Theories across the Globe: An Introduction to Project GLOBE," *Journal of World Business*, Spring 2002, p 4.
[26] See J C Kennedy, "Leadership in Malaysia: Traditional Values, International Outlook," *Academy of Management Executive*, August 2002, pp 15–26; M Javidan and A Dastmalchian, "Culture and Leadership in Iran: The Land of Individual Achievers, Strong Family Ties, and Powerful Elite," *Academy of Management Executive*, November 2003, pp 127–42; and M Javidan, G K Stahl, F Brodbeck, and C P M Wilderom, "Cross-Border Transfer of Knowledge: Cultural Lessons from Project GLOBE," *Academy of Management Executive*, May 2005, pp 59–76.
[27] Adapted from the list in House, Javidan, Hanges, and Dorfman, "Understanding Cultures and Implicit Leadership Theories across the Globe," pp 5–6.
[28] R.J. House, Paul J. Hanges, M. Javidan, P.W. Dorfman, and V. Gupta, Culture, Leadership and Organizations—Thousand Oaks, CA: Sage Publications, 2004.
[29] 2007 International Leadership Association Conference—Nov 1, 2007 – Key Note Speaker: Mansour Javidan—*Leadership and Culture: The GLOBE Findings On Universal and Culturally Specific Attributes of Outstanding Leadership*.
[30] Data from Trompenaars and Hampden-Turner, *Riding the Waves of Culture: Understanding Cultural Diversity in Global Business*, Ch 5. For relevant research evidence, see J Allik and A Realo, "IndividualismCollectivism and Social Capital," *Journal of Cross-Cultural Psychology*, January 2004, pp 29–49; A K Lalwani, S Shavitt, and T Johnson, "What Is the Relation Between Cultural Orientation and Socially Desirable Responding?" *Journal of Personality and Social Psychology*, January 2006, pp 165–78; C Robert, W C Lee, and K Chan, "An Empirical Analysis of Measurement Equivalence with the INDCOL Measure of Individualism and Collectivism: Implications for Valid Cross-Cultural Inference," *Personnel Psychology*, Spring 2006, pp 65–99; and W McEwen, X Fang, C Zhang, and R Burkholder, "Inside the Mind of the Chinese Consumer," *Harvard Business Review*, March 2006, pp 68–76.
[31] Trompenaars and Hampden-Turner, *Riding the Waves of Culture: Understanding Cultural Diversity in Global Business*, p 56. The importance of "relationships" in Eastern and Western cultures is explored in S H Ang, "The Power of Money: A Cross-Cultural Analysis of Business-Related Beliefs," *Journal of World Business*, Spring 2000, pp 43–60.
[32] See M Munter, "Cross-Cultural Communication for Managers," *Business Horizons*, May–June 1993, pp 69–78.
[33] I Adler, "Between the Lines," *Business Mexico*, October 2000, p 24.
[34] Millan, Kras, Jacques, et al Business Quarterly, *Doing Business In Mexico: The Human Resource Challenges* Sept. 22, 1995.
[35] R W Moore, "Time, Culture, and Comparative Management: A Review and Future Direction," in *Advances in International Comparative Management*, vol. 5, ed S B Prasad (Greenwich, CT: JAI Press, 1990), pp 7–8.
[36] See A C Bluedorn, C F Kaufman, and P M Lane, "How Many Things Do You Like to Do at Once? An Introduction to Monochronic and Polychronic Time," *Academy of Management Executive*, November 1992, pp 17–26.
[37] "Multitasking" term drawn from S McCartney, "The Breaking Point: Multitasking Technology Can Raise Stress and Cripple Productivity," *The Arizona Republic*, May 21, 1995, p D10.
[38] See M Archer, "Too Busy to Read This Book? Then You Really Need To," *USA Today*, April 17, 2006, p 10B.
[39] O Port, "You May Have To Reset This Watch—In a Million Years," *BusinessWeek*, August 30, 1993, p 65.
[40] See M Toda and K Morimoto, "Ramadan Fasting—Effect on Healthy Muslims," *Social Behavior and Personality*, no. 1, 2004, pp 13–18.

41 See T Scandura and P Dorfman, "Leadership Research in an International and Cross-Cultural Context," *The Leadership Quarterly*, April 2004, pp 277–307; M Javidan and N Lynton, "The Changing Face of the Chinese Leadership," *Harvard Business Review*, December 2005, pp 28, 30; and M Javidan, P W Dorfman, M S de Luque, and R J House, "In the Eye of the Beholder: Cross Cultural Lessons in Leadership from Project GLOBE," *Academy of Management Perspectives*, February 2006, pp 67–90.

42 J Guyon, "David Whitwam," *Fortune*, July 26, 2004, p 174.

43 Siemens Corporate Information—2008 Annual Report www.siemens.com

44 Stephen Cryne, *Foreign Assignments Increasing, Along With Employee Resistance* Canadian HR Reporter September 27, 2004 http://www.canadianhrreporter.com/ArticleView.aspx?l=1&articleid=3416

45 Wallace Immen, *Ready To Work Abroad?* Globe and Mail November 12, 2003. www.globeandmail.com

46 Stephen Cryne, *Foreign Assignments Increasing, Along With Employee Resistance* Canadian HR Reporter September 27, 2004, Carswell Business Publication, Toronto.

47 These insights come from Tung, "American Expatriates Abroad: From Neophytes to Cosmopolitans"; P M Caligiuri and W F Cascio, "*Can We Send Her There?* Maximizing the Success of Western Women on Global Assignments," *Journal of World Business*, Winter 1998, pp 394–416; T L Speer, "Gender Barriers Crumbling, Traveling Business Women Report," *USA Today*, March 16, 1999, p 5E; G Koretz, "A Woman's Place Is . . . ," *BusinessWeek*, September 13, 1999, p 28; and L K Stroh, A Varma, and S J Valy-Durbin, "Why Are Women Left at Home: Are They Unwilling to Go on International Assignments?" *Journal of World Business*, Fall 2000, pp 241–55. Also see S Bates, "Are Women Better for International Assignments?" *HR Magazine*, December 2003, p 16.

48 An excellent reference book on this topic is J S Black, H B Gregersen, and M E Mendenhall, *Global Assignments: Successfully Expatriating and Repatriating International Managers* (San Francisco: Jossey-Bass, 1992). Also see M B Hess and P Linderman, *The Expert Expatriate: Your Guide to Successful Relocation Abroad* (Yarmouth, Maine: Intercultural Press, 2002); and E Gundling, *Working GlobeSmart: 12 People Skills for Doing Business across Borders* (Palo Alto, CA: Davies-Black Publishing, 2003).

49 Wallace Immen, *Ready To Work Abroad?* Globe and Mail November 12, 2003. www.globeandmail.com; Cigna International Expatriate Benefits, Mercer Human Resource Consulting and International SOS of Canada.

50 Ibid.

51 Ibid.

52 Ibid.

53 See J Carter, "Globe Trotters," *Training*, August 2005, pp 22–28; M A Shaffer, D A Harrison, H Gregersen, J S Black, and L A Ferzandi, "You Can Take It With You: Individual Differences and Expatriate Effectiveness," *Journal of Applied Psychology*, January 2006, pp 109–125; and Y Gong and J Fan, "Longitudinal Examination of the Role of Goal Orientation in Cross-Cultural Adjustment," *Journal of Applied Psychology*, January 2006, pp 176–184.

54 See K Roberts, E E Kossek, and C Ozeki, "Managing the Global Workforce: Challenges and Strategies," *Academy of Management Executive*, November 1998, pp 93–106.

55 J S Lublin, "Younger Managers Learn Global Skills," *The Wall Street Journal*, March 31, 1992, p B1.

56 See D Stamps, "Welcome to America: Watch Out for Culture Shock," *Training*, November 1996, pp 22–30; L Glanz, R Williams, and L Hoeksema, "Sensemaking in Expatriation—A Theoretical Basis," *Thunderbird International Business Review*, January–February 2001, pp 101–19; E Marx, *Breaking Through Culture Shock: What You Need to Succeed in International Business* (London: Nicholas Brealey Publishing, 2001); G K Stahl and P Caligiuri, "The Effectiveness of Expatriate Coping Strategies: The Moderating Role of Cultural Distance, Position Level, and Time on the International Assignment," *Journal of Applied Psychology*, July 2005, pp 603–15; and R Takeuchi, M Wang, and S V Marinova, "Antecedents and Consequences of Psychological Workplace Strain During Expatriation: A Cross-Sectional and Longitudinal Investigation," *Personnel Psychology*, Winter 2005, pp 925–48.

57 See H H Nguyen, L A Messe, and G E Stollak, "Toward a More Complex Understanding of Acculturation and Adjustment," *Journal of Cross-Cultural Psychology*, January 1999, pp 5–31.

58 For more, see S Overman, "Mentors Without Borders," *HR Magazine*, March 2004, pp 83–86; and E Krell, "Budding Relationships," *HR Magazine*, June 2005, pp 114–18.

59 See Black, Gregersen, and Mendenhall, *Global Assignments: Successfully Expatriating and Repatriating International Managers*, p 227. Also see H B Gregersen, "Commitments to a Parent Company and a Local Work Unit During Repatriation," Personnel Psychology, Spring 1992, pp 29–54; and H B Gregersen and J S Black, "Multiple Commitments upon Repatriation: The Japanese Experience," *Journal of Management*, no. 2, 1996, pp 209–29.

60 Ibid., pp 226–27

61 See L K Stroh, H B Gregersen, and J S Black, "Closing the Gap: Expectations versus Reality among Repatriates," *Journal of World Business*, Summer 1998, pp 111–24; and K Tyler, "Retaining Repatriates," *HR Magazine*, March 2006, pp 97–102

PHOTO CREDITS

GLOSSARY

NAME AND COMPANY INDEX

A

Aberle, 82
Ability Beyond Disability, 109
A.C. Jetz, 268
Acadia University, 218
ACE Aviation Holdings, 268
Acordia Inc., 253
Acton, Lord, 193
A.D. Williams Engineering, 231–232
Adams, J. Stacy, 102
Adecco SA, 144, 145
Aerospace Industries Association of
    Canada, 250
Aflac, 82
AIG, 236
Air Canada, 268, 278
Albanese, Tom, 292
Alberta-Pacific (Al-Pac) Forest Industries
    Inc., 126
Albin Engineering Services, Inc., 98
Albin, Marc, 98–99
Alcon, 323
Alderfer, Clayton, 97
Allen & Overy, 14
Allen, Natalie, 81
Aon, 143
Apple, 246
Arcis Corp., 281
As You Like It, 124
Association of Image Consultants, 40
Association of Psychological Science, 225
Atlantic Coastal Action Program (ACAP), 283
Aziz, Amanda, 42
Azjen, Icek, 77, 78

B

Bagley, Constance, 208
Baichwal, Jennifer, 1
Ballmer, Steve, 59, 279
Balsillie, James, 12
Bandura, Albert, 46, 47, 50, 52, 53
Bargaining Council of B.C., 97
Bateman, Thomas S., 55
Bayer Inc., Canada, 373
BCE Inc., 94
Bell Aliant, 218
Bell Canada, 94, 218
Berg, Matt, 321
Bernhard, Wolfgang, 195
Bethlehem Steel, 108
Bhasin, Roberta, 200
Bitheads Inc., 281
Black, Conrad, 12, 199
Blackberry, 12, 13
Blake, Phil, 373
Blanchard, Kenneth, 233
Block, Walter, 328

Boeing, 253
Bombardier, Joseph-Armand, 245
Boucher, Patti, 169
Brewer, Montie, 268
Bristol-Myers Squibb, 74
Bromiley-Meier, Lisa, 24
Brown, Greg, 198
Buckley, Chris, 192
Burghardt, Sarah, 231–232
Burke, Warner, 300
Burns, Sean, 82
Burns, Tom, 281, 283
Burtynsky, Edward, 1
Business Week, 24, 131, 171, 247, 253, 279

C

Cadbury Schweppes, 101
Canadian Airlines, 278
Canadian Auto Workers (CAW), 182, 192
Canadian Business Magazine, 132, 192
Canadian Centre for Justice Statistics, 33
Canadian Centre for Occupational Health
    and Safety (CCOHS), 113
Canadian Charter of Rights and Freedoms, 30
Canadian Employee Relocation Council, 331
Canadian Federation of Students, 42
Canadian HR Reporter, 323
Canadian Human Rights Act, 75
Canadian Human Rights Commission, 10, 97
Canadian International Development
    Agency (CIDA), 39
Canadian Medical Association (CMA), 12
Canadian Policy Research Networks
    (CPRN), 42
Canadian Taxpayers Association, 192
Canadian Tire Corporation, 218, 219
Canon, 177
Career Edge, 99
Carlyle, Robert, 143
Carothers, Chuck, 79, 80
Casserra, Jessica, 360–365
Chambers, John, 59, 128, 256
Chevron, 160
Chouinard, Yvon, 366, 367
Christensen, Clayton, 7
Chrysler, 192
Cirque du Soleil, 375–376
Cisco Systems, 59, 128, 256
Citizenship and Immigration Canada, 317
City of Townsville, 351–355
Clark, Lana, 345–346
Clinician Assessment for Practice Program
    (CAPP), 11
Clitheroewas, Eleanor (Ellie), 367–368
Cloke, Kenneth, 171
Coch, Lester, 303
College of Physicians and Surgeons of
    Nova Scotia, 11

Collins, Francis, 57
Conover, John, 84
Construction Labour Relations Association
    (CLRA), 97
The Container Store, 81
Corace, Charles, 376
Cora's Breakfast & Lunch, 365
Corporate Knights, 284
Countryside Construction, 346
Countryside Environmental Services (CES),
    346–351
Courville, Isabelle, 218, 219
Covey, Stephen R., 51
Crant, J. Michael, 55
Criminal Code, 48
Crooke, Michael, 366

D

Daft, Richard, 151, 277
Daniels, Nathan, 355, 358–360
Day, Brian, 12
D'Cruz, Joseph, 268
DeBakey, Michael, 31, 32
Dell Inc., 74, 204, 295
Dell, Michael, 204
Deloitte Services LP, 261
Deutsche Telekom, 98
Diebold, 147
Dimon, Jamie, 230, 254
Disney Imagineering, 374
Disney, Walt, 374
Disney World, 374
Disneyland, 374
Drabinsky, Garth, 12
Drucker, Peter, 227
Dunn, Patricia C., 253, 254

E

EA Canada, 250
Eastman Kodak Company, 314–316
Ebbers, Bernard, 12, 199
Ecole Polytechnique de Montreal, 218
Edmonton Journal, 328
The 8ʰ Habit, 51
Eisner, Michael, 224
Emotional Intelligence, 61
Employment Equity Act, 10
Enron Corporation, 24
Epcot Center, 374
Equal Opportunity for Women in the
    Workplace Agency (EOWA), 327
European Commission, 33
European Union (EU), 33
Evans, Dick, 292

F

Falconbridge, 292

SUBJECT INDEX

decision tree, 208, 209*f*

decoding, 147

decoding barrier, 148

defensiveness, 155

Delphi technique, 212

demographic characteristics, 294–295

departmentation
 customer, 273
 defined, 272
 functional, 272
 geographic, 273
 hybrid, 273
 matrix, 273
 product, 272–273
 structures, 272*f*

developmental networks
 mentoring, 258–260
 model of, 259*f*
 types of, 259–260

developmental practices, 11, 11*t*

developmental relationship strength, 259

dependency, 199

directive leadership, 229

directive style of decision making, 206

disability stereotypes, 34

discerning listeners, 156

discrepancies, 83, 84

dispositional/genetic components, 84–85

distinctiveness, 34

distributive negotiation, 181

diversity
 appreciating and valuing, 9
 challenges around, 12
 defined, 8
 diversity wheel, 8*f*
 layers of, 8, 8*f*, 10
 work teams and, 135
 workplace, 8, 10–12

diversity management
 accountability practices, 10–11, 11*t*
 common diversity practices, 11*t*
 development practices, 11, 11*t*
 defined, 8
 recruitment practices, 11, 11*t*

diversity of developmental relationships, 258

division of labour
 bureaucracy, 275
 growth of an organization, 271
 organization, 270

dominating, 179

dysfunctional conflict, 172

E

e-business, 13
 defined, 13
 implications for OB, 13
 and Internet revolution, 13

effective listening, 156, 157*t*

effectiveness, 128
 see also organizational effectiveness

effort, 270

ego, 149

electronic communication
 blogs, 161

email (electronic mail), 159–160
 extranet, 159
 handheld devices, 160–161
 Internet, 159
 intranet, 159
 social networking, 161–162
 sustaining effective communication, 163
 teleworking, 162–163
 video conferencing, 162

electronic mail. *See* email

email, 159–160

emotional contagion, 60

emotional intelligence
 defined, 61–62
 developing, 62

emotional labour, 61

emotional stability, 54

emotional trust, 133

emotions
 defined, 60
 emotional intelligence (EI), 61–62
 emotional labour, 61
 and goals, 60
 moods, 60–61
 negative, 60, 60*f*
 positive, 60, 60*f*
 research on, 60–61

empathetic listeners, 156

employee assistance programs (EAPs), 310

employee counselling, 310

employee motivation. *See* motivation

employees
 accommodating, 99
 global, 321, 323

employment equity, 10

empowering, 129

empowerment, 196–198

employment equity, 10

enacted values, 248

encoding, 25–26, 145–146

encoding barrier, 148

encounter phase of organizational socialization, 256

entrepreneurial developmental network, 260

environmental factors, 34, 229

environmental scanning, 342

environmental sensitivity, 310

environmental stimuli, 25

equity, 84

equity sensitivity, 102

equity theory of motivation
 defined, 102
 dynamics of perceived inequity, 102
 individual-organization exchange relationship, 102
 negative and positive inequity, 102, 103*f*
 reducing inequity, 103
 thresholds of equity and inequity, 102–103

ERG theory, 97

escalation of commitment
 defined, 209
 reasons for, 209
 reducing, 210

escape strategy, 307

espoused values, 247

ethical decision making, 208–209

ethical decision tree, 208–209, 209*f*

ethical OB dilemmas
 Behaviour and Integrity towards Policy, 19–20
 Break It Up!, 190–191
 Call Centre Lay Offs, 242
 Can We Talk About Your Body Art?, 40–41
 Finding the Right Recruits for the RCMP, 266–267
 Group Dynamics—Dare to Disagree, 141–142
 I Think My Boss Is Sick—What Should I Do?, 316
 Life in a Virtual Organization—Close Supervision or "Snoopervision"?, 290–291
 The Motivation to Cheat, 118
 Open Communication or Censorship?, 168
 3M Tries to Make a Difference in Russia, 340
 Valuing Truth on the Job, 93
 When Emotional Intelligence is Lacking, Job Satisfaction Can Suffer, 67
 You Say You Never Lie? That's a Lie!, 217

ethics
 business, 12
 challenge of, 12–13
 and decision making, 208–209
 decision tree, 208–209, 209*f*
 defined, 12
 pitfalls in negotiation, 183, 183*t*
 use of power, 198–199

ethnic stereotypes, 32–34

ethnocentrism, 321

European Union (EU), 33

eustress, 304

evaluative listeners, 156

event memory, 26

Everywhere Display, 112

exchange, 196

exercise, 310

existence needs, 97

expatriate, 330

expatriate managers, 13

expatriate workers, 331

expectancy, 104

expectancy theory of motivation
 application of, 105
 defined, 103
 described, 102–103
 expectancy, 104
 instrumentality, 104
 managerial implications, 105–106, 105*f*
 research, 105
 valence, 104–105
 Vroom's expectancy theory, 105

expert power, 195

expertise, 207

external factors
 causal attributions, 34
 intrinsic motivation, 110
 organizational behaviour, 3

incivility, 174
individual-level stressors, 305–306
individualistic culture, 327
inductive reasoning, 58
Industrial Revolution, 6, 275
influence
  environmental, 277
  outcomes, 196
  tactics, 196
influence sharing, 198*f*
informal communication channel, 156
informal groups, 121
information overload, 159
information processing, 148
information richness, 151
ingratiation, 196
inherent morality, 134
initiating structure, 226
innovation, 210
innovative change, 296
inputs, 102
inspirational appeals, 196
institutional collectivism, 325
instrumental values, 71
instrumentality, 104
insufficient resources, 296
integrating, 179
integrative negotiation, 181
intelligence
  bodily-kinesthetic, 58
  defined, 57
  emotional, 61–62
  interpersonal, 58
  intrapersonal, 58
  linguistic, 58
  logical-mathematical, 58
  multiple, 58–59
  musical, 58
  naturalistic, 58
  performance and, 57–59
  practical, 59
  spatial, 58
intentions
  attitudes affect behaviour via, 77–79
  determinants of, 78
  lessons and implications of, 78–79
intergroup conflict, 175–176, 177*f*
internal factors
  causal attributions, 34
  motivation, 95–96, 101
  self-serving bias, 35
internal forces for change
  defined, 295
  human resources problems or prospects, 295–296
  insufficient resources, 296
  managerial preferences or decisions, 296
  organizational process, systems, structure, or culture, 296
internal locus of control, 56, 307
internal processes, 279
international consultants, 177
international organizational behaviour
  board of directors, 122
  cross-cultural differences, 54

cross-cultural relationships, 178
decentralized integrated coastal management, 283
employees' job satisfaction, 84
GLOBE research findings, 224
global campus placement, 14
outsourcing, 197
perceptual errors, 33
resistance to building a highway in India, 302
reverse brain drain, 334
social network site, 162
trusting employees, 98
Walmart culture in Germany, 247
Internet, 13, 159
interpersonal communication
  active listening, 155–156
  aggressive style, 152, 154
  assertive style, 152
  communication styles, 154*t*
  gender differences, 155
  grapevine, 156–158
  non-assertive style, 154
  non-verbal communication, 154–155
  quality of, 152
interpersonal influence, 28
interpersonal intelligence, 58
interpersonal trust, 148
intranet, 159
intrapersonal intelligence, 58
intrinsic (internal) motivation, 110
intuition, 207
invulnerability, 134

J

jargon, 150
job assignment, and self-efficacy, 47
job characteristics model, 109–110, 110*f*
job design
  biological approach, 112
  defined, 108
  and employee motivation, 108–110, 112–113
  job characteristics model, 109–110, 110*f*
  job enlargement, 109
  job enrichment, 109
  job rotation, 109
  mechanistic approach, 108
  motivational approaches, 108–110, 112
  motivator-hygiene model, 100*f*
  perceptual-motor approaches, 112–113
  self-efficacy, 47
job dissatisfaction, 100, 101
job enlargement, 109
job enrichment, 109
job involvement
  defined, 82
  job satisfaction and, 85
  managerial implications of, 82
  performance and, 82–83
job performance, 87
job rotation, 109
job satisfaction
  absenteeism and, 86
  defined, 83

discrepancies and, 83
dispositional/genetic components and, 84–85
equity and, 84
job involvement and, 85
job performance and, 87
major causes of, 83–85
motivation and, 85
need fulfillment and, 83
organizational citizenship behaviours and, 85–86
perceived stress and, 87
relationship to other factors, 85–
turnover and, 87
value attainment and, 83–84
withdrawal cognitions and, 86
journey, 171
judgmental heuristics, 205

K

Kotter's steps for leading organizational change, 299–301, 300*t*

L

laboratory study, 341
language source, 151
law and ethics at work
  barrier-removal legislation, 30
  building employee self-efficacy, 48
  civility and safety in the workplace, 175
  communicating notice to employees, 146
  corporate social responsibility (CSR), 324
  Employment Equity Act, 10
  fostering ethics in business, 208
  Hewlett-Packard's culture, 253
  internal processes in a family business, 280
  mandating counselling, 308
  paying leaders when companies fail, 236
  religious accommodation in the workplace, 75
  safe work environment, 97
  social deviance in virtual teamwork, 133
leader characteristics, 223*t*
leader-member relations, 228
leader trait, 222
leadership
  achievement-oriented leadership, 229
  approaches to studying, 221, 222*t*
  corporate, 225
  culture and, 224
  defined, 221
  directive leadership, 229
  emotional intelligence
  gender and, 224–225
  GLOBE leadership project, 224
  improving effectiveness of, 227
  versus managing, 221
  managerial implications, 27–28
  motivation, 228
  participative leadership, 229
  and self-efficacy, 48
  shared, 231
  styles, 233, 233*f*
  supportive leadership, 229
  teams and, 128

tips, 155
touching, 155
normative commitment
    defined, 81
    increasing, 82
norming, 123
norms
    defined, 126
    developing, 126
    enforcing, 126, 127t
    group, 126
numerical ability, 58
nutritional awareness, 310

O

OB in Action case studies
    Communication Barriers Everywhere, 167
    Consolidated Products, 240–242
    Designing a Motivating Job Using the JCM, 116
    Eastman Kodak, 314–316
    Google's Culture is Truly Unique, 264–266
    How Should We Help Shelly?, 189–190
    It Takes A Village—and a Consultant, 338–339
    Let's Get Together, 139–141
    Managing the Winter Games, 18–19
    Portrait of a Canadian Advisor, 39–40
    Valuing Work: Life Balance, 91–92
    What Should Margarita Deville Do?, 215
    Who Should We Hire?, 66
    The Woody Manufacturing Company, 289–290
obliging, 179
observable artefacts, 246–247
occupational stress
    described, 304
    model, 304–307, 305f
    moderators of, 307–308, 310
    stress-reduction techniques, 310
ombudsman, 180
open system
    biological, 277
    cognitive, 277–278
    defined, 277
openness to experience, 54
opportunistic developmental network, 259
opportunity, 171
optimizing, 205
organic organizations, 281
organization
    as biological system, 277
    as cognitive system, 277
    contemporary structures, 273–274, 274f
    creation of, 270
    defined, 270
    departmentation, 272–273
    growth of, 270–271
    learning organization, 278
    mechanistic organization, 281
    as military/mechanical bureaucracies, 275–277
    modern organizational metaphors, 275–278

network, 273
    new-style, 283–284, 284t
    old-style, 283–284, 284t
    as open system, 277
organic organization, 281
    structure of, 270, 272f
    virtual organizations, 273–274
organization chart
    defined, 270
    division of labour, 271
    hierarchy of authority, 271
    line positions, 272
    sample, 271f
    span of control, 271
    staff positions, 272
organization development (OD)
    characteristics, 300–301
    defined, 299
    interventions, 300–301
    managerial implications, 301
    research, 301
organizational behaviour (OB)
    benefits of studying, 4
    contemporary issues in, 8, 10–14
    and contingency approach, 7–8
    cultural influences on, 320f
    defined, 3
    and e-business, 13
    and ethics, 12–13
    evolution of field of, 5–8
    and globalization, 13–14
    history of, 5–8
    and human relations movement, 6–7
    Internet and e-business revolution, 13
    international. See international organizational behaviour
    learning, 14
    model of, 3f
    research sources, 341
    and scientific management, 6
    and workplace diversity, 8, 10–12
organizational change, 297
organizational citizenship behaviours (OCBs), 85–86
organizational commitment
    defined, 80
    increasing, 81–82
    model of, 80–81, 80f
    practical applications of, 81
    research on, 81
organizational conflict. See conflict
organizational creativity, 210
organizational culture
    basic assumptions, 248
    change, 252–254
    collective commitment, 249
    conceptual framework for, 245f
    competing values framework, 249–251, 250f
    context, 245–246
    defined, 245
    dynamics of, 246–252
    embedding a culture, 257–260
    enacted values, 248
    espoused values, 247

functions of, 248–249
    layers of, 246–248
    mentoring, 257–260
    merging with societal cultures, 320
    observable artefacts, 246–247
    organizational density, 248–249
    outcomes, 251–252
    shaping behaviour, 249
    social system stability, 249
    socialization processes, 254, 256–257
    societal culture and, 319–320
    types of, 249–251
contingency design. See contingency approach to organizational design
organizational effectiveness
    dimensions of, 279f
    generic effectiveness criteria, 278–281
    goal accomplishment, 278
    internal processes, 279
    mixing effectiveness criteria, 280–281
    resource acquisition, 279
    strategic constituencies satisfaction, 279–280
organizational identity, 248–249
organizational moles, 158
organizational politics
    coalition, 201
    defined, 199
    fundamentals of, 199–202
    impression management, 201
    political action, levels of, 200–201, 201f
    political tactics, 201–202, 202t
    triggers of political behaviour, 200
    uncertainty, 200
organizational processes, 296
organizational socialization
    anticipatory socialization phase, 254, 256
    change and acquisition phase, 256
    defined, 254
    encounter phase, 256
    Feldman's model, 254, 256
    managerial implications, 256
    research, 256
    tactics, 257t
organizational stressors, 306
organizational structure, 270
organizing a firm, 342
outcomes
    employee, 102
    encoding, 26
outsourcing structure, 273
outputs, 299
overall trust, 133

P

participative goals, 107
participative leadership, 229
participative management, 196
path-goal theory
    contingency factors, 229
    described, 229–230
    general representation of, 230f
    leadership behaviours, 231t
    managerial implications, 233
    research, 233

work/family conflict, 73–74
resilience to change, 303
resistance, 196
resistance to change
    defined, 3011
    management of, 301–304
    reasons for, 301–302
    research, 303
    strategies for overcoming, 303
    understanding, 301–304
resource acquisition, 279
respect, 133
response, 27
retention, 26
retrieval, 27
reward power, 194
rewards, 48
roles
    defined, 124
    group member, 124–126
    maintenance, 125, 125t
    task, 125,125t

S

salient stimuli, 25
sample survey, 341
satisficing, 206
schema, 26
schemata, 26
scientific management approach
    defined, 6
    mechanistic approach, 108
scouting, 129
secondary appraisal, 306
selection, and self-efficacy, 47
selective attention, 25
self-assessment exercises
    appreciating and valuing diversity, 9
    business etiquette, 153
    decision-making style, 203
    ethnocentrism, 322
    intrinsic motivation, 111
    leadership role, 220
    mechanistic versus organic
        organizations, 282
    self-monitoring, 49
    socialization, 255
    taking perspective, 23
    Type A-B behaviour continuum, 309
    value, 70
    work group autonomy, 130
    workplace incivility, 174
self-censorship, 134
self-concept
    defined, 44
    self-efficacy, 45–48
    self-esteem, 44–45
    self-management, 50–53
    self-monitoring, 48, 50
    understanding, 44–53
self-efficacy
    defined, 45
    employers building employees', 48
    managerial implications, 47–48
    mechanisms of, 46–47

model of, 46f
self-esteem
    cross-cultural perspective, 45
    defined, 44
    employment and, 44–45
    improving, 45
    organization-based, 44
self-improvement habits, 52t
self-managed teams, 128–129, 131
self-management
    arranging support for psychological self,
        52–53
    changing behaviour, 50–51
    consequences, 53
    Covey's eight habits, 52t
    managing situational cues, 51
    self-efficacy, 47
    social learning model, 50–53, 51f
self-monitoring
    defined, 48
    degree of, 50
    research insights and practical
        recommendations, 50
self-perception, 44
self-responsibility, 310
self-serving bias, 35
self-talk, 52–53
semantic barriers to communication, 150
semantic memory, 26
semantics, 150
sender, 145
sender barrier, 148
sense-making device, 249
separation costs, 87
sex-role stereotype, 31
shaping, 59
shared leadership, 231
simplification, 25–26
situation analysis, 342
situational control, 228
situational leadership theory (SLT), 233,
    233f
situational theories
    Fiedler's contingency model, 227–229,
        229f
    path-goal theory, 229–233, 230f
    situational leadership theory (SLT), 233,
        233f
sizing up, 342
skill variety, 110
skills and best practices
    behavioural tendencies to avoid, 28
    building a mentoring network, 260
    communication during change, 304
    developing emotional intelligence, 62
    effective management skills, 4
    improving leadership effectiveness, 227
    international experience, 321
    linking performance and rewards, 106
    managing geographically dispersed
        employees, 275
    managing your email, 160
    preventing groupthink, 134
smoothing, 179
social cognition, 24

social deviance, 133
social learning model, 50–53, 51f
social loafing, 135
social networking, 161–162
social perception
    communication and interpersonal
        influence, 28
    encoding and simplification, 25–26
    hiring, 27
    managerial implications, 27–28
    model, 25f
    performance appraisal, 27
    physical and psychological well-being, 28
    retrieval and response, 27
    selective attention and comprehension, 25
    storage and retention, 26
    workplace aggression, bullying, and
        antisocial behaviour, 28
social power, 194
social pressures, 295
social support, 307
social system stability, 249
socialization tactics, 257t
socialized power, 194
societal culture
    cultural onion, 319
    defined, 319
    merging with organizational cultures, 320
    model of societal and organizational
        cultures, 319–320
spamming, 159
span of control, 271
spatial ability, 58
spatial intelligence, 58
staff personnel, 272
stereotyped views of opposition, 134
stereotypes
    age, 31–32
    defined, 29
    disability, 34
    formation and maintenance, 29–34
    and perceptual errors, 28–34
    personal barriers, 148
    process, 30
    racial and ethnic, 32–34
    sex-role, 31
storage, 26
storming, 123
strategic constituencies satisfaction, 279–280
strategic constituency, 279
strategic plan, 252, 299
stress
    defined, 304
    eustress, 304
    foundations of
    model of occupational stress, 304–307, 305f
    moderators. See stress moderators
    occupational, 304–308, 310
    outcomes of, 307
    perceived stress, 87
    reducing, 310
    stressors, 305–307
stress moderators
    coping, 306–307
    described, 307

hardiness, 307
social support, 307
Type A behaviour pattern, 307–308, 310
stress reduction techniques, 310
stressors
cognitive appraisal of, 306
coping strategies, 306–307
defined, 305
extra-organizational stressors, 306
group-level stressors, 306
individual-level stressors, 305–306
organizational stressors, 306
stronger relationships, 173
support, 133
sustainability, 247
SWOT analysis, 342
symbolic coding, 52
symptom management strategy, 307
systematic soldiering, 108
systems model of change, 298–299, 298*f*

T

target elements of change, 299
task identity, 110
task roles, 125, 125*t*
task significance, 110
task structure, 228
team building, 131–132
teams
characteristics of effective teams, 128
cross-functional teams, 129
defined, 127
and diversity, 136
versus groups, 127–128
self-managed teams, 128–131
threats to effectiveness of, 134–135
trust, 132–133
virtual teams, 131
technological advancements, 295
teleconferencing, 162
teleworking, 162–163
terminal values, 71
theories of motivation

content, 96–101
defined, 95
process, 101–108
Theory X, 7, 7*t*
Theory Y, 7, 7*t*
360-degree feedback, 135
threshold, 112
touching, 155
traditional developmental network, 259
training and development, 47
trait theory, 222–226
transactional leadership, 233–234
transformational leadership
defined, 234
managerial implications, 236–237
model of, 235*f*
research, 236–237
transactional leadership, 233
transforming followers, 2335
trust
building, 133
defined, 133
dimensions of, 133
interpersonal, 148
teamwork, 132–133
turnover, 87
Type A behaviour pattern, 307–308, 310

U

uncertainty avoidance, 325
unfreezing stage, 297
unity of command principle, 270

V

valence, 104–105
value attainment, 83–84
value conflicts
handling through values clarification, 72
individual-organization, 72
interpersonal, 72
intrapersonal, 71–72
types of, 71–72
value congruence, 72, 73

value similarity, 73
value system, 71
values
defined, 71, 247
enacted, 248
espoused, 247
general life, 72–73
instrumental, 71
organizational culture, 247–248
personal, 71–75
terminal, 71
verbal comprehension, 58
video cases. *See* CEOTV.com video cases
video conferencing, 162
virtual organizations, 273–274
virtual teams
defined, 131
practical applications, 131
research, 131
social deviance in, 133
vision, 252
Vroom's expectancy theory, 105

W

withdrawal cognitions, 86
women
see also gender
glass ceiling, 10
word fluency, 58
work attitudes
job involvement, 82–83
job satisfaction, 83–87
organizational commitment, 80–82
work-related musculoskeletal disorders
(WMSDs), 113
work vs. family life conflict
organizational response to, 74–75
research insights about, 73–74
values-based model, 72–73, 73*f*
workplace aggression, 28
workplace bullying, 169
workplace diversity. *See* diversity
workplace incivility, 174–175

share.

www.mcgrawhillconnect.ca